ADA
Yearbook 1995

Studies in
Computer and Communications Systems

Volume 8

Editors

Arvind (MIT)
Ulrich Herzog (Universität Erlangen)
Richard Muntz (UCLA)
Brigitte Plateau (IMAG, Grenoble)
Ken Sevcik (University of Toronto)
Statish Tripathi (University of Maryland)

Previously published in this series

Vol. 1. A.K. Agrawala et al. (Eds.), Mission Critical Operating Systems
Vol. 2. A. Burns (Ed.), Towards Ada 9X
Vol. 3. K. Lyytinen and V.-P. Tahvanainen (eds.), New Generation
CASE Tools
Vol. 4. W.J. Taylor (Ed.), ADA in Transition
Vol. 5. C. Loftus (Ed.), ADA Yearbook 1993
Vol. 6. L. Collingbourne (Ed.), Ada: Towards Maturity
Vol. 7. C. Loftus (Ed.), ADA Yearbook 1994

ISSN: 0927-5444

ADA
Yearbook 1995

Edited by

Mark Ratcliffe

University of Wales, Aberystwyth
for ADA Language UK, Ltd.

1995

IOS
Press

Ohmsha

Amsterdam, Oxford, Tokyo, Washington, DC

ISBN 90 5199 218 1 (IOS Press)
ISBN 4 274 90043 6 C3000 (Ohmsha)

Publisher
IOS Press
Van Diemenstraat 94
1013 CN Amsterdam
Netherlands

Distributor in the UK and Ireland
IOS Press/Lavis Marketing
73 Lime Walk
Headington
Oxford OX3 7AD
England

Distributor in the USA and Canada
IOS Press, Inc.
P.O. Box 10558
Burke, VA 22009-0558
USA

Distributor in Japan
Ohmsha, Ltd.
3-1 Kanda Nishiki - Cho
Chiyoda - Ku
Tokyo 101
Japan

LEGAL NOTICE
The publisher is not responsible for the use which might be made of the following information.

PRINTED IN THE NETHERLANDS

Contents

List of trademarks

Teamwork is a trademark of Cadre Technologies.

VAX, VMS, ULTRIX, MicroVAX, DECstation are trademarks of Digital Equipment Corporation.

AIX, OS/2, PC/AT, RISC SYSTEM/6000, MVS, VM/CMS are registered trademarks of International Business Machines Corporation.

X Window System is a trademark of the Massachusetts Institute of Technology.

MS-DOS is a registered trademark of Microsoft Corporation.

Rational Environment is a trademark of Rational.

SunOS, SunView are trademarks of Sun Microsystems Incorporated.

UNIX is a registered trademark of UNIX Systems Laboratories Corporation.

All other products and brand-names are trademarks of their respective companies or organisations.

Ada UK

Ada UK is the commonly-used name of Ada Language UK Limited, which is a not-for-profit company registered in the United Kingdom. The objectives of the company include promoting the development and use of Ada, and representing the needs and interests of its users. Membership is open to anyone, regardless of nationality.

Further details about the benefits of membership may be obtained from Helen Byard, the Ada UK Administrator:

PO Box 322
York
YO1 3GY
UK
Tel: +44 (0) 1904 412740
Fax: +44 (0) 1904 426702

Preface

This is the fifth issue of the annual publication organised by Ada UK, complementary to the quarterly, *Ada User*. Many of the chapter headings are the same as in previous issues, especially so in Part Two; for example Chapter 16 is an update of last year's Ada Bindings chapter.

The audience for the Yearbook is aimed to be wide, including managers (needing contact addresses and access to information about Ada products), and software and systems engineers using Ada or those intending to use it, requiring detailed technical information about the language. Moreover, those new to Ada will be able to gain useful insights about the language and its evolution.

Reading material can be found in Part One, in addition to a general introduction, Ada UK sponsorship information and letters from Ada organisations. Subsequently, Part Two contains reference material including a list of validated Ada compilers, surveys of Ada related products (including training) and information on Ada bindings.

Readers with comments or suggestions should not hesitate to contact me at the address on the feedback page at the back of the book.

Finally, I would like to acknowledge and thank all those who contributed in some way to the Yearbook:

- To **Helen Byard** for her reports on the status of Ada UK sponsorship and for encouraging sponsors into sending me their sponsorship information.

- Within my department I would like to thank **Chris Loftus**, the editor of the Yearbook for the last two years, for his help and advice. Also, secretaries, **Ruth Scott**, **Menna Davies** and **Margaret Anthony** who keyboarded some of the material, and the computer support staff, **Tim Cairnes**, **Adrian Rixon** and **Thomas Lucas** who succeeded in keeping the machines running.

- Finally, I would like to thank the team at IOS Press for the quality of production of last year's publication, and, I hope you will agree, the present Yearbook also.

Mark Ratcliffe,
Aberystwyth

Part One

Reading material

1

Introduction

Some 16 years ago, the gnomic proclamation Green is Ada announced to the world that the language developed by Ichbiah and his colleagues had been chosen as the new DoD standard language. The similarly cabbalistic formula $X=5$ now heralds confirmation of the new Ada standard: Ada9X will be Ada95. This announcement ushers in a critical period in the life of Ada. There have been recent signs that the use of Ada has started to expand substantially. Either Ada95 will reinforce this trend, leading within the next two or three years to a very much wider use of Ada, or Ada will remain forever a language largely restricted to large systems, usually safety critical, for which high quality is mandated.

Why should we, the readers, the writers, and the editors of this book, care? Most of us come from the world of large systems. No one will prevent us from using Ada; indeed, it is likely to continue to be mandated for most, if not all, of the systems we are involved with. On a purely pragmatic level, of course, we should be concerned about the supply of Ada products. A major reason for the comparatively slow take-up of Ada has been the lack of bindings to other widely used products. The more widely used Ada becomes, the more supporting products will become available.

Much more important, however, is our belief that Ada is, of all the properly supported programming languages, the one most suited to the needs of the professional software developer; other things being equal, for a given expenditure of resources, the use of Ada will result in higher quality software than the use of any other programming language. The widespread use of Ada would show that commerce and industry are beginning to understand the need for high quality software and, at the same time, facilitate its production.

How far we are from a general public awareness of the importance of software quality is illustrated by a company that I recently came across. It produces automotive components, many of which contain embedded microprocessors. The software development group has no standards or procedures; all software is written in assembler; and management discourages staff from designing software before starting to code, on the grounds that they are wasting their time if they're not coding*. The company is accredited to ISO9001 but at no stage have the quality auditors visited the group or commented on its lack of standards and procedures. That such a company can exist and that a standards certification body should certify it show how far we have failed to convince society and perhaps our colleagues in other branches of engineering of the importance of software quality.

And we have also failed to persuade our colleagues that high quality systems cannot be built using low quality tools. We try to make the systems we build as nearly foolproof as possible but we build them with programming languages that invite the fool to indulge his folly. Our software may do a great deal to prevent pilot error but is often written in languages

---

*No kidding! And this is 1995.

that positively promote programmer error despite the fact that the pilots are often better trained than the programmers.

If Ada95 fails to become widely used it will not be for any technical failings. It will be because we, the software engineering profession, have failed. We shall have failed to make society understand the importance of software quality well enough to demand it. And we shall have failed to make our colleagues understand what is needed to achieve it.

To more domestic matters. Ada Language UK is delighted that Ada Europe has agreed to provide a copy of this 1995 Year Book, free of charge to all its members. At the same time, the production of the Year Book has now been properly integrated into the management structure of Ada UK, through an editorial committee; we hope that this will allow us to give our hard-working editors the support that they need but have so often lacked, while at the same time enabling us to improve the coverage and quality of the Year Book.

Frank Bott
University of Wales, Aberystwyth
Chairman, Year Book Editorial Committee

2

Ada UK sponsors

Sponsors of Ada UK are organisations who wish to be prominently associated with the aim of Ada UK to promote the effective use of the Ada programming language.

2.1 Alsys

Alsys
Partridge House
Newtown Road
Henley-on-Thames
Oxon
RG9 1EN
UK

Contact: Ian Campbell

Tel: +44 (0) 1491 579090
Fax: +44 (0) 1491 571866

Alsys was founded in 1980 by Jean Ichbiah following the selection of his team's design for the Ada language. The company has grown steadily and now has offices in USA, UK, France, Germany, Sweden and Japan. Alsys' global presence is augmented by a number of carefully selected distributor channels.

In 1991, Alsys was strategically acquired by Thomson-CSF becoming part of the CASE Division. At the end of 1992, Alsys merged with Telesoft to form the world's largest independent Ada products and services company. Alsys and Telesoft's Ada and CASE products and services are now supplied under the Alsys banner.

Alsys' product lines provide software solutions and tools for a wide variety of application domains including C3I systems, real-time embedded systems, mission critical systems, process control systems, business systems, avionics, aerospace, transportation, utilities, telecommunications and advanced computing architectures.

Ada Development Environments

Alsys offers a wide range of Ada development environments for a broad range of workstation and embedded architectures. Native environments are available for RISC workstations (HP 9000/700 & 800, SUN Sparc and IBM RS/6000), Intel based UNIX (including Solaris, SCO UNIX and LynxOS), Windows, Windows NT, DOS PCs and Digital VAX.

Cross environments target the Motorola MC680X0 and CPU32 families, Intel 80X86 family, MIPs, MIL-STD-1750A and Inmos transputer from a wide range of host platforms. Enabling technologies in the form of packages and bindings are also available to support host and target communication between processes, embedded file handling and interface to SQL databases, OSF X/Motif and POSIX.

Graphical User Interface Builder

In addition, Alsys offers TeleUSE, a graphical user interface (GUI) builder, which increases the productivity of developers to design, prototype, evaluate, code and maintain OSF/Motif based GUIs. TeleUSE/Ada is an optional product which can generate Ada code directly from the TeleUSE description of the application GUI for subsequent compilation.

Alsys also offers a range of services including Ada, X/Motif and product training courses and project consultancy.

Safety Critical Systems

The quality of safety-critical systems and product liability are issues focusing the attention of the Software Industry on the way in which software is produced. International standards organisations such as the BSI have been working on standards for the development and performance of safety-critical systems. Recognising and reacting to the needs of this market, Alsys can now offer a Certifiable Small Ada Run Time (CSMART) which has been tested and documented to a standard that is acceptable to certification authorities on both sides of the Atlantic. CSMART is currently available for Motorola and Intel processors and being used on a number of avionics and utilities applications.

Continuing our commitment to the Ada language, Alsys has been heavily involved in the Ada 95 language review process. Our knowledge and understanding of the new Ada 95 language has been instrumental in our ability to be the first Ada vendor to bring an Ada 95 featured Ada development environment, known as ObjectAda, to market.

2.2   BAeSEMA Ltd

BAeSEMA Ltd
Biwater House
Portsmouth Road
Esher
Surrey
KT10 9SJ
UK

Contact: Mike Christie

Tel: +44 (0) 1372 466660
Fax: +44 (0) 1372 466566

BAeSEMA was formed by British Aerospace and Sema Group in 1991, combining the Scientific and YARD Divisions of Sema Group with Dowty-Sema and staff from British Aerospace. BAeSEMA is a leading supplier of integrated systems, engineering and support services to a wide range of markets.

The 1500 staff of BAeSEMA have a unique mix of skills and experience proven across the world. These range from the core ship design skills of marine engineering and naval architecture to the experience and project management capability needed to support large scale developments. Our systems capabilities encompass systems engineering, advanced software development methods, structured design techniques and over 1000 man-years of Ada software development. We also possess skills in a wide range of engineering disciplines which provide design, management and consultancy to the oil and gas offshore industry, electricity generation, rail transport and large defence infrastructure projects.

Ada based command and control systems

BAeSEMA is a world leader in the design, development and supply of naval command systems, including the Submarine Command System (SMCS), to be fitted widely in the Royal Navy submarine flotilla, and the Surface Ship Command System (SSCS) for the new Royal Navy Type 23 Frigate. In addition to these current fits, studies for future ships and submarines are already underway.

Both SMCS and SSCS are distributed systems using a fibre optic LAN which connects server nodes and a variable number of intelligent display console nodes. Each node is itself a multiprocessor system and all the software for the system, over a million lines of code, is written in Ada. The server nodes are configured in master/slave pairs. The Ada software is designed so that the tasks on the slave can take over automatically, without a pause, in the event of a fault on the master, thus providing extremely high reliability.

These systems are based on a common Ada infrastructure, which has been produced by BAeSEMA to simplify the job of writing Ada software for distributed systems. Its features include:

- resilient message passing;

- real-time task synchronisation;

- distributed database;

- code generated Ada queries of the database;

- resilient transaction handling.

It was originally developed to run on Intel 386/486 processors with TeleSoft's Ada run-time executive, and BAeSEMA is now developing a version to provide these same real-time facilities on top of UNIX operating systems.

In the UNIX environment this infrastructure software is extended to link to a toolkit for providing Combat Systems displays on top of X-Windows. It also has the ability to link bespoke Ada software with Commercial-Off-The-Shelf (COTS) software.

Tactical support systems

For both the UK and foreign navies, BAeSEMA provides systems to evaluate the tactical implications of oceanographic and meteorological data. Many of these models have been written in Ada, and BAeSEMA's Naval Environmental Command Tactical Aid (NECTA) links these around a high performance Object-Oriented database, and X-Windows displays.

BAeSEMA also specialises in software intensive systems for communications, mine warfare systems and electronic warfare.

2.3   CADRE Technologies Ltd

CADRE

CADRE Technologies Ltd
Edenfield
London Road
Bracknell
Berkshire
RG12 2XH
UK

Contact: Joanne Cooling
           Support Manager

Tel: +44 (0) 1344 300003
Fax: +44 (0) 1344 360079

Team*work*

Thirteen years old in 1995, Cadre Technologies develop and market the Team*work* range
of Software Development Automation Solutions. Teamwork provides complete life cycle
support for the development of complex software systems in Ada, from conception and
requirements analysis to design, code generation and test.

Requirements Analysis

Team*work*/Analysis is a family of integrated solutions that support the critical aspects of
requirements analysis and functional specification for high performance multi-processing embedded or complex client server systems. It is based on three proven products. Team*work*/SA
is a powerful structured analysis tool which helps gather and analyse functional requirements.
The second, Team*work*/RT, is an extension to Team*work*/SA for control flow modelling of
event driven or real-time software. Finally, Team*work*/IM models entities, relationships and
attributes of data structures.

Dynamic Analysis

System performance is an important measure of a project's success. Estimating software
performance in a complex system is particularly challenging, because it often incorporates
distributed multi-processing architectures. Team*work*/Dynamic Analysis helps determine
system behaviour, estimate performance and conduct high level verification of specifications.

Requirements Management

Requirements are complex collections of textual descriptions; often ambiguous, rarely complete and frequently changing. DOORS - Dynamic Object Oriented Requirements System

- can help meet the challenge of ensuring the system developed meets the requirements by providing a structured requirements repository and facilities to map requirements onto project deliverables.

Ada Program Design

Ada is a language incorporating advanced programming features to support concepts such as multi-tasking and abstracted data types. Team*work*/Ada is specifically for Ada design.

Team*work*/Ada lets developers build Ada design elements graphically, capturing both system architecture and behaviour. Notation is based on Dr Buhr's Ada Structure Graphs (ASG). Graphic representation allows the user to minimise dependencies among components and avoid race and deadlock conditions between tasks.

Transition from Design to Ada Code

Keeping design representations in step with the related Ada code is a major challenge as developers iterate between design and coding. Team*work*/Ada incorporates design sensitive source code editing, code generation and automated capture of source within the design model.

Team*work*/DSE design sensitive editing capability allows users to develop Ada code within the context of the design developed using Team*work*/Ada. The source code generator then produces Ada code from the architectural designs. Finally, modifications made to the code within the debugging environment can be automatically captured as updates to the design model.

Object Oriented Analysis and Design

As the Ada 95 project comes to fruition, with support for object oriented programming concepts in the language, Cadre's ObjectTeam family provides full support for object oriented analysis and design. Two leading methods are supported; Shlaer Mellor OOA/Recursive Design and Rumbaugh *et al.* Object Modelling Technique.

The Team*work* Environment

All Cadre's Team*work* solutions work within a common tool environment, incorporating network based multi user client-server access to the design object repository. The tools use a graphical user interface common across all platforms, including DEC VMS & Ultrix, Solaris, HP-UX & Domain, IBM AIX and Silicon Graphics IRIX. Team*work*'s design object repository features an application programmable interface, facilitating integration of Team*work* to other tools and environments. The graphical user interface is extensible through the use of user defined menus.

2.4   Electronic Data Systems (EDS)

EDS
Pembroke House
Pembroke Broadway
Camberley
Surrey
GU15 3XD
UK

Contact: Dave Jacobs

Tel: +44 (0) 1276 415000
Fax: +44 (0) 1276 415333

EDS has been at the forefront of software engineering and languages technology since the late 1970s, during which time a range of effective products and services have been developed. The experience positions EDS as a reliable supplier of proven practical technology, in particular the XD Ada development environment and PORTOS, a fully-compliant PCTE implementation.

XD Ada – High Quality, Low Risk

Together with Digital Equipment Corporation, EDS has developed the world's premier family of Ada cross-development toolsets, XD Ada. Since its launch in 1989, XD Ada has offered the most productive development environment for the production of embedded Ada applications.

XD Ada relates directly to project requirements: its unmatched performance provides faster development turnaround; its completeness promotes good software engineering and provides comprehensive support. The net results are high quality, maintainable applications, increased programmer productivity and reduced development time-scales and risk.

XD Ada is based on proven components in use on major projects across the world. In Europe the product is the standard Ada development cross-compiler for the four-nation Eurofighter consortia. In the USA, it has been selected by Boeing for 777 and F-22 applications.

Integration

As a result of the close development relationship with Digital, XD Ada is fully integrated with Digital's OpenVMS operating system, DEC Ada the unmatched OpenVMS Debugger and the Digital DECset CASE tools, providing a unique and comprehensive software development environment. The product is also certified for use with Digital's ASD/SEE (Aerospace & Defence/Software Engineering Environment).

High Performance

XD Ada is targeted to the Motorola M68000 family (including the MC683xx microcontrollers) and the MIL-STD-1750A microprocessor architecture. A significant number of product options exist for further runtime support, for multiprocessor support and for emulator and simulator support.

XD Ada produces excellent code quality through the use of powerful global optimisation techniques. Real project use substantiates industry-accepted benchmark results and proves that XD Ada delivers outstanding performance.

PORTOS – The Open Repository Standard

Announced in conjunction with Digital Equipment Corporation and Sun Microsystems Computer Corporation last year, PORTOS from EDS is a high quality, portable and secure open repository implemented across a range of development platforms. In addition to providing a full implementation of the important ISO PCTE (Portable Common Tool Environment) standard, practical support and interfaces for other international standards such as CORBA and CDIF reduce the significant risks associated with large-scale software development, and offer cost and time to market savings to both tool developers and end users.

EDS has demonstrated industry-standard data and tool integration with PORTOS, in particular integrated with Digital's COHESIONworX multivendor UNIX software development environment.

For the first time, both tool developers and end users can develop a variety of systems in a platform independent manner. PORTOS offers the freedom to pick and choose development tools to suit business goals without locking in to proprietary systems and without abandoning previous investments.

Customer support

EDS' Ada production and development activity is fully supported by a support services operation, with on-line and telephone support. Support packages are tailored to meet a customer's needs and can include areas such as training, installation, target re-configuration and project validation.

EDS

EDS is the world's leader in providing information technology and management services, with more than 30 years experience. In 1993, EDS reported revenues of $8.6b and currently employs more than 70,000 people in 35 countries, applying information technology to meet the needs of businesses and governments around the world.

2.5   Encore Computer (UK) Limited

COMPUTER

Encore Computer (UK) Limited
Marlborough House
Mole Business Park
Leatherhead
Surrey
KT22 7BA
UK

Contact: Vincent Rich

Tel. +44 (0) 1372 363363
Fax. +44 (0) 1372 362926

Encore Computer is the dominant supplier of high performance real-time Ada systems. Encore products include super-minicomputers, operating systems, Ada programming support environments and a wide range of interface cards and supporting software.

Encore offer two complementary families of real-time computers; the RSX proprietary architecture computer and the Infinity R/T real-time open systems based computer.

The Infinity R/T comprises three models; two are based on the Motorola 88000 family of microprocessors and the third is based on the Digital Alpha AXP processor. Motorola based systems incorporate up to four 88110 processors per node and up to eight nodes can be tightly coupled using Encores' patented Reflective Memory system.

Multiple processors within each node can concurrently execute multiple Ada tasks comprising a single Ada program. If a processor becomes blocked during execution of a task then that processor will be context switched to the next highest priority Ada task. The Encore Ada runtime system provides automatic load balancing, a non-blocking tasking model and direct connection of interrupts to Ada tasks. Multiple nodes can be used to construct high availability systems.

Encore Alpha AXP systems utilise 150 MHz and 275 MHz processors. Up to eight processors can be tightly coupled resulting in peak processing performance of 4400 MIPS (Millions of Instructions Per Second). The Encore computer architecture incorporates large cache memories, wide data busses and an I/O co-processor which offloads interrupt processing from the Alpha processor. Each Alpha processor is provided with dedicated SCSI, VME and PCI busses for maximum I/O bandwidth.

Encore Alpha systems are binary compatible with Digital Equipment OSF/1 based Alpha systems and support both the Verdix Ada Development System (VADS) and the Digital Ada compiler.

Encore Computer is a part of the $15 billion Tokyo based Japan Energy Corporation and operates sales and support offices throughout North America, Europe and the Pacific

rim. Encore computers and Ada related products are used in simulation, energy management, transportation, aerospace, military and research applications worldwide. For further
information please contact Encore Computer at Leatherhead.

2.6   Ferranti Naval Systems

Ferranti Naval Systems
A division of GEC-Marconi Limited
Mountbatten House
Jackson Close
Cosham
Hampshire
PO6 1UD
UK

Contact: John Bennett

Tel: +44 (0) 1705 383101
Fax: +44 (0) 1705 326589

The company will be moving to a new site during the spring of 1995 to:
Fitzherbert Road
Farlington
Hampshire

Tel: +44 (0) 1705 701701

Ferranti Naval Systems (FNS) is a leader in the design, development, production and supply of Maritime Command and Control Systems and is a recently acquired division of GEC Marconi Limited.

For 30 years the company has been evolving command and control systems that gather, organise and correlate large quantities of complex, multi-source data. Systems present a clear tactical picture to the ship's commanders in real time, before recommending and initiating split second, critical responses. Ferranti systems integrate fully with other fully autonomous sensors and weapons, dramatically enhancing the effectiveness of the management system itself and that of the sub-systems by two way sharing and co-ordination of data. Ferranti currently has over 100 systems in service in several navies worldwide, including Korea, Brazil, Kenya, New Zealand and Egypt.

Ferranti command systems are operational within the UK Royal Navy, on the Invincible class CVSG Aircraft Carriers, the Type 42 Air Defence Destroyers (ADAWS), Type 22 ASW and multi purpose Frigates (CACS) and the Hunt Class Mine Countermeasures Vessels (CAAIS). Additionally, Ferranti systems are also fitted to UK Royal Naval nuclear SSN/SSBN (Polaris) submarines and the 4 conventional diesel boats. Recently, the company has won competitions to fit ADAWS colour command systems to the new Royal Naval Helicopter support vessel (LPH), HMS Ocean and to the Landing Dock Replacement Vessels (LPD(R)) which are currently being procured.

Within the command systems arena, the company has developed applications for the UK MoD, using the latest Artificial Intelligence techniques, including Data Fusion for Tactical Picture Compilation and Intelligent Knowledge Based techniques for Tactical Threat Evaluation and Weapon Assignment. These techniques are implemented in Ada. The Company is also employing new Ada code, interfaced with legacy languages, to provide evolutionary enhancement and lifetime extension to proven, in service systems.

In addition to command systems products, Ferranti also carries out Prime Contract Project Management on behalf of customers. These programmes range from feasibility studies to full scale development and production.

2.7   Harris Computer Systems Ltd

Harris Computer Systems Ltd
Riverside Way
Watchmoor Park
Camberley
Surrey
GU15 3YD
UK

Contact: Andrew Clarke
           UK Marketing Manager

Tel: +44 (0) 1276 686886
Fax: +44 (0) 1276 678733

Harris Computer Systems Limited is the UK subsidiary of Harris Computer Systems Corporation which designs, manufactures, distributes and supports the Night Hawk family of UNIX-based real-time computer systems for simulation, data acquisition and secure computing applications.

Harris Computer Systems is committed to long-term support of its customer base. This commitment ensures that Harris will continue to provide the highest quality products and support today and in the future. Night Hawk systems were the first open-architecture real-time computer systems. Designed around industry standards, this open architecture prevents customers from being locked into proprietary solutions. Adherence to standards ensures compatibility between Night Hawk and other standards-based systems, system components and software manufactured by different vendors. The Night Hawk family consists of the Series 5000 (MC88110 RISC processor) and the Series 6000 (PowerPC RISC processor) multiprocessor computer systems. The UNIX operating system used by the Night Hawk is compliant with the POSIX 1003.1 and POSIX 1003.1b-1993 Real-time standards. Harris is also compliant with the POSIX 1003.5 Ada Binding standard which defines an operating system interface for Ada programmers.

Real-time Ada Tools include:

- Real-time data monitoring;

- Real-time Ada task monitoring;

- Real-time event tracing;

- Harris Frequency Based Scheduler (FBS);

- Performance monitor.

A certified E3, F-B1 secure solution which provides a Secure UNIX operating system, a Secure Local Area Network and Secure X Windows is available.

Harris Ada Programming Support Environment

The Ada environment includes the Harris Ada Programming Support Environment (HAPSE) which consists of the Harris Basic Ada Runtime System (BART) and an Ada Real-time Multi-processing System (ARMS), an executive designed for critical real-time tasking applications. ARMS provides a real-time multiprocessor/parallel execution environment for standard Ada tasking as defined by ANSI/MIL-STD-1815A.

ARMS implements all tasks as individual threads of execution sharing a common physical memory image. Since each task can execute on different processors within the Night Hawk computer, ARMS provides true concurrence among tasks. ARMS is hosted on the Night Hawk real-time UNIX operating system, CX/UX, thereby combining the advantages of standard UNIX system computing with parallel run-time capabilities. Additionally, ARMS reduces software development efforts by implementing standard Ada tasking for multiple processors without imposing system-dependent methodologies on application designers. For user convenience, ARMS provides automatic task load balancing and assumes full utilisation of all available CPUs. For greater real-time control, ARMS also provides pragmas for explicit control of CPU assignment, task prioritisation and task time slice duration.

Ada Bindings

As well as the POSIX 1003.5 Ada bindings, other bindings include, AXI, Ada X-Windows and Motif bindings. AXI is an Ada interface to the X window system that allows Ada Programmers full use of X-Window's display services and the graphical user interface (GUI) standard. This means that Ada applications with graphics requirements can interface to the X window system through an interface that is completely Ada.

Night Hawk systems provide the NightStar toolkit for software development and execution which compliment advanced-technology compilers, the Harris Ada Programming Support Environment (HAPSE) and graphics and database systems.

One tool within the NightStar toolkit is NightTrace. In an application that has been instrumented with NightTrace, the current value of a variable or expression can be logged at every point where a NightTrace trace-event-logging routine has been inserted. Using a GUI display tool this provides a complete and accurate picture of the application. NightTrace is also an information analysis tool. The trace-event logs that are created when the application is running can be analyzed textually and graphically. Within the Ada tasking executive, NightTrace enables a wide range of tasking information such as data on tasking rendezvous, delays, interrupts, signals and exceptions to be recorded. Support tools within ARMS result in a high-level graphical picture of application tasking information. In keeping with Harris' pre-planned product improvement philosophy, Harris Ada solutions will follow advances in machine and operating system architecture as the Night Hawk family of high-performance computers continues to evolve.

An open systems approach to providing solutions reduces both the cost and time associated with developing and maintaining real-time programs.

2.8   IDE UK Ltd

**INTERACTIVE
DEVELOPMENT
ENVIRONMENTS**

Interactive Development Environments (IDE) UK Ltd
1 Stirling House
Stirling Road
The Surrey Researh Park
Guildford
Surrey
GU2 5RF
UK

Contact: Adrian Jones

Tel: + 44 (0) 1483 579000
Fax: + 44 (0) 1483 31272
Email: adrian@ideuk.co.uk

Software through Pictures (StP) is a family of graphical products that enable the use of Structured and Object-Oriented software methodologies in the development and implementation of software applications. StP tools are built around a core technology that centralises all of the information about an application. This unique architecture therefore provides all StP products with common features, functionality and benefits such as:

- An intuitive interface that is consistent across the whole family of products;

- A multi-user shared repository, so all editors are fully integrated;

- Customisable editor technology that allows the user to tailor or extend the tools to improve their own development process;

- Automatic documentation which uses a scripting language to produce top quality customer presentable documentation;

- Extendible syntax, semantic and consistency checking;

- An open architecture that allows other tools to be easily integrated. In fact, many of the most popular tools have already been integrated.

Software through Pictures for the Object Modelling Technique (StP/OMT) and for Booch (StP/Booch) are a set of graphical editors that help the user design and implement object-oriented applications. StP "understands" object technology along with the complete OMT or Booch diagrams and notation, so it assists in developing a complete and coherent application:

- Helping to define requirements early in the lifecycle with models that mirror the real world and a requirements editor that can capture the business requirements and link them to design objects;

- StP/OMT and StP/Booch are faithful to the object paradigm supporting encapsulation, inheritance and polymorphism;

- StP/OMT integrates all the fundamental OMT models including the later additions of "Use Cases" and event trace scenarios;

- Both StP/OMT and StP/Booch share common functionality and features, and are well prepared for future methods development.

Code Generation

To support user needs and the application needs, both StP/OMT and StP/Booch offer several options for incremental/automatic code generation:

- Support for Ada 83 by generating Ada package specifications from object models. By using object concepts, StP ensures that Ada's unique language features are exploited to the greatest benefit. And when when the time comes, transition to Ada 95 will be easier.

- Support for ANSI 3.0, ARM and cfront C++. Support for class templates is provided, and the user has many options for naming interface and definition files as well as selecting where inline code is generated.

- Support for ParcPlace Smalltalk code generation and capture, allowing a full round trip from code to design or vice versa.

Automatic Checking and consistency

StP/OMT and StP/Booch store the semantics of all diagrams in a multi-user, shared repository built upon a commercial DBMS. Using the repository as an integration link, both products assure the correctness and consistency of user models, so the user is free to focus exclusively on the problem domain.

StP/OMT will also assure consistency throughout the user model by transporting items such as events defined within scenario diagrams to state transitions within the dynamic model.

Specification based testing is also integrated into the architecture allowing for automatic test case generation.

Documentation

All StP products include an automatic documentation facility that allows the user to target quality documentation including text, graphic, tabular and external infromation, towards popular DTP products. Pre-written templates already exist for the generation of 2167A documentation, mandated by the US Department of Defense.

2.9   i-Logix UK Ltd

i-Logix UK Ltd
1 Cornbrash Park
Bumpers Way
Chippenham
Wilts
SN14 6RA
UK

Contact: Harry Hughes

Tel: +44 (0) 1249 446448
Fax: +44 (0) 1249 447373

i-Logix was founded in 1986, evolving out of the consulting and development efforts of two world renowned experts in systems design specification, Dr Amir Pnueli and Dr David Harel of the Weizmann Institute of Science in Israel.

Over the past seven years, i-Logix has developed a significant customer base in industries such as electronics, communications, transportation, aerospace and defence, and government, including companies such as: IBM, Hewlett-Packard, Fujitsu, Motorola, AT&T, Ford Motor Company, Lockheed, NASA, British Rail, Rover, BMW, Siemens and British Aerospace.

To meet the needs of its customer base, i-Logix has created a suite of system design automation tools that enable the design engineer to create system level graphical representations that are mathematically rigorous and that can be analysed and simulated. As a result, the underlying mathematically formalised models can also be used to automatically generate Ada, C, VHDL and Verilog HDL code.

Statemate

Statemate allows design engineers to graphically capture their design specifications and requirements. Once captured, the design can be easily simulated and analysed allowing rapid iteration between design capture, simulation, analysis and modification.

i-Logix's tools also allow the designer to create a soft prototype of the design. This allows customers to validate the design and concept at the earliest possible point in the design process, in order to demonstrate system concepts to end users prior to actual, detailed development and implementation.

Within the Statemate family of products, i-Logix has developed Express-Ada, Express-C and ExpressV-HDL. These tools use the graphical models to generate the code needed to move downstream in the design process — through either software or hardware. Once the design engineer is satisfied with a graphical model provided by these tools, the code generator can automatically generate Ada and C code for software design, or VHDL and Verilog for hardware design. This code is correct by construction. By using i-Logix's products, customers are experiencing between a 2-to-1 to 7-to-1 decrease in the time necessary to get from concept to design and/or code. Users can add code from existing designs to the automatically generated code as well as optimise the code after it has been generated.

Beyond generating code, i-Logix has formed partnerships with leading industry vendors in both the EDA and CASE markets. These vendors include: Synopsys, Cadence Design, Mentor Graphics, Viewlogic Systems and Cadre Technologies, Inc. i-Logix uses these partnerships to maintain the insight necessary to generate code that is optimised to the design engineer's specific EDA or CASE environment, allowing the designer to take advantage of the powerful features of each tool.

Statemate Analyzer: Provides tools for the creation, simulation and analysis of an executable system specification. It includes three graphic editors, one for each graphical view of the specification model (Activity chart, State chart, Module chart). The tools allow the dynamic analysis and behavioural validation of the specification model once it is created. It includes interactive and batch simulation features, dynamic reachability, deadlock and non-determinism testing.

Statemate PrototyperAda: Is a tool for the creation of an executable specification model and the automatic rapid prototyping of the systems under development. The tool translates the Statemate model into an Ada program that can be compiled and run on the workstation or in the target environment. It includes the Panel Graphics Editor (PGE) which allows the engineer to build a graphic mock-up of the system being developed and interactively link to and "test-drive" the specification model using the Prototyper generated code.

ExpressAda: Is a single user toolset for the creation of a graphical executable system specification and the complete simulation, analysis, prototyping and Ada code generation for the system under development incorporating all the functionality of Statemate Analyzer and Prototyper.

Statemate Documenter: Is a tool for creating documentation from the specification model by assembling text and graphics to a user-specified template or a pre-defined DOD-STD-2167A template (provided). It includes Statemate Dataport, which is a subroutine library for extracting all entities defined in a Statemate database. It allows users to write programs and to extract and transfer information to other applications.

Statemate Requirements Traceability (RT): Is a tool within Statemate 5.0 that is tightly integrated into the Statemate Environment. RT allows users to take textual requirements in electronic format and have them automatically entered into RT. Users can create, edit, browse and link derived as well as original requirements to any design element in a Statemate model.

Bi-Directional Interfaces to Software Design tools: With Statemate 5.0 i-Logix also introduces a bi-directional interface between Statemate and Team*work* SA/RT tools. This capability allows users to move Team*work* models into Statemate for simulation and code generation, as well as allowing users to move from System Engineering with Statemate to Software Development with Team*work*.

ExpressV-HDL: Is a tool for the creation and analysis of graphical behavioural models for the system ASIC or circuit being developed. It then automatically generates IEEE-1076 VHDL code or Verilog code that is optimised for leading simulation and synthesis tools.

2.10   IPL

Information Processing Limited
Eveleigh House
Grove Street
Bath
BA1 5LR
UK

Contact: Mr Ian Gilchrist
                 Software Product Consultant

Tel: +44 (0) 1225 444888
Fax: +44 (0) 1225 444400

IPL is one of the UK's leading software houses, with a turnover of £9 million and a professional complement of over 200 staff. The Company has supplied Ada-based software systems for defence, aerospace and a variety of commercial applications.

IPL has been using Ada since 1984, and to date almost one half of the Company's technical staff have had experience of Ada developments. The skills available to clients range from programming to project management, with all staff available on a fixed price or a time and materials basis.

Consultancy services

IPL's consultants have extensive Ada project experience. Clients have used this in a wide range of Ada-related assignments:

- Feasibility studies;

- Proposal preparation and tender evaluation;

- Requirements definition;

- Methodology and tool evaluation;

- Project audits;

- Definition of standards and procedures.

The European Space Agency commissioned IPL to define a dynamically reconfigurable distributed Ada architecture for the COLUMBUS manned space station. A prototype of the distributed architecture was successfully implemented in collaboration with Matra Espace, prime contractor for the COLUMBUS Data Management System.

Implementation services

IPL supplies experienced Ada staff and complete Ada systems to major defence and aerospace contractors and directly to procurement agencies.

The Company's excellent reputation within the defence industry is based on the successful completion of complex operation systems, engineered to the highest software quality and safety standards.

Among the numerous Ada-based systems which IPL has helped develop are:

- A global positioning system (GPS) satellite receiver;

- Military C3I graphics workstations;

- A low-level reconnaissance image processing and analysis system;

- A secure communications terminal;

- An electronic warfare passive sensing system;

- An aircraft engine monitoring system.

AdaTEST

IPL's commitment to quality has led to the development of tools to support the verification and testing of software. Among these is AdaTEST; the UK's leading Ada verification tool, which is now used by many major Ada developers.

AdaTEST provides an integrated set of facilities for the dynamic testing, coverage analysis and static analysis of Ada. The tool has been designed to support both host-based and cross-development environments.

AdaTEST can be used in the verification of any Ada software, from a single procedure to a complex multi-tasking system. The tool is being used successfully to support high integrity and safety critical Ada development to standards such as: Def Stan 00-55, RTCA/DO-178B, IEC/WG9 and RIA 23.

Clients

While IPL's Ada experience is rooted firmly in defence applications, the Company has recently been involved in Ada developments for commercial, safety-critical and high-integrity systems.

Organisations, who have used IPL's Ada expertise include the Civil Aviation Authority, Computing Devices Corporation, DESC, European Space Agency (ESA), Matra, MOD, Nuclear Electric, Thorn EMI and Westinghouse Brake & Signal.

Software quality

IPL's approach to software development is specified within the Company's Quality Management System (QMS). The QMS lays down procedures and recommendations for all stages of the software life-cycle to ensure high and consistent standards.

IPL has been accredited to ISO 9001 (under TickIT), and AQAP 1/13.

2.11   Integral Solutions Ltd

Integral Solutions Ltd.
3 Campbell Court
Bramley
Basingstoke
RG26 5EG
UK

Contact: Ben Rabau

Tel: + 44 (0) 1256 882028
Fax: + 44 (0) 1256 882182
Email: benr@isl.co.uk

Integral Solutions Limited was founded in 1989 with the aim of becoming the UK's leading independent supplier of advanced software technology.

Advanced software technologies, for example, Object Oriented Programming, promise dramatic increases in capability and productivity, but early products were expensive and difficult to integrate with existing systems and development practice. Yet business and research users are making unprecedented demands for IT systems which are more responsive and adaptable, more robust, and able to tackle ever more complex problems. With the combination of new technologies, and ever increasing on-desk power, traditional models of software development are giving way to highly interactive styles incorporating rapid prototyping, animation, use of declarative and higher-level languages, and incremental development.

Today ISL is meeting these users' demands by providing business-oriented applications which encapsulate advanced software, and power development tools which allow advanced technologies to be deployed cost-effectively.

ISL is committed to ongoing technology transfer, through investing in collaborative R&D projects, by discovering "best of breed" products, and bringing new results from academic and industrial laboratories into the market place.

ISL is headed by Alan Montgomery whose Ada experience dates back to the days when Ada was known as Green. The company has unique strengths in integrating Ada's rigorous engineering approach with advanced symbolic, logic, or list-processing languages required to add "intelligence" to Ada Systems.

ISL's Ada products:

- SunSoft's leading Ada language system for the SPARC platform. SPARCompiler Ada is a highly optimised Ada compiler that complies with ANSI/MIL-STD-1815A and is validated by the Ada Joint Program Office. It includes advanced features such as the sharing of DIANA (Descriptive Intermediate Attributed Notation for Ada) information across multiple source files and dynamic linking of shared system libraries.

- SPARCworks/iMPact Ada provides true concurrent Ada tasking, even on non- multi-processing systems by simply recompiling a standard, portable Ada source. SPARC-works/iMPact Ada extends SPARCworks and SPARCompiler functionality with support for Solaris threads.

- SPARCworks/Ada enhances productivity by speeding and simplifying the task programmers do most. The symbolic debugger provides a non-intrusive Ada model that allows programmers to walk through code and examine data structures. It uses DIANA-based information eliminating the need for debug options on the compiler. The LRMtool offers full text search and hypertext browsing of the Ada Language Reference Manual.

- SPARCompiler Ada Libraries include STANDARD, XView, X, Xt, strings, I/O, floating point maths and UNIX system calls.

- SunSoft WorkShop for Ada is an integrated suite of tools designed to speed software development for individuals and teams. It includes SPARCworks/Ada, SPAR-Cworks/iMPact Ada tools, SPARCompiler Ada and ANSI C language systems and SPARCworks/TeamWare code management tools.

ISL's other flagship products include:

- ISS, a world-class reactive scheduling and simulation system for semiconductor wafer fabrication, and similar demanding manufacturing applications. ISS is used by leading manufacturers, and exploits C++ object programming and ISO standards-based factory modelling.

- Clementine, the first data-mining tool designed for use by business professionals. In data-mining sophisticated analysis techniques help users to discover high-value knowledge buried in high-volume data. Clementine's visual programming approach makes it as simple to learn and use as a spreadsheet.

- Poplog and the Integral Toolset. Poplog is ideal for complex applications in which different components require different techniques such as object orientation, logic programming, pattern-matching, symbolic reasoning, graphics, or machine learning.

- SunSoft Development Tools. ISL is a UK distributor of the SPARCworks toolsets for C, C++, FORTRAN, and Pascal, and also for Prolog by BIM. Each of these products products offers the highest performance on SPARC platforms.

- SunSoft Solaris for x86 Development Tools. ISL is also a distributor of the Solaris x86 Operating System as well as the ProWorks toolsets for C, C++ and FORTRAN. With this ISL brings 32-bit UNIX performance to the Intel PC's.

ISL backs its products with the highest quality service based on in-depth knowledge of the products and technologies we offer. This includes bespoke applications development, training, and support and maintenance services to a world-wide user base.

ISL's 400-strong client list includes DRA, Rolls Royce, BAe, GEC Marconi, BT, Alsthom, Thompson, EDS, GEC Plessey Semiconductors and Philips.

2.12   Integrated Systems Inc Ltd

Integrated Systems Inc. Ltd.
Gatehouse
Fretherne Road
Welwyn Garden City
Hertfordshire
AL8 6NS
UK

Contact: Hamid Mirab

Tel: + 44 (0) 1707 331199
Fax: + 44 (0) 1707 391108

Integrated Systems Inc. is the leading provider of control and embedded software design tools used for real world applications. The company's MATRIXx Product Family offers a complete graphical solution for rapidly designing, simulating and testing microprocessor-based control systems. The pSOSystem real-time operating system environment has gained market share through expediting development of embedded software-based end products.

Integrated Systems Inc. focuses on six world-wide embedded system markets: aerospace, automotive, communications, multimedia/entertainment, office/retail automation and industrial process control.

MATRIXx Product Family: Offers the most advanced, high performance products for systems design available today. Integrated Systems provides a complete end-to-end environment for capturing ideas using graphical block diagrams, analysing and simulating them to eliminate errors and testing them on real-time hardware to guarantee performance.

Xmath: Design & Analysis - Xmath software is an advanced open architecture mathematical analysis and visualisation tool with object oriented scripting language, programmable graphical user interface, 2-D colour graphics and windowed interface. Modules include: Control Design, Robust Control, Optimization, Signal Analysis, Model Reduction, Interactive Control Design and Interactive System Identification.

SystemBuild: Modelling & Simulation - SystemBuild software is a graphical programming and simulation environment which accelerates the design and debugging of both linear and non-linear dynamic systems. Based on block diagramming paradigm with hierarchical structuring, the SystemBuild environment offers a library of over 100 predefined building blocks, as well as the capability to define your own. Using the mouse driver editor, a user can quickly build a model, simulate it and verify the results. Modules include: RT/Fuzzy, RT/Expert, Interactive Animation, HyperBuild and State Transition Diagram.

AutoCode: Real-Time Code Generator - AutoCode software automatically translated SystemBuild block diagrams into a real-time source code implementation. Any continuous, discrete or hybrid system can be converted to standard C or Ada source code.

DocumentIt: Automatic Documentation Generator - DocumentIt software automatically generates fast, accurate, high-quality documentation from SystemBuild models.

RealSim: Rapid Prototyping & Implementation System - The RealSim real-time hardware platform features one or more high performance CPUs integrated with analog and digital I/O to allow any SystemBuild model to be run in real-time and interface to the outside world. A hardware connections editor provides a simple, flexible methods of assigning inputs and outputs and the Interactive Animation (IA) module provides a graphical interface to monitor and control the operation of the model running on the RealSim system. Communication between the host workstation and RealSim hardware is via ethernet. This provides for downloading the model, uploading acquired data and interaction with the model through the IA module.

pSOSystem Product Family: Is grounded on an integrated software component architecture which provides outstanding performance, bullet-proof reliability and supple flexibility. Individual components, grouped around real-time kernels, connectivity facilities and development tools can be collected into families, suites or entire development/deployment environments. Through this building block approach pSOSystem can scale to meet application needs from minimal resource stand-alone devices to complex object-oriented distributed systems. Since all pSOSystem components are small and light, they integrated cleanly and efficiently into tight embedded spaces.

pSOSystem is complete, including kernel, networking, file system, distributed systems, graphics and development system components. Users can create all species of embedded systems working from within a single, scaleable product line. In addition pSOSystems pARTNERS+ third party products program offers developers and array of pSOSystem-compatible hardware and software from a blue ribbon list of independent vendors.

2.13 Program Analysers Ltd

Program Analysers

Program Analysers Limited/LDRA
56A Northbrook Street
Newbury
Berkshire
RG13 1AN
UK

Contact: Jim Kelly

Tel: +44 (0) 1635 528 828
Fax: +44 (0) 1635 528 657
Email: sales@ldra.com

Program Analysers is part of the LDRA Group of companies who develop, market and support the code analysis toolset - LDRA*Testbed*. LDRA's vast wealth of experience in the field of software testing, having produced Software Testing Tools for over twenty years, can also be utilised through other services, such as consultancy and training courses.

LDRA*Testbed*

LDRA*Testbed* is at the forefront of quality software testing, available on all major platforms and analysing eleven major languages both statically and dynamically. LDRA*Testbed* is highly flexible and offers incomparable support in testing strategies taking host/target testing, real-time testing, unit testing, regression testing, *etc*. in its stride. All the accumulated test results can be easily understood and communicated to management, or international regulatory bodies through either textual reports, export file, or LDRA*Testbed*'s graphics package. Graphics currently available on LDRA*Testbed* implementations include: histograms; Active/Static/Dynamic Flowgraphs; Call Trees And Kiviat Diagrams. These facilities allow users to analyse the information on source code effortlessly, and allows instant visual assimilation of metrics, test coverage, adherence to a quality model, and all important code visualisation.

   LDRA*Testbed* also offers extensive documentation of the internal workings of source code including data flow, unreachability, procedure interfaces, structured programming verification, *etc*. This makes the tool much more than a simple pass/fail facility (although this is available), therefore offering developers and managers alike, the code analysis facilities they require, either at unit, system or sub-system level.

DO178B Coverage and Validation Requirements.

LDRA*Testbed* offers analysis facilities to allow testing to the DO178B and other standards. In addition to LDRA*Testbed*'s standard facilities, *TBsafe*, can be purchased to test high integrity code to the highest safety critical standards. Subcondition coverage, variable dependency checking, enforcement of safe subsets, and exact semantic analysis all mean that LDRA*Testbed* has the most comprehensive set of analysis methods available.

Test Harness Generation with *TBrun*.

TBrun allows the execution of individual source code modules or units and organises both the test data and corresponding results to simplify both unit and regression testing. *TBrun* may be utilised for either black box or white box testing.

LDRA Dual System for Valid Ada.

High integrity Ada code is often well tested, but today's highly optimising compilers can alter code functionality to an extent that the machine code requires testing again. LDRA*Testbed* can be used to prove equivalence and that all test paths have been identified and tested. LDRA's Dual System is the only product available to test functionality has not been altered. This level of testing is now a requirement of DO178B.

2.14   Program Validation Ltd

Program Validation Ltd
26 Queen's Terrace
Southampton
Hants
SO1 1BQ
UK

Contact: Dr. Bernard Carre

Tel: +44 (0) 1703 330001
Fax: +44 (0) 1703 230805

Program Validation Ltd specialises in languages, methods and tools for the development and verification of high-integrity software. Founded in 1983 by researchers from the University of Southampton after many years of successful collaboration with the Royal Signals and Radar Establishment in Malvern, PVL has played a pioneering role in the application of formal methods in industry and enjoys a worldwide reputation for its expertise.

Activities

PVL maintains its position of excellence in the field through a balanced programme of consultancy on industrial problems, research on rigorous program construction and verification methods, development of software tools and training:

- *Preparation of Standards for Safety-Critical Systems:* PVL has participated in the production of guidelines and standards for various organisations, e.g. the International Atomic Energy Agency and the Civil Aviation Authority, and under the EEC DRIVE programme.

- *Consultancy:* PVL provides advice on all aspects of high-integrity system development, from the choice of specification and design methods, programming languages and target processors, to code verification techniques. PVL assists in the preparation and assessment of formal specifications.

- *Software Validation:* PVL undertakes independent verification and validation of software on behalf of end-users. A substantial part of this work is machine-assisted formal verification of code.

- *Software Tools:* PVL produces and supports tools for high-integrity software development, in particular the SPADE program analysis tools, the SPADE Proof Checker, the SPARK (Ada subset) Examiner and tools ancillary to these.

- *Training:* PVL provides training in software engineering using the SPARK Ada subset, and in the formal specification, flow analysis and verification of SPARK programs. Courses are often tailored to meet clients' particular requirements.

Application areas in which PVL's services have been used include aerospace, railway signaling, energy, automobiles, medical equipment and banking.

SPARK

SPARK is an unambiguous sub-language of Ada, supplemented by annotations (formal comments), for high-integrity programming. It retains considerable expressive power but it has relatively simple semantics: SPARK includes the packages, library units, private types, unconstrained arrays and functions with structured results of Ada, but excludes its access types, generic units, user-defined exceptions and tasks. The annotation system of SPARK eliminates language insecurities; it also allows the inclusion in program texts of design information and formal specifications. A formal definition of SPARK is being constructed by PVL, under contract to the Defence Research Agency.

The use of SPARK is supported by a software tool, the SPARK Examiner. As well as checking conformance to the rules of SPARK, the Examiner facilitates systematic design and implementation of SPARK programs, their static path analysis (as specified in the MoD Interim Defence Standard 00-55), and formal code verification. SPARK is employed in major projects, both civil and military. Use of the SPARK Examiner is mandated by Eurofighter Jagdflugzeug GmbH for all its Risk Class 1 (safety-critical) software.

2.15   Rational Software Corporation

Rational Software Corporation
Olivier House
18 Marine Parade
Brighton
East Sussex
BN2 1TL
UK

Contact: Ian Pascoe

Tel: +44 (0) 1273 624814
Fax: +44 (0) 1273 624364

Rational Software Corporation is a publicly quoted company, which was formed in April
1994 from the merger of the former Rational and Verdix corporations. The world's leading
Ada vendor, Rational's mission is to provide innovative software engineering products, com-
plemented by professional services and support, to companies whose commercial success is
dependent upon software-intensive systems.

Rational's proven approach, supported by technically advanced products, consultancy and
training, has consistently improved the productivity of development teams whilst increasing
quality, reliability and maintainability of the resultant software systems.   Use of the OO
paradigm allied to an iterative process model has enabled Rational to build and deliver
products comprising more than two million lines of Ada code.

Customers are counted amongst the largest aerospace, commercial and government organisations in Europe, the USA and the Asia-Pacific region. Rational's products are field-proven
through use on many of the world's most challenging Ada projects. Lockheed chose Rational
as the core development facility for NASA's Space Station Freedom; IBM chose the Rational
environment for development of the UK CAA's NERC air traffic control system; CelsiusTech
in Sweden has successfully developed a profitable line-of-business command and control
system using Ada and the Rational environment.

Apex

Rational Apex is an innovative software engineering toolset which is hosted on Digital's
Alpha/OSF1, Hewlett Packard's 9000, IBM's RS/6000 and Sun's SparcStation platforms.
Apex provides an integrated, interactive, distributed software development environment for
total lifecycle control of Ada projects. Apex enables projects to reduce development time
by providing the essential syntactic and semantic links which provide support for the logical
decomposition of the system, incremental recompilation and automatic rebuilding without
loss of visibility or control. Apex supports industry standard protocols which simplifies

integration with new and existing project tools. Extensions include support for the new Ada 95 language standard and mixed language working. When used in conjunction with the VADS range of cross compilers, Apex provides unparalleled support for the development of embedded systems targeted to an extensive range of microprocessors. Use of the Compilation Integrator allows any third-party compiler to be integrated with, and controlled by, the Apex environment.

VADS Compilers

Rational's VADS product line is an extensive family of mature, production-quality optimising Ada cross-compilers and related tools which support the production, debugging, tuning and delivery of sophisticated applications. Built from a common code base, all VADS products offer a common user interface and functionality across an unequalled range of host and target combinations. Where appropriate, VADS can be offered with the VxWorks runtime executive to support applications running on off-the-shelf VME hardware.

Rose

Rational Rose is a graphical software-engineering tool that supports object-oriented development. Rose/Ada enables Ada code to be generated from the design model and supports reverse engineering of an existing Ada application into a module diagram, based on the Booch notation. Using Ada representations stored within the Apex environment, Rose/Ada assists in the creation of a valid and consistent software architecture and will support re-use of existing software components. Planned extensions include support for the OMT method, as pioneered by Jim Rumbaugh, a new industry-standard notation which will result from joint studies to be completed by Booch and Rumbaugh, and the new Ada 95 language standard.

SoDA

Lifecycle support for the documentation process is provided through the SoDA tool, which substantially reduces the effort required to complete quality documentation. SoDA can be customised to support any documentation standard and works with tools supporting any programming language. Whereas the traditional methods of producing software documentation are both labour intensive and result in inconsistent representations, SoDA uses hypertext traversal techniques to ensure automatic traceability and on-line access into the development domain.

Professional Services

Rational has extensive experience in assisting and training software developers to apply object-oriented techniques and realise the benefits to be gained from adopting Rational's iterative development process. Rational can offer consultancy services either to support investigations into software process changes or training in new concepts and techniques. A range of training courses are available, either arranged directly on-site for individual clients, or as open-enrolment courses through the public domain.

2.16   SQL Software Ltd

SQL Software Ltd
Northbrook House
John Tate Road
Hertford
SG13 7NN
UK

SQL Software Inc
8500 Leesburg Pike
Suite 405
Vienna
VA 22182
USA

Contact: John Palmer

Tel.: +44 (0) 1992 501414
Fax: +44 (0) 1992 501616

Tel.: +1 703 760 0448
Fax: +1 703 760 0446

The market leader in process configuration management (CM), SQL Software is a privately held company, with its European headquarters in Hertford, UK and operates German subsidiaries in Munich and Frankfurt, along with a network of distributors across Europe. SQL Software has established its North American and Asian headquarters in Vienna, USA and also has offices in Chicago and Pleasanton. SQL Software's International Customer Response Centers providing "Hotline Support" are located in Hertford, UK and Vienna, USA. Founded in 1989 by Tani Haque, SQL Software has installations in Europe, North America, Asia, and Australia.

The Customers

SQL Software counts upwards of 8,000 users in the greater Fortune 1,000 caliber companies worldwide. Blue chip clients feature Motorola, General Electric, Lockheed, CSC, McDonnell Douglas, Harris Lanier, Unisys, Martin Marrietta, Boeing, E-Systems, U.S. Department of Defence, Siemens, Saab, Bull, UK Inland Revenue, ICL, BT, Glaxo, and Ant (Bosch).

The Product

SQL Software markets its PCMS product line, which enables companies to organise, and orderly manage the changes affecting their software, hardware, and documentation assets more efficiently. Process Configuration Management Software provides an in-line solution for organisations to better manage and build different versions of product components, tracking their pending changes, location, status, and relationships intuitively.

PCMS is also the underlying CM system in the DEC supplied software engineering environment ASD/SEE (Aerospace and Defence Software Engineering Environment) as supplied to the DoD F22 project. PCMS is also available encapsulated in HP SoftBench.

PCMS provides integrated CM support for system engineering including change management, release management, with comprehensive baseline and configuration build facilities.

With special functionality for Ada CM (PCMS*Ada).The system is user configurable, allowing working practices and procedures to be defined in a 'control plan' to conform to any predefined standards such as DoD 2167A, as in the case of the F22 project. The application of control is achieved via the application of lifecycles and role responsibilities that apply to all CM items and change documents declared to PCMS.

PCMS key features include:

Process Lifecycle & Role Management	Version Management & Build
Product Structuring	Parallel & Concurrent Development
Problem Management & Defect Tracking	SQL Relational Database
	Release Management
Support of SEI, DOD2167A & ISO9000 Standards	MOTIF, character & command line interfaces
Document Configuration Management	Full API support for integration
Closed loop change control	Windows Client Support

The PCMS suite of products includes:

PCMS*NLS Allows PCMS to run transparently in a heterogeneous networked environment.

PCMS*ART Adds powerful Archive, Retrieval and Transfer facilities to PCMS.

PCMS*SII Supports the whose who need to establish an interface between their own application software and PCMS.

X*PCMS Implemented using X11 and Motif, X*PCMS provides a consistent intuitive graphical user interface on all supported PCMS platforms.

PCMS*Softbench PCMS is available as an encapsulated tool within the Hewlett-Packard SoftBench environment.

PCMS*CTS An Enterprise wide Change and Problem Management Solution.

PCMS*Helpbench Supports the Help Desk functions of recording, and managing the closure of incidents through a process of workflow.

PCMS*PCwin The Microsoft Windows and Windows NT PC Client for PCMS.

PCMS*Ada PCMS for Ada Projects.

2.17   TLD Ada Compiler Systems

TLD Systems
3625 Del Amo Blvd. Suite 100
Torrance
CA 90503
USA

Contact: Bob Risinger

Tel: +1 310 542 5433
Fax: +1 310 542 6323
Email: tld@cerf.net

1995 sees TLD is in its thirteenth year of operation as an independent software vender. We specialise in cross and native compiler systems, software development environments, and real time operating systems. Our products are designed to support real-time applications.

TLD licenses software products and provides support services worldwide. Our customer base includes many large and small companies in North America, Europe, Asia, and Australia.

Our reputation for high quality, dependable products and the increasing use of Ada as the language of choice for space and commercial applications, in addition to military applications, contributes to our continued growth and stability. Our widely-acclaimed Ada Compiler has been used to develop and deliver fully tested production systems since 1984. We currently offer a variety of Ada Compiler Systems used for cross and native development. Expanding to meet the needs of our customers, TLD is currently developing additional targets and hosts for the Ada Compiler System.

Each officer and senior manager of our highly-qualified staff is experienced in design and development of languages, compilers, operating systems, file management systems, networking, and related software. Our staff has developed products for over sixty different host and target computers supporting eighteen different languages. As a team, we have produced and maintained compiler related software for native and cross-development environments, multiple hosts, and multiple targets.

Our reliability and expertise in real time development tools were instrumental in securing many retargeting and rehosting contracts supporting major defence and space programs. TLD implements project-customised features critical to the success of the programs we support.

i960 Ada Compiler System

The i960 TLDacs is now being used by the contractors of US Army's Comanche Helicopter program to develop embedded software. Our product is supporting the MX, XA, and MC models of the Intel i960. The product is Validated under TLD's Comanche contract. A few of the product's features are stated below:

- TLDada exploits the i960's local and global register characteristics for parameter passing and register dedication, selection, and protection.

- TLDlnk supports four gigabytes of memory addressing and multiple domain applications. User defined attributes can be associated with relocatable object control sections to mark segments of code for different regions or domains.

- TLDdbg is designed to support many test board configurations. The Tronix i960 and Intel EVB boards are currently supported.

- Hardware debugging features of the i960 are supported.

- The i960 Real Time Executive utilises the i960's process management hardware feature and supports more than 32 tasks.

- TLD's implementation of Ada tasking utilises process management hardware features.

- TLDrtx may be configured in a user-supervisor model or a tagged domain model. Three application designs are supported: a single Ada program, one or more Ada programs where each program is independently linked to reside in Region 3, and one or more Ada programs where each program is independently linked as an i960 domain (MX and XA only).

- All i960 types are directly supported by TLDrtx.

- TLDacs supports these additional hardware features: Virtual Memory Management, Floating Point Unit, Interprocess Synchronisation (semaphores, hooks, interface), Type Definition Object, Interrupts, Protection, Interprocess Communication (ports).

- TLDacs supports dynamic program services such as allocate memory space for a program, start a program, terminate a program, and release memory space for a program.

- Main program parameters, a feature related to the dynamic program support, is also supported.

1750 Ada Compiler System

TLD's 1750 Ada Compiler System comprises the Ada Info Display, Macro Assembler, Linker, Symbolic Debugger, Simulator, and Run Time System supporting all implementations conforming to MIL-STD-1750A including BIFs, all implementations conforming to MIL-STD-1750B including Type I, II, and III instructions, and Generalised VHSIC Spaceborne Computer (GVSC) implementations including extensions to MIL-STD-1750A ISA as implemented by Honeywell and IBM. 1750 TLDacs is formally validated as fully compliant with MIL-STD-1815A.

TLDada incorporates full global optimisation with thorough, 1750-oriented code optimisation. TLDada supports language defined pragmas plus many TLD-defined pragmas supporting microprocessor hardware features and embedded programming features such as dynamic code replacement and automatic in-lining.

TLDaid provides a capability to extract information from TLDacs' data base files to aid the programmer in a variety of ways including automatic production of technical documentation in either 2167/2168 or user-defined format. This information may be used for design support, reverse engineering, debugging, training, maintenance, and verification and validation testing.

TLD's Symbolic Debugger provides the capability to monitor execution of one or more Ada programs. These programs can execute on one or more Target Test Boards or Emulators or they can execute through interpretive computer simulation. Support is provided for execution control flow tracing and event trapping. TLDdbg supports functions such as EXAMINE HEAP for heap memory utilisation analysis. Through commands such as SHOW TASK, TLDdbg displays detailed information on the status of an Ada task.

2.18   Tartan Inc

European Sales Office   Pittsburgh Corporate Office
Little Langtree   300 Oxford Drive
Hill Bottom   Monroeville
Whitchurch Hill   PA 15146
Reading   USA
RG8 7PU
UK   Tel: +1 412 856 3600
                                   Fax: +1 412 856 3636

Contact: Martyn Jordan

Tel: +44 (0) 1734 843260
Fax: +44 (0) 1734 841014

Tartan Inc. was founded in 1981 and develops markets and supports optimising Ada cross-compilation systems and related software tools for developers of real-time embedded applications. Tartan's products support popular embedded processors controlling military and commercial systems and run on some of the most widely used development platforms.

Tartan's expertise lies in optimisation and the development of extremely efficient run-time techniques which deliver high performing generated code with the smallest run-time overheads. Because of this reputation Tartan has been subcontracted by Motorola, Intel and Texas Instruments to develop Ada cross-compilers for their Microprocessors and Digital Signal Processors (DSP's).

Tartan, in partnership with TRW, was also selected by the US Air Force to build compilers for evaluating the new Ada 95 language enhancements for the real-time i960 MC target. As a result of this research Tartan will deliver the first release of its Ada 95 real-time capabilities in 1994 to its customers as part of the normal maintenance upgrade process.

Tartan Ada development systems

All development systems are hosted on Digital Equipment's VAX family of computers and the Sun Microsystems SPARC workstation.

Ada VMS/1750A. Ada SPARC/1750A. The MIL-STD-1750A 16-bit military processor is the target. The 1750A is the only processor certified by the government to fly in space and is being used on the space shuttle and all military satellites. This product was developed under contract to TI.

Ada VMS/C3x. Ada SPARC/C3x. Texas Instrument's 320C30 and 'C31 DSP's are the targets. The 'C30 is the first DSP processor in the industry offered with validated Ada support. The 'C31 is a TI DSP chip targeted for cost-sensitive high-volume applications requiring 32-bit real-time performance. Either the 'C30 or the 'C31 can be selected by the application developer using a command-line switch.

Ada VMS/C40. Ada SPARC/C40. Texas Instrument's 320C40 Digital Signal Processing chip is the target. The 'C40 is TI's new DSP chip aimed at parallel processing. The product was developed under contract to TI.

Ada VMS/i960 MC. Ada SPARC/i960 MC. Ada RS6000/i960 MC. Intel's JIAWG standard 32-bit i960 MC processor is the target. The IBM RS/6000 is an additional host machine. Tartan offers two support options, Physical Mode and Virtual Mode, to provide developers with a variety of ways to use the i960 MC depending on the requirements of their application. Intel's i960 MC RISC chip has been selected as the standard on both the Light Helicopter and the Advanced Tactical Fighter programs. An Intel contract supported development of this product.

Ada VMS/68xxx. Ada SPARC/68xxx. Motorola's 68040, 68030, 68020, 68332 and 68340 are the target systems for this switch-selectable development system; any of the five targets can be selected by a command-line switch. The 68xxx combination is unique in the Motorola 68000 family market. Motorola supported the development of the 68040, 68332 and 68340 functionality.

The core components of Tartan Ada Development Systems are:

- The highly optimised compiler;

- The Tartan Ada Librarian supporting multiple libraries and multiple access;

- The modular, customisable Tartan Ada Runtime system;

- ARTClient, the Tartan Runtime client package giving access to tasking data structures and operations;

- Intrinsics Packages providing access to target hardware facilities;

- A library of pre-defined Standard Ada Packages;

- Inter-Processor Support allowing coordination of Ada programs and tasks within a program among different C3x, C40 and 68xxx processors via shared memory;

- Math Package including elementary math functions that meet the specifications of the SIGAda and Ada-Europe Numerics Working Groups (c3X, c40, I960 mc, 68xxx);

- The Tartan Linker that precisely controls memory layout and eliminates unused program and run-time sections;

- AdaScope — Tartan's window-oriented, customisable, source- and machine-level symbolic debugger;

- The Tartan Tool Set including the AdaList and Checksum utilities, object file librarian, and file conversion utilities;

- Board Retargeting Kit, a facility to customise the debug kernel to a specific board configuration by modifying a small target-resident program;

- The Help Facility, including on-line help for the compiler, library, and AdaScope;

- Complete Documentation for all components of the system.

Optional components of Tartan Ada development systems

- **Expanded Memory** supporting multiple 64K code segments that address up to 8 million words, allows segmentation of larger applications, provides protection of applications sharing the same processor and is reconfigurable (1750A).

- **Simulator and Emulator Support** including Tartan's 1750A simulator and support for the HP 64000, Tektronix 8540A, TASCO MDC 281, Honeywell's PDU emulators (1750A), Intel's in-circuit emulator for the i960 MC processor and a simulator for the 'C30 and 'C40 products.

- **Maths Package** including elementary math functions that meet the specifications of SIGAda and Ada-Europe Numerics Working Groups (1750A).

- **Run Time Enhancement Package** providing all Ada and assembly language source code for the Tartan Ada Run Time system plus a detailed Implementor's Guide.

- **Assembler** for the 1750A and the i960 MC targets.

- **Assembler Interface** to the TI C30 cross-assembler, including conversion of the output to Tartan's Object File Format (C3x).

- **SPOX Math Package** an extensive math package developed by Spectron Microsystems for DSP applications (C3x and C40).

- **Stand-Alone AdaScope** an advanced version of Tartan's unique debugger offered as a stand-alone product (as well as bundled with each development system) permitting debugging away from program development.

- **Retargeting Kits for AdaScope** facilities to adapt the interface between AdaScope and a different communications link configuration or communications protocol to conform to unique requirements.

- **Consulting Services** for custom modifications.

2.19   Ultra Electronics Command and Control Systems

Ultra Electronics Command and Control Systems
Knaves Beech Business Centre
Loudwater
High Wycombe
Buckinghamshire
HP10 9UT
UK

Contact: Keith Hardy

Tel: +44 (0) 1628 530000
Fax: +44 (0) 1628 524557

Ultra Electronics Command and Control Systems (UECCS), a member of the Ultra Electronics Group, is part of the consortium currently developing two of the largest real-time Ada based systems for the MoD. The Submarine Command System (SMCS) is being fitted on all Royal Naval Submarines and the Surface Ship Command System (SSCS) will be fitted to all Type 23 Frigates and Auxiliary Oiler Replenishment Ships.

Both systems have been designed to meet stringent performance requirements and are based upon a common distributed architecture using Multibus II standard computer cards developed by Ultra. In developing these cards Ultra have used their own very large scale ASIC technology and have adopted Intel 80386 microprocessor and Inmos Transputer technologies. In addition, a high performance CPU card based on the Intel 80486 microprocessor has been produced as part of a joint development with Concurrent Technologies.

The system architecture has been under development since 1985 and the high content of Ada software in both systems has enabled Ultra to gain extensive expertise in the design of large high performance Ada systems and in the management of complex Ada technology. As part of both developments thorough evaluations of leading Ada toolsets were undertaken and this has enabled Ultra to establish a comprehensive evaluation test write based upon the British Standards Institute (BSI) Ada Evaluation System (AES) and now encompassing some 1000 tests. This gives Ultra a unique capability in establishing the quality of not only Ada compilers but complete Ada toolsets.

High Quality Ada Productivity Tools

Our commitment to developing high quality Ada productivity tools has enabled Ultra to form a strategic alliance with TeleSoft whereby Ultra have secured the engineering rights to the TeleGen2 Ada Intel 386 targeted cross development toolset. This alliance has enabled Ultra to significantly enhance the product particularly in respect of the run-time performance and distributed debugging facilities. The current release of the toolset is now validated for both

386 and 486 target environments and includes a complete set of tools for developing 386/486 targeted applications from a VAX/VMS host. The tools include a validated Ada compiler, a library manger, source-level debugger, profiler, linker, downloader/receiver and a suite of language productivity tools including automatic recompilation tools. The cross development system also includes the TeleAda-Exec real-time executive.

As part of the alliance Ultra are now providing full world-wide technical support for the TeleGen2 Ada Intel 386 targeted cross development toolset and includes support to customers in the United Kingdom, France, Israel, Singapore, Canada and the USA. The alliance now continues with Alsys as part of the recent TeleSoft/Alsys merger. In addition, Ultra are able to provide Ada Training and Consultancy addressing both the technical and management aspects of large Ada based systems.

2.20 VSEL Electronics and Software Products

VSEL Electronics and Software Products
Barrow-in-Furness
Cumbria
LA14 1AF
UK

Contact: Peter Fitzpatrick

Tel: +44 (0) 1229 873993
Fax: +44 (0) 1229 874747

VSEL's Electronic and Software Products Group has undertaken a wide variety of projects including the design and production of military networks, complex real-time simulators, CASE tool development, systems analysis facilities, data distribution equipment and specialist test equipment.

New products

In the past year VSEL have delivered a number of major Ada systems spanning a range from high performance embedded systems to workstation based analysis tools.

Outfit INB. Outfit INB provides data distribution facilities for all navigation sensors fitted on the Type 42 Destroyers and Aircraft Carriers, providing information to other equipments via the Combat System Highway. This is the **only** Ada based data distribution system in service with the Royal Navy.

System Trials Analysis Facility. VSEL provide both the recording and analysis systems used in current submarines. The System Trials Data Recorder provides the means to record all data passed between equipments on the submarines Combat System LAN.

The System Trials Analysis Facility (STAF) provides support for the analysis of complex naval trials. STAF provides the means to collate, analyse and display data from major equipments within the Combat System such as the Sonar, Command System, Navigation System and other sensors. Information can be displayed in a wide number of tabular and graphical forms. Again, this is the only such system in service with the Royal Navy to utilise either Ada and X-Windows and provides a five fold increase in performance compared to systems currently in use.

Future Data Highway. VSEL have demonstrated the viability of a fibre optic FDDI network running at 100 MBit/sec for future naval vessels. As part of the contract VSEL used Ada to develop a Conformance Test Equipment which provides the means to test all equipment which intends to use the network.

Vanguard Command Team Trainer. VSEL delivered all the simulations required for the training of the command room staff of the Vanguard submarine and also provided an independent simulation of the Submarine Command System SMCS. This simulation was provided before the real equipment entered service with the Royal Navy.

Type 42 Shore Development Facility. VSEL provided the Scenario Generator system for the Type 42 SDF and simulators for all the firing weapons fitted to the platform. The Scenario Generator provides 1400 simultaneous contacts into the system under test, with the weapon simulators providing concurrent simulations of multiple missiles and torpedoes.

Integrated Modelling Environment. The Integrated Modelling Environment has been developed under MoD sponsorship to provide Computer Aided System Engineering in support of the analysis and design of large complex systems such as Naval Combat Systems.

The IME has been used for the design of Combat Systems for most recent Royal Navy platforms and for the design of large equipment subsystems, and uses "Open Systems" technology including X-Windows and an SQL database providing a user-friendly and expandable toolset.

Support is provided for system analysis and design using a complete set of graphical and textual tools conforming to the Yourdon (Ward/Mellor) notation, including Ada based tools which generate dynamic models of the behaviour of the system being designed.

Electronic products

The group produces high integrity data buses (military networks), simulation and stimulation equipment and custom designed test and analysis equipment.

Experience in the use of 80X86, 8031/51, AMD 29000 and 680X0 microprocessor technology, together with Multibus and VME backplanes has been gained over the past fifteen years. This basic technology has been used to develop standard system elements such as interface cards (including B(P), B(S), synchro, resolver, Def Stan 00-18, NES 1024, STANAG 4156, S-cubed and RS 422) and interface processors.

This technology has been used to develop real-time systems using Ada, C++, C and assembler, together with a wide variety of interface test equipment for MIL-STD-1553B networks and other interfaces.

These systems have been built and tested for rugged environments including those defined in compliance with Naval Engineering Standards

Software products

The group has delivered a wide range of software-intensive systems including real-time simulators, CASE tools and mission-critical software. The group's software engineers develop software-intensive systems which meet the customer's requirements using Structured Analysis/Design and Object-Oriented techniques. All software is developed in accordance with recognised quality standards, in particular AQAP A013 and BS A05750 ISO 9001.

The group has used the Ada language since 1984, and since then have produced more than one million lines of Ada code — much of which has been re-used in later projects. Although Ada forms the basis of the group's Software Engineering strategy, other languages are used where more appropriate, and systems have been delivered using Pascal, C and Fortran in addition to Ada. Expertise also exists in the development of Oracle database applications.

The use of Ada and other Open Systems software technologies such as X-Windows has enabled the group to port and develop software for a wide range of platforms including VAX, Sun, 680X0, 80X86 and RISC processors.

The group's ability to deliver working software which meets the customer's requirements is demonstrated by the support costs of VSEL's software-intensive systems being less than 3% of total development costs.

Electronic and software technology

The Electronic and Software Products Group have developed a set of re-usable system elements — both hardware and software — which conform to International Standards where feasible and have been used to develop a number of systems.

- Backplane system elements conform to Multibus and VME standards.

- Network interfaces conform to standards such as Ethernet, FDDI, 1553B and Combat System Highway (Def Stan 00-18 and Def Stan 00-19).

- Both International and Defence Standard point-to-point interfaces are available, including RS 232, RS 422, RS 485, NES 1024, B(P), B(S), Synchro, Resolver, STANAG 4156 and S-cubed.

- Military standard processor boards conform to relevant NES standards.

- Industry standard operating systems such as UNIX, VMS, MS-DOS and VRTX/ARTX are used where applicable.

- Open Systems software components are used where feasible, including X-Windows, OSF/Motif, Open Look and TCP/IP.

- Re-usable software elements have been developed, with examples ranging from specialist mathematical libraries, through re-usable software components, to complete simulation systems.

2.21   York Software Engineering Limited

York Software Engineering

York Software Engineering Limited
University of York
York
YO1 5DD
UK

Contact: Ron Pierce

Tel: +44 (0) 1904 433741
Fax: +44 (0) 1904 433744

York Software Engineering Limited (YSE) offers consultancy services and products in the area of high integrity systems development, with an emphasis on object oriented analysis and design techniques for assuring dependability, formal methods and Ada.Although the company is an independent organisation, it has strong links with the Computer Science Department at the University of York and is able to transfer the benefit of state-of-the-art research and development to an industrial and commercial context. Major customers of YSE include the UK government departments, defence and aerospace organisations, and nuclear utilities. The chairman of YSE is Geoff Holmes, formerly deputy chairman of SD-Scicon plc and a past president of the Computer Services Association; the technical directors are Professor John McDermid and Professor Ian Wand, both of whom have internationally distinguished reputations in the formal methods and Ada areas respectively.

Development Process Improvement

YSE has an excellent understanding of the best available practices in software development for both safety critical and mission critical applications. By means of training, consultancy support and pilot projects, we can help organisations to improve both the cost-effectiveness of the development process and the quality of the delivered software. The company's services include:

- Audit of the current software development processes;

- Recommendations for process improvement in terms of project standards, methods and tools, including the introduction of appropriate industry standards such as MoD IDS 00-55, IEC 65A and RTCA DO-178B;

- Transition to object-oriented analysis and design methods;

- Introduction of formal methods;

- Introduction of high level programming languages including Ada;

- Advice on the use of safe language subsets including SPARK Ada;

- Static analysis of software for functional, timing and resource usage behaviour;

- Advice on selection and evaluation of CASE tools, compilers, static and dynamic analysers and other software development tools.

Independent Inspection and Verification Services

YSE can provide inspection and verification services for software, including independent test design, testing and static analysis. The company's capabilities include:

- Hazard analysis of software functions in a system context;

- Independent Verification and Validation services;

- MoD Independent Safety Auditor role.

Software Design and Implementation

YSE is able to undertake the development of software systems using the most modern and effective design, implementation and verification techniques, supported by the best available tools from appropriate suppliers.

CADiZ

CADiZ Computer Aided Design in Z, is a UNIX based suite of tools which checks and typesets specifications produced in the Z language. CADiZ also supports previewing and interactive investigation of the properties of Z specifications, and produces professional quality documentation containing English prose, diagrams and the formal specifications themselves. Theorem proving facilities have recently been added. With its low cost and ease of use, CADiZ is rapidly establishing itself as a market leader in Z support tools and is in use on practical projects. A PC/Windows version of CADiZ is under development. The Zeta extension of CADiZ supports the development of Ada programs in the SPARK Ada subset of formal refinement of Z specifications into Ada code. Refinement proof obligations are generated automatically by the tool.

STAMP

STAMP is a tool which calculates worst case code execution times and supports the generation of tests to exercise worst cast times. STAMP operates on executable image files in IEEE-695 format and is initially available for Motorola 68020 processors.

York ACE

York Ada Compiler Environment (ACE) was the original product introduced by YSE and offers low cost, high performance Ada compilation for UNIX environments. A version of York ACE which provides the Ada 95 protected object semantics and supports static worst case execution time and task schedulability analysis has been developed for the European Space Agency. This system is currently being used as the basis for the development of a trustworthy Safety Kernel for safety critical tasking programs.

3

Letters from Ada organisations

3.1 From Ada UK

Ada UK is one of the longest established national Ada organisations having been founded in 1980. It is an independent non-profit limited company whose main goal is the dissemination of information about the Ada language in particular and good software engineering practices in general. It is controlled by a management committee comprising a number of Directors plus the Administrator. There is an annual general meeting at which Directors are elected. All Directors offer their services on a voluntary basis.

The main activities are organised by a number of subcommittees each of which is chaired by a Director and whose members are drawn from the Ada community at large. Activities are funded by membership fees and by sponsorship.

Ada UK has two publications. One is the quarterly, Ada User Journal, which has been published since 1980 (originally as Ada UK News). The other publication is the Ada Year Book which you are reading and which is now in its fifth year.

The major event in the Ada UK calendar is the annual conference which was held in York for many years. The last three conferences were held in London after two years in Brighton. It seems clear that London is a popular venue for reasons of accessibility and in 1995 the conference is being held for the third time in the Gloucester Road area in West London.

The 1994 conference was again successful showing a continued resurgence of interest in Ada. This is no doubt partly caused by the advent of Ada 95 and also because of a growing realisation that Ada is an excellent foundation for developing software that really matters.

Ada UK continues to provide an active forum for discussion of Ada 95. An important event in January 1994 was the academic seminar arranged at Brighton with the goal of disseminating information on Ada 95 to senior staff of computer science departments in the UK in order to encourage the expansion of the teaching of Ada in our universities. This was very successful and is likely to be repeated. The GNAT 9X compiler (including a version for DOS) is also available through Ada UK.

A recent initiative was the establishment of a committee with a specific goal of marketing both Ada and Ada UK. It is all too easy to preach to the converted and so a prime goal has been attendance at other conferences and exhibitions. Four were attended in 1994: Object Expo Europe, Embedded Systems, Software Development 94 and ERA Avionics. An Ada Knowledge pack has been assembled containing information of interest to potential new users; this pack is available to anyone who wishes to learn more about the use of Ada or wishes to persuade others.

The work of Ada UK would not be possible without the financial support of our sponsoring organisations. We are much indebted to them for their contribution. A description of their activities will be found elsewhere in this book.

For further information please contact our administrator, Helen Byard or any other member of the Committee of Management. The members are listed below and their full addresses can be found in the reference section of this book.

John Barnes
Chairman, Ada UK

Committee of Management:

John Barnes,	Chairman
Frank Bott,	Year Book
Helen Byard,	Administrator
Peter Fitzpatrick,	
Garth Glynn,	Company Secretary
Keith Hardy,	
Ian Pascoe,	
Michael Pickett,	Treasurer
Dan Simpson,	
Bill Taylor,	
Brian Tooby.	

3.2   Ada Europe - An overview

Karlotto Mangold
Ada-Europe Secretary
c/o ATM Computer GmbH,
Bücklestr.1-5
D 78467 Konstanz
Germany

Tel: +49-7531-807-235
Fax: +49-7531-807-363
Email: ada-euro@atm.aeg.kn.daimlerbenz.com

What is Ada-Europe?

Ada-Europe is an international organisation, set up to promote the use of Ada. It aims to spread the use and the knowledge of Ada and to promote its introduction into academic and research establishments. Above all, Ada-Europe intends to represent European interests in Ada and Ada-related matters.

In its current form Ada-Europe was established in 1988. As there is no European legal framework to govern such organisations, it was established according to Belgian Law. Currently these are: Ada Belgium, Ada in Denmark, Ada Deutschland, Ada France, Ada Greece, Ada Italy, Ada Ireland, Ada Nederland, Ada i Norge, Ada Scotland, Ada Spain, Ada in Sweden, Ada in Switzerland and Ada UK. Individual members of these organisations can become indirect members of Ada-Europe.

At the moment Ada-Europe has about 800 indirect members. About 300 of these are members of Ada in Sweden, about 100 belong to the Belgium, French, British and Spanish organisations, and Germany, Italy and Switzerland supply about 25 members each. The subscription fee for indirect members in 1995 will be 20 ECU.

What does Ada-Europe do?

The best-known of Ada-Europe's activities is its annual conference.   The last one took place in Copenhagen in September 1994 and was organised in cooperation with Eurospace. The next conference will be held — also together with Ada in Aerospace — in Germany in September 1995. These conferences attract usually 150 to 250 participants. They involve three days of lectures and presentations, and provide the perfect opportunity to discuss new information and exchange experiences with fellow Ada users. As well as the usual conference features, delegates have the opportunity to attend an additional two days of tutorials dealing with specialist Ada matters. The conference also hosts an exhibition, where Ada-related products — in their latest version — are presented.

Ada-Europe provides a framework for setting up working groups and task groups to discuss and investigate technical aspects of using Ada on an European basis.

Indirect members of Ada-Europe receive a quarterly Newsletter. This contains details of Ada-Europe activities, as well as news on Ada standardisation, experiences of using Ada, reports from conferences and tutorials, and reviews of new publications and products. The Newsletter is usually distributed via the national organisations, but can also be mailed directly at additional postage costs.

For more details please contact the Ada-Europe secretary. Ada-Europe is chaired by a board of 8 members elected at the General assembly by the associated member bodies. Since the last general assembly in Copenhagen there are the following board members:

John Barnes,   President
Luc Bernard,   Vice-president
Lars Asplund,   Treasurer
Karlotto Mangold,   Secretary
Xavier Crusset   Conference Organiser
Bjoern Kaellberg
Albert Llamosi   Newsletter
Alfred Strohmeier

3.3   From Ada in Denmark

Ada in Denmark (AiD) is the Danish national Ada organisation affiliated to Ada-Europe.

AiD acts mainly as a distribution point for information from Ada-Europe to the Danish members. There are no formal working groups within AiD, but the members have individually pursued an interest in maintaining the existing Ada standard as well as in the development of Ada 95.

For further information please contact:

Mr. Jorgen Bundgaard
Ada in Denmark
c/o DDC-I A/S
Gl. Lundtoftevej 1B
DK-2800 Lyngby
Denmark

Tel: +45 45 87 11 44
Fax: +45 45 87 22 17
Email: jb@ddci.dk

3.4   From Ada-France

Ada-France is the French group of Ada users. It operates as a working group of AFCET, the French Computer Society, and gathers about 100 members. It is the French associate member to Ada-Europe.

Our activities include monthly informal meetings, where users gather, discuss and exchange experiences on various topics. Current meetings address the new features of Ada 95 and how to best utilise them.

After organising the '93 Ada-Europe conference in Paris, Ada-France will hold its annual French-speaking conference in Spring '95.

Ada-France has been also very active in the field of Ada 95, by sending comments and having members participating in the various ISO meetings. It maintains a close liaison with AFNOR (French standardisation body).

Ada usage is growing in France. Ada is now the preferred language for military software; transportation, aerospace, and power industries are more and more committed to using it.

Contact Points:

AFCET
156, Bld. Pereire
75017 Paris
France

Tel: +33 1 47 66 24 19
Fax: +33 1 42 67 93 12

J-P. Rosen (Chairman)
ADALOG
27, av. de Verdun
92170 Vanves
France

Tel: +33 1 46 45 51 12
Fax: +33 1 46 45 52 49

3.5   From Ada-Italy

Ada-Italy was formed in Pisa in April 1992. Currently its President is:

Paolo Panaroni
Intecs Sistemi S.p.A.
Via Gereschii 32
56126 Pisa
Italy

Tel: +39 50 545233
Fax: +39 50 545200
Email: paolo@pisa.intecs.it

Its Treasurer is:

Mario Mariotti
Sytek - Torino

Tel: +39 11 9884111
Fax: +39 11 9951487
Email: mario@sytek.it

Its Vice-President is:

Marco Gajetti
ALENIA Spazio - Torino

Tel: +39 11 7180201
Fax: +39 11 723307
Email: mgajetti@alsto.alenia.it

The Board of the Association consists of 11 Members who currently are:
Paolo Panaroni (President)

Mario Mariotti (Tresaurer/Secretary)
Marco Gajetti (Vice-President)

Giovanni Cantone
Univerita' Tor Vergata - Roma

Tel: +39 6 72594495
Fax: +39 6 2020519
Email: cantone@info.utovrm.it

Mario Fusani
IEI CNR Pisa

Tel: +39 50 593400 (593478)
Fax: +39 50 554342
Email: fusani@iei.pi.cnr.it

Franco Mazzanti
IEI CNR - Pisa

Tel: +39 50 593400 (593447)
Fax: +39 50 554342
Email: mazzanti@iei.pi.cnr.it

Omar Morales
CESVIT / CQ_WARE - Firenze

Tel: +39 55 4796425
Fax: +39 55 480512
Email: morales@ingfi1.ing.unifi.it

Marcello Barbato
NATO Comm. and Infor. Sys. School - Latina

Tel: +39 773 677072
Fax: +39 773 662467

Stefano Genolini
TXT - Milano

Tel: +39 2 27001001
Fax: +39 2 2578994
Email: genolini@txt.it

Pier Angelo Mariani
SIA - Torino

Tel: +39 11 7794844
Fax: +39 11 725679
Email: mariani@cdc.sia-av.it

Franco Tortarolo
FIAT Avio - Torino

Tel: +39 11 6858490
Fax: +39 11 6858486

This board will remain in charge until July 1996. Ada-Italy currently has 25 members, including the following Collective Members:

Agusta Eli S.r.l. - Agusta Sistemi (Varese)
Alenia Spazio S.p.A (Torino)
Applicazioni Ricerche Informatica S.r.l. (Bari)
Intecs Sistemi S.p.A. (Pisa)
Marconi Olivetti Defense Information Systems S.p.A. (Pisa)
Societa' Italiana Avionica S.p.A. (Torino)
Sytek S.r.l (Torino)
TXT Ingegneria Informatica S.p.A. (Milano)

Ada-Italy is an Associate Member of Ada-Europe. Most of its members are reachable by e-mail. This is a point which is considered extremely important within the association and efforts are being made to increase the number of members having access to this facility.

An "information forwarding service" of the most interesting Ada topics collected all over the internet world is currently provided to all members.

Among the periodic events supported by the Association there is a General Assembly usually held in June/July and a one-day workshop usually held in the autumn. For the autumn of 1994, a special workshop was organised, dedicated to Distributed Real-Time Systems with particular regard to the use of Ada in High Speed transportation systems such as Trains and Planes. Ada-Italy also has its own newsletter.

1994 was dedicated to the dissemination of the Ada technology into the school environment. To date this has involved Rome University, and the Turin Postgraduate school.

To obtain the Statutes of Ada-Italy and a full list of current members or any other information please contact the address given.

Marco Gajetti

3.6   From Ada in Norway

Ada in Norway was founded on February 16th, 1988, and the purpose of the association is:

- – to collect and distribute information about Ada technology and its development;

- – to establish contact with international, and other national Ada bodies;

- – to actively promote the use of Ada in Norway.

In order to fulfill our goals, Ada in Norway publishes a newsletter three to four times a year, and hosts Ada technical seminars twice a year.

Ada in Norway has experienced a positive trend in the membership situation, and as of January 1, 1993 the association numbered 67 personal members, eight corporate members, and eight supporting members.

Points of contact for Ada in Norway are:

Chairman:	Secretary:
Anton B. Leere	Fridtjov Backer
Norwegian Defence Research	Ada in Norway
Establishment	FTD
P.O. Box 25	Oslo mil/Akershus
N-2007 Kjeller	N-0015 Oslo 1
Norway	Norway
Tel: +47 6 807394	Tel: +47 2 402683
Fax: +47 6 807212	Fax: +47 2 402530
Email: leere@ndre.no	

For the coming year we will as usual host two seminars, one in April and one in the October/November time-frame. The topics for these seminars are yet to be selected. We have in the past been very successful in arranging the seminars in co-operation with Ada in Sweden. This is in order to reduce the cost of the seminars.

Ada in Norway is also working actively together with the academic community, in order to promote Ada in education. This is done both by giving presentations at educational institutions, and sponsoring students to attend our seminars.

3.7   From Ada-Spain

Ada-Spain was founded in Madrid on July 1987 by 120 people from about 30 different industrial and academic organisations throughout Spain. Founding president was Angel Alvarez from the Technical University of Madrid.

From the start Ada-Spain wanted to fulfill the need for an easily identifiable contact point within Spain for the international Ada community. As evidence of their desire to actively contribute to the promotion of Ada in the international sense, Ada-Spain hosted the 1989 Ada-Europe Conference. Some 500 delegates gathered in Madrid for this event, making it the largest attended Ada-Europe Conference ever.

Currently Ada-Spain has nine institutional members and some 350 individual members. A good proportion of these individual members are computer professionals who do not work in Ada technology but would desire to do so. Ada-Spain aims to promote Ada related industrial and research efforts within Spain as a means to enlarge the size of the national Ada market.

The association publishes a quarterly newsletter, SpAda which is distributed freely to its members, and holds an annual seminar where members from the local Ada community take turns in teaching the different parts of the language to beginners. Furthermore, other more advanced seminars are organised occasionally to host both international and national experts of the Ada technology. A small library of Ada related documents is also managed for the benefit of its members.

To help spread the use and education of Ada among the Spanish academic centers, Ada-Spain awards an annual prize to the best academic project on Ada technology. Last but not least, the association has been organising an 'Ada-day' for the past three years in Madrid. Its fourth edition will take place in February 1995.

For any additional information regarding Ada-Spain, please contact its Secretary:

Francisco Perez-Zarza
Ada-Spain
P.O. Box 50.403
E-28080 Madrid
Spain

Fax: +34 1 656 5887
Email: fperez@ada.es

3.8   From Ada in Switzerland

Ada in Switzerland is a special interest group of the Swiss Informaticians Society, constituted with its own distinct membership, fees and budget. Ada in Switzerland has about 80 individual members and 15 collective members.

Ada in Switzerland is a forum for persons and parties interested in the Ada Programming Language, in its applications and in Ada-related technologies, such as Software Engineering Methodologies, Environments and Tools. Ada in Switzerland promotes contacts and information exchange among its members and interested parties. It organises meetings, workshops, conferences and other activities related to its purpose. It collaborates with other national and international organisations pursuing similar objectives, e.g. Ada-Europe.

The first meeting of Ada in Switzerland took place in Lausanne on the 13th of October 1988; it was hosted by the Swiss Federal Institute of Technology in Lausanne and organised by Prof. Alfred Strohmeier. Ada in Switzerland usually organises two one-day meetings each year. Each of the meetings attracts 50 or so participants.

Point of contact for Ada in Switzerland is:

Mr. Magnus Kempe
Chair, Ada in Switzerland
Swiss Federal Institute of Technology in
Lausanne
EPFL-DI-LGL
CH–1015 Lausanne, Switzerland

Tel: +41 21 693 2580
Fax: +41 21 693 5079
Email: Magnus.Kempe@di.epfl.ch

3.9   Ada in the European Space Agency

Ada is the recommended language for space software applications in ESA. It has been adopted by the majority of current ESA projects for the development of critical on-board software. However, there are strong constraints imposed by space applications:

- limitations in memory space,

- use of radiation-hard processors, with limited processing speed,

- real-time and reliability requirements of safety critical applications.

Those constraints, together with the lack of mature software development techniques and tools, lead to limited use of powerful facilities provided by the Ada language, such as tasking or exception handling. This has resulted in ESA setting up a number of R&D projects in order to provide suitable hardware and software infrastructure to software development.

Ada is being used in the following ESA projects:

ENVISAT-1. In this Earth observation project, the on-board control software of around 10 different scientific instruments aboard the Polar Platform satellite shall be developed in Ada, with more than 100,000 lines of embedded Ada code.

POLAR PLATFORM. The On-Board Data Handling (OBDH) software, and the Attitude and Orbit Control Subsystem (AOCS) of the PPF satellite have been coded in Ada.

ARTEMIS. The OBDH software, and the AOCS of the ARTEMIS satellite have been coded in Ada.

SILEX. The control software of this important telecommunications instrument aboard the ARTEMIS satellite is written in Ada

ISO (Infrared Space Observatory). The ISO OBDH software, and the AOCS of the ISO scientific satellite have been coded in Ada.

CLUSTER. The On-Board Data Handling software of the CLUSTER satellites has been coded in Ada.

SOHO (SOlar and Heliospheric Observatory). The COBS (Central On-Board Software), controlling critical functions of the mission and the control software of some of the scientific instruments aboard have been implemented in Ada.

COLUMBUS. This was the pioneer project in ESA proposing Ada as the implementation language. Now it includes more than half a million lines of Ada code. They mainly correspond to the ground segment (CGS), including mission preparation, verification, integration and check-out software and simulation software.

SIMSAT. The new satellite simulation infrastructure at ESOC (European Space Operations Centre) is being developed in Ada.

It is important to note that most of the Ada code has been, or is being designed with HOOD (Hierarchical Object-Oriented Design), a method which was initially developed by ESA, and which is now a widely accepted design method for Ada in Europe.

ESA R&D in Software Engineering related to Ada technology includes the following:

ESSDE (European Space Software Development Environment). It is the development environment recommended by ESA for its software projects. It has been implemented with commercial-off-the-shelf tools, and includes the following features:

- Coverage of all software life cycle phases with a strong support for ESA recommended methods and language (IDEF0, HOOD, Ada).

- Smooth transition between the different life-cycle phases, in particular between the design (HOOD objects) and the coding phase (Ada modules).

- Extensive and homogeneous support to global activities of the life cycle: Configuration Management, Documentation,Process Modelling, Traceability and Navigation among the different software objects.

- Customised (but not restricted) to support the ESA Software Engineering Standards.

Future versions of the ESSDE (currently under development) will be based on the PCTE standard.

Development of reusable on-board software. Reusability is recognised as a key factor for reducing the costs of software development. In ESA on-board control systems (OBDH, scientific instruments control) there is a big potential for reusing software, since the requirements are usually very similar. Therefore studies have been and are being conducted in order to set up a set of reusable on-board software components, facilitating their reuse in early stages of the development (analysis, design) and providing the necessary tool infrastructure.

Hard Real-Time Systems and Ada. The work performed in previous years around hard real-time systems has led to the definition of state-of-the-art real-time techniques, and an extension to the HOOD method (HRT-HOOD) for the design of Ada software. These new techniques have been experimented using real applications, and some prototype tools have been developed. It is planned to provide full support to this technology in specific Software Development Environments (SDEs) for on-board software. Furthermore, it is planned to define a general strategy for the development of real-time software in ESA, based on object-oriented technology, Ada 95 and international standards such as POSIX.

Hardware support for Ada. The development of an Ada tasking coprocessor (ATAC) is about to finish. It will support Ada tasking facilities at speeds of about 10 times faster than normal Run-Time Systems. It has been designed to be compatible with the new standard Ada 95.

Ada 95 technology. The transition to Ada 95 is being evaluated in the frame of various contracts, stressing the new object-oriented features, real-time support, and its better interface to other languages and standards.

As a conclusion, Ada can be considered as the main language for ESA on-board software, although its use in ground applications is limited. However, the use of a good language such as Ada is not enough to face the challenge of space applications. Noticeable effort is being done in providing adequate support to Ada software development: the ESSDE, reusable software components and hard real-time techniques. Run-time support, such as that provided by ATAC, is also seen as a key issue for ESA's Ada research.

A safe transition to Ada 95 will be assured by early trade-offs of the language's capabilities and tools availability. Ada 95 is expected to meet many requirements of ESA software, and a good integration of Ada 95 technology in ESA's software development process and its recommended methods (e.g. HOOD) and tools is envisaged.

For any further information concerning Ada in ESA, please contact:

Jorge Amador-Monteverde
Software Engineering &
    Standardisation Section (WME)
ESA-ESTEC
P.O. Box 299
2200 AG Noordwijk
The Netherlands

Tel. +31 1719 84388
Fax +31 1719 85420
Email: amador@wm.estec.esa.nl

Best regards,
Jorge Amador-Monteverde

3.10   International Ada Liaison Committee (IALC)

The ACM Special Interest Group for Ada is facilitating for the formation of the International Ada Liaison Committee (IALC.).

The mission statement for the IALC follows:

> The mission of the IALC is to promote and increase the viability, well being, and growth of Ada technology and use on a worldwide basis. The IALC balances, encourages, and focuses the interests of Ada business, technology, academia, and growth.
>
> The primary activity of the IALC is to maintain a work plan of action to improve the Ada technology base, broaden and grow Ada awareness, and maintain a focal point for present and future Ada-related activities.

Gathering information regarding:

- opportunities for new products and new markets;

- avenues for new distribution and awareness channels for existing and emerging products and services;

- sources of problems, discomfort, and areas needing improvement;

- feedback and awareness of communities external to Ada which could provide future opportunities as described above.

Strategic analysis and work item generation

The gathered information will be analyzed and a strategic work plan formulated. Formulation maps the needs onto a combination of existing and imminent products and services, as well as identifying future research, development, and marketing activities. Needs and actions will be prioritised as required to conform to the resources available. This implementation planning and subsequent oversight is a vital part of the strategic planning of the IALC.

Implementation of the workplan

Assess the availability of resources to be applied to the generated work items. Provoke and persuade available community resources to accept responsibility for the action. If no resources accept assigned responsibility, IALC will "adopt" the work item and become the home for the work responsibility.

Up to three meetings are planned during calendar year 1995.

For further information, contact:

Mark Gerhardt, IALC Convenor   Garth Glynn, IALC Secretary
Tel: +1 408734-6325   Tel: +44 1273 642563
Email: gerhardt_mark@srs.loral.com   Email: jgg@unix.brighton.ac.uk

There is an international mailing list of the IALC members. They may be addressed at ialc@ajpo.sei.cmu.edu

4

The Ada WWW Server

Magnus Kempe
Software Engineering Lab
Institute of Technology in Lausanne
Switzerland

Email: Magnus.Kempe@di.epfl.ch

4.1 Contents

- Introduction

- What's on the server?

- What is WWW?

- Some WWW browsers

- WWW by e-mail

- Copying this FAQ

4.2 Introduction

The Ada WWW Server is a hypertext information server to help disseminate information about the Ada programming language. It is alive and heavily used. The Ada WWW server is managed by Magnus Kempe and located at the Software Engineering Lab of the Swiss Federal Institute of Technology in Lausanne, Switzerland.

In this article you will find: an overview of the contents of the Ada WWW server, general information on WWW, references to some available WWW browsers, and directions to access WWW through e-mail.

The latest version of this FAQ is always accessible through WWW as
   http://lglwww.epfl.ch/Ada/FAQ/ada-www-server.html
The URL of the Ada WWW Server is
   http://lglwww.epfl.ch/Ada/
[don't forget the trailing '/', and it's 'Ada', not 'ADA' or 'ada'].

The Ada WWW Server keeps growing. All comments, ideas, contributions, and requests for additions or corrections, are most welcome.

Email should be directed to the maintainer, "Magnus.Kempe@di.epfl.ch".

4.3   What's on the server?

The Ada WWW Server provides Ada-related information and hypertext access in areas including (the following is a non-exhaustive list):

- Reference Manuals

  - hypertext versions of LRM 83 and of (draft 4.0) RM 95 + text of LRM 83 and RM 95

  - text of the rationales for Ada 83 and 95 & State of Ada 95 Revision Process

- Resources

  - standards

  - bindings

  - tools and components

  - software repositories

  - books, articles, and online papers

  - research activities

  - current list of validated compilers

  - cheap and free compilers

  - educational discounts

  - CD-ROMs

- Intellectual Ammunition

  - some facts about the language

  - Ada 95

  - Ada in academia

  - Ada in industry

  - special interest groups

  - debunking some myths

- Historical Notes on Ada

  - the Lady and the programming language

- Introductory Material

  - design goals and summary of the language + textbooks

  - free compilers

- Frequently Asked Questions–with Answers

  - comp.lang.ada

  - Ada WWW

  - Team-Ada

- FTP Sites–and Mirrors

- Ada-related News and Events

  - conferences, workshops

  - calendar

  - press releases

  - technical and other news

- Ada Picture Gallery

- CS Technical Reports

For instance, you will find the list of schools using Ada in CS1 or CS2, an article on commercial success stories, information about software components, as well as hypertext versions of the Ada reference manual (both 83 and draft 95).

4.4   What is WWW?

The World Wide Web (WWW) is what Fortune Magazine ("The Internet And Your Business," March 7, 1994, pp. 86-96) called the "killer application" that will make the Internet indispensable to anyone in the 1990's just as the spreadsheet did for the PC in the 1980's.

WWW is like a distributed hypermedia encyclopedia. It is a database and communications protocol, it is multimedia, distributed, and hypertext. Clicking on links takes the user from document to document, from site to site, world-wide. WWW was originally developed by researchers at CERN, Geneva, Switzerland.

The basic concepts used in WWW are hypertext – text that is not constrained to be linear – and multimedia – information that is not constrained to be text. With hypertext, documents can contain links to other documents, or another reference within the same document. With multimedia, documents can contain objects that are not necessarily text – sounds, movies, and interactive sessions are all possible.

WWW has also attracted attention from Business Week (two articles, March 28, 1994, pp. 170 and 180), Byte ("Data Highway", March 1994), Scientific American ("Wire Pirates", March 1994), German Der Spiegel (March 1994), and British PC Week (March 15, 1994). In March 1994, WWW was featured on CNN's FutureWatch.

For more information, read the WWW FAQ, available in hypertext at

http://sunsite.unc.edu/boutell/faq/www_faq.html,

and in the FTP archive of news.answers:

ftp://rtfm.mit.edu/pub/usenet/news.answers/www/faq.

4.5   Some WWW browsers

WWW browsers are available for all major platforms (VMS, Windows, DOS, UNIX, VM, NeXTstep, and Macintosh). Here is some information about some of them.

For instance, Mosaic is the name of an application which lets users navigate through the Internet and browse through the Web; this software –distributed free to anyone who requests it and available for UNIX workstations, Macintosh systems, and MS Windows – was developed at NCSA, Champaign-Urbana, Illinois. The Mosaic binaries are FTP-able from

ftp://ftp.ncsa.uiuc.edu/Mosaic/Mosaic-binaries,
ftp://ftp.ncsa.uiuc.edu/Mac/Mosaic, and
ftp://ftp.ncsa.uiuc.edu/PC/Mosaic.

Lynx is a full screen browser for vt100 terminals; precompiled binaries are available from
ftp://ftp2.cc.ukans.edu/pub/lynx.

Cello is a client for PCs running Windows, available from
ftp://fatty.law.cornell.edu/pub/LII/Cello.

W3 is an Emacs subsystem, available from
ftp://cs.indiana.edu/pub/elisp/w3.

If you work on a UNIX machine, a WWW browser might already be installed, so you may try to execute
xmosaic http://lglwww.epfl.ch/Ada/ or
Mosaic http://lglwww.epfl.ch/Ada/

If you do not yet have a WWW browser, you can go over the Internet with
telnet info.cern.ch

which will bring you to the WWW Home Page at CERN. You are now using a simple line-mode browser. To move around the Web, enter the number given after an item. To go to the Ada WWW Server, enter
go http://lglwww.epfl.ch/Ada/

4.6   WWW by e-mail

If you do not have direct Internet access (i.e. ftp, telnet, etc.), you can still retrieve WWW documents by e-mail: send a message to
test-list@info.cern.ch with one or more lines of the form
send [http-address]
e.g. send http://lglwww.epfl.ch/Ada/

At the bottom of the message that you will be sent, you will find all links of the document that you requested. Note that your mail system must be gatewayed to Internet mail.

For more information on how to access the Web, read the WWW FAQ (mentioned above).

5

Ada and software quality

Ian Pascoe
Rational Software Corporation
2A Portersbridge Mews
Romsey
Hampshire
SO51 8DJ
UK

Tel: +44 1794 514388
Email: ianp@rational.com

5.1 Introduction

It is a fact of life that the 'Q' word has become very over-exposed within a relatively short space of time. 'Quality' has become rather like 'Art' - a concept that is almost impossible to define in absolute terms but each observer has a clear and personal preference when presented with examples. Such is especially true of software. Is it indeed possible to define a piece of quality software without any ambiguity? Whilst some relatively trivial measures such as layout, readability and documentation might suffice at one level, metrics such as freedom from bugs, reusability and the ability of the software to meet the specification are more relevant but are neither extensive nor complete.

This paper examines some of the issues which surround this complex topic and suggests that the use of the Ada language does add considerable benefit to the software development process.

5.2 Software quality must improve

There are few finished products around today that do not depend upon software for a large part of their functionality - from domestic goods such as washing machines, electric razors and food processors, to ultra sophisticated transportation and communications systems. Whilst hailed in many quarters as the new Industrial Revolution and offering solutions to many of the world's requirements for increasingly sophisticated products, software has its problems and its sceptics. To observers outside the industry it must appear that software successes are few, since failures are widely publicised whether or not the fault can be directly attributed to a software malfunction.

The move away from centralised computing facilities to distributed, workstation-based environments has resulted in lower licensing costs for software tools, which is even more evident in the rapidly changing PC marketplace. For the price of a modest PC and a handful of software tools, a software development factory can be established without any requirement for licensing of the facility or registration and training of the staff. It is this availability, backed up by a growing management demand for least-cost tooling that is providing unlimited potential to ruin industries wholesale. In an ever-increasing number of companies, directors are betting their companies' futures and their personal reputations through the acquisition of low-cost development tools chosen by in-house practitioners for their 'toy' value. Why are software tools not considered in the same light as any other factory or production investment, since a business decision to develop a line-of-business approach justifies, as a minimum, a realistic assessment of the tooling and preparation costs?

Other reasons which could force organisations to re-assess the impact of software tooling decisions and quality range from external customer and commercial pressures to internal financial and project constraints. However, one further external pressure might yet become the most compelling - the threat of legal action resulting from a product failure directly attributable to software faults. As yet, no one person or company has been sued in the UK for poor quality software but cases have been brought elsewhere and the law is being given provisions to ensure success in future prosecutions.

5.3   Current legislation

So who cares about this? Any company that currently indulges in the development, supply or use of software as a main business activity should already be aware of its obligations and liabilities under the existing Acts, under the Law of Contract where such is in place for a specific piece of work, or under a tort of negligence to an injured third party on whom the onus of proof rests. Product liability under the 1987 Consumer Protection Act imposes the most rigorous test on a manufacturer and the definition of "product" within this Act could be interpreted to include software. The booklet entitled "Product Liability and Computer Software"[1] is recommended for further background reading.

Liability under the Health and Safety at Work Act applies to employers who make equipment available for use by their employees, although some liability could be passed back up to higher-level suppliers. However, this Act does have some impact on equipment design and operation, in that errors must not lead to dangerous situations and any interaction between operator and any control system must be "user-friendly" and not exacerbate any potentially dangerous situation.

However, changes are underway, particularly as a result of continuing European Union (EU) pressure. It was such pressure which resulted in the Consumer Protection Act replacing previous legislation and it is the EU which is causing further changes to the 1992 Supply of Machinery (Safety) Regulations Act. It is this Act which could have most impact on the software industry and current practitioners are well advised to obtain copies of the current law and track the changes which are being proposed. Each change is an opportunity for legislation to catch up on the need to control the impact of software, particularly as understanding and awareness increases. Legislation will expand to impact more and more upon the software development process, particularly as the number of Standards Bodies and Accreditation Centres increases and thoughts about employee certification begin to gain momentum. The unassailable argument is - why train professional such as pilots and doctors so rigorously if their direction and control is circumvented by computer systems developed by unaccredited and unlicensed practitioners?

5.4   Key elements

It is accepted that software development is a complex activity, whether represented as a classic "Waterfall", as a V-model or as an iterative process. A number of stages, typically specification of requirements, design, development, testing and validation, have to be completed and integrated with various control activities. The "invisibility" of software until a level of identifiable base functionality is achieved makes it hard to understand or assess the rate of progress, much less appreciate what level of quality is being attained. There are, however, a number of measures that can be adopted which can improve matters considerably. From observations of a number of projects over many years, the four key elements which affect quality and overall project performance appear to be as follows:

- Choice of programming language;

- Use of quality metrics;

- Adequate testing;

- Control of the production process.

The decision on computer language is crucial, particularly for those safety or event-critical applications. Choice of language has a bearing on the selection of testing tools which provide better visibility of software quality and test coverage, particularly if the language is supported by a compiler that is incapable of checking anything! It is also strange that techniques which have been developed to control the mechanical engineering development processes have not been either amended to fit the software development process, or that the software development hasn't changed to fit the mechanical engineering model. There are a wealth of good techniques which are backed up by good software packages, some of which must be capable of translation to support a software production system. But by whatever means, overall control of the production activity is vital to success.

5.5   Language requirements

For managers concerned with the overall development process there are four criteria that any language should meet, if profitability, timescales and quality considerations are to be met:-

- Support for "software engineering";

- "Programming in the Large";

- High and low level support;

- Controlled language standard.

Support for software engineering includes such features as good code readability, strong typing, information hiding and data abstraction, all of which promote code reliability.

Features such as object-oriented design, separate compilation units, library management systems and modularity promote and enable software development by teams rather than individuals - the concept of "Programming in the Large".

It is a fact of life that not all computing tasks can be performed entirely by a high-level language, particularly for the development of embedded systems. The facility to incorporate assembly code inserts should be easy to implement within the chosen language and by the particular compiler.

From the overall management perspective, the last point is the most important. Not only must the language standard be closely controlled but the tools which support the standard must also be very closely monitored to ensure consistency and repeatability. No Ada compiler, for example, can be sold without first passing the mandated suite of some 4,500 separate tests. By comparison, the lack of an overall C++ standard means that each C++ compiler is essentially a different language, which does not encourage either code portability or staff mobility.

Given that these criteria are important and essential to the success of the organisation, the reasons for choosing Ada in the majority of cases should be self-evident. The arguments in favour of Ada are contained in the materials that Ada UK sends out in response to enquiries and acknowledged in numerous publications. As a definitive text, the book "Programming in Ada"[2] is recommended.

Apart from meeting these criteria, Ada also supports other areas of the development lifecycle. More of the system design can be captured in Ada than in any other language. A good Ada compiler will enforce programming standards and detect errors at a much earlier point in the process. Reliable code means that it is feasible to consider building re-usable modules and components. "If it compiles it will probably work" is the Ada axiom, whereas with other languages integration problems really start after compilation. It is this development discipline which, with access to the program library system and intermediate language representation, provides a mechanism for integrating compilers within a production control environment such as Apex. The use of an integrated suite of software tools offers considerable benefits to the responsible software engineer and project manager.

5.6   Quality metrics requirements

Without stating any particular preferences for specific metrics, it is important to recognise that there are certain checks that should be completed on both source and object code on a regular basis throughout the development activity.

Static analyses are those checks carried out on source code, regardless of application or language. Given adequate tool support, static checks should include an assessment of the written source code against programming standards, including any particular in-house standards that developers are required to follow. In addition, measurements of dataflow and complexity should also be carried out on a regular basis, to ensure that there are no unassigned variables, for example, and that the developed code is neither too convoluted or complex to allow adequate and comprehensive testing.

Dynamic analyses are completed on the executable code to provide evidence of test coverage and testing effectiveness. Depending on the scope of the analysis tool, it may be impossible to complete timing tests due to the intrusive nature of the coverage analysis. However, and particularly where event critical applications are concerned, it is essential to determine and confirm how effective the test cases have been in exercising all areas of the executable code.

The use of static and dynamic analysis tools is even more essential for some languages than others, particularly where compiler syntax, error recovery and run-time checks are rudimentary. The availability of suitable tools means that there is no excuse for not completing such assessments, whatever the project or application.

5.7   Automated testing

It is a sad fact of life that the statement "testing gets done if the project has some contingency left..." is more true than not. Even organisations and projects which do subscribe to a defined testing process are often unable to quantify the percentage of test coverage that is being achieved by the test data. If this state of affairs is linked back to the expected pressure from emerging legislation, a defence against software failure is likely to be the use of best practice in the development process. However, if there is no commitment to testing and testing effectiveness is not being recorded, where is the defence? Automated testing, as a defined, repeated and measured process performed with tools to prove that software either functions as specified or fails to function, must surely become part of the overall development activity.

"As specified" the important rider, not "as written". Experience suggests that, where testing is carried out, testing against the agreed specification is rare, whilst using junior programmers to develop test cases to prove that what has been written works is a common practice which achieves very little. Quantitative measurements are still lacking in the majority of projects - a formal recording of the percentages of statements, branches and test paths covered by the test data. In addition to current revisions in the legislation, further legal extensions are being considered to require testing at the machine code level, particularly for safety-critical real-time applications, which will require even more rigorous procedures.

The first successful prosecution is likely to open the floodgates for other cases. A wise course of action will be to prepare against any eventuality, with a documented commitment to the training of dedicated testing staff, developing and deploying testing standards and use of formal testing tools, in addition to an ability to provide documented evidence on tests completed and coverage metrics achieved.

5.8   Production control requirements

The problems of software development are exacerbated by the sheer number of tasks to be completed during a project by people of varying disciplines. Controlling this production process is now a vital activity which is all too often ignored, or "solved" using a variety of unintegrated and unproved CASE tools. New technology, such as PCTE, is being held up as a possible panacea which will allow every vendor's PCTE-compatible toolsets to be plugged into the environment according to taste and requirement. This reasoning, and the possible emergence of other so-called standards, are responsible for masking and delaying the pressing need for control. Integrated environments are available now on open-systems platforms which offer support for Ada and which have been proven to deliver business benefits across a wide range of projects.

Controlling the process demands consistent information to prevent the re-introduction of errors through mis-keying. Time spent in re-iterative activities such as compilation, debugging and selective recompilation must be automated within the environment. Above all, every item of code must be subjected to rigorous configuration management and version control to minimise system errors and ensure that reliable project information is available. Given that production teams may well be geographically separated either within a site or across multiple sites, any chosen environment must support distribution of the development process without loss of control or direction.

The need to adopt and use such integrated toolsets will be driven by impending legislation which will force organisations to focus on the development process and put the onus on developers to use "best practice". In addition, a requirement for software component traceability cannot be far away. This can only be achieved through rigorous configuration management and version control. Ultimately what counts most is the need to succeed, either as an organisation or as an individual. Whilst every professional is concerned about what has to be done and the need to achieve results, unnecessary worry and concern is counter-productive. Good quality information is a necessary counter-balance which helps to control the process and which, ultimately, imparts the "feel-good" factor and frees the manager from any lingering doubts that short-cuts may have been taken that could result in warranty claims or lawsuits.

5.9   Conclusions

So, what for the future? Given that a vast proportion of the world's software has yet to be written, there is no doubt that standards must rise in order that systems and products can be developed with confidence, not only in the production phase, but also within the user community. For those brave souls currently contemplating a development project, the following brief checklist provides an aide-memoire of the topics which should be considered:-

- Is software a vital component for this project/product?

- What are the safety and/or security aspects of this activity?

- Have all measures been documented that will ensure use of "best practice" for this activity?

- Have all the issues which impact process traceability been considered?

- Are plans in place to ensure that 100% testability can be achieved?

Within each topic there are a number of issues which should be debated and reviewed. Not all relate to the use of tools and choice of language but all contribute to the overall issue of improving quality. If software is to fulfil its promise and deliver the functionality that is required, great steps must be made to ensure that the development activity becomes a reliable and reproducible process. For that to be achieved, management decisions should be made within the context of longer-term business issues, with the recognition that adequate tooling costs are a necessary pre-requisite to achieving optimal component reuse which will be necessary to achieve line-of-business profitability. Within this framework, Ada has much to offer, both as a language and as an aid to quality improvement. Ada demands serious consideration but, when used in conjunction with the other elements discussed, could save your company from the effects of litigation in the event that software fails to function as specified.

References

[1] Eversheds, Hepworth & Chadwick. *Product Liability and Computer Software*. Cloth Hall Court, Infirmary Street, Leeds LS1 2BJ. 1994

[2] J.G.P. Barnes. *Programming in Ada Plus an Overview of Ada 9X*. Addison Wesley. 1994.

6

Ada 9X standard approved

James W. Moore
The MITRE Corporation
7525 Colshire Boulevard
W534 McLean
Virginia 22102
USA

Tel: +1 703 883 7396
Email: moorej@ajpo.sei.cmu.edu

"X" was supposed to have been "4", yet the result was still in doubt.

As the delegates to ISO-IEC JTC1/SC22/WG9 convened for their first 1994 meeting, March 14-18 in Villars-sur-Ollon, Switzerland, they knew that they and the Ada 9X Project Team had met, perhaps improbably, the milestones of an ambitious schedule formulated 21 months before. Nevertheless, the goal of timely standardisation remained just beyond their grasp as they learned that the administrative procedures of ISO standardisation would delay completion of the standard until 1995. Although the difference in time, about 3 months, might be small, the political impact on the credibility of the revision could be great. Further adjustments were necessary. The French delegation noted a recent change in ISO procedures permitting a four-month ballot period at the JTC1 level (the final ISO ballot) and the Mapping Revision Team (MRT) promised to send representatives to ISO Central Secretariat in Geneva, Switzerland so that the final text of the standard could be "walked through" enabling the final publication of the standard. The time gained might be just enough to achieve publication in December 1994 if the technical work could be completed rapidly.

At the Villars meeting, the results of the first round of ballots in both ANSI (American National Standards Institute) and ISO (International Organisation for Standardisation) were known. In the ISO ballot of nations participating in Subcommittee 22 (SC22), only a single national body, New Zealand, had voted against the so-called Committee Draft, although nearly every national body had suggested improvements. The ANSI canvass group had voted overwhelmingly in favor of the draft standard, albeit with a large number of comments. So, prospects for eventual approval looked excellent. The dissenting nation, New Zealand, would not even participate at the next (and final) level of ISO balloting because it was not a member of Joint Technical Committee 1 (JTC1), the parent body of SC22. Nevertheless, ISO protocol demanded that WG9 deal with the comments of New Zealand and every other national body which had offered them. The ANSI canvass had been so overwhelmingly affirmative that ANSI standardisation could have been sought immediately, but that would have abandoned the synchronisation process intended to produce identical ANSI and ISO standards.

During the few months since the completion of the ballots, the Ada 9X Project Office, managed by Christine Anderson, had targeted the Villars meeting of WG9 to perfect the technical aspects of the language revision. The MRT, led by Tucker Taft of Intermetrics, had modified its draft to deal with issues exposed by the balloting and by other technical exercises. The modifications had been discussed and refined, via electronic mail and via meetings, with the members of WG9's 9X Rapporteur Group (XRG), chaired by Erhard Ploedereder. The result was a series of Language Study Notes (LSN) which would be considered and resolved by WG9 during its Villars meeting. The MRT could then make the final changes to the draft and submit it for the last round of balloting during summer 1994.

Under the leadership of its convener, Robert Mathis, WG9 had followed a careful process to reach this point. Nearly two years before, the landmark WG9 meeting in Frankfurt had established the revision's technical baseline by refining and adopting Anderson's "Zero-Based Budget". Sixteen months before, the Salem meeting had established the "look" of the long-awaited Object-Oriented Programming portions of the revision. Seven months before, the Boston meeting had resolved the major issues regarding internationalisation of character sets and had repackaged the predefined environment and annexes to emphasise their role as libraries of useful functionality. As a result of the rapid maturation of the revision proposal, the issues for the Villars meeting seemed to be distinctly more academic than the grand issues of previous meetings; the Villars issues stemmed primarily from the ramifications and interactions of those grand decisions.

One example is an issue which came to be known by the phrase "non-binary moduli". There was a long-established and well-known need for systems programmers to have binary types which "wrap around" at a particular bit-length boundary. Some thought, though that confining such moduli to powers of two seemed an unnecessary restriction. Furthermore, non-binary moduli can be useful in certain numerical algorithms and in applications such as hashing. So, the discussion dealt with the trade-off among simplicity of specification, extent of usefulness and cost of implementation in a portion of the language that nearly all would regard as minor. In the end, the MRT described an approach to implementation which gained a narrow vote of approval and the feature was placed in the language.

Another example is an issue known by the phrase "downward closures". The MRT had long ago found a safe way to correct one of the most criticised omissions of Ada 87, a straight-forward mechanism for passing subprograms as parameters to other subprograms. In exploring its use, though, early users of the revised language had discovered that they occasionally wished to pass as a parameter a subprogram which was more deeply nested. The proposed revision provided no facility for this, yet early users claimed that one could program oneself "into a corner" if they didn't have such a facility. The meeting discussed various changes which might accommodate the needs of these users and finally settled, again by a narrow vote, upon a mechanism which was already in the language, a particular use of generic formal subprograms.

Even if the grand issues were settled, many pedestrian ones remained. By narrow votes in previous meetings, the legality of a trailing underscore in the name of an identifier had been approved. No one really liked the look of such a thing, but it provided a straightforward way to change existing programs containing identifiers which clashed with the new key words introduced by Ada 9X. The change had drawn a surprising amount of criticism in the balloting process, though. Thoroughly tired of the issue, WG9 after only a few minutes of discussion, decided to revert to the rules of Ada 87 and never to discuss the issue again.

Perhaps the most bedeviling of issues was the naming of the subprogram to make any needed changes to a new value of a controlled object following its assignment. For months, the operation had been known by the mundane and inappropriate name of "Split" while the MRT and the committee waited for a better name to surface. Throughout the week, WG9 delegates, hoping for inspiration, added suggestions, both serious and whimsical, to a chart posted in the back of the room. In the final vote a name, appropriate if equally mundane, was adopted – "Adjust".

Aside from perfecting both the obscure and the ordinary portions of the revision, though, the delegates to WG9 did find themselves with a new set of issues resulting from the balloting process. The balloting had revealed a substantial and persuasive body of sentiment that Ada 87 had made it just too hard to perform straightforward operations that other languages could do very simply, like return an exit status code from a main program. Furthermore, teachers and text book authors complained that difficult portions of the language, like generics, had to be taught before simple operations, like text input/output, could be illustrated in examples. So, the Villars meeting found itself dealing with a number of individual issues lumped into the general category of "environmental friendliness". The group added a package providing facilities for getting parameters from the command line and for setting a status code upon exit. Predefined instantiations of the generic packages for numeric text I/O were added (at Villars and at the later meeting in Baltimore) so that users (and text book writers) did not have to deal with generics in order to perform simple I/O. Facilities were added to text input/output to make it easier for users to perform interactive character-at-a-time I/O or to write their own customised I/O packages.

The facilities for interoperability with other languages received a great deal of attention as it becomes clearer that modern Ada systems will probably be multi-lingual integrations of existing components and off-the-shelf products. Mechanisms for linking Ada object modules with those produced by COBOL, Fortran and C were completed.

Improvements to Ada's information systems processing capabilities continued to receive its share of attention. One issue was the provision of COBOL-like picture clauses for the editing of output strings. Ben Brosgol and his colleagues had found that the working group's direction to make Ada picture formats "just like" the COBOL picture, except for certain improvements, contained a dilemma. It turned out to be very hard to precisely specify the editing performed by picture strings. (The COBOL standard contains pages of inscrutable text which has accumulated over history.) So, the Ada standard could simply make a reference to the difficult COBOL standard, noting specific changes, or the Ada standard could, with appropriate changes, copy the text from the COBOL standard. Both solutions left the reader of the standard with little usable guidance. During the discussion, Brosgol mentioned that he had been able to rewrite the COBOL rules in a more compact and readable fashion that seemed to produce identical results in all but the most obscure of areas. WG9 seized on that solution and directed the MRT to implement it. Ironically, the resulting specification is now being considered by the COBOL standardisation committee for incorporation in their next revision.

The other specialised needs areas were modified in response to balloting comments. Numerics, led by Ken Dritz, made changes to the discrete random number generator in order to improve its soundness. Anthony Gargaro's Distributed Systems annex was changed to better specify the behavior of tagged types shared among partitions. Small but important changes were made to the Real-time and Systems Programming annexes, edited by Offer Pazy and Ted Baker, to meet the needs of various real-time communities. The Safety & Security annex, edited by Brian Wichmann, received little attention in the WG9 meeting; balloting comments on its contents were minor.

The Villars meeting of WG9 ended with the delegates optimistic that the remainder of the standardisation process would complete during 1994. A set of summary resolutions encouraged compiler implementors to begin the incorporation of 9X features in their products, encouraged the validation authorities to permit this, and encouraged users to begin the transition process.

At WG9's second meeting of the year, convened November 11 in Baltimore, the optimism appeared to be justified. The newest revision of the standard had been overwhelmingly approved by the second ballot of the ANSI canvass group. The national body members of ISO JTC1 had approved it by a vote of eighteen in favor and none opposed with two abstentions. Nevertheless, minor revisions were needed to deal with the comments provided by the various national bodies. Because the XRG had carefully prepared proposed resolutions in a prior meeting, WG9 was able to quickly deal with the few remaining issues and turn its attention from the 9X revision to its other business.

The Numerics Rapporteur Group reported that two of their proposed standards, on Elementary Mathematical Functions and on Primitive Mathematical Functions, had completed their ISO balloting process and had been sent to the Secretariat for publication. The SQL Rapporteur Group reported that their proposed standard, the SAMeDL (SQL/Ada Module Design Language), had achieved the same result. The Real-Time Rapporteur Group reported that their Technical Report on Ada Real-Time Facilities had been approved by SC22 and submitted to JTC1 for its final ISO ballot.

The convener announced that SC22, at its previous meeting, had approved withdrawing the work items for the Ada Rapporteur Group, which provides interpretations to the Ada 87 standard, and the Uniformity Rapporteur Group, which facilitates uniformity of implementations, on the grounds that the work of these groups was now completed. WG9 reconstituted the two groups to perform the analogous functions for the new 9X standard. New Rapporteur Groups were formed to work in the areas of Verification and Bindings.

At the conclusion of the meeting (and as of this writing, November 28, 1994) it remains unclear whether ISO publication of the Ada 9X standard will occur before year-end 1994. Representatives of the MRT are in Geneva to assist in accelerating the process. In any case, Ada 9X will be distinguished as the first object-oriented language to be internationally standardised. At a banquet on November 10, the various key contributors to Ada 9X were assembled to celebrate the success of their contributions. The Honorable Emmett Paige Jr., Assistant Secretary of Defense and key Ada proponent in the U.S. Department of Defense, lauded the participants and announced his intention to award Chris Anderson the highest civilian award available to Defense employees for her leadership in bringing the program to its completion.

The new Ada Standard is to be published in 1995. Its designation will be "ISO/IEC 8652:1995" - *Editor*

7

Highlights of Ada 95*

John Barnes
John Barnes Informatics
11 Albert Road
Caversham
Berkshire
RG4 7AN

Tel: +44 1734 474125
Fax: +44 1734 483474

The brightest highlights of Ada 95 are its inherent reliability and its ability to provide abstraction through the package and private type. These features already exist in Ada 83 and so in a real sense Ada 83 already contains the best of Ada 95. Indeed, Ada 83 is already a very good language. However, time and technology do not stand still, and Ada 95 is designed to meet increased requirements which have arisen from three directions. These are: feedback from the use of existing paradigms; additional market requirements to match evolving hardware capability; and increased fundamental understanding which has introduced new paradigms. As we will see, Ada 95 follows on from the tradition of excellence of Ada 83 and meets these additional requirements in an outstanding manner.

One of the great strengths of Ada 83 is its reliability. The strong typing and related features ensure that programs contain few surprises; most errors are detected at compile time and of those remaining many are detected by runtime constraints. This aspect of Ada considerably reduces the costs and risks of program development compared for example with C or its derivatives such as C++.

However, Ada 83 has proved to be somewhat less flexible than might be desired in some circumstances. For example, it has not always proved straightforward to interface to non-Ada systems. Moreover, the type model coupled with the flat library mechanism can cause significant costs through the need for apparently unnecessary recompilation.

A prime goal of the design of Ada 95 has thus been to give the language a more open and extensible feel without losing the inherent integrity and efficiency of Ada 83. That is to keep the Software Engineering but allow more flexibility.

The additions in Ada 95 which contribute to this more flexible feel are type extension, the hierarchical library and the greater ability to manipulate pointers or references.

As a consequence, Ada 95 incorporates the benefits of Object Oriented languages without incurring the pervasive overheads of languages such as SmallTalk or the insecurity brought

---

*This paper was received after the announcement that Ada 9X is to be Ada 95.

by the weak C foundation in the case of C++. Ada 95 remains a very strongly typed language but provides the prime benefits of all key aspects of the Object Oriented paradigm.

Another area of major change in Ada 95 is in the tasking model where the introduction of protected types allows a more efficient implementation of standard problems of shared data access. This brings the benefits of speed provided by low-level primitives such as semaphores without the risks incurred by the use of such unstructured primitives. Moreover, the clearly data-oriented view brought by the protected types fits in naturally with the general spirit of the Object Oriented paradigm.

Other improvements to the tasking model allow a more flexible response to interrupts and other changes of state.

Ada 95 also incorporates numerous other minor changes reflecting feedback from the use of existing features as well as specific new features addressing the needs of specialised applications and communities.

This paper highlights the major new features of Ada 95 and the consequential benefits as seen by the general Ada user.

7.1   Programming by extension

The key idea of programming by extension is the ability to declare a new type that refines an existing parent type by inheriting, modifying or adding to both the existing components and the operations of the parent type. A major goal is the reuse of existing reliable software without the need for recompilation and retesting.

Type extension in Ada 95 builds upon the existing Ada 83 concept of a derived type. In Ada 83, a derived type inherited the operations of its parent and could add new operations; however, it was not possible to add new components to the type. The whole mechanism was thus somewhat static. By contrast, in Ada 95 a derived type can also be extended to add new components. As we will see, the mechanism is much more dynamic and allows greater flexibility through late binding and polymorphism.

In Ada 95, record types may be extended on derivation provided that they are marked as tagged. Private types implemented as record types can also be marked as tagged. As the name implies, a tagged type has an associated tag. The word *tag* is familiar from Pascal where it is used to denote what in Ada is known as a discriminant; as we shall see later, the Ada 95 tag is effectively a hidden discriminant identifying the type and so the term is very appropriate.

As a very simple example suppose we wish to manipulate various kinds of geometrical objects which form some sort of hierarchy. All objects will have a position given by their x- and y-coordinates. So we can declare the root of the hierarchy as

```
type Object is tagged
    record
        X_Coord: Float;
        Y_Coord: Float;
    end record;
```

The other types of geometrical objects will be derived (directly or indirectly) from this type. For example we could have

```
type Circle is new Object with
    record
        Radius: Float;
    end record;
```

and the type `Circle` then has the three components X_Coord, Y_Coord and Radius. It inherits the two coordinates from the type `Object` and the component `Radius` is added explicitly.

Sometimes it is convenient to derive a new type without adding any further components. For example

```
type Point is new Object with null record;
```

In this last case we have derived `Point` from `Object` but naturally not added any new components. However, since we are dealing with tagged types we have to explicitly add `with null record;` to indicate that we did not want any new components. This has the advantage that it is always clear from a declaration whether a type is tagged or not. Note that `tagged` is of course a new reserved word; Ada 95 has a small number (six) of such new reserved words.

A private type can also be marked as tagged

```
type Shape is tagged private;
```

and the full type declaration must then (ultimately) be a tagged record

```
type Shape is tagged
    record ...
```

or derived from a tagged record such as `Object`. On the other hand we might wish to make visible the fact that the type `Shape` is derived from `Object` and yet keep the additional components hidden. In this case we would write

```
package Hidden_Shape is
    type Shape is new Object with private;      -- client view
        ...
private
    type Shape is new Object with               -- server view
        record

            -- the private components

        end record;
end Hidden_Shape;
```

In this last case it is not necessary for the full declaration of `Shape` to be derived directly from the type `Object`. There might be a chain of intermediate derived types (it could be derived from `Circle`); all that matters is that `Shape` is ultimately derived from `Object`.

Just as in Ada 83, derived types inherit the operations which "belong" to the parent type these are called *primitive operations* in Ada 95. User-written subprograms are classed as primitive operations if they are declared in the same package specification as the type and have the type as parameter or result.

Thus we might have declared a function giving the distance from the origin

```
function Distance(O: in Object) return Float is
begin
    return Sqrt(O.X_Coord**2 + O.Y_Coord**2);
end Distance;
```

The type `Circle` would then sensibly inherit this function. If however, we were concerned with the area of an object then we might start with

```
function Area(O: in Object) return Float is
begin
    return 0.0;
end Area;
```

which returns zero since a raw object has no area. This would also be inherited by the type `Circle` but would be inappropriate; it would be more sensible to explicitly declare

```
function Area(C: in Circle) return Float is
begin
    return Pi*C.Radius**2;
end Area;
```

which will override the inherited operation.

It is possible to "convert" a value from the type `Circle` to `Object` and vice versa. From Circle to Object is easy, we simply write

```
O: Object := (1.0, 0.5);
C: Circle := (0.0, 0.0, 12.2);
...
O := Object(C);
```

which effectively ignores the third component. However, conversion in the other direction requires the provision of a value for the extra component and this is done by an extension aggregate thus

```
C := (O with 46.8);
```

where the expression O is extended after `with` by the values of the extra components written just as in a normal aggregate. In this case we only had to give a value for the radius.

We now consider a more practical example which illustrates the use of tagged types to build a system as a hierarchy of types and packages. We will see how this allows the system to be extended without recompilation of the central part of the system. By way of illustration we start by showing the rigid way this had to be programmed in Ada 83 by the use of variants.

Our system represents the processing of alerts (alarms) in a ground mission control station. Alerts are of three levels of priority. Low level alerts are merely logged, medium level alerts cause a person to be assigned to deal with the problem and high level alerts cause an alarm bell to ring if the matter is not dealt with by a specified time. In addition, a message is displayed on various devices according to its priority.

First consider how this might have be done in Ada 83

```
with Calendar;
package Alert_System is

    type Priority is (Low, Medium, High);
    type Device is (Teletype, Console, Big_Screen);

    type Alert(P: Priority) is
        record
            Time_Of_Arrival: Calendar.Time;
            Message: Text;
            case P is
```

```
                      when Low => null;
                      when Medium | High =>
                          Action_Officer: Person;
                          case P is
                              when Low | Medium => null;
                              when High =>
                                  Ring_Alarm_At: Calendar.Time;
                          end case;
                  end case;
              end record;

          procedure Display (A: in Alert; On: in Device);
          procedure Handle (A: in out Alert);
          procedure Log (A: in Alert);
          procedure Set_Alarm (A: in Alert);

      end Alert_System;
```

Each alert is represented as a discriminated record with the priority as the discriminant. Perhaps surprisingly, the structure and processing depend on this discriminant in a quite complex manner. One immediate difficulty is that we are more or less obliged to use nested variants because of the rule that all the components of a record have to have different identifiers. The body of the procedure Handle might be

```
procedure Handle(A: in out Alert) is
begin
    A.Time_Of_Arrival := Calendar.Clock;
    Log(A);
    Display(A, Teletype);
    case A.P is
        when Low => null;         -- nothing special
        when Medium | High =>
            A.Action_Officer := Assign_Volunteer;
            Display(A, Console);
            case A.P is
                when Low | Medium => null;
                when High =>
                    Display(A, Big_Screen);
                    Set_Alarm(A);
            end case;
    end case;
end Handle;
```

One problem with this approach is that the code is curiously complex due to the nested structure and consequently hard to maintain and error-prone. If we try to avoid the nested case statement then we have to repeat some of the code.

A more serious problem is that if, for example, we need to add a further alert category, perhaps an emergency alert (which would mean adding another value to the type Priority), then the whole system will have to be modified and recompiled. Existing reliable code will then be disturbed with the risk of subsequent errors.

In Ada 95 we can use a series of tagged types with a distinct procedure Handle for each one. This completely eliminates the need for case statements or variants and indeed the type Priority itself is no longer required because it is now inherent in the types themselves (it is implicit in the tag). The package specification now becomes

```
with Calendar;
```

```
package New_Alert_System  is

    type Device is (Teletype, Console, Big_Screen);

    type Alert is tagged
        record
            Time_Of_Arrival: Calendar.Time;
            Message: Text;
        end record;

    procedure Display(A: in Alert; On: in Device);
    procedure Handle(A: in out Alert);
    procedure Log(A: in Alert);

    type Low_Alert is new Alert with null record;

    type Medium_Alert is new Alert  with
        record
            Action_Officer: Person;
        end record;

    -- now override inherited operation
    procedure Handle(MA: in out Medium_Alert);

    type High_Alert is new Medium_Alert  with
        record
            Ring_Alarm_At: Calendar.Time;
        end record;

    procedure Handle(HA: in out High_Alert);
    procedure Set_Alarm(HA: in High_Alert);

end New_Alert_System;
```

In this formulation the variant record is replaced with the tagged type Alert and three types derived from it. Note that Ada 95 allows a type to be derived in the same package specification as the parent and to inherit all the primitive operations but we cannot add any new primitive operations to the parent after a type has been derived from it. This is different to Ada 83 where the operations were not derivable until after the end of the package specification. This change allows the related types to be conveniently encapsulated all in the same package.

The type Low_Alert is simply a copy of Alert (note with null record;) and could be dispensed with although it maintains equivalence with the Ada 83 version; Low_Alert inherits the procedure Handle from Alert. The type Medium_Alert extends Alert and provides its own procedure Handle thus overriding the inherited version. The type High_Alert further extends Medium_Alert and similarly provides its own procedure Handle. Thus instead of a single procedure Handle containing complex case statements the Ada 95 solution distributes the logic for handling alerts to each specific alert type without any redundancy.

Note that Low_Alert, Medium_Alert and High_Alert all also inherit the procedures Display and Log but without change. Finally, High_Alert adds the procedure Set_Alarm which is not used by the lower alert levels and thus it seems inappropriate to declare it for them.

The package body is as follows

```
package body New_Alert_System  is
```

```
    procedure Handle(A: in out Alert)  is
    begin
        A.Time_Of_Arrival := Calendar.Clock;
        Log(A);
        Display(A, Teletype);
    end Handle;

    procedure Handle(MA: in out Medium_Alert)  is
    begin
        Handle(Alert(MA));              -- handle as plain alert
        MA.Action_Officer := Assign_Volunteer;
        Display(MA, Console);
    end Handle;

    procedure Handle(HA: in out High_Alert)  is
    begin
        Handle(Medium_Alert(HA));   -- conversion
        Display(HA, Big_Screen);
        Set_Alarm(HA);
    end Handle;

    procedure Display(A: in Alert; On: in Device) is separate;
    procedure Log(A: in Alert) is separate;

    procedure Set_Alarm(HA: in High_Alert) is separate;

  end New_Alert_System;
```

Each distinct body for Handle contains just the code relevant to the type and delegates additional processing back to its parent using an explicit type conversion. Note carefully that all type checking is static and so no runtime penalties are incurred with this structure (the variant checks have been avoided).

In the Ada 95 model a new alert level (perhaps Emergency_Alert) can be added without recompilation (and perhaps more importantly, without retesting) of the existing code.

```
with New_Alert_System;
package Emergency_Alert_System is

    type Emergency_Alert is
        new New_Alert_System.Alert with priv' ';

    procedure Handle(EA: in out Emergency_Alert);

    procedure Display(EA: in Emergency_Alert;
                      On: in New_Alert_System.Device);

    procedure Log(EA: in Emergency_Alert);

private
      ...
end Emergency_Alert_System;
```

In the Ada 83 model extensive recompilation would have been necessary since the variant records would have required redefinition. Thus we see that Ada 95 truly provides Programming by Extension.

7.2   Class wide programming

The facilities we have seen so far have allowed us to define a new type as an extension of an existing one. We have introduced the different kinds of alerts as distinct but related types. What we also need is a means to manipulate *any* kind of alert and to process it accordingly. We do this through the introduction of the notion of class-wide types.

With each tagged type T there is an associated type T'Class. This type comprises the union of all the types in the tree of derived types rooted at T. The values of T'Class are thus the values of T and all its derived types. Moreover a value of any type derived from T can be implicitly converted to the type T'Class.

Thus in the case of the type Alert the tree of types is as shown in Figure 1.

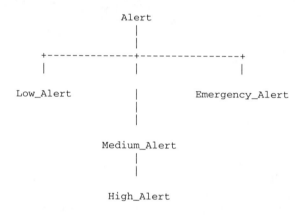

Figure 1: A Tree of Types

A value of any of the alert types can be implicitly converted to Alert'Class. Note carefully that Medium_Alert'Class is not the same as Alert'Class; the former consists just of Medium_Alert and High_Alert.

Each value of a class-wide type has a tag which identifies its particular type from other types in the tree of types at runtime. It is the existence of this tag which gives rise to the term tagged types.

The type T'Class is treated as an unconstrained type; this is because we cannot possibly know how much space could be required by any value of a class-wide type because the type might be extended. As a consequence, although we can declare an object of a class-wide type we must initialize it and it is then constrained by the tag.

However, we can declare an access type referring to a class-wide type in which case the access could designate any value of the class-wide type from time to time. The use of access types is therefore a key factor in class-wide programming. Moreover, a parameter of a procedure can also be of a class-wide type. There is a strong analogy between class-wide types and other unconstrained types such as array types.

We can now continue our example by considering how we might buffer up a series of alerts and process them in sequence. The whole essence of the problem is that such a central routine cannot know of the individual types because we need it to work (without recompilation) even if we extend the system by adding a new alert type to it.

The central routine could thus take a class-wide value as its parameter so we might have

```
procedure Process_Alerts(AC: in out Alert'Class) is
    ...
begin
    ...
    Handle(AC); -- dispatch according to tag
    ...
end Process_Alerts;
```

In this case we do not know which procedure `Handle` to call until runtime because we do not know which specific type the alert belongs to. However, `AC` is of a class-wide type and so its value includes a tag indicating the specific type of the value. The choice of `Handle` is then determined by the value of this tag; the parameter is then implicitly converted to the appropriate specific alert type before being passed to the appropriate procedure `Handle`.

This runtime choice of procedure is called *dispatching* and is key to the flexibility of class-wide programming.

Before being processed, the alerts might be held on a heterogeneous queue using an access type

```
type Alert_Ptr is access Alert'Class;
```

and the central routine could manipulate the alerts directly from such a queue

```
procedure Process_Alerts is
    Next_Alert: Alert_Ptr;
begin
    ...
    Next_Alert :=   -- get next alert
    ...
    Handle(Next_Alert.all);   -- dispatch to appropriate Handle
    ...
end Process_Alerts;
```

In this case, the value of the object referred to by `Next_Alert` is of a class-wide type and so includes a tag indicating the specific type. The parameter `Next_Alert.all` is thus dereferenced, the value of the tag gives the choice of `Handle` and the parameter is then implicitly converted as before and then passed to the chosen procedure `Handle`.

Dispatching may be implemented as a simple indirect jump through a table of subprograms indexed by the primitive operations such as `Handle`. This is generally much more efficient than the alternative of variant records and case statements, with their attendant variant checks.

7.3   Abstract types and subprograms

The final topic to be introduced in this brief introduction to the Object Oriented features of Ada 95 is the concept of abstract tagged types and abstract subprograms. These are marked as abstract in their declaration. The purpose of an abstract type is to provide a common foundation upon which useful types can be built by derivation. An abstract subprogram is a sort of place holder for an operation to be provided (it does not have a body).

An abstract tagged type can have abstract primitive subprograms and these dispatch. An abstract type on its own is of little use because we cannot declare an object of an abstract type.

Upon derivation from an abstract type we can provide actual subprograms for the abstract subprograms of the parent type (and it is in this sense that we said they were place holders). If all the abstract subprograms are replaced by proper subprograms then the type need not be declared as abstract and we can then declare objects of the type in the usual way. (The rules ensure that dispatching always works.)

Returning now to our example of processing alerts we could reformulate this so that the root type Alert was just an abstract type and then build the specific types upon this. This would enable us to program and compile all the general infrastructure routines for processing all alerts such as Process_Alerts in the previous section without any concern at all for the individual alerts and indeed before deciding what they should contain.

The baseline package could then simply become

```
package Base_Alert_System  is
    type Alert is abstract tagged null record;
    procedure Handle(A: in out Alert) is abstract;
end Base_Alert_System;
```

in which we declare the type Alert as a tagged null record with just the procedure Handle as an abstract subprogram; this does not have a body. (Note the abbreviated form for a null record declaration which saves us having to write record null ; end record ;).

We can now develop our alert infrastructure and then later add the normal alert system containing the three levels of alerts thus

```
with Calendar;
with Base_Alert_System;
package Normal_Alert_System  is

    type Device is (Teletype, Console, Big_Screen);

    type Low_Alert is new Base_Alert_System.Alert with
        record
            Time_Of_Arrival: Calendar.Time;
            Message: Text;
        end record;

    -- now provide actual subprogram for abstract one
    procedure Handle(LA: in out Low_Alert);

    procedure Display(LA: in Low_Alert; On: in Device);
    procedure Log(LA: in Low_Alert);

    type Medium_Alert is new Low_Alert with
        record
            Action_Officer: Person;
        end record;

    procedure Handle(MA: in out Medium_Alert);

    type High_Alert is new Medium_Alert with
        record
            Ring_Alarm_At: Calendar.Time;
        end record;

    procedure Handle(HA: in out High_Alert);
    procedure Set_Alarm(HA: in High_Alert);

end Normal_Alert_System;
```

In this revised formulation we must provide a procedure Handle for Low_Alert to meet the promise of the abstract type. The procedures Display and Log now take a parameter of Low_Alert and the type Medium_Alert is more naturally derived from Low_Alert.

Note carefully that we did not make `Display` and `Log` abstract subprograms in the package `Base_Alert_System`. There was no need; it is only `Handle` that is required by the general infrastructure such as the procedure `Process_Alerts` and to add the others would weaken the abstraction and clutter the base level.

Corresponding changes are required to the package body; the procedure `Handle` previously applying to `Alert` now applies to `Low_Alert` and in the procedure `Handle` for `Medium_Alert` we need to change the type conversion in the call to the "parent" `Handle` which is of course now the procedure `Handle` for `Low_Alert`. The two procedures thus become

```
procedure Handle(LA: in out Low_Alert) is
begin
    LA.Time_Of_Arrival := Calendar.Clock;
    Log(LA);
    Display(LA, Teletype);
end Handle;

procedure Handle(MA: in out Medium_Alert) is
begin
    Handle(Low_Alert(MA)); -- handle as low alert
    MA.Action_Officer := Assign_Volunteer;
    Display(MA, Console);
end Handle;
```

When we now add our `Emergency_Alert` we can choose to derive this from the baseline `Alert` as before or perhaps from some other point in the tree picking up the existing facilities of one of the other levels.

7.4   Summary of type extension

The key points we have seen are as follows.

Ada 95 introduces the notion of tagged types. Only record (and private) types can be tagged. Values of tagged types carry a tag with them. The tag indicates the specific type. A tagged type can be extended on derivation with additional components.

Primitive operations of a type are inherited on derivation. The primitive operations are those implicitly declared, plus, in the case of a type declared in a package specification, all subprograms with a parameter or result of that type also declared in the package specification. Primitive operations can be overridden on derivation and further ones added.

A tagged type can be declared as abstract and can have abstract primitive subprograms. An abstract subprogram does not have a body but one can be provided on derivation. An abstract type provides a foundation for building specific types with some common protocol.

`T'Class` denotes the class-wide type rooted at `T`. Implicit conversion is allowed to values of `T'Class`. Objects and parameters of `T'Class` are treated as unconstrained. An appropriate access type can designate any value of `T'Class`.

Calling a primitive operation with an actual parameter of a class-wide type results in dispatching: that is the runtime selection of the operation according to the tag. This is often called late binding a key property of Object Oriented languages.

Another term commonly encountered is polymorphism. Class-wide types are said to be polymorphic because their values are of different "shapes" (from the Greek *poly*, many, and *morphe*, form). Polymorphism is another property of Object Oriented languages.

One of the main advantages of type extension is that it can be done without recompiling and retesting an existing stable system. This is perhaps the most important overall characteristic of Object Oriented languages.

7.5   Dynamic selection

In the previous section we mentioned late binding; this simply means that the procedure to be called is identified late in the compile-link-run process. All procedure calls were bound early in Ada 83 and this was one reason why the language felt so static; even the generic mechanism only deferred binding to instantiation which is still essentially a compile time process.

There were a number of reasons for taking such a static approach in Ada 83. There was concern for the implementation cost of dynamic binding, it was also clear that the presence of dynamic binding would reduce the provability of programs, and moreover it was felt that the introduction of generics where subprograms could be passed as parameters would cater for practical situations where formal procedure parameters were used in other languages.

However, the absence of dynamic binding in Ada 83 has been unfortunate. It is now realized that implementation costs are trivial and not necessarily pervasive; provability is not a relevant argument because we now know that in any safety-critical software where mathematical provability is a real issue, we only use a small subset of the language. And furthermore, the generic mechanism has proved not to be a sufficiently flexible alternative anyway.

We have seen how dispatching in Ada 95 is one mechanism for late binding. Another is provided by the manipulation of subprogram values through an extension of access types.

In Ada 95 an access type can refer to a subprogram; an access-to-subprogram value can be created by the Access attribute and a subprogram can be called indirectly by dereferencing such an access value. Thus we can write

```
type Trig_Function is access function(F: Float) return Float;
T: Trig_Function;
X, Theta: Float;
```

and T can then "point to" functions such as Sin, Cos and Tan. We can then assign an appropriate access-to-subprogram value to T by for example

```
T := Sin'Access;
```

and later indirectly call the subprogram currently referred to by T as expected

```
X := T(Theta);
```

which is really an abbreviation for

```
X := T.all(Theta);
```

Just as with many other uses of access types the .all is not usually required but it would be necessary if there were no parameters.

The access to subprogram mechanism can be used to program general dynamic selection and to pass subprograms as parameters. It allows program call-back to be implemented in a natural and efficient manner.

There are a number of rules which ensure that access to subprogram values cannot be misused. Conformance matching ensures that the subprogram always has the correct number and type of parameters and there are rules about accessibility that ensure that a subprogram is not called out of context. Flexibility is thus gained without loss of integrity.

Simple classic numerical algorithms can now be implemented in Ada 95 in the same way as in languages such as Fortran but with complete security. Thus an integration routine might have the following specification

```
type Integrand is access function(X: Float) return Float;

function Integrate(F: Integrand; From, To: Float;
                   Accuracy: Float := 1.0E-7) return Float;
```

and we might then write

```
Area := Integrate(Log'Access, 1.0, 2.0);
```

which will compute the area under the curve for *log(x)* from 1.0 to 2.0. Within the body of the function Integrate there will be calls of the actual subprogram passed as a parameter; this is a simple form of call-back.

A common paradigm within the process industry is to implement sequencing control through successive calls of a number of interpreter actions. A sequence compiler might interactively build an array of such actions which are then obeyed. Thus we might have

```
type Action is access procedure;
Action_Sequence: array(1 .. N) of Action;

... -- build the array
    -- and then obey it
for I in Action_Sequence'Range loop
    Action_Sequence(I).all;
end loop;
```

It is of course possible for a record (possibly private) to contain components whose types are access to subprogram types. Consider the following example of a package which provides facilities associated with the actions obtained when we press keys on our keyboard or perhaps click our mouse on a window button.

```
package Push_Buttons  is

    type Button is private;

    type Button_Response is access
                   procedure(B: in out Button);

    function Create(...) return Button;

    procedure Push(B: in out Button);

    procedure Set_Response(B: in out Button;
                           R: in Button_Response);

    procedure Default_Response(B: in out Button);

    ...

private
    type Button  is
```

```
          record
              Response: Button_Response := Default_Response'Access;
                   ... -- other aspects of the button
          end record;
   end Push_Buttons;
```

A button is represented as a private record containing a number of components describing properties of the button (position on screen for example). One component is an access to a procedure which is the action to be executed when the button is pushed. Note carefully that the button value is passed to this procedure as a parameter so that the procedure can obtain access to the other components of the record describing the button. The procedure Create fills in these other components and other functions (not shown) provide access to them. The procedure Push invokes the action of clicking the mouse and an appropriate default procedure is provided which warns the user if the button has not been set. The body might be as follows

```
   package body Push_Buttons  is

       procedure Push(B: in out Button)  is
       begin
           B.Response(B);      -- indirect call
       end Push;

       procedure Set_Response(B: in out Button;
                                 R: in Button_Response)  is
       begin
           B.Response := R;    -- set procedure value in record
       end Set_Response;

       procedure Default_Response(B: in out Button)  is
       begin
           Put("Button not set");
           Monitor.Beep;
       end Default_Response;

       ...
   end Push_Buttons;
```

We can now set the specific actions we want when a button is pushed. Thus we might want some emergency action to take place when a big red button is pushed.

```
   Big_Red_Button: Button;

   procedure Emergency(B: in out Button)  is
   begin
       -- call fire brigade etc
   end Emergency;
   ...
   Set_Response(Big_Red_Button, Emergency'Access);
   ...
   Push(Big_Red_Button);
```

The reader will realize that the access to subprogram mechanism coupled with the inheritance and dispatching facilities described earlier enable very flexible yet secure dynamic structures to be programmed.

7.6   Other access types

We have just seen how access types in Ada 95 have been extended to provide a means of manipulating subprogram values. Access types have also been extended to provide more flexible access to objects.

In Ada 83, access values could only refer to objects dynamically created through the allocator mechanism (using new). It was not possible to access objects declared in the normal way. This approach was inherited from Pascal which had similar restrictions and was a reaction against the very flexible approach adopted by Algol 68 and C which can give rise to dangerous dangling references.

However, the ability to manipulate pointers is very valuable provided the risks can be overcome. The view taken by Ada 83 has proved unnecessarily inflexible, especially when interfacing to external systems possibly written in other languages.

In Ada 95 we can declare a general access type such as

```
type Int_Ptr is access all Integer;
```

and we can then assign the "address" of any variable of type `Integer` to a variable of type `Int_Ptr` provided that the designated variable is marked as aliased. So we can write

```
IP: Int_Ptr;
I: aliased Integer;
...
IP := I'Access;
```

and we can then read and update the variable I through the access variable IP. Note once more the use of 'Access. Note also that aliased is another new reserved word.

As with access to subprogram values there are rules that (at compile time) ensure that dangling references cannot arise.

A variation is that we can restrict the access to be read-only by replacing all in the type definition by constant. This allows read-only access to any variable and also to a constant thus

```
type Const_Int_Ptr is access constant Integer;
CIP: Const_Int_Ptr;
I: aliased Integer;
C: aliased constant Integer := 1815;
```

followed by

```
CIP := I'Access;   -- access to a variable, or
CIP := C'Access;   -- access to a constant
```

The type accessed by a general access type can of course be any type such as an array or record. We can thus build chains from records statically declared. Note that we can also use an allocator to generate general access values. Our chain could thus include a mixture of records from both storage mechanisms.

Finally note that the accessed object could be a component of a composite type. Thus we could point into the middle of a record (provided the component is marked as aliased). In a fast implementation of Conway's Game of Life a cell might contain access values directly referencing the component of its eight neighbors containing the counter saying whether the cell is alive or dead.

```
type Ref_Count is access constant Integer range 0 .. 1;
type Ref_Count_Array is array (Integer range <>) of Ref_Count;

type Cell is
    record
        Life_Count: aliased Integer range 0 .. 1;
        Total_Neighbor_Count: Integer range 0 .. 8;
        Neighbor_Count: Ref_Count_Array(1 .. 8);
        ...
    end record;
```

We can now link the cells together according to our model by statements such as

```
This_Cell.Neighbor_Count(1) := Cell_To_The_North.Life_Count'Access;
```

and then the heart of the computation which computes the sum of the life counts in the neighbors might be

```
C.Total_Neighbor_Count := 0;

for I in C.Neighbor_Count'Range loop
    C.Total_Neighbor_Count :=
        C.Total_Neighbor_Count + C.Neighbor_Count(I).all;
end loop;
```

Observe that we have given the type Ref_Count and the component Life_Count the same static subtypes so that they can be checked at compile time; this is not essential but avoids a run-time check that would otherwise be required if they did not statically match.

General access types can also be used to program static ragged arrays as for example a table of messages of different lengths. The key to this is that the accessed type can be unconstrained (such as String) and thus we can have an array of pointers to strings of different lengths. In Ada 83 we would have had to allocate all the strings dynamically using an allocator.

In conclusion we have seen how the access types of Ada 83 have been considerably enhanced in Ada 95 to allow much more flexible programming which is especially important in open systems while nevertheless retaining the inherent security missing in languages such as C and C ++.

7.7   Hierarchical libraries

One of the great strengths of Ada is the library package where the distinct specification and body decouple the user interface to a package (the specification) from its implementation (the body). This enables the details of the implementation and the clients to be recompiled separately without interference provided the specification remains stable.

However, although this works well for smallish programs it has proved cumbersome when programs become large or complex. There are two aspects of the problem: the coarse control of visibility of private types and the inability to extend without recompilation.

There are occasions when we wish to write two logically distinct packages which nevertheless share a private type. We could not do this in Ada 83. We either had to make the type not private so that both packages could see it with the unfortunate consequence that all the client packages could also see the type; this broke the abstraction. Or, on the other hand, if we wished to keep the abstraction, then we had to merge the two packages together and this resulted in a large monolithic package with increased recompilation costs. (We discount as naughty the use of tricks such as Unchecked_Conversion to get at the details of private types.)

The other aspect of the difficulty arose when we wished to extend an existing system by adding more facilities to it. If we add to a package specification then naturally we have to recompile it but moreover we also have to recompile all existing clients even if the additions have no impact upon them.

In Ada 95 these and other similar problems are solved by the introduction of a hierarchical library structure containing child packages and child subprograms. There are two kinds of children: public children and private children. We will just consider public children for the moment; private children are discussed in the next section.

Consider first the familiar example of a package for the manipulation of complex numbers. It might contain the private type itself plus the four standard operations and also subprograms to construct and decompose a complex number taking a cartesian view. Thus we might have

```
package Complex_Numbers is

    type Complex is private;

    function "+" (Left, Right: Complex) return Complex;
    ... -- similarly "-", "*" and "/"

    function Cartesian_To_Complex(Real, Imag: Float)
            return Complex;

    function Real_Part(X: Complex) return Float;

    function Imag_Part(X: Complex) return Float;

    private
    ...
end Complex_Numbers;
```

We have deliberately not shown the completion of the private type since it is immaterial how it is implemented. Although this package gives the user a cartesian view of the type, nevertheless it certainly does not have to be implemented that way.

Some time later we might need to additionally provide a polar view by the provision of subprograms which construct and decompose a complex number from and to its polar coordinates. In Ada 83 we could only do this by adding to the existing package and this forced us to recompile all the existing clients.

In Ada 95, however, we can add a child package as follows

```
package Complex_Numbers.Polar is

    function Polar_To_Complex(R, Theta: Float)
            return Complex;
    function "abs" (Right: Complex) return Float;
    function Arg(X: Complex) return Float;

end Complex_Numbers.Polar;
```

and within the body of this package we can access the private type Complex itself.

Note the notation, a package having the name P.Q is a child package of its parent package P. We can think of the child package as being declared inside the declarative region of its parent but after the end of the specification of its parent; most of the visibility rules stem from this model. In other words the declarative region defined by the parent (which is primarily both the specification and body of the parent) also includes the space occupied by the text of the children; but it is important to realize that the children are inside that region and do not just extend it. Observe that the child does not need a with clause for the parent and that the entities of the parent are directly visible without a use clause.

In just the same way, library packages in Ada 95 can be thought of as being declared in the declarative region of the package Standard and after the end of its specification. Note that a child subprogram is not a primitive operation of a type declared in its parent's specification because the child is not declared in the specification but after it.

The important special visibility rule is that the private part (if any) and the body of the child have visibility of the private part of their parent. (They naturally also have visibility of the visible part.) However, the visible part of a (public) child package does not have visibility of the private part of its parent; if it did it would allow renaming and hence the export of the hidden private details to any client; this would break the abstraction of the private type (this rule does not apply to private children as explained later).

The body of the child package for our complex number example could simply be

```
package body Complex_Numbers.Polar is
    -- bodies of Polar_To_Complex etc
end Complex_Numbers.Polar;
```

In order to access the procedures of the child package the client must have a with clause for the child package. However this also implicitly provides a with clause for the parent as well thereby saving us the burden of having to write one separately. Thus we might have

```
with Complex_Numbers.Polar;
package Client is
    ...
```

and then within Client we can access the various subprograms in the usual way by writing Complex_Numbers.Real_Part or Complex_Numbers.Polar.Arg and so on.

Direct visibility can be obtained by use clauses as expected. However, a use clause for the child does not imply one for the parent; but, because of the model that the child is in the declarative region of the parent, a use clause for the parent makes the child name itself directly visible. So writing

```
with Complex_Numbers.Polar; use Complex_Numbers;
```

now allows us to refer to the subprograms as Real_Part and Polar.Arg respectively.

We could of course have added

```
use Complex_Numbers.Polar;
```

and we would then be able to refer to the subprogram Polar.Arg as just Arg.

Child packages thus neatly solve both the problem of sharing a private type over several compilation units and the problem of extending a package without recompiling the clients. They thus provide another form of programming by extension.

A package may of course have several children. In fact with hindsight it might have been more logical to have developed our complex number package as three packages: a parent containing the private type and the four arithmetic operations and then two child packages, one giving the cartesian view and the other giving the polar view of the type. At a later date we could add yet another package providing perhaps the trigonometric functions on complex numbers and again this can be done without recompiling what has already been written and thus without the risk of introducing errors.

The extension mechanism provided by child packages fits neatly together with that provided by tagged types. Thus a child package might itself have a private part and then within that part we might derive and extend a private type from the parent package. This is illustrated by the following example which relates to the processing of widgets in a window system.

```
package XTK is
    type Widget is tagged private;
    type Widget_Access is access Widget'Class;
    ...
private
    type Widget is tagged
        record
            Parent: Widget_Access;
            ...
        end record;
end XTK;

-- now extend the Widget


package XTK.Color is
    type Colored_Widget is new Widget with private;
    ...
private
    type Colored_Widget is new Widget with
        record
            Color: ...
        end record;
end XTK.Color;
```

An interesting point with this construction is that clients at the parent level (those just withing XTK) only see the external properties common to all widgets, although by class-wide programming using Widget_Access, they may be manipulating colored widgets. However, a client of XTK.Color also has access to the external properties of colored widgets because we have made the extended type visible (although still private of course). It should be noted that in fact the private part of XTK.Color does not actually access the private part of XTK although it has visibility of it. But of course the body of XTK.Color undoubtedly will and that is why we need a child package.

Another example is provided by the alert system discussed in section 7.1. It would probably be better if the additional package concerning emergency alerts was actually a child of the main package thus

```
package New_Alert_System.Emergency is

    type Emergency_Alert is new Alert with private;
    ...
end New_Alert_System.Emergency;
```

The advantages are manifold. The commonality of naming makes it clear that the child is indeed just a part of the total system; this is emphasized by not needing a with clause for the parent and that the entities in the parent are immediately visible. In addition, although not required in this example, any private mechanisms in the private part of the parent would be visible to the child. The alternative structure in section 7.3 where the baseline used an abstract type could also be rearranged.

The benefit of just the commonality of naming is very important since it prevents the inadvertent interference between different parts of subsystems. This is used to good advantage in the arrangement of the Ada 95 predefined library as will be seen in section 7.13.

Finally, it is very important to realize that the child mechanism is hierarchical. Children may have children to any level so we can build a complete tree providing decomposition of facilities in a natural manner. A child may have a private part and this is then visible from its children but not its parent.

With regard to siblings a child can obviously only have visibility of a previously compiled sibling anyway. And then the normal rules apply: a child can only see the visible part of its siblings.

A parent body may access (via with clauses) and thus depend upon its children and grandchildren. A child body automatically depends upon its parent (and grandparent) and needs no with clause for them. A child body can depend upon its siblings (again via with clauses).

7.8   Private child units

In the previous section we introduced the concept of hierarchical child packages and showed how these allowed extension and continued privacy of private types without recompilation. However, the whole idea was based on the provision of additional facilities for the client. The specifications of the additional packages were all visible to the client.

In the development of large subsystems it often happens that we would like to decompose the system for implementation reasons but without giving any additional visibility to clients.

Ada 83 had a problem in this area which we have not yet addressed. In Ada 83 the only means at our disposal for the decomposition of a body was the subunit. However, although a subunit could be recompiled without affecting other subunits at the same level, any change to the top level body (which of course includes the stubs of the subunits) required all subunits to be recompiled.

Ada 95 also solves this problem by the provision of a form of child unit that is totally private to its parent. In order to illustrate this idea consider the following outline of an operating system.

```
package OS is
    -- parent package defines types used throughout the system
    type File_Descriptor is private;
    ...
private
    type File_Descriptor is new Integer;
end OS;

package OS.Exceptions is
    -- exceptions used throughout the system
    File_Descriptor_Error,
    File_Name_Error,
    Permission_Error: exception;
end OS.Exceptions;

with OS.Exceptions;
package OS.File_Manager is
    type File_Mode is (Read_Only, Write_Only, Read_Write);
```

```
function Open(File_Name: String; Mode: File_Mode)
    return File_Descriptor;

procedure Close(File: in File_Descriptor);
    ...
end OS.File_Manager;

procedure OS.Interpret(Command: String);

private package OS.Internals is
    ...
end OS.Internals;

private package OS.Internals_Debug is
    ...
end OS.Internals_Debug;
```

In this example the parent package contains the types used throughout the system. There are then three public child units, the package OS.Exceptions containing various exceptions, the package OS.File_Manager which provides file open/close routines (note the explicit with clause for its sibling OS.Exceptions) and a procedure OS.Interpret which interprets a command line passed as a parameter. (Incidentally this illustrates that a child unit can be a subprogram as well as a package. It can actually be any library unit and that includes a generic declaration and a generic instantiation.) Finally we have two private child packages called OS.Internals and OS.Internals_Debug.

A private child (distinguished by starting with the word private) can be declared at any point in the child hierarchy. The visibility rules for private children are similar to those for public children but there are two extra rules.

The first extra rule is that a private child is only visible within the subtree of the hierarchy whose root is its parent. And moreover within that tree it is not visible to the specifications of any public siblings (although it is visible to their bodies).

In our example, since the private child is a direct child of the package OS, the package OS.Internals is visible to the bodies of OS itself, of OS.File_Manager and of OS.Interpret (OS.Exceptions has no body anyway) and it is also visible to both body and specification of OS.Internals_Debug. But it is not visible outside OS and a client package certainly cannot access OS.Internals at all.

The other extra rule is that the visible part of the private child can access the private part of its parent. This is quite safe because it cannot export information about a private type to a client because it is not itself visible. Nor can it export information indirectly via its public siblings because, as mentioned above, it is not visible to the visible parts of their specifications but only to their private parts and bodies.

We can now safely implement our system in the package OS.Internals and we can create a subtree for the convenience of development and extensibility. We would then have a third level in the hierarchy containing packages such as OS.Internals.Devices, OS.Internals.Access_Rights and so on.

It might be helpful just to summarize the various visibility rules which are actually quite simple and mostly follow from the model of the child being located after the end of the specification of its parent but inside the parent's declarative region. (We use "to with" for brevity.)

- A specification never needs to with its parent; it may with a sibling except that a public child specification may not with a private sibling; it may not with its own child (it has not been compiled yet!).

- A body never needs to with its parent; it may with a sibling (private or not); it may with its own child (and grandchild...).

- The entities of the parent are accessible by simple name within a child; a use clause is not required.

- The context clause of the parent also applies to a child.

- A private child is never visible outside the tree rooted at its parent. And within that tree it is not visible to the specifications of public siblings.

- The private part and body of any child can access the private part of its parent (and grandparent...).

- In addition the visible part of a private child can also access the private part of its parent (and grandparent...).

- A with clause for a child automatically implies with clauses for all its ancestors.

- A use clause for a library unit makes the child units accessible by simple name (this only applies to child units for which there is also a with clause).

These rules may seem a bit complex but actually stem from just a few considerations of consistency. Questions regarding access to children of sibling units and other remote relatives follow by analogy with an external client viewing the appropriate subtree.

We conclude our discussion of hierarchical libraries by considering their interaction with generics. Genericity is also an important tool in the construction of subsystems and it is essential that it be usable with the child concept.

Any parent unit may have generic children but a generic parent can only have generic children. If the parent unit is not generic then a generic child may be instantiated in the usual way at any point where it is visible.

On the other hand, if the parent unit is itself generic, then a generic child can be instantiated outside the parent hierarchy provided the parent is first instantiated and the child is mentioned in a with clause; the instantiation of the child then refers to the instantiation of the parent. Note that although the original generic hierarchy consists of library units, the instantiations need not be library units.

As a simple example, we might wish to make the package Complex_Numbers of the previous section generic with respect to the underlying floating point type. We would write

```
generic
    type Float_Type is digits <>;
package Complex_Numbers is
    ...
end Complex_Numbers;

generic package Complex_Numbers.Polar is
    ...
end Complex_Numbers.Polar;
```

and then the instantiations might be

```
with Complex_Numbers;
package Real_Complex_Numbers is new Complex_Numbers(Real);

with Complex_Numbers.Polar;
package Real_Complex_Numbers.Real_Polar is
    new Real_Complex_Numbers.Polar;
```

We thus have to instantiate the generic hierarchy (or as much of it as we want) unit by unit. This avoids a number of problems that would arise with a more liberal approach but enables complete subsystems to be built in a generic manner. In the above example we chose to make the instantiated packages into a corresponding hierarchy but as mentioned they could equally have been instantiated as local packages with unrelated names. But an important point is that the instantiation of the child refers to the instantiation of the parent and not to the generic parent. This ensures that the instantiation of the child has visibility of the correct instantiation of the parent.

The reader will now appreciate that the hierarchical library system of Ada 95 provides a very powerful and convenient tool for the development of large systems from component subsystems. This is of particular value in developing bindings to systems such as POSIX in a very elegantly organized manner.

7.9   Protected types

The rendezvous model of Ada 83 provided an advanced high level approach to task synchro-nisation which avoided the methodological difficulties encountered by the use of low-level primitives such as semaphores and signals. As is well-known, such low-level primitives suffer from similar problems as gotos; it is obvious what they do and they are trivial to implement but in practice easy to misuse and can lead to programs which are difficult to maintain.

Unfortunately the rendezvous has not proved entirely satisfactory. It required additional tasks to manage shared data and this often led to poor performance. Moreover, in some situations, awkward race conditions arose essentially because of abstraction inversion. And from a methodological viewpoint the rendezvous is clearly control oriented and thus out-of-line with a modern object oriented approach.

In Ada 95 we introduce the concept of a protected type which encapsulates and provides synchronised access to the private data of objects of the type without the introduction of an additional task. Protected types are very similar in spirit to the shared objects of the Orca language developed by Bal, Kaashoek and Tanenbaum of Amsterdam [Bal 92].

A protected type has a distinct specification and body in a similar style to a package or task. The specification provides the access protocol and the body provides the implementation details. We can also have a single protected object by analogy with a single task.

As a simple example consider the following

```
protected Variable is
    function Read return Item;
    procedure Write(New_Value: Item);
private
    Data: Item;
end Variable;

protected body Variable is

    function Read return Item is
    begin
        return Data;
    end Read;

    procedure Write(New_Value: Item) is
    begin
        Data := New_Value;
    end Write;
```

```
end Variable;
```

The protected object `Variable` provides controlled access to the private variable `Data` of some type `Item`. The function `Read` enables us to read the current value whereas the procedure `Write` enables us to update the value. Calls use the familiar dotted notation.

```
X := Variable.Read;
...
Variable.Write(New_Value => Y);
```

Within a protected body we can have a number of subprograms and the implementation is such that (like a monitor) calls of the subprograms are mutually exclusive and thus cannot interfere with each other. A procedure in the protected body can access the private data in an arbitrary manner whereas a function is only allowed read access to the private data. The implementation is consequently permitted to perform the useful optimisation of allowing multiple calls of functions at the same time.

By analogy with entries in tasks, a protected type may also have entries. The action of an entry call is provided by an entry body which has a barrier condition which must be true before the entry body can be executed. There is a strong parallel between an accept statement with a guard in a task body and an entry body with a barrier in a protected body, although, as we shall see in a moment, the timing of the evaluation of barriers is quite different to that of guards.

A good illustration of the use of barriers is given by a protected type implementing the classic bounded buffer. Consider

```
protected type Bounded_Buffer is
    entry Put(X: in Item);
    entry Get(X: out Item);
private
    A: Item_Array(1 .. Max);
    I, J: Integer range 1 .. Max := 1;
    Count: Integer range 0 .. Max := 0;
end Bounded_Buffer;

protected body Bounded_Buffer is

    entry Put(X: in Item) when Count < Max is
    begin
        A(I) := X;
        I := I mod Max + 1; Count := Count + 1;
    end Put;

    entry Get(X: out Item) when Count > 0 is
    begin
        X := A(J);
        J := J mod Max + 1; Count := Count - 1;
    end Get;

end Bounded_Buffer;
```

This provides a cyclic bounded buffer holding up to `Max` values of the type `Item` with access through the entries `Put` and `Get`. We can declare an object of the protected type and access it as expected

```
My_Buffer: Bounded_Buffer;
...
My_Buffer.Put(X);
```

The behavior of the protected type is controlled by the barriers. When an entry is called its barrier is evaluated; if the barrier is false then the call is queued in much the same way that calls on entries in tasks are queued. When My_Buffer is declared, the buffer is empty and so the barrier for Put is true whereas the barrier for Get is false. So initially only a call of Put can be executed and a task issuing a call of Get will be queued.

At the end of the execution of an entry body (or a procedure body) of the protected object all barriers which have queued tasks are reevaluated thus possibly permitting the processing of an entry call which had been queued on a false barrier. So at the end of the first call of Put, if a call of Get had been queued, then the barrier is reevaluated thus permitting a waiting call of Get to be serviced at once.

It is important to realize that there is no task associated with the buffer itself; the evaluation of barriers is effectively performed by the runtime system. Barriers are evaluated when an entry is first called and when something happens which could sensibly change the state of a barrier with a waiting task.

Thus barriers are only reevaluated at the end of an entry or procedure body and not at the end of a protected function call because a function call cannot change the state of the protected object and so is not expected to change the values of barriers. These rules ensure that a protected object can be implemented efficiently.

Note that a barrier *could* refer to a global variable; such a variable might get changed other than through a call of a protected procedure or entry it could be changed by another task or even by a call of a protected function; such changes will thus not be acted upon promptly. The programmer needs to be aware of this and should not use global variables in barriers without due consideration.

It must be understood that the barrier protection mechanism is superimposed upon the natural mutual exclusion of the protected construct thus giving two distinct levels of protection. At the end of a protected call, already queued entries (whose barriers are now true) take precedence over other calls contending for the protected object. On the other hand, a new entry call cannot even evaluate its barrier if the protected object is busy with another call until that call (and any processible queued calls) have finished.

This has the following important consequence: if the state of a protected resource changes and there is a task waiting for the new state, then this task will gain access to the resource and be guaranteed that the state of the resource when it gets it is the same as when the decision to release the task was made. Unsatisfactory polling and race conditions are completely avoided.

Protected objects are very similar to monitors in general concept; they are passive constructions with synchronisation provided by the language runtime system. However, they have a great advantage over monitors in that the protocols are described by barrier conditions (which are fairly easy to prove correct) rather than the low-level and unstructured signals internal to monitors as found in Modula.

In other words protected objects have the essential advantages of the high level guards of the rendezvous model but without the overhead of an active task.

Protected types enable very efficient implementations of various semaphore and similar paradigms. For example a counting semaphore might be implemented as follows

```
protected type Counting_Semaphore (Start_Count: Integer := 1) is
    entry Secure;
    procedure Release;
```

```
        function Count return Integer;
    private
        Current_Count: Integer := Start_Count;
    end Counting_Semaphore;

    protected body Counting_Semaphore is

        entry Secure when Current_Count > 0 is
        begin
            Current_Count := Current_Count - 1;
        end Secure;

        procedure Release is
        begin
            Current_Count := Current_Count + 1;
        end Release;

        function Count return Integer is
        begin
            return Current_Count;
        end Count;

    end Counting_Semaphore;
```

This implements the general form of Dijkstra's semaphore. It illustrates the use of all three forms of protected operations: a function, a procedure and an entry. The entry `Secure` and the procedure `Release` correspond to the P and V operations (from the Dutch Passeren and Vrijmaken) and the function `Count` gives the current value of the semaphore. This example also illustrates that a protected type can have a discriminant which is here used to provide the initial value of the semaphore or in other words the number of items of the resource being guarded by the semaphore.

It is important to note that a task type may also have a discriminant in Ada 95 and this can similarly be used to initialize a task. This can for example be used to tell a task who it is (perhaps from among an array of tasks) without introducing a special entry just for that purpose.

Our final example introduces the ability to requeue a call on another entry. It sometimes happens that a service needs to be provided in two parts and that the calling task has to be suspended after the first part until conditions are such that the second part can be done. Two entry calls are then necessary but attempts to program this in Ada 83 usually run into difficulties; race conditions can arise in the interval between the calls and there is often unnecessary visibility of the internal protocol.

The example is of a broadcast signal. Tasks wait for some event and then when it occurs all the waiting tasks are released and the event reset. The difficulty is to prevent tasks that call the wait operation after the event has occurred, but before the signal can be reset, from getting through. In other words, we must reset the signal in preference to letting new tasks through. The requeue statement allows us to program such preference control. An implementation is

```
    protected Event is
        entry Wait;
        entry Signal;
    private
        entry Reset;
        Occurred: Boolean := False;
    end Event;
```

```
protected body Event is

    entry Wait when Occurred is
    begin
        null;   -- note null body
    end Wait;

    entry Signal when True is -- barrier is always true
    begin
        if Wait'Count > 0 then
            Occurred := True;
            requeue Reset;
        end if;
    end Signal;

    entry Reset when Wait'Count = 0 is
    begin
        Occurred := False;
    end Reset;

end Event;
```

Tasks indicate that they wish to wait for the event by the call

```
Event.Wait;
```

and the happening of the event is notified by some task calling

```
Event.Signal;
```

whereupon all the waiting tasks are allowed to proceed and the event is reset so that future calls of Wait work properly.

The Boolean variable Occurred is normally false and is only true while tasks are being released. The entry Wait has no body but just exists so that calling tasks can suspend themselves on its queue while waiting for Occurred to become true.

The entry Signal is interesting. It has a permanently true barrier and so is always processed. If there are no tasks on the queue of Wait (that is no tasks are waiting), then there is nothing to do and so it exits. On the other hand if there are tasks waiting then it must release them in such a way that no further tasks can get on the queue but then regain control so that it can reset the flag. It does this by requeuing itself on the entry Reset after setting Occurred to true to indicate that the event has occurred.

The semantics of requeue are such that this completes the action of Signal. However, remember that at the end of the body of a protected entry or procedure the barriers are reevaluated for those entries which have tasks queued. In this case there are indeed tasks on the queue for Wait and there is also a task on the queue for Reset (the task that called Signal in the first place); the barrier for Wait is now true but of course the barrier for Reset is false since there are still tasks on the queue for Wait. A waiting task is thus allowed to execute the body of Wait (being null this does nothing) and the task thus proceeds and then the barrier evaluation repeats. The same process continues until all the waiting tasks have gone when finally the barrier of Reset also becomes true. The original task which called signal now executes the body of Reset thus resetting Occurred to false so that the system is once more in its initial state. The protected object as a whole is now finally left since there are no waiting tasks on any of the barriers.

Note carefully that if any tasks had tried to call `Wait` or `Signal` while the whole process was in progress then they would not have been able to do so because the protected object as a whole was busy. This illustrates the two levels of protection and is the underlying reason why a race condition does not arise.

Another consequence of the two levels is that it still all works properly even in the face of such difficulties as timed and conditional calls and aborts. The reader may recall, for example, that by contrast, the `Count` attribute for entries in tasks cannot be relied upon in the face of timed entry calls.

A minor point to note is that the entry `Reset` is declared in the private part of the protected type and thus cannot be called from outside. Ada 95 also allows a task to have a private part containing private entries.

The above example has been used for illustration only. The astute reader will have observed that the condition is not strictly needed inside `Signal`; without it the caller will simply always requeue and then immediately be processed if there are no waiting tasks. But the condition clarifies the description. Indeed, the very astute reader might care to note that we can actually program this example in Ada 95 without using requeue at all. A more realistic classic example is the disk scheduler where a caller is requeued if the head is currently over the wrong track.

In this section we have outlined the main features of protected types. There are a number of detailed aspects that we have not covered. The general intent, however, should be clear. Protected types provide a data-oriented approach to synchronisation which couples the high-level conditions (the barriers) with the efficiency of monitors. Furthermore the requeue statement provides a means of programming preference control and thus enables race conditions to be avoided.

It must be remembered, of course, that the existing task model remains; the rendezvous will continue to be a necessary approach in many circumstances of a general nature (such as for directly passing messages). But the protected object provides a better paradigm for most data-oriented situations.

7.10   Task scheduling and timing

A criticism of Ada 83 has been that its scheduling rules are unsatisfactory especially with regard to the rendezvous. First-in-first-out queuing on entries and the arbitrary selection from several open alternatives in a select statement lead to conflict with the normal preemptive priority rules. For example, priority inversion occurs when a high priority task is on an entry queue behind a lower priority task.

Furthermore, mode changes may require the ability to dynamically change priorities and this conflicts with the simple static model of Ada 83. In addition, advances in the design of scheduling techniques based on Rate Monotonic Scheduling prescribe a variety of techniques to be used in different circumstances according to the arrival pattern of events; see [Sha 90a] and [Klein 93].

Ada 95 allows much more freedom in the choice of priority and scheduling rules. However, because this is a specialised area (and may not be appropriate on some host architectures), the details are contained in the Real-Time Systems annex to which the reader is referred for more details.

Timing is another important aspect of scheduling and the delay statement of Ada 83 has not proved adequate in all circumstances.

For example, an attempt to wait until a specific time by a sequence such as

```
Next_Time: Time;
...
Next_Time := time_to_be_woken_up;
delay Next_Time - Clock;
```

which is intended to stop the task until the time given by the variable Next_Time, is not foolproof. The problem is that there is a race condition. Between calling the function Clock and issuing the delay statement, it is possible for the task to be preempted by a higher priority task. The result is that when the delay is finally issued, the Duration value will be inappropriate and the task will be delayed for too long.

This difficulty is overcome in Ada 95 by the introduction of a complementary delay until statement which takes a Time (rather than a Duration) as its argument. We can then simply write

```
delay until Next_Time;
```

and all will be well.

The final new tasking facility to be introduced in this section is the ability to perform an asynchronous transfer of control. This enables an activity to be abandoned if some condition arises (such as running out of time) and an alternative sequence of statements to be executed instead. This gives the capability of performing mode changes.

This could of course be programmed in Ada 83 by the introduction of an agent task and the use of the abort statement but this was a heavy solution not at all appropriate for most applications needing a mode change.

Asynchronous transfer of control is achieved by a new form of select statement which comprises two parts: an abortable part and a triggering alternative. As a simple example consider

```
select
    delay 5.0;                  -- triggering alternative
    Put_Line("Calculation did not complete");
then abort
    Invert_Giant_Matrix(M);   -- abortable part
end select};
```

The general idea is that if the statements between then abort and end select do not complete before the expiry of the delay then they are abandoned and the statements following the delay executed instead. Thus if we cannot invert our large matrix in five seconds we give up and print a message.

The statement that triggers the abandonment can alternatively be an entry call instead of a delay statement. If the call returns before the computation is complete then again the computation is abandoned and any statements following the entry call are executed instead. On the other hand if the computation completes before the entry call, then the entry call is itself abandoned.

The entry call can, of course, be to a task or to a protected object as described in the previous section. Indeed, Ada 95 allows an entry call to be to a protected object or to a task in all contexts.

Other refinements to the Ada tasking model include a better description of the behavior of the abort statement and a more useful approach to shared variables by the introduction of a number of pragmas.

7.11   Generic parameters

The generic facility in Ada 83 has proved very useful for developing reusable software particularly with regard to its type parameterisation capability. However, there were a few anomalies which have been rectified in Ada 95. In addition a number of further parameter models have been added to match the object oriented facilities.

In Ada 83 the so-called contract model was broken because of the lack of distinction between constrained and unconstrained formal parameters. Thus if we had

```
generic
    type T is private;
package P is ...

package body P is
   X: T;
    ...
```

then in Ada 83 we could instantiate this with a type such as `Integer` which was fine. However we could also supply an unconstrained type such as `String` and this failed because when we came to declare the object T we found that there were no constraints and we could not declare an object as an unconstrained array. The problem was that the error was not detected through a mismatch in the instantiation mechanism but as an error in the body itself. But the whole essence of the contract model is that if the actual parameter satisfies the requirements of the formal then any body which matches the formal specification will work. The poor user might not have had access to the source of the body but nevertheless found errors reported in it despite the instantiation apparently working.

This serious violation of the contract model is repaired in Ada 95. The parameter matching rules for the example above no longer accept an unconstrained type such as `String` but require a type such as `Integer` or a constrained type or a record type with default discriminants (these are collectively known as definite types in Ada 95).

If we wish to write a generic package that will indeed accept an unconstrained type then we have to use a new form of notation as follows

```
generic
    type T(<>) is private;
package P ...
```

In this case we are not allowed to declare an (uninitialized) object of type T in the body; we can only use T in ways which do not require a constrained type. The actual parameter can now be any unconstrained type such as `String`; it could, of course, also be a constrained type.

Other new parameter models are useful for combining genericity with type extension and for writing class-wide generic packages. The formal declaration

```
type T is tagged private;
```

requires that the actual type be tagged.

We can also write

```
type T is new S;
```

or

```
type T is new S with private;
```

In both cases the actual type must be S or derived directly or indirectly from S. If we add with private then both S and the actual type must be tagged. (Remember the rule that all tagged types have tagged or with in their declaration.)

In all these cases we can also follow the formal type name with ($<>$) to indicate that the actual may be unconstrained (strictly, indefinite to use the terminology introduced above). Furthermore if we follow is by abstract then the actual type can also be abstract (but it need not be).

The last new kind of formal generic parameter is the formal generic package. This greatly simplifies the composition of generic packages. It allows one package to be used as a parameter to another so that a hierarchy of facilities can be created.

Examples are inevitably a bit long but consider first the following two packages in Ada 83. The first defines a private type for complex numbers and the basic operations upon them. The second builds on the first and provides various vector operations on complex numbers. The whole system is generic with respect to the underlying floating point type used for the complex numbers.

```
generic
    type Float_Type is digits <>;
package Generic_Complex_Numbers is
    type Complex is private;
    function "+" (Left, Right: Complex) return Complex;
    function "-" (Left, Right: Complex) return Complex;
    -- etc
end Generic_Complex_Numbers;

generic
    type Float_Type is digits <>;
    type Complex is private;
    with function "+" (Left, Right: Complex)
        return Complex is <>;
    with function "-" (Left, Right: Complex)
        return Complex is <>;
    -- and so on
package Generic_Complex_Vectors is

    -- types and operations on vectors

end Generic_Complex_Vectors;
```

and we can then instantiate these two packages by for example

```
package Long_Complex is
    new Generic_Complex_Numbers(Long_Float);
    use Long_Complex;

package Long_Complex_Vectors is
    new Generic_Complex_Vectors(Long_Float, Complex);
```

In this Ada 83 formulation we had to pass the type Complex and all its operations exported from Complex_Numbers back into the vector package as distinct formal parameters so that we could use them in that package. The burden was somewhat reduced by using the default mechanism for the operations but this incurred the slight risk that the user might have redefined one of them with incorrect properties (it also forced us to write a use clause or lots of renamings).

This burden is completely alleviated in Ada 95 by the ability to declare generic formal packages. In the generic formal part we can write

```
with package P is new Q(<>);
```

and then the actual parameter corresponding to P must be any package which has been obtained by instantiating Q which must itself be a generic package.

Returning to our example, in Ada 95, having written Generic_Complex_Numbers as before, we can now write

```
with Generic_Complex_Numbers;
generic
    with package Complex_Numbers is
        new Generic_Complex_Numbers (<>);
package Generic_Complex_Vectors is

    -- as before

end Generic_Complex_Vectors;
```

where the actual package must be any instantiation of Generic_Complex_Numbers. Hence our previous instantiations can now be simplified and we can write

```
package Long_Complex is
    new Generic_Complex_Numbers(Long_Float);

package Long_Complex_Vectors is
    new Generic_Complex_Vectors(Long_Complex);
```

The key point is that we no longer have to import (explicitly or implicitly) the type and operators exported by the instantiation of Generic_Complex_Numbers. Hence the parameter list of Generic_Complex_Vectors is reduced to merely the one parameter which is the package Long_Complex obtained by the instantiation of Generic_Complex_Numbers. We no longer even have to pass the underlying type Long_Float.

Although this example has been couched in terms of a numerical application, the general approach is applicable to many examples of building a hierarchy of generic packages.

7.12   Other improvements

We have now covered most of the major improvements which give Ada 95 so much extra power over Ada 83. But the discussion has not been complete; we have omitted important facilities such as the introduction of controlled types giving initialization, finalization and user defined assignment and the use of access discriminants to give the functionality of multiple inheritance.

There are also a number of minor changes which remove various irritations and which together make Ada 95 a major improvement within existing paradigms. We will now briefly mention the more notable of these improvements.

The attribute T'Base can now be used as a type mark. So if Float_Type is a generic formal parameter we can then declare

```
Local: Float_Type'Base;
```

and any constraints imposed by the actual parameter will not then apply to the working variable `Local`. This is important for certain numeric algorithms where we wish to be unconstrained in intermediate computations.

The underlying model for the numeric types is slightly changed by the introduction of fictitious types *root_integer* and *root_real*. This brings a number of simplifications and improvements regarding implicit type conversions and one is the removal of the notorious irritation that

```
for I in -1 .. 100 loop
```

was not allowed in Ada 83. It is allowed in Ada 95.

The rule distinguishing basic declarative items from later declarative items has been removed (this essentially said that little declarations cannot follow big declarations and was intended to prevent little ones getting lost visually but it backfired). As a consequence declarations can now be in any order. This often helps with the placing of representation clauses.

Another irritation in Ada 83 was the problem of use clauses and operators. There was a dilemma between, on the one hand, disallowing a use clause and then having to use prefix notation for operators or introduce a lot of renaming or, on the other hand, allowing a use clause so that infixed operators could be used but then allowing visibility of everything and running the risk that package name prefixes might be omitted with a consequent serious loss of readability. Many organisations have imposed a complete ban on use clauses and burdened themselves with lots of renaming. This is solved in Ada 95 by the introduction of a use type clause. If we have a package `Complex_Numbers` which declares a type `Complex` and various operators `"+"`, `"-"` and so on, we can write

```
with Complex_Numbers; use type Complex_Numbers.Complex;
```

and then within our package we can use the operators belonging to the type `Complex` in infix notation. Other identifiers in `Complex_Numbers` will still have to use the full dotted notation so we can see from which package they come. Predefined operators such as `"="` are also made directly visible by an appropriate use type clause.

Concerning `"="` the rules regarding its redefinition are now completely relaxed. It may be redefined for any type at all and need not necessarily return a result of type `Boolean`. The only remaining rule in this area is that if the redefined `"="` does return a result of type `Boolean` then a corresponding `"/="` is also implicitly declared. On the other hand, `"/="` may itself be redefined only if its result is not type `Boolean`.

The rules regarding static expressions are improved and allow further sensible expressions to be treated as static. A static expression may now contain membership tests, attributes, conversions and so on. Moreover, an expression which looks static but occurs in a context not demanding a static expression will be evaluated statically; this was surprisingly not the case in Ada 83 an expression such as $2+3$ was only required to be evaluated at compile time if it occurred in a context demanding a static expression. Note also that rounding of odd halves is now defined as away from zero so `Integer(1.5)` is now 2.

A small change which will be welcomed is that a subprogram body may now be provided by renaming. This avoids tediously writing code which merely calls another subprogram. Renaming is now also allowed for generic units and a library unit may now be renamed as a library unit; these facilities will be found to be particularly useful with child units.

Another change which will bring a sigh of relief is that `out` parameters can now be read. They are treated just like a variable that happens not to be explicitly initialized; this change will save the introduction of many local variables and much frustration. A related change is that the restriction that it was not possible to declare a subprogram with out parameters of a limited type is also lifted.

Some restrictions regarding arrays are also relaxed. It is now possible to deduce the bounds of a variable (as well as a constant) from an appropriate initial value, such as in

```
S: String := Get_Message; -- a function call
```

which avoids having to write the tedious

```
Message: constant String := Get_Message;
S: String(Message'Range) := Message;
```

It is also possible to use a named aggregate with an "others" component as an initial value or in an assignment. Sliding is now permitted for subprogram parameters and function results in return statements which are treated like assignment with regard to array bound matching.

There are also improvements in the treatment of discriminants. A private type can now have a discriminated type with defaults as its full type thus

```
package P is
     type T is private;
private
     type T(N: Natural := 1) is
     ...
end P;
```

Infuriatingly this was not allowed in Ada 83 although the corresponding problem with matching generic parameters was eliminated many years ago.

An important improvement in exception handlers is the ability to access information regarding the occurrence of an exception. This is done by declaring a "choice parameter" in the handler and we can then use that to get hold of, for example, the exception name for debugging purposes. We can write

```
when Event: others =>
    Put_Line("Unexpected exception: " & Exception_Name(Event));
```

where the function Exception_Name returns the name of the exception as a string (such as 'Constraint_Error'). Other functions provide further useful diagnostic information regarding the cause of the exception.

An important improvement which will be a great relief to systems programmers is that the language now includes support for unsigned integer types (modular types). This provides shift and logical operations as well as modular arithmetic operations and thus enables unsigned integer values to be manipulated as sequences of bits.

Another improvement worth mentioning in this brief summary concerns library package bodies. In Ada 83 a package body was optional if it was not required by the language (for providing subprogram bodies for example). However, this rule, which was meant to be a helpful convenience, seriously misfired sometimes when a library package was recompiled and bodies which just did initialization could get inadvertently lost without any warning. In Ada 95, a library package is only allowed to have a body if it is required by language rules; the pragma Elaborate_Body is one way of indicating that a body is required.

Finally, in order to meet the needs of the international community, the type Character has been changed to the full 8-bit ISO set (Latin-1) and the type Wide_Character representing the 16-bit ISO Basic Multilingual Plane has been added. The type Wide_String is also defined by analogy.

7.13 The predefined library

There are many additional predefined packages in the standard library which has been re-structured in order to take advantage of the facilities offered by the hierarchical library. As mentioned above, root library packages behave as children of Standard. There are just three such predefined child packages of Standard, namely System, Interfaces and Ada and these in turn have a number of child packages. Those of System are concerned with intrinsic language capability such as the control of storage. Those of Interfaces concern the interfaces to other languages. The remaining more general predefined packages are children of the package Ada.

An important reason for the new structure is that it avoids potential name conflicts with packages written by the user; thus only the names Ada and Interfaces could conflict with existing Ada 83 code. Without this structure the risk of conflict would have been high especially given the many new predefined packages in Ada 95.

The existing packages such as Calendar, Unchecked_Conversion and Text_IO are now child packages of Ada. Compatibility with Ada 83 is achieved by the use of library unit renaming (itself a new feature in Ada 95) thus

```
with Ada.Text_IO;
package Text_IO renames Ada.Text_IO;
```

We will now briefly summarize the more notable packages in the predefined library in order to give the reader an appreciation of the breadth of standard facilities provided.

The package Ada itself is simply

```
package Ada is
    pragma Pure(Ada);   -- as white as driven snow!
end Ada;
```

where the pragma indicates that Ada has no variable state; (this concept is important for sharing in distributed systems).

Input-output is provided by the packages Ada.Text_IO, Ada.Sequential_IO, Ada.Direct_IO and Ada.IO_Exceptions plus a number of new packages. The package Ada.Wide_Text_IO is identical to Text_IO except that it handles the types Wide_Character and Wide_String. General stream input-output is provided by Ada.Streams and Ada.Streams.Stream_IO; these enable heterogeneous files of arbitrary types to be manipulated (remember that Direct_IO and Sequential_IO manipulate files whose items are all of the same type). The package Ada.Text_IO.Text_Streams gives access to the stream associated with Text_IO; this allows mixed binary and text input-output and the use of the standard files with streams.

There are also nongeneric versions of the packages Text_IO.Integer_IO and Text_IO.Float_IO for the predefined types such as Integer and Float. Their names are Ada.Integer_Text_IO and Ada.Float_Text_IO and so on for other predefined types; there are also corresponding wide versions. These nongeneric packages will be found useful for training and overcome the need to teach genericity on day one of every Ada course.

The package Ada.Characters.Handling provides classification and conversion functions for characters. Examples are Is_Letter which returns an appropriate Boolean value and To_Wide_Character which converts a character to the corresponding wide character. The package Ada.Characters.Latin_1 contains named constants in a similar style to Standard.ASCII which is now obsolescent.

General string handling is provided by the package Ada.Strings. Three different forms of string are handled by packages Strings.Fixed, Strings.Bounded and Strings.Unbounded. In addition, packages such as Strings.Wide_Fixed perform similar operations on wide strings.

Extensive mathematical facilities are provided by the package Ada.Numerics. This parent package is just

```
package Ada.Numerics is
    pragma Pure(Numerics);
    Argument_Error: exception;
    Pi: constant := 3.14159_26535_ ... ;
    e: constant} := 2.71828_18284_ ... ;
end Ada.Numerics;
```

and includes the child package Ada.Numerics.Generic_Elementary_Functions which is similar to the corresponding standard ISO/IEC 11430:1994 for Ada 83 [ISO 94a]. There are also nongeneric versions such as Ada.Numerics.Elementary_Functions for the predefined types Float and so on. Facilities for manipulating complex types and complex elementary functions are provided by other child packages defined in the Numerics annex.

The package Ada.Numerics.Float_Random enables the user to produce streams of pseudo-random floating point numbers with ease. There is also a generic package Ada.Numerics.Discrete_Random which provides for streams of discrete values (both integer and enumeration types).

The package Ada.Exceptions defines facilities for manipulating exception occurrences such as the function Exception_Name mentioned above.

The package System has child packages System.Storage_Elements and System.Storage_Pools which are concerned with storage allocation.

The package Interfaces contains the child packages Interfaces.C, Interfaces.COBOL and Interfaces.Fortran which provide facilities for interfacing to programs in those languages. It also contains declarations of hardware supported numeric types. Implementations are encouraged to add further child packages for interfacing to other languages.

7.14   The specialized needs annexes

There are six Specialized Needs annexes. In this summary we cannot go into detail but their content covers the following topics:

Systems Programming This covers a number of low-level features such as in-line machine instructions, interrupt handling, shared variable access and task identification. This annex is a prior requirement for the Real-Time Systems annex.

Real-Time Systems As mentioned above this annex addresses various scheduling and priority issues including setting priorities dynamically, scheduling algorithms and entry queue protocols. It also includes detailed requirements on the abort statement for single and multiple processor systems and a monotonic time package (as distinct from Calendar which might go backwards because of time-zone or daylight-saving changes).

Distributed Systems The core language introduces the idea of a partition whereby one coherent "program" is distributed over a number of partitions each with its own environment task. This annex defines two forms of partitions and inter-partition communication using statically and dynamically bound remote subprogram calls.

Information Systems The core language extends fixed point types to include basic support for decimal types. This annex defines a number of packages providing detailed facilities for manipulating decimal values and conversion to external format using picture strings.

Numerics This annex addresses the special needs of the numeric community. One significant change is the basis for model numbers. These are no longer described in the core language but in this annex. Moreover, model numbers in 95 are essentially what were called safe numbers in Ada 83 and the old model numbers and the term safe numbers have been abandoned. Having both safe and model numbers did not bring benefit commensurate with the complexity and confusion thereby introduced. This annex also includes packages for manipulating complex numbers.

Safety and Security This annex addresses restrictions on the use of the language and requirements of compilation systems for programs to be used in safety-critical and related applications where program security is vital.

7.15   Conclusion

This discussion has been designed to give the reader a general feel for the scope of Ada 95 and some of the detail. Although we have not addressed all the many improvements that Ada 95 provides, nevertheless, it will be clear that Ada 95 is an outstanding language.

Ada 95 brings all the benefits of object oriented languages such as C++ within the secure engineering framework provided by Ada 83. In addition Ada 95 addresses the needs of many specialised communities (such as real-time) in a cohesive and high-level manner not provided by any other language at all.

Ada 95 deserves the attention of all members of the computing profession. It is a coherent and reliable foundation vehicle for developing the major applications of the next decade.

7.16   Acknowledgements

This paper is based on Chapter II of Part One of the Ada 95 Rationale [Rat 95] with alterations as follows: the conclusion has been extended and internal subheading numbers and references have been changed as appropriate for a self standing paper.

The Ada 95 Rationale contains the following copyright notice:

7.17   References

Bal 92 H. E. Bal, M. F. Kaashoek, and A. S. Tanenbaum. *Orca: A Language for Parallel Programming of Distributed Systems.* IEEE Transactions on Software Engineering, 18(3): 190-205, March 1992.

ISO 94a International Standards Organization. *Generic Package of Elementary Functions for Ada.* ISO-IEC/JTC 1 11430:1994.

Klein 93 M. H. Klein, T. Ralya, B. Pollak, R. Obenza, and M. G. Harbour. *A Practitioner's Handbook for Real-Time Analysis: Guide to Rate Monotonic Analysis for Real-Time Systems.* Klewer Academic Publishers, 1993.

Rat 95 *Ada 95 Rationale.* Intermetrics Inc, January 1995.

Sha 90a L. Sha, and J. B. Goodenough. *Real-Time Scheduling Theory and Ada.* Computer 23(4): 53-62, April, 1990.

8

Random number generation in Ada 95

K. W. Dritz *
Argonne National Laboratory
Argonne
IL 60439
USA

Email: dritz@mcs.anl.gov

The generation of random numbers[†] is central to many kinds of scientific study, especially those involving simulation or modeling. Most libraries of mathematical software have one or more *random number generators* (RNGs), encapsulating the best techniques for random number generation that have been reported in the literature, and at least rudimentary capabilities for generating random numbers are intrinsically provided in particular programming languages (among them, C and Fortran 90). The lack of a predefined RNG in Ada has inhibited the portability of application programs that need random numbers. With Ada 95, that problem will cease to exist, at least for the vast majority of such applications.

The facilities for random number generation can be found in the Predefined Language Environment (Annex A) of Ada 95 [2], where they take the form of a pair of children of the predefined package `Ada.Numerics`. The package `Ada.Numerics.Float_Random` defines types and operations for the generation of floating-point random numbers, while the generic package `Ada.Numerics.Discrete_Random` plays a similar rôle for the generation of random integers (actually, random values of an arbitrary user-specified discrete subtype).

The content of these two packages underwent many changes after the initial proposal for an RNG facility, which did not even include the latter package. Perhaps more than for any other mathematical library routine, preconceived opinions about the form that the RNG should take ran strong, and many compromises were made before the final RNG was formulated. Nevertheless, certain goals for the design of the facility remained constant throughout the development process:

- The facility should be easy to use; it should appeal to the application programmer migrating from Fortran and should not require a major investment in learning new

*This chapter was written with financial support from Intermetrics, Inc., to Argonne National Laboratory under proposal No. P-91122.

[†]Technically, of course, we mean to say *pseudo-random numbers*, numbers in an algorithmically generated sequence that do not *appear* to be correlated and that satisfy some of the same statistical properties that truly random numbers satisfy.

concepts unique to Ada.

- It should be possible to obtain a repeatable sequence of random numbers for use during program testing. When one is trying to understand aberrant program behaviour, one needs to be able to rule out differences in the random numbers generated from one run to the next.

- It should be possible to obtain a unique sequence of random numbers in each production run of an application program. Changing from the repeatable mode to the unique mode should be straightforward.

- It should be possible to have multiple random number sequences, for those applications that require it. It should be possible to have separate RNGs in each task, as well as multiple RNGs in a single task. It should be possible to make multiple generators generate the same sequence or different sequences.

- It should be possible to save the state of an RNG and to restore an RNG to a previously saved state. This supports certain debugging requirements as well as the checkpointing and restarting of long-running applications.

- For testing purposes, it should be possible to examine the state of an RNG in an interactive debugger without advanced planning.

We discuss below how these goals have been realised in the Ada 95 RNG facility.

Implementations are free to exploit advances in the theory of random number generation, because Ada 95 does not prescribe the algorithm to be used. In order to provide some assurance that the algorithm used is minimally acceptable, the language prescribes tests of uniformity and randomness that must be satisfied by the implementation, and it also prescribes a lower bound on the periodicity of the RNG algorithm. Several popular RNG algorithms are known to pass the tests, including the venerable multiplicative linear congruential generator with multiplier 7^5 and modulus $2^{31} - 1$ of Lewis, Goodman, and Miller [4] and both the add-with-carry and subtract-with-borrow Fibonacci generators of Marsaglia and Zaman [5]. Other algorithms that would be expected to pass, but which have not been explicitly tested, include the combination generators of Wichmann and Hill [6] and L'Ecuyer [3] and the x^2 mod N generators of Blum, Blum, and Shub [1]. In order to allow users to assess the suitability of the algorithm for their particular application, the implementation must describe the algorithm it uses and must document some of its properties.

The predefined floating-point RNG package has the specification shown in Figure 8.1. The first point to note about this package is that it defines both *basic facilities*, which are expected to be needed by all or most applications of random numbers, and *advanced facilities*, which are expected to be needed only by those few applications having advanced or specialised needs. Most programmers will need to learn and use only the basic facilities. In fact, to get started, one need only "with" and "use" the package, declare a generator, and invoke the Random function on the generator, as illustrated in Figure 8.2. Another point to note is that only uniformly distributed random numbers are provided, and they lie in the customary range of 0.0 to 1.0.[‡] The uniform distribution is the one most commonly encountered in practice;

[‡] Some implementations may be incapable of generating either or both endpoints of the range, but application programmers are forewarned by a note in the reference manual not to depend on that. The subtleties of mapping this range into a particular range of integers was one of the motivations for providing a separate discrete random number generator package.

```
package Ada.Numerics.Float_Random is

   -- Basic facilities

   type Generator is limited private;

   subtype Uniformly_Distributed is Float range 0.0 .. 1.0;
   function Random (Gen : Generator)
      return Uniformly_Distributed;

   procedure Reset (Gen       : in Generator;
                    Initiator : in Integer);
   procedure Reset (Gen       : in Generator);

   -- Advanced facilities

   type State is private;

   procedure Save  (Gen        : in  Generator;
                    To_State   : out State);
   procedure Reset (Gen        : in  Generator;
                    From_State : in  State);

   Max_Image_Width : constant := -- impl. defined integer;

   function Image (Of_State    : State)  return String;
   function Value (Coded_State : String) return State;

private

   ...  -- not specified by the language

end Ada.Numerics.Float_Random;
```

Figure 8.1. Specification of Ada.Numerics.Float_Random

```
with Ada.Numerics.Float_Random; use Ada.Numerics.Float_Random;
procedure Simple_Application is

   RNG : Generator;
   X : Float;
   ...

begin

   loop

      ...
      X := Random(RNG);
      ...

   end loop;

end Application;
```

Figure 8.2. Example of a simple use of `Ada.Numerics.Float_Random`

other distributions can be obtained from the uniform distribution by techniques covered in standard textbooks.

The example in Figure 8.2 shows that random number generators in Ada 95 are associated with objects of the type `Generator`. Each such object should be regarded as the source of a sequence of random numbers, successive elements of which can be obtained by applying the `Random` operation (as a function) to the object. The current "position" in the sequence is internal state information that is hidden from the user by virtue of the fact that `Generator` is a private type.

As the example illustrates, the ease with which one can begin to use the floating-point random number generator is likely to appeal to novice application programmers, who may have some experience with Fortran but little or none with Ada. In particular, it is not necessary for the programmer to learn how to use generics in order to use the floating-point random number generator, and this feature goes a long way toward meeting the first design goal. Floating-point random numbers are provided only in the predefined type `Float`, which programmers migrating from Fortran are likely to use instinctively; random numbers of some other floating-point type can be obtained by explicit conversion.[§]

The second design goal, provision for obtaining repeatable sequences of random numbers

---

[§]We decided that learning how to perform explicit numeric conversions was less of a challenge to inexperienced programmers than learning how to use generics. In most cases, such conversions will serve merely to satisfy the strong typing requirements and will not affect the value of the random number; but if the conversion is to a type with greater or lesser precision, the value may be affected. The decision to avoid generics, thereby giving the user no direct way to request random numbers of different precisions, was also made partly on the basis of the implementation burden that it would have created. Floating-point random numbers of exceptionally high precision are required by only a few very specialised applications, and it is reasonable to expect those applications to shoulder the burden of providing high-precision random numbers. They can do so by building on the facilities that have been provided; for example, they can scale and combine the results of two or more calls to Random to obtain a single high-precision random number.

(for program testing), is met by making that the default behaviour of generator objects. That is, each generator is implicitly initialised to the same fixed state. One has to go a little out of the way to obtain a unique sequence of random numbers in each run. Thus, during the initial stages of program testing, when one has not thought to turn on all the bells and whistles, there is no danger of obtaining nondeterministic behaviour (which could confound the testing process).

When one has progressed far enough in program testing to want a unique sequence of random numbers in each run, one merely needs to insert a call to the "time-dependent reset operation" in the program before the first call to `Random`. The `Reset` procedure comprises three overloadings, all of which reset the state of the generator given as a parameter; they differ in the nature of the resetting that is performed. When `Reset` is called with no parameters other than a generator, the action is to reset the generator to a time-dependent state; an example is shown in Figure 8.3. According to the reference manual, two calls to the time-dependent reset operation are guaranteed to establish different states if the calls are made at least one second apart, and not more than fifty years apart; this is certainly sufficient for priming a generator to yield unique sequences in different runs of the application. The time-dependent reset operation supports the third design goal.

One may declare any number of generator objects, and they can be aggregated into arrays or made components of other objects with arbitrary structure. Thus, multiple generators can be created trivially, either within a single task or in each of several tasks.¶ Unless one of the reset operations is used, however, all such generators will be started in the same state and will yield the same sequence. While that result may well be what is desired, it is more likely that each generator is intended to yield a different sequence. To satisfy that need, which is expressed by the fourth design goal, we provide an "initiator-dependent reset operation" as one of the overloadings of the `Reset` procedure, the one that takes an integer parameter named `Initiator` in addition to a generator. The idea is to reset each generator with a distinct initiator value before using any of them to generate random numbers; for example, if there are n generators, each may be reset by a different initiator value in the range 1 to n. The semantics of the initiator-dependent reset operation are such that, if the characteristics of the implementation permit, each possible value of the initiator will initiate a sequence of random numbers that does not, in a practical sense, overlap the sequence initiated by any other value. If this is impossible to achieve in a given implementation, then the mapping between initiator values and generator states is required, at least, to be a rapidly varying function of the initiator value.

This technique for starting multiple generators in different states suffices when repeatable program behaviour is desired in each run. A more elaborate technique is required when, in addition to being different from each other, one desires the initial generator states to be unique in different runs. For example, one might generate the initiator values randomly, using the discrete random number generator, after having initialised the latter to a time-dependent state. If a wide enough range is requested during the instantiation of the discrete random number generator package, only a small probability exists that a given initiator value will be generated more than once; nevertheless, it would be wise to filter out any duplicates that do happen to be generated, so that each of the floating-point generators can definitely be started in a unique state.

The advanced facilities of `Ada.Numerics.Float_Random` are concerned with sav-

¶We considered an alternative design that uses generics and associates a single, implicit generator with each instance. Having certain advantages as well as disadvantages, the alternative was rejected because it does not allow for generators to be components of other objects, such as arrays, or be allocated dynamically—capabilities that might reasonably be needed in some advanced applications.

ing and restoring generator states and with examining or manipulating generator states in the form of (implementation-defined) strings. Because Ada 95 does not prescribe the RNG algorithm to be used, it also imposes no requirements on the representation of generator states.

The fifth design goal addresses a long-running application's need to checkpoint its state so that it can later be restarted from the same state. Since the state of a random number generator (which is part of the application's state) is implicit, or hidden from the user, operations have been provided to obtain the state from a generator (by means of the `Save` procedure) and to reset a generator to a previously obtained state (by means of the third overloading of the `Reset` procedure). To store a state explicitly, one needs to declare a variable of the type `State`. One way that these advanced facilities can be used to checkpoint and restart a generator's state is illustrated in Figure 8.3.[||]

It should be emphasised that simple applications, like that illustrated in Figure 8.2, will have no need to declare variables of type `State`.

Since `State` is a private type, there is no way to examine or manipulate a state that has been exported from a generator. However, in some circumstances, particularly in advanced applications, there may be a need to do so, as enunciated by the sixth design goal. For this purpose, we have provided `Image` and `Value` functions, which are functions that convert state values to string values, and vice versa. The named number `Max_Image_Width` gives an upper bound on the size of the string representation of a state.

Even though the string representation of a state is implementation defined, one can perform some tasks with these strings portably. For example, the strings can be printed. Thus, if one observes aberrant behaviour while using a symbolic debugger for program testing, one can obtain the current state of a generator, print its image on the terminal, and write it down for later reference. One can reverse the process by entering interactively a valid state in its string form, converting it to the corresponding state, and then resetting a generator to that state.

In more demanding applications, perhaps involving experimentation with random number generators, one can use information provided by the implementation on how it maps between strings and states to construct an arbitrary state by assembling the corresponding string. Note that the `Value` function must validate the string it is given, and must raise `Constraint_Error` if given a string that is not the image of a state. But this is the only time that state information must be checked for validity. In the more usual type of RNG design, the state information is exposed and often defined in detail, thereby creating the possibility of corruption or, alternatively, requiring that the operation for generating the next random number validate the state each time it is invoked.

The predefined discrete RNG package, `Ada.Numerics.Discrete_Random`, has an almost identical specification (not shown here). The main difference is that it is generic and must be instantiated with a discrete subtype before use. It exports the same entities as `Ada.Numerics.Float_Random`, with the exception that its `Random` function delivers a value of the generic formal subtype `Result_Subtype`, instead of the `Uniformly_Distributed` subtype of `Float`.

Although it is not difficult to convert, or map, floating-point random numbers in the range 0.0 to 1.0 into integers in some range, or into the range of any other discrete subtype, some subtleties arise at the endpoints 0.0 and 1.0 with certain techniques. `Ada.Numerics.Discrete_Random` is provided partly to head off those potential problems and partly to allow implementations to gain efficiency, when the end goal is random integers, by staying entirely within the integer domain. Nevertheless, some unusual applications may not be well served by the discrete RNG package, because it cannot readily be used to generate (say) random integers

---

[||] For the sake of simplicity, the file in which the generator's state is saved between runs is assumed to exist, in this example.

```ada
with Ada.Numerics.Float_Random; use Ada.Numerics.Float_Random;
with Ada.Sequential_IO;
procedure Checkpoint_Restart_Application is

   RNG : Generator;
   X : Float;
   RNG_State : State;
   type Run_Types is (Fresh_Start, Restart);
   Type_Of_This_Run : Run_Types;

   package State_IO is new Ada.Sequential_IO (State);
   use State_IO;
   State_File : File_Type;

begin

   Type_Of_This_Run := ...;
   case Type_Of_This_Run is
   when Fresh_Start =>
      Reset (RNG);   -- Time-dependent reset
   when Restart =>
      Open (State_File, In_File, Name => ...);
      Read (State_File, RNG_State);
      Close (State_File);
      Reset (RNG, RNG_State);   -- Reset from saved state
   end case;

   ...
   X := Random(RNG);
   ...

   -- Checkpoint the generator

   Save (RNG, RNG_State);   -- Save current generator state
   Open (State_File, Out_File, Name => ...);
   Write (State_File, RNG_State);
   Close (State_File);

end Checkpoint_Restart_Application;
```

Figure 8.3. Example of checkpointing and restarting a generator state

in a different range on each call; the range of the Random function is fixed at instantiation time. An application that has such a requirement would be better off generating random floating-point numbers and mapping them into the desired dynamically varying range. A note in the reference manual gives a reliable technique for performing that mapping. If FG is a floating-point generator and M has an integer value greater than zero, then the expression Integer(Float(M) * Random(FG)) mod M yields an integer uniformly distributed in the range 0 to M − 1.

References

[1] L. Blum, M. Blum, and M. Shub. *A Simple Unpredictable Pseudo-Random Number Generator*. SIAM Journal of Computing 15(2):364–383, 1986.

[2] ISO/IEC DIS 8652. *Information technology — Programming languages — Ada*.

[3] P. L'Ecuyer. *Efficient and Portable Combined Random Number Generators*. Communications of the ACM 31(6):742–749, 774, 1988.

[4] P. A. Lewis, A. S. Goodman, and J. M. Miller. *A Pseudo-Random Number Generator for the System/360*. IBM System Journal 8(2):136–146, 1969.

[5] G. Marsaglia and A. Zaman. *A New Class of Random Number Generators*. Annals of Applied Probability 1(3):462–480, 1991.

[6] B. A. Wichmann and I. D. Hill. *An Efficient and Portable Pseudo-Random Number Generator*. Applied Statistics 31:188–190, 1982.

9

Formal methods in the design of Ada 95

David Guaspari *
Odyssey Research Associates
Ithaca
NY 14850
USA

Email: davidg@oracorp.com

Several advisory groups have been established to provide suggestions and criticism to the Ada 9X Mapping Revision Team, the small design team that is revising the definition of the Ada programming language. One such group, the Language Precision Team, based its criticisms on attempts to construct formal mathematical models of the design. This paper reports on the first phase of that work.

9.1   Introduction

Formal, mathematical methods are most useful when applied early in the design and implementation of a software system—that, at least, is the familiar refrain. I will report here on a modest effort to apply formal methods at the earliest possible stage, namely, in the design of the Ada 9X programming language itself. This paper is an "experience report" that provides brief case studies illustrating the kinds of problems we worked on, how we approached them, and the extent (if any) to which the results proved useful (section 9.4). It also derives some lessons and suggestions for those undertaking future projects of this kind (section 9.5). A detailed technical account of any of these case studies is beyond the scope of this paper, and the interested reader in the technical details is referred to [14, 15].

9.2   Background

Ada 9X* is the interim name for the first revision of Ada 83, which is the current standard for the Ada programming language. The revision has been in progress since 1988, when the

*©1994 IEEE. Reprinted, with permission, from *Proceedings of the Ninth Annual Conference on Computer Assurance, COMPASS '94*, Gaithersburg, MD, June, 1884, pages 29–37. This work was supported by the U.S. Department of the Air Force under Contract No. FO8635-90-C-0308. The views and conclusions contained in this paper are those of the author and should not be interpreted as necessarily representing the official policies, either expressed or implied, of the Ada 95 Project Office or the U.S. Government.

*From here on to be referred to as Ada 95 -*Editor*.

Ada Joint Programming Office first asked the Ada Board to recommend a plan for revising the Ada standard. The first step in the revision was to solicit criticisms of Ada 83. A set of requirements [7] for the new language standard, based on those criticisms, was published in 1990. A small design team, the Mapping Revision Team (MRT), became exclusively responsible for revising the language standard to satisfy those requirements. The MRT, from Intermetrics, is led by S. Tucker Taft.

The Ada 95 design includes support for object-oriented programming, improved support for real-time programming, and adjustments to features of Ada 83 that have proven inconvenient. It defines a core language (a highly but not fully compatible extension of Ada 83) that must be supported by all validated compilers, together with annexes for specialized applications. A vendor may choose to validate its compiler for one or more annexes.

Several changes are of special interest to those concerned with assured computing:

- The semantics of the language has been tightened so that the effects of programs containing certain kinds of programming errors—such as the reading of an uninitialized scalar—are more predictable than they were in Ada 83.

- An annex for safety and security defines and standardizes requirements on compilers intended for use in critical applications.

  The annex for safety and security includes several requirements that make execution more predictable, simplify the generation of object code and implementation of the run-time environment, make the object code more suitable for manual review, and facilitate testing. This annex is principally the work of John McHugh and Brian Wichmann.

- Mathematical methods were applied (on a small scale) to the language design itself. Those applications are the subject of this paper.

The work of the MRT has regularly been subject to independent review and criticism by a committee of Distinguished Reviewers and by several advisory teams—for example, by two User/Implementor teams, each consisting of an industrial user (attempting to make significant use of the new language on a realistic application) and a compiler vendor (undertaking, experimentally, to modify its current implementation in order to provide the necessary new features). One novel decision established the Language Precision Team (LPT), which investigated language proposals from a mathematical point of view.

The LPT has applied formal mathematical analysis to help improve the design of Ada 95 (e.g., by clarifying the language proposals) and to help promote its acceptance (e.g., by identifying a verifiable subset that would meet the needs of safety-critical applications). This paper reports on the first LPT project, which ran from the fall of 1990 until the end of 1992. That project produced studies of several language issues: optimization, sharing and storage, tasking and protected records, overload resolution, the floating point model, distribution, program errors, and object-oriented programming. (A second LPT project, which is still underway, began at the end of 1993.)

The membership of the LPT consisted of experts in Ada 83, formal methods, security, and safety: David Guaspari, Douglas Hoover, K.T. Narayana, and Mark Saaltink (all of Odyssey Research Associates); David Goldschlag, Michael K. Smith, and Matthew Wilding (all of Computational Logic, Inc.); Bill Easton (Peregrine Systems); Wolfgang Polak (an independent consultant); and John McHugh (Portland State University). Brian Wichmann, of Britain's National Physical Laboratory, served as an external reviewer.

9.3   The approach

The LPT could hope to influence the design of Ada 95 only by starting with a realistic idea about what we could reasonably hope to achieve. I will briefly review the history of mathematical work in Ada and then sketch the LPT's approach.

9.3.1   Previous studies of Ada

Ada 83 is one of the most intensively studied real-world programming languages. This scrutiny has included formal definitions covering almost all of the language and the implementation of automated support for specifying and reasoning about language subsets.

Language definitions.   We know of four substantial projects aimed at developing a mathematical definition of Ada 83.

A definition of the sequential part of Preliminary Ada was published in [8], but seems to have had little effect on the design of Ada 83. That project labored under many handicaps: mathematical techniques suitable for modeling concurrency were lacking at the time; and the designers of Ada 83 seem to have regarded the work as an add-on, thus reducing its influence by definition.

Dansk Datamatik [2] formally defined parts of Preliminary Ada and used their definition in developing their family of commercial Ada compilers.

The first of all validated Ada compilers evolved from a formal definition project at New York University [6]. The original goal of that project was to define Ada in the very high-level programming language SETL. This project resulted in the first validated Ada compiler.

A draft formal definition of (virtually) the entire Ada Reference Manual, sponsored by the European Economic Community, appeared in 1987 [5].* The published rationale for this project suggested many potential uses for this after-the-fact definition, including tool sets for browsing through the definition, and an interpreter capable of executing it. This work is a virtuoso exercise in the development and application of formal techniques on a large scale. The resulting model provides an unambiguous interpretation of the reference manual, but is complex and does not seem particularly suited to analysis—that is, the task of proving theorems *about* the model seems difficult. Much of the complexity may fairly be ascribed to intrinsic complexities in Ada—particularly those introduced by tasking (which, as the formal definition makes clear, has a pervasive influence on the dynamic semantics of the language).

Reasoning systems.   Several mathematical models of subsets of Ada 83 have been devised for the sake of reasoning about Ada 83 programs (e.g., [3, 9, 10, 12]) and have been used as the basis of machine-supported verification systems. The underlying formalisms differ, as each was chosen for its suitability to support a particular technique of formal reasoning. Members of the LPT have been involved in the development of two of these systems (Penelope and AVA).

9.3.2   The LPT

This large body of mathematical work has had some practical payoff—particularly on the development of commercial compilers—but had little influence on the design of Ada 83 itself. It seemed that the LPT could most usefully contribute to the design of Ada 95 by

---

*The implementation-dependent features of chapter 13 are omitted.

working "in the small"—using mathematical techniques to attack design problems chosen opportunistically. Accordingly, most of the LPT reports attempt to provide a rigorous version of the informal, intuitive modeling that goes on as a normal part of thinking about design alternatives.

The small-scale, opportunistic approach had several obvious advantages:

- We did not spend effort on well-understood aspects of the language (as would be required if we undertook to model the entire language).

- Each problem could be attacked from a point of view, and at a level of abstraction, that seemed best suited to it.

- We could more easily adapt to changes in the mapping proposals.

Opportunism in action.   Here is a simple concrete example. An early mapping proposal would have allowed a user-defined subtype T to be associated with a user-supplied default expression e. Any object x of such a subtype T declared would, in the absence of an explicit initialization, be initialized by evaluating e and assigning its value to x.[†]

One reason for this innocuous looking proposal was to guarantee that (something like) the following innocuous looking property should be true

> (*) If T is a scalar subtype with a default expression and x is any object of subtype T, then x will always have a defined value.

Now consider some implications of (*).

(1) If we have

```
type A is range 1..10 := 1;
       -- default initialization
type AR is
  record
      x: boolean;
      y: A;
  end record;
procedure Q(u : out AR) is
begin
   ...
end;
```

then, within the body of Q, (*) should imply that u.y always has a defined value. So, in order to preserve (*), the semantics of out parameters must guarantee that certain of their components are initialized at the beginning of a subprogram call.

(2) Subtype conversions become problematic:

```
type not_init is range 1..10;
type A1 is array(foo) of not_init;

subtype init is not_init := 1;
type init_array is array(foo) of init;
```

[†]This idea was eventually abandoned, but that makes it no less useful as an example.

```
x1: A1;
x2: init_array := init_array(x1);
```

The explicit initialization of x2 makes its components *uninitialized*. Since those components are objects of subtype `init`, property (*) fails.

Instead of accumulating an *ad hoc* catalogue of such troublesome examples, we would like to understand the essence of the problem: what abstract properties of a programming language suffice to guarantee that it satisfies (*)? We can capture such a collection of properties axiomatically. Here is a (simplified) sketch. The constituents of the model are

- Labels—a label is an abstract version of a type mark and indicates, in particular, whether that type mark is associated with a default initialization expression.

- Objects—each object has a unique label. We write $y < x$ if object y is a subobject (component) of x, and we say that a set C of objects *covers* x if every scalar subobject of x whose label has a default initialization is also a subobject of an element of C.

- Values—each value has a unique label. A value is *bad* if it has any subcomponent that lacks a defined value, but whose label is associated with a default initialization.

- States—a state consists of a set of objects, a subobject and covering relation, and a store assigning a value to each object. A state must satisfy the invariant $(\mathcal{G})$ that if the value of object x is good, so are the values of all its subobjects.

The dynamic semantics of this model represents execution as a sequence of events, where the events are of two kinds:

- "$x \leftarrow e$" Assign the value e to x, where e is an expression formed by applying operations from some predefined set O to the values in existing objects. An important assumption about O is noted below.

- "*create* $x : C \leftarrow V$" Create object x and assign to the objects in C (which is a covering set for x) the values defined by V (where V is a map from C into values).

The effect of an event on the state is characterized by a small set of axioms, such as

- If $y < x$, and e is a good value, and x has a good value, then after the event "$y \leftarrow e$" the value of x is still good.

- The event "*create* $x : C \leftarrow V$" may occur only in a state in which x does not exist. If all the values in V are good, then after this event the value of x is good.

It follows trivially from these axioms that, so long as the values on the right-hand side of an event are good values, an occurrence of the event preserves $(\mathcal{G})$ as an invariant. In addition, the axioms imply all the instances we need of a kind of converse to $(\mathcal{G})$: If all the objects in a cover for x have good values, then the value of x is good.

To be sure that the right-hand values of events are good it will be enough to know that each operation $o \in O$ is applied only on the domain of inputs in which o is *non-decreasing* in the following sense: If all the arguments to o are good, then so is its result.

To apply our axiomatics to proposed Ada 95 rules, we define a set O of non-decreasing operations and ask which executions can be modeled by an atomic sequence of events using the operations of O. Example 1 amounts to asking whether the proposed language rules permit parameter passing to be represented by appropriate *create* events. Example 2 amounts to asking whether all subtype conversions (more precisely, all non-erroneous subtype conversions that do not raise exceptions) are non-decreasing operations on values.

As we proceeded to examine other language rules, additional qualifications arose. For example, we must reformulate (*) to ask only about the values of objects in states that arise during executions in which no erroneous execution has yet occurred—hardly a surprising observation. We also see that the assumed atomicity of events can be violated by certain pathologies, such as the abortion of a task in the middle of a copy operation.

The moral of this example is simply that the model made it straightforward to evaluate (informally, but rigorously) the effect of any particular language proposal on property (*). The default initialization proposal was dropped during a phase that attempted to reduce the sheer scale of the revision by eliminating any nontrivial change that was nonessential. As the examples have shown, the proposal would not have been a "point" change.

The limits of opportunism.   The limitations of this small-scale approach are also plain. The only way to axiomatize a problem in isolation is to make assumptions about what has been left out. There is no way to *prove* that those assumptions are true (i.e., that the axioms apply) without embedding it in a model of the entire programming language. Our model of initialization can be, and was, applied informally to the English-language definitions in the reference manual and mapping proposals. The results were informative, but not iron-clad.

Further, some of the most vexing problems in language design concern the interactions of seemingly remote features, and those problems cannot be attacked without large-scale models of the kind that have been attempted in the past. Consequently, one LPT report developed a draft framework for a large-scale "natural semantics" definition of the sequential part of Ada 95, by which we hoped to clarify the interactions of the object-oriented features, finalization, distribution, etc.

9.4   Some case studies

9.4.1   Overload resolution

The most enthusiastically received LPT report provided an analysis of overload resolution. Ada permits subprogram names to be overloaded and also permits a certain collection of operator symbols (including + and =) to be overloaded and used as infix operators. The Ada 83 rules for visibility and overload resolution are complex—the demonstration that overload resolution could be implemented in only two passes was a nontrivial achievement— and few people, if any, understand them fully. Knowledge of the fine points of these rules is rarely necessary, and programmers typically ignore them until a surprise forces names to be written in some inconvenient and awkward way. Because the fine points are not consistently interpreted by compilers, subtle portability problems can result.

One special source of trouble has been the "use" clause. A compilation unit Comp becomes a client of a compilation unit P if the declaration of Comp is prefaced by the clause "with P." That is, the with-clause makes P and its exports visible to Comp, and Comp may therefore refer to an entity Q exported by package P under its full name, P.Q. If Comp is also prefaced by the use-clause "use P" then Q may refer to this operation by its simple name, Q, as well.

A use-clause increases the supply of entities potentially nameable by their simple names, and therefore increases the possibility of name conflicts, which the overloading rules must either resolve or make illegal. A use-clause can sometimes make a program more difficult to read by making it harder to associate an occurrence of a name with the declaration that introduced that name. In addition, the Ada 83 rules inadvertently admitted a pathology, commonly called a "Beaujolais effect," whereby adding or removing a use-clause could change the resolution of names so as to transform one legal program into another legal program with a different meaning. (The key point about a Beaujolais effect is that both programs are legal, and therefore compilable, which means that the user will not be warned that the program's meaning has changed.)

As a result, some programming projects have gone so far as to forbid use-clauses. Unfortunately, without a "use P" clause, the operator symbols exported by P are available to a client only in prefix form—thus, for example, forcing a client to write an equality test in the unpleasant notation P. "=" (x, y).* In the world view of Ada, the primary objection to this notation is not that it requires a few more key strokes than x = y, but that it is much less readable.

The LPT report on overload resolution† considered several interrelated problems:

- The Ada 83 rules for overload resolution are complex and contain unpleasant surprises.

- To make infix operators more easily available to clients, the MRT originally suggested introducing special visibility rules for operators, called "primitive visibility rules." There was controversy over the desirability of these rules and some confusion about what the rules actually were. In particular, neither the description in the mapping documents nor the implementation suggested in [1] was precise.

- The incompatibilities between various new proposals and the Ada 83 rules were not fully understood.

This report used Z [13] to define a conceptual scheme in which alternatives could be formulated precisely—a general abstract model of overload resolution parameterized by certain key decisions about which interpretations of symbols are possible and which, given a choice, are to be preferred. This uniform description of a set of alternatives is a "classic" use of formalism for the sake of clarity.

Furthermore, because the model was economical—pitched at a level of abstraction that presented only the relevant details—it could be analyzed. For any particular set of rules, we could pose and answer questions such as the following:

1. Do the rules permit "Beaujolais effects"?

2. Can a legal Ada 83 program become a legal Ada 95 program with a different meaning—that is, one in which the resolution of names changes?

3. Can the overload resolution rules be implemented by an algorithm requiring only local information?

The most desirable answers are (in order) no, no, and yes. The MRT's proposed rules did not quite meet these goals; but by analyzing formally what would be necessary to meet them, we were able to suggest slight modifications to those rules that would do the trick. The modified rules would not be fully upward compatible; a small number of legal Ada 83

---

*In the absence of a use-clause the prefix form can be obtained by explicitly renaming P. "=" to an infix operator, but large lists of renamings are themselves error prone.

†By Bill Easton of Peregrine Systems.

programs would become illegal in Ada 95, but the model permits a precise characterization of such programs. The essentials of the MRT's proposal have been incorporated into the Ada 95 standard.

This example illustrates all the hoped-for benefits of our approach: The formalism was chosen to fit the problem and could therefore be easily explained to its intended audience; it clarified the problem, suggested a new solution, and was used to prove correctness properties of proposed solutions; and its results, being timely, influenced the thinking of the MRT.

Note some of the things that helped to make this piece of work successful. First, its author was ideally qualified—a mathematician by training and an Ada lawyer by trade. Second, overload resolution is a very suitable problem, because it can in fact be modeled in isolation from other parts of the language. Finally, the work addressed an acknowledged difficulty, and attempts to address the problem were floundering.

9.4.2   Tasking and real-time

The Ada 83 rendezvous provides a very general model of synchronous communication. For some applications, this generality entailed unacceptably high overhead costs and an unacceptably complex run-time environment. The MRT therefore proposed a new construct, the *protected record*, that could be efficiently used to synchronize access to a shared data structure. No separate thread of control is implied by a protected record, for nothing happens to its state between accesses. The addition of protected records is a significant change to the language.

A more specialized change addresses problems in interprocess communication through shared objects—especially communication between an Ada program and some concurrent non-Ada process implemented either in software or on a hardware device. The Ada 83 mechanisms supporting shared variables are somewhat weak and their semantics is obscure, so the MRT proposed replacing the Ada 83 pragma SHARED by the two pragmas ATOMIC (loads and stores of objects so marked should be indivisible) and VOLATILE (objects so marked may be updated asynchronously—e.g., by a hardware device).

The LPT undertook three separate studies associated with the tasking and real-time features of Ada 95, and pursued them in very different ways.

A timed model.   We undertook to model a tasking subset, taking into account its quantitative time behavior, using a timed denotational semantics.[‡] Mathematical formalisms for real-time systems are very much a research topic, and in January 1992 a version of our model was presented at an academic meeting [11]. The model was complex and, despite its theoretical interest, not immediately helpful to the MRT—although it did uncover some difficulties, particularly in the rules for calculating priorities. We decided that this work was becoming a pure research effort with insufficient payoff to Ada 95 and stopped working on it.

An untimed model.   In addition to the timed model, we produced an untimed model of (a subset of) the protected record constructs.[§] This model, formulated in Unity [4], is quite simple and can be used to describe the effects of all possible orders in which a collection of tasks might acquire and release a protected record.

To achieve this simplicity, we deliberately chose a language subset corresponding to the expected uses of the construct: Access to the operations of a protected record is controlled

---

[‡]By K.T. Narayana, of ORA.

[§]By David Goldschlag, of Computational Logic, Inc.

by boolean guards called entry barriers (functioning like the conditions in a selective wait statement). We assumed that these booleans depend only on the state of the protected record and not, e.g., on the states of global variables that can be asynchronously updated by external processes or modified by side effects resulting from the evaluation of other entry barriers.

The model could be used straightforwardly to prove the correctness of, e.g., a standard implementation of "producers and consumers" in which accesses are synchronized by a protected record. In some early meetings, the Distinguished Reviewers found it helpful to organize their discussions around this precise definition of protected records—another "classic" application of a formal definition.

A model of shared variables.   Like most of the LPT studies, the model of shared variables[¶] provides a formalism addressed specifically to one problem. Of our three models of real-time and tasking features, it seems to have been the most useful to the MRT.

Ada 83 permits tasks to share variables, placing the burden for synchronizing access to such variables on the programmer. The programmer's responsibility is expressed in terms of "assumptions" that the compiler is allowed to make. (Some of these responsibilities are transferred to the implementation if the programmer invokes pragma SHARED). Ada 95 introduces a new way in which tasks can communicate, via protected records, and replaces pragma SHARED by the pragmas ATOMIC and VOLATILE.

The Ada 95 rules about the use of shared variables were originally expressed in terms of implementation strategies such as "keeping local copies" and "direct-to-memory writing." Two problems arose: devising what the rules should be, and devising a description of the rules at the proper semantic level (one that avoids references to implementation details).

The MRT first considered the POSIX model, which is formulated in terms of a notion of precedence, a *partial* ordering of events according to which, intuitively, "x precedes y" means that x is guaranteed to finish before y starts. This vocabulary was not quite appropriate: The attempt to define protected operations solely in terms of the POSIX model resulted in a semantics whose implementations would be unnecessarily inefficient. (In particular, after every protected action, implementations would have to discard local copies of shared variables and flush all caches.)

The MRT suggested that a more suitable model could be formulated in terms of a strengthened precedence relation that they called *signaling*. Roughly speaking, an event of one task signals an event of another task if the tasks are synchronized (in the sense of [ARM 9.11]) between the two events.

This model, however, had problems of its own: In some circumstances the model was too weak to guarantee that the result of successive accesses to components of protected records would be predictable. The LPT proposed a model that generalized and incorporated both models—including notions of precedence (slightly varied) and signaling, and the relations between them. This axiomatic framework could be used to express and explore various semantic rules for protected records and could also be used to show that certain implementation strategies (e.g., decisions about when to flush caches) would satisfy the rules. We also proposed specific rules for protected records, in terms of this model, that seemed to meet the needs for efficiency and predictability.

A variant of the LPT's framework is used in the latest version of the Ada 95 rules, and many of the specific Ada 95 rules are closely related to rules proposed in the LPT model. The LPT report identified some problems with preliminary versions of these rules. All such problems have been addressed in the Draft Standard. For example, the original rule describing

---

[¶] By Mark Saaltink, of ORA Canada.

signaling between actions on a protected record was very difficult to formulate precisely, and would have been difficult for a programmer to use; the MRT revised this rule to make it simpler in both respects. The MRT has formulated an elegant narrative description of their rules that is much more readable than a simple transcription of the mathematical description into English would have been.

9.4.3   Object-oriented programming

The LPT has begun to identify a verifiable subset of Ada 95. We were interested, in particular, whether methods used in the Penelope system [9] for reasoning about Ada 83—a predicate transformer semantics based on ordinary first-order logic—could be naturally extended to Ada 95. The introduction of object-oriented constructs is a significant extension to the language, so we set ourselves the task of devising a specification notation and a proof formalism for reasoning about an interesting subset of these features.

The work[||] resulted in a draft specification notation and a demonstrably sound proof formalism for the basic object-oriented mechanisms of inheritance and dispatching—omitting generics and private types (for reasons of time), and tasking (because tasking is not yet handled by formal reasoning tools for Ada 83). These results show that the OOP features of Ada 95 are semantically clean and provide a useful beginning at the definition of a verifiable subset. Sections 9.4.3 and 9.4.3 briefly describe this project.

Background

Tagged types.   Ada 83 provides a notion of type derivation. If type D is derived from type T, then

- The set of values of D is an isomorphic copy of the set of values of T.

- Explicit type conversion between D and T is possible.

- D inherits certain operations of T (called the *derivable* operations of T).

  More precisely, each derivable operation of T gives rise to a corresponding, implicitly declared, operation of D. The default implementation of such an inherited operation is the result of calling the corresponding operation of T with each argument of type D converted to T. The user may override the default implementation of an inherited operation by explicitly providing a body for it.

Ada 95 generalizes this mechanism to provide basic features of object-oriented programming: extension, inheritance, and dispatching (run-time binding). A type is "tagged" if it is a record type whose declaration contains the key word `tagged` or if it is derived from a tagged type. A type D derived from a tagged type T may extend T by containing extra components and will inherit the *primitive operations* of its parent type T. A value of a type descended from T contains an implicit component—a "tag"—that identifies which descendant of T it comes from. The default implementation of an inherited operation is, as in Ada 83, the result of calling the corresponding operation of T with each argument of type D converted to T; and, also as before, the user may override this default by explicitly supplying a body for the inherited operation.

These mechanisms make it possible to achieve run-time binding (dispatching) of subprogram calls: A primitive operation of a tagged type T may be applied to an operand of some

---

[||]By David Guaspari, of ORA.

type known statically to be *descended* from T, but whose actual type may not be known until run-time. At run-time the tag of the value is then used to identify its type and thereby to invoke the corresponding primitive operation on that type.

The state of the art.   Specifying and reasoning about OOP is a research topic. An initial survey of the literature turned up nothing directly useful, although we did obtain some relevant manuscripts, in draft, a few months before the LPT project ended. Our approach to this problem could not be a matter of applying an existing body of theory.

As a result, we had to devote considerable time to general problems in reasoning about OOP that were not specific to the Ada 95 proposals. In fact, we decided that it would first be necessary to formalize the static binding provided by Ada 83 generics, as a kind of warm-up exercise. These difficulties, and the volatility of the language proposals about OOP, may suggest that this subject was inappropriate for the LPT. On the other hand, we made progress. It is rare for a real-world OOP language to claim any kind of support from formal reasoning.**

Opportunities.   Some initial attempts at addressing technical design problems, in the spirit of the other LPT reports, came to nothing. If we missed some opportunities, at least part of the reason is that the LPT was not part of the design team: Because the OOP proposals were in a state of rapid flux and because the rationale for certain decisions was not always apparent in the design documents the MRT issued for external consumption, only a group more intimately involved in the design would have been able to identify good opportunities.

In addition, many of the MRT's immediate problems concerned pragmatic design decisions, and not the underlying semantics. For example, they needed to choose

- The best syntax for declaring a tagged type or a type extension.

- The static semantics for dispatching calls (to help users understand what operations their calls should be dispatching to).

  Our proof formalism works from a "resolved" language in which a first pass of static analysis has answered these questions (insofar as they can be decided statically).

- A design that could be implemented without "distributed overhead"—that is, one in which a program not using the OOP features would pay no performance penalty.

These considerations suggested that the most useful work we could do would be prospective—to identify a significant verifiable subset of the OOP constructs.

Working with the MRT

Our discussions with the MRT about the OOP design centered on two kinds of questions: Did we really understand the proposals? Was our subset misleadingly simple because it omitted some essential idioms?

We based our first formalism on a miscellany of examples that had been produced and circulated by the MRT and other teams. After reviewing this work, the MRT asked whether the formalism accommodated "redispatching," which was not used in the examples we originally studied: At run-time the tag on one operand may be used to select (dispatch to) a primitive operation, and that primitive operation itself may use the tag on some other operand to dispatch again.

**We know of draft formal specification languages for C++ and Modula-3, but neither is supported by a reasoning system.

To accommodate redispatching, we had to revise the formalism radically, after which the model was no longer fully compositional: It did not support extending a tagged type by adding components that were themselves of tagged types. The MRT said flatly that this limitation was unacceptable. To remove the limitation we spent a months groping with pure questions of formal logic, but the result seemed in the end acceptable: a formal model of (and a reasoning system for) what the MRT regarded as the basic OOP mechanisms. The formalism is expressed in terms of predicate transformers using (essentially) first-order logic and extends the existing Penelope formalism for reasoning about the sequential part of Ada 83. We had time to apply the method only to very simple examples, so the adequacy of the specification notation and the tractability of our proof techniques have not been demonstrated.

9.5   Conclusions

The fate of previous formal work on Ada, and the constraints on the design of Ada 95, suggested that the LPT should proceed opportunistically—identifying problems that seemed both useful and approachable, applying whatever formal techniques (Z, Unity, denotational semantics, predicate transformers) seemed most suitable to each problem. The success of such a strategy depends on how well opportunities are identified. Although the members of the MRT have consistently been open to and interested in whatever help the LPT could offer and are much more sophisticated consumers of mathematical information than typical industrial clients, our record here was mixed: It was difficult to decide on the best "assignments" for the LPT. It was not always clear to the MRT what kinds of help the LPT might be able to give, and the MRT lacked the resources to tutor us and keep us current enough to spot opportunities as they flew past. An attempt to solve this problem institutionally—by designating one member of the MRT to be a liaison with the LPT—could not bear the weight of these demands.

These difficulties reaffirm a commonplace: that mathematical methods are most successful when they form an integral part of the working methods of a project. To that extent, the LPT suffered from being an add-on. Another practical problem with an add-on project is that, as a purely contractual matter, such a separate effort must be accountable for some specified set of products, such as mathematical models of particular language features. Yet some of the most helpful mathematical analysis can be work that is completely consumed in the course of the design—e.g., a detailed analysis of a road not taken, making it plain why that road is a dead end. The Ada 95 Project Office, through which the LPT was funded, has been open-minded about such matters and helped make the best of a situation that is intrinsically flawed.

Another choice that bears examination is the decision to constitute the LPT from a widely scattered membership. Significant work was done in California, Texas, North Carolina, West Virginia, New York, and Canada. This arrangement provided the most outright technical expertise. Because we were so spread out, and because the LPT was contractually obligated to consider a large number of topics, each member of the team assumed responsibility for one or more reports and used the other members not as collaborators but as reviewers. The administrative details were very awkward, but e-mail, telephone, and a shared "mathematical culture" made the arrangement workable, if not pleasant. The fact that we were physically separated from one another was less important than the fact that we were functionally separated from the MRT.

One last consideration is sociological: the differences in culture between the MRT and the LPT. The MRT has naturally been concerned with a great number of design decisions that are matters of taste, politics, etc., and from which the LPT was glad to be free. On purely technical matters it seems fair to say that the LPT customarily approaches problems by way of a semantic model, while the MRT and the other advisory teams customarily approach problems from the point of view of implementations (their efficiency, cost, etc.). For example, a mathematical approach often concerns itself with pathologies to a degree that some would consider unseemly—treating them as evidence that a simple model of the language, or some desirable language property, has failed. From other points of view pathologies may seem like uninteresting marginal cases requiring at most ad hoc rules that will make some particularly doubtful usages illegal. Such differences in viewpoint are desirable. Members of the LPT differed in their ability to bridge the differences, to elicit from the MRT the problems that needed to be formalized, and to adapt their own concerns to those of the MRT. Those abilities proved as important as purely technical skills.

I believe that the LPT work has been useful to the MRT and to those Distinguished Reviewers who have studied it, and that some of its contributions were unlikely to have come from any other source—that is, from any source not approaching the problems in a formal mathematical way. I also believe that we have made a useful start on identifying a verifiable subset of Ada 95 and showing how to reason about it. I would like to think that, sooner rather than later, work like this will not be the province of a separate group of consultants, but will be part of the standard operating procedure in language design, as it is part of the practice of every mature engineering discipline.

References

[1] Ada 9X Mapping/Revision Team. Ada 9X implementation modules I. Technical report, Intermetrics, Inc., January 1991.

[2] D. Bjorner and O. N. Est. Towards a formal description of Ada. volume 98 of *Lecture Notes in Comput. Sci.*, Berlin, 1980. Springer-Verlag.

[3] B.A. Carré and T.J. Jennings. SPARK—the SPADE Ada Kernel. Technical report, University of Southampton, Dept. of Electronics and Computer Science, 1988.

[4] K.M. Chandy and J. Misra. *Parallel Program Design: A Foundation.* Addison Wesley, Massachusetts, 1988.

[5] The draft formal definition of Ada. Technical Report AdaFD/DDC/25, Dansk Datamatic Center, Denmark, 1987.

[6] Robert B. K. Dewar, Philippe B. Kruchten, and Brian Siritzky. Ada/Ed interpreter, Executable semantic model for Ada. Technical report, Dept. of Computer Science, Courant Institute, New York, 1984.

[7] Ada 9X Requirements. Technical report, Office of the Undersecretary of Defense for Acquisition, 1990.

[8] V.D. Donzeau-Gouge, G. Kahn, and B. Lang. Formal definition of the Ada programming language. *INRIA*, November 1980.

[9] David Guaspari, Carla Marceau, and Wolfgang Polak. Formal verification of Ada programs. *IEEE Transactions on Software Engineering*, 16:1058–1075, September 1990.

[10] David F. Martin and Jeffrey V. Cook. Adding Ada program verification capability to the State Delta Verification System (SDVS). In *11th National Computer Security Conference*, October 1988.

[11] K. T. Narayana. Formal techniques in real time and fault tolerant systems. Lecture Notes in Computer Science, *to appear.*

[12] Michael K. Smith. The AVA reference manual. Technical Report 64, Computational Logic, Inc., Austin, Texas, 1992.

[13] J. M. Spivey. *The Z Notation: A Reference Manual.* Prentice Hall International Series in Computer Science. Prentice Hall, 1989.

[14] Language Precision Team. Formal studies of Ada 9X, Final report. Technical report, Odyssey Research Associates, December 1992.

[15] Language Precision Team. Formal studies of Ada 9X, Interim report. Technical report, Office of the Undersecretary of Defense for Acquisition, January 1992.

10

The GNAT Project: A GNU-Ada 9X Compiler

The paper "The GNAT Project: A GNU-Ada 9X Compiler" originally appeared in the proceedings of "Tri-Ada 94: Architecting Systems for the '90's and Beyond".

The GNAT Project: A GNU-Ada 9X Compiler

Edmond Schonberg   Bernard Banner

New York University   New York University
Courant Institute   Courant Institute
251 Mercer Street   251 Mercer Street
New York, NY 10012   New York, NY 10012
schonberg@cs.nyu.edu   banner@cs.nyu.edu

Abstract

We describe the general organization of the GNAT compiler, its relationship to the GCC multilanguage compiler system, and some of the architectural details of the system. This paper serves as an introduction to the following papers in this session.

Introduction: Ada 9X and the GNAT Project

The Ada community has proposed a number of explanations for the relative lack of success of Ada vis-a-vis of C and more recently C++, in spite of the clear superiority of Ada as a language for software engineering. At least one reason for the slow spread of Ada through the software community has been the absence of a cheap (or even free) high-quality compiler that can run on a variety of platforms and is usable both for training and serious software construction. The imminent introduction of Ada 9X presents us with a new opportunity. The language offers up-to-date tools for object-oriented programming, for information systems, for distributed systems, for interfacing with other languages, for hierarchical system decomposition, etc. If a free, high-quality compiler were to appear at the same time as the standardization of the language is completed, it would assist considerably in spreading the knowledge of the new language, and in encouraging comparisons with existing languages (in which we can expect Ada 9X to show its superiority).

The GNAT project aims to produce such a compiler. GNAT (an acronym for GNU NYU Ada Translator), is a front-end and runtime system for Ada 9X that uses the successful GCC [GCC94a] back-end as a retargetable code

This work has been supported in part by the Ada 9X Program Office through Air Force Contract FO8630-92-C-0019.

generator. GNAT is thus part of the GNU software, and is distributed according to the guidelines of the Free Software Foundation. GNAT will be a complete compiler, but will not be validated by New York University. Successively more complete versions of GNAT have been distributed over the last 18 months. The availability of sources for the system is allowing language designers and implementors to participate in the construction of GNAT itself. As a result, many members of the Ada community are contributing software packages for portions of GNAT, in particular for the language annexes.

In the following sections we give a technical overview of the structure of GNAT. We then discuss some of the more interesting features of the system, from the user point of view. Finally, we describe the status of the annexes, the GNU licenses and some of the ongoing collaborations involving the GNAT team and others.

1. GCC: An industrial-strength compiler

GCC is the compiler system of the GNU environment. GNU (a self-referential acronym for "GNU is Not Unix") is a Unix-compatible operating system, being developed by the Free Software Foundation, and distributed under the GNU General Public License (GPL). GNU software is always distributed with its sources, and the GPL enjoins anyone who modifies GNU software and then redistributes the modified product to supply the sources for the modifications as well. In this fashion, enhancements to the original software benefit the software community at large. GCC is today the centerpiece of the GNU software. GCC is a retargetable and rehostable compiler system, with multiple front-ends and a large number of hardware targets. Originally designed as a compiler for C, it now includes front-ends for C++, Modula-3, Fortran, Objective-C, and most recently Ada.

2. The organization of GNAT

The first decision to be made was the language in which GNAT should be written. GCC is fully written in C, but for technical reasons as well as non-technical ones, it was inconceivable to use anything but Ada for GNAT itself. We started using a relatively small subset of Ada 83, and in typical fash-

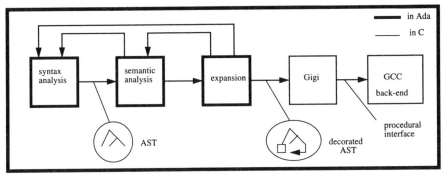

Figure 1

ion extended the subset whenever new features became implemented. Six months after the coding started in earnest, we were able to bootstrap the compiler, and abandon the commercial compiler we had been using up to that point. As Ada 9X features are implemented, we are now able to write GNAT in Ada 9X. In fact, the definition of the language depends heavily on hierarchical libraries, and cannot be given except in Ada 9X, so that it is natural for the compiler and the environment to use child units throughout. Figure 1 shows the overall structure of the GNAT compiler.

The front-end of the GNAT compiler is thus written in Ada 9X. The back-end of the compiler is the back-end of GCC proper, extended to meet the needs of Ada semantics. The front-end comprises four phases, which communicate by means of a rather compact Abstract Syntax Tree (AST). The implementation details of the AST are hidden by several procedural interfaces that provide access to syntactic and semantic attributes. The layering of the system, and the various levels of abstraction, are the obvious benefits of writing in Ada, in what one might call "proper"Ada style. It is worth mentioning that strictly speaking GNAT does not use a symbol table. Rather, all semantic information concerning program entities is stored in defining occurrences of these entities directly in the AST. The GNAT structures are thus close in spirit to those of DIANA [DIANA83], albeit more compact. It appears that the AST will be adequate to support an ASIS interface, [ASIS91] but we have not examined the design of such an interface in any detail yet.

GNAT includes three other modules which are not involved in code generation but are an integral part of any Ada compilation system. These are the runtime and tasking executive, the library manager, and the binder. These components are also written in Ada 9X.

Before presenting some details about the compiler proper, we want to highlight two user-friendly aspects of the GNAT system that are particularly relevant to its use in the early days of Ada 9X.

2.1 A compiler for everyone: character sets

One interesting aspect of GNAT is its support for foreign language character sets. GNAT fully implements the new standard in this respect, and in fact goes well beyond the stated minimum requirements.

Latin-1 is fully supported, including its use in identifiers, as described in the RM. In addition, optional switches allow localization of the identifier character set to Latin-2, Latin-3, Latin-4, the IBM PC set, the restricted (Ada 83) 7-bit set, or the full upper half without case equivalence (useful for some languages like Thai, where there is no upper/lower case equivalence). Types wide character and wide string are fully supported, and a compiler switch allows the use of wide characters in identifiers. Several different encoding methods are implemented for wide characters, including the EUC and Shift-JIS encodings in common use in Japan. We envision adding in the future other representations such as an interface to the Unicode encoding scheme.

2.2 A compiler to ease the transition: 83/9X modes

Two modes of compilation are offered in GNAT. Ada 83 mode allows programs to be compiled using Ada 83 rules. This is most useful for programs which might be incompatible with Ada 9X rules such as those using the new reserved words like **tagged** as identifiers in their programs. This mode will also flag as errors those constructs which are allowed in Ada 9X but not in Ada 83 such as basic declarative items appearing after later declarative items, unconstrained variable declarations, among others. Special recognition of Ada 9X constructs takes place so that when new features (tagged types or requeue statements, say) are encountered in Ada 83 mode, appropriate error messages are issued, instead of treating them as unrecognizable text (as would be the case for a typical Ada 83 compiler).

Of course the Ada 9X mode is the default. While we have tried to be faithful in our Ada 83 mode, the introduction in Ada 9X of some real upward incompatibilities makes it very hard to remove all 9X semantics from the implementation, so that programs that GNAT considers legal Ada 83 may in fact include some minor 9X extensions. Examples of these include the use of the Ada 9X Text_IO, which has added Append_Mode to File_Type. Given that our chief goal is to provide an *Ada 9X* compiler, these small departures from strict Ada 83 behavior are benign. We envision having a mode which will warn users of constructs in their Ada 83 programs which might introduce incompatibilities in Ada 9X along the lines discussed in [PLOEDEREDER92].

3. Syntax analysis in GNAT

The parser is a hand-coded recursive descent parser. It includes a sophisticated error recovery system, which among other things takes indentation into account when attempting to correct scope errors. In our experience, the recovery is superior to that of other compilers, and the parser is remarkably stable in the presence of badly mangled programs. This is especially important in a student oriented setting. All GNU compilers heretofore had used LALR(1) parsers generated with Bison (The GNU equivalent of YACC). The choice of a handwritten parser at this date may seem surprising, but is amply justified by the following:

(a) **Clarity**. The parser follows carefully the grammar given in the Ada 9X reference manual.This has clear pedagogical advantages, but precludes the use of a table-driven parser, given that the grammar as given is not LALR(k).

(b) **Performance**. Even though the overall performance of the system is bounded by the speed of the code generator, it does not hurt that the parser of GNAT is faster than any table-driven one.

(c) **Error messages**. The most important reason is the quality of the error reporting. Even in case of serious structural errors, such as an interchange of ";" and "is" between specification and body of a subprogram, GNAT generates a precise and intelligible message. Bottom-up parsers have serious difficulties with such errors.

3.1 Some friendly error recovery

It is expected that many of the people that will evaluate GNAT will be users of other languages like C and Pascal. The error detection of GNAT recognizes some of the classical mistakes that these users are expected to make, such as using != or <> for inequality and == for equality; it informs them that the proper token should be /= or =.

The parser tries to make use of the casing of identifiers in the program, and assumes that the user has some consistent policy regarding the casing convention used to distinguish keywords from user-defined entities. The parser deduces this convention from the first keyword and identifier that it encounters. In the example given in figure 2, the compiler makes use of the upper/lower case rule for identifiers to treat **exception** as an intended identifier rather than the beginning of an exception handler.

```
procedure Wrong1 is
   Exception : Integer;
   |
   reserved word "exception" cannot be used as identifier
begin
   ...
end;
```

Figure 2

Special treatment is given to particularly common mistakes such as using a positional aggregates with a single component (instead of the required named association), as shown in figure 3. Needless to say, this recovery requires semantic information:

```
1.  procedure Wrong2 is
2.     type R is record
3.        M : Integer;
4.     end record;
5.     Vr : R;
6.  begin
7.     Vr := 1;
        |
     expected type "r" declared at line 2:9
     found type "universal_integer"

8.     Vr := (1);
        |
     positional aggregate cannot have one component.
9.  end;
```

Figure 3

The next example given in figure 4 makes use of indentation to match if statements.

```
1.  procedure Wrong3 is
2.  begin
3.     if a > b then
4.        null;
5.
6.end;
   |
   "end if;" expected for "if" at line 3:4
```

Figure 4

Note that a more conventional approach to error recovery would have produced two errors: it would have identified the "end" with the if-statement, complained about a missing "if", and then complained about the missing end for the procedure itself.

4. Semantic analysis and expansion

These two interlinked phases have the following purpose: Semantic analysis performs name and type resolution, decorates the AST with various semantic attributes, and as a by-product performs all static legality checks on the program.

The semantic analysis follows the rule that all modifications to the AST allow recovery of the original source program. The expander is not bound by such a rule. As a consequence, the output of the semantic pass is the proper interface to an ASIS tool.

The expander modifies the AST in order to simplify its translation into the GCC tree. Most of the expander activity results in the construction of additional AST fragments. Given that code generation requires that such fragments carry all semantic attributes, every expansion activity must be followed by additional semantic processing on the generated tree. This recursive structure is carried further: some predefined operations such as exponentiation are defined by means of a generic procedure, for which the run-time library holds instantiations for the various predefined types. The expansion of the operation results in the loading and compilation of the required instantiation, followed by a call to the corresponding function. Aggregates, initialization procedures, equality on composite types, boolean operations on arrays, and tasking operations are typical expansions.

4.1 Expansion: an example

A typical task of the expander is the construction of initialization procedures for composite types. For arrays, the initialization procedures expand into loops whose body invokes the initialization procedure for the component type. For records the initialization procedure invokes the corresponding procedures for each component type, or else assigns the default expression present in the record type declaration. In either case it is simpler to build the AST for the procedure, and invoke (recursively) the semantic analysis on this AST, which may lead to further expansion and analysis, rather than to laboriously generate a low-level representation for the operations involved.

There is a further unusual recursive aspect to the structure of GNAT. The program library (described in greater detail below) does not hold any intermediate representation of compiled units. As a result, package declarations are analyzed whenever they appear in a context clause. Furthermore, if a generic unit, or an inlined unit G, is defined in a package P, then the instantiation or inlining of G in the current compilation requires that the body of P be analyzed as well. Thus the library manager, the parser, and the semantic analyzer can be activated from within semantic analysis.

4.2 Invoking Run-Time routines

The possibility of analyzing other units in the middle of semantic analysis gives GNAT a powerful mechanism to interface with run-time routines without having to know their internals. The front-end has a map that associates various run-time library items with the library files that contain them. If the compiler needs to generate a call to one of these items (say, a tasking support routine) or make a reference to library data, it can retrieve the corresponding file and analyze it, thereby generating the proper external symbol in the

user program. It is even possible for the compiler to inline run-time procedures in the user program without having to embed the details of the runtime in the compiler proper. For a compiler that is intended to be portable, and therefore depend on different run-time libraries, this is an obvious asset.

Two aspects of the semantic processing deserve additional discussion: the handling of generic units, and the implementation of tagged types and object-oriented features. The latter is described in [TAG94]. We proceed to describe briefly the implementation of generic units.

4.3 Generic units

Traditionally, there are two implementation techniques for generic instantiations: in-line expansion (often called "macro" expansion) and direct compilation of generic units, also known as shared generics. The latter model is known to be fraught with difficulties, and GNAT, like most other compilers, implements generics by expansion. Following the source-based model of the compiler, [LIB94], generic specifications are analyzed each time they appear in a context clause, and there is no code nor intermediate representation produced by such analysis. The analysis of the unit performs name resolution and all the required semantic checks, and the syntax tree is annotated with semantic information. There is no tree expansion performed on a generic unit, except insofar as some expansion is intrinsic to semantic processing (e.g. the transformation of a range attribute into a discrete range). The semantic analysis is performed on a copy of the original tree, which retains the unanalyzed structure of the parsed source text. After semantic analysis, all references in the generic unit that are not local are copied onto the original generic tree.

At the point of generic instantiation, the tree for the generic unit is copied, and the new tree is treated as a regular (non-generic) unit which is analyzed and for which code is generated. Note that name resolution has captured all non-local references at the point of generic declaration. These references are not analyzed anew. On the other hand, local references in the generic unit are resolved as local references in the instance. The mechanism can be pictured as below in figure 5.

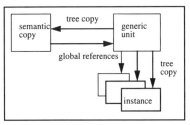

Figure 5

4.4 Generic bodies

The instantiation of generic bodies is done on a separate pass, after all semantic analysis of the main unit is completed. By delaying the instantiation of bodies, it becomes possible to compile legal programs that present difficult order-of-elaboration problems to other compilers. For example, consider the program fragments given in figure 6.

Conventional compilation schemes either reject these instantiations as circular (even though they are not) or are forced to use an indirect linking approach to the instances, which is inefficient. In GNAT, the instantiated bodies are placed in-line in the tree. If the instantiation precedes textually the appearance of the generic body, then the instantiated body is placed immediately after the generic. Otherwise the instantiated body is placed in the tree at the point of instantiation.

5. Gigi and code generation

The phase labeled Gigi (Gnat to Gnu) interfaces the front-end with the GCC code generator. Gigi traverses the decorated and expanded AST, in order to build the corresponding GCC tree, which is then input to the code generator proper. More precisely, the activities of GCC tree construction and code generation are interspersed, so that after each code generation activity, the GCC tree fragment can be discarded. At no time is a full tree built (there is no such notion in GCC). This is in line with the one-pass model of compilation used for C, and is memory-efficient.

In order to bridge the semantic gap between Ada and C, several code generation routines in GCC have been extended, and others added, so that the burden of translation is also assumed by Gigi and GCC whenever it would be awkward or inefficient to perform the expansion in the front-end. For example, there are code generation actions for exceptions, for variant parts, and for access to unconstrained types. As a matter of GCC policy, the code generator is extended only when the extension is likely to be of benefit to more than one language. Such examples of this include discriminated records, unconstrained arrays, checked arithmetic and exceptions. A full description of the implementation of these is given in [GCC94b].

5.1 Two languages, one data structure

Gigi traverses the AST produced by the front-end, and emits calls to the generators that build GCC trees. The AST is constructed by an Ada program, and described by means of a series of Ada access functions. Given that Gigi is written in C, it must be provided with a view of the AST which is isomorphic with that held by the front-end. This is achieved by means of header files that are automatically generated from the Ada specifications for the AST. Several utility programs, which are part of the compiler-construction machinery, perform this task. These utilities are invoked whenever one of the AST specifications is updated.

5.2 Exceptions

The exception mechanism is intended to be usable by all GCC languages that have exceptions: Ada, C++, and Modula-3. The mechanism should be sufficiently uniform to allow multi-language programs to function in the presence of language-specific exceptions and exception handlers: for example, an Ada exception may propagate from a C++ module to an Ada handler. The mechanism should also be zero cost, that is to say, there should be no run-time cost attached to the mere presence of a handler, only to the actual occurrence of an exception. The design of exception handling is closely related to the semantics of finalization and is explained in full detail in [GCC94b].

6. The Runtime: GNARL

The most important activities of the run-time have to do with task management: creation, activation, rendez-vous, termination. The runtime maintains the data structures needed to manage, schedule, and synchronize tasking activities. In order to make GNAT easily portable, the runtime is written in Ada (with some very small assembly glue) and two procedural interfaces, GNARLI and GNULLI, are used to isolate the compiler from the runtime, and the runtime from the underlying operating system.

GNARLI (GNU Ada Run-time Library Interface) is the interface between the compiler and the run-time. Each Ada construct that applies to tasks or protected objects is implemented by one or more subprograms in the run-time. The

```
package A is                          package B is
   generic ...                          generic ...
   package G_A  is ...                  package G_B is ...
end A;                                end B;
.................................................................
with B;                               with A;
package body A                        package body B is
   package N_B is new B.G_B (...);      package N_A is new A.G_A (...);
end A;                                end B;
```

Figure 6

expander transforms each occurrence of such constructs into the corresponding series of calls. The packages that constitute the run-time are treated as any other unit of the context of the compilation, and analyzed when needed. This obviates the need to place run-time information in the compiler itself, and allows a knowledgeable user to modify the run-time if he/she so chooses.

GNULLI (GNU Low Level Interface) provides the interface between the run-time and the underlying operating system. The design of GNULLI makes use of a few POSIX-like threads primitives, and assumes the existence of such primitives in the host OS. A threads package that emulates those primitives is supplied for systems that do not have them, e.g. conventional Unix systems. Otherwise the implementation of GNULLI is straightforward on modern operating systems such as Solaris, Mach, OS/2 and Windows NT. The design and implementation of GNARL have been carried out at Florida State University by the group directed by Ted Baker and Ted Giering, and follows their design of previous portable Ada runtimes, notably CARTS and MRT-SI. The design of GNARL is described in detail in [RTS94]

7. Library management

The notion of program library is seen justifiably as one of the fundamental contributions of Ada to software engineering. The library guarantees that type safety is maintained across compilations, and prevents the construction of inconsistent systems by excluding obsolete units. In all Ada compilers to date, the library is a complex structure that holds intermediate representations of compiled units, information about dependences between compiled units, symbol tables, etc. The Ada 83 RM strongly suggested that such a structure was mandatory, but in fact a monolithic library is not required to implement rigorously the semantics of separate compilation. Furthermore, the monolithic library approach is ill-adapted to multi-language systems, and has been responsible for some of the awkwardness of interfacing Ada to other languages.

We have chosen a completely different approach in GNAT. The library itself is implicit, and object files depend only on the sources used to compile them, and not on other objects. There are no intermediate representations of compiled units, so that the declarations of the units appearing in the context clause of a given compilation are always analyzed anew. Dependency information is kept directly in the object files (in fact, they are kept in a small separate file, conceptually linked to the object file), and amounts to a few hundred bytes per unit. The binder can be used to verify the consistency of a system before linking, and is also used to determine the order of elaboration. Given the speed of the front-end, our approach is no less efficient than the conventional library mechanism, and has three important advantages over it:

(a) Compilation of an Ada unit is identical to compilation of a module or file in another language: the result of the compilation of one source is one object file, period. Given that object files only depend on sources, not on other objects, there is no longer a required order of compilation. All the components of a system can be compiled in any order. Only the modification of a source program may obsolete a compiled unit. A well-known dreaded phenomenon of previous Ada systems, namely the accidental recompilation of one unit that obsoletes a slew of other units in the library, even when the source is unchanged, is thus avoided completely.

(b) Inlining works in a much more flexible way than in normal compilers. Given that compiling, and thus inlining, is always done from the source, there is no requirement that the entities to be inlined should be compiled first. It is even possible for two bodies to inline functions defined in each other, without fear of circularities.

(c) The absense of any forced order of compilation facilitates the parallel compilation of a large system on different processors.

It is gratifying that this flexible model is fully conformant with the prescribed semantics given in the Ada Reference Manual, and at the same time comfortable for programmers used to the behavior of make and similar tools. The GNAT model simplifies the construction of multi-language programs and makes Ada look more familiar to programmers in other languages. It even makes it possible to write multi-language programs with Ada components, whose main program is not itself written in Ada. Note that in such cases the binder will still be required, in order to construct the series of calls to the elaboration procedures of the Ada components.

The source-based organization of the library is the most novel aspect of the GNAT architecture. Details of the library mechanism and its use are found in [LIB94]

8. The Binder

The role of the binder is twofold: to check the consistency of the objects that are to be assembled into an executable, and to construct the program that is executed by the environment task. The binder determines a valid order of elaboration for the units in the program, and packages the calls to the corresponding elaboration procedures into a single procedure. This binding procedure then invokes the main program itself. The binding procedure includes the outermost exception handler that notifies the user when an otherwise unhandled exception terminates program execution.

The binder makes use of the information created when each unit is compiled. This information includes the semantic dependencies of each unit, the date of latest modification of their sources, the presence of various elaboration and categorization pragmas, and whether a given unit may be a main program.

The binder has been designed with flexibility in mind. In one mode, it can verify that all objects depend on a consistent set of sources. Given that time stamps of the sources used for a compilation are kept in the object files, this check does not require that sources themselves be present, which is an advantage in commercial settings for software distribution. Another mode of operation is to verify that the system is up-to-date, that is to say that no source was modified after compilation. In all cases, possible inconsistencies are diagnosed and treated either as fatal errors or as warnings.

9. Evolving tools

Even though the goal of the project does not encompass a full programming environment, there are number of basic programming tools built around the compiler proper that exist or are under development.

9.1 Cross-Reference

The GNAT system provides a stand-alone tool, GNATF, which performs syntax and semantics checking only. This is considerably faster than using the full compiler since tree expansion and code generation are not performed. GNATF also generates cross reference and feature summary information.

The cross reference information produced falls into the following categories:

- Precise information about all declared entities, i.e. where they are defined and where they are used (traditional cross reference table).
- Warnings about entities declared but never used.
- Warnings about **with** clauses that are unnecessary, misplaced, or redundant.

Cross reference information can be gathered on entire programs, or on isolated units. Distinction is made between entities that appear directly in the compiled unit and those that are referenced in the compiled unit but are defined elsewhere.

The features summary facility of GNATF lists the names of Ada 9X features that are used in the source program, such as features restricted in Ada 83 (use of Latin_1, Ada 9X later declaration ordering) as well as major 9X constructs like child units, type extension and new pragmas. This will be useful in environments that want to control the introduction of Ada 9X features, and also to estimate the coverage of test suites such as the new ACVC suite.

9.2 Interfacing with the debugger

One of the critical features of GCC is the integration of all its translators with the symbolic debugger gdb. In order to make gdb usable with Ada, the front-end must generate the proper symbol table information, and gdb must become cognizant of various aspects of ada syntax and semantics. Work is under way to enhance gdb along the following lines:

- Understand Ada 9X data types, including arrays and discriminated records.
- Accept near-Ada syntax in expressions.
- Support setting of breakpoints and stepping-through in specific instantiations of generic units

- Permit "relatively convenient" reference to overloaded functions.
- Handle dispatching calls.

There should also be access to exception-handling and tasking, but this will be through explicit, ordinary gdb calls to designated runtime routines, and will not (initially) involve any enhancements to gdb itself.

9.3 A style checker

The GNAT front-end includes facilities to verify that the program obeys specific layout rules. For now, these are rules established for the text of GNAT itself, but we envision a system in which the user can specify various layout attributes that he/she wants enforced, such as:

- Indentation levels.
- Spacing requirements around tokens
- Uniform casing rules between definition and uses of identifiers
- Capitalization conventions for user-defined entities, reserved words and pragmas.
- Maximum line length.
- Presence of program unit names following the **end** keyword.

9.4 An Ada-specific make utility

The source-based organization of the compiler, and the dependency information used by the binder, can serve as the foundation for an intelligent Make program, which minimizes the amount of recompilation required after the modification of some component of a system. The design of such a tool is described in [FAST94].

10. Some statistics

The system is currently composed of 200,000 lines of Ada text and comments, distributed among 642 files. The parser is 18,000 lines, semantics comprises 37,000 lines, the expander 16,000, child units of System (including the tasking library) take 25,000 lines. The scanner, utilities, predefined libraries (child units of Ada) complete the count. Gigi comprises 10,000 lines of C. Roughly half of the Ada source lines are internal documentation and blank lines. The GCC back-end component of GNAT is approximately 220,000 lines of C. GNAT compiles its own front-end in about 20 minutes, on a 60 Mhz Pentium machine.

11. Conclusions

Compiler quality means different things to different users. For students and beginners, GNAT intends to be user-friendly, provide lucid error messages, and fast turn-around for small programs. For a software engineer, code quality is paramount, and GNAT can rely on the proven performance of the GCC back-end. For the embedded-systems developer, the existence of cross-compilation tools is critical, and here as well GCC provides the necessary functionality. For the language researcher and the compiler writer, the existence of sources of a full compiler is invaluable.

Starting from its earliest, very incomplete releases, the GNAT system has had a growing and dedicated group of users. The cooperative spirit fostered by the activities of the Free Software Foundation is striking: days after the first release of GNAT, several ports to unexpected machines were reported, and offers were made to the project of important software components: bindings to Mach, to X-windows, implementation of various language annexes, etc. This synergy within the Ada community is a rewarding by-product of the GNAT project.

Appendix I: How to obtain GNAT

GNAT is available via anonymous ftp from cs.nyu.edu (128.122.140.24), in the directory pub/gnat. This directory contains a README file, as well as the source for GNAT and binaries for various machines. These files can also be found on the Public Ada Library (PAL) and its mirror sites. Users are invited to submit any comments, bug reports or other communication to gnat-report@cs.nyu.edu.Those without Internet access can find GNAT on the various Ada CDROMs now being commercially distributed.

Appendix II: Status of Standard Libraries and Annexes

GNAT will eventually include a full implementation of the standard libraries described in Annex A, as well as all the specialized needs annexes. This section gives some details of the current status as of 8/94, and describes our technical approach.

Annex A: Predefined Language Environment

Most of the facilities in this section are already provided in GNAT in the form of standard Ada packages and subprograms. Some of the coding for the string functions was originally inspired by a version of the ADAR (Ada Decimal-Associated Reusabilia) package [ADAR94], but the code has been substantially revised to improve efficiency. Throughout, the intention is to achieve the best possible implementation, consistent with the requirement of maintaining maximum target independence. At the time of writing, the major omissions are the Input-Output packages other than Text_IO.

Annex B: Interface to Other Languages

The interface to C is fully implemented. We intend to complete the Fortran interface, including support for arrays stored in the Fortran column-major order. The interface to COBOL is more problematical, since many of the GCC targets lack significant COBOL compilers, and those that are available often have incompatible formats. As described in a subsequent section, we do intend to fully implement the information systems annex, with the intention of making Ada a viable language for fiscal calculations and other information systems tasks, in environments which often lack good compiler tools in this area.

Annex C: Systems Programming

This is substantially complete now, and all features will eventually be incorporated into GNAT. In particular, we will couple the package MACHINE_CODE capability to the existing support for code statements in GCC, and provide full support for all representation clauses and pragmas.

Annex D: Real-Time Systems

The complete implementation of the GNARL interface includes full support of all features in the real-time systems annex. This support is predicated on complete support of the GNULLI layer. On some systems, this may simply not be practical, and on those, we will not be able to meet some of the performance and behavior criteria of the Annex. For example, on a system like OS/2, which does not have asynchronous inter-task cancellation, we probably cannot provide ATC in a form that meets the requirements of this annex.

Annex E: Distributed Systems

There are three main facets of the implementation of the Distributed Systems annex: stream I/O, stub expansion for remote call interface packages, and the communication subsystem. The first is part of the core language, and its implementation is underway. The design of the stub expansion has been done by collaborators at Texas A&M and at ENST-Bretagne, and we plan to implement their design in GNAT. The same groups are also collaborating on the implementation of the communication subsystem, for which prototypes using TCP/IP and PVM already exist. We will provide an implementation of this annex on at least two targets: a network of SPARC workstations, and the IBM SP1 multiprocessor.

Annex F: Information Systems

We intend to provide a full implementation of the information systems Annex, including support of both binary decimal and packed decimal formats. The implementation of the picture editing packages will use standard Ada packages, with the possibility of specializing on machines providing special support for decimal operations or editing operations. We have chosen the Intel format for packed decimal, but this is defined in a single runtime module that is easily modified if some other format is preferred.

Annex G: Numerics

Most of the numerics capability is already supported in GNAT. We anticipate that accurate target-dependent support of the accuracy requirements will require significant modifications to the GCC backend, which at the moment does not do much worrying about floating-point accuracy (for example, the accuracy of conversion of floating-point constants is left to the assembler being used).

Annex H: Safety and Security

GNAT will include full support for the safety and security annex at least on certain specified machines. The hard part of the requirement is the need to provide fully annotated assembly listings. It is not very much in the Unix style for compilers to provide listings at all, let alone elaborately annotated listings, so it is not surprising that GCC has no capabilities in this area. One possible approach to the implementation is to write an external tool which uses the GDB interface to obtain debugging information (including line numbers, variable names etc.), and a modified version of GAS (the GNU assembler) to obtain the assembly listing with code and offsets

Appendix III: The GNU Licenses

Much confusion has arisen over the exact effect and restrictions of the GNU public license (common known as "copyleft"). This section is intended to clarify the import of copyleft. The GNAT compiler itself is covered by the GPL, the GNU General Public License [GPL91]. The intention of this license is to ensure that the compiler is freely available and freely copyable. It can still be sold, but the buyer can always copy it freely, so the general expectation is that it is sold for reasonable charges, like typical public domain (PD) software. Indeed one might ask why not simply place GNAT in the public domain to achieve this effect.

The trouble with PD software is that there is nothing to stop someone making (possibly minor) modifications, and then copyrighting the result and protecting it as fully proprietary software. This has happened to a number of important software products in the past. A government grant pays for the development of the software, which is initially in the public domain, and the PD version is still freely available. However, a commercial company forms, and continued maintenance applies only to a proprietary version, and soon everyone is paying for something that was intended to be free.

The GPL is precisely designed to preclude such an occurrence. It enjoins anyone that modifies GNAT to either keep the modifications entirely to themselves, or to distribute these modifications retaining the GPL, thus ensuring that the technology remains in the domain of free software. It is of course possible for companies to provide software support services, but no one can ever claim proprietary rights to GNAT or any program derived from GNAT.

Given the aim of producing a freely available Ada compiler, the use of the GPL makes good sense, and our contract with the government requires us to release the compiler under the GPL for this reason. However, there is often concern that the GPL will restrict what people can use the compiler *for* as opposed to what they can *do* with the compiler itself.

It is definitely *not* the case that any software that is generated by use of the GNAT compiler is "contaminated" by the GPL, and itself becomes freely distributable. Code generated by the compiler certainly is owned by whoever owns

the source code. Library routines present a slightly different issue. If the library routines and runtime were covered by the GPL, then it would indeed be the case that all programs generated by the GNAT compiler would be covered by the GPL, and thus the use of the compiler would be greatly restricted. To avoid this, and to ensure the widest possible sphere of use for GNAT, the library and runtime are covered by the LGPL, the GNU Library General Public License [LGPL91]. This provides for free distribution of the runtime in programs, even if they are proprietary. The only requirement is that such programs be made available in a form that permits linking with different versions of the library routines, e.g. by distributing object files.

An example may prove more effective in making this point than a discussion of the legal details. NEXT Corp. uses GCC as the compiler technology for the NextStep system, using the Objective C front end. This front end, being married to the GCC backend, is covered by the GPL, and is freely distributed with sources. NextStep itself is certainly *not* freely distributed, and the sources are proprietary. (In fact, the NextStep sources and resulting proprietary executable operating systems are the primary capital of Next Inc.)

Although it is possible, as we have described, to use GNAT to create proprietary software, we remain committed to the ideal of free software, and hope that the full availability of GNAT with sources will encourage research and teaching using Ada, and will also encourage members of the worldwide Ada community to continue enhancing GNAT and thus to add to its value as a robust industrial tool in software development.

Acknowledgments

Because of space limitations we cannot mention the names of all of those whose messages, bug reports, suggestions for enhancements, and software contributions have added to the completeness and robustness of GNAT, but we must identify some collaborative efforts underway to complete the implementation of the various language annexes. First and foremost, a group at Florida State University (Ted Baker, Ted, Giering, Frank Mueller, Dong-ik Oh) is implementing the Systems Programming and the Real-Time annexes. Groups at Texas A&M University (Richard Volz, Ron Theriaux, Gary Smith) and ENST, France (Yvon Kermarrec, Laurent Pautet) are designing and implementing the Distributed Systems annex.

Ben Brosgol, Dave Emery, and Robert Eachus at Mitre are developing the Information Systems Annex. Jon Squire at Westinghouse Corp. and Ken Dritz at Argonne National Laboratories have contributed several modules of the Numerics Annex. Jean-Pierre Rosen is developing the real-time annex for OS/2. Doug Rupp at the University of Washington is maintaining the DOS and Windows NT ports of GNAT as well as writing Ada bindings to certain Windows NT libraries.

Franco Gasperoni and Patrick Bazire, at ENST Paris, have implemented the GNAT cross-reference facility and are developing a fast recompilation (intelligent MAKE) for the system. Paul Hilfinger at UC Berkeley is enhancing gdb to give it the functionality described in section 9.2 above. Bill Yow has contributed bindings to the OS/2 presentation manager. We want to thank them all, as well as all users whose reports and whose patience with a rapidly evolving system have been a constant source of encouragement.

The GNAT team at New York University, whose work is summarized here, includes: Bernard Banner, Cyrille Comar, Robert Dewar, Sam Figueroa, Richard Kenner, Gail Schenker Morgulis, Brett Porter, Ed Schonberg, and Chien-Chang Sheng. Past members of the project are Bruno Leclerc and Cyril Crozes.

Special thanks to Chris Anderson, head of the Ada 9X project, for her constant support and encouragement.

References

[ADA83] Reference Manual for the Ada Programming Language, ANSI/MIL STD 1815A, AJPO, 1983

[ADA94] Tucker Taft et al, Programming Language Ada, Language and Standard Libraries, Draft 5.0 (proposed ISO/ANSI standard), IR-MA-1363-4, Intermetrics Inc., June 1994

[ADAR94] Ben Brosgol, Robert Eachus and Dave Emery, Information Systems Development in Ada. In *Proceedings of WAdaS '94*, 1994.

[ASIS91] J.B. Bladen et al, Ada Semantic Interface Specification (ASIS). In *Proceedings of Tri-Ada '91*, San Jose, California, 1991

[DIANA83] G.Goos, W.A.Wulf, A.Evans, Jr. and K.J.Butlet. *DIANA - An Intermediate Language for Ada*, Lecture Notes in Computer Science, number 161, Springer-Verlag, 1983

[FAST94] Franco Gasperoni and Patrick Bazire, Smart Recompilation and the GNAT Compiler. In *Proceedings of Tri-Ada '94*, Baltimore, Maryland, 1994 (this volume)

[GCC94a] Richard Stallman, *Using and Porting GNU CC*, Free Software Foundation, 1994

[GCC94b] Richard Kenner. Integrating GNAT into GCC. In *Proceedings of Tri-Ada '94*, Baltimore, Maryland, 1994 (this volume)

[GPL91] GNU General Public License, Free Software Foundation, 1991

[LGPL91] GNU Library General Public License, Free Software Foundation, 1991

[LIB94] Robert B.K. Dewar. The GNAT Model of Compilation. In *Proceedings of Tri-Ada '94*, Baltimore, Maryland, 1994 (this volume)

[PLOEDEREDER92] Erhard Ploedereder. "How to Program in Ada 9X", *ACM Ada Letters, Volume XII, Number 6*, (Nov/Dec 1992)

[RTS94] E.W. Giering, F. Mueller and T.P.Baker. Features of the GNU Ada Runtime Library. In *Proceedings of Tri-Ada '94*, Baltimore, Maryland, 1994 (this volume)

[TAG94] Cyrille Comar and Brett Porter. The GNAT Implementation of Tagged Types. In *Proceedings of Tri-Ada '94*, Baltimore, Maryland, 1994 (this volume)

11

Smart recompilation: pitfalls & opportunities

Patrick Bazire
Télécom Paris – ENST
Département Informatique
and
Cyrille Comar
Computer Science Department
New York University
Email: comar@cs.nyu.edu
and
Franco Gasperoni
Télécom Paris – ENST
Département Informatique
Email: gasperon@inf.enst.fr

Abstract

Despite tremendous progress in hardware speed, compilation remains a time consuming activity. Programmers tend to adopt unorthodox tricks to minimise recompilation needs, thus tainting a system's design with pernicious compromises motivated by compilation efficiency.

The goal of smart recompilation is to reduce compilation costs by capitalising on previous compilations. To achieve this objective, a smart recompilation system monitors the effects of source changes on the set of previously compiled modules. In this article we describe the design of a smart recompilation system that is being implemented in the realm of the GNAT compiler [5]. A preliminary version of this work was presented in [3]. The current article revisits the notion of smart recompilation and incorporates a number of radical design changes which are the consequence of a first prototype implementation completed in November 94.

11.1   Smart recompilation: opportunities

When developing or maintaining software, the typical programmers' life-cycle is

update sources/recompile/test

Current recompilation schemes, whether based on `make` or other automatic tools, tend to recompile sources very conservatively. For instance, changing a comment in an Ada package spec entail the recompilation of all the units directly or indirectly depending on the spec. Likewise, deleting an empty line in a C header file implies the recompilation of all the C files directly or indirectly `#include`-ing the header file. Such recompilations are clearly unnecessary, but cannot be avoided in systems that automatically re-build object modules based on the time stamps of their sources.

Generally speaking, more meaningful package modification, such as deletions, additions or modifications of program entities, such as functions or procedures, will force the recompilation of all (Ada) sources which directly or indirectly depend on the modified specs, even though some are totally unaffected by these changes.

What is the impact of these useless recompilations on programmer's productivity? This depends on the amount of useless recompilations and speed of the underlying compiler.

We will show that today's programmers spend more than half of their compilation time performing useless recompilations. Given that the execution speed of today's Ada compilers, be they Alsys, Verdix or GNAT [5] is on the order of a few hundred lines per second, wasted recompilation time adds up for industrial-strength software projects*.

Wasted recompilation time is just the tip of the iceberg. A more serious problem is the fact that, to avoid lengthy recompilations, developers often resort to unorthodox programming tricks which spoil the cleanness of the system's design [4]. At best, programmers refrain from keeping up-to-date comments stored in system specs. Little by little, the system becomes hopelessly undocumented.

The objective of this paper is to show how the smart recompilation system being implemented on top of the GNAT compiler can help alleviate this problem. The goal of smart recompilation is to reduce recompilation costs by capitalising on previous compilations. To achieve this objective, a smart recompilation system bases its recompilation decisions on actual source changes, rather than source file time stamps. System's safety is enforced by recompiling sources which are potentially affected by such changes. For one thing, such system will allow programmers to freely update comments in a system's specs without requiring recompilation.

Smart recompilation is not a novel technique. Ticky, in 1986, was one of the first to experiment with this approach in the realm of C and Pascal [6]. Similar experiments were performed in Norway in the mid 80's on the Chill compiler. Brett introduced it in the Dec Ada compiler [1].

11.2   Pitfalls of smart recompilation

Although smart recompilation is a well known and useful concept, it has not yet found wide spread usage. Why?

1. To decide whether to recompile a source file, current systems need only look at the time stamps of a small number of files. This can be done extremely quickly. A smart recompilation system needs to further look inside these files to decide the actual effect of the changes. If the infrastructure put forth to this effect is bulky, it will out-weigh the gains over plain recompilation.

---

*All measurements mentioned in this paper have been performed on a Sun sparc 10 with 32 Meg of RAM.

2. Software bugs are unavoidable. The more convoluted a software system is, the greater the chances. The risk of bugs in a smart recompilation system grows with its level of sophistication. A very sophisticated smart recompilation system might save a great deal of recompilations at the expense of system's safety. Specifically, it may decide not to compile a source file, whereas it should have.

These two potential pitfalls bring us to one of the crucial point of this paper:

> What is the right trade-off in a smart recompilation system between recompilation effectiveness and design simplicity?

We have tried to answer this question in the context of the GNAT compiler in today's technological reality. It is important to understand that the very need of smart recompilation is very technology dependent. A 100,000 lines/sec code generator may obviate its need all-together.

11.3 Smart recompilation opportunities & their cost

In this section we examine various types of source file modifications, their impact on recompilation and the cost to detect them and implement them in a smart recompilation system based on GNAT. GNAT always compiles or recompiles a source file when asked to. Specifically,

```
gcc -c file.adb
```

always generates the corresponding object file `file.o` and the Ada library file `file.ali`. `file.ali` contains the list of `with`-ed units as well as the names and time stamps of all the sources loaded during the compilation of `file.adb` [2]. `.ali` files are used by the Ada binder to orchestrate elaboration order and to verify system's consistency at link time.

Whereas GNAT always generates code from scratch, smart GNAT is permitted not to recompile a source file if it thinks it is unnecessary. Specifically,

```
gcc -c -<smart-switch> file.adb
```

may or may not compile `file.adb` according to the obsolescence of `file.o` with respect to the current sources.

11.3.1 Format changes

The simplest source file modification that can be envisioned is a change in format. There are two types of format changes:

1. Changes in comments, spacing, case of the identifiers, etc.

2. Syntactic format changes such as

   procedure P(X,Y:Float); ⇒ procedure P(X:Float;Y:Float);

   another example could be

```
                         ⇒
        procedure T is    procedure T is
          X,Y: Float;        X: Float;
                             Y: Float;
```

While the first type of modification does not require syntactic analysis the second one does. Lets us first examine the cost of determining pure format modification.

To detect whether two source files differ only in comments, spacing, or case of the identifiers, one can use the command "`diff -w -i`" augmented with Ada comment information. The speed of "`diff -w -i`" is about 22,000 lines/sec[*].

To detect more sophisticated syntactic format changes, parsing is needed. More specifically, after the two source files are parsed their corresponding abstract syntax trees (ASTs) need to be compared. The cost of parsing plus building the AST is roughly 1,700 lines/sec for bodies and 5,000 lines/sec for specs. These figures have been taken with all GNAT's consistency checks on, and should be expected to triple or quadruple when all such checks are disabled. Thus, the final and overall cost of comparing two ASTs should be around 8,000 lines/sec for specs and 3,000 lines/sec for bodies.

These figures indicate that the overhead for finding syntax-related format changes would be acceptable for specs, but may be less acceptable for bodies. In addition, it is important to notice that syntactic format changes are likely to alter debugging line information in bodies and thus are likely to entail recompilation. In light of these facts we have decided to:

- Detect simple format changes for specs and bodies;

- Fail to recognise syntactic format changes for either specs or bodies. Even though recognising syntactic format changes for specs, we have decided not to, since such type of format change is not very frequent in specs.

11.3.2 Sophisticated changes in bodies

The cost of semantically analysing a body in GNAT is around 150 lines/sec. Again this figure will be boosted by a factor three or four after all of GNAT's consistency checks are disabled. The overall speed of the compiler including code generation is about 100 lines/sec. It is therefore unrealistic to bother detecting sophisticated changes in bodies such as:

```
                        ⇒
for J in 1..100 loop    for I in 1..100 loop
    A(J):=0;                A(I):=0;
end loop;               end loop;
```

Speed is one inhibiting factor for the detection of sophisticated changes in bodies. Even if this was not the case, obsolescence of debugging information is most of the time unavoidable. A programmer will certainly be displeased not to be able to print I's value while stepping through the new version of the loop.

11.3.3 Sophisticated changes in specs

Our approach for changes in specs is to detect the entities which have been:

- added;

- deleted;

- modified.

---

[*]All measurements mentioned in this paper have been performed on a Sun sparc 10 with 32 Meg of RAM.

Semantic processing for specs costs about 2,500 lines/sec. Again with an optimised GNAT we may expect a figure around 10,000 lines/sec. Thus in our initial design [3] we had planned to compare ASTs to obtain the list of such entities. After our tree comparison prototype implementation which took around 4,000 lines of Ada, we realised that we would have had a number of difficulties in informally proving that the code was correct. In addition every change to the GNAT AST structure would have entailed maintenance on smart GNAT.

We have therefore scaled down our initial objective and plan to detect entity changes only for objects and subprograms declared in a spec. This only requires that we implement an extremely crude parser which need not build an AST. We estimate such tasks to be less than 2,000 lines of Ada. Note, however, that the following design of smart GNAT is completely independent of the actual kind of entities which are detected as added, deleted or modified.

11.3.4   Impact of spec changes on bodies

To evaluate the recompilation consequences of an entity change in a spec with respect to a particular body we could perform semantic analysis. Again this would be too time consuming. We have therefore looked into a much simpler solution relying on an Ada cognisant version of "`grep -i -w`" which searches for the occurrence of a given identifier in a source file. The speed of such a tool is on the order of 76,000 lines/sec.

This approach is certainly not foolproof, but it is safe. If the name of an entity E does not appear in a source file `Target` we are certain that changes affecting E do not affect `Target`. On the other hand if E's name appears in `Target` it is not necessarily the case that `Target` is affected by changes in E. This would be the case if E is an overloaded entity. Only semantic resolution will be able to tell for sure whether `Target` is affected by modifications to E.

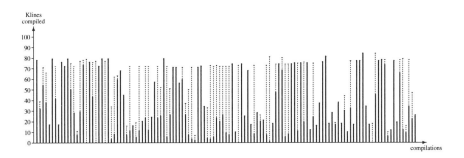

Figure 11.1. Lines compiled in GNAT Jan. 1-Apr. 6, 1994: 7 Mlines (plain), 4.4 Mlines (smart).

11.4   Effectiveness of Smart GNAT

Before describing the design of smart GNAT we intend to demonstrate its effectiveness. The following three charts have been obtained with a prototype implementation of smart GNAT. The experiment performed was as follows. We have taken 9 months of the software development effort of GNAT involving over 7 Meg of sources and have investigated recompilation impacts of source modifications. After each set of modifications by one of the GNAT teammates, we have measured the plain and smart recompilation impacts. We have omitted from the charts all plain compilations less than 10 Klines.

The three charts portrayed (see figures 11.1, 11.2, 11.3), contain a number of vertical lines whose lower part is plain and whose upper part is dashed. The overall line length indicates the number of lines that had to be recompiled after a related set of source modifications by one of the GNAT teammates. The lower part of the line (shown as plain) indicates the number of lines that smart recompilation would have recompiled, and the upper-part of the line (shown as dashed) the number of lines that have been compiled but didn't need to.

As the figures show, smart recompilation often cuts compilation costs by a factor 8 to 10. We believe that when smart compilation will be operational this ratio is likely to increase, since a programmer will take advantage of such a feature.

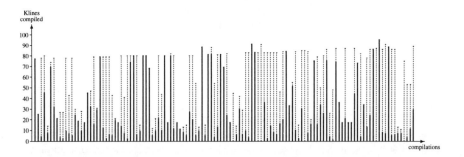

Figure 11.2. Lines compiled in GNAT Apr. 6-Jun. 16, 1994: 7.4 Mlines (plain), 3.4 Mlines (smart).

11.5   Design of Smart GNAT

In light of the considerations previously mentioned, the source changes which we have decided to track are:

1. Simple format changes in specs and bodies;

2. Changes in the entities (subprograms and objects) declared in a spec. Such changes can be additions, deletions or modifications.

All changes which do not fall in either of these categories will entail full recompilation of the affected sources and their dependents.

Apart from reducing recompilation costs, smart recompilation allows a crude form of an Ada make facility. Assuming that * . adb denotes the set of bodies in the system being constructed, typing

```
gcc -c -<smart-switch> *.adb
```

will have the effect of compiling or recompiling the compilation units which have been meaningfully affected by the latest set of source changes.

11.5.1   Integration constraints of Smart GNAT

To facilitate smooth integration of smart recompilation in day-to-day development activities, smart recompilation should have the same look & feel of plain compilation. Thus:

```
gcc -c file.adb
```

and

```
gcc -c -<smart-switch> file.adb
```

should generate exactly the same `file.o` and `file.ali`. In particular:

```
gcc -c -g file.adb
```

and

```
gcc -c -g -<smart-switch> file.adb
```

should generate the same `file.o`.

Another important constraint on smart recompilation is its ability to inter-operate with plain compilation. This means that it should be possible to bind and link modules compiled with smart and plain compilation. This objective seems a direct consequence of the above "look & feel" constraint. However, since smart recompilation may need to save some additional history that plain "`gcc -c`" need not save, we must ensure that intermixing calls to plain "`gcc -c`" and to "`gcc -c -<smart-switch>`" does not confuse "`gcc -c -<smart-switch>`".

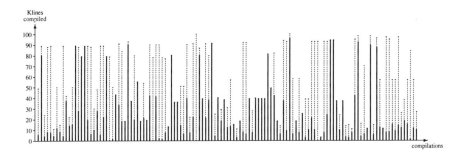

Figure 11.3. Lines compiled in GNAT Jun. 16-Sep. 20, 1994: 7.3 Mlines (plain), 3.4 Mlines (smart).

11.5.2   The smart recompilation process

Our stereotypical scenario involves a programmer working on a set of sources. One or several directories contain the object files of the various versions of the system. When the programmer invokes the command:

```
gcc -c -<smart-switch> file.adb
```

in the context of a given object file directory, the smart recompilation system must answer the following question:

"Given the current set of source files and the current `file.o` and `file.ali` do I need to recompile `file.adb` or can I get away with just updating `file.ali`?"

To answer this question the high-level steps undertaken by "`gcc -c -<smart-switch>`" are:

1. Retrieve the old sources used to produce `file.o`;

2. Compare the current sources with the old ones;

3. Decide whether the differences between current and old sources have an impact on the validity of the current `file.o`. If they have, recompile `file.o`;

4. If no fresh compilation is necessary update `file.ali`.

The following sections will explicit the approach adopted for each these four steps. Specifically section 11.5.3 will address issue 1, retrieving the old sources. As the reader will see, our approach will maintain a history of file changes for each source in the system. Section 11.5.4 explains how the history files are used by smart recompilation to address 3 and 4 above. Finally section 11.5.5 explains how smart recompilation history files are kept up to date by comparing two successive versions of a source. This answers issue 2 above.

Our smart recompilation system capitalises only on simple algorithms employing `diff`-like and `grep`-like tools. As previously mentioned, we have purposely avoided employing sophisticated AST comparison algorithms for several reasons:

- Make the implementation effort as straightforward as possible and in as few lines as possible (eventually it would be nice to have an informal guarantee that smart recompilation is safe);

- Keep the smart recompilation overhead to a minimum;

- Be free to keep smart recompilation as a stand alone tool or to integrate it into GNAT.

11.5.3   Retrieving the sources: history files

The problem with simple approaches

To retrieve the sources with which an object file `file.o` was compiled, one can envision either one of the following simple possibilities:

1. Every time a file `file.adb` is compiled we save next to `file.o` the entire set of sources used to generate the object file;

2. Look into the current `file.ali` and find the list of sources along with their time stamps which participated in the creation of `file.o`. Then search in a source control system, such as RCS, for these files with these precise time stamps.

The first is certainly the easiest approach. It has the enormous disadvantage of requiring a potentially quadratic amount of space. It also attaches a set of sources to each object file. If one keeps several directories each with different versions of the object files, the duplication of the set of sources is that much worse.

For what concerns the source control approach, if any of the time stamps of the searched files is missing from the source control system, then we have to recompile, no matter what. An approach solely based on the existence of a source control system has to be ported to a number of such systems, RCS, SCCS, etc.

As stated, both approaches have another disadvantage. They are potentially slow. Suppose, for instance, that some low level package spec is modified. Then, when rebuilding the whole system we certainly do not want to compare the current version of such spec 200 times with 200 previous versions (most of which, if not all will be the same).

Keeping the history of changes

Our first remark is that, if we are able to log the changes between one instance and the next of a source file, we will be able to quickly pinpoint whether the current changes affect a specific object file.

Thus, in the case where a low-level spec s.ads is modified, the first time we smart recompile a file which needs s.ads, we compare the old and new s.ads and we log in some history file, say s.hs, the entities which have been added, deleted or modified in the new version. When the next smart recompilation involving s.ads comes along, no comparisons are necessary. The smart recompilation system will just need to look into s.hs.

If this sounds like some sort of primitive source control to you, you are absolutely right. The big difference here is that the changes which smart GNAT needs to keep track of amount to a list of time stamps and names of the entities which have been added, deleted or modified. The details will be given in a few paragraphs. What is important to notice is that this takes very little space.

In order to be able to update the smart recompilation history of a file it is necessary to retrieve the latest version of the source. How one retrieves this source is not particularly important. We may for instance save the file along with the history information. This last option is my preferred mode of operation since smart recompilation should work in the absence of source control systems.

The overall space cost is at most the total size of the sources. In GNAT this is about 5.4 meg for bodies and 2.4 meg for specs. If you do not save the comments and replace them by newlines, then the specs only take about 400K and the bodies only 2.7 megs. This can be further reduced by 1 meg for bodies by getting rid of spaces.

Smart recompilation history file

The purpose of this section is to detail the contents of a smart recompilation history file. Given a file Source, the general format of its history file is

$$T_n \cdots T_2 \, T_1$$
$$T_d$$
$$T_m$$

$entity\_name \; T_j$ (only for specs)

$\cdots$

$entity\_name \; T_k$ (only for specs)

%

latest version of Source
as seen by smart recompilation
(its time stamp is T_n *).*

where

- $T_n \cdots T_2\ T_1$: is the set of time stamps of Source as seen by the smart recompilation system (an example will clarify this). The more recent time stamps come first. T_n is the time stamp of Source when it was copied in its history file. To keep history files reasonably short only the last 10 of these time stamps will be saved.

- T_d: is one of $T_n \cdots T_2\ T_1$. It is the latest time stamp when the debugging info of Source has been affected.

- T_m is one of $T_n \cdots T_2\ T_1$. It is the latest time stamp when a non format modification occurred in Source. For bodies T_m is T_1.

- *entity_name* T is an entity name, whose last update time (addition, deletion, direct or indirect modification) is T. T is one of $T_n \cdots T_2\ T_1$. In our first implementation we will not consider entities other than subprograms or objects. This list of entity names is only present for specs. For overloaded entities there is only one instance of *entity_name*. Thus if a spec contains two overloaded functions with name "<", the spec's history will contain an entry with *entity_name* "<" if either one of the two overloaded procedures is modified.

Note that every time stamp appearing in the history file is one of $T_n \cdots T_2\ T_1$. Thus, when updating this history, if smart recompilation decides to eliminate the oldest one to shorten the file, all *entity_name* with that time stamp will be purged from the history.

As an example, consider the following package spec and its evolution:

```
-- time t1          -- time t2          -- time t3
package Spec is      package Spec is      package Spec is
   procedure P1;        procedure P1;        procedure P2;
                        procedure P2;
end Spec;            end Spec;            end Spec;


-- time t4          -- time t5          -- time t6
package Spec is      package Spec is      package Spec is
   procedure P2;        function P2          procedure P2;
   -- comment             return Float;      procedure P3;
end Spec;            end Spec;            end Spec;
```

Assuming that spec.ads is involved in a smart recompilation after each one of the above changes, and that it did not exist before t1, the smart recompilation history file spec.hs will look like:

```
spec.hs after t1     spec.hs after t2     spec.hs after t3
t1                   t2 t1                t3 t2 t1
t1                   t2                   t3
t1                   t2                   t3
                     p2 t2                p2 t2
                                          p1 t3


spec.hs after t4     spec.hs after t5     spec.hs after t6
t4 t3 t2 t1          t5 t4 t3 t2 t1       t6 t5 t4 t3 t2 t1
t3                   t5                   t6
t3                   t5                   t6
```

```
p2 t2                  p2 t5                  p2 t6
p1 t3                  p1 t3                  p1 t3
                                              p3 t6
```

11.5.4   The smart recompilation algorithm

After having introduced the information saved by smart recompilation between compilations, we are ready to explain the "gcc -c -<smart-switch>" algorithm. To smart recompile a file Target (Target can be a spec or a body) we proceed as follows:

1. Compiling Target does not generate an .ali file

   If Compiling Target does not generate an .ali file (Target is a sub-unit or a spec with a corresponding body), we do not try to be smart and we always compile Target. This means only performing semantic analysis. After compiling Target we update its smart recompilation history. Section 11.5.5 will explain how such an update is performed.

   Note : All smart recompilation history updates in this and the following points entail no syntactic or semantic analysis. Before updating the history of changes of a source file, smart recompilation makes sure the source file is semantically correct. This is, for instance, achieved by performing the updates after a successful compilation, or after having invoked semantic analysis. If a compilation or semantic analysis is attempted and some syntactic or semantic errors are detected, the smart recompilation process is halted without further ado.

2. Target has never been compiled

   If compiling Target generates an .ali file and we cannot find it, Target needs to be compiled. After compiling Target, we update the smart recompilation history of each source loaded during the compilation of Target.

3. Target has already been compiled

   (a) Check if Target's .ali file is up-to-date.

      If the time stamps of the sources in Target's .ali file match their current time stamp, no compilation is necessary. If this last compilation of Target was not performed with smart recompilation, then update the history of loaded sources.

   (b) Target's .ali is not up-to-date. Determine any immediate recompilation impact.

      - Update the history of each Source loaded during Target's last compilation. Let T_{ali} be the time stamp of Source in Target's .ali file. If T_{ali} is not listed in the history file of Source, then some major changes must have occurred since T_{ali} and we must recompile.
      In fact, when smart recompilation detects major changes in a source file it re-initialises its history from scratch by wiping out all but the latest one of the time stamps recorded. Note that T_{ali} may not be listed in the history of Source because the last compilation of Target may have been done with plain "gcc -c" instead of "gcc -c -<smart-switch>" and therefore smart recompilation has no idea of the changes that Source has incurred since T_{ali}.

- If the spec of `Target` or any of the bodies loaded during the last compilation of `Target` have incurred a change affecting debug information and we want to preserve such info in `Target`'s object file we need to recompile.

- Ditto, if the spec of `Target` has incurred non format modifications since T_{ali}.

(c) Determine the transitive impact of spec changes.

Let `Source` be one of the sources loaded during `Target`'s last compilation, T_{ali} the time stamp of `Source` in `Target`'s .`ali` file and E_{set} the names of all entities which have been added, deleted or modified since T_{ali} in specs explicitly or implicitly with-ed by `Source`.

- If the name of any entity in E_{set} occurs in `Source` then a change in one of the sources loaded during `Target`'s last compilation may potentially affect another such source. This may or may not have further transitive effects on `Target`. To be on the safe side we recompile `Target` and update the history of loaded sources.

    Keeping track of transitive effects between specs is certainly possible. We have chosen not to in order to keep our design as simple as possible. Furthermore if the only entity changes that smart recompilation detects are objects and subprograms, transitive modification effects between specs will probably be limited.

(d) No need to recompile, update `Target`'s .`ali` file.

If smart recompilation has detected that no recompilation is necessary perform a semantic analysis of the specs that have incurred a non-format change to ensure the latest spec changes are valid and then update `Target`'s .`ali` file by saving the current time stamp of all the sources listed therein.

11.5.5   Updating history files

After having explained the contents of the history files and the way they are used in smart recompilation, we turn now to the algorithm which updates these history files. Let `Source` be a source file whose history needs to be updated. The algorithm proceeds as follows:

1. If there is no history of `Source`, then create it and return.

2. If `Source`'s history is already up-to-date, that is its current time stamp has already been recorded, there is nothing to do.

3. In all other cases start by recording `Source`'s current time stamp in its history file.

    If the number of time stamps recorded in `Source`'s history file is longer than a certain threshold, then remove the oldest time stamp recorded in `Source`'s history file, along with the names with that time stamp. This manipulation is performed to keep history files reasonably short.

    Compare the current version of `Source` with the version saved in its recompilation history. One of five things may happen:

    (a) If there has been only a format change which does not affect debugging information, then return with nothing to do.

(b) If there has been a format change affecting debugging information, update T_d and return.

(c) If Source is a spec and the only change incurred by Source concerns the initial value of some non constant objects declared in Source, update T_d and T_m, then return.

(d) If Source is a spec and the only changes incurred by Source concerns the addition, deletion or modification of entities declared in Source (for the time being we only consider subprograms and objects), then update T_d and T_m and add each of these entities to the smart recompilation history of Source, along with Source's current time stamp.

(e) If Source is a body and has incurred any non format modification, or Source is a Spec and has incurred a non format modification which involves things beyond subprograms and objects (for instance the set of with or use clauses has changed, or a type declared in Source has been added, deleted or modified, etc.) then reinitialise the history file of Source.

Note: The algorithm that compares Source with its previous version capitalises on the fact that the old version of Source is syntactically and semantically correct. Because the only changes allowed are objects and subprograms it is easy to enrich a diff-like routine with a primitive knowledge of Ada syntactic rules for objects and subprograms. Thus, the routine that compares two source files need not fully parse or semantically analyse any of the sources. If the comparison algorithm is puzzled by a source change it will decree that the source has incurred major modifications.

11.5.6   The smart recompilation cost

Our initial implementation effort estimate is around 4,000 lines of code. The code itself should be pretty straight-forward, no overly sophisticated algorithms are to be implemented.

The time consuming operations of smart recompilation are updating the history files and searching for entity names in source files. Because these operations will be based respectively on enhanced versions of "diff" and "grep" whose respective performance is roughly 22,000 lines/sec and 76,000 lines/sec on a sparc 10 we expect the overhead of smart recompilation to be negligible.

11.6   Conclusion

The smart recompilation project started out as being very ambitious. We were planning to use sophisticated AST-based algorithms to detect all sorts of programmer modifications. Fortunately during the prototyping stage we realised the pitfalls & opportunities that have been evoked at the beginning of this article and we have completely revisited our effort.

We believe the approach presented here to be a reasonable compromise between smart recompilation effectiveness & safety, cost, and implementation simplicity.

11.7   Acknowledgement

We wish to express our heart-felt gratitude to Robert Dewar, Ed Schonberg and the whole GNAT team for uncountably many enriching discussions.

References

[1] B.R. BRETT, *Smart Recompilation: What is It? Its Benefits for the User, and its Implementation in the DEC Ada Compilation System*, in Conference Proceedings of Tri-Ada'93, 1993, pp. 277-287.

[2] R.B.K. DEWAR, *The compilation model of GNAT*, in Conference in Proceedings of TRI-Ada'94, pp. 58-70, November 1994.

[3] F. GASPERONI AND P. BAZIRE, *Smart recompilation and the GNAT compiler*, in Conference in Proceedings of TRI-Ada'94, pp. 104-111, November 1994.

[4] D. HOLDSWORTH, T.G. DAWSON AND A. MCKAY, *1334 Compilation Units, Ada in the Large*, in "Ada into the 90s", Mitchell and Simpson editors, Chapman Hall, pp. 179–187.

[5] E.SCHONBERG AND B.BANNER, *The GNAT Project: A GNU-Ada 9X Compiler*, in Conference Proceedings of TRI-Ada'94, pp. 48-57, November 1994.

[6] W.F. TICKY, *Smart Recompilation*, ACM Transactions on Programming Languages and Systems, vol. 8, no. 3, July 1986, pp. 273-291.

Part Two

Reference material

12

Validated Ada compilers

12.1 An introduction to the validation process[*]

An 'Ada implementation' is comprised of an Ada compiler, linker and any other necessary software, its host computer (on which the compiler is run), and the target computer (on which the generated code will be run).

The purpose of validation is to encourage conformity of Ada implementations with the standard — the Ada programming language, ANSI/MIL-STD-1815A (1983). Compliance is measured only within the limits of the collection of test programs contained in the Ada Compiler Validation Capability (ACVC). Characteristics not specified by the standard, such as performance or suitability for a particular application, are outside the scope of Ada validation.

The validation process is carried out by the Ada certification body. This body consists of the Ada Joint Program Office, (AJPO), technical and contracting support organizations, and Ada Validation Facilities (AVFs). The AJPO, a component of the Department of Defense, establishes policies of the Ada certification system, issues validation certificates for AVF-tested Ada implementations and registers Ada implementations that are untested by an AVF. The Ada certification body operates in conjunction with the U.S. Department of Commerce which has the responsibility for establishing and maintaining a certification system for the Federal Information Processing Standards (FIPS).

The Ada Compiler Validation Capability (ACVC)

The Ada Compiler Validation Capability (ACVC) is a suite of programs and support software designed to test whether an Ada implementation complies with the Ada programming language. The current version is ACVC 1.11.

Validation by AVF testing

In order to obtain a validation certificate, the following six steps must be completed by the customer and the Ada certification body:

1. A formal validation agreement between the customer and an AVF is required in order to obtain validation services.

2. Prevalidation, consisting of customer testing, submission of results to the AVF, and resolution of any test issues (e.g. a missing or incomplete result to a test) must precede the actual validation.

3. Validation testing will be performed by an AVF at the customer's site.

---

[*]Extracted from the AdaIC Bulletin Board file containing the list of validated Ada compilers as of 1st December 1994.

4. A Declaration of Conformance must then be completed and signed by the customer no later than at the time of validation testing.

5. A Validation Summary Report (VSR) will be prepared by the AVF to document the validation.

6. A Validation certificate will then be issued to the customer by the authority of the AJPO for a successfully tested Ada implementation.

Validation by registration

An Ada implementation may be 'derived' from a base implementation which has been previously validated by testing. The implementer of a derived compiler may request that it be validated by registration rather than by AVF testing.

For an implementation to be considered 'derived', the following four criteria must be met:

1. The Ada compiler was obtained from the Ada compiler of the base implementation by changes that are within the scope of accepted software maintenance practices.

2. The target machine of the base and derived Ada implementation have compatible instruction sets and operating systems or kernels.

3. The Ada compiler has been tested with the customized test suite that was used to validate the base implementation.

4. The 'result profile' for the derived implementation is either the same as the base implementation or, if there are differences, these differences are justified as being within the scope of accepted software maintenance practices.

Registration requests must comply with the format and content of the sample given in Appendix D of the Validation Procedures (version 3.1), and may be sent directly to the Ada Validation Organization (AVO), a technical support organization of the Ada certification body.

Information regarding a derived compiler that is accepted by the AVO will be forwarded to the AJPO to be added to the public list of validated Ada compilers.

For further information

For further information, see "Ada Compiler Validation Procedures, Version 3.1, August 1992". An electronic copy of the document is available on the AdaIC Bulletin Board as file VALPROC.HLP. Access to the menu-driven bulletin board requires a computer terminal or personal computer and modem. Users should set their telecommunications package with the following parameters: Baud rate= 300-9600 baud; Data Bits= 8; Parity= none; Stop Bits= 1. Then dial +1 703 614 0215 (Commercial) or 224 0215 (Autovon). First-time users will be prompted to register for an account.

Most files have been compressed using PKZIP and must be uncompressed after downloading. PKZIP is available on the bulletin board and can be obtained by downloading the file PKZ101.EXE. Macintosh Plus users can download the file UNZIP101.SIT.

Copies may also be obtained by purchase from the Defense Technical Information Center (DTIC) and the National Technical Information Service (NTIS) with accession number AD A257 705. NTIS sells documents to the public. DTIC distributes documents only to Military, government, or defense contractors who are registered with them.

National Technical Information Service (NTIS)

National Technical Information Service
U.S. Department of Commerce
5285 Port Royal Road

Springfield
Virginia 22161
USA
Tel: +1 703 487 4650

Defense Technical Information Center (DTIC)

Defense Technical Information Center
Cameron Station
Alexandria
Virginia 22314
USA
Tel: +1 703 274 7633 AV 284 763

Ada validation facility managers

The following Ada Validation Facilities (AVFs), chartered by the Ada Joint Program Office, perform
Ada Compiler Validation Capability testing and related support functions.

Dr. William Dashiell
National Institute of Standards
and Technology
Computer Systems Lab
Software Standards Validation Group
Building 255, Room A266
Gaithersburg, MD 20899
USA
Tel: +1 301 975 2490
Fax: +1 301 948 6213, 301 948 1784
Email: nist-avf@ajpo.sei.cmu.edu,
        dashiell@ecf.ncsl.nist.gov

Mr. Dale Lange
Ada Validation Facility
Language Control Facility
645 C-CSG/SCSL
Area B, Building 676
Wright-Patterson AFB
OH 45433-6503
USA
Tel: +1 513 255 4472
Fax: +1 513 255 4585
Email: langed@ss1.sews.wpafb.af.mil

Mr. Jon Leigh
Mr. Dave Bamber
The National Computing Centre, Ltd.
Oxford Road
Manchester
M1 7ED
UK
Tel: +44 161 228 6333
Fax: +44 161 236 9877
Email: ncc-avf@ncc.co.uk,
        uk-avf@ajpo.sei.cmu.edu

Mr. Alphonse Philippe
AFNOR
Tour Europe, Cedex 7
F-92080 Paris la Defence
France
Tel: +33 1 42 91 5960
Email: afnor@ajpo.sei.cmu.edu

Mr. Michael Tonndorf
IABG, Dept ITE
Einsteinstraße 20
D-85521 Ottobrunn
Germany
Tel: +49 89 6088 2477
Fax: +49 89 6088 3418
Email: tonndorf@ite.iabg.de,
        tonndorf@ajpo.sei.cmu.edu

For further information on the AVFs or validation policies and procedures, contact:

Ada Validation Office
Attn: Ms. Audrey A. Hook
Institute for Defense Analysis
1801 North Beauregard Street
Alexandria, VA 22311
USA
Tel: +1 703 845 6639
Fax: +1 703 845 6848
Email: hook@ida.org

12.2 Introduction to the list

The data were extracted from:

> File VAL-COMP.HLP: List of Validated Ada
> Compilers for December 1994
> Form G/V10-1294;
> Ada Information Clearinghouse,
> Tel: +1 703 685 1477

The following are Ada compilers that have been validated by the Ada Joint Program Office (AJPO). The list is updated monthly, and presently includes 377 base compilers and 446 compilers derived from base implementations. For the most current information on validated Ada compilers, please contact the Ada Information Clearinghouse on +1 703 685 1477.

The entries are shown in the following format:

Host machine architecture including operating system
　　vendor and compiler
　　target machine, if different from the host
　　(certificate number)

The host machine architecture details are not repeated if they are identical to the previous entry.

The certificate number has the following form:

(#YYMMDDFX.XXNNN): YYMMDD is the date on-site testing was completed; F is the Ada Validation Facility; X.XX is the ACVC Version; NNN is a unique sequence number that is assigned by the AVO.

For example, the certificate number #901120W1.11087 means the compiler completed on-site testing November 20, 1990, at Wright-Patterson AFB under ACVC 1.11.

12.3   Alphabetical list

AETECHXAda Ver. 6.1
Any computer system comprising: cpu:
Intel 80386 or 80486; fpu: Optional;
memory: 8 MByte RAM; disk: 160 MByte
hard drive (under SCO Unix 3.2, Solaris
X86, ESIX System V, Release 4.0, &
Interactive Unix System V, Release 3.2)
(BASE #901129W1.11086)

AETECHXAda Version 6.1
Any computer system comprising: cpu:
Intel 80386 or 80486; fpu: optional;
memory: 8 MByte RAM; disk: 160 MByte
hard drive (under Univel UnixWare
Version 1.0.3a)
(BASE #901129W1.11086)

**AETECH, Inc.AETECH POSIX Compiler
Version 5.1.0**
Any Computer System Comprising: cpu:
Intel 80386 & 80486; fpu: optional;
memory: 4 MByte RAM; disk: 60 MByte
hard drive (under ESIX System V,
Release 4.0)
(BASE #901129W1.11086)

**AETECH, Inc.AETECH POSIX Compiler,
Version 5.1.0**
Any Computer System Comprising: cpu:
Intel 80386 & 80486, fpu: optional,
memory: 4 MByte RAM, disk: 60 MByte
hard drive (under Interactive Unix System
V, Release 3.2)
(BASE #901129W1.11086)

AETECH, Inc.IntegrAda 386 5.1.0
Northgate 386/25 (under Phar Lap/DOS
3.3)
Northgate 386/25 (under MS DOS 3.3)
(#901120W1.11087) Any Computer System
Comprising: cpu: Intel 80386, fpu:
optional, memory: 4 MByte RAM, disk: 40
MByte hard drive (under Phar Lap/DOS
3.3)
*Any Computer System Comprising: cpu: Intel
80386, fpu: optional, memory: 4 MByte RAM,
disk: 40 MByte hard drive (under MS DOS
3.3)*
(BASE #901120W1.11087)

AETECH, Inc.IntegrAda 386 Ver 6.2
Any Computer System Comprising: cpu:
Intel 80386 & 80486; fpu: optional;
memory: 4 MByte RAM; disk: 40 MByte
hard drive (under MS DOS 3.3, 5.0, & 6.0)
(BASE #901120W1.11087)

AETECH, Inc.IntegrAda 5.1.0 POSIX
Unisys PW/2 386 (under SCO Unix 3.2)
(#901129W1.11086)

AETECH, Inc.IntegrAda DOS Ver 6.1
Any Computer System Comprising: cpu:
Intel 80x86 series; fpu: optional; memory:
640 KByte RAM; disk: 40 MByte hard
drive (under MS DOS 3.3, 5.0, & 6.0)
(BASE #901120W1.11087)

**AETECH, Inc.IntegrAda for Windows Ver
1.2**
Any Computer System Comprising: cpu:
Intel 80386 & 80486; fpu: optional;
memory: 4 MByte RAM; disk: 40 MByte
hard drive (under MS DOS 3.3, 5.0, & 6.0,
with Windows 3.1)
(BASE #901120W1.11087)

AETECH, Inc.IntegrAda Posix 5.1.0
Any Computer System Comprising: cpu:
Intel 80386, fpu: optional, memory: 4
MByte RAM, disk: 60 MByte hard drive
(under SCO Unix 3.2)
(BASE #901129W1.11086)

**Aitech Defense Systems, Inc.AI-ADA/88K
Version 2.4**
VAXstation 3100 Cluster (under VMS 5.3)
*Tadpole TP880V (88100-based VME board)
(bare machine)*
(#900930W1.11030)

**Aitech Defense Systems, Inc.AI-ADA/88K,
Version 2.4**
All DEC MicroVAX, VAXstation,
VAXserver, VAX-11, VAX 8xxx & VAX
6xxx series (under VMS versions 5.0, 5.1,
5.2 & 5.3, as supported)
*Tadpole TP880V (88100-based VME board) &
Motorola MVME181 (88100-based VME
board) (bare machines)*
(BASE #900930W1.11030)

**Aitech Defense Systems, Inc.AI-ADA/96K,
Version 3.0**
VAXstation 3100 Cluster (under VMS 5.3)
DSP96002 ADS board (bare machine)
(#911012W1.11224) Sun-4/330 (under
SunOS 4.1.1)
DSP96002 ADS board (bare machine)
(#911012W1.11225)

Alenia Aeritalia & Selenia S.p.ADACS 80x86PM, Version 4.60
DEC VAX-11, VAXserver, VAXstation, MicroVAX, VAX 4000, VAX 6000, VAX 8000, & VAX 9000 Series of computers (under VMS 5.4)
Alenia MARA 80386- & 80486-based computers (under Alenia Operating System 8.6)
(BASE #920509S1.11259)

Alenia Aeritalia & Selenia S.p.ADACS VAX/VMS to 80x86 PM MARA Ada Cross Compiler, Version 4.6
MicroVAX 4000/200 (under VMS Version 5.4)
Alenia MARA (80286-based) (under Alenia Operating System, Version 8.6 System)
(#920509S1.11259)

Alliant Computer Systems Corporation Alliant FX/Ada Compiler, Version 2.3
Alliant FX/80 (under Concentrix Release 5.7)
(#901218W1.11106)

Alliant Computer Systems Corporation Alliant FX/Ada-2800 Compiler, Version 1.0
Alliant FX/2800 (under Concentrix Release 2.0)
(#901218W1.11105)

Alsys (formerly TeleSoft)TeleGen2 Ada Cross Development System for Sun-4 to 68k, Version 4.1aS (or V1A_S)
Sun Microsystems Sun-4, SPARCstation, & SPARCserver series of computers (under SunOS 4.1)
DY 4 Systems SVME-122 (bare machine, using TeleAda-Exec)
(BASE #921218I1.11304)

Alsys / German MoDNATO SWG on APSE Compiler for Sun3/SunOS to MC68020, Version S3CM1.82
Sun-3/60 (under SunOS Version 4.0.3, with CAIS Version 5.5E)
Motorola MVME133XT (MC68020) (bare machine)
(#920728I1.11261)

Alsys / German MoDNATO SWG on APSE Compiler for Sun3/SunOS, Version S3C1.82-02
Sun-3/60 (under SunOS Version 4.0.3, with CAIS Version 5.5D)
Sun-3/60 (under SunOS Version 4.0.3)
(#911016I1.11233)

Alsys / German MoDNATO SWG on APSE Compiler for VAX/VMS to MC68020, Version VCM1.82-02
VAX 8350 (under VMS Version 5.4-1, with CAIS Version 5.5E)
Motorola MVME133XT (MC68020) (bare machine)
(#920306I1.11248)

Alsys / German MoDNATO SWG on APSE Compiler for VAX/VMS, Version VC1.82-02
VAX 8350 (under VMS Version 5.4-1, with CAIS Version 5.5E)
VAX 8350 (under VMS Version 5.4-1)
(#911118I1.11236)

AlsysAlsyCOMP_002 Version 5.5.1
HP 9000 Series 300 & 400 (all models) (under HP-UX 8.0)
(BASE #901022A1.11046)

AlsysAlsyCOMP_002, Version 5.3
HP 9000s350 (under HP-UX 6.5)
(#901022A1.11046) HP 9000 Series 300, all models (under HP-UX 6.5 & 7.0)
(BASE #901022A1.11046)

AlsysAlsyCOMP_003 Version 5.1
HP Vectra RS/25C (under MS-DOS 3.30)
(#901102W1.11058) Zenith Z-248 Model 50 (under MS-DOS 3.30)
(#901102W1.11059) Any Computer System that executes the Intel 80286, 80386, or 80486 instruction set (under MS/DOS 5.0)
(BASE #901102W1.11058)

AlsysAlsyCOMP_003, Version 5.1
Unisys Desktop III (under MS-DOS 3.30)
(BASE #901102W1.11058) HP Vectra ES/12; and IBM PC/AT (all models) (under MS-DOS 3.30)
(BASE #901102W1.11059) ICS SB286SC/12 (under MS-DOS 3.30)
(BASE #901102W1.11059)

AlsysAlsyCOMP_004 Version 5.5.1
HP Apollo 9000 Series 400 (under Domain/OS SR10.4)
(BASE #901022A1.11044)

AlsysAlsyCOMP_004, Version 5.3
Apollo DN4000 (under Domain/OS SR10.2)
(#901022A1.11044) Apollo DN3000, DN3500, DN4000 & DN4500 (under Domain/OS SR10.2 & SR10.3)
(BASE #901022A1.11044)

AlsysAlsyCOMP_005 Version 5.5.1
Sun Microsystems Sun-3 computer family
(under SunOS 4.1.1)
(BASE #901022A1.11047)

AlsysAlsyCOMP_005, Version 5.3
Sun-3/260 (under SunOS 3.2)
(#901022A1.11047) Sun 3/50, /60, /75, /80,
/160, /260, /280, /470 & /480 (under
SunOS 3.2, 3.5, 4.0 & 4.1)
(BASE #901022A1.11047)

AlsysAlsyCOMP_006, Version 5.3
IBM 9370 Model 90 (under VM/IS CMS
release 5.1)
(#901125N1.11071)

AlsysAlsyCOMP_011 Version 5.3.1
DEC VAX-11, VAXserver, VAXstation,
MicroVAX, VAX 4000, VAX 6000, VAX
8000, & VAX 9000 series of computers
(under VMS 5.2, 5.3, & 5.4, as supported)
Motorola MVME101 (68000), MVME121
(68010), MVME133XT & MVME135-1
(68020), & MVME147-1 (68030) (bare
machines, using ARTK 5.3.1)
(BASE #901127A1.11069)

AlsysAlsyCOMP_011 Version 5.5.1
DEC VAX-11, VAXserver, VAXstation,
MicroVAX, VAX 4000, VAX 6000, VAX
8000, & VAX 9000 computer series (under
VMS 5.4)
Motorola MVME 131, MVME133,
MVME133XT, MVME135, & MVME147
(68020 & 68030 cpu.s) (bare machines, using
VRTX32); Motorola MVME101, MVME121,
MVME131, MVME133, MVME133XT,
MVME135, M68332EVS, MVME147, &
MVME167 (68000, 68010, 68020, 68030, &
68040 cpu.s) (bare machines, using ARTK
Version 5.5.1)
(BASE #901127A1.11069)

AlsysAlsyCOMP_011, Version 5.3
VAX 6210 (under VMS 5.2)
Motorola MVME135-1 (68020/68881) (bare
machine, using ARTK Version 5.3)
(#901127A1.11069) DEC VAX-11,
VAXserver, VAXstation, MicroVAX, VAX
4000, VAX 6000, VAX 8000 & VAX 9000
Series of computers (as supported) (under
VMS 5.2, 5.3 & 5.4)
Motorola MVME101 (68000), MVME121
(68010), MVME135-1 (68020/68881) &
MVME147-1 (68030/68882) (bare machines,
using ARTK 5.3)
(BASE #901127A1.11069)

AlsysAlsyCOMP_012 Version 5.5.1
HP 9000 Series 400 (all models) (under
HP-UX 8.0)
Motorola MVME 131, MVME133,
MVME133XT, MVME135, & MVME147
(68020 & 68030 cpu.s) (bare machines, using
VRTX32); Motorola MVME101, MVME121,
MVME 131, MVME133, MVME133XT,
MVME135, MVME147, & MVME167 (68000,
68010, 68020, 68030, & 68040 cpu.s) (bare
machines, using ARTK Version 5.5.1)
(BASE #901116A1.11066)

AlsysAlsyCOMP_012, Version 5.3
HP 9000s350 (under HP-UX 6.5)
Motorola MVME101 (68000) (bare machine,
using ARTK Version 5.3)
(#901116A1.11066) HP 9000 Series 300
(all models) (under HP-UX 6.5 & 7.0)
Motorola M68332EVS Evaluation System
Customers (CPU32) (bare machine, using
ARTK 5.3)
(BASE #901116A1.11066) HP 9000 Series
300, Models 340, 345, 360, 370 & 375
(under HP-UX 6.5 & 7.0)
Motorola MVME101 (68000), MVME121
(68010), MVME135-1 (68020/68881) &
MVME147-1 (68030/68882) (bare machines,
using ARTK 5.3)
(BASE #901116A1.11066)

AlsysAlsyCOMP_015 Version 5.5.1
Sun Microsystems Sun-3 computer family
(under SunOS 4.1.1)
Motorola MVME 131, MVME133,
MVME133XT, MVME135, & MVME147
(68020 & 68030 cpu.s) (bare machines, using
VRTX32); Motorola MVME101, MVME121,
MVME131, MVME133, MVME133XT,
MVME135, M68332EVS, MVME147, &
MVME167 (68000, 68010, 68020, 68030, &
68040 cpu.s) (bare machines, using ARTK
Version 5.5.1)
(BASE #901116A1.11068)

AlsysAlsyCOMP_015, Version 5.3
Sun 3/260 (under SunOS 3.2)
Motorola MVME121 (68010) (bare machine,
using ARTK Version 5.3)
(#901116A1.11068) Sun 3/50, /60, /75, /80,
/160, /260, /280, /470 & /480 (under
SunOS 3.2, 3.5, 4.0 & 4.1)
Motorola MVME101 (68000), MVME121
(68010), MVME135-1 (68020/68881) &
MVME147-1 (68030/68882) (bare machines,
using ARTK 5.3)
(BASE #901116A1.11068)

AlsysAlsyCOMP_016 Version 5.1
Compaq Deskpro 386 (under MS-DOS
3.30, Phar Lap 2.0)
(#901102W1.11055) CompuAdd 320 (under
MS-DOS 3.30, Phar Lap 2.0)
(#901102W1.11056) ALR Power Veisa 486
(under MS-DOS 3.30, Phar Lap 2.0)
(#901102W1.11057) Any Computer System
Comprising: cpu: Intel 80386; fpu:
optional; memory: 5 MByte RAM; disk: 10
MByte (under MS-DOS 3.30, Phar Lap
2.0)
(BASE #901102W1.11056)

AlsysAlsyCOMP_016 Version 5.1.1
Any Computer System that executes the
Intel 80386 or 80486 instruction set (under
MS/DOS 5.0 & Phar Lap 4.0)
(BASE #901102W1.11055)

AlsysAlsyCOMP_016, Version 5.1
HP Vectra RS/20, RS/20C, RS/25 &
RS/25C; AST Premium 386; and Unisys
386 & Desktop III (under MS-DOS 3.30,
Phar Lap 2.0)
(BASE #901102W1.11056)

AlsysAlsycomp_017 Version 5.4.3
MicroVAX II (under VMS V5.3)
*INMOS T425 transputer on a B403 TRAM
(bare), using the Host running INMOS Iserver
V1.42i for file-server support via a CAPLIN
QT0 board link and INMOS T800 transputer
on a B405 TRAM (bare), using the Host
running INMOS Iserver V1.42i for file-server
support via a CAPLIN QT0 board link*
(BASE #901118N1.11064)

AlsysAlsyCOMP_017, V5.3
MicroVAX II (under VMS V5.3)
*INMOS T425 transputer on a B403 TRAM
(bare) using the Host running INMOS Iserver
1.3 for file-server support via a CAPLIN QT0
board link; INMOS T800 transputer on a B405
TRAM (bare) using the Host running INMOS
Iserver 1.3 for file-server support via a
CAPLIN QT0 board link*
(BASE #901118N1.11064)

AlsysAlsyCOMP_017, Version 5.2
MicroVAX II (under VMS V5.3)
*INMOS T425 transputer on a B403 TRAM
(bare) using the Host running INMOS Iserver
1.3 for file-server support via a CAPLIN QT0
board link*
(#901118N1.11064)

AlsysAlsyCOMP_018 Version 5.2
MicroVAX 3100 (under VMS 5.3)
(#901120A1.11070)

AlsysAlsyCOMP_018, Version 5.2
DEC VAX-11, VAXserver, VAXstation,
MicroVAX, VAX 4000, VAX 6000, VAX
8000 & VAX 9000 Series of computers (as
supported) (under VMS 5.2 & 5.4)
(BASE #901120A1.11070)

AlsysAlsyCOMP_019 Version 5.3.1
CompuAdd 433 (under MS-DOS 5.0
running Phar Lap 4.0)
Intel iSBC 186/100 (bare machine)
(#921210W1.11302) CompuAdd 433 (under
MS-DOS 5.0 running Phar Lap 4.0)
*Any 80C186EB- & 80C188EB-based
single-board computers (bare machines)*
(BASE #921210W1.11302)

AlsysAlsyCOMP_023, Version 5.3
IBM 370 3084Q (under MVS/XA release
3.2)
(#901125N1.11072)

AlsysAlsyCOMP_024 V5.4
IBM RISC System 6000 (all models)
(under AIX 3.2)
(BASE #910809W1.11195)

AlsysAlsyCOMP_024, Version 5.3
IBM RISC System 6000, model 520
(under AIX v3.1)
(#910809W1.11195)

AlsysAlsyCOMP_025, Version 1.83
MIPS M/120-5 (under RISC/os, Version
4.0)
(#900814I1.11041)

AlsysAlsyCOMP_026, Version 1.82
Sun-3/60 (under SunOS, Version 4.0.3)
(#900814I1.11040)

AlsysAlsyCOMP_028 Version 5.3
Compaq Deskpro 386/20 (under DOS
3.31 & 5.0)
*Motorola MVME101, MVME121, MVME131,
MVME133, MVME133XT, MVME135-1,
MVME147-1, M68332EVS (68000, 68010,
68020, & 68030 cpu.s) (bare machine, using
ARTK Version 5.3)*
(BASE #901127A1.11069)

AlsysAlsyCOMP_029 Version 5.3.1
Any Computer System that executes the
Intel 80386 or 80486 instruction set (under
MS-DOS 5.0 or higher version, and
PharLap v4.0)
*Any Intel486 DX2 single board computer
(bare machine, using ARTK 5.3)*
(BASE #910323W1.11132)

AlsysAlsyCOMP_029, Version 5.3
CompuAdd 325 (under DOS 3.31)
Intel iSBC 386/116 (bare machine, using ARTK 5.3)
(#910323W1.11131)

AlsysAlsyCOMP_029, Version 5.3.1
Any Computer System that executes the Intel 80386 or 80486 instruction set (under MS-DOS version 5.0 & Phar Lap version 4.0)
Any 80486 single board computer (bare machine, using ARTK 5.3)
(BASE #910323W1.11131)

AlsysAlsyCOMP_030 Version 5.3.1
MicroVAX II (under VMS 5.2)
Any Intel486 DX2 single board computer (bare machine, using ARTK 5.3)
(BASE #910323W1.11132)

AlsysAlsyCOMP_030, Version 5.3
MicroVAX II (under VMS 5.2)
Intel iSBC 386/31 (bare machine, using ARTK 5.3)
(#910323W1.11132)

AlsysAlsyCOMP_030, Version 5.3.1
MicroVAX II (under VMS 5.2)
Any 80386 single board computer (bare machine, using ARTK 5.3)
(BASE #910323W1.11132)

AlsysAlsyCOMP_032, 5.5
CompuAdd 433 (under IBM OS/2, Version 2.1 + Threads)
(#931208W1.11333)

AlsysAlsyCOMP_033, Version 5.3
Sun 3/140 (under SunOS 4.1)
Intel iSBC 386/12 (bare machine, using ARTK 5.3)
(#910323W1.11133)

AlsysAlsyCOMP_034 Version 5.1
IBM PS/2 Model 80 (under LynxOS Version 2.0 + Threads Release 11)
(#910129W1.11113) Any Computer System that executes the Intel 80386 or 80486 instruction set (under SCO Open Desktop 1.1 & SCO Unix 3.2, SCO Open Desktop 2.0 & SCO Unix 3.2.4, Interactive Unix 3.2.2, and AT&T Unix System V Release 4.0)
(BASE #901221W1.11103)

AlsysAlsyCOMP_034 Version 5.1.2
SAIC LCU V2 (under SCO Open Desktop 2.0 (SCO Unix 3.2.4))
(BASE #901221W1.11103)

AlsysAlsyCOMP_034 Version 5.5
Any computer system that executes the Intel 80386 or i486 instruction set (under SCO Open Desktop 2.0 with SCO Unix version 3.2.4, Interactive Unix 3.2.2, or AT&T Unix System V Release 4.0)
(BASE #901221W1.11103)

AlsysAlsyComp_034 Version 5.5.6
IBM PS/2 Model 80 series (under LynxOS v2.2)
(BASE #910129W1.11113)

AlsysAlsyCOMP_034, Version 5.1
Multitech 1100 (under SCO Unix 3.2)
(#901221W1.11103) Everex AGI 3000D, Compaq Deskpro 386 & SAI Technologies Army Lightweight Computer Unit (LCU V2) (under Interactive Unix 3.2)
Each Host, self-targetted
(BASE #901221W1.11103) Any Computer System comprising: cpu: Intel 80386 or 80486; fpu: optional (under a Unix 3.2-based OS)
Each Host, self-targetted
(BASE #901221W1.11103) Prime MBX (under Prime Unix V.4)
(BASE #901221W1.11103) IBM PS/2 Models 70-xxx & 80-xxx (under LynxOS Version 2.0 Release 15)
(BASE #910129W1.11113)

AlsysAlsyCOMP_034, Version 5.1.2
Zenith Data Systems Z-Station 433 DEh (under SCO Unix 3.2.4 running SecureWare CMW+ Version 2.2)
(BASE #901221W1.11103)

AlsysAlsyCOMP_035 Version 5.5.1
CETIA Unigraph models 1000/325; 2000/50, /250, /325; 3000/325-333; 6000/325-333; 7000/325/ 8000/325; & 9000 (under Unigraph/X 3.2c.1)
(BASE #901022A1.11048)

AlsysAlsyCOMP_035, Version 5.3
CETIA Unigraph 6000 (under Unigraph/X 3.1)
(#901022A1.11048) Unigraph 1000/325, 2000/50, 2000/250, 2000/325, 3000/325-333, 6000/325-333, 7000/325, 8000/325 & 9000 (under Unigraph/X 3.1 & 3.1.1)
(BASE #901022A1.11048)

AlsysAlsyCOMP_036 Version 5.5.1
HP 9000 Series 400 (all models) (under DomainOS SR 10.4)
Motorola MVME101, MVME121, MVME131, MVME133, MVME133XT, MVME135,

M68332EVS, MVME147, & MVME167
(68000, 68010, 68020, 68030, & 68040 cpu.s)
(bare machines, using ARTK Version 5.5.1)
(BASE #901116A1.11067)

AlsysAlsyCOMP_036, Version 5.3
Apollo DN4000 (under Domain/OS
SR10.2)
*Motorola MVME147-1 (68030/68882) (bare
machine, using ARTK Version 5.3)*
(#901116A1.11067) Apollo DN 3000, 3500,
4000 & 4500 (under Domain/OS SR10.2 &
SR10.3)
*Motorola MVME101 (68000), MVME121
(68010), MVME135-1 (68020/68881) &
MVME147-1 (68030/68882) (bare machines,
using ARTK 5.3)*
(BASE #901116A1.11067)

AlsysAlsycomp_037 Version 5.4.2
INMOS T800 transputer on a B405 TRAM
board (bare), with an INMOS B008
Communications link implemented in an
IBM PC/AT (under MS-DOS 3.1 and
INMOS Iserver V1.42h)
*INMOS T800 transputer on a B405 TRAM
(bare), using an IBM PC/AT under MS-DOS
3.1 running INMOS Iserver V1.42h for
file-server support via an INMOS B008 board
link and INMOS T425 transputer on a B403
TRAM (bare), using an IBM PC/AT under
MS-DOS 3.1 running INMOS Iserver V1.42h
for file-server support via an INMOS B008
board link*
(BASE #901114N1.11065)

AlsysAlsyCOMP_037, V5.3
INMOS T800 transputer on a B403 TRAM
(bare) with an INMOS B008
Communications link implemented in an
IBM PC/AT (under MS-DOS 3.1 and
INMOS Iserver V1.3)
*INMOS T800 transputer on a B405 TRAM
(bare) using an IBM PC/AT under MS-DOS
3.1 running INMOS Iserver 1.3 for file-server
support via an INMOS B008 board link;
INMOS T425 transputer on a B403 TRAM
(bare) using an IBM PC/AT under MS-DOS
3.1 running INMOS Iserver 1.3 for file-server
support via an INMOS B008 board link*
(BASE #901114N1.11065)

AlsysAlsyCOMP_037, Version 5.2
INMOS T800 transputer on a B405 TRAM
(bare) with an INMOS B008
Communications link implemented in an
IBM PC/AT (under MS-DOS 3.1 and
INMOS Iserver V1.3)
*INMOS T800 transputer on a B405 TRAM
(bare) using an IBM PC/AT under MS-DOS*

*3.1 running INMOS Iserver 1.3 for file-server
support via an INMOS B008 board link*
(#901114N1.11065)

AlsysAlsyCOMP_040, Version 5.3
HP Vectra RS/25C (under DOS 3.30)
Unisys B39 (under BTOS II, v3.2.0)
(#910809W1.11197)

AlsysAlsyCOMP_042, Version 5.3
IBM 9370 Model 90 (under AIX/370
Version 1.2)
(#900627N1.11013)

AlsysAlsyCOMP_043, Version 5.3
Apple Macintosh IIcx (under Macintosh
System Software 6.0.5)
(#901221W1.11104)

AlsysAlsyCOMP_046, Version 5.3
Sony NEWS NWS-1850 (under
NEWS-OS 3.3)
(#901022A1.11043) Sony NEWS series
1250, 15xx, 17xx, 18xx & 19xx (under
NEWS-OS versions 3.3 & 3.4)
(BASE #901022A1.11043)

AlsysAlsyCOMP_048 Version 5.5.1
Sun SPARCstation & SPARCserver
computer families; SPARCcenter 2000
(under SunOS 4.1.2); Solbourne Series
5/100, /530, /600, /670, /800, 5E/900; &
S4000 (under OS/MP 4.1A.1)
*Motorola MVME101, MVME121, MVME131,
MVME133, MVME133XT, MVME135,
M68332EVS, MVME147, & MVME167
(68000, 68010, 68020, 68030, & 68040 cpu.s)
(bare machines, using ARTK Version 5.5.1)*
(BASE #901116A1.11066)

AlsysAlsyCOMP_048, V5.5.2
Sun Microsystems Sun-4, SPARCstation,
& SPARCserver series of computers; and
SPARCcenter 2000 (under SunOS 4.1.2)
*Motorola MVME10, MVME121, MVME131,
MVME133, MVME133XT, MVME135,
MVME147, MVME167, & MEN A4 (68332)
(bare machines, using ARTK 5.5.2)*
(BASE #901116A1.11066)

AlsysAlsyCOMP_049, Version 1.83
VAX 8530 (under VMS Version 5.3-1)
*Integrated Device Technology IDT7RS301
System (R3000/R3010) (bare machine)*
(#910407I1.11144)

AlsysAlsyCOMP_049, Version 1.83-01
VAX 8530 (under VMS 5.3-1)
*Lockheed Sanders STAR MVP (R3000/R3010)
(bare machine)*
(BASE #910407I1.11144)

AlsysAlsyCOMP_049, Version 1.84
DEC VAX-11, VAXserver, VAXstation,
MicroVAX, VAX 4000, VAX 6000, VAX
8000, & VAX 9000 series of computers
(under VMS 5.3 & 5.4)
Lockheed Sanders STAR MVP board
(R3000/R3010) (bare machine)
(BASE #910407I1.11144)

AlsysAlsyCOMP_050, Version 5.3
Bull DPX/2 320 (under B.O.S. 02.00.05)
(#901022A1.11045) Bull DPX 2/210, /220,
/320, /340 & /360 (under BOS 02.00.05 &
2.00.10)
(BASE #901022A1.11045)

AlsysAlsyCOMP_052 Version 5.3.1
Sun Microsystems Sun-4, SPARCstation,
& SPARCserver computer families (under
SunOS 4.1)
Any Intel486 DX2 single board computer
(bare machine, using ARTK 5.3)
(BASE #910323W1.11132)

AlsysAlsyCOMP_052, Version 5.3.1
Sun Microsystems Sun-4, SPARCserver,
& SPARCstation computer families (under
SunOS 4.1)
Intel iSBC 386/31, iSBC 386/1xx, iSBC
486/1xx (bare machines, using ARTK 5.3)
(BASE #910323W1.11133)

AlsysAlsyCOMP_053, Version 1.82
VAX 8530 (under VMS, Version 5.1)
(#900509I1.11009)

AlsysAlsyCOMP_055, Version 1.82
VAX 8530 (under VMS, Version 5.3-1)
KWS EB68020 (under OS-9/68020, Version
2.3)
(#910201I1.11128)

AlsysAlsyCOMP_056, Version 1.82
Sun 3/60 (under SunOS, Version 4.0.3)
KWS EB68020 (under OS-9/68020, Version
2.3)
(#910131I1.11127)

AlsysAlsyCOMP_057, Version 1.83
DECstation 3100 (under ULTRIX Version
4.0)
(#910625I1.11193)

AlsysAlsyCOMP_057, Version 1.83-01
DEC DECstation & DECsystem computer
families (under ULTRIX 4.0 & 4.2)
(BASE #910625I1.11193)

AlsysAlsyCOMP_058, Version 5.3
Unisys B39 (under BTOS II, v3.2.0)
(#910809W1.11196)

AlsysAlsyCOMP_061, Version 1.83
DECstation 3100 (under ULTRIX Version
4.2)
Lockheed Sanders STAR MVP board
(R3000/3010) (bare machine)
(#920429I1.11251)

AlsysAlsyCOMP_061, Version 1.84
DEC DECstation & DECsystem computer
families (under ULTRIX 4.2)
Lockheed Sanders STAR MVP board
(R3000/R3010) (bare machine)
(BASE #920429I1.11251)

AlsysAlsyCOMP_061, Version 1.84-01
DEC DECstation & DECsystem computer
families (under ULTRIX 4.2)
Lockheed Sanders STAR MVP board
(R3000/R3010), Integrated Device Technology
IDT7RS385 board (R3081E) (bare machines)
(BASE #920429I1.11251)

AlsysAlsyCOMP_062 Version 5.35
HP 9000 Series 800 Model 827 (under
HP-UX Version 8.02)
(#921118N1.11298) HP 9000 Series 700,
all models (under HP-UX, Version A.B8.05
(release 8.05)); HP 9000 Series 800, all
models (under HP-UX, Version A.B8.00
(release 8.00))
HP 9000 Series 700, all models (under
HP-UX, Version A.B8.05 (release 8.05))
(BASE #911107W1.11227) HP 9000 Series
700, all models (under HP-UX, Version
A.B8.05 (release 8.05)); HP 9000 Series
800, all models (under HP-UX, Version
A.B8.00 (release 8.00))
HP 9000 Series 800, all models (under
HP-UX, Version A.B8.00 (release 8.00))
(BASE #911107W1.11228) HP 9000 Series
800 Models 807, 817, 847, & 867 (under
HP-UX B-Level Security Operating
System, Version A.08.08)
(BASE #911107W1.11228)

AlsysAlsyCOMP_062 Version 5.5.1
HP 9000 Series 700, all models (under
HP-UX, Version 9.01); HP 9000 Series
800, all models (under HP-UX, Version
9.0)
HP 9000 Series 700, all models (under
HP-UX, Version 9.01)
(BASE #911107W1.11227) HP 9000 Series
700, all models (under HP-UX, Version

9.01); HP 9000 Series 800, all models
(under HP-UX, Version 9.0)
HP 9000 Series 800, all models (under
HP-UX, Version 9.0)
(BASE #911107W1.11228)

AlsysAlsyCOMP_062 Version 5.5.2
HP 9000 Series 700, all models (under
HP-UX, Version 9.01); HP 9000 Series
800, all models (under HP-UX, Version
9.0)
HP 9000 Series 700, all models (under
HP-UX, Version 9.01)
(BASE #911107W1.11227)

AlsysAlsyCOMP_062, V5.5.2A
HP 9000 series 700, all models (under
HP-UX, Version 10.0)
(BASE #911107W1.11227)

AlsysAlsyCOMP_062, Version 5.35
HP 9000 Series 700 Model 720 (under
HP-UX, Version A.B8.05 (release 8.05))
(#911107W1.11227) HP 9000 Series 800
Model 835 (under HP-UX, Version
A.B8.00 (release 8.00))
(#911107W1.11228)

AlsysAlsyCOMP_063 Version 5.5.1
HP 9000 Series 700 (all models) (under
HP-UX 9.0)
Motorola MVME101, MVME121,
M68332EVS, MVME131, MVME133,
MVME133XT, MVME135, MVME147, &
MVME167 (68000-, 68010-, 68020-, 68030-,
& 68040-based single-board computers) (bare
machines, using ARTK 5.5.1)
(BASE #901116A1.11066)

AlsysAlsyCOMP_065, Version 5.3
Sun Microsystems Sun-4, SPARCserver,
and SPARCstation computer families
(under SunOS 4.1)
Any Intel 8086, 80186, or 80286 single-board
computer (bare machine, running ARTK 5.3)
(BASE #921210W1.11302)

AlsysAlsyCOMP_068, Version 1.83
Control Data 4680 (under EP/IX 1.4.3)
(#930125I1.11310)

AlsysAlsyCOMP_069, Verison 1.83-02A
Control Data 4000 series of computers
(under EP/LX 1.3)
(BASE #920730I1.11262)

AlsysAlsyCOMP_069, Version 1.83
Control Data 4336 (under TC/IX 1.0.2)
(#920730I1.11262) Control Data 4000
series of computers (under TC/IX 1.0.2 &

1.1)
(BASE #920730I1.11262) Control Data
4000 series of computers (under TC/IX
1.2)
(BASE #920730I1.11262)

AlsysAlsyCOMP_069, Version 1.83-02B
Control Data 4000 Series of computers
(under EP/LX 1.3)
(BASE #920730I1.11262)

AlsysAlsyCOMP_070 Version 5.5.3
Any computer system that executes the
Intel 80386 or i486 instruction set (under
LynxOS, Version 2.1)
(BASE #910129W1.11113)

AlsysAlsyCOMP_072 Version 5.37
Sun SPARCstation 2 (under SunOS 4.1.1)
(#911119A1.11231)

AlsysAlsyCOMP_072 Version 5.5.1
Solbourne Series 5/500, /530, /600, /670,
/800, & 5E/900; & S4000 (under OS/MP
4.1)
(BASE #911119A1.11231) SPARCstation
ELC, IPC, & IPX; SPARCserver 330, 370,
390, 490, 690MP, 670MP, & 690MP
(under SunOS 4.1.1)
(BASE #911119A1.11231) Sun
Microsystems Sun-4, SPARCstation, &
SPARCserver computer series (all
models) (under Solaris 2.1)
(BASE #911119A1.11231)

AlsysAlsyCOMP_072 Version 5.5.2
Sun Microsystems Sun-4, SPARCstation,
& SPARCserver computer families (under
Solaris 2.3)
(BASE #911119A1.11231)

AlsysAlsyCOMP_072, Version 5.37
Solbourne Series 5/500, /530, /600, /670,
/800 & 5E/900; and S4000 (under OS/MP
4.1)
(BASE #911119A1.11231) Sun
SPARCstation ELC, IPC & IPX;
SPARCserver 330, 370, 390, 470, 490,
630MP, 670MP & 690MP (under SunOS
4.1.1)
(BASE #911119A1.11231)

AlsysAlsyCOMP_076, Version 5.5.2
HP 9000 Series 700, all models (under
HP-UX, Version 9.1)
HP 9000/742 RT VME board (under HP-RT,
Version 1.1)
(BASE #911107W1.11227)

AlsysAlsyCOMP_083, 5.5
CompuAdd 466 (under Windows NT,
Version 3.1 + Threads)
(#931208W1.11334)

AlsysAlsyComp_084 Version 5.5.1
Sun Microsystems Sun-4, SPARCstation,
& SPARCserver computer families (under
Solaris 2.1)
Intel iSBC 386/31, iSBC 386/1xx, & iSBC
486/1xx (bare machines, using ARTK 5.3)
(BASE #910323W1.11133)

AlsysAlsyCOMP_085, V5.1.3
Any computer that executes the Intel
80386, 80486, or Pentium instruction set
(under MS-DOS 6.20 & Phar Lap TNT 6.1,
with MS-Windows 3.1)
(BASE #901102W1.11055)

AlsysAlsyCOMP_79, V5.5.2
IBM RS/6000 models M20, 220/22S/22W,
230/23S/23W, 34H, 355, 360, 365, 370,
375/37T, 55L, 570, 580, 58H, 590, 97B,
98B, & 990; CETIA models SBW 225,
2225, 2230, 334H, 3355, 3360, 3365,
3370, 3375, 5580, 558H, 5590, & 9990
(under AIX Version 3.2)
Motorola MVME101, MVME121, MVME131,
MVME133, MVME133XT, MVME135,
MVME147, MVME167, & MEN A4 (68332)
(bare machines, using ARTK 5.5.2)
(BASE #901116A1.11066)

AlsysAlsys Ada Software Development
Environment for HP 9000 Series 600, 700 &
800, Version 5.35
HP 9000 Series 800 Model 807 (under
HP-UX BLS Version A.08.08)
(#930115S1.11305) HP 9000 Series 800
Model 817 (under HP-UX BLS Version
A.08.08)
(#930115S1.11306) HP 9000 Series 800
Model 847 (under HP-UX BLS Version
A.08.08)
(#930115S1.11307) HP 9000 Series 800
Model 867 (under HP-UX BLS Version
A.08.08)
(#930115S1.11308)

AlsysAlsys Ada Software Development
Environment for HP 9000 Series 700/800,
Version 5.35
Zenith Data Systems Z-Station 433 DEh
(under SCO Unix 3.2 running SecureWare
CMW+ Version 2.2 w/MaxSix)
(#930115S1.11309)

AlsysAlsysCOMP_062 Version 5.5.2
HP 9000 Series 700, all models (under
HP-UX, Version 9.01); HP 9000 Series
800, all models (under HP-UX, Version
9.0)
HP 9000 Series 800, all models (under
HP-UX, Version 9.0)
(BASE #911107W1.11228)

AlsysAlsysCOMP_063, V5.5.2
Hewlett-Packard HP9000 Series 700
(under HP-UX 9.0)
Motorola MVME101, MVME121, MVME131,
MVME133, MVME133XT, MVME135,
MVME147, MVME167, MEN A4 (68332)
(bare machines, using ARTK 5.5.2)
(BASE #901116A1.11066)

AlsysAlysCOMP_073, Version 5.3
IBM ES/9000 Model 610 (under AIX/ESA
Version 2)
(#921126N1.11300)

AlsysAlysCOMP_17 Version 5.4.10
VAXstation 4000 Model 60 (under VMS
5.5-2)
INMOS T9000 transputer Gamma D02 on an
INMOS VME TestBoard (bare machine)
(#940826N1.11375)

AlsysAlysCOMP_69, Version 1.83-02A
Control Data 4000 series of computers
(under EP/LX 1.3)
(BASE #920730I1.11262)

AlsysTeleGen2 Ada Cross Development
System for SUN-4 to eMIPS, Version 2a
Sun-4/690 (under SunOS 5.3)
Algorithmics p-4000i (R4000) (bare machine)
(BASE #921029I1.11295)

AlsysTeleGen2 Ada Host Development
System for MacII Systems, Version 4.1
Macintosh IIx & IIfx (under A/UX 3.0
Secure)
(BASE #910721I1.11194)

AlsysTeleGen2 Ada Host Development
System for SPARCsystems, Version 2a
Sun-4/690 (under SunOS release 5.3)
(BASE #901128W1.11090)

AlsysVAX/VMS to INMOS T800 Ada
BSMART cross compiler, V5.4.8
VAXstation 4000 Model 60 (under VMS
5.5-2)
INMOS T800 transputer implemented on a
B417 TRAM (bare), using the Host running

*INMOS Iserver 1.5 for file-server support via
an INMOS B300 TCPlink*
(BASE #901118N1.11064)

**ATLAS ELEKTRONIK GmbHATLAS
ELEKTRONIK Ada Compiler VVME 1.82**
VAX 6000-410 (under VMS Version 5.2)
*ATLAS ELEKTRONIK GmbH MPR 2300
(under MOS 2300, Version 2.1)*
(#910324I1.11136)

**Concurrent Computer CorporationC3 Ada
Version 1.0v**
Concurrent Computer Corporation 8400
(MIPS R3000/3010) (under RTU Version
5.1)
(#901130W1.11109)

**Concurrent Computer CorporationC3 Ada
Version 1.1v**
Concurrent Computer Corporation 6650
with Super Lightning Floating Point (under
RTU Version 5.0C)
(#901130W1.11107) Concurrent Computer
Corporation 6650 with MC68882 Floating
Point (under RTU Version 5.0C)
(#901130W1.11110)

**Concurrent Computer CorporationC3 Ada
Version 3.0**
Concurrent Computer Corporation
MAXION Multiprocessor System with
MIPS R4400 & Internal Floating Point (all
models) (under RTU Version 6.2)
(BASE #901130W1.11109)

**Concurrent Computer CorporationC3 Ada
Version R03-00V**
Concurrent Computer Corporation
3280MPS (under OS/32 Version
R08-03.2)
(#901130W1.11108)

**Concurrent Computer CorporationC3 Ada
Versions 2.0bV4 & 2.0bV4c**
Concurrent Computer Corporation Series
7000 (MC68040) (under RTU Version
6.1A)
(BASE #901130W1.1110)

**Concurrent Computer CorporationC3 Ada,
Version 1.0**
Concurrent Computer Corporation Series
8000 (MIPS R3000/3010) (under RTU
Versions 5.1A, 5.1B & 6.0)
(BASE #901130W1.11109)

**Concurrent Computer CorporationC3 Ada,
Version 1.0v**
Concurrent Computer Corporation Series
8000 (all models) (under RTU Versions
5.1, 5.1A & 5.1B)
(BASE #901130W1.11109)

**Concurrent Computer CorporationC3 Ada,
Version 1.1**
Concurrent Computer Corporation Series
6000 (MC68030, with Super Lightning
Floating Point) & Series 5000 (MC68020,
with Lightning Floating Point) (under RTU
Versions 5.0A, 5.0B, 5.0C & 6.0)
(BASE #901130W1.11107) Concurrent
Computer Corporation Series 6000
(MC68030/MC68882) & Series 5000
(MC68020/MC68881) (under RTU
Versions 5.0A, 5.0B, 5.0C & 6.0)
(BASE #901130W1.11110)

**Concurrent Computer CorporationC3 Ada,
Version 1.1v**
Concurrent Computer Corporation Series
6000 with Super Lightning Floating Point,
and Series 5000 with Lightning Floating
Point (all models) (under RTU Version
5.0A, 5.0B & 5.0C)
(BASE #901130W1.11107) Concurrent
Computer Corporation Series 6000 with
an MC68882 fpu, and Series 5000 with an
MC68881 fpu (all models) (under RTU
Versions 5.0A, 5.0B & 5.0C)
(BASE #901130W1.11110)

**Concurrent Computer CorporationC3 Ada,
Version 1.2 & 2.0b**
Concurrent Computer Corporation Series
7000 (MC68040) (under RTU Version 6.1)
(BASE #901130W1.11110)

**Concurrent Computer CorporationC3 Ada,
Version 2.0b**
Concurrent Computer Corporation Series
8000 (MIPS R3000/3010) (under RTU
Version 6.0)
(BASE #901130W1.11109) Concurrent
Computer Corporation Series 7000
(MC68040) (under RTU Version 6.1)
(BASE #901130W1.11110)

**Concurrent Computer CorporationC3 Ada,
Version 2.0p**
Concurrent Computer Corporation Series
8000 (R3000/3010), all models (under
RTU Versions 5.1A, 5.1B & 6.0)
(BASE #901130W1.11109)

Concurrent Computer CorporationC3 Ada, Version R03-00V
Concurrent Computer Corporation Series 3200: 3200 MPS, 3203, 3205, 3210, 3220, 3230, 3250, 3230XP, 3250XP, 3230MPS, 3260MPS, Micro4, and Micro5 (under OS/32 Versions R08-03, R08-03.1 & R08-03.2)
(BASE #901130W1.11108)

Concurrent Computer CorporationC3Ada Version R03-00
Concurrent Computer Corporation System Bus Processor family of computers (under Trusted OS/32 and MTM Version R08-03.3S, and OS/32 Versions R08-03.2, R09-01.1OS/32, & R09-02)
(BASE #901130W1.11108)

Concurrent Computer CorporationC3Ada, Version 0.5
Concurrent Computer Corporation 8400 (MIPS R3000/3010) (under RTU Version 5.1)
(#900427I1.11008) Concurrent Computer Corporation 8500 (MIPS R3000/R3010) (under RTU Version 5.1)
(BASE #900427I1.11008)

Control Data Systems, Inc.NOS/VE Ada, Version 1.4
CYBER 180-930-31 (under NOS/VE, Level 826)
(#931217S1.11336)

CONVEX Computer Corporation CONVEX Ada, Version 2.0
CONVEX C220 (under ConvexOS 8.1) (#900910W1.11027) CONVEX C120, C201, C202, C210, C210i, C220, C220i, C230, C230i, C240, C3210, C3220, C3230, C3240, C3410, C3420, C3430, C3440, C3450, C3460, C3470, C3480, C3810, C3820, C3830, C3840, C3850, C3860, C3870, C3880 (under ConvexOS versions 8.1, 9.0, 9.1 & 10.0)
Each Host, self-targetted
(BASE #900910W1.11027) CONVEX C120, C201, C202, C210, C220, C230, C240, C210i, C220i & C230i (under ConvexOS, Versions 8.1 and 9.0)
(BASE #900910W1.11027)

CONVEX Computer Corporation CONVEX Ada, Version 2.1
CONVEX C120, and C2xx, C32xx, C34xx, & C38xx computer series (under ConvexOS, Versions 8.1, 9.0, 9.1, 10.0, &

10.1; and ConvexOS/Secure Versions 9.5 & 10.0)
(BASE #900910W1.11027)

Cray Research Inc.Cray Ada Compiler Release 3.1
CRAY X-MP/EA & X-MP (all models) (under UNICOS Releases 6.1 & 7.0)
(BASE #901112W1.11116) CRAY Y-MP & Y-MP EL (all models) (under UNICOS Releases 6.1 & 7.0)
(BASE #901112W1.11117) CRAY CRAY-2/4-128 (all models) (under UNICOS Releases 6.1 & 7.0)
(BASE #911006W1.11223)

Cray Research, Inc.Cray Ada Compiler 3.0
X-MP/EA (all models) (under UNICOS Release 6.1)
(BASE #901112W1.11116) CRAY Y-MP & Y-MP EL (all models) (under UNICOS Releases 6.1)
Each Host, self-targeted
(BASE #901112W1.11117) CRAY-2/4-128 (all models) (under UNICOS Release 6.1)
Each Host, self-targeted
(BASE #911006W1.11223)

Cray Research, Inc.Cray Ada Compiler 3.1
CRAY C-90 (in Y-MP mode) (under UNICOS 7C.0)
(BASE #901112W1.11117)

Cray Research, Inc.Cray Ada Compiler Release 2.0
Cray X-MP/EA (under UNICOS Release 5.0)
(#901112W1.11116) Cray Y-MP (under UNICOS Release 5.0)
(#901112W1.11117) CRAY-2/4-128 (under UNICOS Release 6.1)
(#911006W1.11223) CRAY X-MP & X-MP/EA, all models (under UNICOS Releases 5.1, 6.0 & 6.1)
Each Host, self-targeted
(BASE #901112W1.11116) CRAY Y-MP EL (under UNICOS Releases 6.0 & 6.1)
(BASE #901112W1.11117) Cray Y-MP, all models (under UNICOS Releases 5.1, 6.0 & 6.1)
Each Host, self-targeted
(BASE #901112W1.11117) CRAY-2 (all models) (under UNICOS Release 6.1)
Each Host, self-targeted
(BASE #911006W1.11223)

**DDC International A/SDACS 80386
DMS/OS Ada Compiler System, Version 4.6**
IBM PS/2 Model 80-311 (under LynxOS
386/PS2, Version 2.0A)
(#901129S1.11112)

**DDC International A/SDACS 80386 UNIX
V Ada Compiler System, Version 4.6**
ICL DRS300 (under DRS/NX, Version 3.2
(UNIX System V/386 release 3.2))
(#901129S1.11075)

**DDC International A/SDACS Sun-3/SunOS
to 68030 Bare Ada Cross Compiler System,
Version 4.6.4, MRI IEEE 695
(BASIC_MODE)**
Sun-3/50 (under SunOS Release
4.0_Export)
Motorola MVME143 board (68030/68882)
(bare machine)
(#910502S1.11159)

**DDC International A/SDACS Sun-3/SunOS
to 68030 Bare Ada Cross Compiler System,
Version 4.6.4, MRI IEEE 695
(SECURE_MODE)**
Sun-3/50 (under SunOS Release
4.0_Export)
Motorola MVME143 board (68030/68882)
(bare machine)
(#910502S1.11160)

**DDC International A/SDACS Sun3/SunOS
Native Ada Compiler System, Version 4.6**
Sun-3/60 (under SunOS, Version
4.0_Export)
(#901129S1.11076)

**DDC International A/SDACS VAX/VMS
Native Ada Compiler System, Version 4.6**
VAX 8530 (under VMS Version 5.3)
(#901129S1.11050)

**DDC International A/SDACS VAX/VMS to
68020 Bare Cross Compiler System, Version
4.6**
MicroVAX 3100 (under VMS Version 5.3)
Motorola MVME133 board (68020/68881)
(bare machine)
(#901129S1.11051)

**DDC International A/SDACS VAX/VMS to
80186 Bare Ada Cross Compiler System
with Rate Monotonic Scheduling, Version
4.6**
VAX 8530 (under VMS Version 5.3)
Intel iSBC 186/03 (bare machine)
(#901129S1.11077) DEC VAX-11,
VAXserver, VAXstation, MicroVAX, VAX

6000, VAX 8000 & VAX 9000 Series of
computers, including Raytheon Military
VAX computer model 860 (under VMS
Version 5.3)
Intel iSBC 186/03 (bare machine)
(BASE #901129S1.11077)

**DDC International A/SDACS VAX/VMS to
80186 Bare Ada Cross Compiler System,
Version 4.6**
VAX 8530 (under VMS Version 5.3)
Intel iSBC 186/03 (bare machine)
(#901129S1.11079) DEC VAX-11,
VAXserver, VAXstation, MicroVAX, VAX
6000, VAX 8000 & VAX 9000 Series of
computers, including Raytheon Military
VAX computer model 860 (under VMS
Version 5.3)
Intel iSBC 186/03 (bare machine)
(BASE #901129S1.11079)

**DDC International A/SDACS VAX/VMS to
80286 Bare Ada Cross Compiler System
with Rate Monotonic Scheduling, Version
4.6**
DEC VAX-11, VAXserver, VAXstation,
MicroVAX, VAX 6000, VAX 8000 & VAX
9000 Series of computers, including
Raytheon Military VAX computer model
860 (under VMS Version 5.3)
Intel iSBC 286/12 (bare machine)
(BASE #901129S1.11077)

**DDC International A/SDACS VAX/VMS to
80286 Bare Ada Cross Compiler System,
Version 4.6**
DEC VAX-11, VAXserver, VAXstation,
MicroVAX, VAX 6000, VAX 8000 & VAX
9000 Series of computers, including
Raytheon Military VAX computer model
860 (under VMS Version 5.3)
Intel iSBC 286/12 (bare machine)
(BASE #901129S1.11079)

**DDC International A/SDACS VAX/VMS to
80286 PM Bare Ada Cross Compiler
System with Rate Monotonic Scheduling,
Version 4.6**
DEC VAX-11, VAXserver, VAXstation,
MicroVAX, VAX 6000, VAX 8000 & VAX
9000 Series of computers, including
Raytheon Military VAX computer model
860 (under VMS Version 5.3)
Intel iSBC 286/12 in Protected Mode (bare
machine)
(BASE #901129S1.11077)

**DDC International A/SDACS VAX/VMS to
80286 PM Bare Ada Cross Compiler**

System, Version 4.6
DEC VAX-11, VAXserver, VAXstation,
MicroVAX, VAX 6000, VAX 8000 & VAX
9000 Series of computers, including
Raytheon Military VAX computer model
860 (under VMS Version 5.3)
*Intel iSBC 286/12 in Protected Mode (bare
machine)*
(BASE #901129S1.11079)

**DDC International A/SDACS VAX/VMS to
80386 Bare Ada Cross Compiler System
with Rate Monotonic Scheduling, Version
4.6**
VAX 8530 (under VMS Version 5.3)
Intel iSBC 386/21 (bare machine)
(#901129S1.11078)

**DDC International A/SDACS VAX/VMS to
80386 PM Bare Ada Cross Compiler
System, Version 4.6**
VAX 8530 (under VMS Version 5.3)
Intel iSBC 386/21 (bare machine)
(#901129S1.11074)

**DDC International A/SDACS VAX/VMS to
8086 Bare Ada Cross Compiler System with
Rate Monotonic Scheduling, Version 4.6**
DEC VAX-11, VAXserver, VAXstation,
MicroVAX, VAX 6000, VAX 8000 & VAX
9000 Series of computers, including
Raytheon Military VAX computer model
860 (under VMS Version 5.3)
Intel iSBC 86/35 (bare machine)
(BASE #901129S1.11077)

**DDC International A/SDACS VAX/VMS to
8086 Bare Ada Cross Compiler System,
Version 4.6**
DEC VAX-11, VAXserver, VAXstation,
MicroVAX, VAX 6000, VAX 8000 & VAX
9000 Series of computers, including
Raytheon Military VAX computer model
860 (under VMS Version 5.3)
Intel iSBC 86/35 (bare machine)
(BASE #901129S1.11079)

**DDC International A/SDACS VAX/VMS to
80860 Bare Ada Cross Compiler System,
Version 4.6.1**
VAX 8530 (under VMS Version 5.3)
*Tadpole Technology plc TP860M (bare
machine)*
(#910502S1.11158)

**DDC-I A/SDACS Sun SPARC/SunOS to
80486 PM Bare Ada Cross Compiler
System, Version 4.6.4**
Sun Microsystems Sun-4, SPARCserver,
SPARCclassic, and SPARCstation

computer families (under SunOS Version
4.1)
*Intel 80486 DX4 based in IBM PS/ValuePoint
desktop (operated as a bare machine)*
(BASE #940325S1/11350)

**DDC-I A/SDACS Sun-3/SunOS to 68030
Bare Ada Cross Compiler System, Version
4.6.9j, MRI IEEE 695 (BASIC-MODE)**
Sun Microsystems Sun-3 computer
families (under SunOS Version 4.0)
*Motorola MVME143 (68030/68882) board
(bare machine)*
(BASE #910502S1.11159)

**DDC-I A/SDACS Sun-3/SunOS to 68030
Bare Ada Cross Compiler System, Version
4.6.9j, MRI IEEE 695 (SECURE_MODE)**
Sun Microsystems Sun-3 computer
families (under SunOS Version 4.0)
*Motorola MVME143 (68030/68882) board
(bare machine)*
(BASE #910502S1.11160)

**DDC-I, Inc.DACS DECstation/ULTRIX to
MIPS R3000 Bare Ada Cross Compiler
System, Release 2.1-16**
DECstation 3100 (under ULTRIX Version
4.0)
*Integrated Device Technology IDT7RS301
R3000/R3010 Board (bare machine)*
(#920805S1.11264)

**DDC-I, Inc.DACS MIPS R3000 bare Ada
Cross Compiler System, Version 4.7.1**
Sun SPARCstation IPX (under SunOS,
Release 4.1.3)
*DACS Sun SPARC/SunOS to MIPS R3000
Bare Instruction Set Architecture Simulator,
Version 4.7.1, executing on the Host (bare
machine simulation)*
(#931119S1.11332)

**DDC-I, Inc.DACS MIPS RISC/os to MIPS
R3000 Bare Ada Cross Compiler System,
Release 2.1-16**
MIPS M/120-5 (under RISC/os Version
4.50)
*Lockheed Sanders STAR MVP R3000/R3010
Board (bare machine)*
(#920805S1.11263)

**DDC-I, Inc.DACS Sun SPARC/Solaris
Native Ada Compiler System, Version 4.6.2**
Sun SPARCclassic (under Solaris,
Release 2.1)
(#940325S1.11354)

DDC-I, Inc.DACS Sun SPARC/Solaris to
80186 Bare Ada Cross Compiler System w/
Rate Monotonic Scheduling, 4.6.4
Sun SPARCclassic (under Solaris,
Release 2.1)
Intel iSBC 186/100 (bare machine)
(#940325S1.11344)

DDC-I, Inc.DACS Sun SPARC/Solaris to
80186 Bare Ada Cross Compiler System,
Version 4.6.4
Sun SPARCclassic (under Solaris,
Release 2.1)
Intel iSBC 186/100 (bare machine)
(#940325S1.11343)

DDC-I, Inc.DACS Sun SPARC/Solaris to
80386 PM Bare Ada Compiler System w/
Rate Monotonic Scheduling, 4.6.4
Sun SPARCclassic (under Solaris,
Release 2.1)
Intel iSBC 386/116 (bare machine)
(#940325S1.11349)

DDC-I, Inc.DACS Sun SPARC/Solaris to
80386 PM Bare Ada Cross Compiler
System, Version 4.6.4
Sun SPARCclassic (under Solaris,
Release 2.1)
Intel iSBC 386/116 (bare machine)
(#940325S1.11348)

DDC-I, Inc.DACS Sun SPARC/Solaris to
Pentium PM Bare Ada Cross Compiler Sys.
w/Rate Monotonic Scheduling, 4.6.4
Sun SPARCclassic (under Solaris,
Release 2.1)
*Intel Xpress Desktop (product #
XBASE6E4F-B, with Pentium cpu), operating
as a bare machine (bare machine)*
(#940325S1.11353)

DDC-I, Inc.DACS Sun SPARC/Solaris to
Pentium PM Bare Ada Cross Compiler
System, Version 4.6.4
Sun SPARCclassic (under Solaris,
Release 2.1)
*Intel Xpress Desktop (product #
XBASE6E4F-B, with Pentium cpu), operating
as a bare machine (bare machine)*
(#940325S1.11352)

DDC-I, Inc.DACS Sun SPARC/SunOS
Native Ada Compiler System, Version 4.6.1
SPARCstation 2 (under SunOS, Version
4.1.1)
(#920805S1.11265)

DDC-I, Inc.DACS Sun SPARC/SunOS to
680x0 Bare Ada Cross Compiler System
(BASIC_MODE), Version 4.6.9
Sun SPARCstation IPX (under SunOS,
Release 4.1.1)
Lynwood j435TU (68030) (bare machine)
(#940325S1.11346)

DDC-I, Inc.DACS Sun SPARC/SunOS to
680x0 Bare Ada Cross Compiler System
(SECURE_MODE), Version 4.6.9
Sun SPARCstation IPX (under SunOS,
Release 4.1.1)
Lynwood j435TU (68030) (bare machine)
(#940325S1.11347)

DDC-I, Inc.DACS Sun SPARC/SunOS to
680x0 Bare Ada Cross Compiler System,
Version 4.6.9
Sun SPARCstation IPX (under SunOS,
Release 4.1.1)
*Motorola MVME143 (68030/68882) (bare
machine)*
(#940325S1.11345)

DDC-I, Inc.DACS Sun SPARC/SunOS to
80186 Bare Ada Cross Compiler System w/
Rate Monotonic Scheduling, 4.6.4
Sun SPARCstation IPX (under SunOS,
Release 4.1.2)
Intel iSBC 186/100 (bare machine)
(#940325S1.11342)

DDC-I, Inc.DACS Sun SPARC/SunOS to
80186 Bare Ada Cross Compiler System,
Version 4.6.4
Sun SPARCstation IPX (under SunOS,
Release 4.1.2)
Intel iSBC 186/100 (bare machine)
(#940325S1.11341)

DDC-I, Inc.DACS Sun SPARC/SunOS to
80386 PM bare Ada Cross Compiler
System, Version 4.6.4
Sun SPARCstation 1+ (under SunOS,
Release 4.1.1)
Intel iSBC 386/116 (bare machine)
(#931119S1.11331)

DDC-I, Inc.DACS Sun SPARC/SunOS to
Pentium PM Bare Ada Cross Compiler
System w/Rate Monotonic Scheduling, 4.6.4
Sun SPARCstation IPX (under SunOS,
Release 4.1.2)
*Intel Xpress Desktop (product #
XBASE6E4F-B, with Pentium cpu), operating
as a bare machine (bare machine)*
(#940325S1.11351)

DDC-I, Inc.DACS Sun SPARC/SunOS to Pentium PM Bare Ada Cross Compiler System, Version 4.6.4
Sun SPARCstation IPX (under SunOS, Release 4.1.2)
Intel Xpress Desktop (product # XBASE6E4F-B, with Pentium cpu), operating as a bare machine (bare machine)
(#940325S1.11350)

DDC-I, Inc.DACS VAX/VMS to 80486 PM Bare Ada Cross Compiler System, Version 4.6
VAX 8530 (under VMS Version 5.3)
Intel iSBC 486/125 (bare machine)
(BASE #901129S1.11074)

DDC-Inter, Inc.InterACT Ada 1750A Compiler System, Release 3.5
MicroVAX 3100 Cluster (under VMS 5.2)
InterACT MIL-STD-1750A Instruction Set Architecture Simulator Release 2.3 (bare machine simulation)
(#910705S1.11191)

DDC-Inter, Inc.InterACT Ada MIPS Cross-Compiler System, Release 2.0
MicroVAX 3100 Cluster (under VMS 5.2)
Lockheed Sanders STAR MVP R3000/R3010 Board (bare machine)
(#910705S1.11192)

DDC-Inter, Inc.InterACT Ada MIPS Cross-Compiler System, Release 2.1
MicroVAX 3100 Cluster (under VMS 5.2)
Lockheed Sanders STAR MVP R3000/R3010 Board (bare machine)
(BASE #910705S1.11192)

DECS Ltd.VME Ada Compiler VA3.25
ICL Series 39 Level 80 (all models) (under VME with VMEB Environment Option Version SV293)
ICL Series 39 Level 80 & Series 39 SX Processor families (under VME with VMEB Environment Option Version SV293)
(BASE #921008N1.11293)

DESC Ltd.VME Ada Compiler VA3.25
ICL Series 39 Level 80 (under VME with VMEB Environment Option Version SV292)
(BASE #921008N1.11293)

DESC Ltd.VME Ada Compiler VA3.20
ICL Series 39 Level 80 (under VME with VMEB Environment Option Version SV292)
(BASE #921008N1.11293)

Digital Equipment CorporationDEC Ada for DEC OSF/1 AXP Systems, Version 3.1
DEC 3000 Model 400 (under DEC OSF/1, Version 1.3)
(#931029S1.11330) DEC 2000 Sever, 3000 Workstation and Server models, 4000, 7000, & 10000 series of AXP computers (under DEC OSF/1 Version 1.3)
(BASE #931029S1.11330)

Digital Equipment CorporationDEC Ada for DEC OSF/1 AXP Systems, Version 3.2
DEC 3000 Model 400 AXP Workstation (under DEC OSF/1, Version 3.0 with patch OSFV30-010-1)
(#940929S1.11378) DEC 2000 Server, 3000 Workstation and Server models, 4000, 7000, & 10000 series of AXP computers (under DEC OSF/1 Version 3.0 with patch OSFV30-010-1)
(BASE #940929S1.11378)

Digital Equipment CorporationDEC Ada for OpenVMS AXP Systems, Version 3.0-5
DEC 3000 Model 400 (under OpenVMS AXP Operating System, Version 1.0)
(#930319S1.11315) DEC 3000 Workstation and Server models, 4000, 7000, & 10000 series of AXP computers (under OpenVMS Version 1.0)
(BASE #930319S1.11315)

Digital Equipment CorporationDEC Ada for OpenVMS AXP Systems, Version 3.0A-7
DEC 2000 Server, 3000 Workstation and Server models, 4000, 7000, & 10000 series of AXP computers (as supported) (under OpenVMS AXP Operation System Version 1.5)
(BASE #930319S1.11315)

Digital Equipment CorporationDEC Ada for OpenVMS AXP Systems, Version 3.0A-9
VAXft, VAX 4000, 6000, 8000, 9000, & 10000; MicroVAX II, 2000, & 3000; VAXstation II, 2000, 3000, 4000; VAXserver 3000, 4000, & 6000; and VAX-11 series of computers (as supported) (under OpenVMS VAX Operating System Version 5.5)
(BASE #930319S1.11316)

Digital Equipment CorporationDEC Ada for OpenVMS VAX Systems, Version 3.0-7
VAXstation 4000 Model 60 (under VMS Version 5.5)
(#930319S1.11316) VAXstation 4000 Model 60 (under VMS Version 5.5)
VAXstation 3100 Model 48 (under VAXELN Version 4.4, using VAXELN Ada Version 2.2)
(#930319S1.11317) VAXft, VAX 4000, 6000, 8000, 9000, & 10000; MicroVAX II, 2000, & 3000; VAXstation II, 2000, 3000, 4000; VAXserver 3000, 4000, & 6000 series of computers (as supported) (under VMS Version 5.4 & 5.5)
(BASE #930319S1.11316) VAXft, VAX 4000, 6000, 8000, 9000, & 10000; MicroVAX II, 2000, & 3000; VAXstation II, 2000, 3000, 4000; VAXserver 3000, 4000, & 6000 series of computers (as supported) (under VMS Version 5.4 & 5.5)
VAX 4000, 6000, & 9000; MicroVAX II, 2000, 3000; KA620-BA, KAV30 VME SBC, KA800-M; rtVAX 300, 1000, 3000, 4000, 6000, 9000, & rtVAXstation 3100; IVAX 620 & 630; VAXstation II, 2000, 3000, & 4000; VAXserver 3000, 4000, & 6000 series of computers (as supported) (under VAXELN Version 4.4, using VAXELN Ada Version 2.2)
(BASE #930319S1.11317)

Digital Equipment CorporationDEC Ada, Version 1.0
DECstation 5000 Model 200 (under ULTRIX 4.2)
(#911025S1.11226) DECstation 2100, 3100, 3100s, 5000 Models 120/125, 120/125CX, 120/125PXG, 120/125PXG TURBO, 200, 200CX, 200PX, 200PXG, 200PXG TURBO; and DECsystem 3100, 5000 Model 200, 5100, 5400, 5500, 5810, 5820, 5830 & 5840 (under ULTRIX Versions 4.0, 4.1 & 4.2)
(BASE #911025S1.11226) DEC DECstation 2100, 3100, & 5000, and DECsystem 5000, 5100, 5400, 5500, 5800, & 5900 series of computers (under ULTRIX Versions 4.0, 4.1, 4.2, & 4.2A)
(BASE #911025S1.11226)

Digital Equipment CorporationDEC Ada, Version 1.1
DECstation 2100, 3100, & 5000; and DECsystem 3100, 5000, 5100, 5400, 5500, 5810, 5820, 5840, & 5900 series of computers (under Ultrix Version 4.2)
(BASE #911025S1.11226)

Digital Equipment CorporationVAX Ada Version 2.2
DEC VAX-11, VAXserver, VAXstation, VAXft, MicroVAX, VAX 4000, VAX 6000, VAX 8000 & VAX 9000 Series of computers (as supported); Ratheon Military VAX Computer Model 860; and Norden MilVAX Computer Model MilVAX II (under VMS Version 5.4)
(BASE #901109S1.11053) DEC VAX-11, VAXserver, VAXstation, VAXft, MicroVAX, VAX 4000, VAX 6000, VAX 8000 & VAX 9000 Series of computers (as supported); Ratheon Military VAX Computer Model 860; and Norden MilVAX Computer Model MilVAX II (under VMS Version 5.4)
VAX 4000 Models 200 & 300; VAX 6000 Series 200, 300 & 400; VAX 8200, 8250, 8500, 8530, 8550, 8700, 8800 & 8810; VAX-11/730 & /750; MicroVAX II, 2000, 3100, 3300, 3400, 3500, 3600, 3800 & 3900; VAXstation 2000, 3100, 3150, 3200, 3500 & II/GPX; VAXserver 3100, 3300, 3400, 3500, 3600, 3800, 3900; VAXserver 4000-300; VAXserver 6000 Models 210, 220, 310, 320, 410 & 420; Ratheon Military VAX Computer Models 810 & 860; Norden MilVAX Computer Model MilVAX II, IVAX 620 & 630; VAX RTA; KA620-BA & KA800-M; rtVAX 300, 1000, 3200, 3300, 3305, 3400, 3500, 3600, 3800, 4000 Model 300, 8550, 8700, rtVAX 6000 Models 200, 300 & 400 Series and rtVAXstation 3100 Models 30 & 38 (under VAXELN Version 4.2, using VAXELN Ada Version 2.2)
(BASE #901109S1.11054) VAX 6000 Model 200, 300 & 400 Series; VAX 8200, 8250, 8300, 8350, 8500, 8530, 8550, 8600, 8650, 8700, 8800, 8810, 8820, 8830, 8840, 8842, 8974 & 8978; VAX-11/730, /750, /780, /785; MicroVAX II, 2000, 3100, 3300, 3400, 3500, 3600, 3800 & 3900; VAXstation II, 2000, 3100 series, 3200, 3500, 3520, 3540 & 8000; VAXserver 3100, 3300, 3400, 3500, 3600, 3602, 3800, 3900; VAXserver 6000-310, 6000-410 & 6000-420; Ratheon Military VAX Computer Model 860 (under VMS Version 5.4)
VAX 6000 Model 200, 300 & 400 Series; VAX 8200, 8250, 8500, 8530, 8550, 8700, 8800 & 8810; VAX-11/730 & /750; MicroVAX II, 2000, 3100, 3300, 3400, 3500, 3600, 3800 & 3900; VAXstation 2000, 3100, 3150, 3200, 3500 & II/GPX; VAXserver 3100, 3300, 3400, 3500, 3600, 3602, 3800, 3900; VAXserver 6000 Models 210 220, 310, 320, 410 & 420; Ratheon Military VAX Computer Models 810 & 860; Norden Systems: Mil Vax II, IVAX 620 & 630; VAX RTA; KA620-BA, rtVAX 300,

1000, 3200, 3300, 3305, 3400, 3500, 3600,
3800, 8550, 8700, rtVAX 6000 Model 200, 300
& 400 Series & rtVAXstation 3100 Models 30
& 38 (under VAXELN Version 4.1 using
VAXELN Ada Version 2.2)
(BASE #901109S1.11054)

**Digital Equipment CorporationVAX Ada
Version 2.3**
All VAX, MicroVAX, VAXstation,
VAXserver series of computers (as
supported) (under VMS Versions 5.4 &
5.5)
(BASE #901109S1.11053) All VAX,
MicroVAX, VAXstation, VAXserver series
of computers (as supported) (under VMS
Versions 5.4 & 5.5)
VAX 4000, 6000, & 9000 series of computers;
MicroVAX II, 2000, & 3000 series of
computers; VAXstation II, 2000, 3000, & 4000
series of computers; VAXserver 3000, 4000, &
6000 series of computers; IVAX 620 & 630;
KA620-BA, KA800-M, & KAV30 VME SBC;
rtVAX 300, 1000, 3000, 4000, 6000, & 9000
series of computers; and rtVAXstation 3100
series of computers; (under VAXELN Version
4.4, using VAXELN Ada Version 2.2)
(BASE #901109S1.11054)

**Digital Equipment CorporationVAX Ada,
Version 2.2**
VAX 8800 (under VMS Version 5.4)
(#901109S1.11053) VAX 8800 (under VMS
Version 5.4)
MicroVAX II (under VAXELN Version 4.1,
using VAXELN Ada Version 2.2)
(#901109S1.11054)

**Dowty Maritime LimitedTeleGen2 Ada
Cross Development System, Version 3.2 for
VAX/VMS to 386**
DEC VAX-11, MicroVAX, VAXserver,
VAXstation, VAXft; and VAX 4000, 6000,
7000, 8000, 9000, & 10000 series of
computers (under VMS 5.5-2)
All members of the Intel iSBC 386 & iSBC 486
model series (bare machines, using
TeleAda-EXEC 3.2)
(BASE #910325I1.11139)

**E-Systems/ECI DivisionTolerant Ada
Development System, Version 6.0**
Tolerant Eternity (under TX, 5.4.0)
(#901003W1.11039)

**EDS Defence LimitedXD Ada CPU32
Version 1.3-13**
MicroVAX 3100 (under VMS 6.0)
Motorla M68340EVS Evaluation System
(MC68340) CPU32, with 128K additional

RAM & MC68881 fpu (bare machine)
(BASE #901007N1.11042)

**EDS Defence LimitedXD Ada
CPU32/MC68332 Version 1.3-15**
DECstation 3100 (under ULTRIX 3.1)
(BASE #901007N1.11042) MicroVAX 3100
(under VMS 6.0)
Motorla M68332EVS Evaluation System
(MC68332) CPU32, with 128K additional
RAM & MC68881 fpu (bare machine)
(BASE #901007N1.11042)

**EDS Defence LimitedXD Ada MC68000
V1.3-12**
MicroVAX 3100 (under VMS 6.0)
Motorola MC68000 on an MVME117-3FP
MPU VME module using an MC68881 fpu
(bare machine)
(BASE #910314N1.11134)

**EDS Defence LimitedXD Ada MC68020
Version 1.3-10**
MicroVAX 3100 (under VMS 6.0)
Motorola MVME133XT board (68020/68882)
(BASE #901007N1.11042)

**EDS Defence LimitedXD Ada
MC68020/ARTX V1.3-23**
MicroVAX 3100 (under VMS 6.0)
Motorola MVME147S-1 (68030) (bare
machine, using ARTX Real Time Executive)
(BASE #910911N1.11199)

**EDS Defence LimitedXD Ada MC68040
V1.3-37**
MicroVAX 3100 (under VMS 6.0)
Motorola MVME167 MPU VMEmodule
(68040) (bare machine)
(BASE #911128N1.11230)

**EDS Defence Ltd.XD Ada MC68020/EFA
Version 1.3-28**
MicroVAX 3100 (under VMS 6.0)
Motorola MVME135-1 board (68020/68881)
(bare machine)
(BASE #901007N1.11042)

**EDS Defence Ltd.XD Ada MC68040/ARTX
Version 1.3-24**
MicroVAX 3100 (under VMS 6.0)
Motorola MVME167 (68040) (bare machine,
using ARTX Real Time Executive)
(BASE #921112N1.11297)

**EDS Defense LimitedXD Ada
CPU32/MC68332 Version 1.3-15**
MicroVAX 3100 (under VMS 6.0)
Motorola M68332EVS Evaluation System
(MC68332) CPU32, with 128K additional

RAM & MC68881 fpu (bare machine)
(BASE #901007N1.11042)

**EDS Defense LimitedXD Ada
MC68000/EFA V1.3-27**
MicroVAX 3100 (under VMS 6.0)
*Motorola MC68000 on an MVME117-3FP
MPU VME module using an MC68881 fpu
(bare machine)*
(BASE #910314N1.11134)

**EDS Defense LimitedXD Ada MC68020/
ARTX V1.3-23**
MicroVAX 3100 (under VMS 6.0)
*Motorola MVME147S-1 (680 30) (bare
machine, using ARTX Real Time Executive)*
(BASE # 910911N1.11199)

**EDS-Scicon Defence LimitedXD Ada
MC68040/ARTX Version 1.2**
Local Area VAX Cluster (comprising
VAXserver 3600, MicroVAX 2000 (2), &
MicroVAX II machines) (under VMS 5.5)
Motorola MVME167 (68040) (bare machine)
(#921112N1.11297)

**Encore Computer CorporationParallel Ada
Development System, Revision 1.0**
Encore 91 Series Model 91-0340 (under
UMAX 3.0)
(#910130W1.11114) Encore 91 Series
Model 91-0340 (under UMAX 3.0)
*Encore 91 Series Model 91-0430 (under
uMPX 1.0)*
(#910130W1.11115) Encore 91 Series, all
models (under UMAX 3.0)
(BASE #910130W1.11114) Encore 91
Series, all models (under UMAX 3.0)
*Encore 91 Series, all models (under
microMPX 1.0)*
(BASE #910130W1.11115)

**Encore Computer CorporationParallel Ada
Development System, Revision 2.0**
Encore 91, 93, & 94 Series, all models
(under UMAX 3.0)
(BASE #910130W1.11114) Encore 91
Series, all models (under UMAX 3.0)
*Encore 91 Series, all models (under
microMPX 1.0 & microARTE 1.0)*
(BASE #910130W1.11115)

**Encore Computer CorporationParallel Ada
Development System, Revision 2.2.0**
Encore 91 Series, all models (under
UMAX 3.0.X)
(BASE #910130W1.11114) Encore 93
Series, all models (under UMAX 3.1.X)
(BASE #910130W1.11114) Encore Infinity
90 Series, all models (under UMAX 3.0.X)
(BASE #910130W1.11114) Encore 91
Series, all models (under UMAX 3.0.X)
(BASE #910130W1.11115) Encore 93
Series, all models (under UMAX 3.1.X)
(BASE #910130W1.11115)

**Encore Computer CorporationParallel Ada
Development System, Revision 2.3.0**
Encore 91 Series, all models (under
UMAX 3.0.X)
(BASE #910130W1.11114) Encore Infinity
90 Series, all models (under UNMAX
3.0.X)
(BASE #910130W1.11114) Encore Infinity
R/T series, all models (under UMAX 3.0.X)
(BASE #910130W1.11114) Encore 91
Series, all models (under UMAX 3.0.X)
(BASE #910130W1.11115) Encore Infinity
R/T series, all models (under UMAX 3.0.X)
(BASE #910130W1.11115)

**Green Hills Software, Inc.Green Hills
Optimizing Ada Compiler, 1.8.7**
SPARCstation 10 (under SunOS, Release
4.1.3)
(#940223W1.11338) SPARCstation 10
(under SunOS, Release 4.1.3)
*Force CPU-40 (68040) (bare machine using
VxWorks, 5.1)*
(#940223W1.11339)

Green Valley SoftwareC_Ada, Version 1.1
ZENY 386 (under UNIX System V/386,
Release 3.2)
(#930927S1.11328)

**GSE Gesellschaft fur Software-Engineering
Meridian Ada, Version 4.1**
MIPS M/120 RISComputer (under UMIPS
4.51)
(#910711W1.11180) IBM RISC System
6000/520 (under AIX Version 3)
(#910711W1.11182) HP 9000 Series 400
Model 400T (under HP-UX 7.03)
(#910711W1.11184) Concurrent Computer
Corporation M6000 Model 6450 (under
RTU 5.0C)
(#910711W1.11186) Concurrent Computer
Corporation M8000 Model 8500 (under

RTU 5.1A)
(#910711W1.11187) Data General AViiON
400 Model 402 (under DG/UX 4.31)
(#910711W1.11188) HP 9000 Series 700
Model 720 (under HP-UX 8.01)
(#910711W1.11190)

**Harris CorporationHarris Ada Compiler,
version 6.2**
Harris NH-4400, NH-4800, & NH-5800
(under CX/UX 6.1, CX/RT 6.1, CX/SX 6.1,
& CX/SX 6.2)
(BASE #900918W1.11028)

**Harris CorporationComputer Systems
Division Harris Ada 5.1**
Harris NH-4400 (under CX/UX 5.1)
(#900918W1.11028) 1.1
(#900918W1.11029) Harris NH-4400 (under
CX/UX 5.1, CX/RT 5.1, OR CX/SX 5.1)
(BASE #900918W1.11028) Harris NH-3800
(under CX/UX 5.1)
(BASE #900918W1.11029)

**Harris CorporationComputer Systems
Division Harris Ada 5.1.1**
Harris NH-4400 & NH-4800 (under CX/UX
5.3, CX/RT 5.3 & CX/SX 5.3)
(BASE #900918W1.11028) NH-1200,
NH-3400 & NH-3800 (under CX/UX 5.2,
CX/RT 5.2 & CX/SX 5.2)
(BASE #900918W1.11029)

**Harris CorporationComputer Systems
Division Harris Ada Compiler 5.1.1**
NH-4400 & NH-4800 (under CX/UX 6.1,
CX/RT 6.1, & CX/SX 6.1)
(BASE #900918W1.11028) NH-4400,
NH-4800, & NH-5800 (under CX/UX 6.2,
CX/RT 6.2, & CX/SX 6.2)
(BASE #900918W1.11028) Harris NH-1200,
NH-3400 & NH-3800 (under CX/UX 5.3,
CX/RT 5.3 & CX/SX 5.3)
(BASE #900918W1.11029)

**Harris CorporationComputer Systems
Division Harris Ada Compiler, Version 5.1**
Harris NH-4400 (under CX/UX 5.2, CX/RT
5.2 & CX/SX 5.2)
(BASE #900918W1.11028) Harris NH-1200,
NH-3400 & NH-3800 (under CX/UX 5.1,
CX/RT 5.1, OR CX/SX 5.1)
(BASE #900918W1.11029)

**Harris CorporationComputer Systems
Division Harris Ada Compiler, version 6.2**
Harris NH-4400, NH-4800, & NH-5800
(under CX/UX 6.2 & CX/RT 6.2)
(BASE #900918W1.11028)

**Harris CorporationComputer Systems
Division Harris Ada Compiler, version 7.1**
Harris NH-4400, NH-4800, & NH-5800
(under CX/UX 7.1 & CX/RT 7.1)
(BASE #900918W1.11028)

**Harris CorporationComputer Systems
Division Harris Ada version 5.2**
Harris NH-4400, -4800, & -5800 (under
CX/UX 6.2, CX/RT 6.2, & CX/SX 6.2)
Harris NH-4400, NH-4800, & NH-5800
(Harris Ada runtime System & ARMS Runtime
System)
(BASE #900918W1.11028)

**Harris CorporationComputer Systems
Divison Harris Ada Compiler, Version 7.**
Harris NH-4400, NH-4800, & NH-5800
(under CX/UX 7.1 & CX/RT 7.1)
(BASE #900918W1.11028)

**Hewlett-Packard Co.Apollo Systems
Division Domain Ada V6.0m**
Harris NH-1200, NH-3400, & NH-3800
(under CX/UX 6.1, CX/RT 6.1, & CX/SX
6.1)
(#910411W1.11137)

**Hewlett-Packard Co.Apollo Systems
Division Domain Ada V6.0p**
DN4500 (under Domain/OS SR10.3)
(#910411W1.11138)

**Hewlett-Packard CompanyHP 9000 Series
300 Ada Compiler, Version 5.35**
DN10000 (under Domain/OS SR10.3.p)
(#901022W1.11049) HP 9000 Series 300
Model 370 (under HP-UX, Version
A.07.00)
(BASE #901022W1.11049)

**Hewlett-Packard CompanyHP 9000 Series
300 Ada Compiler, Version 5.35t**
HP 9000 Series 300 & 400, all models
(under HP-UX, Version A.B7.03)
(BASE #901022W1.11049)

**IBM Canada, Ltd. (now OC Systems)OCS
Legacy Ada/370 MVS Version 2.0**
RISC System/6000, model 7013-520
(under AIX 3.2)
(BASE #910612W1.11169)

**IBM Canada, Ltd. (now OC Systems)OCS
Legacy Ada/6000 Version 1.4**
IBM 937x, 43xx, 308x, 3090, & ES/9000
processors (under MVS/ESA 3.1.0, 4.1.0,
& 4.3.0; & MVS/SP XA 2.2)
(BASE #920121W1.11234)

IBM Canada, Ltd.AIX Ada/6000 Internal Development Version
RISC System/6000 models 7013-320, -520, -530, -540, -550, -730, & -930 (under AIX 3.1 & 3.2)
(#920121W1.11234)

IBM Canada, Ltd.AIX Ada/6000 Release 2, Preliminary Version
HP 9000 Series 300 & 400, all Models (under HP-UX, Versions A.B7.00 (release 7.0), A.B7.03 (release 7.3), A.B7.05 (release 7.5) & A.B8.00 (release 8.0), as supported)
(#901127W1.11085)

IBM Canada, Ltd.AIX Ada/6000 Release 2.0
RISC System/6000 model 7013-530 (under AIX 3.1)
(BASE #901127W1.11085)

IBM Canada, Ltd.AIX Ada/6000 Release 2.2
RISC System/6000 models 7013-320, -520, -530, -540, -550, -730 & -930 (under AIX 3.1)
(BASE #901127W1.11085)

IBM Canada, Ltd.AIX Ada/6000 Release 3.0
RISC System/6000 model 7012-320 (under AIX 3.2)
(BASE #920121W1.11234)

IBM Canada, Ltd.XL Ada/6000 Internal Development Version
RISC System/6000, all models (under AIX 3.2)
(#921119W1.11299)

Intel CorporationiPSC/860 Ada Release 6.1.0(E) Unix System V/860 Release 4 Version 3, 312425-0001
IBM RS/6000 series (all models) (under AIX Version 3.2)
Intel iPSC/860 (under Ada-NX, Release 3.3.1)
(#920513W1.11255)

Intermetrics Inc.RISCAE Honeywell RH32-targeted Ada Compiler, 1.0
VAXstation 4000 (under VMS 5.5)
RISCAE Honeywell RH32 Simulator (bare machine simulation, executing on the Host)
(#930901W1.11322)

Intermetrics Inc.RISCAE TRW RH32-targeted Ada Compiler, 1.0
Amdahl 5890/180E (under MVS/XA Release 2.2)
RISCAE TRW RH32 Simulator (bare machine simulation, executing on the Host)
(#930901W1.11321)

IntermetricsIntermetrics MVS Ada Compiler, Version 8.1
Intel i860 Station (under Unix System V/860, Version 4)
(BASE #910622W1.11170)

Intermetrics, Inc.Intermetrics MVS Ada Compiler, Version 7.0
IBM 3083 (under UTS 580 Release 1.2.3)
(#910622W1.11170)

Intermetrics, Inc.UTS Ada Compiler, Version 302.03
VAXstation 4000 (under VMS 5.5)
(#910425W1.11141)

International Business Machines Corporation IBM Ada/370 MVS Compiler, Version 1.4.0
IBM 4381 (under MVS/ESA 3.1.0)
IBM 937x, 43xx, 308x 8090, & ES/9000 processors (under same OS as Host)
(BASE #910612W1.11169)

International Business Machines Corporation IBM Ada/370, Version 1.1.0
Amdahl 5890/180E (under MVS/XA Release 2.2)
(#901128W1.11091) IBM 3090 (under VM/SP Release 6.0 HPO 60)
(#901128W1.11092) IBM 3083 (under VM/SP HPO Release 5.0)
(BASE #901128W1.11091) IBM 3084 (under VM/ESA Release 1.0 370 Feature)
(BASE #901128W1.11091) IBM 3090 (under VM/ESA Release 1.0 ESA Feature)
(BASE #901128W1.11091) IBM 3090 (under VM/XA Release 2.1)
(BASE #901128W1.11091) IBM 4381 (under MVS/XA Release 3.8)
(BASE #901128W1.11092)

International Business Machines Corporation

IBM Ada/370, Version 1.2.0 & 1.3.0
IBM 4381 (under MVS/ESA Release 3.1)
IBM 937x, 43xx, 308x, 3090 & ES/9000
processors (under MVS/SP XA 2.2)
(BASE #910612W1.11169) IBM 3083
(under VM/SP HPO Release 5.0)
IBM 937x, 43xx, 308x, 3090 & ES/9000
processors (under VM/SP HPO 6.0)
(BASE #910612W1.11168) IBM 3084
(under VM/ESA 1.1.0 (370 Feature))
IBM 937x, 43xx, 308x, 3090 & ES/9000
processors (under VM/ESA 1.1.0 (ESA
Feature))
(BASE #910612W1.11168) IBM 3090
(under VM/ESA 1.1.0 (ESA Feature))
IBM 937x, 43xx, 308x, 3090 & ES/9000
processors (under VM/ESA 1.1.1)
(BASE #910612W1.11168) IBM 3090
(under VM/SP HPO 6.0)
IBM 937x, 43xx, 308x, 3090 & ES/9000
processors (under VM/XA 2.1)
(BASE #910612W1.11168) IBM 3090
(under VM/XA 2.1)
IBM 937x, 43xx, 308x, 3090 & ES/9000
processors (under VM/ESA 1.1.0 (370
Feature)))
(BASE #910612W1.11168) IBM 3090
(under MVS/ESA Release 4.1.0)
IBM 937x, 43xx, 308x, 3090 & ES/9000
processors (MVS/ESA Release 4.2.0)
(BASE #910612W1.11169) IBM 3090
(under MVS/SP XA 2.2)
IBM 937x, 43xx, 308x, 3090 & ES/9000
processors (MVS/ESA Release 4.1.0)
(BASE #910612W1.11169)

International Business Machines Corporation
IBM Ada/370, Version 1.2.0 (optimized)
IBM 3090 (under MVS/ESA Release 4.1)
(#910612W1.11166) IBM 3083 (under
VM/SP HPO Release 5.0)
(#910612W1.11167)

International Business Machines Corporation
IBM Ada/370, Version 1.2.0 (unoptimized)
IBM 4381 (under MVS/ESA Release 3.1)
(#910612W1.11168) IBM 3084 (under
VM/ESA 1.1.0(370 Feature)); IBM 3090
(under VM/ESA 1.1.0(ESA Feature),
VM/ESA 1.1.1, VM/XA 2.1, & VM/SP HPO
5.0 & 6.0)
(#910612W1.11169)

International Business Machines Corporation

IBM Ada/370, Version 1.3.0
IBM 3090 (under MVS/ESA 4.1.0 & 4.2.0)
IBM 937x, 43xx, 308x, 3090, & ES/9000
computers (under same OS as Host)
(BASE #910612W1.11169) IBM 3090
(under MVS/ESA Release 4.2.0)
IBM 937x, 43xx, 308x, 3090, & ES/9000
computers (under same OS as Host)
(BASE #910612W1.11169)

International Business Machines Corporation
IBM Ada/370, VM/CMS Ada Compiler,
Version 1.4.0
IBM 3090 (under VM/ESA 1.1.1)
IBM 937x, 43xx, 308x 8090, & ES/9000
processors (under same OS as Host)
(BASE #910612W1.11168)

International Computers LimitedVME Ada
Compiler VA3,00
IBM 3090 (under MVS/ESA 3.1.0, 4.1.0, &
4.2.0, & MVS/SP XA 2.2)
(#911003N1.11222)

International Computers LimitedVME Ada
Compiler VA3.10
ICL Series 39 Level 80 (under VME with
VMEB Environment Option Version
SV291)
(#921008N1.11293)

Irvine Compiler CorporationICC Ada for
HP 9000 Series 300/400, Version 7.4
HP 9000 Model 400 (under HP-UX
Release 7.03)
(BASE #910510W1.11147)

Irvine Compiler CorporationICC Ada for
HP 9000 Series 700/800 7.4
HP 9000 Series 700 & 800, all Models
(under HP-UX Version A.B8.05 (release
8.05))
(BASE #910510W1.11145)

Irvine Compiler CorporationICC Ada for
HP 9000 Series 700/800, Version 7.4
HP 9000 Model 720 (under HP-UX
Release 8.01)
(BASE #910510W1.11145)

Irvine Compiler CorporationICC Ada for
i960MC 7.4
DEC VAX-11, VAXserver, VAXstation,
MicroVAX, VAX 4000, VAX 6000, VAX
8000, VAX 9000, & VAX 10000 series of
computers (under VMS 5.4)
Intel i960MC, with/without ICE 960, on an
EXV80960MC board; any single-board

computer using the i960 chip; and Intel i060
simulator, executing on the Host (bare
machines)
(BASE #910510W1.11148) HP 9000 Series
300 & 400, all models (under HP-UX
Version 8.0, all releases)
Intel i960MC, with/without ICE 960, on an
EXV80960MC board; any single-board
computer using the i960 chip; and Intel i060
simulator, executing on the Host (bare
machines)
(BASE #910510W1.11148) HP 9000 Series
700, all models (under HP-UX Version 8.0,
all releases)
Intel i960MC, with/without ICE 960, on an
EXV80960MC board; any single-board
computer using the i960 chip; and Intel i060
simulator, executing on the Host (bare
machines)
(BASE #910510W1.11148) Sun
Microsystems Sun-3 computers, all
models (under SunOS version 4.1.2 &
Solaris version 1.0.1, all releases)
Intel i960MC, with/without ICE 960, on an
EXV80960MC board; any single-board
computer using the i960 chip; and Intel i060
simulator, executing on the Host (bare
machines)
(BASE #910510W1.11148)

**Irvine Compiler CorporationICC Ada for
i960MC, Version 7.4**
VAXstation 3100 Model M38 (under VMS
5.3-1)
Intel i960MC with or without ICE960 on an
Intel EXV80960MC board; any single-board
computer that uses the i960 chip; Intel i960
simulator (executing on the Host) (bare
machine)
(BASE #910510W1.11148)

**Irvine Compiler CorporationICC Ada for
i960MM and i960MX Version 7.4**
DEC VAX-11, VAXserver, VAXstation,
MicroVAX, VAX 4000, VAX 6000, VAX
8000, VAX 9000, & VAX 10000 Series of
computers (under VMS 5.4)
Intel i960MM & i960MX, with/without ICE
960, on a TRONIX PI960MX-JXV JIAWG
Execution Vehicle board; any single-board
computer using the i960MM/MX superscalar
chip; and Intel i060 simulator, executing on
the Host (bare machines)
(BASE #920520I1.11260) HP 9000 Series
300 & 400, all models (under HP-UX
Version 8.0, all releases)
Intel i960MM & i960MX, with/without ICE
960, on a TRONIX PI960MX-JXV JIAWG
Execution Vehicle board; any single-board

computer using the i960MM/MX superscalar
chip; and Intel i060 simulator, executing on
the Host (bare machines)
(BASE #920520I1.11260) HP 9000 Series
700, all models (under HP-UX Version 8.0,
all releases)
Intel i960MM & i960MX, with/without ICE
960, on a TRONIX PI960MX-JXV JIAWG
Execution Vehicle board; any single-board
computer using the i960MM/MX superscalar
chip; and Intel i060 simulator, executing on
the Host (bare machines)
(BASE #920520I1.11260) Sun
Microsystems Sun-3 computers, all
models (under SunOS version 4.1.2 &
Solaris version 1.0.1, all releases)
Intel i960MM & i960MX, with/without ICE
960, on a TRONIX PI960MX-JXV JIAWG
Execution Vehicle board; any single-board
computer using the i960MM/MX superscalar
chip; and Intel i060 simulator, executing on
the Host (bare machines)
(BASE #920520I1.11260)

**Irvine Compiler CorporationICC Ada for
i960MX and i960MM, Version 7.4**
VAXstation 3100 Model M38 (under VMS
Version 5.3-1)
Intel i960MM & i960MX on a TRONIX
PI960MX-JXV JIAWG Execution Vehicle
board; any single-board computer that uses
the i960MM/MX superscalar chip; Intel i960
simulator (executing on the Host) (bare
machine)
(BASE #920520I1.11260)

**Irvine Compiler CorporationICC Ada for
i960XA, Version 7.5**
Sun Microsystems Sun-4, SPARCstation,
& SPARCserver computers, all models
(under SunOS version 4.1.2 & Solaris
version 1.0.1, all releases)
Intel i960XA with or without ICE960 on an
Intel EXV80960XA board; any single-board
computer that uses the i960XA chip; Intel
i960XA simulator (executing on the Host)
(bare machine)
(BASE #910510W1.11148)

**Irvine Compiler CorporationICC Ada for
Sun3, Version 7.4**
Sun 3/50 (under SunOS V4.0)
(BASE #910510W1.11146)

**Irvine Compiler CorporationICC Ada
v7.0.0**
ICL Series 39 Level 80 (under VME with
VMEB Environment Option Version

SV292)
(#910510W1.11145) HP 9000 Series 700 & 800, all models (under HP-UX Versions 8.0 & 9.0, all releases; and HP-UX BLS Version 8.0, all releases)
(#910510W1.11146) Sun Microsystems Sun-3 computer family (under SunOS 4.0 & 4.1)
(#910510W1.11147) HP 9000 Series 300 & 400, all Models (under HP-UX Version A.B8.05 (release 8.05))
Intel i80960MC (bare machine)
(#910510W1.11148)

Irvine Compiler CorporationICC Ada v7.4.0
DEC VAX-11, MicroVAX, VAXserver, VAXstation, VAXft; and VAX 4000, 6000, 7000, 8000, 9000, & 10000 series of computers (under VMS 5.4)
Intel i960MX in Hughes DMV running in tagged mode (bare machine, using CHKSYS kernel version 104)
(#920520I1.11260)

Meridian Software Systems, Inc.Meridian Ada, Version 4.1
Sun Microsystems Sun-4, SPARCstation, & SPARCserver computers, all models (under SunOS version 4.1.2 & Solaris version 1.0.1, all releases)
(#900909W1.11031) Sun-3/260 (under SunOS, Version 4.1)
(#900909W1.11032) Sun Microsystems Sun-4, SPARCserver & SPARCstation computer families (under SunOS Versions 4.1 & 4.1.1)
(#900909W1.11033) DECstation 2100, 3100 & 5000 (under Ultrix 3.0)
(#900909W1.11034) Any Computer System Comprising: cpu: any that executes the Intel 80286, 80386, or 80486 instruction set; fpu: Intel 80287, 80387, or equivalent, as appropriate; memory: 640 KByte RAM; disk: 20 MByte hard drive (under IBM PC-DOS 3.30)
(#900909W1.11035) Any Computer System Comprising: cpu: any that executes the Intel 8086 instruction set; fpu: Intel 8087 or equivalent, as appropriate; memory: 640 KByte RAM; disk: 20 MByte hard drive (under IBM PC-DOS 3.30)
(#900909W1.11036) Any Computer System Comprising: cpu: any that executes the Intel 80286, 80386, or 80486 instruction set; fpu: Intel 80287, 80387, or equivalent, as appropriate; memory: 1.5 MByte RAM; disk: 20 MByte hard drive (under MS-DOS

3.20/OS286)
(#900909W1.11037) Any Computer System Comprising: Cpu: any that executes the Intel 80386 or 80486 instruction set; Fpu: Intel 80387 or equivalent, for 80386 cpu; Memory: 2 or greater MByte RAM; Disk: 40 MByte hard drive (under SCO Unix 3.2 or INTERACTIVE UNIX System V/386 Release 3.2)
(#900909W1.11038) Apple Macintosh SE 30 (under System 6.0.3)
(#901108W1.11060) Apple Macintosh II (under A/UX 2.0)
(#901108W1.11061) Stardent Titan P3 (under Stardent/Unix 3.0)
(#901108W1.11062) MicroVAX 3100 (under Ultrix 3.1)
(#901108W1.11063) Any Computer System Comprising: cpu: any that executes the Intel 80386 or 80486 instruction set; fpu: Intel 80387 or equivalent, as appropriate; memory: 1.5 MByte RAM; disk: 20 MByte hard drive (under IBM PC-DOS 3.30/OS386)
(#911002W1.11219) NeXTstation (under System Release 2.0)
Mercury MC860 VM (under MC/OS, Version 2.0)
(#911002W1.11220) SGI PowerSeries 4D/310S (under IRIX Sys V 3.3.2)
Mercury MC860 VM (under MC/OS, Version 2.0)
(#911002W1.11221) Sun Microsystems Sun-4/110, /150, /260 & /280; SPARCserver 330, 370, 390, 470 & 490; and SPARCstation 2, IPC & IPX (under SunOS Versions 4.1 & 4.1.1) and SPARCengine 1E (under SunOS Version 4.1e)
(#911216W1.11232) Sun-4/110 (under SunOS, Version 4.1)
(BASE #900909W1.11032) DECstation 3100 (under Ultrix, Version 3.0)
(BASE #900909W1.11033) IBM PS/2 Model 60 (with Floating-Point Co-Processor) (under IBM PC-DOS 3.30)
(BASE #900909W1.11034) IBM PS/2 Model 30 (with Floating-Point Co-Processor) (under IBM PC-DOS 3.30)
(BASE #900909W1.11035) ITT XTRA/286 (with Floating-Point Co-Processor) (under MS-DOS 3.20/OS286)
(BASE #900909W1.11036) 80 Data 386/25 (under 386/ix 1.0.6)
(BASE #900909W1.11037) Any Computer System comprising: cpu: any that executes the Intel 80386 or 80486 instruction set, fpu: optional Intel 80387 or equivalent, for 80386 cpu, memory: 2

MByte RAM minimum, disk: 40 MByte hard drive, OS: SCO Unix 3.2 or Interactive 386/ix 1.0.6
(BASE #900909W1.11037) Apple Macintosh II (under System 6.0.3)
(BASE #900909W1.11038) SGI PowerSeries 4D/310S (under IRIX Sys V 3.3.2)
Mercury MC860VB & MC860VM (under MC/OS, Version 2.0)
(BASE #911002W1.11220) SGI PowerSeries 4D/310S (under IRIX Sys V 3.3.2)
Mercury MC860VS (under MC/OS, Version 2.VS)
(BASE #911002W1.11220) Sun-4/110 (under SunOS, Version 4.1)
Mercury MC860VB & MC860VM (under MC/OS, Version 2.0) and Mercury MC860VS (under MC/OS, Version 2.VS)
(BASE #911002W1.11221)

Meridian Software Systems, Inc.Meridian Ada, Version 4.1.1
MicroVAX II (under VMS 5.2)
(#911002W1.11218) Any Computer System comprising: cpu: any that executes the Intel 80286, 80386, or 80486 instruction set, fpu: Intel 80287, 80387, or equivalent, as appropriate, memory: 640 KByte RAM minimum, disk: 20 MByte hard drive, OS: IBM PC-DOS 3.30
(BASE #900909W1.11034) Any Computer System comprising: cpu: any that executes the Intel 8086 instruction set, fpu: Intel 8087 or equivalent, as appropriate, memory: 640 KByte RAM minimum, disk: 20 MByte hard drive, OS: IBM PC-DOS 3.30
(BASE #900909W1.11035) Any Computer System comprising: cpu: any that executes the Intel 80286, 80386, or 80486 instruction set, fpu: Intel 80287, 80387, or equivalent, as appropriate, memory: 1.5 MByte RAM minimum, disk: 20 MByte hard drive, OS: MS-DOS 3.20/OS286
(BASE #900909W1.11036) Sequent Symmetry 2000/40, /200, /400 & /700 (under DYNIX/ptx V1.2.0)
(BASE #900909W1.11037)

Meridian Software Systems, Inc.Meridian Ada, Version 4.1.3
Sequoia Series 400 (under Topix, Version 6.5)
(#920915W1.11266) InterGraph InterPro Series C300- & C400-based models

(under CLIX, System 5 Release 3.1)
(#920915W1.11267) Essence 836 (under DOS 5.0, running Microsoft Windows 3.0)
(#920915W1.11268) BBN TC2000 (under nX 3.0.1)
BBN TC2000 (under pSOS+/88k)
(#920915W1.11269) BBN TC2000 (under nX 3.0.1)
(#921202W1.11301) HP 9000/827 (under HP-UX 8.02)
(#930401W1.11313) Motorola VME 167-68040 (under OS/9 68K, v2.4)
ADSP-21020 (bare machine)
(#930401W1.11314) Intergraph Interpro 2400 (under CLIX System 5, Release 3.1)
(BASE #920915W1.11266)

Meridian Software Systems, Inc.Meridian Ada, Version 4.1.4
Any Computer System Comprising: Cpu: any that executes the Intel 80286, 80386, or 80486 instruction set; Fpu: Intel 80287, 80387, or equivalent, as appropriate; Memory: 640 or greater KByte RAM; Disk: 20 MByte hard drive (under IBM PC-DOS 3.30)
(BASE #900909W1.11034) Any Computer System Comprising: Cpu: any that executes the Intel 8086 instruction set; Fpu: Intel 8087 or equivalent, as appropriate; Memory: 640 or greater KByte RAM; Disk: 20 MByte hard drive (under IBM PC-DOS 3.30)
(BASE #900909W1.11035) Any Computer System Comprising: Cpu: any that executes the Intel 80286, 80386, or 80486 instruction set; Fpu: Intel 80287, 80387, or equivalent, as appropriate; Memory: 1.5 or greater MByte RAM; Disk: 20 MByte hard drive (under MS-DOS 3.30/OS286)
(BASE #900909W1.11036) IBM PS/2 Model 80 (with Floating Point Co-Processor) (under IBM PC-DOS 3.30/OS386)
(BASE #911002W1.11218)

MIPS Computer SystemsMIPS Ada 3.0
MIPS M/2000 (under RISC/os 4.50)
(#900619W1.11011)

MIPS Computer SystemsMIPS ASAPP 3.0
Essence 486 (under MS-DOS 5.0)
R3200-6 CPU board (bare machine)
(#900619W1.11010)

Multiprocessor Toolsmith Inc. CASEWorks/RT Ada v1.1 for Sun SPARCStation
MIPS M/2000 (under RISC/os 4.50)
(BASE #930722W1.11318) Sun Microsystems SPARCstation series

(under SunOS 4.11, 4.1.2, & 4.1.3)
Any MC68020-, MC68030-, &
MC68040-based single-board computer (bare
machines, using Unison 3.1)
(BASE #930722W1.11319)

Multiprocessor Toolsmiths Inc.
CASEWorks/RT Ada for the Sun
SPARCStation, 1.1
Sun Microsystems SPARCstation series
(under SunOS 4.11, 4.1.2, & 4.1.3)
(#930722W1.11318)

Multiprocessor Toolsmiths Inc.
CASEWorks/RT Ada i860, Version 1.1
Sun SPARCstation 10 (under SunOS
4.1.3)
CSPI Supercard II (Intel 80860) with VSB
daughterboard (bare machine)
(#930722W1.11320)

Multiprocessor Toolsmiths Inc.
CASEWorks/RT Ada MC680x0, Version 1.1
Sun SPARCstation 10 (under SunOS
4.1.3)
Motorola MVME147 (bare machine)
(#930722W1.11319)

Multiprocessor Toolsmiths Inc.
CASEWorks/RT Ada v1.1 for i860
Sun SPARCstation 2 (under SunOS 4.1.1)
CSPI Supercard 2 with VSB daughterboard,
CSPI Supercard 3 with VSB daughterboard,
CSPI Supercard 3XL with VSB daughterboard,
& CSPI Supercard 4 with VSB daughterboard
(bare machines, using Unison/pSOS+ 3.1)
(BASE #930722W1.11320)

NEC CorporationNEC Ada Compiler
System for EWS-UX/V (Rel 4.0) to
V70/RX-UX832, Version 1.0
NEC EWS4800/60 (under EWS-UX/V
R8.1)
NEC MV4000 (under RX-UX832 V1.6)
(BASE #910918S1.11217)

NEC CorporationNEC Ada Compiler
System for EWS-UX/V (Release 4.0),
Version Release 2.1(4.6)
Sun Microsystems SPARCstation series
(under SunOS 4.11, 4.1.2, & 4.1.3)
(#910918S1.11216)

NEC CorporationNEC Ada Compiler
System for EWS-UX/V to V70/RX-UX832,
Version 1.0
UP4800 Series models 520, 605, 620,
625, 630, & 635 (under UP-UX/V R4.1)
EWS4800 Superstation RISC Series (all

EWS RISC models, only) (under
EWS-UX/V(R4.0) R6.2 &
EWS-UX/V(R4.2) R7.1, as supported)
NEC MV4000 (under RX-UX832 V1.6)
(#910918S1.11217)

NEC CorporationNEC Ada Compiler
System for EWS-UX/V(Rel 4.0) to
V70/RX-UX832 version R4.1(V4.6.4)
All RISC (MIPS R3000- & R4000-based)
models of the EWS4800 series (under
EWS-UX/V (4.0) R2.1)
NEC MV4000 (under RX-UX832 V1.63)
(BASE #910918S1.11217)

NEC CorporationNEC Ada Compiler
System, Version R4.1 (4.6.4)
NEC EWS4800/220 (under EWS-UX/V
(Release 4.0) R2.1)
(BASE #910918S1.11216)

North China Institute of Computing Technology
C_Ada, Version 1.0
EWS4800 Superstation RISC Series
(under EWS-UX/V(R4.0) R6.2)
(#910902N1.11198)

Proprietary Software Systems, Inc.PSS
VAX/ZR34325 Compiler Version XB-01.000
MicroVAX II (under ULTRIX 3.0)
PSS Zoran ZR34325 Digital Signal Processor
AdaRAID Version XK-01.000 (bare machine
simulation, executing on the Host)
(#920423I1.11250)

R.R. Software, Inc.Janus/Ada 2.2.0 Phar
Lap/DOS
VAX 8350 (under VMS Version 5.4)
IBM PS/2 Model 80 (under MS DOS 3.3)
(#901120W1.11088) IBM PS/2 Model 80
(under Phar Lap/DOS 3.3)
Any Computer System Comprising: cpu: Intel
80386, fpu: optional, memory: 4 MByte RAM,
disk: 40 MByte hard drive (under MS DOS
3.3)
(BASE #901120W1.11088)

R.R. Software, Inc.Janus/Ada 2.2.0 Unix
Any Computer System Comprising: cpu:
any that executes the Intel 80386
instruction set; fpu: optional; memory: 2
MByte RAM; disk: 40 MByte hard drive
(under Phar Lap / MS-DOS 3.3)
(#901129W1.11089)

R.R. Software, Inc.Janus/Ada 2.2.0 UNIX
Northgate 386/25 (under SCO Unix 3.2)
(BASE #901129W1.11089)

R.R. Software, Inc.Janus/Ada 2.2.1 DOS
Any Computer System Comprising: cpu:
Intel 80386, fpu: optional, memory: 4
MByte RAM, disk: 40 MByte hard drive
(under Phar Lap/DOS 3.3)
(BASE #901120W1.11088)

R.R. Software, Inc.Janus/Ada 2.2.2 386 to DOS
Any Computer System Comprising: cpu:
any that executes the Intel 8086/8088
instruction set; fpu: optional; memory: 640
KByte RAM; disk: 20 MByte hard drive
(under MS-DOS 3.3)
(BASE #901120W1.11088)

R.R. Software, Inc.Janus/Ada 2.2.2 DOS
Any Computer System Comprising: cpu:
any that executes Intel 8086/8088
instructions; fpu: optional; memory: 640
KByte RAM; disk: 20 MByte hard drive
(under MS DOS 3.3)
(BASE #901120W1.11088)

R.R. Software, Inc.Janus/Ada 2.2.2 UNIX
Any Computer System Comprising: cpu:
Intel 80386, fpu: optional, memory: 4
MByte RAM, disk: 60 MByte hard drive
(under SCO Unix 3.2)
(BASE #901129W1.11089)

RationalM68020/Bare Cross-Development Facility, Version 7
R1000 Series 300 (under Rational
Environment Version D_12_24_0)
Motorola MVME135 (68020) (bare machine)
(#901116W1.11083)

RationalM68020/OS-2000 Cross-Development Facility, Version 7
Any Computer System Comprising: cpu:
any that executes the Intel 80386
instruction set; fpu: optional; memory: 4
MByte RAM; disk: 40 MByte hard drive
(under SCO Unix 3.2)
Phillips PG2100 (OS-2000 Release 2.0)
(#901116W1.11081)

RationalM68020/Unix Cross-Development Facility, Version 7
R1000 Series 300 (under Rational
Environment Version D_12_24_0)
*HP 9000 Model 370MH (under HP-UX
Version 7.0)*
(#901116W1.11082)

RationalRational Environment, D_12_24_0
R1000 Series 300 (under Rational
Environment Version D_12_24_0)
(#901116W1.11084)

Rational Software CorporationApex 1.4.1
Any Computer that executes the Intel
80486 instruction set (under Interactive
UNIX System V/386 Release 3.2)
(#940608W1.11356) SPARCstation 10/51
(under SunOS 4.1.3)
(#940608W1.11357) SPARCstation 10/51
(under Solaris 2.3)
(#940608W1.11358)

Rational Software CorporationDADScross Sun4 => MIPS R3000, Product #2100-01451, Version 6.2
IBM RS/6000 Model 41T (under AIX 3.2.5)
*Heurikon HKMIPS/V3500 (MIPS R3000)
(bare machine)*
(#940630W1.11366)

Rational Software CorporationDADScross Sun4 => Paragon, Product #2100-01452, Version 6.2
Sun SPARCstation 10/512 (under Solaris
2.3)
Intel Paragon (under OSF/1 Release 1.1.4)
(#940630W1.11368)

Rational Software CorporationMeridian Ada, v4.1.4
R1000 Series 300 (under Rational
Environment Version D_12_24_0)
(BASE #900909W1.11038)

Rational Software CorporationSilicon Graphics VADS, VAda-2100-00732, Version 6.2
DEC 3000 Model 500 AXP (under OSF/1,
V1.3)
(#940630W1.11361)

Rational Software CorporationSun Microsystems iMPact Ada 1.0
Sun Microsystems SPARCclassic,
SPARCcluster, SPARCcenter,
SPARCstation, SPARCserver, &
SPARCsystem computer families (under
Solaris 2.4)
(BASE #921004W1.11290)

Rational Software CorporationSun Microsystems SPARCompiler Ada2.1
AT&T 3B2/600GR UNIX System V
Release 4, Product #2100-01449, Version
6.2
(BASE #921004W1.11289)

Rational Software CorporationVADS 386/486, VAda-110-3737, Version 6.2
Sun Microsystems Sun-4, SPARCstation,
& SPARCserver computer family (under

SunOS 4.13)
(BASE #910517W1.11157)

Rational Software CorporationVADS
AT&T 3B2/600GR UNIX System V Release
4, Product #2100-01449, Version 6.2
DG AViiON G70592-A (88110) (under
UNIX System V Release 4)
AT&T 3B2/600GR (under System V, Release
4.0)
(#940630W1.11373)

Rational Software CorporationVADS IBM
RS/6000 => PowerPC, Product
#2100-01445, Version 6.2
IBM RS/6000 Model 250 (under AIX 3.2.5)
Motorola MVME1601 (PowerPC 601) (bare
machine)
(#940630W1.11364)

Rational Software CorporationVADS
PowerPC => PowerPC, Product
#2100-01445, Version 6.2
Silicon Graphics Challenge (4IP19 @
100MHz) (under IRIX 5.2)
Motorola MVME1601 (PowerPC 601) (bare
machine)
(#940630W1.11363)

Rational Software CorporationVADS
PowerPC SELF, Product #2100-01443,
Version 6.2
IBM RS/6000 Model 530 (under AIX 3.2.5)
(#940630W1.11365) IBM RS/6000 Model
250 (under AIX 3.2.5)
(BASE #940630W1.11365)

Rational Software CorporationVADS Sun4
=> PowerPC Simulator, Product
#2100-01455, Version 6.2
Sun SPARCcenter 2000 (under Solaris
2.3)
VADS PowerPC Instruction Set Simulator,
executing on the Host (bare machine
simulation)
(#940630W1.11370)

Rational Software CorporationVADS Sun4
=> PowerPC, Product #2100-01444, Version
6.2
Sun SPARCstation 10 (under SunOS
4.1.3)
Motorola MVME1601 (PowerPC 601) (bare
machine)
(#940630W1.11369)

Rational Software CorporationVADS
System V/88 Release 4, VAda-110-8383,

Product #2100-00736, Version 6.2
Sun SPARCstation 2 (under SunOS 4.1.2)
Same As Host
(#940630W1.11371)

Rational Software CorporationVADS
System V/88 Release 4, VAda-110-8484,
Product #2100-01464, Version 6.2
Motorola Series 900 Model 911 (M88110)
(under UNIX System V Release 4)
Same As Host
(#940630W1.11372)

Rational Software CorporationVADScross
IBM RISC System/6000 AIX 3.2.3 => MIPS
R4000, Version 6.2
Silicon Graphics Challenge (4IP19 @
100MHz) (under IRIX 5.2)
SGI Indigo XS4000 (MIPS R4000), operating
as a bare machine (bare machine)
(#940630W1.11362)

Rational Software CorporationVADScross
Sun-4 => GA040-1, Version 3.0
Apple Macintosh II Family of computers
(under System 7.1)
General Atronics GA040-1 (MC68040-based
single-board computer) (bare machine)
(BASE #910517W1.11152)

Rational Software CorporationVADScross
Sun4 Solaris 2.3 => MIPS R4000, Version
6.2
Sun SPARCstation 10 (under SunOS
4.1.3)
SGI Indigo XS4000 (MIPS R4000) (operating
as a bare machine)
(#940630W1.11367)

Rational Software CorporationVADSself
for DEC Alpha AXP OSF/1, Product
#2100-01439, Version 6.2
RS/6000 model 350 (under AIX 3.2.5)
(#940630W1.11359)

Rational Software CorporationVASDself
for DEC Alpha AXP OSF/1, Product
#2100-01439, Version 6.2
DEC 4000 Model 610 AXP (under OSF/1,
V2.0)
(#940630W1.11360)

Rockwell International Corporation
DDC-Based Ada/CAPS Compiler System,
Version 6.3
DEC VAX-11, VAXserver, VAXstation,
MicroVAX, VAX 6000, VAX 8000 & VAX

9000 Series of computers (under VMS
Versions 5.3-1 & 5.4)
*CAPS/AAMP2 & CAPS/AAMP3 (bare
machines)*
(BASE #910306W1.11130)

**Rockwell International Corporation
DDC-Based Ada/CAPS Compiler, Version
6.0**
Sun Microsystems SPARCclassic,
SPARCclusters, SPARCcenter,
SPARCstation, SPARCserver, &
SPARCsystem computer families (under
Solaris 2.4)
CAPS/AAMP1 (bare machine)
(#910306W1.11129) DEC VAX-11,
VAXserver, VAXstation, MicroVAX, VAX
6000, VAX 8000 & VAX 9000 Series of
computers (under VMS Versions 5.3-1 &
5.4)
CAPS/AAMP2 (bare machine)
(#910306W1.11130)

**Rockwell International Corporation
DDC-Based Ada/CAPS Compiler, Version
6.1**
VAX 8650 (under VMS, Version 5.3-1)
CAPS/AAMP1 (bare machine)
(BASE #910306W1.11129) VAXstation 3100
Model 30 (under VMS 5.4)
CAPS/AAMP2 (bare machine)
(BASE #910306W1.11130)

**SD-Scicon UK LtdXD Ada CPU32 Version
1.2**
VAX Cluster (comprising VAXserver 3600,
MicroVAX 2000 (2) & MicroVAX II
machines) (under VMS 5.4)
*Motorola M68340EVS Evaluation System
CPU32 (bare machine)*
(BASE #901007N1.11042)

**SD-Scicon UK LtdXD Ada
CPU32/MC68332 Version 1.2**
VAX Cluster (comprising VAXserver 3600,
MicroVAX 2000 (2), & MicroVAX II
machines) (under VMS 5.4)
*Motorola M68332EVS Evaluation System
CPU32 (bare machine)*
(BASE #901007N1.11042)

**SD-Scicon UK LtdXD Ada MC68000,
Version 1.2**
Local Area VAX Cluster (comprising
VAXserver 3600, MicroVAX 2000 (2) &
MicroVAX II machines) (under VMS 5.3)
*Motorola MC68000 on an MVME117-3FP
board (bare machine)*
(#910314N1.11134)

**SD-Scicon UK LtdXD Ada MC68000/EFA,
Version 1.2**
Local Area VAX Cluster (comprising
VAXserver 3600, MicroVAX 2000 (2) &
MicroVAX II machines) (under VMS 5.4)
*Motorola MC68000 on an MVME117-3FP
board (bare machine)*
(BASE #910314N1.11134)

**SD-Scicon UK LtdXD Ada MC68020
MVME135 & MVME147, Version 1.2A**
VAX Cluster (comprising VAXserver 3600,
MicroVAX 2000 (2) & MicroVAX II
machines) (under VMS 5.4)
*Motorola MVME135-1 (MC68020) &
MVME147S-1 (MC68030) boards (bare
machines)*
(BASE #901007N1.11042)

**SD-Scicon UK LtdXD Ada MC68020
Version 1.2**
VAX Cluster (comprising VAXserver 3600,
MicroVAX 2000 (2) & MicroVAX II
machines) (under VMS Version 5.3)
*Motorola MVME135-1 board (MC68020) and
Motorola MVME147S-1 board (MC68030)
(bare machines)*
(BASE #901007N1.11042)

**SD-Scicon UK LtdXD Ada MC68020,
Version 1.2**
DEC VAX-11, VAXserver, VAXstation,
MicroVAX, VAX 4000, VAX 6000, VAX
8000, VAX 9000, & VAX 10000 series of
computers (under VMS 5.5-2)
*Motorola MVME133XT board (MC68020)
(bare machine)*
(#901007N1.11042)

**SD-Scicon UK LtdXD Ada MC68020,
Version 1.2A**
VAX Cluster (comprising VAXserver 3600,
MicroVAX 2000 (2) & MicroVAX II
machines) (under VMS 5.3)
*Motorola MVME133XT board (MC68020)
(bare machine)*
(BASE #901007N1.11042)

**SD-Scicon UK LtdXD Ada
MC68020/ARTX, Version T1.2**
Local Area VAX Cluster (comprising
VAXserver 3600, MicroVAX 2000 (2) &
MicroVAX II machines) (under VMS 5.4)
*Motorola MVME147S-1 (MC68030) (bare
machine)*
(#910911N1.11199)

SD-Scicon UK LtdXD Ada MC68020/EFA, Version 1.2A
VAX Cluster (comprising VAXserver 3600, MicroVAX 2000 (2) & MicroVAX II machines) (under VMS 5.4)
Motorola MVME135-1 board (MC68020) (bare machine)
(BASE #901007N1.11042)

SD-Scicon UK LtdXD Ada MC68040, Version 1.2
Local Area VAX Cluster (comprising VAXserver 3600, MicroVAX 2000 (2) & MicroVAX II machines) (under VMS 5.4)
Motorola MVME165 (MC68040) (bare machine)
(#911128N1.11230) Local Area VAX Cluster (comprising VAXserver 3600, MicroVAX 2000 (2), & MicroVAX II machines) (under VMS 5.5)
Motorola MVME167 (68040) (bare machine)
(BASE #911128N1.11230)

SD-Scicon UK LtdXD Ada MC68040/FORCE CPU-40, Version 1.2
Local Area VAX Cluster (comprising VAXserver 3600, MicroVAX 2000 (2) & MicroVAX II machines) (under VMS 5.4)
FORCE CPU-40 (MC68040) (bare machine)
(BASE #911128N1.11230)

SD-Scicon UK LtdXD Ada MIL-STD-1750A, Version 1.2
VAX Cluster (comprising VAXserver 3600, MicroVAX 2000 (2), & MicroVAX II machines) (under VMS 5.4)
Fairchild F9450 on a SBC-50 board (MIL-STD-1750A) (bare machine)
(#901214N1.11080)

Siemens Nixdorf Informations- systeme AG Ada (SINIX) V4.1
SIEMENS NIXDORF 7.530, 7.536, 7.541, 7.550, 7.551, 7.560, 7.561, 7.570, 7.571, 7.580 & 7.590; 7.500-C30, -C40, -H60, -H90 & -H120 (under BS2000 V9.5 & V10.0)
(#910711W1.11181) Siemens Nixdorf WX200 (SINIX-ODT) (under SINIX-ODT V1.5)
(#920325I1.11249) Siemens Nixdorf PC (under SINIX Version V5.41)
(#920922I1.11276) Siemens Nixdorf WX200 (SINIX-ODT) (under SINIX-ODT V1.0)
(BASE #910711W1.11181) Siemens Nixdorf MX300i (under SINIX Version V5.41)
Each Host, self targeted
(BASE #920325I1.11249) Siemens Nixdorf WX200 & MX500i (under SINIX Version

5.41)
(BASE #920325I1.11249) Siemens Nixdorf RM600 (under SINIX Version V5.41)
(BASE #920922I1.11276)

Siemens Nixdorf Informations- systeme AG SIEMENS NIXDORF BS2000 Ada Compiler V2.1
Local Area VAX Cluster (comprising VAXserver 3600, MicroVAX 2000 (2), & MicroVAX II machines) (under VMS 5.5)
(#901119I1.11111) SIEMENS NIXDORF 7.590G (under BS2000 V9.5)
(BASE #901119I1.11111)

Silicon Graphics Computer Systems4D ADA 3.0
Siemens Nixdorf RM400 (under SINIX Version V5.41)
(#900703W1.11014) Iris-4D/380 (under IRIX Release 4D-3.3)
(#900703W1.11015) Iris-4D/220S (under IRIX Release 4D-3.3)
(#900703W1.11016)

Silicon Graphics, Inc.VADS SGI-Irix, SC4-ADA-4.0, Version 6.1
Iris-4D/25 (under IRIX Release 4D-3.3)
(#910920W1.11203) IRIS Indigo, Personal IRIS 4D, IRIS 4D series of computers (under Irix V4.0)
(#910920W1.11204) SGI Indigo (under Irix V4.0)
(BASE #910920W1.11203)

SKY Computers, Inc.Meridian Ada, Version 4.1
SGI 4D/440 (under Irix V3.3)
SKYbolt 8116-V (under SKYbolt kernel version 2.33)
(#910711W1.11183) SGI Personal Iris W-4D25 (under Irix System V 3.3)
SKYstation 8117-P (under SKYstation kernel version 2.33)
(#910711W1.11185) SPARCstation 1 (under SunOS release 4.1)
(#910711W1.11189)

SKY Computers, Inc.SKYvec ADA Release 3.6
SGI Personal Iris W-4D25 (under Irix System V 3.3)
SKYbolt Model 8146-V (under SKYmpxrt release 3.6)
(#940803W1.11374)

Software Leverage, Inc.Parallel-Leverage d Ada, 6.1.0.2
SPARCstation 10 Model 402 (under SunOS 4.1.3)
(#940411W1.11355) Sequent Symmetry S27 (under DYNIX/ptx, 1.2)
(BASE #940411W1.11355)

Stratus Computer, Inc.Stratus Ada, Version 6.1
Unisys U6000/7x & U6000/8x series, and Unisys Commercial Secure U6000/7x & U6000/8x series, all models (under DYNIX/ptx 1.2)
(#921015W1.11294)

Stratus Computer, Inc.Stratus Ada, Version 6.1.0.5
Stratus XA/R20 (under FTX, 2.0.1)
(BASE #921015W1.11294)

Sun MicrosystemsSun Microsystems Sun Ada, SunOS, ADE-1.0-4-4-21, Version 1.0
Stratus XA/R series of computers (under FTX 2.3)
(BASE #900510W1.11006)

Sun MicrosystemsSun Microsystems Sun Ada, SunOS, ADE-1.1-4-4-21, Version 1.1
Sun Microsystems Sun-4, SPARCserver, & SPARCstation computer families; SPARCserver 600MP Series; & 4600MP-64 (under SunOS Version 4.2 releases 4.1 & 4.1.2, as supported)
(BASE #900510W1.11006)

Sun MicrosystemsSun Microsystems Sun Ada, SunOS, ADE-1.1-4-4-21, Versions 1.0 & 1.1
Sun Microsystems Sun-4, SPARCserver, SPARCstation, & SPARCengine computer families; SPARCserver 600MP Series; & 4600MP-64 (under SunOS Version 4.2 release 4.1.2)
(BASE #900510W1.11006)

Sun Microsystems, Inc.Sun Microsystems SPARCompiler Ada 2.1
Sun Microsystems Sun-4, SPARCserver, & SPARCstation computer families (under SunOS 4.1.3)
(BASE #921004W1.11289)

Sun Microsystems, Inc.Sun Microsystems SPARCworks iMPact Ada 1.0
Sun-4, SPARCserver, & SPARCstation computer families (under Solaris 2.0, 2.1, 2.2, & 2.3)
(BASE #921004W1.11290)

Tartan, Inc.Tartan Ada RS6000/960mc, Version 4.2.2
SPARCstation ELC (under SunOS Version 4.1.1)
Intel EXV80960MC board (bare machine)
(BASE #920313I1.11247)

Tartan, Inc.Tartan Ada SPARC 1750a Version 4.2.1
SPARCstation ELC (under SunOS version 4.1.1)
Fairchild F9450 on an SBC-50 board (bare machine)
(BASE #920313I1.11245)

Tartan, Inc.Tartan Ada SPARC 1750a, Version 4.2
SPARCstation ELC (under SunOS version 4.1.1)
Fairchild F9450 on an SBC-50 board (MIL-STD-1750A) (bare machine)
(#920313I1.11245)

Tartan, Inc.Tartan Ada SPARC 680X0, Version 4.2
Sun SPARCstation ELC (under SunOS 4.1.1)
Motorola MVME134 (MC68020) (bare machine)
(#920313I1.11246)

Tartan, Inc.Tartan Ada SPARC 960mc, Version 4.2
SPARCstation ELC (under SunOS version 4.1.1)
Intel EXV80960MC board (bare machine)
(#920313I1.11247)

Tartan, Inc.Tartan Ada SPARC 960mc, Version 4.2.2
SPARCstation ELC (under SunOS version 4.1.1)
Intel EXV80960MC board (bare machine)
(BASE #920313I1.11247)

Tartan, Inc.Tartan Ada SPARC C30, Version 4.2
VAXstation 3100 (under VMS 5.5)
Texas Instruments TMS320C30 Application Board (bare machine)
(#920313I1.11244)

Tartan, Inc.Tartan Ada SPARC C3X, Version 4.3
SPARCstation ELC (under SunOS version 4.1.1)
Texas Instruments TMS320C30 Application Board, & Atlanta Signal Processors Elf TMS320C31 board (bare machines)
(BASE #920313I1.11244)

Tartan, Inc.Tartan Ada SPARC/1750A, Version 4.3
SPARCstation ELC (under SunOS version 4.1.1)
Texas Instruments STL VHSIC 1750A, & Fairchild F9450 on an SBC-50 (MIL-STD-1750A) (bare machines)
(BASE #920313I1.11245)

Tartan, Inc.Tartan Ada SPARC/68XXX Version 4.3
SPARCstation ELC (under SunOS version 4.1.1)
Motorola MVME134 (68020), MVME143 (68030), MVME165 (68040), MC68332 (CPU32), & MC68340 (CPU32) (bare machines)
(BASE #920313I1.11246)

Tartan, Inc.Tartan Ada SPARC/960MC/PMRT, Version 4.3
SPARCstation ELC (under SunOS version 4.1.1)
Cyclone CVME962 board, Intel EXV80960MC board, & PI-960MX-JXV board (bare machines)
(BASE #920313I1.11247)

Tartan, Inc.Tartan Ada SPARC/960MC/SVMRT , Version 4.3
IBM RISC System/6000 Model 320H (under AIX Version 3.2)
Cyclone CVME962 board, & Intel EXV80960MC board (bare machines)
(BASE #920313I1.11247)

Tartan, Inc.Tartan Ada SPARC/C40, Version 4.3
VAXstation 4000 Model 60 (under VMS 5.5)
Texas Instruments TMS320C40 Parallel Develpment System (bare machine)
(BASE #921030I1.11296)

Tartan, Inc.Tartan Ada Sun/960MC, Version 4.0
VAXstation 3100 (under VMS 5.5)
Intel ICE960/25 on an Intel EXV80960MC board (bare machine)
(#901210I1.11122)

Tartan, Inc.Tartan Ada Sun/C30 Version 4.0
VAXstation 3100 (under VMS 5.5)
Texas Instruments TMS320C30 Application Board (bare machine)
(#901212I1.11123)

Tartan, Inc.Tartan Ada Sun/C30, Version 4.1.1
Sun 3/50 (under SunOS Version 4.0.3)
Texas Instruments TMS320C30 Application Board (bare machine)
(BASE #901212I1.11123)

Tartan, Inc.Tartan Ada Sun/Sun, Version 4.0
Sun 3/60 (under SunOS Version 4.0.3)
(#901211I1.11118)

Tartan, Inc.Tartan Ada Sun/Sun, Version 4.1
Sun 3/60 (under SunOS Version 4.0.3)
(BASE #901211I1.11118)

Tartan, Inc.Tartan Ada Sun/Sun, Version 4.2
Sun 3/60 (under SunOS Version 4.0.3)
(BASE #901211I1.11118)

Tartan, Inc.Tartan Ada VMS/1750A, Version 4.0
Sun 3/50 (under SunOS Version 4.0.3)
Texas Instruments STL VHSIC 1750A (bare machine)
(#901213I1.11119)

Tartan, Inc.Tartan Ada VMS/1750A, Version 4.1
VAXstation 3200 (under VMS 5.2)
Texas Instruments STL VHSIC 1750A (bare machine)
(BASE #901213I1.11119)

Tartan, Inc.Tartan Ada VMS/1750A, Version 4.3
VAXstation 3200 (under VMS 5.2)
Texas Instruments STL VHSIC 1750A, & Fairchild F9450 on an SBC-50 (MIL-STD-1750A) (bare machines)
(BASE #901213I1.11119)

Tartan, Inc.Tartan Ada VMS/680X0, Version 4.1
VAXstation 3100 (under VMS 5.5)
Motorola MVME134 (MC68020) (bare machine)
(#910613I1.11171)

Tartan, Inc.Tartan Ada VMS/680X0, Version 4.1.1
VAXstation 3100 (under VMS 5.2)
Motorola MVME134 (MC68020), MVME143 (MC68030), & MVME165 (MC68040) (bare machines)
(BASE #910613I1.11171)

Tartan, Inc. Tartan Ada VMS/680X0/IPS, Version 4.1.2
VAXstation 3100 (under VMS 5.2)
Motorola MVME134 (MC68020) (bare machine)
(BASE #910613I1.11171)

Tartan, Inc. Tartan Ada VMS/68XXX Version 4.3
VAXstation 3100 (under VMS 5.2)
Motorola MVME134 (68020), MVME143 (68030), MVME165 (68040), MC68332 (CPU32), & MC68340 (CPU32) (bare machines)
(BASE #910613I1.11171)

Tartan, Inc. Tartan Ada VMS/960MC, Version 4.0
Sun 3/60 (under SunOS Version 4.0.3)
Intel ICE960/25 on an Intel EXV80960MC board (bare machine)
(#901212I1.11120)

Tartan, Inc. Tartan Ada VMS/960MC, Version 4.1
VAXstation 3100 (under VMS 5.2)
Intel EXV80960MC board, & Intel ICE960/25 on an Intel EXV80960MC board (bare machines)
(BASE #901212I1.11120)

Tartan, Inc. Tartan Ada VMS/960MC, Version 4.2.1
VAXstation 3100 (under VMS 5.2)
Intel ICE960/25 on an Intel EXV80960MC board (bare machine)
(BASE #901212I1.11120) VAXstation 3100 (under VMS 5.2)
Intel EXV80960MC board (bare machine)
(BASE #901212I1.11120)

Tartan, Inc. Tartan Ada VMS/960MC, Version 4.2.2
VAXstation 3100 (under VMS 5.2)
Intel EXV80960MC board (bare machine)
(BASE #901212I1.11120)

Tartan, Inc. Tartan Ada VMS/960MC/PMRT, Version 4.3
VAXstation 3100 (under VMS 5.5)
Cyclone CVME962 board, Intel EXV80960MC board, & PI-960MX-JXV board (bare machines)
(BASE #901212I1.11120)

Tartan, Inc. Tartan Ada VMS/960MC/SVMRT, Version 4.3
VAXstation 3100 (under VMS 5.2)
Cyclone CVME962 board, & Intel EXV80960MC board (bare machines)
(BASE #901212I1.11120)

Tartan, Inc. Tartan Ada VMS/C30, Version 4.0
Sun-4, SPARCserver, & SPARCstation computer families (under Solaris 2.0, 2.1, 2.2, & 2.3)
Texas Instruments TMS320C30 Application Board (bare machine)
(#901210I1.11121)

Tartan, Inc. Tartan Ada VMS/C30, Version 4.1
VAXstation 3100 (under VMS 5.2)
Texas Instruments TMS320C30 Application Board (bare machine)
(BASE #901210I1.11121)

Tartan, Inc. Tartan Ada VMS/C30, Version 4.1.1
VAXstation 3100 (under VMS 5.2)
Texas Instruments TMS320C30 Application Board, NAVY SEM-D Key Code ADSP (bare machines)
(BASE #901210I1.11121)

Tartan, Inc. Tartan Ada VMS/C30/IPS, Version 4.1.2
VAXstation 3100 (under VMS 5.2)
Texas Instruments TMS320C30 (bare machine)
(BASE #901210I1.11121)

Tartan, Inc. Tartan Ada VMS/C3X Version 4.3
VAXstation 3100 (under VMS 5.2)
Texas Instruments TMS320C30 Application Board, & Atlanta Signal Processors Elf TMS320C31 board (bare machines)
(BASE #901210I1.11121)

Tartan, Inc. Tartan Ada VMS/C40 v4.2.1
SPARCstation ELC (under SunOS version 4.1.1)
Texas Instruments TMS320C40 Parallel Processing Development System (bare machine)
(#921030I1.11296)

Tartan, Inc. Tartan Ada VMS/C40, Version 4.3
SPARCstation ELC (under SunOS version 4.1.1)
Texas Instruments TMS320C40 Parallel Develpment System (bare machine)
(BASE #921030I1.11296)

**Tartan, Inc.TartanWorks Ada 68xxx
Version 4.3.1**
VAXstation 3100 (under VMS 5.5)
*Motorola MVME167 (68040) (bare machine,
using VxWorks 5.1)*
(#940221I1.11340)

**TeleGen2Ada Cross Development System
for VAX/VMS to 68K, Version 4.1**
DEC VAX-11, VAXserver, 6000, VAX 8000
& VAX 9000 Series of computers (under
VMS Versions 5.0, 5.1, 5.2, 5.3 & 5.4, as
supported)
(68040) board families (bare machines)
(BASE #910121I1.11124)

TeleSoft68K, Version 4.1
MicroVAX 3800 (under VAX/VMS Version
5.2)
*Motorola board series Force CPU-30,
CPU-31, CPU-32 & CPU-37 (bare machines)*
(BASE #910121I1.11124)

**TeleSoftSystem for VAX/VMS to 68K,
Version 4.1**
DEC VAX-11, VAXserver, VMS Versions
5.0, 5.1, 5.2, 5.3 & 5.4, as supported)
*Motorola board series machines, using
TeleAda-Exec)*
(BASE #910121I1.11124)

**TeleSoftTeleGen2 Ada Compilation System
for VAX to 80960, Version 4.1**
MicroVAX 3800 (under VMS Version 5.4)
*Intel EXV 960 MC-MIL (i960 XA) (bare
machine, using Hughes O.S. Ada RTS
interface)*
(#911213I1.11235)

**TeleSoftTeleGen2 Ada Cross Development
System Version 4.1.1 for SUN-4 to eMIPS**
MicroVAX 3800 (under VMS Version 5.4)
*Integrated Device Technology IDT7RS301
System (R3000/R3010) (bare machine)*
(#921029I1.11295)

**TeleSoftTeleGen2 Ada Cross Development
System, Version 3.1**
VAX 6210 (under VMS 5.3)
*Intel iSBC 486/133SE board (bare machine,
using TeleAda-EXEC 1.0)*
(BASE #910325I1.11139)

**TeleSoftTeleGen2 Ada Cross Development
System, Version 3.1 for SPARC to 68K**
VAX 4000-300 (under VMS 5.4-3)
*Motorola MVME147 (68030) (bare machine,
using TeleAda-EXEC 1.0)*
(#910325I1.11140)

**TeleSoftTeleGen2 Ada Cross Development
System, Version 3.1 for VAX/VMS to 386**
Sun-3/480 (under Sun UNIX, Release 4.1)
*Intel iSBC 386-120 (80386/387) (bare
machine, using TeleAda-EXEC 1.0)*
(#910325I1.11139)

**TeleSoftTeleGen2 Ada Cross Development
System, Version 4.1, for SUN-3 to 68K**
MicroVAX 3800 (under VAX/VMS Version
5.2)
*Motorola MVME135-1 (MC68020) (bare
machine)*
(#910125I1.11126)

**TeleSoftTeleGen2 Ada Cross Development
System, Version 4.1, for VAX/VMS to 68K**
Sun Microsystems Sun-4, SPARCserver,
& SPARCstation computer families (under
Solaris 2.1)
*Motorola MVME133A-20 (MC68020) (bare
machine)*
(#910121I1.11124)

**TeleSoftTeleGen2 Ada Cross Development
System, Version 4.1, for VAX/VMS to MIPS**
VAXstation, MicroVAX, VAX 6000, VAX
8000 & VAX 9000 Series of computers (as
supported) (under VMS Versions 5.0, 5.1,
5.2, 5.3 & 5.4)
*Integrated Device Technology IDT7RS301
System (R3000/R3010) (bare machine)*
(#910123I1.11125)

**TeleSoftTeleGen2 Ada Development System
for VAX to 1750A, Version 3.25**
Apple Macintosh II family, & SE/30 (under
A/UX Release 2.0)
*MIL-STD-1750A ECSPO ITS RAID Simulator,
Version 6.0 (bare machine simulation,
executing on the Host)*
(#911028I1.11229)

**TeleSoftTeleGen2 Ada Host Development
System for MacII Systems, Version 4.1**
Apple Macintosh IIfx (under A/UX 2.0)
(BASE #910721I1.11194)

**TeleSoftTeleGen2 Ada Host Development
System for SPARCSystems, Version 4.1**
Sun Microsystems Sun-4, SPARCserver,
SPARCstation, & SPARCengine computer
families (under SunOS 4.2, release 4.1)
(BASE #901128W1.11090) Sun-4/280
(under Sun UNIX 4.2, Release 4.1)
(BASE #901128W1.11090)

TeleSoftTeleGen2 Ada Host Development
System for SPARCSystems, Version 4.1.1
Solbourne Series 5 & 5E; and S4000
(under OS/MP 4.1)
(BASE #901128W1.11090)

TeleSoftTeleGen2 Ada Host Development
System, Version 4.1, for MacII Systems
(#910721I1.11194)

TeleSoftTeleGen2 Ada Host Development
System, Version 4.1, for SPARCSystems
Sun-3/280 (under Sun UNIX 4.2, Release
4.0.3)
(#901128W1.11090)

TeleSoftTeleGen2 Sun-3 Ada Development
System, Version 4.01
SPARCstation ELC (under SunOS 4.3.1)
(#900525I1.11012)

TeleSoftTeleGen2(tm) Ada Cross
Development System for Sun-4 to e68k,
Version 4.1c
Sun-4/690 (under SunOS Release 4.1.2)
*Motorola MVME147S-1 (68030/68882) (bare
machine)*
(#921218I1.11304)

TeleSoftTeleGen2(tm) Ada Cross
Development System for Sun-4 to i960,
Version 4.1.1
Sun-4/690 (under SunOS Release 4.1.2)
*CVME962 System (i960XA board with MC
Processor) (bare machine)*
(#921218I1.11303)

Texas InstrumentsMIPS-Ada, Version 3.0
Sun-4/690 (under SunOS Release 4.1.2)
*TI DP32 R3000 Processor (bare machine,
using TI DP32 RTE Version 1.0)*
(#901030W1.11052)

Texas InstrumentsTI Ada, Version 1.0
MIPS M/2000 (under RISC/os 4.02)
*TI DP32 R3000 Processor (bare machine,
using TI Executive and Runtime Services
(EARS) Version 1.0)*
(#910403W1.11135)

TISOFT, Inc.Green Hills Optimizing Ada
Compiler, Version 1.8.7 with Patch ID 1
MicroVAX 3400 (under VMS 5.3-1)
Same As Host
(#941012S1.11379) Compaq ProLiant 2000
Model 5/66 (under SCO UNIX Release 3.2
Version 4.2)
(BASE #941012S1.11379)

TLD Systems, Inc.TLD Comanche
VAX/i960 Ada Compiler System, Version
4.1.1
DEC VAX-11, VAXserver, VAXstation,
MicroVAX, VAX 4000, VAX 6000, VAX
8000, & VAX 9000 Series of computers
(under VMS 5.5)
*Various hardware & software implementations
of the Intel i960 hardware architecture,
including: TLDmps i960 Multiple Processor
Simulator (executing on a host), Tronic JIAWG
i960 MX/XA Execution Vehicle, Intel EXV
960MX Execution Vehicle, and Westinghouse
Data Processing System (containing multiple
i960 MX/XA boards) (bare machines or bare
machine simulation, using TLDrtx Real Time
Executive, Version 4.1.1)*
(BASE #940305W1.11335)

TLD Systems, Inc.TLD Comanche
VAX/MIL-STD-1750A Ada Compiler
System, Version 3.4.C
Compaq ProLiant 1000 & 2000 Series
Servers using Intel 486DX2/66,
Pentium/66, & Pentium/90 processors
(under SCO UNIX Release 3.2 Version
4.2, with/without SCO MPX
Multi-Processor Extension Release 3.0)
*TLDmps MIL-STD-1750A Multiple Processor
Simulator, executing on the Host (bare
machine simulation, using TLDrtx Real Time
Executive, 3.4.C)*
(BASE #931012W1.11329)

TLD Systems, Ltd.TLD Comanche
VAX/i960 Ada Compiler System, Version
4.1.1
VAXstation 4000 Model 60 (under VMS
5.5)
*Tronix JIAWG Execution Vehicle (i960MX)
(bare machine using TLD Real Time Executive
(TLDrtx), (Domain Configuration), Version
4.1.1)*
(#940305W1.11335)

TLD Systems, Ltd.TLD Comanche
VAX/MIL-STD-1750A Ada Compiler
System, Version 3.4.C
HP 9000/350 (under HP-UX, Version 7.0)
*TLD MIL-STD-1750A Multiple Processor
Simulator (TLDmps), executing on the Host
(bare machine simulation, using TLD Real
Time Executive (TLDrtx), 3.4.C)*
(#931012W1.11329)

TLD Systems, Ltd.TLD HP
9000/MIL-STD-1750 A Ada Compiler
System, Version 2.9.0
DEC VAX-11, VAXserver, VAXstation,
MicroVAX, VAX 4000, VAX 6000, VAX

8000, & VAX 9000 Series of computers (under VMS 5.4)
TLDmps MIL-STD-1750A Multiple Processor Simulator (bare machine simulation, using TLDrtx Real Time Executive, Version 1.0.0, and executing on the Host)
(#920319W1.11243)

TLD Systems, Ltd.TLD MV/MV Ada Compiler System, Version 2.9.0
Sun-4/75 (under SunOS, Version 4.1.1)
(#920319W1.11238)

TLD Systems, Ltd.TLD RISC6000/MIL-STD- 1750A Ada Compiler System, Version 2.9.0
Sun-4/75 (under SunOS, Version 4.1.1)
TLDmps MIL-STD-1750A Multiple Processor Simulator (bare machine simulation, using TLDrtx Real Time Executive, Version 1.0.0, and executing on the Host)
(#920319W1.11241) IBM RISC System 6000, Model 530 (under AIX, Version 3.1)
IBM User Console with IBM Generic VHSIC Spaceborne Computer (bare machine, using TLDrtx Real Time Execution, Version 1.0.0)
(BASE #920319W1.11241)

TLD Systems, Ltd.TLD Sun-4/MIL-STD-175 0A Ada Compiler System, Version 2.9.0
DEC VAX-11, VAXserver, VAXstation, MicroVAX, VAX 4000, VAX 6000, VAX 8000, & VAX 9000 Series of computers (under VMS 5.5)
Rockwell International RI-1750AB Brassboard Development System (bare machine, using TLDrtx Real Time Executive, Version 1.0.0)
(#920319W1.11237) Data General MV/32 20000-2 (under AOS/VS II, Version 2.03)
Honeywell Program Development Unit (PDU) with Honeywell Generic VHSIC Spaceborne Computer (GVSC) MIL-STD-1750A (bare machine, using TLDrtx Real Time Executive, Version 1.0.0)
(#920319W1.11239) Sun-4/75 (under SunOS, Version 4.1.1)
TLD MIL-STD-1750A Multiple Processor Simulator (bare machine simulation, using TLDrtx Real Time Executive, Version 1.0.0, and executing on the Host)
(#920319W1.11240)

TLD Systems, Ltd.TLD VAX/MIL-STD-1750A Ada Compiler System, Version 2.9.0
IBM RISC System 6000 series (under AIX, Version 3.1)
TLD MIL-STD-1750A Multiple Processor Simulator (bare machine simulation, using

TLDrtx Real Time Executive, Version 1.0.0, and executing on the Host)
(#920319W1.11242) MicroVAX 3500 (under VMS, Version 5.1)
IBM User Console with IBM Generic VHSIC Spaceborne Computer (bare machine, using TLDrtx Real Time Execution, Version 1.0.0)
(BASE #920319W1.11242) Sun-4/60 (under SunOS 4.1)
board families (bare machines, optionally using TeleAda_Exec 2.0)
(BASE #910325I1.11140)

U.S. Air ForceAFCAS 1750A Ada Compiler, Version 1.0
DEC Local Area Network VAX Cluster (comprising 2 MicroVAX 3100 Model 90 machines) (under VMS 5.5)
Air Force RAID MIL-STD-1750A simulator (bare machine simulation, executing on the Host)
(#910425W1.11142)

U.S. Air ForceAFCAS 1750A Ada Compiler, Version 1.1
VAXstation 3100 (under VMS Version 5.3)
Air Force RAID MIL-STD-1750A simulator (bare machine simulation, executing on the Host)
(BASE #910425W1.11142)

U.S. Air ForceAFCAS 1750A/XMEM Ada Compiler, Version 1.0
DEC VAXstation 3100 (under VMS Version 5.4)
Air Force RAID MIL-STD-1750A simulator (bare machine simulation, executing on the Host)
(#910425W1.11143)

U.S. Air ForceAFCAS 1750A/XMEM Ada Compiler, Version 1.1
VAXstation 3100 (under VMS Version 5.3)
Air Force RAID MIL-STD-1750A simulator (bare machine simulation, executing on the Host)
(BASE #910425W1.11143)

U.S. NAVYAda/L, Version 4.0 (/OPTIMIZE)
VAX-11/785 (under VMS Version 5.3)
AN/UYK-43 (single cpu) (bare machine)
(#910626S1.11172) VAX 8550 (under VMS Version 5.3)
AN/UYK-43 (EMR) (bare machine)
(#910626S1.11173) VAX 8550 (under VMS Version 5.3)
AN/UYK-43 (single cpu) (bare machine)
(#910626S1.11176) VAX-11/785 (under VMS Version 5.3)
AN/UYK-43 (EMR) (bare machine)
(#910626S1.11177)

U.S. NAVYAda/M, Version 4.0 (/OPTIMIZE)
VAX 8550 (under VMS Version 5.3)
AN/UYK-44 (EMR) (bare machine)
(#910626S1.11174) VAX 8550 (under VMS Version 5.3)
AN/AYK-14 (bare machine)
(#910626S1.11175) VAX-11/785 (under VMS Version 5.3)
AN/UYK-44 (EMR) (bare machine)
(#910626S1.11178) VAX-11/785 (under VMS Version 5.3)
AN/AYK-14 (bare machine)
(#910626S1.11179)

U.S. NAVYAda/M, Version 4.5 (/NO_OPTIMIZE)
VAX Cluster (comprising VAX 8550, 8600, & 8650 machines) (under VMS Version 5.3)
Enhanced Processor (EP) AN/UYK-44 (bare machine)
(#920918S1.11274) VAX Cluster (comprising VAX 8550, 8600, & 8650 machines) (under VMS Version 5.3)
VHSIC Processor Module (VPM) AN/AYK-14 (bare machine)
(#920918S1.11275)

U.S. NAVYAda/M, Version 4.5 (/OPTIMIZE)
VAXstation 4000 (under VMS Version 5.5)
Enhanced Processor (EP) AN/UYK-44 (bare machine)
(#920918S1.11272) VAX Cluster (comprising VAX 8550, 8600, & 8650 machines) (under VMS Version 5.3)
VHSIC Processor Module (VPM) AN/AYK-14 (bare machine)
(#920918S1.11273)

U.S. NAVYAdaVAX, Version 5.0 (/NO_OPTIMIZE)
VAX 8600 (under VMS Version 5.3)
(#910517S1.11163) VAX-11/785 (under VMS Version 5.3)
(#910517S1.11165)

U.S. NAVYAdaVAX, Version 5.0 (/OPTIMIZE)
DEC VAXstation 3100 (under VMS Version 5.4)
(#910517S1.11162) VAX 8600 (under VMS Version 5.3)
(#910517S1.11164)

U.S. NAVYAdaVAX, Version 5.5 (/NO_OPTIMIZE)
VAXstation 4000 (under VMS Version 5.5)
(#920918S1.11271)

U.S. NAVYAdaVAX, Version 5.5 (/OPTIMIZE)
VAX-11/785 (under VMS Version 5.3)
(#920918S1.11270)

UNISYS CorporationUCS Ada, Version 1R1
VAX Cluster (comprising VAX 8550, 8600, & 8650 machines) (under VMS Version 5.3)
(#910510S1.11161) UNISYS 2200/600 (under OS1100, Version 43R2)
(BASE #910510S1.11161)

Verdix CorporationSPARCompiler Ada Porting Kit, Version 2.0
SPARCstation LX 4/30 (under Solaris 2.1)
(BASE #921004W1.11285)

Verdix CorporationSPARCworks Professional Ada, Version 2.0
Sun Microsystems Sun-4, SPARCstation, & SPARCserver computer families (under Solaris 2.1)
(BASE #921004W1.11285)

Verdix CorporationVAda-110-0202, Version 6.0
Digitial Equipment Corp. DECstation & DECsystem series of MIPS-based computers (under ULTRIX 3.1, 4.0, 4.1, 4.2, & 4.3)
(#900228W1.11002) DEC VAX-11, MicroVAX, VAXserver, VAXstation, VAX 6000, VAX 8000 & VAX 9000 series (under ULTRIX 4.0)
(BASE #900228W1.11002) VAXsystem 3100 (under ULTRIX 3.1)
(BASE #900228W1.11002)

Verdix CorporationVAda-110-4040, Version 6.0
Sun 4/280 (under SunOS 4.0)
(BASE #900510W1.11006)

Verdix CorporationVAda-110-6161, Version 6.0.2
UNISYS 1100/90, 2200/100, /200, /400, /600, & /900 (under OS 1100, Versions 43R2 & 43R3, as supported)
(#900228W1.11001) DECstation 3100 (under ULTRIX 3.1)
(BASE #900228W1.11001)

Verdix CorporationVADS 386/486 System V, Rel. 3.2, VAda-110-3232, Version 6.0
Zenith Z-486/33E (under SCO UNIX i386 release 3.2)
(BASE #910517W1.11155)

Verdix CorporationVADS 386/486 System V, Rel. 3.2, VAda-110-3232, Version 6.1
Intel 402 (under SCO UNIX 3.2v2.e)
(BASE #910517W1.11157)

Verdix CorporationVADS 386/486, VAda-110-3232, Version 6.2
Hewlett-Packard HP 9000 Series 300 (under HP-UX 7.0)
(BASE #910517W1.11157)

Verdix CorporationVADS AT&T 3B2/600G UNIX System V, Release 3.2.2, VAda-110-5151, Version 6.0
Sun-4/20, /65, /110, /150, /260 & /280; SPARCserver 330, 370, 390, 470 & 490; SPARCstation SLC, 1, 1+, 2, 330 & 370; and SPARCengine 1 VME (under SunOS 4.1)
(#901129W1.11099)

Verdix CorporationVADS AT&T 3B2/600GR UNIX System V, Release 4.0, VAda-110-6363, Version 6.1
Sun Microsystems Sun-3 computer family (under SunOS 4.1)
(#920513W1.11252)

Verdix CorporationVADS BCS => 88K, VAda-110-80680, Version 6.1
IBM RISC System/6000 series of computers (under AIX 3.1 & 3.2)
Motorola MVME187 (88000) (bare machine)
(#920513W1.11254)

Verdix CorporationVADS BCS/88K AViion DGUX 5.4, VAda-110-8080, Version 6.1
DG AViiON Models 4000, 4000GHI, 4020, 4100, 4120, 5010, 5200, 5220, 5240,

5300, 5310, 5400, 5402, 5410, 5412, 6200 & 6220 (under DG/UX 4.3)
(BASE #901129W1.11101)

Verdix CorporationVADS BCS/88K, AViion DGUX 4.3, VAda-110-8080, Version 6.1
Hewlett-Packard HP 9000 Series 300 (under HP-UX 7.0 & 8.0)
(#901129W1.11101) Data General AViiON Model 5120 (under DG/UX 4.3)
(BASE #901129W1.11101)

Verdix CorporationVADS BCS/88K, AViion DGUX 4.3, VAda-110-8080, Versions 6.1 & 6.2
Motorola 8000 Delta Series (MC88000), all models (under Unix System V/88, R32V3)
(BASE #901129W1.11101)

Verdix CorporationVADS BCS/88K, VAda-110-8080, Version 6.1
Data General AViiON Models 4000, 4000GHI, 4020, 4100, 4120, 5010, 5200, 5220, 5240, 5300, 5310, 5400, 5402, 5410, 5412, 6200 & 6220; MODCOMP Real Star Family (under DG/UX 5.4)
(BASE #901129W1.11101) MODCOMP Real Star Family (under REAL/IX C.0.2)
(BASE #901129W1.11101)

Verdix CorporationVADS DEC-RISC => , 68K, Ultrix 4.0, VAda-110-61125, Version 6.0
DECstation 3100 (under Ultrix 3.1)
Cyclone CVME 44, CVME 46 & CVME 48; Force CPU 21, CPU 29, CPU 30, CPU 31, CPU 32, CPU 37 & Golden Triangle Firepower; Heurikon HK68/V30 Series, V2E Series & V2F Series; Integrated Solutions VME68K20, VME68K30, VME68225 & Liberator SBC; Matrix MS-CPU220 & MS-CPU320; Mizar MZ7120, MZ7122, MZ7124, MZ7130, MZ8120 & MZ8130; Sun Microsystems 3E Board Set; Motorola MVME147 Series (MC68030), MVME133 Series, MVME134 & MVME135 (MC68020); Tadpole TP32V & TP33M (bare machines)
(BASE #900726W1.11024)

Verdix CorporationVADS DEC-RISC => 88k, VAda-110-61680, Version 6.1
Sun Microsystems Sun-4, SPARCserver, & SPARCstation omputer families (under SunOS 4.0, 4.1, & 4.2)
Motorola MVME181 (bare machine)
(#910517W1.11153) DECstation 2100 (under ULTRIX V4.0)
Motorola MVME181 (88000) (bare machine)
(BASE #910517W1.11153)

**Verdix CorporationVADS DEC-RISC =>
88k, VAda-110-61680, Versions 6.1 & 6.2**
DEC DECstation & DECsystem computer
families (under ULTRIX 4.0)
*Hughes Realtime Embedded Ada Processor
(REAP) (bare machine)*
(BASE #910517W1.11153)

**Verdix CorporationVADS DEC-RISC =>
MIPS R3000, VAda-110-61620, Version 6.1
& 6.2**
DEC DECstation & DECsystem computer
families (under ULTRIX 4.0)
*Heurikon HKMIPS/V3500; LSI Logic
LR33000/LR33050 Pocket Rocket; any MIPS
R2000-based & R3000-based computers;
Omnibyte VR3000; and Pulsar 3000 (bare
machines)*
(BASE #910517W1.11150) Sun
Microsystems Sun-3 computer family
(under SunOS 4.1)
*Lockheed Sanders STAR MVP (R3000) (bare
machine)*
(#910517W1.11150) DECstation 5000-200
(under ULTRIX V4.0)
*Lockheed Sanders STAR MVP (R3000) (bare
machine)*
(BASE #910517W1.11150)

**Verdix CorporationVADS DEC-RISC,
Ultrix 4.0, VAda-110-6161, Version 6.0**
DECstation 2100, 5000; DECsystem
5400, 5810, 5820, 5830, 5840 (under
ULTRIX 3.1)
(BASE #900228W1.11001)

**Verdix CorporationVADS DEC-RISC,
Ultrix 4.1, VAda-110-6161, Version 6.0**
DECstation 2100, 3100, 5000 & 5200; and
DECsystem 3100, 5000, 5100, 5200,
5400, 5500, 5810, 5820, 5830 & 5840
(under ULTRIX 4.0)
(BASE #900228W1.11001)

**Verdix CorporationVADS DEC-RISC,
Ultrix 4.2, VAda-110-6161, Version 6.0**
DECstation 2100, 3100, 5000 & 5200; and
DECsystem 3100, 5000, 5100, 5200,
5400, 5500, 5810, 5820, 5830 & 5840
(under ULTRIX 4.1)
(BASE #900228W1.11001)

**Verdix CorporationVADS DEC-RISC,
VAda-110-6161, Verisons 6.0, 6.1, & 6.2**
DECstation 2100, 3100, 5000 & 5200;
DECsystem 3100, 5000, 5100, 5200,
5400, 5500, 5810, 5820, 5830 & 5840
(under Ultrix 4.2)
(BASE #900228W1.11001)

**Verdix CorporationVADS
DEC-RISC=>68K, Ultrix 3.1,
VAda-110-61125, Versions 6.0, 6.1, 6.2**
DECstation 2100, 3100, 5000 & 5200; and
DECsystem 3100, 5000, 5100, 5200,
5400, 5500, 5810, 5820, 5830 & 5840
(under ULTRIX 4.0)
*Cyclone CVME 48; Force CPU 21, CPU 29,
CPU 30, CPU 31, CPU 32, CPU 37; Heurikon
HK68/V2Fb Series, HK68/V30 Series, &
HK68/V3E Series; Matrix MS-CPU220,
MD-CPU320, & MD-CPU330; Mizar
MZ7122, MZ7124, MZ7130, MZ8120, &
MZ8130; Motorola MVME133 Series,
MVME134, MVME135, & MVME147 Series;
Radstone CPU-2A; SBE VCOM-24; and
Tadpole TP32V (bare machines)*
(BASE #900726W1.11024)

**Verdix CorporationVADS
DEC-RISK=>68k, Ultrix 3.1,
VAda-110-61125, Version 6.0**
DEC VAX-11, VAXserver, VAXstation,
MicroVAX, VAX 6000, VAX 8000, & VAX
9000 Series of computers (under Ultrix
4.0, 4.1, & 4.2)
*Motorola MVME147 (MC68030) (bare
machine)*
(#900726W1.11024)

**Verdix CorporationVADS HP 9000 Series
700/800, VAda-110-7575, Version 6.2**
HP 9000/720 (under HP-UX 8.0.7)
(BASE #930226W1.11311)

**Verdix CorporationVADS HP 9000/300,
HP-UX 7.0, VAda-110-1515, Version 6.0**
IMB RISC System/6000 series of
computers (under AIX 3.1 & 3.2)
(#900726W1.11018) HP 9000/350 (under
HP-UX 7.0)
(BASE #900726W1.11018)

**Verdix CorporationVADS HP 9000/300,
VAda-110-1515, Version 6.0**
Any computer that executes the Intel
80386 or 80486 instruction set (under 486
SCO ODT v1.1.1 & v2 R3.1, NCR UNIX
System V Release 4.0, and UNIX System
V/486 Release 4.0)
(BASE #910517W1.11157)

**Verdix CorporationVADS HP-9000/300 =>
68K, HP-UX 7.0 , VAda-110-15125, Version
6.0**
AT&T 3B2/600G (under UNIX System V,
Release 3.2.2)
Motorola MVME133A (68020) (bare machine)
(#901129W1.11100)

**Verdix CorporationVADS HP-9000/300 =>
68K, HP-UX 7.0, VAda-110-15125, Version
6.0**
HP 9000 Model 350 (under HP-UX 7.0)
*Cyclone CVME 44, CVME 46 & CVME 48;
Force CPU 21, CPU 29, CPU 30, CPU 31,
CPU 32, CPU 37 & Golden Triangle
Firepower; Heurikon HK68/V30 Series, V2E
Series & V2F Series; Integrated Solutions
VME68K20, VME68K30, VME68225 &
Liberator SBC; Matrix MS-CPU220 &
MS-CPU320; Mizar MZ7120, MZ7122,
MZ7124, MZ7130, MZ8120 & MZ8130; Sun
Microsystems 3E Board Set; Motorola
MVME147 Series (MC68030), MVME133
Series, MVME134 & MVME135 (MC68020);
Tadpole TP32V & TP33M (bare machines)*
(BASE #901129W1.11100)

**Verdix CorporationVADS HP-9000/300 =>
68K, VAda-110-15125, Version 6.0**
HP 9000 Series 300 Models 310, 320,
330, 340, 350, 360 & 370 (under HP-UX
7.0)
*Cyclone CVME 48; Force CPU 21, CPU 29,
CPU 30, CPU 31, CPU 32, CPU 37; Heurikon
HK68/V2Fb Series, HK68/V30 Series, &
HK68/V3E Series; Matrix MS-CPU220,
MS-CPU320, & MS-CPU330; Mizar MZ7122,
MZ7124, MZ7130, MZ8120, & MZ8130;
Motorola MVME133 Series, MVME134,
MVME135, & MVME147 Series; Radstone
CPU-2A; SBE VCOM-24; and Tadpole TP32V*
(BASE #901129W1.11100)

**Verdix CorporationVADS IBM PS/2 AIX
=> 68K, VAda-110-35125, Version 6.0**
IBM PS/2 Model 80 (under AIX 1.1)
*Motorola MVME133A-20 (MC68020) (bare
machine)*
(#900510W1.11005)

**Verdix CorporationVADS IBM PS/2 AIX
=> Intel 80386, VAda-110-35315, Version 6.0**
Sun-3/50, /60, /80, /150, /160, /260, /280,
/470 & /480 (under SunOS 4.0 & 4.1)
Intel iSBC 386/12 (bare machine)
(#900510W1.11004)

**Verdix CorporationVADS IBM PS/2, AIX
1.1, VAda-110-3535, Version 6.1**
Sun Microsystems Sun-4, SPARCstation,
& SPARCserver computer families (under
SunOS 4.0, 4.1., & 4.2)
(#910920W1.11208)

**Verdix CorporationVADS IBM RISC
System/6000 => IBM RISC System/6000,**

VAda-110-71710, Version 6.2
AT&T 3B2/600GR (under UNIX System V,
Release 4.0)
*IBM RISC System/6000 Model 320 (bare
machine)*
(#920513W1.11253)

**Verdix CorporationVADS IBM RISC
System/6000 AIX => 68020/30 ARTX,
VAda-110-71120, Version 6.0**
Sun Microsystems Sun-4, SPARCstation,
& SPARCserver computer families (under
SunOS 4.0, 4.1, & 4.2)
Motorola MVME147 (68030) (bare machine)
(#910920W1.11212) IBM RISC
System/6000 Model 530 (under AIX 3.1)
Motorola MVME147 (68030) (bare machine)
(BASE #910920W1.11212)

**Verdix CorporationVADS IBM RISC
System/6000 VAda-110-7171, Version 6.2**
DECstation & DECsystem (MIPS-based)
computer families (under ULTRIX 4.1, 4.2,
& 4.3)
(BASE #921004W1.11278)

**Verdix CorporationVADS IBM RISC
System/6000, AIX 3.1, VAda-110-7171,
Version 6.0**
Sun-3/50, /60, /80, /150, /160, /260, /280,
/470 & /480 (under SunOS 4.0 & 4.1)
(#900726W1.11017) IBM RISC
System/6000 Model 530 (under AIX 3.1)
(BASE #900726W1.11017) IBM RISC
System/6000 Models 320, 520, 540, 730
& 930 (under AIX 3.1)
(BASE #900726W1.11017)

**Verdix CorporationVADS IBM RISC
System/6000, VAda-110-7171, Version 6.2**
IBM RISC System/6000 models 230 &
570 (under AIX 3.2 & AIX BI/CMW)
(#921004W1.11278E) IBM RISC
System/6000 model 220 (under AIX 3.2)
(#921004W1.11279)

**Verdix CorporationVADS IBM RISC
System/6000, VAda-110-7171, Versions 6.0,
6.1, & 6.2**
IBM RISC System/6000 Models 220, 320,
320H, 340, 350, 520, 520H, 530H, 540,
550, 560, 730, 930, & 950 (under AIX 3.2)
(BASE #900726W1.11017)

**Verdix CorporationVADS IBM RISC
System/6000, VAda-110-71710, Version 6.2**
IBM RISC System/6000 Model 530 (under
AIX 3.2)
(BASE #920513W1.11253)

Verdix CorporationVADS IBM RISC System/6000=>386, AIX 3.1, VAda-110-71315, Version 6.0
IBM RISC System/6000 series of computers (under AIX 3.1 & 3.2)
Intel iSBC 386/116 (bare machine)
(#900726W1.11026) IBM RISC System/6000 Model 530 (under AIX 3.1)
Intel iSBC 386/116 (bare machine)
(BASE #900726W1.11026) IBM RISC System/6000 Models 320, 520, 540, 730 & 930 (under AIX 3.1)
Intel iSBC 486/125 (bare machine)
(BASE #900726W1.11026)

Verdix CorporationVADS IBM RISC System/6000=>68k, AIX 3.1, VAda-110-71125, Version 6.0
Digital Equipment Corp. DECstation & DECsystem series of MIPS-based computers (under ULTRIX 3.1, 4.0, 4.1, 4.2, & 4.3)
Motorola MVME147 (MC68030) (bare machine)
(#900726W1.11025)

Verdix CorporationVADS IBM RISC System/6000=>68K, AIX 3.1, VAda-110-71125, Version 6.0
IBM RISC System/6000 Model 530 (under AIX 3.1)
Cyclone CVME 44, CVME 46 & CVME48; Force CPU 21, CPU 29, CPU 30, CPU 31, CPU 32, CPU 37 & Golden Triangle Firepower; Heurikon HK68/V30 Series, V2E Series & V2F Series; Integrated Solutions VME68K20, VME68K30, VME68225 & Liberator SBC; Matrix MS-CPU220 & MS-CPU320; Mizar MZ7120, MZ7122, MZ7124, MZ7130, MZ8120 & MZ8130; Sun Microsystems 3E Board Set; Motorola MVME133 Series, MVME134, MVME135 & MVME147 Series; and Tadpole TP32V & TP33M (bare machines)
(BASE #900726W1.11025)

Verdix CorporationVADS IBM RISC System/6000=>68K, VAda-110-71125, Versions 6.0, 6.1, & 6.2
DEC VAX-11, VAXserver, VAXstation, MicroVAX, VAX 6000, VAX 8000, VAX 9000 Series of computers (under VMS 5.0, 5.2, & 5.3)
Cyclone CVME 48; Force CPU 21, CPU 29, CPU 30, CPU 31, CPU 32, CPU 37; Heurikon HK68/V2Fb Series, HK68/V30 Series, & HK68/V3E Series; Matrix MS-CPU220, MS-CPU320, & MS-CPU330; Mizar MZ7122, MZ7124, MZ7130, MZ8120, & MZ8130;

Motorola MVME133 Series, MVME134, MVME135, & MVME147 Series; Radstone CPU-2A; SBE VCOM-24; and Tadpole TP32V (bare machine)
(BASE #900726W1.11025) Sun Microsystems Sun-4, SPARCserver & SPARCstation computer families (under SunOS 4.1)
Ironics IV9001 board (AMD 29000) (bare machine)
(BASE #910517W1.11156)

Verdix CorporationVADS IBM RS/6000 => MIPS R3000, VAda-110-71620, Version 6.1
DEC VAX-11, VAXserver, VAXstation, MicroVAX, VAX 6000, VAX 8000, & VAX 9000 Series of computers (under VMS 5.3)
IDT 7RS302 (R3000) (bare machine)
(#910920W1.11202)

Verdix CorporationVADS IBM RS/6000 => MIPS R3000, VAda-110-71620, Versions 6.1 & 6.2
IBM RISC System/6000 Models 320, 520, 540, 730, & 930 (under AIX 3.1)
Heurikon HKMIPS/V3500; LSI Logic LR33000/LR33050 Pocket Rocket; any MIPS R2000-based & R3000-based computers; Omnibyte VR3000; and Pulsar 3000 (bare machines)
(BASE #910920W1.11202)

Verdix CorporationVADS IBM RS/6000 AIX 3.1, VAda-110-71620, Version 6.1
IBM RISC System/6000 Model 530 (under AIX 3.1)
IDT 7RS302 (R3000) (bare machine)
(BASE #910920W1.11202)

Verdix CorporationVADS MIPS => MIPS R3000, VAda-110-62620, Version 6.1
IBM PS/2 Model 80 (under AIX 1.1)
Lockheed Sanders STAR MVP (R3000) (bare machine)
(#910920W1.11209)

Verdix CorporationVADS MIPS => MIPS R3000, VAda-110-62620, Versions 6.1 & 6.2
MIPS RC3230 (under RISC/os 4.52)
Heurikon HKMIPS/V3500; LSI Logic LR33000/LR33050 Pocket Rocket; any MIPS R2000-based R3000-based computers Omnibyte VR3000; and Pulsar 3000 (bare machines)
(BASE #910920W1.11209)

**Verdix CorporationVADS MIPS,
VAda-110-6262, Version 6.1**
Any computer that executes the Intel
80486 instruction set (under SCO UNIX
3.2v4.2)
(#910920W1.11200)

**Verdix CorporationVADS MP Silicon
Graphics, VAda-110-6565, Version 6.2**
Silicon Graphics IRIS 4D/440 (under IRIX
4.0.1)
(#921004W1.11292)

**Verdix CorporationVADS MP Sun SPARC
Solaris 2.1, VAda-110-4141, Version 6.2**
Sun SPARCserver 690 (under Solaris 2.1)
(#921004W1.11290)

**Verdix CorporationVADS MP Sun SPARC,
Solaris 2.0, VAda-110-4141, Version 6.2**
Sun SPARCserver 690 (under Solaris 2.1)
(BASE #921004W1.11290)

**Verdix CorporationVADS Prime EXL/320,
UNIX System V/386 3.2, VAda-110-3232,
Version 6.0**
HP 9000 Series 300 Models 310, 320,
330, 340, 350, 360 & 370 (under HP-UX
7.0)
(#900726W1.11019)

**Verdix CorporationVADS Sequent Balance
DYNIX V3.0, VAda-110-2323, Version 6.0**
Any computer that executes the Intel
80386 or 80486 instruction set (under
NCR UNIX System V Release 4.0, UNIX
System V/486 Release 4.0, 486 Sunsoft
Interactive UNIX Release 4.0, 486
Interactive UNIX Release 3.01R3.2)
(#901129W1.11096)

**Verdix CorporationVADS Silicon Graphics
Self, VAda-110-6464, Version 6.2**
Sun Microsystems Sun-4, SPARCserver,
& SPARCstation computer families (under
Solaris 2.0 & 2.1)
(#921004W1.11291)

**Verdix CorporationVADS Sun SPARC =>
386, VAda-110-40315, Version 6.2**
Sun Microsystems Sun-4, SPARCserver,
& SPARCstation computer families (under
SunOS 4.0, 4.1, & 4.2)
Intel iSBC 386/20p (bare machine)
(#920513W1.11258) Sun Microsystems
Sun-4, SPARCserver, & SPARCstation
computer families (under SunOS 4.1 &
4.2)
Intel iSBC 486/133 & 486/166 (bare machines)
(BASE #920513W1.11258)

**Verdix CorporationVADS Sun SPARC =>
386/486, VAda-110-40315, Version 6.2
under SunOS4.x**
Sun-4/260 (under SunOS, Version 4.1.2)
*Any single-board computer that executes the
Intel 80386 or i486 instruction set (bare
machine)*
(BASE #920513W1.11258)

**Verdix CorporationVADS Sun SPARC
Solaris 2.1, VAda-110-4040, Version 6.2**
NCR model 3550 (under NCR UNIX SVR4
MP-RAS Release 2)
(#921004W1.11284) Sun Microsystems
Sun-4, SPARCstation, & SPARCserver
computer families (under Solaris 2.1 & 2.2)
(#921004W1.11286) SPARCstation 10
model 30 (under Solaris 2.1)
(#921004W1.11287) SPARCstation 10
model 41 (under Solaris 2.1)
(#921004W1.11288) SPARCstation 10
model 42 (under Solaris 2.1)
(#921004W1.11289)

**Verdix CorporationVADS Sun-3 Sun OS,
VAda-110-1313, Version 6.0**
Sun 3/280 (under SunOS 4.0)
(BASE #900510W1.11003)

**Verdix CorporationVADS Sun-3 SunOS =>
68020/30 ARTX, VAda-110-13120, Version
6.0**
MIPS RC3230 (under RISC/OS 4.5)
Motorola MVME147 (68030) (bare machine)
(#910920W1.11210)

**Verdix CorporationVADS Sun-3 SunOS =>
68k, VAda-110-13140, Version 6.0**
Sun Microsystem Sun-4, SPARCstation, &
SPARCserver computer families (under
SunOS 4.0, 4.1, & 4.2)
Motorola MVME165 (68040) (bare machine)
(#910517W1.11149) Sun 3/260 (under
SunOS Release 4.0)
*Motorola MVME 165 (MC68040) (bare
machine)*
(BASE #910517W1.11149)

**Verdix CorporationVADS Sun-3 SunOS =>
AMD 29K, VAda-110-13525, Version 6.04**
DEC VAX-11, VAXserver, VAXstation,
MicroVAX, VAX 6000, VAX 8000, & VAX
9000 Series of computers (under VMS

5.3)
*Ironics IV9001 board (AMD 29000) (Am29000
bare VME machine)*
(#910920W1.11215) Sun-3/180 (under
SunOS 4.1.1)
*Ironics IV9001 board (AMD 29000) (Am29000
bare VME machine)*
(BASE #910920W1.11215)

**Verdix CorporationVADS Sun-4 => CPU32,
SunOS, VAda-110-40150, Versions 6.0 & 6.2**
Sun Microsystems Sun-4, SPARCserver,
SPARCstation, & SPARCengine computer
families (under SunOS 4.1)
*Motorola CPU32-68331, -68332, -68333, &
-68340 Evaluation Systems (bare machines)*
(BASE #910920W1.11207)

**Verdix CorporationVADS Sun-4 =>
MC68000/10, SunOS 4.1, VAda-110-40128,
Version 6.0**
Sun Microsystems Sun-4, SPARCserver,
& SPARCstation computer families (under
SunOS 4.1)
*Motorola 68302, Philips-Signetics 68070, &
Toshiba 68301 (bare machines)*
(BASE #910920W1.11206)

**Verdix CorporationVADS Sun-4 =>
MC68000/10, SunOS, VAda-110-40128,
Versions 6.0, 6.1, & 6.2**
Sun Microsystems Sun-4, SPARCserver,
SPARCstation, & SPARCengine computer
families (under SunOS 4.1)
*Motorola MVME101, Motorola 68302,
Philips-Signetics 68070, & Toshiba 68301
single-board computers (bare machines)*
(BASE #910920W1.11206)

**Verdix CorporationVADS Sun-4 => MIPS
R3000, VAda-110-40620, Version 6.1 & 6.2**
Sun Microsystems Sun-4, SPARCserver,
& SPARCstation computer families (under
SunOS 4.1)
*Heurikon HKMIPS/V3500; LSI Logic
LR33000/LR33050 Pocket Rocket; any MIPS
R2000-based & R3000-based computer;
Omnibyte VR3000; and Pulsar 3000 (bare
machines)*
(BASE #910920W1.11205) IBM
RISC/System 6000 Series of computers
(under AIX 3.1 & 3.2)
*LSI LR33000 Pocket Rocket Evaluation board
(R3000) (bare machine)*
(#910920W1.11205) SPARCserver 490
(under SunOS Release 4.1)
*LSI LR33000 Pocket Rocket Evaluation board
(R3000) (bare machine)*
(BASE #910920W1.11205)

**Verdix CorporationVADS Sun-4 => Sun-3,
Sun OS 4.0, VAda-110-4013, Version 6.0**
Sun Microsystems Sun-4, SPARCserver,
SPARCstation, & SPARCengine computer
families (under SunOS 4.1)
Sun-3/260 (under SunOS 4.0)
(#901129W1.11098) Sun-4/260 (under
SunOS 4.0)
*Sun-3/50, /60, /80, /150, /160, /260, /280, /470
& /480 (under SunOS 4.1)*
(BASE #901129W1.11098)

**Verdix CorporationVADS Sun-4 Solaris 2.1,
VAda-110-4040, Version 6.2**
RDI Britelite IPX Laptop (under Solaris
2.1)
(#921004W1.11285)

**Verdix CorporationVADS Sun-4 SunOS =>
68040, VAda-110-40140, Versions 6.0 & 6.2**
Sun Microsystems Sun-4, SPARCserver &
SPARCstation computer families (under
SunOS 4.1)
*DY 4 Systems SVME-144; Force CPU-40
Series/Eagle I; Motorola MVME165,
MVME167, MVME167A; PEP Modular
Computer VM40; and Tadpole TP41V*
(BASE #910517W1.11152)

**Verdix CorporationVADS Sun-4 SunOS =>
68k, VAda-110-40140, Version 6.0**
DEC VAX-11, VAXserver, VAXstation,
MicroVAX, VAX 6000, VAX 8000, & VAX
9000 Series of computers (under VMS
5.0, 5.2, & 5.3)
Motorola MVME165 (68040) (bare machine)
(#910517W1.11152)

**Verdix CorporationVADS Sun-4 SunOS =>
AMD 29K, 6.0 VAda-110-40525, Version 6.0**
Any computer that executes the Intel
80386 or 80486 instruction set (under
SCO UNIX Release 3.2 running
SecureWare CMW+/386 v2)
*Ironics IV9001 board (AMD 29000) (bare
machine)*
(#910517W1.11156)

**Verdix CorporationVADS Sun-4 SunOS =>
AMD 29K, VAda-110-40525, Versions 6.0,
6.1, & 6.2**
Sun Microsystems Sun-4, SPARCstation,
& SPARCserver of compters (under
SunOS 4.0, 4.1, & 4.2)
*Ironics IV9001 board (AMD 29000) (bare
machine)*
(BASE #910517W1.11156)

**Verdix CorporationVADS Sun-4 SunOS =>
CPU32, VAda-110-40150, Version 6.0**
Sun Microsystems Sun-4, SPARCstation,
& SPARCserver computer families (under
SunOS 4.0, 4.1, & 4.2)
*Motorola CPU32 - M68332EVS Evaluation
System (68332) (bare machine)*
(#910920W1.11207) Sun Microsystems
Sun-4, SPARCserver, & SPARCstation
computer families (under SunOS 4.1)
*Motorola CPU32-68331, -68333, & -68340
Evaluation Systems (bare machines)*
(BASE #910920W1.11207) Sun-4/280
(under SunOS Release 4.0.3)
*Motorola CPU32 - M68332EVS Evaluation
System (68332) (bare machine)*
(BASE #910920W1.11207)

**Verdix CorporationVADS Sun-4 SunOS =>
MC68000/10, VAda-110-40128, Version 6.0**
Sun Microsystems Sun-4, SPARCstation,
& SPARCstation, & SPARCserver series
of computers (under SunOS 4.0, 4.1, &
4.2)
*Motorola MVME101 (68000) with
MVME222-1 memory board (bare machine)*
(#910920W1.11206)

**Verdix CorporationVADS Sun-4 SunOS,
VAda-110-4040, Version 6.0**
IBM PS/2 Model 80 (under AIX 1.1)
(#900510W1.11006)

**Verdix CorporationVADS Sun3 SunOS =>
68020/30 ARTX, VAda-110-13120, Version
6.0**
Sun-3/280 (under SunOS Release 4.0)
*Cyclone CVME 44, 46, & 48; Force CPU 21,
CPU 29, CPU 30, CPU 31, CPU 32, CPU 37,
& Golden Triangle Firepower; Heurikon
HK68/V2E Series, /V2F Series, & /V30 Series;
Integrated Solutions VME68K20, 68K30,
68225, & Liberator SBC; Matrix MS-CPU220
& MS-CPU320; Mizar MZ7122, MZ7124,
MZ7130, MZ8120, & MZ8130; Motorola
MVME133 Series, MVME134, MVME135,
MVME136, MVME141, & MVME147 Series;
Sun Microsystems 3E board set; and Tadpole
Technology TP32V & TP32M (bare machines)*
(BASE #910920W1.11210)

**Verdix CorporationVADS Sun3 SunOS =>
68K, VAda-110-13125, Version 6.0**
Sun-4/20, /65, /110, /150 & /260;
SPARCserver 310, 330, 370, 390, 470 &
490; SPARCstation SLC, 1, 1+, 2, 310,
330 & 370; and SPARCengine 1 VME

(under SunOS 4.1)
*Motorola MVME147 (MC68030) (bare
machine)*
(#900510W1.11007) Sun 3/280 (under
SunOS 4.0)
*Cyclone CVME 44, CVME 46 & CVME 48;
Force CPU 21, CPU 29, CPU 30, CPU 31,
CPU 32, CPU 37 & Golden Triangle
Firepower; Heurikon HK68/V30 Series, V2E
Series & V2F Series; Integrated Solutions
VME68K20, VME68K30, VME68225 &
Liberator SBC; Matrix MS-CPU220 &
MS-CPU320; Mizar MZ7120, MZ7122,
MZ7124, MZ7130, MZ8120 & MZ8130; Sun
Microsystems 3E Board Set; Motorola
MVME147 Series & MVME141 (MC68030),
MVME133 Series, MVME134, MVME135 &
MVME136 (MC68020), MVME-110,
MVME-165 & MVME-167; Tadpole TP32V &
TP33M (bare machines)*
(BASE #900510W1.11007)

**Verdix CorporationVADS Sun3 SunOS,
VAda-110-1313, Version 6.0**
DEC VAX-11, VAXserver, VAXstation,
MicroVAX, VAX 6000, VAX 8000 & VAX
9000 Series of computers (under ULTRIX
4.2)
(#900510W1.11003)

**Verdix CorporationVADS Sun4 => 68K,
Sun OS 4.0, VAda-110-40125, Version 6.0**
Sequent Balance 8000 (under DYNIX
Version 3.0)
Motorola MVME147 (68030) (bare machine)
(#901129W1.11097) Sun-4/260 (under
SunOS 4.0)
*Cyclone CVME 44, CVME 46 & CVME 48;
Force CPU 21, CPU 29, CPU 30, CPU 31,
CPU 32, CPU 37 & Golden Triangle
Firepower; Heurikon HK68/V30 Series, V2E
Series & V2F Series; Integrated Solutions
VME68K20, VME68K30, VME68225 &
Liberator SBC; Matrix MS-CPU220 &
MS-CPU320; Mizar MZ7120, MZ7122,
MZ7124, MZ7130, MZ8120 & MZ8130; Sun
Microsystems 3E Board Set; Motorola
MVME110 (MC68000), MVME133 Series,
MVME134, MVME135 & MVME136
(MC68020), MVME147 Series & MVME141
(MC68030), MVME-165 & MVME-167
(MC68040); Tadpole TP32V & TP33M (bare
machines)*
(BASE #901129W1.11097)

**Verdix CorporationVADS Sun4 => 68K,
Sun OS 4.1, VAda-110-40125, Version 6.0**
Sun-4/20, /65, /110 & /150; SPARCserver
330, 370, 390, 470 & 490; SPARCstation

SLC, 1, 1+, 2, 330 & 370; and
SPARCengine 1 VME (under SunOS 4.1)
Cyclone CVME 44, 46, & 48; Force CPU 21,
CPU 29, CPU 30, CPU 31, CPU 32, CPU 37,
& Golden Triangle Firepower; Heurikon
HK68/V2E Series, /V2F Series, & /V30 Series;
Integrated Solutions VME68K20, 68K30,
68225, & Liberator SBC; Matrix MS-CPU220
& MS-CPU320; Mizar MZ7120, MZ7122,
MZ7124, MZ7130, MZ8120, MZ8130, &
CPU330; Motorola MVME133 Series,
MVME134, MVME135, & MVME147 Series;
Sun Microsystems 3E board set; and Tadpole
Technology TP32V & TP33M (bare machines)
(BASE #901129W1.11097)

Verdix CorporationVADS Sun4 => 68K,
SunOS 4.0, VAda-110-40125, Version 6.0 &
6.2
IBM RISC System/6000 Models 220, 320,
320H, 340, 350, 520, 520H, 530H, 540,
550, 560, 730, 930, & 950 (under AIX 3.2)
Cyclone CVME 48; Force CPU 21, CPU 29,
CPU 30, CPU 31, CPU 32, CPU 37; Heurikon
HK68/V2Fb Series, HK68/V30 Series, &
HK68/V3E Series; Matrix MS-CPU220,
MD-CPU320, MD-CPU330; Mizar MZ7122,
MZ7124, MZ7130, MZ8120, & MZ8130;
Motorola MVME133 Series, MVME134,
MVME135, & MVME147 Series; Radstone
CPU-2A; SBE VCOM-24; and Tadpole TP32V
(BASE #900726W1.11097)

Verdix CorporationVADS Sun4 =>
MC68000/10, VAda-110-40128, Version 6.0
Sun-4/280 (under SunOS Release 4.0.3)
Motorola MVME101 (68000) with
MVME222-1 memory board (bare machine)
(BASE #910920W1.11206)

Verdix CorporationVADS Sun4 => MIPS
R3000, VAda-110-42620, Version 6.0
Sun Microsystems Sun-4, SPARCstation,
& SPARCserver computer families (under
SunOS 4.0, 4.1, & 4.2)
Lockheed Sanders STAR MVP (R3000) (bare
machine)
(#930901W1.11323)

Verdix CorporationVADS Sun4 => MIPS
R4000, VAda-110-40630, Version 6.2
Sun SPARCstation 2 (under Solaris 2.2)
Silicon Graphics Indigo XS4000 used as a
MIPS R4000 board (bare machine)
(#930901W1.11324)

Verdix CorporationVADS Sun4 =>
PARAGON, VAda-110-40782, Version 6.2
Sun SPARCstation 2 (under SunOS 4.1.2)
Intel PARAGON Supercomputer (under OSF/1
Release 1.0.3 Server 1.1 PT10.7.6(T10.4))
(#930901W1.11325)

Verdix CorporationVADS Sun4 => SPARC,
Sun OS 4.1, VAda-110-40440, Version 6.0
Data General AViiON computer series
(under DG/UX 4.3 & 5.4)
SPARCengine 1E (bare machine)
(#901129W1.11102)

Verdix CorporationVADS Sun4 SunOS =>
68020/30 ARTX, VAda-110-40120, Version
6.0
Sun Microsystems Sun-3 computer family
(under SunOS 4.1)
Motorola MVME147 (68030) (bare machine)
(#910920W1.11211) SPARCstation 2
(under SunOS Release 4.1.1)
Motorola MVME147 (68030) (bare machine)
(BASE #910920W1.11211)

Verdix CorporationVADS Sun4 SunOS =>
68020/30 ARTX, VAda-110-40120, Versions
6.0 & 6.2
Sun Microsystems Sun-4, SPARCserver,
& SPARCstation computer families (under
SunOS 4.1)
Cyclone CVME 48; Force CPU 21, CPU 29,
CPU 30, CPU 31, CPU 32, CPU 37; Heurikon
HK68/V2Fb Series, HK68/V30 Series, &
HK68/V3E Series; Matrix MS-CPU220,
MS-CPU320, & MS-CPU330; Mizar MZ7122,
MZ7124, MZ7130, MZ8120 & MZ8130;
Motorola MVME133 Series, MVME134,
MVME135, & MVME147 Series; Radstone
CPU-2A; SBE VCOM-24; and Tadpole TP32V
(bare machines)
(BASE #910920W1.11211)

Verdix CorporationVADS Sun4 SunOS =>
68k, VAda-110-40140, Version 6.0
Sun 4/280 (under SunOS Release 4.0)
Motorola MVME165 (68040) (bare machine)
(BASE #910517W1.11152)

Verdix CorporationVADS Sun4 SunOS =>
AMD 29K, VAda-110-40525, Version 6.0
Sun 4/280 (under SunOS 4.0.3)
Ironics IV9001 board (AMD 29000) (bare
machine)
(BASE #910517W1.11156)

Verdix CorporationVADS Sun4=>SPARC, Sun OS 4.1, VAda-110-40440, Version 6.0
Sun-4/490 (under SunOS 4.1)
SPARCengine 1E (bare machine)
(BASE #901129W1.11102)

Verdix CorporationVADS Sun4=>SPARC, Sun OS4.1, VAda-110-40440, Version 6.0 & 6.1
Sun-4/20, /65, /110, /150 & /260;
SPARCserver 330, 370, 390, 470 & 490;
and SPARCstation SLC, 1, 1+, 2, 330 & 370 (under SunOS 4.1)
SPARCengine 1E & Ironics IV-SPARC-33A. (bare machines)
(BASE #901129W1.11102)

Verdix CorporationVADS System V/386/486, VAda-110-3232, Version 6.1
IBM RISC System/6000 model 530H (under AIX 3.2)
(#921004W1.11280) ASL 486/33 (under UNIX System V, Release 3.2)
(#921004W1.11281) AST Premium 486 (under UNIX System V, Release 4.0)
(#921004W1.11282) NCR model 3450 (under NCR UNIX SVR4 MP-RAS Release 2)
(#921004W1.11283)

Verdix CorporationVADS SYSTEM V/860 RELEASE 4, VAda-110-9090, Version 6.1
IBM RISC System/6000 Models 320, 520, 540, 730, & 930 (under AIX 3.1)
(#910920W1.11213)

Verdix CorporationVADS SYSTEM V/88 RELEASE 4, VAda-110-8080, Version 6.2
Motorola Delta 8640 (under UNIX System V/88 Release 4.0)
(#930901W1.11327)

Verdix CorporationVADS SYSTEM V/88 RELEASE, VAda-110-8080, Version 6.2
Sun SPARCstation 2 (under SunOS 4.1.3)
(#930901W1.11326)

Verdix CorporationVADS UNIX System V/386, Rel. 4, VAda-110-3232, Version 6.0
DEC VAX-11, VAXserver, VAXstation, MicroVAX, VAX 6000, VAX 8000 & VAX 9000 Series of computers (under VMS 5.3)
(#901129W1.11095)

Verdix CorporationVADS UNIX System V/386/486, VAda-110-3232, Versions 6.0, 6.1, & 6.2
NCR 3000, 3320, 3335, 3345, 3445, 3447, 3450, & 3550 (under NCR UNIX System

V, Release 4.0); AST Premium 486/33 (under UNIX System V/486, Release 4.0)
(BASE #901129W1.11095)

Verdix CorporationVADS UNIX System V/486, Rel. 4, VAda-110-3232, Version 6.0
Intel 302 System (under UNIX System V/386, Release 4)
(BASE #901129W1.11095)

Verdix CorporationVADS UNIX System V/486, Rel.4, VAda-110-3232, Version 6.0
NCR 3000, 3320, 3335, 3345, 3445, 3447, 3450, & 3550 (under UNIX System V/486, Release 4)
(BASE #901129W1.11095)

Verdix CorporationVADS UNIX System V/486, SCO UNIX 3.2, VAda-110-3232, Version 6.0
Sun Microsystems Sun-4, SPARCserver & SPARCstation computer families (under SunOS 4.1)
(#910517W1.11155) Zenith Z-486/25E (under SCO UNIX i386 release 3.2)
(BASE #910517W1.11155)

Verdix CorporationVADS UNIX System V/486, SCO UNIX 3.2, VAda-110-3232, Version 6.0, 6.1, & 6.2
Any Computer System Comprising: cpu: any that executes the Intel 80386/i486 instruction set (under Any operating system compatible with Unix System V Release 3.2)
(BASE #910517W1.11155)

Verdix CorporationVADS UNIX System V/486, SCO UNIX 3.2, VAda-110-3232, Version 6.1
Sun Microsystems Sun-4, SPARCstation, & SPARCserver series of computers (under SunOS 4.0, 4.1, & 4.2)
(#910517W1.11157)

Verdix CorporationVADS UNIX System V/486, SCO UNIX 3.2, VAda-110-3232, Versions 6.1, & 6.2
Any Computer System Comprising: cpu: any that executes the Intel 80386/i486 instruction set (under Any operating system compatible with Unix System V Release 3.2)
(BASE #910517W1.11157)

Verdix CorporationVADS VAda-110-6262, Version 6.1
MIPS RC3230 (under RISC/os 4.52)
(BASE #910920W1.11200)

Verdix CorporationVADS VAX VMS =>
AMD 29K, VAda-110-03525, Version 6.04
MicroVAX 3600 (under VMS 5.2)
Ironics IV9001 board (AMD 29000) (Am29000
bare VME machine)
(BASE #910920W1.11214)

Verdix CorporationVADS VAX/ULTRIX =>
68K, ULTRIX 3.1, VAda-110-02125,
Version 6.0
MicroVAX 3100 (under Ultrix 3.1)
Cyclone CVME 44, CVME 46 & CVME 48;
Force CPU 21, CPU 29, CPU 30, CPU 31,
CPU 32, CPU 37 & Golden Triangle
Firepower; Heurikon HK68/V30 Series, V2E
Series & V2F Series; Integrated Solutions
VME68K20, VME68K30, VME68225 &
Liberator SBC; Matrix MS-CPU220 &
MS-CPU320; Mizar MZ7120, MZ7122,
MZ7124, MZ7130, MZ8120 & MZ8130; Sun
Microsystems 3E Board Set; Motorola
MVME147 Series & MVME141 (MC68030),
MVME133 Series, MVME134 & MVME135
(MC68020); Tadpole TP32V & TP33M (bare
machines); Tektronix MV System, MV 68020
Support System using TekDB Version 5.0.2
emulation software (bare machine simulation)
(BASE #900726W1.11023)

Verdix CorporationVADS
VAX/Ultrix=>68k, Ultrix 3.1,
VAda-110-02125, Version 6.0
DEC VAX-11, VAXserver, VAXstation,
MicroVAX, VAX 6000, VAX 8000 & VAX
9000 Series of computers (under VMS
5.3)
Tektronix MV System, MV 68020 Support
System, using TekDB Version 5.0.2 emulation
software (bare machine simulation)
(#900726W1.11023)

Verdix CorporationVADS
VAX/ULTRIX=>68K, ULTRIX 3.1,
VAda-110-02125, Version 6.0
DEC VAX-11, VAXserver, VAXstation,
MicroVAX, VAX 6000, VAX 8000 & VAX
9000 Series of computers (under Ultrix
3.1)
Cyclone CVME 48; Force CPU 21, CPU 29,
CPU 30, CPU 31, CPU 32, CPU 37; Heurikon
HK68/V2Fb Series, HK68/V30 Series, &
HK68/V3E Series; Matrix MS-CPU220,
MS-CPU320, & MS-CPU330; Mizar MZ7122,
MZ7124, MZ7130, MZ8120, & MZ8130;
Motorola MVME133 Series, MVME134,
MVME135, & MVME147 Series; Radstone
CPU-2A; SBE VCOM-24; Tadpole TP32V;
and Tektronix MV System, MV 68020 Support
System using TekDB Version 5.0.2 emulation

software (bare machine simulation) (bare
machines)
(BASE #900726W1.11023)

Verdix CorporationVADS VAX/VMS 5.2 =>
Intel 80386/WEITEK 3167,
VAda-110-03315, Version 6.0
Sun Microsystems Sun-4, SPARCstation,
& SPARCserver computer families (under
SunOS 4.0, 4.1, & 4.2)
Intel iSBC 386/116 using a WEITEK 3167 fpu
(bare machine)
(#901129W1.11094)

Verdix CorporationVADS VAX/VMS 5.2,
VAda-110-0303, Version 6.0
Prime EXL/320 (under UNIX System
V/386 3.2)
(#900726W1.11020)

Verdix CorporationVADS VAX/VMS 5.2,
VAda-110-0303, Versions 6.0 & 6.2
DEC VAX-11, VAXserver, VAXstation,
MicroVAX, VAX 6000, VAX 8000 & VAX
9000 Series of computers (under VMS
5.3)
(BASE #900726W1.11020)

Verdix CorporationVADS VAX/VMS 5.3 =>
Intel 80386/WEITEK 3167,
VAda-110-03315, Version 6.0
MicroVAX 3100 (under VMS Version 5.2)
Intel iSBC 386/116 using a WEITEK 3167 fpu
(bare machine)
(BASE #901129W1.11094)

Verdix CorporationVADS VAX/VMS 5.3,
VAda-110-0303, Version 6.0
MicroVAX 3100 (under VAX/VMS V5.2)
(BASE #900726W1.11020)

Verdix CorporationVADS VAX/VMS =>
68040, VAda-110-03140, Version 6.0
MIPS RC3xxx & RC4xxx series of
computers (under RISC/OS 4.5)
Motorola MVME165 (68040) (bare machine)
(#910920W1.11201) MicroVAX 3100 (under
VMS 5.3)
Motorola MVME165 (68040) (bare machine)
(BASE #910920W1.11201)

Verdix CorporationVADS VAX/VMS =>
68K, VMS 5.2, VAda-110-03125, Version 6.0
MicroVAX 3100 (under VAX/VMS V5.2)
Cyclone CVME 44, CVME 46 & CVME 48;
Force CPU 21, CPU 29, CPU 30, CPU 31,
CPU 32, CPU 37 & Golden Triangle
Firepower; Heurikon HK68/V30 Series, V2E
Series & V2F Series; Integrated Solutions

*VME68K20, VME68K30, VME68225 &
Liberator SBC; Matrix MS-CPU220 &
MS-CPU320; Mizar MZ7120, MZ7122,
MZ7124, MZ7130, MZ8120 & MZ8130; Sun
Microsystems 3E Board Set; Motorola
MVME147 Series & MVME141 (MC68030),
MVME133 Series, MVME134, MVME135 &
MVME136 (MC68020), MVME-165 &
MVME167; Tadpole TP32V & TP33M (bare
machines)*
(BASE #900726W1.11021)

**Verdix CorporationVADS VAX/VMS =>
MIPS R3000, VAda-110-03620, Versions 6.1
& 6.2**
DEC VAX-11, VAXserver, VAXstation,
MicroVAX, VAX 6000, VAX 8000 & VAX
9000 Series of computers (under VMS
5.3)
*Heurikon HKMIPS/V3500; LSI Logic
LR33000/LR33050 Pocket Rocket; any MIPS
R2000-based & R3000-based computers;
Omnibyte VR3000; and Puslar 3000 (bare
machines)*
(BASE #910517W1.11151)

**Verdix CorporationVADS
VAX/VMS=>68K, VAda-110-03125,
Versions 6.0 & 6.2**
IBM RISC System/6000 Models 320, 520,
540, 730 & 930 (under AIX 3.1)
*Cyclone CVME 48; Force CPU 21, CPU 29,
CPU 30, CPU 31, CPU 32, CPU 37; Heurikon
HK68/V2Fb Series, HK68/V30 Series, &
HK68/V3E Series; Matrix MS-CPU220,
MS-CPU320, &MS-CPU330; Mizar MZ7122,
MZ7124, MZ7130, MZ8120, & MZ8130;
Motorola MVME133 Series, MVME134,
MVME135, & MVME147 Series; Radstone
CPU-2A; SBE VCOM-24; and Tadpole TP32V
(bare machine)*
(BASE #900726W1.11025)

**Verdix CorporationVADS VAX/VMS=>68k,
VMS 5.2, VAda-110-03125, Version 6.0**
DEC VAX-11, MicroVAX, VAXserver,
VAXstation, and VAX 6000, 8000, & 9000
series of computers (under VMS 5.0, 5.2,
& 5.3)
*Motorola MVME147 (MC68030) (bare
machine)*
(#900726W1.11021)

**Verdix CorporationVADS
VAX/VMS=>Intel 386, VMS 5.2,
VAda-110-03315, Version 6.0**
DEC VAX-11, VAXserver, VAXstation,
MicroVAX, VAX 6000, VAX 8000 & VAX

9000 Series of computers (under VMS
5.2)
Intel iSBC 386/32 (bare machine)
(#900726W1.11022)

**Verdix CorporationVADS
VAX/VMS=>Intel 386, VMS 5.3,
VAda-110-03315, Version 6.0**
MicroVAX 3100 (under VAX/VMS V5.2)
Intel iSBC 386/32 (bare machine)
(BASE #900726W1.11022)

**Verdix CorporationVADS VMS =>
AMD29000, VAda-110-03525, Version 6.04**
Okidata I860 Workstation (under UNIX
SYSTEM V/860 RELEASE 4 v1.0)
*Ironics IV9001 board (AMD 29000) (Am29000
bare VME machine)*
(#910920W1.11214)

**Verdix CorporationVADS VMS => MIPS
R3000, VAda-110-03620, Version 6.1**
DECstation & DECsystem (MIPS-based)
computer families (under ULTRIX 3.1, 4.0,
4.1, 4.2, & 4.3)
*Integrated Device Technology IDT7RS302
(bare machine)*
(#910517W1.11151) MicroVAX 3600 (under
VMS V5.2)
*Integrated Device Technology IDT7RS302
(bare machine)*
(BASE #910517W1.11151)

**Verdix CorporationVADS Windows
NT/486, VAda-110-36315, Version 6.2**
Data General AViiON Model 530 (under
DG/UX Release 5.4.2)
(#940110W1.11337)

**Verdix CorporationVADSself HP 9000
series 700 VAda-110-7575, Version 6.2**
Silicon Graphics IRIS 4D/440 (under IRIX
4.0.1)
(#930226W1.11311)

**Verdix CorporationVADSworks
DEC-RISC=>MIPS R3000,
VAda-115-61640, Version 2.0**
Sun Microsystems Sun-4, SPARCserver,
& SPARCstation computer families (under
SunOS 4.0, 4.1, & 4.2)
*Lockheed Sanders STAR MVP board (bare
machine, using vxWorks 5.0)*
(#921004W1.11277) DECstation 5000/200
(under Ultrix V4.1)
*Heurikon HKMIPS/V3500; LSI Logic
LR33000/LR33050 Pocket Rocket; any MIPS
R2000-based & R3000-based computers;*

Omnibyte VR3000; and Pulsar 3000 (bare machines, using VxWorks 5.0 & 5.1)
(BASE #921004W1.11277)

Verdix CorporationVADSworks Sun-4 => MIPS R3000 VAda-115-40640, Version 2.0
HP 9000 Series 700 & 800, all models (under HP-UX Versions 8.0 & 9.0, all releases as appropriate)
Heurikon HKMIPS/3500 (R3000) board (bare machine, using vxWorks 5.0)
(#930226W1.11312) Sun-4/20 (under SunOS Release 4.1.1)
Heurikon HKMIPS/V3500; (bare machine, using vxWorks 5.0)
(BASE #930226W1.11312)

Verdix CorporationVADSworks Sun4 => 68k, VAda-115-40800, Version 2.0
DECstation & DECsystem (MIPS-based) computer families (under ULTRIX 3.1, 4.0, 4.1, 4.2, & 4.3)
Motorola MVME147SA (bare machine, using vxWorks 5.0)
(#910517W1.11154)

Verdix CorporationVADSworks Sun4 => 68K, VAda-115-40800, Version 2.0
Motorola 88000 Delta (under R32V3 920117)
Motorola MVME167A (68040) (bare machine, using VxWorks 5.0)
(#920513W1.11256)

Verdix CorporationVADSworks Sun4 => 68k, VAda-115-40800, Version 2.0
Sun 4/20 (under SunOS 4.1.1)
Force CPU 21, CPU 29, CPU 30, CPU 31, CPU 32, CPU 33, CPU 37, & Golden Triangle Firepower; General Micro Systems GMSV17 & GMSV37; Heurikon HK68/V20, /V2E, /V2F, /V2FA, /V30, /V30XE, /V3E, & /V3F; Ironics IV-3201a, 3204, 3220, & 3230; Matrix MS-CPU320; Mizar MZ7122 & MZ7124; Motorola MVME133 Series, MVME135, MVME135A, MVME141, MVME143, & MVME147; Radstone PME 68-25 & 68-31; SBE VLAN-e & VPU30; Sun Microsystems 3E; and Tadpole Technology TP32V-4MB (bare machines, using vxWorks 5.0)
(BASE #910517W1.11154)

Verdix CorporationVADSworks Sun4 => 68K, VAda-115-40800, Version 2.0
Sun-4/20 (under SunOS, 4.1.1)
DY 4 Systems SVME-144; Force CPU-40 Series; Motorola MVME162, MVME165, MVME167, & MVME167A; PEP Modular

Computer VM40; and Tadpole TP41V (bare machine, using vxWorks 5.0)
(BASE #920513W1.11256)

Verdix CorporationVADSworks Sun4 => 68K, VAda-115-40800, Versions 2.0 & 3.0
Sun Microsystems Sun-4, SPARCserver, & SPARCstation computer families (under SunOS 4.0, 4.1, & 4.2)
DY 4 Systems SVME-144; Force CPU-40 Series; Motorola MVME162, MVME165, MVME167, & MVME167A; PEP Modular Computer VM40; Radstone CPU-40; and Tadpole TP41V (bare machine, using vxWorks 5.0)
(BASE #920513W1.11256)

Verdix CorporationVADSworks Sun4 => SPARC, VAda-115-40850, Version 2.0
Sun Microsystems Sun-4, SPARCstation, & SPARCserver computer family (under SunOS 4.0, 4.1, & 4.2)
Sun SPARCengine 1e (bare machine, using VxWorks v5.0)
(#920513W1.11257) Sun-4/20 (under SunOS, 4.1.1)
Sun SPARCengine 1e (bare machine, using vxWorks 5.0)
(BASE #920513W1.11257)

Wang Laboratories, Inc.Wang VS Ada Version 5.00.00
Compudyne 486 (under Windows NT 3.1) (#901129W1.11093) Wang VS 8480 (under Wang VSOS 7.30.02)
(BASE #901129W1.11093)

York Software Engineering LimitedYork Ada Compiler Environment (ACE) Release 5
Wang VS Models: 100 & 300; 5430, 5440, 5450 & 5460; 7010, 7110, 7120, 7150 & 7310; 8220, 8230, 8260, 8430, 8460, 8470 & 8480; and 10050, 10075 & 10100 (under all VS OS versions 7.21.xx & 7.30.xx)
(#901127N1.11073) InterAct 220, 2020, 3050, 6040, 6080, 6240 & 6280 (under CLIX Release 3.1)
(BASE #901127N1.11073) Intergraph InterPro 3050 Workstation (under CLIX R3.1)
(BASE #901127N1.11073) Intergraph Mobile GIS/C2 (under CLIX Release 3.1)
(BASE #901127N1.11073) InterPro 125, 225, 340, 360, 2020, 3070, 6040, 6240, 6080 & 6280 (under CLIX Release 3.1)
(BASE #901127N1.11073) InterServe 200, 300, 2000, 3000, 4200, 5200, 6000, 6105

& 6505 (under CLIX Release 3.1)
(BASE #901127N1.11073) InterView 220 &
3050 (under CLIX Release 3.1)
(BASE #901127N1.11073)

13

Ada suppliers

13.1   Compiler suppliers

AETECH

US contact

5841 Edison Place
Suite 110
Carlsbad
CA 92008
USA

Tel: +1 619 431 7714
Fax: +1 619 431 7714

European contacts

Grey Matter Ltd
Prigg Meadow
Ashburton
Devon
TQ13 7DF
UK

Tel: +44 1364 53499
Fax: +44 1364 53071

LinSoft
Box 634
S-58107 Linkoping
Sweden

Tel: +46 13 11 1588
Fax: +46 13 15 2429

Products

AETECH POSIX Compiler, IntegrAda 386 and IntegrAda for Windows. AETECH Ada Software Development Toolset.

ALENIA Aeritalia & Selenia S.p.A

Via Tiburtina km. 12,4
00131 Roma
Italy

Tel: +39 6 41972520

Products

DACS 80X86PM, DACS VAX/VMS to 80X86 PM
MARA Ada Cross Compiler.

Alliant Computer Systems

1 Monarch Drive
Littleton
MA 01460
USA

Tel: +1 508 486 4950

Products

Alliant FX/Ada Compiler, Alliant FX/Ada-2800 Compiler.

Alsys

European contacts

Alsys
Partridge House
Newtown Road
Henley-on-Thames
Oxfordshire
RG9 1EN
UK

Tel: +44 1491 579090
Fax: +44 1491 571866

Alsys SA
29 ave Lucien-René Duchesne
78170 La Celle-St Cloud
France

Tel: +33 1 30 78 17 17
Fax: +33 1 39 18 26 80

Alsys GmbH
Kleinoberfeld 7
D-76135
Germany

Tel: +49 721 98 65 30
Fax: +49 721 98 65 398

Alsys AB
Utsiktsvägen 10
Box 2014
S-149 02 Nynäshamn
Sweden

Tel: +46 8 520 69010
Fax: +46 8 520 20965

US contact

Alsys, Inc.
Suite 600
11921 Freedom Drive
Reston
Virginia 22090-9606
USA

Tel: +1 703 904 7811
Fax: +1 703 904 7823

Products

Ada compilation systems for a wide range of host and target machines including SPARC workstations, HP 9000 series 700 and 800, VAX/VMS and Intel and Motorola processors. Details of training courses can be found in Chapter 14.

ATLAS ELEKTRONIK GmbH

Sebaldsbruecker Heerstr. 235
P.O. Box 44 85 45
W-2800 Bremen 44
Germany

Tel: +49 291 457 3058

Products

ATLAS ELEKTRONIK Ada Compiler VVME.

Concurrent Computer Corporation

US contact

2 Crescent Place
Oceanport
NJ 07757
USA

Tel: +1 908 870 5936
Fax: +1 908 870 5860

Other contacts

227 Bath Road
Slough
Berkshire
SL1 4AX
UK

Tel: +44 1753 77777
Fax: +44 1753 24657

Australia:	+61 2 887 1000
Hong Kong:	+852 880 0802
Japan:	+81 3 3864 5713
Singapore:	+65 339 8877
France:	+33 1 30 85 37 00
Germany:	+49 89 85 60 30
Holland:	+31 18 203 8000

Products

C^3 Ada Language System.

CONVEX Computer BV

European contact

CONVEX Computer BV
Europalaan 514
3526 KS Utrecht
Postbus 3267
3502 GG Utrcht
The Netherlands

Tel: +31 30 888368
Fax: +31 30 892942

US contact

CONVEX Computer Corp.
3000 Waterview Parkway
P.O. Box 833851
Richardson
TX 75083
USA

Tel: +1 214 497 4346

Products

CONVEX Ada compilation system.

Cray Research

US contacts

500 Montezuma
Suite 118
Santa Fe
NM 87501
USA

Tel: +1 505 988 2468

655A Lone Oak Drive
Eagan
Minnesota 55121
USA

European contact

Cray Research Europe Ltd
Oldbury
Bracknell
Berkshire
RG12 4TQ
UK

Tel: +44 1344 485971
Fax: +44 1344 426319

Products

Cray Ada 3.1.

DDC International

European contact

DDC-I International A/S
Gl. Lundtoftevej 1B
DK-2800 Lyngby
Denmark

Tel: +45 45 87 11 44
Fax: +45 45 87 22 17

First Matrix Limited
Old Lion Court
High Street
Marlborough
Wiltshire
UK

Tel: +44 1672 515 510
Fax: + 44 1672 515 514

US contacts

DDC-I, Inc.
410 N. 44th Street
Phoenix
AZ 85008
USA

Tel: +1 602 275 7172
Fax: +1 602 275 7502

DDC-I, Inc.
5930 LBJ Freeway
Suite No. 400
Dallas
TX 75240
USA

Tel: +1 214 458 9611
Fax: +1 214 458 9606

DDC-I, Inc.
24 Pleasant Run
Merrimack
NH 03054
USA

Tel: +1 603 424 6620
Fax: +1 603 424 8289

Products

DDC-I Ada compilers, Ada debuggers, and Ada tools
for native and cross development. Re-seller of Ada
tools, including BEOLOGIC tool for control and
surveillance systems, and KeyOne CASE toolset for
the design, programming, and documentation phases
of Ada software products.

DESC Ltd

Jays Close
Viables Industrial Estate
Basingstoke
Hampshire
RG22 4BY
UK

Tel: +44 1256 819711

Products

VME Ada Compiler - Limited availability.

Digital Equipment Corporation

US contact

MS: ZK2-1/M11
110 Spit Brook Road
Nashua
NH 03062
USA

Tel: +1 603 881 0247

UK contact

PO Box 115
Worton Grange
Imperial Way
Reading
Berkshire
RG2 0TL
UK

Tel: +44 1734 868711

Products

DEC Ada, VAX Ada, XD Ada Cross-Development
System.

EDS

European contacts

Pembroke House
Pembroke Broadway
Camberley
Surrey
GU15 3XD
UK

Tel: +44 1276 415000
Fax: +44 1276 683511

XD Ada is also distributed and supported throughout Europe by Digital Equipment Corporation. For more information, contact your local Digital Sales Representative.

US contact

8 New England Executive Park
Burlington
MA 01803
USA

Tel: +1 617 273 3030

Products

EDS, the world's premier IT services company, offers proven software development toolkits and services, providing high quality, high performance products for M68000 and MIL-STD-1750A systems developers.

Together with Digital Equipment Corporation, EDS has developed the XD Ada product family, which has become established as the highest quality and highest performance Ada cross-development toolset in the market today.

The combination of real performance, integration and overall product quality represents a low risk solution, offering increased programmer productivity and reduced development costs.

E-Systems, Inc.

ECI Division
1501 72nd Street North
St. Petersburg
FL 33733
USA

Tel: +1 813 381 2000

Products

Tolerant Ada Development System.

EII SOFTWARE

315 Bureaux de la Colline
92213 Saint-Cloud
France

Tel: +33 1 49117328
Fax: +33 1 49117531

Products

Entreprise II software engineering environment. Enterprise II is a PCTE based framework and repository product from EII SOFTWARE running on UNIX workstations on heterogeneous LANs. The underlying repository technology and surrounding utilities are based on Emeraude PCTE from TRANSTAR. The user interface is based on X-Windows/MOTIF.

Encore Computer Corporation

US contact

6901 W. Sunrise Blvd.
Ft. Lauderdale
FL 33313
USA

Tel: +1 305 587 2900

UK contact

Marlborough House
Mole Business Park
Randalls Road
Leatherhead
Surrey
KT22 7BA
UK

Tel: +44 1372 363363
Fax: +44 1372 362926

Products

Parallel Ada, MicroARTE and the Real-Time Process Monitor.

First Matrix

Old Lion Court
High Street
Marlborough
Wiltshire
SN8 1HQ
UK

Tel: +44 1672 515 510
Fax: +44 1672 515 514

Products

U.K. Distributors of Ada 83, Ada 95 Compilers & Development Environments: DACS Ada cross compilers, TBGEN Ada test harness generator, TCMON Ada test coverage monitor, KeyOne Ada syntax directed editor.

GSE Software Engineering GmbH

Brabanter Straße 4
D-80805 Munich
Germany

Tel: +49 89 3 60 08 0
Fax: +49 89 3 60 08 141

Products

Verdix Ada Development System. SunSoft SPARCworks Professional Ada development environment. IPL AdaTEST tool. Tartan Optimising Ada Compilers. Tartan AdaScope debugging tool. OIS Screen Machine - Ada GUI Builder. Training courses and consultancy in these and other products.

Harris Systems

US contact

Harris Computer Systems Corporation
2101 West Cypress Creek Road
Fort Lauderdale
Florida 33309
USA

Tel: +1 305 974 1700
Fax: +1 305 977 5580

European contacts

Harris Systemes Electroniques S.A.
Computer Systems Division
2-4 Avenue de l'Europe
78140 Velizy
France

Tel: +33 1 34 65 40 50
Fax: +33 1 34 65 40 59

Harris GmbH
Computer Systems Division
Koenigswinterer Strasse 554
D-53227 Bonn
Germany

Tel: +49 228 970 230
Fax: +49 228 970 23 50

Harris Systems Ltd
Computer Systems Division
Riverside Way
Watchmoor Park
Camberley
Surrey
GU15 3YD
UK

Tel: +44 1276 686886
Fax: +44 1276 678733

Products

Harris Ada Programming Support Environment (HAPSE) and Ada Real-Time Multiprocessor System (ARMS). S3410 HAPSE training course (five days).

Hewlett-Packard Company

US contact

19447 Pruneridge Ave.
MS: 47LH
Cupertino
CA 9501
USA

Tel: +1 408 447 5742

UK contact

Hewlett-Packard Ltd
Cain Road
Bracknell
Berkshire
RG12 1HN
UK

Tel: +44 1344 360000
Fax: +44 1344 361240

Products

Domain Ada and compilers for the HP 9000.

IBM Canada Ltd

844 Don Mills
North York
Ontario
M3C 1V7
Canada

Tel: +1 416 448 3659

Products

AIX Ada/6000, IBM Ada/370, VME Ada Compiler.

Intel Corporation

Supercomputer Systems Division
15201 NW Greenbrier Parkway
Beaverton
OR 97006
USA

Tel: +1 503 629 7600

Products

Ada for the iPSC/860 Parallel Supercomputer Ada for
the Paragon XP/S and XP/E Supercomputers.
Note: The Ada we sell for our supercomputers is developed by Verdix.

ICL (UK) Ltd

Eskdale Road
Winnersh
Wokingham
Berkshire
RG11 5TT
UK

Tel: +44 1734 693131
Fax: +44 1734 693131 Extn. 6004

Products

VME Ada Compiler.

Intermetrics

Intermetrics, Inc.
733 Concord Avenue
Cambridge
MA 02138
USA

Tel: +1 617 661 1840

Products

Intermetrics MVS Ada Compiler, UTS Ada Compiler.
SQL Ada Module Description Language (SAMeDL)
Compiler.

Irvine Compiler Corporation

Hewlett-Packard distributes and supports ICC compilers hosted on HP computers.
For other products contact:

Irvine Compiler Corporation
34 Executive Park
Suite 270
Irvine
CA 92714
USA

Tel: +1 714 250 1366
Fax: +1 714 250 0676
Email: info@irvine.com

Products

ICC Ada.

Meridian Software Systems, Inc.

US contact

10 Pasteur Street
Irvine
CA 92718
USA

Tel: +1 714 727 0700
Fax: +1 714 727 3583

European contacts

N.A. Software Ltd
Roscoe House
62 Roscoe Street
Liverpool
L1 9DW
UK

Tel: +44 151 7094738
Fax: +44 151 7095645

Verdix Europe
123 Rue du Chateau
92100 Boulogne
France

Tel: +33 1 49 09 10 10
Fax: +33 1 46 04 17 19

Products

Meridian Ada development system.

MIPS Computer Systems

928 Arques Ave.
Sunnyvale
CA 94086
USA

Tel: +1 408 524 8095

Products

MIPS Ada and MIPS ASAPP Ada compilation systems.

NEC Corporation

Environment Systems Department
C&C Common Software
    Development Laboratory
Shibaura 2-11-5
Minato-ku
Tokyo 108
Japan

Tel: +81 3 5476 1107

Products

NEC Ada Compiler System.

North China Institute of Computing Technology

Beijing Green Valley Software
3 Floor CITIC Building
19 Jianguomenwai Dajie
Beijing 100004
China

Tel: +86 1 500 4372

Products

C_Ada.

Proprietary Software Systems

429 Santa Monica Blvd.
Suite 430
Santa Monica
CA 90401
USA

Tel: +1 310 394 5233
Fax: +1 310 393 3122

Products

PSS VAX/ZR34325 Compiler. PSS AdaRAID Symbolic Interactive Debugger. PSS VAX/VMS 1750A Ada compiler.

Rational

US contact

Rational
Corporate Headquarters
2800 San Tomas Expressway
Santa Clara
CA 95051-0951
USA

Tel: +1 408 496 3600
Fax: +1 408 496 3636

European contacts

Rational SARL
Immeuble Delalande
1, Place Charles de Gulle
78180 – Montigny le Bretonneux
France

Tel: +33 1 30 12 09 50
Fax: +33 1 30 12 09 66

Rational GmbH
Rosenstraße 7
D-82049 Pullach Im Isartal
Munich
Germany

Tel: +49 89 797 021
Fax: +49 89 799 343

Rational Technology Ltd
First Floor, Olivier House
18 Marine Parade
Brighton
East Sussex
BN2 1TL
UK

Tel: +44 1273 624814
Fax: +44 1273 624364

Rational AB
Veddestavaegen 24
S-175, 62 Jaerfaella
Sweden

Tel: +46 8 761 0600
Fax: +46 8 760 0026

Artificial Intelligence Software S.P.A.
11 Via Rombon
I-201134 Milano
Italy

Tel: +39 2 264 0107
Fax: +39 2 264 10744

Desarrollo y Macroinformacion S.A.
C/General PerWn, 6-2-B
28020 Madrid
Spain

Tel: +34 1 571 39 62
Fax: +34 1 571 41 29

Products

Rational is a leading provider of innovative products and services to support quality software engineering. Rational Apex is an Ada-specific development environment, running on open-systems platforms (IBM RISC System/6000 and Sun SPARC), that supports the compilation, configuration management, test and metrication of Ada or mixed language projects from thousands to millions of lines of code.

Rational Rose is a graphical CASE tool supporting the Booch method of object-oriented analysis and design via notation checking and round-trip engineering.

Rational Rose/C++ is a graphical, object-oriented, software-engineering tool that supports the iterative development of C++ applications.

TestMate is a comprehensive set of testing tools integrated with Rational Apex that reduce the cost of software testing and maintenance and improve the quality of software.

VADS is a production-quality software development system that includes a high-performance compiler, a debugger, library-management tools, a performance analyzer, a coverage analyzer, a task-event trace/analysis tool, and a runtime system.

DADS is a distributed application development system that allows automatic and transparent distribution of Ada objects in a single Ada program across a homogeneous network.

R.R. Software

P.O. Box 1512
Madison
WI 53701
USA

Tel: +1 608 251 3133
Fax: +1 608 251 3340

Products

Janus/Ada Ada development system.

Rockwell International

Mail Station 124-211
400 Collins Rd. NE
Cedar Rapids
IA 52498
USA

Tel: +1 319 395 1729

Products

DDC-Based Ada/CAPS Compiler.

Siemens Nixdorf Informationssysteme AG

Informationssysteme AG
Otto-Hahn-Ring 6
D-81730
Munich
Germany

Tel: +49 89 636 47691
Fax: +49 89 636 44352
Email: hans.stenger@mch.sni.de

Products

SIEMENS NIXDORF BS2000 Ada Compiler.

Silicon Graphics

US contact

2011 N. Shoreline Blvd.
P.O. Box 7311
Mountain View
CA 94039-7311
USA

Tel: +1 415 960 1980

European contact

Veldzigt 2
3454 PW de Meern
The Netherlands

Tel: +31 3406 21711
Fax: +31 3406 21454

Products

4D ADA 3.0 and SC4-ADA-4.0 compilation systems. Bindings to standards such as GL and X Window System.

SKY Computers, Inc.

10480 Little Patuxent Parkway
Suite 500
Columbia
MD 21044
USA

Tel: +1 301 740 5675

Products

Meridian Ada.

Stratus Computer

55 Fairbanks Blvd.
Marlboro
MA 01752-1298
USA

Tel: +1 508 460 2695

Products

Stratus Ada compilation system.

SunSoft

US contact

2550 Garcia Avenue
Mountain View
CA 94043
USA

European contacts

13 avenue Morane Saulnier
78142 Vélizy Cedex
France

Tel: +33 1 30 67 52 02
Fax: +33 1 30 67 54 73

Bretonischer Ring 3
Postfach 1336
8011 Grassbrunn 1
Germany

Bagshot Manor
Green Lane
Bagshot
Surrey
GU19 5NL
UK

Tel: +44 1276 451440
Fax: +44 1276 453803

Products

SunSoft WorkShop for Ada, an integrated suite of tools for Ada includes: SPARCworks/Ada development tools for building, testing, debugging, and tuning applications; SPARCompiler Ada and C language systems to help build high-performance Ada and ANSI C applications; SPARCworks/Ada iMPact tools to easily develop multiprocessing/multithreading applications; SPARCworks/TeamWare code management tools to speed and simplify project integration, system builds, software version control, and release management.

The Sun Ada Development Environment is the most complete, high-performance development environment for Solaris 1 and includes: Sun Ada, an ANSI/MIL-STD-1815A validated Ada language system; SPARCworks/Ada development tools - AdaVision, dbtool, LRMTool, and EditTool; GXV-Ada, and Ads source code builder for the OpenWindows Developer Guide.

Tartan, Inc.

300 Oxford Drive
Monroeville
PA 15146
USA

Tel: +1 412 856 3600
Fax: +1 412 856 3636

Products

The following Ada compilation systems: Tartan Ada VMS/C30; Tartan Ada VMS/C30/IPS; Tartan Ada Sun/960MC; Tartan Ada Sun/Sun; Tartan Ada VMS/960MC; Tartan Ada Sun/C30; Tartan Ada VMS/1750A; Tartan Ada VMS/680X0; Tartan Ada VMS/680X0/IPS; Tartan Ada SPARC C30; Tartan Ada SPARC 1750A; Tartan Ada SPARC 680X0; Tartan Ada SPARC 960mc; Tartan Ada RS6000/960mc; Tartan Ada VMS/C40.

Texas Instruments

6500 Chase Oaks Blvd.
P.O. Box 869305
Plano
TX 75086
USA

Tel: +1 214 575 5346

Products

MIPS Ada and TI Ada compilation systems.

TLD Systems

3625 Del Amo Boulevard
Suite 100
Torrance
CA 90503
USA

Tel: +1 310 542 5433
Fax: +1 310 542 6323
Email: tld@cerf.net

Products

The TLD Ada Compiler System supports cross development to 16-bit and 32-bit microprocessors, such as 1750 and Intel i960, used in embedded systems. The products are hosted onSun Microsystems, VAX, IBM, and HP host computers. In addition to the Compiler, components include Ada Library Manager, Ada Information Display, Cross Assemblers, Cross Linkers, Symbolic Debugger, Simulators, and complete Run Time Systems. Source code of the Run Time Systems are included. Technical documentation files are automatically produced by TLDacs.

U.S. Air Force

OO-ALC/TISEA
7278 4th Street
Bldg 100
Hill AFB
UT 84056-5205
USA

Tel: +1 801 777 7850

Products

AFCAS 1750A Ada Compiler, AFCAS 1750A/
XMEM Ada Compiler.

U.S. NAVY

U.S. Navy NAVSEA PMS-412
Washington
DC 20362-5101
USA

Tel: +1 703 602 8204

Products

Ada/L, Ada/M, AdaVAX Ada compilation systems.

UNISYS Corporation

Unisys U.S. Information System
P.O. Box 500, MS: B360
Blue Bell
PA 19424
USA

Tel: +1 215 542 6209

Products

UCS Ada.

Verdix Corporation

US contact

Manager, Marketing Communications
Verdix Corporation
14130A Sullyfield Circle
VA 22021 Chantilly
USA

Tel: +1 703 318 5800

European contact

Verdix Europe
123 rue du Chateau
92100 Boulogne
France

Tel: +33 1 46 99 47 77
Fax: +33 1 46 99 47 00

Products

VADS (Verdix Ada Development System); VADScross
for embedded software applications; VADSworks for
microprocessor systems; VADSpro configuration management system; VADS APSE.
OpenAda Windows from Meridian Software Systems
(a Verdix company).

Wang Laboratories

One Industrial Ave.
MS: 019-890
Lowell
MA 01851
USA

Tel: +1 508 967 7002

Products

Wang VS Ada compilation system.

York Software Engineering Limited

University of York
York
YO1 5DD
UK

Tel: +44 1904 433741
Fax: +44 1904 433744

Products

The York Ada Compiler Environment (York ACE) provides a comprehensive UNIX-based Ada environment
comprising a validated compiler and various other utilities, e.g. Ada library management tools, a symbolic
debugger and a cross referencer. YSE also provides
Ada training courses for both managers and techni-
cians (see Chapter 14). In addition, a wide range of
consultancy services are available — the company has
particular expertise in high integrity computing areas.

13.2 Suppliers of Ada-related development tools

ADALOG

27 avenue de Verdun
92170 Vanves
France

Tel: +33 1 46 45 51 12
Fax: +33 1 46 45 52 49

Products

Adalog is operated by Jean-Pierre Rosen, a leading French expert in Ada and object-oriented design. It provides international services in consulting, expertise and training in Ada and Ada-related technologies.

Advanced Methods and Tools

Campus Road
Listerhills Technology Park
Bradford
W. Yorkshire
BD7 1HR
UK

Tel: +44 1274 736895
Fax: +44 1274 736553

Products

A range of object-oriented analysis, design, code generation and testing tools for PC-hosts. Ada courses are detailed in Chapter 14.

ANTYCIP

98 Ter Boulevard Héloise
BP 111
95103 Argenteuil Cedex
France

Tel: +33 1 39 61 14 14
Fax: +33 1 30 76 29 73

Products

VERDIX: Ada compilers and environments for native and cross developments. Sun Ada Development Environment: native Ada compiler for SUN workstations. i-Logix Statemate: system and software specification tools with automatic Ada code generation.

BAeSEMA Ltd

Avonbridge House
Bath Road
Chippenham
Wilts
SN15 2BB
UK

Tel: +44 1249 655015
Fax: +44 1249 655723

Products

LIFESPAN configuration management and change control system. LIFESPAN training courses.

Cadre Technologies

Centennial Court
Easthampstead Road
Bracknell
Berkshire
RG12 1JA
UK

Tel: +44 1344 300003
Fax: +44 1344 360079

Products

Team*work* integrated development environment.

Dassault Electronique

55 quai Marcel Dassault
92214 Saint-Cloud
France

Tel: +33 1 34 81 78 35
Fax: +33 1 34 81 60 70

Products

ILIADE, an integrated software engineering workbench dedicated to Ada and C. DEVISOR, a software test and debug system performing both unit tests and validation tests. It is programming language and target machine independent.

Digital Equipment Co Ltd

PO Box 115
Worton Grange
Imperial Way
Reading
Berkshire
RG2 0TL
UK

Tel: +44 1734 868711

Products

DECset, DECset DEC Software Engineering Tools, VAX DEC/CMS Code Management System, VAX DEC/MMS Module Management System, DEC PCA Performance and Coverage Analyzer, DEC Test Manager, DEC LSE/SCA Language-Sensitive Editor, COHESIONworX for OSF/1 - Software development toolset, Team/See for OSF/1 - Software Engineering Environment (Full lifecycle coverage).

Emeraude

European contact

153 bureaux de la Colline
92213 Saint Cloud
France

Tel: +33 1 49 11 72 68
Fax: +33 1 49 11 72 40

US contact

67 South Bedford Street
Burlington
MA 01803-5152
USA

Tel: +1 617 229 5827
Fax: +1 617 272 0558

Products

Emeraude PCTE framework. Emeraude VCM (Version and Configuration Management on PCTE) PCTE one day seminar. PCTE five day training course (incl. practical work).

EVB Software Engineering, Inc.

5320 Spectrum Drive
Frederick
MD 21701
USA

Tel: +1 301 695 6960
Fax: +1 301 695 7734
Email: info@evb.com

Products

GRACE reusable components. STRATEGIES Heragraph 2D/3D graphics application framework. GRAMMI graphical user-interface builder. Complexity Measures Tool for Ada software. Paradigm Plus/EVB Edition tool that supports EVB's Ada Object Oriented Development method.
For training see Chapter 14.

GEC-Marconi Software Systems

Elstree Way
Borehamwood
Herts
WD6 1RX
UK

Tel: +44 181 732 0238
Fax: +44 181 732 0362

Products

VADS Verdix range of compilers and tools and the Sun Ada Development Environment. SPARCworks Ada programming environment.

Imperial Software Technology

95 London Street
Reading
Berks
UK

Tel: +44 1734 587055
Fax: +44 1734 589005
Email: acl@ist.co.uk

Products

X-Designer, a Graphical User Interface builder for Motif.

Instrumatic UK Ltd

First Ave
Globe Park
Marlow
Bucks
SL7 1YA
UK

Tel: +44 1628 476741
Fax: +44 1628 474440

Products

McCabe Toolset — Testing and Metrics, Reverse Engineering/Reuse.
PCMS — Product Configuration Management System.
Training and consultancy on methods and tools.

Integrated Software Environments

32 Acre End Street
Eynsham
Oxford
OX8 1PA
UK

Tel: +44 1865 880080
Fax: +44 1865 883817

Products

ADAGRAPH design and reverse engineering tool.

Interactive Development Environments

American contacts

Interactive Development Environments
595 Market Street
San Francisco
CA 94105
USA

Tel: +1 415 543 0900
Fax: +1 415 543 0145

IDE Canada
4145 North Service Road
Burlington
Ontario
L7L 6A3
Canada

Tel: +1 416 336 8954
Fax: +1 416 332 3007

European contacts

IDE France
7ter rue de la porte de Buc
78000 Versailles
France

Tel: +33 1 39 02 26 02
Fax: +33 1 39 02 05 37

IDE GmbH
Fraunhoferstraße 11
8054 Ismaning
Germany

Tel: +49 89 996 5440
Fax: +49 89 961 2246

IDE UK Ltd
1 Stirling House
Stirling Road
Surrey Research Park
Guildford
Surrey
GU2 5RF
UK

Tel: +44 1483 579000
Fax: +44 1483 31272

Products

Software through Pictures Object Modeling Technique
for Ada (OMT/Ada).

IPL

Eveleigh house
Grove Street
Bath
BA1 5LR
UK

Tel: +44 1225 444888
Fax: +44 1225 444400
Email: ipl@iplbath.demon.co.uk

Eurogiciel
Technoparc 3
BP 543
31674 LABAGE
France

Tel: +33 61 39 13 21
Fax: +33 61 39 01 15

GSE Software Engineering GmbH
Brabanter Straße 4
D-8000 Munchen 40
Germany

Tel: +49 89 360080
Fax: +49 89 360081 41
Email: mst@gsemchn.uucp

Norsys Technology AB
Finlandsgatan 12
Box 1239
S 16428
KISTA
Sweden

Tel: +46 8 7507575
Fax: +46 8 7039272

Quality Checked Software Ltd
PO Box 6656
Beaverton
Oregon
OR 97007-0656
USA

Tel: +1 503 645 5610
Fax: +1 503 690 0201
Email: qcs@teleport.com

Products

AdaTEST Dynamic Testing, Coverage Analysis and
Static Analysis Ada verification tool.

IPSYS Software

Marlborough Court
Pickford Street
Macclesfield
Cheshire
SK11 6JD
UK

Tel: +44 1625 616722
Fax: +44 1625 616780

Products

IPSYS HOOD Toolset analysis and design toolset. IP-SYS Reverse Engineer reverse engineering tool. The ACTIF tool integration framework environment from Expert Cache Ltd. The Kennedy Carter Intelligent OOA tool which supports the Shlaer Mellor method.

Koning en Hartman B.V.

1, Energieweg
2627 AP Delft
The Netherlands

Tel: +31 15 60 99 06
Fax: +31 15 61 91 94

Products

TeamWork: Ada Software Development Automation. DataViewsataViews: Dynamic Data Visualisation Tool.

LBMS

Evelyn House
62 Oxford Street
London
W1N 9LF
UK

Tel: +44 171 636 4213
Fax: +44 171 636 2708

Products

LBMS System Engineer I-CASE Toolset.

LPS srl

Corso Svizzera, 185
10149 Torino
Italy

Tel: +39 11 77 11 164
Fax: +39 11 74 70 94

Products

KeyOne CASE toolset.

Mark V Systems

16400 Ventura Blvd.
Encino
CA 91436
USA

Tel: +1 818 995 7671
Fax: +1 818 995 4267

Products

ObjectMaker Meta CASE Tool. Pre-programmed with object-oriented and traditional methods. Ada code generation and reverse engineering.

Microtec Research

US contact

Microtec Research, Inc.
2350 Mission College Blvd.
Santa Clara
CA 95054
USA

Tel: +1 408 980 1300
Fax: +1 408 982 8266
Email: support@mri.com

European contact

Microtec Research Ltd
Ringway House
Bell Road
Daneshill
Basingstoke
Hants
RG24 0FB
UK

Tel: +44 1256 57551
Fax: +44 1256 57553

Japanese contact

Nihon Microtec Research, K.K.
Ichiban-cho West Building 3F
10-8 Ichiban-cho
Chiyoda-ku
Tokyo 102
Japan

Tel: +81 3 5210 3050
Fax: +81 3 5210 3180

Products

XRAY cross-development toolset.

NAG Ltd

Wilkinson House
Jordan Hill Road
Oxford
OX2 8DR
UK

Tel: +44 1865 511245
Fax: +44 1865 310139

Products

NAG Library reusable components.

Object Technologies

20 Foresters
Bicester Road
Oakley
Bucks
HP18 9PY
UK

Tel: +44 1844 237530
Fax: +44 121 705 6413

Products

ObjectMaker Meta CASE Tool. Pre-programmed with object-oriented and traditional methods. Ada code generation and reverse engineering.

Objective Interface Systems

Objective Interface Systems, Inc.
1985 Preston White Drive
Suite 250
Reston
Virginia
22091-5448
USA

Tel: +1 703 264 1900
Fax: +1 703 264 1721

Products

OIS products include Screen Machine, a platform independent graphical and character user interface builder. Additionally, OIS develops, supports, and maintains three Sybase products: DB-Library/Ada, Client-Library/Ada, and Ada Workbench. New implementations for Ada 95 scheduled for release this year include CORBA (the Object Managements Group's Common Object Request Broker Architecture) and Fresco (the object oriented graphics toolkit developed for the X Consortium).

PAFEC Ltd

Strelley Hall
Strelley
Nottingham
NG8 6PE
UK

Tel: +44 1159 357055
Fax: +44 1159 390695

Products

HORSES reusable components.

P-E International

Systems Group
161 Fleet Road
Fleet
Hants
GU13 8PD
UK

Tel: +44 1252 625121
Fax: +44 1252 617665

Products

PRO-QUEST program analysis tool. TESTA test tool.

Program Analysers/LDRA

European contacts

56 Northbrook Street
Newbury
Berks
RG13 1AN
UK

Tel: +44 1635 528828
Fax: +44 1635 528657

LDRA Technologie S.A.
Off-Shore Voie No.1 BP 17
Bâtment Stratege
31312 Labége Cedex
France

Tel: +33 61 39 77 77
Fax: +33 61 39 23 22

US contact

LDRA Technology, Inc.
3000-3 Hartley Road
Jacksonville
Florida
USA

Tel: +1 904 268 3267
Fax: +1 904 268 0733

Products

LDRA Testbed software analysis toolset.
LDRA TBrun test harness generator.
LDRA Validada software proving toolset for Ada programs.

Program Validation Ltd

26 Queens Terrace
Southampton
SO1 1BQ
UK

Tel: +44 1703 330001
Fax: +44 1703 230805
Email: pvl@cix.compulink.co.uk

Products

SPARK Examiner is a tool which carries out static semantic checks of Ada source code to ensure that it conforms to the secure and well-defined SPARK subset.
SPADE Proof Checker is an interactive proof assistant which greatly simplifies, and improves the accuracy of, the proof of verification conditions produced by the SPARK Examiner. Training in the above products as well as high-integrity and safety critical software production.

PROSA Software

Tudor House
649 London Road
High Wycombe
Bucks
HP11 1EZ
UK

Tel: +44 1494 473349

Products

PROSA integrated analysis, design and code generation toolset.

Radstone Technology plc

US contact

Radstone Technology Corporation
20 Craig Road
Montvale
NJ 07645-1737
USA

Tel: +1 201 391 2899
Fax: +1 201 391 2899

European contacts

Water Lane
Towcester
Northants
NN12 7JN
UK

Tel: +44 1327 359444
Fax: +44 1327 359662

Radstone Technology SA
Miniparc
6 avenue des Andes
91940 Les Ulis
France

Tel: +33 1 64 46 04 03
Fax: +33 1 69 28 03 40

Radstone Technology GmbH
Bahnhofstraße 38
D-6090 Rüsselsheim
Germany

Tel: +49 6142 6 80 04
Fax: +49 6142 6 38 34

Radstone work closely with all the major Ada vendors to ensure that its hardware products have the widest range of Ada support.

Real-Time Software

118-120 Warwick Street
Leamington Spa
Warwicks
CV32 4QY
UK

Tel: +44 1926 450858

Products

System Architect analysis and design toolset.

SCS Systems & Communication Software

Route de l'Orme
Bât. Homère
Les Algorithmes
91192 Saint Aubin
France

Tel: +33 1 69 41 82 70
Fax: +33 1 69 41 05 47
Email: mathieu@scs.fr

Products

SPARCworks Professional Ada for Solaris 2.0 from SunSoft.
IPSYS HOOD Toolset from IPSYS Software.

XinADA, from Top Graph'X, are software libraries giving access to the X Window System.

TA Consultancy Services Ltd

'The Barbican'
East Street
Farnham
Surrey
GU9 7TB
UK

Tel: +44 1252 711414
Fax: +44 1252 735633

AIKI
4 rue du General Lanrezac
75017 Paris
France

Tel: +33 1 48 88 97 00
Fax: +33 1 48 88 95 96

GPP mbH
Kolpingring 18a
D-8024 Oberhaching b.
Munich
Germany

Tel: +49 89 61304 1
Fax: +49 89 61304 294

Products

MALPAS program analysing toolset and associated training courses.

SOFTIX

9 avenue du Canada
91966 Les Ulis Cedex
France

Tel: +33 1 69 07 02 29
Fax: +33 1 69 07 31 43

Products

Gecomo Plus/Size Plus, AdaNICE, KeyOne, CMF / CM_SX_ADA.

SQL Software Ltd

North Brook House
John Tate Road
Hertford
Hertfordshire
SG13 7NN
UK

Tel: +44 1992 501414
Fax: +44 1992 501616

Products

PCMS*Ada configuration management tool.

STRATEGIES

European contact

41-43 Rue de Villeneuve
Silic 429
Rungis 94583
France

Tel: +33 1 46 87 11 29
Fax: +33 1 46 87 67 24

US contact

EVB Software Engineering, Inc
5303 Spectrum Drive
Frederick
MD 21701
USA

Tel: +1 301 695 6960

Products

Heragraph 2D/3D graphics application framework.

TA Consultancy Services Ltd

Newnhams
West Street
Farnham
Surrey
GU9 7EQ
UK

Tel: +44 1252 711414
Fax: +44 1252 735155

Products

MALPAS program analysing toolset.

Testwell

Kanslerinkatu 8
SF-33720 Tampere
Finland

Tel: +358 31 316 5464
Fax: +358 31 318 3311

Products

TBGEN System is a black-box test harnessing tool for unit and unit integration testing of Ada code. It also supports testing with stubs. TCMON System is a white-box testing tool for finding out test coverage and for program execution monitoring. These tools are available also via DDC-I A/S and its UK distributor First Matrix Limited.

Thornbrook

22 Sinnels Field
Shipton-Under-Wychwood
Oxfordshire
OX7 6EJ
UK

Tel: +44 1993 831333
Fax: +44 1993 831522

Products

The complete range of Tartan Compilers and Tools, in addition to others for use on PCs and by educational establishments. The complete range of Ada Mathematical Libraries from MassTech, Inc. Other Ada based products include software management systems, application development systems and security products.

Top Graph'X

10 Allée de la Mare Jacob
91290 La Norille
France

Tel: +33 1 69 26 97 88
Fax: +33 1 69 26 97 89

Products

XinADA Ada libraries giving access to the X Window System.

Verilog

Verilog SA
15 rue Nicholas Vauquelin
31081 Toulouse
France

Verilog GmbH
Am Haag 10
D-8032 Grafelfing
Munich
Germany

Verilog SA
Associacion Transpirenaica
Toulouse-Barcelona
Johann Sebastian Bach 3
08021 Barcelona
Spain

Verilog UK Ltd
34 The Quadrant
Richmond
Surrey
TW9 1DN
UK

Tel: +44 181 940 2212
Fax: +44 181 940 2933

Products

LOGISCOPE program analysis tool.

West Solutions BV

Bagijnhof 80
2611 AR Delft
The Netherlands

Tel: +31 15 123190
Fax: +31 15 147889

Products

Sun Ada Development Environment.

14

Training companies and courses

14.1   Live courses

ADALOG

Address: 27 avenue de Verdun
92170 Vanves
France

Tel: +33 1 46 45 51 12
Fax: +33 1 46 45 52 49

Contact name: Jean-Pierre Rosen

Course 1

Course title: Ada (in French).
Normal course location: Adalog, Vanves.
Duration: 6 days.
Frequency held: Approx. every 2 months.

The two categories of staff likely to be most interested in this course:
(1) Developers (2) Quality assurance and project managers.

Brief description: This is a full Ada course, covering all aspects of Ada 83, introduction to Object Oriented Design, and some insights on what's coming up with Ada 95. It is split into two 3-day sessions to provide better pedagogical efficiency avoiding the "saturation effect" often found in 5-day courses.

Course 2

Course title: Introduction to Ada 95 (in French).
Normal course location: Adalog, Vanves.
Duration: 1 day.
Frequency held: Approx. every 2 months.

The two categories of staff likely to be most interested in this course:
(1) Developers (2) Quality assurance and project managers.

Brief description: This is a general overview of new Ada 95 features, intended to prepare the transition of existing Ada teams towards Ada 95.

AdaTraining Ltd / High Integrity Systems Ltd

Address: Astra Centre
Edinburgh Way
Harlow

Essex
CM20 2BE
UK

Tel: +44 1279 450000
Fax: +44 1279 429149

Contact name: Pat Moule

Course 1

Course title: Ada Programming.
Normal course location: At company address or at customer site.
Normal duration: 5 days.
Frequency held: Monthly.

This course has practical/lab sessions using the following Ada compiler system(s): Various.

The two categories of staff likely to be most interested in this course:
(1) Programmers/software engineers (2) Programming team leaders.

Brief description: Designed for those who require a working knowledge of Ada, the course combines lectures and practicals and covers the language features.

Course 2

Course title: Advanced Ada Workshop.
Normal course location: At company address or at customer site.
Normal duration: 5 days.
Frequency held: Monthly.

This course has practical/lab sessions using the following Ada compiler system(s): DEC Ada

The two categories of staff likely to be most interested in this course:
(1) Systems/software engineers (2) Group/team leaders.

Brief description: An intensive second-level course which focuses on the design and application of Ada in large embedded systems, and includes a guided mini-project.

Course 3

Course title: Managing Ada Today.
Normal course location: At company address or at customer site.
Normal duration: 1 day.
Frequency held: Monthly.

This course has no practical/lab sessions.

The two categories of staff likely to be most interested in this course:
(1) Technical managers (2) Business managers.

Brief description: Where knowledge of the practical issues involved in using Ada is required, this course provides an objective introduction, with advice on exploiting the benefits of Ada.

Course 4

Course title: Ada Design Seminar.
Normal course location: At company address or at customer site.
Normal duration: 1 day.
Frequency held: Monthly.

This course has no practical/lab sessions.

The two categories of staff likely to be most interested in this course:
(1) Systems/software engineers (2) Consultants.

Brief description: Provides impartial and informed answers to the typical questions raised about the design of Ada software and the selection of appropriate design techniques.

Course 5

Course title: Designing Large Real-Time Systems With Ada.
Normal course location: At company address or at customer site.
Normal duration: 5 days.
Frequency held: Monthly.

This course has no practical/lab sessions.

The two categories of staff likely to be most interested in this course:
(1) Software designers (2) Systems designers.

Brief description: The course teaches real-time object oriented design methods which give equal importance to process abstraction, functional abstraction and data abstraction.

Advanced Methods and Tools (née KBSL)

Address: 1 Campus Road
Listerhills Science Park
Bradford
West Yorks
BD7 1HR
UK

Tel: +44 1274 736895
Fax: +44 1274 736553

Contact name: Dr John Robinson

Course 1

Course title: Ada Programming.
Normal course location: Clients' sites.
Normal duration: 5 days.
Frequency held: On demand.

This course has practical lab sessions: Delegate has extensive opportunity to gain practical, hands-on experience of the Ada language.

The two categories of staff likely to be most interested in this course:
(1) Team leaders (2) Software engineers.

Brief description: Presents the complete Ada 83 language emphasizing how language features should be used to maximise their effectiveness. The course makes extensive use of practical exercises.

AETECH

Address: 5841 Edison Place
Suite 110
Carlsbad
CA 92008
USA

Tel: +1 619 431-7714
Fax: +1 619 431-0860

Contact name: Vince Lombardo

Course 1

Course title: Introduction to Ada.
Normal course location: Customer site.
Normal duration: 5 days.
Frequency held: On demand.

Requirements: Students should have a basic understanding of programming concepts. Uses Air Force's DESKTOP III Ada compiler on PCs. Has extensive practical content.

The two categories of staff likely to be most interested in this course:
(1) Software engineers (2) Managers.

Brief description: A "full-semester" college level curriculum compressed into a "5-day course" to teach basic Ada programming skills that can be used to write Ada applications for all platforms: mainframes, minis, and PCs.

Alsys Ltd

Address: Partridge House
Newtown Road
Henley-on-Thames
Oxon
RG9 1EN
UK

Tel: +44 1491 579090
Fax: +44 1491 571866

Contact name: Ian Campbell

Course 1

Course title: Understanding Ada Seminar and Workshop.
Normal course location: Customer site.
Normal duration: 5 days.
Frequency held: On demand.

This course has practical/lab sessions using the following Ada compiler system(s): Alsys.

The two categories of staff likely to be most interested in this course:
(1) Project leaders (2) Software engineers.

Brief description: Gives a thorough grounding in the theoretical and practical aspects of the Ada language.

Course 2

Course title: Object-Oriented Design and Ada (in conjunction with Napier University).
Normal course location: Customer site.
Normal duration: 5 days.
Frequency held: On demand.

The two categories of staff likely to be most interested in this course:
(1) Project leaders (2) Software engineers.

Brief description: Combines the theoretical parts of the Understanding Ada course with a detailed examination of the OOD paradigm, covering its development from academic roots to its implementation in Ada.

Course 3

Course title: Hierarchical Object-Oriented Design and Ada (in conjunction with Napier University).
Normal course location: Customer site.
Normal duration: 5 days.
Frequency held: On demand.

The two categories of staff likely to be most interested in this course:
(1) Project leaders (2) Software engineers.

Brief description: Combines the theoretical parts of the Understanding Ada course with a detailed examination of the OOD paradigm, covering its development from academic roots to the design of HOOD and its mapping to Ada.

Course 4

Course title: Advanced Ada workshop (in conjunction with Napier University).
Normal course location: Customer site.
Normal duration: 5 days.
Frequency held: On demand.

This course has practical/lab sessions using the following Ada compiler system(s): Alsys.

The two categories of staff likely to be most interested in this course:
(1) Project leaders (2) Software engineers with at least two years' Ada experience.

Brief description: Focuses on the advanced use of the Ada language.

For custom courses designed to suit your individual needs please do not hesitate to contact Alsys Ltd.

Augusta Technology Ltd

Address: Unit 2
The Science Park
Cefn Llan
Aberystwyth
Dyfed
SY23 3AH
UK

Tel: +44 1970 626001
Fax: +44 1970 626665
Email: mbr@uk.ac.aber

Contact name: Mark Ratcliffe

Course 1

Course title: Programming in Ada.
Normal course location: Various.
Normal duration: 5 days.
Frequency held: On demand.

This course is designed for programmers with little if any Ada experience.

The two categories of staff likely to be most interested in this course:
(1) Programmers and software engineers (2) Programming team leaders.

Brief description: This course provides participants with hands-on experience through extensive Ada programming exercises throughout the course.

Course 1

Course title: Ada 95 - A manager's overview.
Normal course location: Various.
Normal duration: 1 day.
Frequency held: On demand.

This course introduces the latest developments in Ada.

The two categories of staff likely to be most interested in this course:
(1) Programming team leaders (2) Programmers and software engineers.

Brief description: While avoiding unnecessary technical detail, this one day seminar describes the impact of the 95 changes on projects wishing to adopt the new standard.

Centre for Advanced Software Design (CASD)

Address: Napier University
219 Colinton Road
Edinburgh
EH14 1DJ
UK

Tel: +44 131 455 4305
Fax: +44 131 443 8161
Email: avril@cs.napier.ac.uk

Contact name: Avril Tobin

Course 1

Course title: Programming with Ada.
Normal course location: Various.
Normal duration: 5 days.
Frequency held: On demand.

This course has practical/lab sessions using the following Ada compiler system(s): Alsys.

The two categories of staff likely to be most interested in this course:
(1) Programmers and software engineers (2) Programming team leaders.

Brief description: This course will provide students with the knowledge and skills to design, code and test programs written in Ada.

Course 2

Course title: Advanced Ada Programming.
Normal course location: Various.
Normal duration: 5 days.
Frequency held: On demand.

This course has practical/lab sessions using the following Ada compiler system(s): Alsys.

The two categories of staff likely to be most interested in this course:
(1) Programmers and software engineers (2) Software project leaders.

Brief description: The purpose of this course is to bring delegates to a high level of proficiency in the Ada programming language which will enable them to implement and maintain real-time systems.

Course 3

Course title: Object-Oriented Design and Ada.
Normal course location: Various.
Normal duration: 3 or 5 days*.
Frequency held: On demand.

This course has practical/lab sessions using the following Ada compiler system(s): Alsys.

The two categories of staff likely to be most interested in this course:
(1) Programmers and software engineers (2) Technical team leaders.

Brief description: The purpose of this course is to describe pragmatically the use of object-oriented design (OOD), and in particular Hierarchical Object-Oriented Design (HOOD), within the context of the software development life-cycle and to show how it can be implemented with Ada.

[*The 5 day version of this course contains extensive practical sessions.]

Course 4

Course title: Hierarchical Object-Oriented Design.
Normal course location: Various.
Normal duration: 3 or 5 days*.
Frequency held: On demand.

This course has practical/lab sessions using the following Ada compiler system(s): IPSYS HOOD toolset.

The two categories of staff likely to be most interested in this course:
(1) Programmers and software engineers (2) Technical project leaders.

Brief description: This course aims to provide the background, scope and use of Hierarchical Object-Oriented Design (HOOD) within the context of the software development life-cycle, and to show how it is implemented in Ada.

[*The 5 day version of this course contains extensive practical sessions.]

Note: All CASD courses are tailored to customer's needs. For example, Courses 3 and 4 may be run in conjunction with an Ada programming course over 1–2 weeks, depending on the number of practical/laboratory sessions.

Datel Technology Ltd

Address: 323 Clifton Drive
Lytham St Annes
Lancs
FY8 1HN
UK

Tel: +44 1253 713311
Fax: +44 1253 714369

Contact name: Steve Williamson

Course 1

Course title: Ada Appreciation.
Normal course location: Poulton-le-Fylde (Blackpool).
Normal duration: 3 days.
Frequency held: 2.5 months.

This course has practical/lab sessions using the following Ada compiler system(s): Meridian Adavantage.

The two categories of staff likely to be most interested in this course:
(1) Managers (2) Engineers and evaluators.

Brief description: Provides an understanding of Ada, an appreciation of Ada structure, 'runtime' aspects, and provides familiarity with the tools used to develop Ada code.

Digital Equipment Co Ltd

Address: Digital Park
Imperial Way
Reading
Berks.
RG2 0TE
UK

Tel: +44 1734 869766

Contact name: Customer Training Support Desk

Course 1

Course title: Programming in Ada, Ref. No. EY-D557E-L0.
Normal course location: At company address (on site) or Digital Reading Training Centre.
Normal duration: 5 days.
Frequency held: Once a quarter.

This course has practical/lab sessions using the following Ada compiler system(s):
VAX/VMS.

The two categories of staff likely to be most interested in this course:
(1) Programmers (2) System programmers.

Brief description: Teaches the syntax, format and structure of the language.

Course 2

Course title: Utilising VMS Features from VAX Ada, Ref. No. EY-A772E-L0.
Normal course location: At company address (on site) or Digital Reading Training Centre.
Normal duration: 5 days.
Frequency held: Subject to demand.

This course has practical/lab sessions using the following Ada compiler system(s):
VAX/VMS.

The two categories of staff likely to be most interested in this course:
(1) Application developers (2) Programmers.

Brief description: Teaches the advantages of the many service libraries and routines available on VMS to maximise the efficiency and productivity of Ada applications.

EDS

Address: Ferneberga House
          Alexandra Road
          Farnborough
          Hants
          GU14 6DQ
          UK

Tel: +44 1252 544444
Fax: +44 1252 371557

Contact name: Sue Tilley

Course 1

Course title: Ada Programming.
Normal course location: Farnborough Training Centre or on-site.
Normal duration: 5 days.
Frequency held: One to two months.

This course has practical/lab sessions using the following Ada compiler system(s): DEC VAX Ada.

The two categories of staff likely to be most interested in this course:
(1) Programmers (2) Designers.

Brief description: Provides delegates with a fundamental grounding in Ada programming.

Encore Computer (UK) Ltd

Address: Marlborough House
Mole Business Park
Randalls Road
Leatherhead
Surrey
KT22 7BA
UK

Tel: +44 1372 363363
Fax: +44 1372 362928

Contact name: David Thompson

Course 1

Course title: Ada support for software engineering principles.
Normal course location: At company address.
Normal duration: 5 days.
Frequency held: Quarterly.

This course has practical/lab sessions.

The category of staff likely to be most interested in this course:
(1) Software and systems engineers.

Brief description: Teaches the skills necessary to develop a modular Ada application, including features of the Ada language that support software engineering principles.

Course 2

Course title: Ada Programming Language Package 1.
Normal course location: At company address.
Normal duration: 5 days.
Frequency held: Quarterly.

This course has practical/lab sessions using the following Ada compiler system(s):
Generic.

The two categories of staff likely to be most interested in this course:
(1) Programmers (2) Systems analysts.

Brief description: Covers the necessary skills to write and execute basic Ada programs.

EVB Software Engineering

Address: 5303 Spectrum Drive
Frederick
MD 21701
USA

Tel: +1 301 695-6960
Fax: +1 301 695-7734

Contact name: Bonnie J. Dancy

Course 1

Course title: Management Overview of Ada.
Normal course location: EVB or customer site.
Normal duration: 1 day.
Frequency held: On demand.

This course has no practical/lab sessions.

The category of staff likely to be most interested in this course:
(1) Managers.

Brief description: This seminar discusses what managers need to know about Ada and its impact on their software development practices. Includes a brief history and overview of the language, education, and management issues.

Course 2

Course title: Introduction to Ada Software Engineering.
Normal course location: EVB or customer site.
Normal duration: 3 days.
Frequency held: On demand.

This course has no practical/lab sessions.

The two categories of staff likely to be most interested in this course:
(1) Software engineers (2) Managers.

Brief description: An overview of the software engineering concepts that influence the design of the Ada language and how those concepts support the language are the focus of this course. Various methods are surveyed in the light of the software engineering concepts they embrace, the life-cycles and life-cycle phases they support, and the metrics for judging their effectiveness.

Course 3

Course title: Ada Programming Workshop I.
Normal course location: EVB or customer site.
Normal duration: 5 days.
Frequency held: On demand.

This course has practical/lab sessions.

The category of staff likely to be most interested in this course:
(1) Software engineers.

Brief description: First part of a two part series which provides a comprehensive introduction to the Ada language within the framework of software engineering principles and practices. In addition to Ada, the fundamentals of object-oriented design are introduced and used in the lab.

Course 4

Course title: Ada Programming Workshop II.
Normal course location: EVB or customer site.
Normal duration: 5 days.
Frequency held: On demand.

This course has practical/lab sessions.

The category of staff likely to be most interested in this course:
(1) Software engineers.

Brief description: Second part of the two part series and focuses in-depth on the more complex and powerful features of the Ada language.

Course 5

Course title: Ada in Embedded Systems.
Normal course location: EVB or customer site.
Normal duration: 5 days.
Frequency held: On demand.

This course has practical/lab sessions. Students should have attended courses 3 and 4 above or have equivalent knowledge of Ada software development.

The two categories of staff likely to be most interested in this course:
(1) Software engineers (2) Systems programmers.

Brief description: Intensive training in developing embedded software using Ada. Topics include Ada tasking, Ada representation clauses and interfacing Ada to other languages. Other issues include cross compilation, scheduling algorithms and testing concurrent software.

Course 6

Course title: Ada Object Oriented Development.
Normal course location: EVB or customer site.
Normal duration: 10 days.
Frequency held: On demand.

This course has practical/lab sessions. About one third of time spent in the lab.

The two categories of staff likely to be most interested in this course:
(1) Software engineers (2) Analysts.

Brief description: Designed to provide necessary information, coupled with practical experience, to enable students to use an object-oriented approach to Ada software development.

Course 7

Course title: Object Oriented Requirements Analysis.
Normal course location: EVB or customer site.
Normal duration: 5 days.
Frequency held: On demand.

This course has practical/lab sessions. About one fifth of time spent in lab.

The two categories of staff likely to be most interested in this course:
(1) Software engineers (2) Analysts.

Brief description: Provides a detailed approach to requirements analysis using an object-oriented approach. Issues covered include the application of OORA to real software design problems, where OORA fits in the software life-cycle, common problems, and how they are overcome, the benefits of OORA, and its impact on reusability of Ada software.

Course 8

Course title: Ada Object Oriented Development.
Normal course location: EVB or customer site.
Normal duration: 5 days.
Frequency held: On demand.

This course has practical/lab sessions. About one half of time spent in the lab.

The two categories of staff likely to be most interested in this course:
(1) Software engineers (2) Analysts.

Brief description: Provides an in-depth understanding of the OO Design methodology as it is used for the development of Ada software.

Course 9

Course title: Software Reuse in Ada.
Normal course location: EVB or customer site.
Normal duration: 2 days.
Frequency held: On demand.

This course has no practical/lab sessions.

The two categories of staff likely to be most interested in this course:
(1) Managers (2) Software engineers.

Brief description: This course answers the question: "How is building software for reusability different from the way software is currently built?" The focus of the course is based on lessons leaned from the experience EVB gained from building the GRACE reusable software component library.

Course 10

Course title: Testing Ada Software.
Normal course location: EVB or customer site.
Normal duration: 3 days.
Frequency held: On demand.

This course has some practical/lab sessions.

The two categories of staff likely to be most interested in this course:
(1) Software engineers (2) Managers.

Brief description: Provides a study of software testing principles with a close look at the impact of the Ada language on testing practices and software quality. A number of effective software testing techniques are introduced.

Course 11

Course title: Developing X Window Applications Using Ada.
Normal course location: EVB or customer site.
Normal duration: 5 days.
Frequency held: On demand.

This course has practical/lab sessions. 40% of time spent in lab.

The category of staff likely to be most interested in this course:
(1) Software engineers.

Brief description: Teaches students to develop X Window applications in most languages. Students will understand the potential traps and pitfalls in developing X Window applications using advanced features of Ada.

GEC-Marconi Software Systems

Address: Elstree Way
Borehamwood
Hertfordshire
WD6 1RX
UK

Tel: +44 181 732 0788
Fax: +44 181 732 0362

Contact Name: David Stuart

Course 1

Course title: Ada Programming and Engineering.
Normal course location: At company address or at customer site.
Normal duration: 5 days.
Frequency held: Bi-quarterly or on demand.

This course has intensive practical sessions which are compiler and method independent.

The two categories of staff likely to be most interested in this course:
(1) Programmers and software engineers (2) Technical team leaders.

Brief Description: Enables delegates to use Ada proficiently and emphasises best practise.

Course 2

Course title: Object Oriented Development **Normal course location:** At company address or at customer site **Normal duration:** 2 days **Frequency held:** Quarterly or on demand.

Requirements: No specific language or tool requirements.

Brief Description: Provides a detailed, pragmatic overview of Object Oriented concepts.

Kennedy Carter

Address: 1 Thornton Road
London
SW19 4NB
UK

Tel: +44 181 947 0553
Fax: +44 181 944 6536

Contact name: Tracy Morgan

Course 1

Course title: The Ada Programming Language.
Normal course location: Wimbledon or client's site.
Normal duration: 5 days.
Frequency held: On demand.

This course has practical/lab sessions using the following Ada compiler system(s): Alsys (or client supplied).

The two categories of staff likely to be most interested in this course:
(1) Software engineers (2) Team leaders.

Brief description: Presents all the language features with an emphasis on exploiting good design principles.

Course 2

Course title: Real-Time Structured Analysis and Structured Design.
Normal course location: Wimbledon or client's site.
Normal duration: 5 days.
Frequency held: Public courses approx. every six weeks; on-site courses on demand.

This course has exercise sessions and a major case study.

The two categories of staff likely to be most interested in this course:
(1) Project engineers (2) System analysts.

Brief description: The RTSA/SD process, notations and strategies are detailed and presented as an essential precursor to object identification and implementation in Ada.

Course 3

Course title: Object-Oriented Design with RTSA and Ada.
Normal course location: Various.
Normal duration: 3 days.
Frequency held: On demand.

This course has exercise sessions and a major case study.

The two categories of staff likely to be most interested in this course:
(1) Project engineers (2) Software designers.

Brief description: This course details the principles of object-oriented design and presents a systematic strategy for the identification and specification of objects and their interdependences. Mappings of the resulting OOD architecture onto Ada are defined.

Course 4

Course title: Object-Oriented Analysis: Information, State and Process Modelling.
Normal course location: Wimbledon.
Normal duration: 5 days.
Frequency held: Bi-monthly.

This course has exercise sessions and a major case study.

The two categories of staff likely to be most interested in this course:
(1) Project engineers (2) System analysts.

Brief description: This project technology course presents the full Shlaer Mellor OOA covering information models, state models and process models.

Course 5

Course title: Recursive Design.
Normal course location: Various.
Normal duration: 5 days.
Frequency held: Public courses approx. once a quarter; on-site courses on demand.

This course has exercise sessions and a major case study.

The two categories of staff likely to be most interested in this course:
(1) Project engineers (2) System analysts.

Brief description: This project technology course presents the full Shlaer Mellor recursive design method including domain analysis, OOD architectures and systematic mappings from OOA to OOD.

Program Validation Ltd

Address: Program Validation Ltd
26, Queen's Terrace
Southampton
SO1 1BQ
UK

Tel: +44 1703 330001
Fax: +44 1703 230805
Email: pvl@cix.compulink.co.uk

Contact name: Peter Amey

Course 1

Course title: SPARK Seminar for management.
Normal course location: Southampton or Bath. (On-site courses also available.)
Normal duration: 1 day.
Frequency held: 6 monthly.
Requirements: None.
The category of staff likely to be most interested in this course:
(1) Managers responsible for projects involving high-integrity Ada.

Brief description: This seminar presents the rationale of SPARK, outlines the SPARK language, and indicates the role of the SPARK Examiner in supporting systematic program development and static code analysis.

Course 2

Course title: Software Engineering with SPARK
Normal course location: Southampton or Bath. (On-site courses also available.)
Normal duration: 4 days.
Frequency held: Quarterly.

Requirements: Some experience of Ada or another high-level programming language.
The two categories of staff likely to be most interested in this course:
(1) Project engineers (2) analysts and programmers.

Brief description: This course presents SPARK by delineating its subset of Ada and explaining the purpose of the SPARK annotations. It covers systematic design in SPARK, and static analysis (as required by Interim Def Stan 00-55). "Hands on" experience of the SPARK Examiner is provided through exercises and a design study.

Course 3

Course title: Semantic Analysis and Formal Verification of SPARK Programs.
Normal course location: Southampton or Bath. (On-site courses also available.)
Normal duration: 5 days.
Frequency held: 6 monthly.
Requirements: Previous experience of SPARK programming. Some knowledge of formal specifications is helpful.
The two categories of staff likely to be most interested in this course:
(1) Project engineers (2) analysts and programmers.

Brief description: The course introduces formal specification, the logical basis of proof and formal verification of program code. These methods are then applied to SPARK program development with practical application of the SPARK Examiner. Tuition in planning, performing and managing proof is supplemented by practical work using the SPADE Proof Checker.

Rational

Address: Rational Technology Ltd
Olivier House
18 Marine Parade
Brighton
E. Sussex
BN2 1TL

Tel: +44 1273 624814
Fax: +44 1273 624364

Contact name: Iain Gavin

Course 1

Course title: Introduction to Object-Oriented Technology.
Normal course location: Open enrolment or on-site courses available.
Normal duration: 1 day.
Frequency held: 1 to 2 months.

Requirements: No specific language or tool requirements.
The category of staff likely to be most interested in this course:
(1) Managers or those looking for an overview of OO technology.

Brief description: Provides a thorough overview of what makes OO technology important today and what benefits can be derived from its application. Covers many aspects including client-server usage, management risks, process models, notation, etc.

Course 2

Course title: Object-Oriented Analysis/Object-Oriented Design.
Normal course location: Open enrolment or on-site courses available.
Normal duration: 4/4 days or 4 days combined.
Frequency held: 1 to 2 months.

Requirements: No specific language or tool requirements.
The category of staff likely to be most interested in this course:
(1) Those wanting in-depth training in the Booch method of object-oriented analysis and design.

Brief description: Provides detailed training in object-oriented analysis and design, and in the Booch notation and process.

York Software Engineering Ltd

Address: University of York
Heslington
York
YO1 5DD
UK

Tel: +44 1904 433741
Fax: +44 1904 433744

Contact name: David Jordan

Course 1

Course title: Introduction to Ada: A Course for Experienced Programmers.
Normal course location: York.
Normal duration: 5 days.
Frequency held: Thrice yearly.

This course has practical/lab sessions using the following Ada compiler system(s): York ACE under UNIX.

The two categories of staff likely to be most interested in this course:
(1) Programmers (2) Analysts.

Brief description: Introduces the whole language with practical sessions using the fully validated York Ada Compiler Environment.

Course 2

Course title: Ada Concepts: A Course for Technical Managers.
Normal course location: York.
Normal duration: 1 day.
Frequency held: Every eight weeks.

This course has no practical/lab sessions.

The two categories of staff likely to be most interested in this course:
(1) Technical managers (2) Programmers.

Brief description: Introduces Ada to technical managers unfamiliar with the language, but who need to know how it might be used within their particular environment.

14.2 Media-based courses (no live instructor)

Advanced Methods and Tools (née KBSL)

Address: 1 Campus Road
Listerhills Science Park
Bradford
West Yorks
BD7 1HR
UK

Tel: +44 1274 736895
Fax: +44 1274 736553

Contact name: Dr John Robinson

Course 1

Course title: Design Masters.
Media based on: Video.
Typical duration: 2-hours.
Computer hardware assumed: None.

There is no particular Ada compiler system associated with the course.

The two categories of staff likely to be most interested in this course:
(1) Technical managers (2) Programmers/engineers.

Brief description: A two-hour presentation by Grady Booch, Jim Rumbaugh and Sam Adams providing an overview of the three Object Oriented methods: Booch, OMT and CRC.

Alsys Ltd

Address: Partridge House
Newtown Road
Henley-on-Thames
Oxon.
RG9 1EN
UK

Tel: +44 1491 579090
Fax: +44 1491 571866

Contact name: Ian Campbell

Course 1

Course title: Lessons on Ada.
Media based on: Computer.
Typical duration: 50 hours.
Computer hardware assumed: VAX/VMS or PC DOS or PS/2 DOS.

There are particular Ada compiler system(s) associated with the course: Alsys

The two categories of staff likely to be most interested in this course:
(1) Project leaders (2) Software engineers.

Brief description: A two-volume computer aided instruction course mixing tutorials and exercises and providing a detailed explanation of the full Ada language.

R.R. Software

Address: PO Box 1512
Madison
WI 53701
USA

Tel: +1 608 251-3133
Fax: +1 608 251-3340

Contact name: Customer services

Course 1

Course title: AdaVid Video Training Video Tape.
Media based on: VHS video tapes.
Typical duration: 10 hours.

There are particular Ada compiler system(s) associated with the course: Janus/Ada.

The category of staff likely to be most interested in this course:
(1) Programmers.

Brief description: Introductory training course on nine VHS video tapes. Covers all of the basics of programming in Ada. Experience in programming in another programming language is assumed.

15

Ada 9X Compatibility Guide, January 1995

The report "Ada 9X Compatibility Guide, Version 6.0, 1 January 1995" is reproduced here verbatim. The copyright of the report resides with the U.K. Ministry of Defence and the report is reprinted with their permission.

Ada Compatibility Guide

Version 6.0
1 January 1995

Prepared By:

Bill Taylor
Transition Technology Limited
5 Lark Hill Rise
Winchester
Hants
SO22 4LX
United Kingdom

Tel: +44 1962 877466
Fax: +44 1962 877467

Email: taylorb@sw–eng.falls–church.va.us

Prepared For:

MoD (PE), CIS(Eng)31a
Room 214, Adastral House
Theobalds Road
London
WC1X 8RU
United Kingdom

CONTENTS

CONTENTS (contd)

INTRODUCTION

A major design goal of Ada 95 (the revision to Ada) was to avoid or at least minimise the need for modifying the existing base of Ada 83 software to make it compatible with Ada 95. This involved not only pursuing upward compatibility but also preserving implementation–dependent behaviour that can currently be relied upon. This goal has largely been achieved; the revision has introduced 43 known incompatibilities of which only six are likely to occur in a normal Ada program. Total upward compatibility would not have allowed the correction of certain errors and certainly would not have allowed the enhancements needed to satisfy many of the revision requirements.

The great majority of Ada 83 programs will not be significantly affected by these changes – the most likely incompatibilities being automatically detected at compile–time. Moreover, tools are being developed to aid in the reliable detection of any problems and thereby smooth the process of transition.

This guide is aimed at projects currently writing or intending to write Ada applications where enhancement or maintenance is required beyond 1997. Its purpose is to alert such projects to any upward incompatibilities between Ada 83 and Ada 95 so that Ada 83 software can be written avoiding these incompatibilities long before transitioning to Ada 95 is required. A set of guidelines is included for avoiding all but the obscure incompatibilities.

The guide describes each of the upward incompatibilities in terms of the language change, a rationale for the change, a description and example of the incompatibility, an indication of how it can be avoided in existing Ada 83 programs, and the possibility of its automatic detection and removal. Many of the proposed incompatibilities will not occur in *normal* programs – the Ada 83 semantics being known only to the most erudite of Ada programmers, so each incompatibility is classified according to how likely a normal Ada 83 program of a reasonable size would contain an occurrence of the incompatibility. Incompatibilities are also classified according to whether they cause illegalities at compile–time or different semantics at run–time.

This version of the guide corresponds to the International Standard version of the language, published in early 1995 [2]. The opportunity has been taken to present the incompatibilities in the order of the appropriate section of the Ada 83 Language Reference Manual [1].

REFERENCES

[1] ANSI–MIL–STD–1815A, Reference Manual for the Ada Programming Language, Department of Defense, January 1983

[2] Programming Language Ada, ISO/IEC 8652–1995.

ACKNOWLEDGEMENTS

I am indebted to Tucker Taft (Intermetrics) and Bob Duff for their detailed suggestions for clarifying and correcting earlier drafts. I would particularly like to thank Kathy Gilroy (Software Compositions) for the detailed analysis of the guide made in conjunction with the *Transition Aid* tool, and to Erhard Ploedereder for permission to base the set of guidelines for avoiding transition problems on his paper published in Ada Letters. I also wish to thank John Barnes, Ben Brosgol, Robert Dewar, Dan Eilers, Brian Hanson, Wolfgang Herzog, Kit Lester, Jim Moore, Christine Saunders, Bob Sutherland and Stef Van Vlierberghe for their helpful suggestions.

SUMMARY OF UPWARD INCOMPATIBILITIES

A change (to a given feature) is **upward compatible** if the required behaviour of all legal Ada 83 programs is unaffected by the change. In particular, all legal Ada 83 programs remain legal, with the same meaning. Otherwise the change is **upward incompatible**.

An upward incompatible change is further classified as being:

- **upward consistent** if the semantics of all legal Ada 83 programs that remain legal are unaffected by the change. Some legal Ada 83 programs may become illegal, but those that remain legal have the same meaning.

- **upward consistent if no exceptions** if the semantics of all legal Ada 83 programs that do not raise a exception relating to the feature and that remain legal are unaffected by the change. Some legal Ada 83 programs may become illegal, and some that raised an exception may no longer do so if a meaningful result can be produced.

- **upward inconsistent** if the semantics of some legal, correct Ada 83 programs are affected by the change. In particular, the program may now raise a predefined exception when it didn't in the past, or it may produce a different result.

This section gives a brief description of the upward incompatible changes from Ada 83 to Ada 95 grouped according to the above classification, together with a list of any incompatibilities that cannot be avoided in Ada 83 programs or that cannot be precisely detected.

Upward Inconsistent Incompatibilities

If a legal Ada 83 program contains occurrences of any of the *upward inconsistent* incompatibilities, its run−time behaviour will change as an Ada 95 program. An incompatibility, for which most occurrences would be detected at compile time but where it is theoretically possible (but very unlikely) that it would cause a change in run time behaviour, is listed under *Upward Consistent Incompatibilities* and marked with a diamond (♦).

Derived type inherits all operations of parent − in Ada 95 a derived type inherits all its parent's primitive operations previously declared in the same declarative part, unlike Ada 83 (see Incompatibility 4). It is unlikely that many programs derive from a type in the same package in which it is declared.

Real types may have less precision − the chosen representation of a real type may have less precision in Ada 95 compared to that in Ada 83 (see Incompatibilities 9 and 11). This change will have little impact.

Default *Small* for fixed point subtypes − in Ada 83, the default value of *Small* for a fixed point subtype *S* is defined to be the largest power of two not exceeding *S'Delta*. In Ada 95, it can be a smaller power of two (see Incompatibility 12). Other than affecting the value of *S'Small*, this change will have little impact.

Rounding from real to integer is deterministic − the effect of rounding is defined in Ada 95 where a real number is exactly between two integers (see Incompatibility 16). As the Ada 83 behaviour is implementation−defined, any program which required a deterministic result would have programmed around this problem.

Exact evaluation of static expressions in non−static contexts − in Ada 95, the evaluation is required to be exact. In Ada 83, it is only required to be exact for universal expressions in a static context (see Incompatibility 22). As most implementations use exact evaluation for all static expressions, most programs will be unaffected.

Numeric_Error **renames** *Constraint_Error* − in Ada 95, the declaration for *Numeric_Error* has been changed to a renaming of *Constraint_Error* (see Incompatibility 29). If programs conform to recommended practice (handling *Constraint_Error* and *Numeric_Error* together) no effect will be noticed.

Evaluation order of defaulted generic actual parameters − the order of evaluation of defaulted generic actuals is arbitrary in Ada 95. In Ada 83, defaulted generic actuals are evaluated after all supplied actuals (see Incompatibility 32). It is unlikely that any normal program depends on the Ada 83 behaviour.

Upward Consistent Incompatibilities

If a legal Ada 83 compilation unit contains occurrences of any of the *upward consistent* incompatibilities, it will probably be an illegal Ada 95 compilation and hence the incompatibility would be detected at compile-time. However, where an incompatibility is marked with a diamond (♦), most occurrences of the incompatibility will be detected at compile time, but it is theoretically possible (but very unlikely) that some occurrences will not be detected at compile time, but cause different behaviour at run time.

Upward Consistent Incompatibilities are classified as follows:

* *Likely, Less likely and Unlikely* Incompatibilities – for which it is likely, less likely or unlikely that an existing reasonably-sized Ada 83 program (50–100,000 lines) will exhibit occurrences of the incompatibility. A much larger program is more likely to exhibit a *less likely* incompatibility.

* *Implementation–Dependent* Incompatibilities – where the definition of a new facility in Ada 95 may clash with an implementation–defined use in Ada 83, in which case occurrences of the incompatibility will probably cause a legal Ada 83 program to be an illegal Ada 95 program.

* *Implementation–Choice* Incompatibilities – where an Ada 83 facility is no longer defined in Ada 95, but where an implementation is free to continue supporting it. Otherwise, use of the facility will cause a legal Ada 83 program to be an illegal Ada 95 program.

Likely Incompatibilities

Unconstrained generic actuals – in Ada 95, special syntax must be used in a generic formal parameter to allow unconstrained actuals (see Incompatibility 31).

Less likely Incompatibilities

New Keywords – in Ada 95, six new reserved keywords have been defined (see Incompatibility 2).

♦ **Subtype *Character* has 256 positions** – in Ada 95, subtype *Character* has 256 positions. In Ada 83, it has 128 positions (see Incompatibility 5).

Definition of forcing occurrences tightened – in Ada 95, range constraints on a type after its declaration are treated as forcing occurrences. In Ada 83 they are not (see Incompatibility 7).

Character literals always visible – in Ada 95, character literals are visible everywhere. In Ada 83 they follow the usual rules of visibility (see Incompatibility 25).

Library package bodies illegal if not required – in Ada 95, it is illegal to provide a body for a library package that does not require one (see Incompatibility 28). In Ada 83, it is allowed.

Numeric_Error **renames** *Constraint_Error* – in Ada 95, the declaration for *Numeric_Error* has been changed to a renaming of *Constraint_Error* (see Incompatibility 29).

Unlikely Incompatibilities

Bad pragmas illegal – in Ada 95, a pragma with an error in its arguments makes the compilation illegal. In Ada 83, the pragma is ignored (see Incompatibility 1).

S'Base **not defined for composite subtypes** – in Ada 95, *S'Base* is not defined for a composite subtype S (see Incompatibility 3).

Wide_Character **shares all character literals** – as a result of adding subtypes *Wide_Character* and *Wide_String* to package *Standard*, Ada 83 character literals are always overloaded (see Incompatibility 6) and Ada 83 string literals are always overloaded (see Incompatibility 13).

Static matching of subtypes – in Ada 95, matching of subtypes is performed statically instead of at run-time (as in Ada 83) in array conversions (see Incompatibility 18) and generic instantiations (see Incompatibility 33).

Preference for universal numeric operators – in Ada 95, the overload resolution rules have been changed to simplify them and remove occurrences of the *Beaujolais* effect (see Incompatibility 19).

Explicit constraints illegal in uninitialised allocators designating access types – in Ada 95 it is illegal for an explicit constraint to be supplied for an uninitialised allocator if the subtype designates an access type. In Ada 83, the constraint is ignored (see Incompatibility 20).

Exceptions in static expressions cause illegalities – in Ada 95 it is illegal for an exception to be raised whilst evaluating a static expression (at compile–time). In Ada 83 the exception renders the expression non–static (see Incompatibility 21).

Functions returning local variables containing tasks – in Ada 95 it is illegal or *Program_Error* is raised if a function with a result type with a task subcomponent returns a local variable. In Ada 83, it is erroneous to return a variable containing a local task (see Incompatibility 23).

Illegal to use value of deferred constant – in Ada 95 it is illegal to use the value of a deferred constant before it is set. In Ada 83 it is erroneous (see Incompatibility 24).

Assume worst when checking generic bodies – Ada 83 generic contract–model violations have been overcome in Ada 95 by assuming the worst case in a generic body (see Incompatibility 30).

Definition of forcing occurrences tightened – in Ada 95, occurrences in pragmas are treated as forcing occurrences. In Ada 83 they are not treated as forcing occurrences (see Incompatibility 34).

Illegal to change representation of types containing tasks – in Ada 95, it is illegal to give a representation item for a derived type containing a task (see Incompatibility 35).

♦ **New identifiers added to package** *System* – new identifiers in package *System* may introduce illegalities into a unit having a use clause for package *System* (see Incompatibility 36).

♦ **New identifiers added to package** *Text_Io* – new identifiers in package *Text_Io* may introduce illegalities into a unit having a use clause for package *Text_Io* (see Incompatibilities 37and 39).

♦ **New identifiers added to package** *Standard* – new identifiers in package *Standard* may clash with existing use–visible identifiers (see Incompatibility 40).

Unlikely Implementation–Dependent Incompatibilities

♦ **New pragmas defined** – the names of new pragmas may clash with implementation–defined pragmas (see Incompatibility 41).

♦ **New attributes defined** – the names of new attributes may clash with implementation–defined attributes (see Incompatibility 42).

New library units defined – the names of new (language–defined) library units may clash with user–defined or implementation–defined library units (see Incompatibility 43).

Unlikely Implementation–Choice Incompatibilities

Real attributes replaced – the Ada 83 attributes for a real subtype *S* (such as *S'Mantissa*) have been replaced by a different set in Ada 95 (see Incompatibility 10).

Certain pragmas removed – some pragmas have been removed from the language and pragma *Priority* has been moved to the Real–Time Annex (see Incompatibility 27).

Error Inconsistencies

Error inconsistencies only affect Ada 83 programs in which a predefined exception is implicitly raised.

Exceeding *'First* or *'Last* of an unconstrained floating point subtype – in Ada 95, the attributes *S'First* and *S'Last* of a floating point subtype *S* declared without a range constraint are treated as minimum bounds and may be exceeded without causing *Constraint_Error* (see Incompatibility 8).

Dependent compatibility checks performed on object declaration – In Ada 95, dependent compatibility checks are performed on object declaration. Under certain circumstances in Ada 83, they are performed on subtype declaration (see Incompatibility 14).

Lower bound of concatenation changed for constrained array types – in Ada 95, the lower bound of the result of concatenation for a constrained array type is defined to be *'First* of the index subtype. In Ada 83, the lower bound of the result is *'First* of the left hand operand, risking *Constraint_Error* (see Incompatibility 15).

Implicit array subtype conversion – Ada 95 allows sliding in more situations than did Ada 83, so *Constraint_Error* might not be raised as in Ada 83 (see Incompatibility 17).

Raising *Time_Error* deferred – in Ada 95, raising *Time_Error* can be deferred until *Split* or *Year* is called, or might not be raised at all. In Ada 83, it is raised on "+" or "−" (see Incompatibility 26).

Input format for real numbers relaxed – in Ada 95, the format for real numbers accepted by *Float_Io* and *Fixed_Io* is relaxed, so that *Data_Error* will not be raised in some cases where it was raised in Ada 83 (see Incompatibility 38).

Detection and Avoidance of Incompatibilities

All upward consistent incompatibilities can be detected in Ada 83 source. Detecting the error inconsistencies is not worthwhile. The remaining inconsistencies are detectable with the exception of:

Real types may have less precision (see Incompatibilities 9 and 11), but the impact is small.

Rounding from Real to Integer is deterministic (see Incompatibility 16), but the possibility of an occurrence of the incompatibility can be warned. Avoidance is possible, but difficult.

Evaluation order of defaulted generic actual parameters (see Incompatibility 32), but the possibility of an occurrence of the incompatibility can be warned. Avoidance is possible.

All the detectable incompatibilities identified can be avoided in Ada 83 source with the exception of:

Subtype *Character* has 256 positions (see Incompatibility 5), where avoidance is possible but can lead to obscure code.

Real attributes replaced (see Incompatibility 10), which can only be avoided if the values yielded can be determined by alternative means.

Unconstrained Generic Actuals (see Incompatibility 31), which cannot be avoided at all.

Append_Mode **added to** *File_Mode* **enumeration** (see Incompatibility 37), where avoidance is possible can lead to obscure code.

DETAILED DESCRIPTIONS

This section lists all the known upward incompatibilities between Ada 83 and Ada 95. They are sorted by section number in the Ada 83 Language Reference Manual [1].

The information for each incompatibility is grouped under the following headings:

(a) Status

Whether the change is **upward consistent, upward consistent if no exceptions** or **upward inconsistent** and the likelihood of the incompatibility occurring in a normal Ada 83 program of a reasonable size and whether its occurrence can be avoided.

(b) References

The **LRM** reference is to the Ada 83 Language Reference Manual [1]. The **RM95** reference is to the Ada 95 Reference Manual [2].

(c) Language Change

A description of the language change.

(d) Rationale

The reason for the change.

(e) Incompatibility

An explanation and example of any incompatibilities introduced.

(f) Avoidance in Ada 83

A description of how to avoid the incompatibility in Ada 83 programs, or where this is not possible, how an Ada 83 program can be converted into a legal Ada 95 program with identical behaviour. The objective is to achieve a single program with the same behaviour in Ada 83 and Ada 95.

(g) Detection and Automated Correction

Whether the incompatibility is detectable and whether it is amenable to automatic conversion. In this respect, a tool would not be expected to analyse a complete program and make "global" decisions, for example to change the name of a library package called *Protected* to one called *Protected_1* (having checked that such a change would be-upward compatible) and make all the consequential changes to units *with*ing package *Protected*. Note that any automated correction assumes that the program is a legal Ada 83 program.

(h) Notes

Any relevant comments.

1. Bad Pragmas Illegal

(a) Status   Upward Consistent – unlikely in normal programs – probably unintentional

(b) References LRM–2.8(9); RM95–2.8

(c) Language Change

In Ada 95, errors in a recognised pragma cause the pragma to be illegal.

(d) Rationale

It is considered more useful to reject a bad pragma than to ignore it.

(e) Incompatibility

In Ada 83, a recognised pragma with an error is ignored, for example:

```
type Bits is array (0 .. 31) of Boolean;
pragma Pack (Bit);                          – – typo!
```

(f) Avoidance in Ada 83

Remove or correct the pragma – it is extremely unlikely that the Ada 83 behaviour was intentional.

(g) Detection and Automated Correction

Detection of a bad pragma is problematic, given that it can be implementation–defined.

(h) Notes

Another change to pragmas in Ada 95 is that an implementation:

(1) *must* have a mode in which unrecognised pragmas are warned,

(2) *may* have a mode in which unrecognised pragmas are ignored,

(3) *may* have a mode in which unrecognised pragmas are treated as errors

2. New Reserved Words

(a) Status Upward Consistent – less likely in normal programs – avoidable

(b) References LRM–2.9(2); RM95–2.9(2)

(c) Language Change

Six new reserved words are introduced in Ada 95: *abstract, aliased, protected, requeue, tagged* and *until*.

(d) Rationale

Alternatives which avoid new reserved words are the use of unreserved keywords (a new concept) and the use of combinations of existing keywords. Neither of these options is preferable to the one–off inconvenience of the proposed incompatibility.

(e) Incompatibility

Any Ada 83 program that uses any of these words as identifiers is an illegal Ada 95 program. For example:

Protected : Boolean := False;

type *Abstract* **is private;**

procedure *Requeue (The_Activity : Activity; On_Queue : Queue);*

(f) Avoidance in Ada 83

Avoid use of these six words as identifiers.

(g) Detection and Automated Correction

Detection of the incompatibility is straightforward. Automated correction is possible but problematic.

3. *S'Base* not defined for Composite Subtypes

(a) **Status**   Upward Consistent – unlikely in normal programs – avoidable

(b) **References** LRM–3.3.3(9);

(c) **Language Change**

In Ada 95, the attribute *S'Base* is not available for composite subtypes.

(d) **Rationale**

In Ada 95, *S'Base* can be used as a subtype mark for elementary subtypes, particularly useful for numeric formal types in generics. However, problems would arise if *S'Base* were allowed as a subtype mark for composite subtypes, for example:

```
type T (X : Integer) is record
    A : String(1..X);
    B : String(1..X);
    C : Float;
end record;

type S is new T (80);
```

A legitimate representation for *S* would omit all overhead associated with the discriminant *X*, squeezing out any internal *dope* for *A* and *B*, since their upper bound is known at compile–time. However, *S'Base* would then be unrepresentable.

In Ada 83, *S'Base* can only be used as a prefix to another attribute – as there are no interesting attributes for a composite subtype (as opposed to a composite object), there are unlikely to be Ada 83 programs that use *S'Base* for a composite subtype.

The only attributes available for a composite subtype are *'Constrained*, *'First*, *'Last*, *'Length*, *'Range* and *'Size*. A generic is unlikely to contain occurrences of *S'Base'Constrained*, since the value is of no practical use. Similarly, the value of *S'Base'Size* is of no practical use. The other attributes are only applicable to constrained array subtypes. *S'Base* for an array subtype is always unconstrained!

(e) **Incompatibility**

An Ada 83 program that uses *S'Base* for a composite subtype *S* is an illegal Ada 95 program.

(f) **Avoidance in Ada 83**

Avoid using *S'Base* for a composite subtype S.

(g) **Detection and Automated Correction**

Detection of the incompatibility is straightforward. Automated correction is possible, if replacing *S'Base* by *S* is acceptable for composite subtypes.

4. Derived Type Inherits all Operations of Parent

(a) **Status**   Upward Inconsistent but detectable – unlikely in normal programs – avoidable

(b) **References** LRM–3.4(11); RM95–3.4(17)

(c) **Language Change**

In Ada 95, a primitive operation of a type becomes derivable at the end of the declaration, unlike in Ada 83 where it only becomes derivable after the end of the visible part in which the type is declared.

(d) **Rationale**

This change is introduced to ensure that a derived tagged type inherits all the operations of its parent type. The change also applies to untagged types for consistency and simplification (it will probably fix more bugs than it creates), especially as in Ada 95 (unlike Ada 83) it is legal to derive from a type which is derived in the same visible part, so what is a rare situation in Ada 83 could be more common in Ada 95.

(e) **Incompatibility**

(1) An inconsistency can arise if a predefined operator is over–ridden, for example:

```
package P is
    type Some_Array is array (1 .. 10) of Integer;
    function "&" (Left, Right : Some_Array) return Some_Array;
    type New_Array is new Some_Array;
end P;
```

In Ada 83, the "&" operator for subtype *New_Array* is the default "&" for array subtypes and not that declared for subtype *Some_Array*. In Ada 95, *New_Array* will inherit the "&" from its parent, *Some_Array*.

(2) an (upward consistent) incompatibility can arise if a primitive operation is defined before the type is derived from, for example:

```
package P is
    type T is (A, B, C, D);
    function F (X : T := A) return Integer;
    type New_T is new T;
end P;
```

A call to *P.F (B)* or to *P.F* will resolve to the *F* for type *T* in Ada 83 (because *New_T* does not inherit *F*), but will be ambiguous in Ada 95 (because both *T* and *New_T* have a function *F*).

(f) **Avoidance in Ada 83**

If the (obscure) Ada 83 behaviour is intentional, the second type should be derived from the first type before the former's primitive operations, thus:

```
package P is
    type Some_Array is array (1 .. 10) of Integer;
    type New_Array is new Some_Array;
    function "&" (Left, Right : Some_Array) return Some_Array;
end P;
```

An alternative avoidance is to derive the two types from a common third subtype.

(g) **Detection and Automated Correction**

Detection that an inconsistency may arise is possible. Manual correction is necessary to determine whether the Ada 83 semantics need to be preserved.

5.   Subtype *Character* has 256 Positions

(a) **Status**   Upward Inconsistent but detectable – unlikely in normal programs – avoidable
Upward Consistent – less likely in normal programs – difficult to avoid

(b) **References** LRM–3.5.2(1); RM95–3.5.2(2)

(c) **Language Change**

In Ada 95, subtype *Character* has 256 positions; in Ada 83, it has 128 positions. Note that this change is also allowed in Ada 83 implementations.

(d) **Rationale**

Although suitable for English–speaking nations, a character type based on ASCII is inappropriate for most of Europe. ISO has defined a number of 256 character standards (such as Latin_1, Latin_2 etc). This change accommodates non–English speaking nations.

(e) **Incompatibility**

An Ada 83 program could be an illegal Ada 95 program if it has a case statement or an array indexed by *Character*, but it could be a legal Ada 95 program with different semantics if it relies on the position number or value of *Character'Last*. For example:

```
type Char_Kind is (Numeric, Alphabetic, Other);
Kind_Array : array (Character) of Char_Kind :=              -- (1)
                 ('0' .. '9' => Numeric,
                  'A' .. 'Z' | 'a' .. 'z' => Alphabetic;
                  others => Other);

case Char is                                               -- (2)
     when Character'Val(0) .. Character'Val(63) => ...
     when Character'Val(64) .. Character'Val(127) => ...
end case;

I : Integer := Character'Pos(Character'Last);              -- (3)
```

Declaration (1) is legal in Ada 95 but probably requires changing.

Statement (2) is illegal in Ada 95

Statement (3) will yield a different value in Ada 95.

(f) **Avoidance in Ada 83**

As it is likely that allowing for 256 characters is outside the scope of the original requirement, avoidance is not the issue – a review of the requirements is necessary.

The upward inconsistency can be avoided by not depending on the position or value of *Character'Last*. Avoiding the other incompatibilities is possible by treating the extra characters identically, via an *others*–choice. However, this can lead to obscure code.

An alternative strategy that avoids all the above problems, but risks raising *Constraint_Error* on character input, is to replace all occurrences of *Character* by a subtype of *Character* covering the first 128 values. However, in most cases such a change is unnecessary and leads to less clear code.

(g) **Detection and Automated Correction**

Detection of the upward consistent incompatibilities is straightforward; detection that an inconsistency may arise is possible. Manual correction is necessary to determine whether the required semantics of the program are those defined by Ada 95. No correction is necessary if the alternative strategy is adopted.

6. All Character Literals Overloaded

(a) Status   Upward Consistent – unlikely in normal programs – avoidable

(b) References   LRM–3.5.2(1); RM95–3.5.2(3)

(c) Language Change

The Ada 95 version of package *Standard* defines a new character subtype, *Wide_Character* (see Incompatibility 5), whose literals include all of those defined for subtype *Character*.

(d) Rationale

Subtype *Wide_Character* is required for non–alphabetic languages, such as Japanese Kanji and Chinese, where 256 literals are insufficient.

(e) Incompatibility

All existing Ada 83 character literals are overloaded in Ada 95, so any expression or subtype conversion using only character literals is ambiguous and hence illegal, for example:

... *Character* ('x') ...

if 'x' = 'y' **then** ...

for *I* **in** 'A' .. 'Z' **loop**

(f) Avoidance in Ada 83

One of the operands needs to be *subtype qualified* (or equivalent), for example:

... *Character'* ('x') ...

if *Character'*('x') = 'y' **then** ...

for *I* **in** *Character* **range** 'A' .. 'Z' **loop**

(g) Detection and Automated Correction

Detection of the incompatibility is straightforward. Automated correction is possible, by assuming the required subtype is *Standard.Character* as above.

(h) Notes

WG9, the ISO Working Group with responsibility for maintaining the Ada standard, has decreed that this change can be introduced into Ada 83 compilers.

7. Range Constraint on Scalar Type is Forcing Occurrence

(a) **Status**   Upward Consistent – less likely in normal programs – avoidable

(b) **References**   LRM–3.5(5); RM95–13.14(11)

(c) **Language Change**

A range constraint on a scalar type (after its declaration) is a forcing occurrence (freezing point in Ada 95), so for example subsequent representation clauses for the type are illegal.

(d) **Rationale**

For discrete subtypes, no evaluation of an expression of a type should be required prior to knowing the representation of the type. If knowledge is required, then this occurrence becomes a freezing point for the type in Ada 95.

For real subtypes, AI–174 recognised that the values of 'First and 'Last depend on the representation chosen for the type. The default representation can be overridden by a representation clause. However, when an intervening subtype or derived type declaration occurs, the chosen representation is not available, so 'First and 'Last are not yet known.

(e) **Incompatibility**

The following example is illegal in Ada 95, because the subtype declaration will be a forcing occurrence of *Volt*.

```
type Volt is delta 0.2 range 0.0 .. 255.0;
subtype Mini_Volt is Volt range 0.0 .. 0.9;
for Volt'Small use 0.125;
```

(f) **Avoidance in Ada 83**

Ensure that a representation clause immediately follows the declaration to which it refers, a good practice for readability.

```
type Volt is delta 0.2 range 0.0 .. 255.0;
for Volt'Small use 0.125;
subtype Mini_Volt is Volt range 0.0 .. 0.9;
```

(g) **Detection and Automated Correction**

Detection of the illegal representation (ie attribute definition) clause is straightforward. Automated correction is possible, by moving the offending representation clause to precede the forcing occurrence.

8.   Exceeding *'First* or *'Last* of an Unconstrained Floating Point Subtype

(a)   Status   Upward Consistent if no Constraint_Error – less likely in normal programs but unlikely to require attention – avoidable

(b)   References LRM–3.5.7(3); RM95–3.5.7(11)

(c)   Language Change

In Ada 95, the attributes *S'First* and *S'Last* for an unconstrained floating point subtype *S*, specify the minimum range supported by the implementation for run–time operations on values of the corresponding numeric subtype.   This means that the range check (which could cause *Constraint_Error* to be raised) on assignment and parameter passing is optional provided the correct value is returned

An unconstrained floating point subtype arises from a floating point type declaration in which no range constraint is given.

(d)   Rationale

In Ada 83, an implementation is required to perform the range check on assignment and parameter passing but is allowed to avoid the range check during evaluation of an expression if the correct result is derived.   This could occur where an intermediate value is held in extended precision (which often gives extended range as well).   Without the rule, extended precision would have to be lost just to enable a (probably) useless range check to be made.   Note that if *'Machine_Overflows* is *False* no overflow checks are made anyway!

In Ada 95 this permission is extended to variables.   *Constraint_Error* would only then be raised if such a variable were assigned to a location where a smaller range can be held.

(e)   Incompatibility

In the following examples, *Constraint_Error* is not guaranteed to occur:

type *F* **is digits** *6;*

Data : Float := Float'Last + Float'Last;
Data2 : F := F'Last + F'Last;

(f)   Avoidance in Ada 83

Do not rely on *Constraint_Error* being raised where expected.

(g)   Detection and Automated Correction

Detection of the incompatibility is not possible.   However, it is unlikely that any change is necessary, as few applications are likely to rely on a range check for bounds in excess of 10^{38}.

Note that if identical Ada 83 behaviour is required, a possible (avoidance and) correction strategy is to introduce a constrained subtype, for example by replacing:

type *F* **is digits** *6;*

with:

type *F_Base* **is digits** *6;*
subtype *F* **is** *F_Base* **range** *F'First .. F'Last;*

9. Floating Point Types may have Less Precision

(a) Status   Upward Inconsistent, Implementation–Dependent – unlikely – avoidable

(b) References   LRM–3.5.7(4); RM95–3.5.7(4) and G.2.1

(c) Language Change

In the Ada 95 core language, the required accuracy of floating point arithmetic is undefined. However in the Numerics Annex in *strict mode*, the model numbers are defined in terms of the hardware radix. In Ada 83, the safe and model numbers are defined in terms of a hypothesised binary radix.

(d) Rationale

For the majority of applications, the accuracy model for floating point arithmetic is an irrelevance – the accuracy provide by the hardware will suffice. For more demanding applications, the accuracy model is defined in the Numerics Annex. It is likely that implementations will obey the rules in the annex anyway.

The rules in the annex differ from those in Ada 83 to allow for implementations where the hardware radix is non–binary (such as some IBM hardware where the radix is 16) – the Ada 83 rules sometimes result in a double precision representation being required even though a single precision representation would satisfy the requirement for model numbers. The change is seen as a desirable correction of an anomaly.

(e) Incompatibility

In Ada 95, a floating point type could be represented in single precision when it was represented in double precision in Ada 83. For example:

> **type** *T* **is digits** *Float'Digits* **range** –*Float'Last* .. *Float'Last;*

With hexadecimal hardware, double precision is used in Ada 83, because *Float* has model and safe numbers with 21 binary digits in their mantissas, as is required to model the hypothesised hexadecimal hardware using a binary radix; thus *Float'Last*, which is not a model number, is slightly outside the range of safe numbers of the single precision type, making that type ineligible for selection as the representation of *T* even though it provides adequate precision. In Ada 95, *Float'Last* (the same value as in Ada 83) is a model number and is in the safe range of *Float* on the hypothesised hardware, making *Float* eligible for the representation of *T*.

(f) Avoidance in Ada 83

The lack of an accuracy model in the core language is unavoidable. Even in implementations conforming to the Numerics Annex, for programs intended for hardware with a non–binary radix, do not use *Float'Last* (or numbers very close to it) in the range specification.

(g) Detection and Automated Correction

In the general case, detection the inconsistency is not possible. No correction is possible (or likely to be necessary).

For the special case described above, detection of is straightforward. Manual correction is necessary as it is likely that no correction is required – ie the inconsistency is generally benevolent.

(h) Notes

In *strict mode*, implementations claiming conformance to the Numerics Annex have to provide guaranteed accuracy requirements. In *relaxed mode*, no such guarantee need be made, just as for the core language. Implementations must support both modes, though they need not differ.

10. Real Attributes Removed

(a) Status   Upward Consistent, Implementation–Choice – unlikely in normal programs –
unavoidable if information required

(b) References   LRM–3.5.8(4–13) and 3.5.10(4–12)

(c) Language Change

In Ada 95, the attributes *S'Mantissa*, *S'Emax*, *S'Large*, *S'Small*, *S'Epsilon*, *S'Safe_Emax*, *S'Safe_Large* and *S'Safe_Small* for a floating point subtype *S* have been removed from the language. A replacement set of attributes is defined in Ada 95 (in A.5.3).

Similarly, the attributes *S'Mantissa*, *S'Large*, *S'Safe_Large* and *S'Safe_Small* for a fixed point subtype *S* have been removed from the language. No replacements are defined in Ada 95.

Implementations are encouraged to retain the Ada 83 attributes (as implementation–defined attributes) with the same values as in Ada 83.

(d) Rationale

Given that the floating and fixed point models have been simplified, the original attributes have been replaced by alternatives with a better defined and more relevant meaning. Given that some of the attributes differ slightly in Ada 95, it is preferable avoid an upward inconsistency by removing the attributes rather than redefining their values.

(e) Incompatibility

An Ada 83 program containing these attribute names is an illegal Ada 95 program, unless an implementation chooses to retain them for upward compatibility. Unless **all** do, portability will be compromised so avoidance/correction is advisable.

(f) Avoidance in Ada 83

None, although it is unlikely that any existing programs (outside the Validation Suite) will use these attributes. Also, if all implementations support these attributes, no change is required anyway!

(g) Detection and Automated Correction

Detection of the use of these attributes is straightforward. Manual correction is necessary.

11. Fixed Point Types may have Less Precision

(a) **Status**   Upward Inconsistent, Implementation–Dependent – unlikely – avoidable

(b) **References** LRM–3.5.9(2); RM95–3.5.9(8) and G.2.3

(c) **Language Change**

In Ada 95, the values of a fixed point type are just the integer multiples of its *small*, and in the core language, the required accuracy of fixed point arithmetic is undefined. The accuracy requirement for *strict mode* of execution is defined in the Numerics Annex.

In Ada 83, the model numbers are the integer multiples of its *small*, but extra values are allowed in between the model numbers.

(d) **Rationale**

The change was made to simplify the fixed point number model.

(e) **Incompatibility**

In Ada 83, an implementation was free to use extra bits available in the representation of a fixed point type for extra accuracy.   In Ada 95, this freedom is removed.   Alternatively, an Ada 95 implementation could make the same decision in Ada 95 as in Ada 83 by choosing a smaller default *small* than was allowed in Ada 83. However, this would also result in an upward inconsistency (see Incompatibility 12).

(f) **Avoidance in Ada 83**

If more accuracy than that provided in Ada 95 is required, then either provide an explicit value for *Small*, or choose a smaller value for *Delta*.

(g) **Detection and Automated Correction**

Detection of the inconsistency is problematic – it depends on individual compiler behaviour and whether *strict mode* has been selected. No correction is possible (or likely to be necessary).

(h) **Notes**

In *strict mode*, implementations claiming conformance to the Numerics Annex have to provide guaranteed accuracy requirements. In *relaxed mode*, no such guarantee need be made, just as for the core language. Implementations must support both modes, though they need not differ.

12. Default *Small* for a Fixed Point Subtype

(a) Status   Upward Inconsistent, Implementation–Choice but detectable – unlikely in normal programs as implementations unlikely to exploit – avoidable

(b) References   LRM–3.5.9 (5); RM95–3.5.9(8)

(c) Language Change

In Ada 95, the default *Small* for a fixed point subtype *S* is always equal to *S'Base'Small*, which is not necessarily the largest power of two not exceeding *S'Delta*.

(d) Rationale

In Ada 83, a fixed point subtype *S* can have a different *Small* than its base type. This is to allow implementations to hold a fixed point number left justified. Ada 83 implementations are allowed to make *S'Base'Small* a smaller power of two (but not many compilers ever exploited this permission). In Ada 95, an implementation can still make *S'Base'Small* smaller than necessary but the default *Small* for a fixed point subtype S must be the same as *S'Base'Small*.

(e) Incompatibility

In Ada 83, the default value for *Small* for a fixed point subtype *S* is required to be the largest power of two not exceeding *S'Delta*. In Ada 95, it could be a smaller power of two. Hence the value of *S'Small* could be different in Ada 95.

(f) Avoidance in Ada 83

Either provide an explicit value for *Small* or avoid using *S'Small* for a fixed point type *S*. Use *S'Delta* if appropriate.

(g) Detection and Automated Correction

Detecting occurrences of *S'Small* for a fixed point subtype *S* without a representation clause for *Small* is straightforward. Automated correction is possible, by providing an attribute definition clause for *S'Small* (with a value of the largest power of two not exceeding *S'Delta*).

13. All String Literals Overloaded

(a) **Status** Upward Consistent – unlikely in normal programs – avoidable

(b) **References** LRM–3.6.3(1); RM95–3.6.3(2)

(c) **Language Change**

The Ada 95 version of package *Standard* defines a new string subtype (*Wide_String*), whose literals include all of those defined for subtype *String*.

(d) **Rationale**

Subtype *Wide_String* is required to enable strings of *Wide_Character*s to be formed (see Incompatibility 6).

(e) **Incompatibility**

All existing Ada 83 string literals are overloaded in Ada 95, so any expressions using only string literals are ambiguous and hence illegal. This situation is unlikely for manually–produced programs, but possible for automatically–generated programs, for example:

    if *"abc"* = *"xyz"* **then** ...

(f) **Avoidance in Ada 83**

One of the operands needs to be *subtype qualified*, for example:

    if *String' ("abc")* = *"xyz"* **then** ...

(g) **Detection and Automated Correction**

Detection of the incompatibility is straightforward. Automated correction is possible, by assuming the required subtype is *Standard.String*.

(h) **Notes**

WG9, the ISO Working Group with responsibility for maintaining the Ada standard, has decreed that this change can be introduced into Ada 83 compilers.

Calls to *Text_Io* operations are not affected as support for I/O of *Wide_Strings* is achieved via a dedicated package (*Wide_Text_Io*) rather than extra declarations in package *Text_Io*.

14. Dependent Compatibility Checks Performed on Object Declaration

(a) Status   Upward Consistent if no Constraint_Error – very unlikely in normal programs – avoidable

(b) References   LRM–3.7.2(5); RM95–3.7.1(10)

(c) Language Change

In Ada 95, *Dependent Compatibility Checks* are deferred until object creation (if any).

(d) Rationale

Performing the check on the subtype declaration is against the spirit of Ada – objects might never be declared.

(e) Incompatibility

In Ada 83, Dependent Compatibility Checks are performed on subtype declaration, for example (assuming that $J > 5$).

```
subtype Sub1 is Integer range J .. 20;
subtype Sub2 is Integer range 1 .. 20;

type T1 (D1 : Sub1) is .....

type T2 (D2 : Sub2) is record
    S : T1 (D2);
end record;

subtype S2 is T2 (5);          -- Constraint_Error raised in Ada 83

X : S2;                        -- Constraint_Error raised in Ada 95
```

In Ada 83, *Constraint_Error* is raised during the elaboration of *S2* because the value of discriminant *S2.T1* is 5, which is outside the range of *Sub1*. The declaration for *X* would never be elaborated.

In Ada 95, *Constraint_Error* is raised during the elaboration of *X* because the discriminant for *X.S* is 5, which is outside the range of *Sub1*.

(f) Avoidance in Ada 83

Do not rely on *Constraint_Error* being raised when expected, although it is difficult to imagine that existing programs depend on this behaviour!

(g) Detection and Automated Correction

It is not worth detecting that a *Constraint_Error* might have been possible in Ada 83.

15. Lower Bound of Concatenation Changed for Constrained Array Types

(a) **Status**   Upward Consistent if no Constraint_Error – unlikely in normal programs and unlikely to require attention – avoidable

(b) **References** LRM–4.5.3(4); RM95–4.5.3(6)

(c) **Language Change**

In Ada 95, the lower bound of the result of concatenation for a constrained array type is defined to be 'First of the index subtype (as opposed to 'First of the left hand operand).

(d) **Rationale**

In Ada 83, concatenation between objects of a constrained array type usually causes *Constraint_Error* to be raised, for example:

    type *A* **is array** *(1..10)* **of** *Integer;*   *– – A is constrained array type*

    X : A;

    X := X (6..10) & X (1..5);   *– – raises Constraint_Error in Ada 83*

    X := X (6) & X (7..10) & X (1..5);   *– – OK, but obscure*

In the first statement, because the lower bound of the left hand operand is "6", the lower bound of result of concatenation will also be "6", causing *Constraint_Error* to be raised (because 6..15 is not within the range of the index subtype).

In Ada 95, constrained array types are not defined in terms of the equivalent unconstrained array type, and so it is reasonable for the rules for concatenation to differ for constrained and unconstrained array types.

(e) **Incompatibility**

In cases such as those above, *Constraint_Error* will not occur in Ada 95, where it did in Ada 83.

(f) **Avoidance in Ada 83**

Do not rely on *Constraint_Error* being raised when expected.

(g) **Detection and Automated Correction**

It is not worth detecting where *Constraint_Error* might be raised in Ada 83.

16. Rounding from Real to Integer is Deterministic

(a) Status Upward Inconsistent, Implementation–Dependent but warnable – unlikely in well–written programs, where the precise effect matters – avoidable with difficulty

(b) References LRM–4.6(7); RM95–4.6(33)

(c) Language Change

When converting a value from a real to an integer type, a value exactly between two integers is rounded away from zero.

(d) Rationale

This is one of the most unnecessary implementation dependencies in Ada 83. It should not be implementation–dependent whether *Integer (1.0/2.0)* yields 0 or 1.

All other ISO languages that define a standard *Round* function define it to round *away* from zero. *Round–to–nearest–even* (a possible alternative) is appropriate when converting from one floating point type to another, or when discarding the extra bits of precision developed during a floating point calculation, since (on a statistical basis) it produces more generally accurate results. However, a conversion from floating point to integer is totally different.

(e) Incompatibility

In Ada 83, the choice of which integer to choose is left implementation–defined, for example:

Flt : Float := 0.5;

Int := Integer (Flt);

In Ada 83, the value of *Int* could be *0* or *1*, depending on the implementation. In Ada 95, the value of *Int* is always *1*.

(f) Avoidance in Ada 83

The implementation–dependence can be avoided by writing portable code, in which case no change of behaviour would occur in Ada 95.

(g) Detection and Automated Correction

Detection of all conversions from real to integer is possible (but not very helpful). Manual intervention would be necessary to achieve a specific rounding algorithm.

(h) Notes

This language change is included in the list of upward incompatible changes, because some Ada 95 implementations will not be able to provide identical behaviour to their Ada 83 implementation.

In Ada 95, *rounding–to–nearest–even* can be obtained by use of the attribute *S'Unbiased_Rounding*. Truncation can be obtained by use of the attribute *S'Truncation*.

17. Implicit Array Subtype Conversion

(a) Status   Upward Consistent if no Constraint_Error – less likely in normal programs but unlikely to require attention – avoidable

(b) References LRM–4.6(11); RM95–4.6(37)

(c) Language Change

In Ada 95, more implicit array subtype conversions (ie sliding) is allowed than in Ada 83, thus avoiding *Constraint_Error*.

(d) Rationale

Such restrictions are unnecessary and counter–intuitive.

(e) Incompatibility

In the following examples, *Constraint_Error* will not occur in Ada 95:

(1)

```
type R1 is record
    S : String (1 .. 10);
end record;

type R2 is record
    S : String (11 .. 20);
end record;

V1 : R1;
V2 : R2 := R2' (S => V1.S);          -- Constraint_Error in Ada 83, slides in Ada 95
V3 : R2 := R2' (S => "abcde" & "efghi");   -- likewise, since 'First of concatenation is 1
```

(2) parameter passing:

```
X : String (5 .. 7);
subtype String_1_3 is String (1 .. 3);
procedure P ( S : String_1_3);

P (X);                               -- raises Constraint-Error in Ada 83, slides in Ada 95
```

(3) an initialised allocator:

```
type A is access String (5 .. 7);
X : A := new String' ("abc");        -- raises Constraint-Error in Ada 83, slides in Ada 95
```

(f) Avoidance in Ada 83

Do not rely on *Constraint_Error* being raised when expected.

(g) Detection and Automated Correction

It is not worth detecting that a *Constraint_Error* might have been possible in Ada 83.

18. Static Matching of Component Subtype in Array Conversions

(a) **Status**   Upward Consistent – unlikely in normal programs – avoidable

(b) **References** LRM–4.6(11); RM95–4.6(12)

(c) **Language Change**

In Ada 95 the component subtypes in an array conversion must match statically – either the subtypes must both be static and matching, or they must be the same subtype.

(d) **Rationale**

Reporting errors at compile–time (rather than run–time) is one of the objectives of the Ada 95 Revision – the incompatibilities are unlikely to occur.

(e) **Incompatibility**

In Ada 83, the check is performed at run–time and *Constraint_Error* raised if the component subtypes did not match.

For example:

type *A1* **is array** *(1 .. 10)* **of** *Integer* **range** *I .. J;*
type *A2* **is array** *(1 .. 10)* **of** *Integer* **range** *K .. L;*

X1 : A1;
X2 : A2 := A2 (X1);

In Ada 83, *Constraint_Error is* raised unless *I=K* and *J=L*.
In Ada 95, the conversion is illegal.

(f) **Avoidance in Ada 83**

Ensure component subtypes match statically. Code relying on the Ada 83 semantics is unnecessarily obscure.

(g) **Detection and Automated Correction**

Detection of the incompatibility is straightforward. Manual correction is necessary however.

(h) **Notes**

There is a similar change for generic matching rules for formal array and access subtypes (see Incompatibility 33).

19. Preference for Universal Numeric Operators

(a) **Status**   Upward Consistent – very unlikely in normal programs – avoidable.

(b) **References** LRM–4.6(15); RM95–8.6(29)

(c) **Language Change**

In Ada 95 preference is given to Universal Numeric operators during overload resolution, as opposed to preference *against* implicit conversion in Ada 83.

(d) **Rationale**

The Ada 83 rule is difficult to understand; implementations have chosen different interpretations. The official interpretation (by WG9's Ada Rapporteur Group) is so difficult to implement that the interpretation is not enforced.

The revised rules are simpler to understand, simpler to implement and eliminate *Beaujolais* effects, for example:

```
package P is
    procedure Q (B : Boolean);                    -- Q1
end P;

with P; use P;
procedure Main is
    function "<" (X, Y : Integer) return Integer is ...
    procedure Q (I : Integer) is ...              -- Q2
begin
    Q (1 < 2);
end Main;
```

In Ada 83, the call to Q resolves unambiguously to a call on $Q1$ (because the call to $Q2$ involves *implicitly* converting the universal integer parameters to Integer), whereas if Q were not declared in package P, the call would resolve unambiguously to a call on $Q2$. This is an example of the (pathological) *Beaujolais* effect – the adding or removing of a declaration has a semantic effect.

(e) **Incompatibility**

In Ada 83, preference during overload resolution is *against* implicit conversion (see LRM–4.6(15)). In Ada 95, this preference *against* has been removed.

If *extra* operators are provided for a numeric type then an Ada 83 program could be an illegal Ada 95 program, but only if it contained a *Beaujolais* effect.

In the above example, the call to Q is ambiguous in Ada 95. If the declaration of $P.Q$ or the *use* clause were removed, the call would resolve to a call on $Q2$ (as in Ada 83).

(f) **Avoidance in Ada 83**

It is difficult to imagine that existing programs depend on this behaviour!

(g) **Detection and Automated Correction**

Detection of the incompatibility is straightforward. Automated correction is possible, by replacing the call to Q by a call to $P.Q$ (in the example).

20. Explicit Constraints Illegal in Uninitialised Allocators Designating Access Types

(a) Status   Upward Consistent – unlikely – avoidable

(b) References   LRM–4.8(4); RM95–4.8(4)

(c) Language Change

In Ada 95 it is illegal to supply a explicit constraint (ie index or discriminant constraint) in an uninitialised allocator if the designated type is an access type. In Ada 83, the constraint is ignored, ie it does not affect the subtype of the allocated object, according to AI–331.

(d) Rationale

Making illegal a constraint that was ignored is a minor improvement to the language.

(e) Incompatibility

The following example is illegal in Ada 95. In Ada 83, the explicit constraint is ignored.

    type String_Ptr is access String;
    type String_Ptr_Ptr is access String_Ptr;

    P: String_Ptr_Ptr := new String_Ptr (1..10);

(f) Avoidance in Ada 83

Do not supply explicit constraints for uninitialised allocators for a subtype that designates an access type.

(g) Detection and Automated Correction

Detection of the incompatibility is straightforward. Automated correction is possible by removing the offending constraint.

21. Exceptions in Static Expressions Cause Illegalities

(a) Status   Upward Consistent – unlikely in normal programs – avoidable

(b) References LRM–4.9(2); RM95–4.9(33)

(c) Language Change

In Ada 95, if the evaluation of a static expression causes an exception (other than overflow), then the expression is illegal. In Ada 83, to qualify as static, an expression must deliver a value (ie not cause an exception). Note that in Ada 95, an implementation is required to evaluate such expressions exactly (see Incompatibility 22).

(d) Rationale

The new rules make the evaluation of static expressions more portable – in Ada 83, it is implementation–dependent whether *Constraint_Error* is raised or the correct value is yielded.

Reporting errors at compile–time (rather than run–time) is one of the objectives of the Ada 95 Revision – only programs which contain logic to ensure that the expression is not evaluated at run–time will suffer.

(e) Incompatibility

In the following examples, *Constraint_Error* will occur in Ada 83 and illegalities in Ada 95:

    I := 999_999;   – – where I is an Integer and Integer'Last < 10**6

    I := 1/0;   – – division by zero

Note that by encapsulating the offending expression into a suitable conditional statement, the exception can be avoided in Ada 83, but the evaluation will still be illegal in Ada 95, for example:

    if Integer'Last >= 10**6 then
        declare
            I : Integer;
        begin
            I := 999_999;
        end;
    end if;

Note also that in the following example, *Constraint_Error* may occur in Ada 83 but not in Ada 95:

    type Short_Int is range –32768 .. 32767;
    I : Short_Int := –32768;   – – run time evaluation in Ada 83 might cause Constraint_Error

(f) Avoidance in Ada 83

Do not rely on *Constraint_Error* being raised during evaluation of static expressions. Additionally, do not try to make code portable by techniques such as the conditional statement above.

(g) Detection and Automated Correction

Detecting that an expression (raising an exception) would cause an illegality in Ada 95 is straightforward (it has to be detected by Ada 95 parsers). Automated correction is possible, by replacing the static expression by a non–static expression, if this is the desired behaviour.

22. Exact Evaluation of Static Expressions in non–Static Contexts

(a) Status   Upward Inconsistency, Implementation–Dependent and warnable – unlikely in
normal programs – avoidable

(b) References LRM–4.9(12) and 4.10(4); RM95–4.9(25,28,29)

(c) Language Change

In Ada 95, an implementation is required to evaluate static expressions in a non–static context exactly. In Ada 83, an implementation can adopt a different strategy (for example, to yield the same result as execution on the target).

(d) Rationale

Leaving the choice undefined is an unnecessary implementation dependency

(e) Incompatibility

In Ada 83, an implementation is allowed to evaluate static expressions in a non–static context exactly, but is free to evaluate them in a manner consistent with the target, for example:

> F : **constant** *Float := 1.0;*
>
> **if** $F/3.0*3.0 = 1.0$ **then** .....

In Ada 95, the value of the boolean expression is always TRUE. In Ada 83 it could be TRUE or FALSE.

(f) Avoidance in Ada 83

The implementation–dependence can be avoided in Ada 83 by ensuring that such expressions only occur in a static context, for example:

> F : **constant** *Float := 1.0;*
> G : **constant** *Float := F/3.0*3.0;*
>
> **if** $G = 1.0$ **then** .....

(g) Detection and Automated Correction

Detection of all static expressions in non–static contexts is possible. Manual intervention is necessary to determine whether a different value might be obtained in Ada 95.

(h) Notes

This language change is included in the list of incompatible changes, because some Ada 95 implementations will not be able to provide identical behaviour to their Ada 83 implementation.

23. Functions returning Local Variables containing Tasks

(a) **Status** Upward Consistent – very unlikely in normal programs – avoidable

(b) **References** LRM–5.8; RM95–6.5(17)

(c) **Language Change**

A function with a limited *by–reference* result type (ie a task, protected or *Limited_Controlled* type or a type having a subcomponent of one of these types) and which attempts to return a local variable or a formal parameter is illegal or raises *Program_Error*. In general, the check can be performed at compile time but within a generic body this may not be possible.

(d) **Rationale**

In Ada 83, the only types that become limited *by–reference* types in Ada 95 are task types and those with task subcomponents. AI 867 defines that if a function returns a local task, further execution is erroneous. It is highly desirable to remove this erroneousness in Ada 95 especially as more types are limited by-reference types in Ada 95. Although this rule might trap a few Ada 83 programs which were not erroneous, alternative rules for removing the erroneousness are less acceptable.

(e) **Incompatibility**

In Ada 83, according to AI 867, if a function returns a locally declared task, further execution is erroneous. In Ada 95 the following cases are illegal, but were legal and not erroneous in Ada 83:

(1) returning a formal parameter containing a task,

(2) returning a local variant record whose current variant does not include a task but which has a task in some other variant, for example:

```
task type Tt is ....
type L (D : Boolean := False) is record
    case D is
        when False => I : Integer;
        when True => T : Tt;
    end case;
end record;

function F return L is
    Local_L : L ;
begin
    return Local_L;
end F;
```

(f) **Avoidance in Ada 83**

Do not return local variables or formal parameters containing tasks from functions.

(g) **Detection and Automated Correction**

Detection of functions returning local variables or formal parameters containing tasks is possible except in generic bodies where an instantiation would be illegal only because of the body – a violation of the contract model. Manual correction is necessary anyway.

24. Illegal to use Value of Deferred Constant

(a) **Status**   Upward Consistent – very unlikely in normal programs – avoidable

(b) **References**   LRM–7.4.3(4); RM95–7.4(9)

(c) **Language Change**

In Ada 95, trying to use the value of a deferred constant (before it has been set) is illegal.

(d) **Rationale**

In Ada 95, deferred constants are more important than in Ada 83: the value can be supplied via a Pragma Import (useful when interfacing to other languages); a child package may wish to export a constant of a private type exported by its parent; deferred constants can be of any type (not just private types) so will be more frequently used. The change is a ramification of the revision to forcing occurrences (see Incompatibility 7). Also, reporting errors at compile–time (rather than treating the program as erroneous) is one of the objectives of the Ada 95 Revision.

(e) **Incompatibility**

In Ada 83, trying to use the value of a deferred constant (before it has been set) is erroneous. An implementation is free to raise *Program_Error* if it can detect this situation.

In the following example, the elaboration of *Storage* requires that *Null_Data* be already elaborated:

```
package Adt is
    type Data is private;
    Null_Data : constant Data;
private
    type Data is range 0 .. 255;
    type Hidden_Data (D : Data := Null_Data) is record .... end record;
    Storage : Hidden_Data;
    Null_Data : constant Data := 0;
end Adt;
```

(f) **Avoidance in Ada 83**

Do not access the value of a deferred constant before its value has been set.

(g) **Detection and Automated Correction**

Detection of the incompatibility is straightforward (it has to be detected by Ada 95 parsers). Automated correction is possible by moving the offending declaration to after the full constant declaration.

25. Character Literals Always Visible

(a) **Status** Upward Consistent – less likely in existing programs – avoidable

(b) **References** LRM–8.7(1); RM95–4.2(3)

(c) **Language Change**

In Ada 95, character literals are resolved using context, rather than content.

(d) **Rationale**

The new rule makes character literals consistent with numeric, null and string literals – they are usable everywhere; string literals are more usable. In Ada 83, visibility of character literals cannot be used to help resolve the type of a string literal, but they nevertheless must be directly visible. For example:

```
with Ebcdic;
package Ebcdic_Strings is
    subtype E_Character is Ebcdic.Character;
    type E_String is array (Positive range <>) of E_Character;
end Ebcdic_Strings;
--------------------------------------------------
with Ebcdic_Strings;
package Const is
    M : constant Ebcdic_Strings.E_String := "this is a string" & " and so is this";
end Const;
```

The above is illegal in Ada 83 and Ada 95. In Ada 95, inserting **"use type** *Ebcdic_Strings.E_String*" makes "&" directly visible, but unless character literals were usable anywhere, a *use*–clause for package *Ebcdic* would be necessary. This would then be the only case where the usability of an operation of one type (namely a string literal) depended on the direct visibility of some other type declaration.

(e) **Incompatibility**

In Ada 83, during overload resolution, only those character literals directly visible are considered. In Ada 95, context must determine the character type, for example:

```
with Ebcdic;
procedure Test is
    procedure Put (C : Character) is ...;
    procedure Put (C : Ebcdic.Character) is ...
begin
    Put ('A');
end Test;
```

In Ada 83, *'A'* resolves to *Standard.'A'*, but in Ada 95 it is ambiguous because there are two candidate *Put* procedures: one which takes a parameter of subtype *Character* and another that takes a parameter of subtype *Ebcdic.Character* – the character *'A'* could be either of these because *Ebcdic.Character* is visible.

(f) **Avoidance in Ada 83**

The character literal needs to be *subtype qualified*, for example:

```
Put (Character'('A'));
```

(g) **Detection and Automated Correction**

Detection of the incompatibility is straightforward. Automated correction is possible, by qualifying the literal with the appropriate subtype.

26. Raising *Time_Error* Deferred

(a) Status Upward Consistent if no Time_Error – unlikely in normal programs and unlikely to require attention – avoidable

(b) References LRM–9.6(6); RM95–9.6(26)

(c) Language Change

In Ada 95, *Time_Error* need only be raised on *"+"* or *"–"* if the time is unrepresentable (ie overflow occurs). Instead it is raised in procedures *Year* and *Split* if the year number is out of range (of subtype *Year_Number*).

(d) Rationale

This change simplifies the implementation of *"+"* and *"–"* by removing the range check (only an overflow check need be made). It also allows consideration of local time zone information to be delayed until *Year* or *Split*.

(e) Incompatibility

In a program for which *Time_Error* was raised during a call to *"+"* or *"–"* in Ada 83, in Ada 95, raising the exception would be deferred until *Year* or *Split* were called or not raised at all.

> *T : Time := Time_Of (2099, 12, 31);*   *– –last day of calendar*
>
> *T := T + Day_Duration'Last;*   *– –Time_Error in Ada 83 (2100, 1, 1)*
>
> *Y : Year_Number := Year (T);*   *– –Time_Error in Ada 95 (Year > 2099)*

In Ada 83, *Time_Error* is raised on the *"+"* because the year number is out of range. In Ada 95, this check is deferred until the need to represent the year number, ie in a call to *Year* or *Split*.

(f) Avoidance in Ada 83

Do not rely on *Time_Error* being raised.

(g) Detection and Automated Correction

It is not worth detecting that a *Time_Error* might have been possible in Ada 83.

27. Certain Pragmas Removed

(a) **Status**   Upward Consistent, Implementation–Choice – unlikely to cause incompatibility

(b) **References**   LRM–9.8(1), 9.11(9), 13.7(4), 13.9(1)

(c) **Language Change**

Pragmas *Interface*, *Memory_Size*, *Shared*, *System_Name* and *Storage_Unit* are undefined in the Ada 95 language; pragma *Priority* is undefined in the Ada 95 core language.

(d) **Rationale**

Pragma *Priority* has been moved to the Real–Time Annex – forcing implementations to give an illusion of supporting priorities is counter–productive.

Pragma *Shared* has been replaced by pragma *Atomic*, which is defined in the Systems Programming Annex.

Pragmas *System_Name*, *Storage_Unit* and *Memory_Size* were introduced in Ada 83 as a mechanism for changing the values of the corresponding named numbers in package *System*. Some Ada 83 implementations allow package *System* to be recompiled, so these pragmas are unnecessary. Other implementations neither allowed package *System* to be recompiled nor supported the pragmas. Only those implementations that did not allow package *System* to be recompiled but supported the pragmas will be affected. These implementations are likely to continue to support the pragmas.

Pragma *Interface* has been replaced by pragma *Import*, with additional functionality.

Leaving the pragmas in the language just to avoid a short–term transition problem would be short-sighted. The language will be simpler without them, and implementations are allowed to continue to support them.

(e) **Incompatibility**

These pragmas are defined in Ada 83. If an Ada 95 implementation does not support them, occurrences of the pragma will be ignored, the program will still be legal (except for pragma *Interface*), but the intended effect will not happen. However, implementations which support the required functionality are unlikely to remove support for the Ada 83 pragmas.

(f) **Avoidance in Ada 83**

Use of pragma *Priority* in a program not requiring support for the Real–Time Annex is unlikely.

Implementations that fully supported pragma *Shared* are likely to continue to do so.

Use of the *System*–related pragmas is unlikely to occur in normal library units – they are usually restricted to being compiled in empty libraries.

Use of pragma *Interface* cannot be avoided (if the functionality is needed).

(g) **Detection and Automated Correction**

Detection of the use of the pragmas in straightforward. Automated correction is possible for pragmas *Interface* and *Shared* – by changing them to pragma *Import* or *Atomic* (as appropriate). For the other pragmas, no change is necessary – any warnings generated by an Ada 95 compiler would need to be addressed.

(h) **Notes**

The named number declarations in package *System* with the same names as the *System*–related pragmas have not been removed.

28. Library Package Bodies Illegal if not Required

(a) Status Upward Consistent – less likely (but risky) in normal programs – avoidable

(b) References LRM–10.1; RM95–7.2(4)

(c) Language Change

In Ada 95, it is illegal to provide a body for a library package that does not require one.

(d) Rationale

This avoids a nasty and not so rare error in Ada 83 – if a body is provided for a library package that does not need one, then if the package specification is subsequently changed, the body becomes obsolete but, as it is optional, subsequent builds incorporating the package will not incorporate the body, unless it is manually recompiled.

(e) Incompatibility

In Ada 83, a body can be provided for a package that does not need one; in Ada 95, such a body would be illegal, for example:

```
package P is
    Global_Variable : Integer;
end P;
- - - - - - - - - - - - - - - - - - - - - - - - - - - - - - - - - - - - - -
package body P is
    function Func return Integer is ...;
begin
    Global_Variable :=Func;
end P;
```

A similar situation can arise where an optional package body declares tasks.

(f) Avoidance in Ada 83

Avoid optional bodies by declaring a spurious procedure or incomplete type in the private part of the package, for example:

```
package P is
    Global_Variable : Integer;
private
    type Body_Required;
end P;
- - - - - - - - - - - - - - - - - - - - - - - - - - - - - - - - - - - - - -
package body P is
    type Body_Required is (Dummy);
    function Func return Integer is ...;
begin
    Global_Variable :=Func;
end P;
```

(g) Detection and Automated Correction

Detection of a non–required library package body is straightforward. Automated correction, by changing its specification may be unwise, due to the non–uniform nature of program (sub)libraries.

(h) Notes

In Ada 95, the illegality can be avoided by adding a pragma *Elaborate_Body* to the package specification – this makes the body required and causes it to be elaborated immediately after the specification.

29. *Numeric_Error* renames *Constraint_Error*

(a) Status   Upward Inconsistent but detectable – unlikely in well–written normal programs as
Ada 83 behaviour is not well defined – avoidable
Upward Consistent – less likely in well–written normal programs as Ada 83
behaviour is not well defined – avoidable

(b) References   LRM–11.1(6); RM95–J.6(2)

(c) Language Change

In Ada 95, the exception *Numeric_Error* is a renaming of *Constraint_Error*, instead of being a distinct exception.

(d) Rationale

In Ada 83, it was not always clear whether *Numeric_Error* or *Constraint_Error* should be raised in certain circumstances, so the ARG issued a non–binding interpretation that allowed an implementation to raise *Constraint_Error* wherever Numeric_Error was specified.

It is less disruptive to existing Ada 83 programs to make *Numeric_Error* a renaming of *Constraint_Error*, rather than remove it from the language (as once proposed).

(e) Incompatibility

If a frame has an explicit handler for *Numeric_Error* or *Constraint_Error* but not both, an occurrence of the other exception would be caught by that handler in Ada 95 but not in Ada 83, a change in behaviour, for example:

```
exception
    when Numeric_Error => Action_1;          -- also catches Constraint_Error in Ada 95
end;

exception
    when Constraint_Error => Action_2;       -- also catches Numeric_Error in Ada 95
    when others => Action_1;                  -- catches Numeric_Error in Ada 83
end;
```

If a frame has different explicit handlers for *Numeric_Error* and *Constraint_Error*, the program will be illegal in Ada 95, for example:

```
exception
    when Numeric_Error => Action_1
    when Constraint_Error => Action_2;
end;
```

Note that a further inconsistency will occur in programs that explicitly raise Numeric_Error.

(f) Avoidance in Ada 83

Always handle *Numeric_Error* and *Constraint_Error* in the same handler (sensible for portability), for example:

```
when Numeric_Error | Constraint_Error => Some_Action;
```

Note, this is legal in Ada 95, due to a language change that allows multiple views of an exception to be choices in the same handler.

(g) Detection and Automated Correction

Detection is possible of situations in which *Numeric_Error* and *Constraint_Error* would be handled differently. Manual correction is necessary to ensure the required behaviour .

30. Assume Worst when Checking Generic Bodies

(a) Status Upward Consistent – unlikely in normal programs – avoidable

(b) References LRM–12.1; RM95–12.3(11)

(c) Language Change

In Ada 95, an array–type formal parameter of a generic formal subprogram is assumed to be unconstrained, precluding the use, in the generic body, of an *others* choice for an aggregate as an actual parameter in a call to the formal subprogram.

(d) Rationale

In Ada 83, it is possible that the legality of a generic instantiation depends on the contents of the generic body, with the implication that changing the body could render existing (legal) instantiations illegal! This change eliminates that possibility. See also Incompatibility 31.

(e) Incompatibility

An Ada 83 generic body in which an aggregate is supplied as an actual array–type parameter in a call to a generic formal subprogram, is illegal in Ada 95 if an *others* choice is supplied. This is because the actual subprogram in the instantiation could have a corresponding unconstrained array subtype (the parameters are only required to have the same base type, not the same subtype!), for example:

```
subtype Small_String is String (1 .. 255);

generic
    with procedure Gp (S : Small_String);
package Gen_Pack is ....;
---------------------------------------------------------------
package body Gen_Pack is
    ....
    Gp ((others => "*"));                        -- illegal in Ada 95
    ....
end Gen_Pack;
---------------------------------------------------------------
procedure P1 (S : Small_String);
procedure P2 (S : String);
package Pack_1 is new Gen_Pack (P1);             -- legal in Ada 83
package Pack_2 is new Gen_Pack (P2);             -- illegal in Ada 83
```

In Ada 83, the instantiation for Pack_2 is illegal because the body of *Gen_Pack* calls *Gp* (ie calls *P2*) with an aggregate with an *others* choice, which is illegal because *P2* has a parameter of an unconstrained array subtype (viz *String*). In Ada 95, the body of *Gen_Pack* is illegal.

(f) Avoidance in Ada 83

Qualify the aggregate with the subtype name:

```
Gp (Small_String'(others => "*"));
```

(g) Detection and Automated Correction

Detection of the incompatibility in the body is straightforward. Automated correction is possible by qualifying the aggregate with the subtype name.

31. Unconstrained Generic Actual Subtypes

(a) **Status**   Upward Consistent – very likely in normal programs – unavoidable

(b) **References** LRM–12.1.2; RM95–12.5.1(6)

(c) **Language Change**

Ada 95 provides new syntax for a generic formal private type to indicate that the actual subtype is allowed to be indefinite (ie unconstrained without defaults). The old syntax is retained, but the meaning is changed to require definite actuals (ie constrained or with defaults).

(d) **Rationale**

In Ada 83, no indication is given in a generic formal type declaration as to whether the actual needs to be constrained, for example because the body declares a variable of the subtype. It is thus possible for a legal instantiation to become illegal if the body is changed.

The alternative of introducing a pragma (such as *Definite*) was considered an inferior solution from a language design perspective.

(e) **Incompatibility**

An Ada 83 program is an illegal Ada 95 program if an indefinite subtype is used as a generic actual parameter. For example the following legal Ada 83 program is illegal in Ada 95 (because *String* is an indefinite subtype).

```
generic
    type Element_Type is private;
package Stack is ....
-----------------------------------------------------------
with Stack;
package String_Stack is new Stack (Element_Type => String);
```

(f) **Avoidance in Ada 83**

None. It is recommended that formal private types be annotated with an appropriate comment, thus:

```
generic

    type Element_Type is private;   -- !! (<>) in Ada 95
package Stack is ...
```

(g) **Detection and Automated Correction**

Detection of the incompatibility is straightforward but does not address future instantiations.

A possible strategy for the (automatic) conversion of an Ada 95 program is to change each occurrence of a generic formal private type to be indefinite, and then check the corresponding body is still legal, for example:

```
generic
    type Element_Type (<>) is private;
package Stack is ....
```

(h) **Notes**

WG9 has recommended that Ada 83 compilers be allowed to accept the new syntax (with or without any semantic effect), in which case lack of use of the new syntax must have no semantic effect.

Some predefined library units in Ada 83 have been changed, such as *Unchecked_Conversion*, *Unchecked_Deallocation* and *Sequential_Io* (but not *Direct_Io*).

32. Evaluation Order of Defaulted Generic Actual Parameters

(a) Status   Upward Inconsistent, Implementation–Choice but warnable – unlikely and
non–portable – avoidable

(b) References LRM–12.3(17); RM95–12.3(20)

(c) Language Change

In Ada 95, the supplied and defaulted actual parameters in a generic instantiation are evaluated in an arbitrary order consistent with any dependencies of defaults on other parameters. In Ada 83, defaulted parameters are evaluated after all supplied parameters.

(d) Rationale

There are no obvious benefits to the existing rule. It is an unnecessary and arbitrary restriction, preventing a *natural* order of evaluation.

(e) Incompatibility

In Ada 83, the order of evaluation of the supplied actual parameters in a generic instantiation is arbitrary, this must then be followed by the evaluation of the default values of any omitted generic associations (if any). It is likely that not many users are aware of this behaviour let alone rely on it!

(f) Avoidance in Ada 83

Do not rely on the order of evaluation of generic parameters. Relying on a particular order is unnecessarily obscure.

(g) Detection and Automated Correction

Detection that an inconsistency may arise is possible. Manual correction is necessary to determine whether the required semantics of the program (ie the Ada 83 defined order) would be met by the Ada 95 semantics. Note that relying on a particular order is a *bounded error*.

(h) Notes

An implementation can avoid the incompatibility by retaining Ada 83 semantics, but any program that relied upon the Ada 83 semantics would be non–portable in Ada 95.

33. Compatibility Checks at Compile–Time

(a) Status   Upward Consistent – unlikely in normal programs – avoidable

(b) References LRM–12.3.2(3), 12.3.4(4), 12.3.5(1); RM95–12.5.1(14), 12.5.3(6,7), 12.5.4(3)

(c) Language Change

In Ada 95, the following checks for matching of actual and formal generic parameters are performed at compile–time:

(1)   for formal private types, that the discriminant subtypes match,

(2)   for formal array types, that the component subtypes match,

(3)   for formal array types, that the index subtypes or ranges match,

(4)   for formal access types, that the designated subtypes match,

(d) Rationale

Reporting errors at compile–time (rather than run–time) is one of the objectives of the Ada 95 Revision. However, the incompatibilities are unlikely to occur in practice.

(e) Incompatibility

In Ada 83, the checks are performed at run–time and Constraint_Error raised if the subtypes do not match.

For example:

> **subtype** *S1* **is** *Integer* **range** *K .. L;*
>
> **generic**
>   **type** *F (D : S1)* **is private***;*
> **package** *P* **is** ....
>
> **type** *S2* **is** *Integer* **range** *I .. J;*
> **type** *A (D : S2)* **is record** ... **end record***;*
>
> **package** *Pp* **is new** *P (A);*

In Ada 83, *Constraint_Error* is raised unless *I=K* and *J=L.*
In Ada 95, the instantiation is illegal.

(f) Avoidance in Ada 83

Ensure subtypes match statically. Code relying on the Ada 83 semantics is unnecessarily obscure.

(g) Detection and Automated Correction

Detection of the incompatibility is straightforward. Manual correction is necessary however.

(h) Notes

See Incompatibility 18 for another example of static matching.

34. Occurrences within Pragmas can be Forcing Occurrences

(a) **Status**   Upward Consistent – unlikely in normal programs – avoidable

(b) **References**   LRM–13.1;   RM95–13.14

(c) **Language Change**

In Ada 95, occurrences within pragmas can be forcing occurrences.

(d) **Rationale**

It is likely that the Ada 95 behaviour will fix more bugs than it will cause given the Ada 83 behaviour.

(e) **Incompatibility**

In Ada 83, occurrences within pragmas that would otherwise be forcing occurrences cause the pragma to be ignored!

In the example below, the occurrence of *Short_Int'Size* in a pragma should be a forcing occurrence but as it occurs inside a pragma, this is not allowed, so the pragmas is ignored.

```
package P is
    type Short_Int is range 1 .. 10;
    task T is
        pragma Priority (Short_Int'Size);
    end T;
private
    for Short_Int'Size use 8;
end P;
```

(f) **Avoidance in Ada 83**

Ensure that a pragma does not precede any representation clauses for the type that would be frozen.

(g) **Detection and Automated Correction**

Detection of the incompatibility is straightforward. Automated correction is possible, by moving such pragmas further down the declarative part, or by moving the representation clause to immediately follow the type definition. Because of placement restrictions on some pragmas, the latter action may not be possible, for example:

```
package P is
    type Short_Int is range 1 .. 10;
    for Short_Int'Size use 8;
    task T is
        pragma Priority (Short_Int'Size);
    end T;
private
    ...
end P;
```

35. Illegal to Change Representation of Types containing Tasks

(a) **Status**   Upward Consistent – unlikely in normal programs – avoidable

(b) **References** LRM–13.6; RM95–13.1(10)

(c) **Language Change**

In Ada 95, it is illegal to give a representation item for a derived type which is a limited *by–reference* type.

(d) **Rationale**

As limited *by–reference* types are required to be passed by reference and returned by reference, it is impossible to change the representation as part of parameter passing. And, since assignment is not defined, any kind of representation change is impossible

(e) **Incompatibility**

In Ada 83, the only types that become limited *by–reference* types in Ada 95 are task types and those with task subcomponents, for example:

```
task type T;

type By_Ref is record
    T_Comp : T;
end record;

type New_By_Ref is new By_Ref;
pragma Pack (New_By_Ref);
```

In Ada 95, the pragma is illegal.

(f) **Avoidance in Ada 83**

Avoidance changing the representation of types with subcomponents of a task type.

(g) **Detection and Automated Correction**

Detection of the incompatibility is straightforward. Manual correction is necessary as the only possible correction is to apply the representation item to the parent subtype.

36. New Identifiers Added to Package *System*

(a) Status Upward Inconsistent, Implementation–Dependent but detectable – unlikely in
   normal programs – avoidable
   Upward Consistent – unlikely in normal programs – avoidable

(b) References LRM–13.7; RM95–13.7(3–18)

(c) Language Change

New identifiers have been added to package *System*.

(d) Rationale

The alternative of adding the identifier to a child package of *System* has been used in many cases, but this is not considered appropriate in all cases.

(e) Incompatibility

- If an Ada 83 program has a *use*–clause for package *System* and has use–visibility of any of these new identifiers (via another package), the program is an illegal Ada 95 program.

  package *Other_Package* **is**
      Word_Size : **constant** *Integer* := 32;
  end *Other_Package;*

  use *System;* **use** *Other_Package;*

  ... Word_Size ...   *– – in Ada 83 refers to Other_Package.Word_Size*
                        – – in Ada 95 neither are visible

- If an implementation has used any of these identifiers in package *System* in a similar way, it is possible that the program is a legal Ada 95 program with different semantics!

The following new identifiers are defined in package *System*:

(1) the numbers: *Max_Base_Digits* (3.5.7), *Max_Binary_Modulus* (3.5.4), *Max_Nonbinary_Modulus* (3.5.4), *Word_Size* (13.7);

(2) the constants: *Null_Address* (13.7), *Default_Bit_Order* (13.7), *Default_Priority* (H.1);

(3) the subtypes: *Any_Priority* (H.1), *Bit_Order* (13.5.2), *Interrupt_Priority* (H.1).

(4) the enumeration literals: *High_Order_First* (13.7), *Low_Order_First* (13.7).

(f) Avoidance in Ada 83

Do not include *use*–clauses for package *System*. This is good practice as implementations have always been free to add identifiers to package *System*.

(g) Detection and Automated Correction

Detection of the incompatibility is straightforward.

If the collision occurs with an identifier (*Word_Size*) declared in another package (*Other_Package*), then automated correction is possible, by replacing *Word_Size* by *Other_Package.Word_Size*.

If the implementation used the identifier in its version of *System*, manual correction is necessary.

37. *Append_File* Added to *File_Mode* Enumeration

(a) Status Upward Inconsistent but detectable – unlikely in normal programs – avoidable

Upward Consistent – unlikely in normal programs – unavoidable

(b) References LRM–14.1(8); RM95–A.8.1(4) and A.10.1(4)

(c) Language Change

In Ada 95, enumeration subtype *File_Mode* in packages *Sequential_Io* and *Text_Io* has an additional literal (*Append_File*).

(d) Rationale

This is the most appropriate way to add *append–to–file* functionality.

(e) Incompatibility

An Ada 83 program could be an illegal Ada 95 program if it had a case statement or an array indexed by *File_Mode*, but it could be a legal Ada 95 program but with different semantics if it relied on the position number of *File_Mode'Last*, for example:

```
Mode_Array : array (Text_Io.File_Mode) of Boolean := (In_File => True,     -- (1)
                                                      Out_File => False);
case Mode is                                                               -- (2)
    when In_File => ...
    when Out_File => ...
end case;

if M = Out_File then
    -- some action for out files
else
    -- some action for in files                                           -- (3)
end if;

for M in Text_Io.File_Mode loop
    Text_Io.Put ("*");                                                    -- (4)
end loop;
```

Declaration (1) is illegal in Ada 95.

Statement (2) is illegal in Ada 95.

Statement (3) will be executed for append files in Ada 95

Statement (4) will have a different effect in Ada 95.

This change has an additional incompatibility for programs that have use clauses for package *Text_Io*. For further details, see Incompatibility 36 for a similar problem in package *System*.

(f) Avoidance in Ada 83

The upward inconsistency can be avoided by not depending on the value of *File_Mode'Last*. The other incompatibilities can be avoided by using an *others* choice to specify the required behaviour for *Append_File*. However, such a change leads to obscure code.

(g) Detection and Automated Correction

Detection of the upward consistent incompatibilities is straightforward; detection that an inconsistency may arise is possible. Manual correction is necessary to determine whether the required semantics of the program are those defined by Ada 95.

38. Input Format for Real Numbers Relaxed

(a) **Status**   Upward   Consistent   if   no   Data_Error   –   unlikely   in   normal   programs   and   unlikely to require attention – avoidable

(b) **References** LRM–14.3.5(10); RM95–A.10.6(6)

(c) **Language Change**

In Ada 95, *Float_IO* and *Fixed_IO* will accept any numeric input that conforms to ISO 6093, which includes numbers with no leading digit, no trailing digit or no decimal point.

(d) **Rationale**

The new rule makes it possible to input data files produced by programs written in other languages (such as Fortran)

(e) **Incompatibility**

In Ada 83, the only acceptable input format for real numbers is to include: a leading digit, a decimal point and a trailing digit. Thus, a program that inputs a number that is acceptable in the Ada 95 rules but not in the Ada 83 rules (such as *.75*), will cause the exception *Data_Error* to be raised as an Ada 83 program but will execute without such an exception as an Ada 95 program.

(f) **Avoidance in Ada 83**

Do not rely on *Data_Error* being raised.

(g) **Detection and Automated Correction**

Detection is not possible, but the need for a correction is extremely unlikely.

(h) **Notes**

The Ada 95 attribute *S'Value* for a real subtype *S* will also accept real numbers conforming to the relaxed syntax.

39. New Identifiers Added to Package *Text_Io*

(a) Status   Upward Consistent – unlikely in normal programs – avoidable

(b) References LRM–14.3.10; RM95–A.10.1(13–21, 43–45)

(c) Language Change

New identifiers have been added to package *Text_Io*.

(d) Rationale

The alternative of adding the identifier to a child package of *Text_Io* has been used in many cases, but this is not considered appropriate in all cases.

(e) Incompatibility

If an Ada 83 program has a *use*–clause for package *Text_Io* and has use–visibility of any of these new identifiers (via another package), the program is an illegal Ada 95 program.

```
package Other_Package is
    type File_Access is ...;
end Other_Package;

use Text_Io; use Other_Package;

... File_Access ...              – – in Ada 83 refers to Other_Package.File_Access
                                 – – in Ada 95 neither are directly visible
```

The following new identifiers are defined in package *Text_Io*:

(1)   the subprograms: *Set_Error*, *Standard_Error*, *Current_Error*, *Flush*, *Is_Open*, *Look_Ahead*, *Get_Immediate*;

(2)   the generic packages: *Modular_Io, Decimal_Io;*

(3)   the subtype: *File_Access;*

(f) Avoidance in Ada 83

Do not apply a *use*–clause for package *Text_Io*.

(g) Detection and Automated Correction

Detection of the incompatibility is straightforward. Automated correction is possible, by replacing (in the example) *File_Access* by *Other_Package.File_Access*.

An alternative strategy is to remove the *use*–clause for package *Text_Io* (and/or *Other_Package*), replacing it with a *use–type*–clause if necessary, and adjusting all references to identifiers declared directly within it.

(h) Notes

The identifier *Append_File* has also been added to package *Text_Io* (see Incompatibility 37)

40. New Identifiers in Package *Standard*

(a) Status Upward Inconsistent but detectable – unlikely in normal programs – avoidable
Upward Consistent – unlikely in normal programs – avoidable

(b) References LRM–C; RM95–A.1(36,41)

(c) Language Change

New identifiers have been added to package *Standard*:

Wide_Character and *Wide_String* (see Incompatibilities 6 and 13).

(d) Rationale

Although such identifiers have been kept to a minimum, there are cases where identifiers need to be directly visible for a new feature to be readily usable.

(e) Incompatibility

If an Ada 83 program has *use*–visibility of any of these new identifiers, it is probable that the program is an illegal Ada 95 program, but it is possible (if the Ada 83 and Ada 95 uses of the identifiers are similar) that the program is a legal Ada 95 program with different semantics!

For example:

```
package My_Characters is
    type Wide_Character is ('A', 'B', 'C', ...);
end My_Characters;
- - - - - - - - - - - - - - - - - - - - - - - - - - -
with Text_Io;
with My_Characters;  use My_Characters;
procedure Example is
    Char : Wide_Character := 'C';
    Pos : Natural := Wide_Character'Pos (Char);
begin
    Text_Io.Put (Integer'Image(Pos));
end Example;
```

In Ada 83, the variable *Char* is of subtype *My_Characters.Wide_Character* and the string "2" will be output. In Ada 95, the variable *Char* is of subtype *Standard.Wide_Character* and the string "67" will be output.

(f) Avoidance in Ada 83

Treat all the identifiers in package Standard as reserved words.

(g) Detection and Automated Correction

Detection of the incompatibility is straightforward. Automated correction is possible, by replacing (for example) *Wide_Character* by *Other_Package.Wide_Character*, where *Other_Package* is the other use–visible package that exports the colliding identifier.

41. New Pragmas Defined

(a) **Status**   Upward Inconsistent, Implementation–Dependent – no known problems
            Upward Consistent, Implementation–Dependent – no known problems

(b) **References** LRM–(various); RM95–(various)

(c) **Language Change**

New pragmas have been defined in Ada 95:

> *All_Calls_Remote* (E.2.3), *Asynchronous* (E.4.1), *Atomic* (C.6), *Atomic_Components* (C.6), *Attach_Handler* (C.3.1), *Convention* (B.1), *Discard_Names* (C.5), *Elaborate_All* (10.2.1), *Elaborate_Body* (10.2.1), *Export* (B.1), *Import* (B.1), *Inspection_Point* (H.3.2), *Interrupt_Handler* (C.3.1), *Interrupt_Priority* (D.1), *Linker_Options* (B.1), *Locking_Policy* (D.3), *Normalize_Scalars* (H.1), *Preelaborate* (10.2.1), *Pure* (10.2.1), *Queuing_Policy* (D.4), *Remote_Call_Interface* (E.2.3), *Remote_Types* (E.2.2), *Restrictions* (13.12), *Reviewable* (H.3.1), *Shared_Passive* (E.2.1), *Task_Dispatching_Policy* (D.2.2), *Volatile* (C.6), *Volatile_Components* (C.6).

(d) **Rationale**

New pragmas are needed to satisfy some of the requirements for Ada 95.

(e) **Incompatibility**

Implementations are free to add pragmas to the language. If an Ada 83 program uses an implementation–defined pragma with the same name, it is probable that the program is an illegal Ada 95 program (see Incompatibility 1), but it is possible (if the Ada 83 and Ada 95 uses of the pragmas are similar) that the program is a legal Ada 95 program with different semantics!

There are no known Ada 83 implementations that have implemented a pragma with the same name as one of the new pragmas, other than with the same semantics.

(f) **Avoidance in Ada 83**

None possible, assuming use of the implementation–defined pragmas is required.   Perhaps implementations will provide an alternative name for the offending pragma long before Ada 95 compilers are available.

(g) **Detection and Automated Correction**

Detection of the use of new Ada 95 pragmas is straightforward. Manual correction is necessary as the semantics of implementation–defined pragmas are unavailable.

(h) **Notes**

The same problem could arise when moving from one Ada 83 implementation to another.

42. New Attributes Defined

(a) **Status**   Upward Inconsistent, Implementation–Dependent – no known problems
Upward Consistent, Implementation–Dependent – no known problems

(b) **References** LRM–(various); RM95–(various)

(c) **Language Change**

New attributes have been defined in Ada 95:

Access (3.10.2), *Adjacent* (A.5.3), *Alignment* (13.3), *Bit_Order* (13.5.3), *Body_Version* (E.3), *Caller* (C.7.1), *Ceiling* (A.5.3), *Class* (3.9), *Component_Size* (13.3), *Compose* (A.5.3), *Copy_Sign* (A.5.3), *Definite* (12.5.1), *Denorm* (A.5.3), *Exponent* (A.5.3), *External_Tag* (13.3), *Floor* (A.5.3), *Fraction* (A.5.3), *Identity* (11.4.1), *Input* (13.13.2), *Leading_Part* (A.5.3), *Machine* (A.5.3), *Max* (3.5), *Max_Size_In_Storage_Elements* (13.11.1), *Min* (3.5), *Model* (A.5.3), *Model_Emin* (A.5.3), *Model_Epsilon* (A.5.3), *Model_Mantissa* (A.5.3), *Model_Small* (A.5.3), *Modulus* (3.5.4), *Output* (13.13.2), *Partition_Id* (E.1), *Read* (13.13.2), *Remainder* (A.5.3), *Round* (3.5.10), *Rounding* (A.5.3), *Safe_First* (A.5.3), *Safe_Last* (A.5.3), *Scale* (3.5.10), *Scaling* (A.5.3), *Signed_Zeros* (A.5.3), *Storage_Pool* (13.11), *Tag* (3.9), *Truncation* (A.5.3), *Unbiased_Rounding* (A.5.3), *Unchecked_ -Access* (13.10), *Valid* (13.9.2), *Version* (E.3), *Wide_Image* (3.5), *Wide_Value* (3.5), *Wide_Width* (3.5), *Write* (13.13.2).

(d) **Rationale**

New attributes are needed to satisfy some of the requirements for Ada 95.

(e) **Incompatibility**

Implementations are free to add attributes to the language. If an Ada 83 program uses an implementation–defined attribute with the same name as an Ada 95 defined attribute, it is probable that the program is an illegal Ada 95 program, but it is possible (if the Ada 83 and Ada 95 uses of the attributes are similar) that the program is a legal Ada 95 program with different semantics!

There are no known Ada 83 implementations that have implemented an attribute with the same name as one of the new attributes.

(f) **Avoidance in Ada 83**

None possible, assuming use of the implementation–defined attributes is required. Perhaps implementations will provide an alternative name for the offending attribute long before Ada 95 compilers are available.

(g) **Detection and Automated Correction**

Detection of the use of new Ada 95 attributes is straightforward. Manual correction is necessary as the semantics of implementation–defined attributes are unavailable.

43. New Library Units Defined

(a) **Status**   Upward Consistent, Implementation–Dependent – no known problems

(b) **References** RM95–A.2(2), B.2(3)

(c) **Language Change**

New library units have been defined in Ada 95:

Ada (A.2), *Interfaces* (B.2).

(d) **Rationale**

New library units are needed to satisfy some of the requirements for Ada 95. The number of new library units required has been minimised by making all language–defined library units child units of packages *Ada*, *Interfaces* or *System*.

(e) **Incompatibility**

Implementations and users are free to define new library units. However, some implementations do not allow the language–defined library units to be redefined, so attempting to compile a user–defined library unit with the same name as a library unit added by Ada 95 could fail. Any Ada 83 program using such a package would probably be an illegal Ada 95 program.

There are no known Ada 83 implementations that supply a package with one of the new names.

(f) **Avoidance in Ada 83**

Avoid naming library units with the same names as Ada 95 defined packages. Where the library unit is implementation–defined, no avoidance is possible, assuming use of the library unit is required. Perhaps implementations will provide an alternative name for the offending library unit long before Ada 95 compilers are available.

(g) **Detection and Automated Correction**

Detection of the definition and/or use of library units with the same name as new Ada 95 library units is straightforward. For user–defined units, automatic correction is possible. For implementation–defined names, manual correction is necessary.

GUIDELINES FOR AVOIDING TRANSITION PROBLEMS

This section describes a set of rules for writing Ada 83 programs to avoid upward incompatibilities when transitioning to Ada 95. They are a simplified version of those described earlier in the guide and avoid all but the obscure incompatibilities.

(1) Do not use the following identifiers:

    (a)   *Abstract, Aliased, Protected, Requeue, Tagged, Until* (see Incompatibility 2);

    (b)   *Wide_Character, Wide_String* (see Incompatibility 40);

    (c)   *Ada, Interfaces* (see Incompatibility 43).

(2) Do not apply a *use*-clause for package *System*[1] (see Incompatibility 36).

(3) Do not apply a *use*-clause for package *Text_Io* nor for instantiations of package *Sequential_Io*[2] (see Incompatibilities 37 and 39).

(4) Do not provide a body for a library package that does not require one[3] (see Incompatibility 28).

(5) Add a distinctive comment[4] to all generic formal private types that can be legally instantiated with indefinite subtypes[5] (see Incompatibility 31).

(6) Place representation clauses for a real type immediately after the type declaration (see Incompatibility 7).

(7) Do not derive from a type in the package declaring the parent type (see Incompatibility 4)[6].

(8) Avoid use of the model-oriented attributes of real types (see Incompatibility 10).

(9) Allow for subtype *Character* to have 256 positions (see Incompatibility 5) and for character literals to be always visible (see Incompatibility 25).

(10) Avoid use of relational operators between character or string literals (see Incompatibilities 6 and 13).

(11) Do not assume *too much* about the state of the computation when exceptions are implicitly raised. Do not knowingly cause implicit exceptions to be raised (see Incompatibilities 8, 14, 15, 17, 26 and 38).

(12) Always handle *Constraint_Error* and *Numeric_Error* in the same exception handler (see Incompatibility 29).

---

[1]Alternatively, avoid using the following identifiers: *Any_Priority, Bit_Order, Default_Bit_Order, Default_Priority, Interrupt_Priority, Max_Base_Digits, Max_Binary_Modulus, Max_Nonbinary_Modulus, Null_Address, Word_Size*

[2]Alternatively, avoid using the following identifiers: *Current_Error, Decimal_Io, File_Access, Flush, Get_Immediate, Is_Open, Look_Ahead, Modular_Io, Set_Error, Standard_Error*;

[3]Alternatively, place a pragma *Elaborate_Body* in the specification – this will be ignored in Ada 83 (unrecognised pragma) but will cause the body to be required (and hence be legal) in Ada 95

[4]such as -- *! (<>) in Ada 95*

[5]ie unconstrained subtypes without defaults

[6]Alternatively, derive any new types before redefining any predefined operations on the parent type.

16

Available Ada bindings*

Preface

This publication is made possible by a unique collaboration among the guest editors, the Ada Information Clearinghouse (AdaIC), the Asset Source for Software Engineering Technology (ASSET), and the Association for Computing Machinery's Special Interest Group on Ada (SIGAda). Each party provides a valuable contribution to the total publication:

- The AdaIC is providing overall administration and editorial control of the document, as well as collecting information on the products that provide Ada bindings to the various standards.

- ASSET is collaborating with AdaIC on the overall production of the document. In addition, ASSET will gather and make available reusable software components identified by the guest editors.

- ACM SIGAda has generously agreed to publish the Available Ada Bindings as a special edition of Ada Letters.

- The guest editors lend their expertise and judgment in writing the individual sections of the document and providing pointers to reusable components and products.

The goal is to provide an authoritative reference that will:

- describe the status of the major standards and bindings available to Ada programmers;

- provide a listing of relevant reusable resources; and

- list vendors supporting commercial implementations.

Note: All brands and product names are the trademarks of their respective holders.

16.1   Introduction

16.1.1   Background

To further the growth of Ada, it is important that Ada applications be able to access whatever resources an end user will wish to control. This frequently requires Ada bindings to other standards and protocols that control such resources.

In general, a software standard defines a set of services that can be provided to an application; and it defines an interface through which those services can be accessed. In order for an Ada program to

---

*Reprinted, almost verbatim, from the May 1994 Ada Information Clearinghouse report of the same name.

use these services, there must be a definition of the interface expressed in terms of the Ada language. That definition is the Ada binding to the standard. These other standards may be formal standards, de-facto standards, or commercial products that have become widely available.

Sometimes a binding effort may take place as part of a formal standardisation program – with public input and representation from both the Ada community and the community most interested in the standard. At other times, a particular organisation or company may write a binding only for a particular product, Ada compiler, or application, etc. The Department of Defense (DoD) and the Ada Joint Program Office (AJPO) have an interest in the evolution of standards; major standards bodies involved include the American National Standards Institute (ANSI), the Institute of Electrical and Electronics Engineers (IEEE), and the International Organisation for Standardisation and International Electrotechnical Commission (ISO-IEC).

As indicated above, a "binding" is essentially conceptual – a definition. The user still needs to be able to obtain a product that implements the binding. Typically, the implementation of the bindings is provided by the same vendor as the implementation of the standard.

Among the caveats to be noted in using this information is that the way in which a binding is designed can affect the portability and reusability of the Ada application that uses it. It should be clearly understood that this report does not address issues of portability and reusability. Users will have to evaluate both the binding itself and any binding product in order to ensure that they meet the needs of a given project. Also, DoD use of the Ada programming language does not imply in any manner that the DoD endorses or favors any commercial Ada product.

16.1.2   Purpose of this document

The purpose of this document is to assist readers in selecting standards and bindings that are suitable for their work. The editors have attempted to provide material that assists readers in making this selection while remaining fair and even-handed in the descriptions. The responsibility to make the selection from alternatives rests with the reader; the editors have provided material to support the reader's decision, not to make the decision for the reader.

16.1.3   Report organisation

Each major standard or family of standards is covered in its own chapter; introductory material is intended to provide information useful in understanding the general subject of standards and bindings. At the end of the document, several appendices provide other useful information – such as how to obtain information from various software libraries, notably ASSET, a collaborator in this project.

Each chapter is divided into three sections. The first section (x.1) is written by an expert guest editor; it describes the history and status of the standards and bindings treated in this article. The second section (x.2) describes software and other softcopy information available from software libraries. The third (x.3) section is a listing of vendor products. The guest editor is responsible only for the contents of the first section. Information in the second section is provided by the software libraries; information in the third section is provided by vendors.

Section x.1

This section describes the history and status of the various standards and bindings treated in the section. If more than one exist, it explains the relationships and differences among them and provides background information to aid a reader in making intelligent selections. In particular, if there are competing standards, the section should assist a reader in selecting one for a particular job. This section may include notes on the availability of conforming products as well as commenting on detailed documentation describing the standards. When appropriate, historical work is briefly described.

Section x.2

This section provides the reader with information on reusable software and softcopy related to the standards being described. As noted above, ASSET has collaborated in producing this document. However, the relevant collections of other reuse libraries are also noted. Most of this material has been provided by the reuse libraries themselves.

Section x.3

This information is provided by vendors and collated by the AdaIC. It has not been verified, and neither the editors nor any of the collaborators should be held liable for its correctness or completeness.

Further, it should be noted that with continuing developments, it is almost certain that some information has been superseded, and more products and services are available than are listed here. The AdaIC is always seeking word of changes and additions to the information given here.

Appendix A provides descriptions of those standards for which no Ada binding products or resources were identified.

Appendix B contains a copy of the Available Ada Bindings questionnaire. Users are encouraged to use this form to report new information to the AdaIC.

Appendix C contains information on the following repositories and software libraries: the AJPO's Internet host, AdaNet, ASSET, COSMIC, DSRS, and the PAL.

16.1.4 Definitions

In order to make the treatment more uniform in the various sections, we have asked editors to make careful distinctions among various terms that are often confused or misused.

First, we need to be careful in making the distinction between a specification and a product that implements the specification.

Specification: A document describing a set of services that can be provided to another user or program. In this context, the specifications are usually provided by some group that is chartered for the purpose of developing and documenting the specification. Sometimes the specification is defined in terms of a specific programming language. In recent years, though, there has been a trend toward defining specifications in a manner that is independent of any particular language. In these cases, one must also define bindings to the various programming languages that are expected to use the services described by the specification.

Product: A piece of software that implements a specification. In our case, products are typically provided by vendors who sell them commercially. Occasionally, they exist in the public domain.

The next important distinction describes the type of interface provided by the product to permit application programs to access the services described by the specification. Broadly speaking, there are two types of interfaces: implementations and bindings.

Implementation: This describes the form of interface where the product or a substantial portion of the product is implemented in the same language as the application program. This permits the application program to use the interface by compiling those portions of the product along with the application program. This form of interface is often found in layered reference models where the layers that are closest to the application program interface are written in the same language as the application.

Binding: This describes the form of interface where the product is implemented in a different pro-gramming language than the application but exports an interface suitable for the desired programming language. In the case of Ada, we often find that the product is implemented in C but exports a set of procedures that may be called by an Ada program.

Unfortunately, the term binding is also used in a more general sense to subsume both of the cases described above. Furthermore, the word binding is often used to describe both the specifications for the interface and the product that implements the interface.

Binding specifications can be characterised in various ways: as thick or thin; and as direct or abstract.

Thick/Thin: Bindings are sometimes described as "thick" or "thin" (These terms should not be confused with "direct" and "abstract" – see below.) Thickness and thinness refer to the method of specifying the semantics in the specifications document. A thick binding combines descriptions of both the syntax and the semantics provided by the binding. When referring to a thick binding, a user would probably refer only to the binding specification and not have to look at the language-independent functional specification. A thin binding specifies only the syntax of how a particular programming language can access a particular service. The reader of a thin binding would have to look at another document, the language-independent functional specification, to determine the semantics associated with the various syntactical constructions.

Direct/Abstract: This concept is often confused with thick/thin. If a language binding generally provides direct access to the functionality of the specification via procedure calls and parameters, then the binding may be called "direct". If, on the other hand, the binding repackages the functionality to exploit the particular characteristics of the language, it may be called "abstract" Access to POSIX pthreads is an interesting and current example. If the standards-writers provide direct Ada procedure calls to create, synchronise and destroy POSIX pthreads, then this will be a direct binding. If, on the other hand, POSIX pthreads are equated to Ada tasks and the pthreads are implicitly manipulated via the language-defined tasking functions, then the binding will be abstract.

Finally, we must be very careful to use the word standard appropriately.

Standard: This word should be used only to describe specifications that have completed the formal standardisation process by an organisation that has the legal authority to create standards. Specifications that have broad industry acceptance, but lack a formal standard may be termed "de facto standards". Specifications that are in a draft stage and have not yet completed the standardisation process may be called "draft standards" or "proposed standards."

16.1.5   Availability of Ada Binding Products

Vendor Support

	ASIS	GPEF	GPPF	GKS	IRDSX	POSIS	PHIG	SQL	XWind	others
Advanced Technology Center				*			*		*	
AETECH, Inc.						*	*	*	*	MS-Windows
Alsys, Inc.	*	*				*		*	*	
Competence Center Informatik GmbH								*		
Convex Computer Corporation		*	*							
Digital Equipment Corporation				*			*	*	*	
EVB Software Engineering, Inc.									*	
Encore Computer Corporation		*	*							
Gallium Software, Inc.				*						
IBM	*							*	*	CICS
Ingres Corporation								*		
Integrated Computer Solutions, Inc.									*	
Intermetrics, Inc.								*		
MassTech, Inc.		*								
Objective Interface Systems, Inc.									*	
Oracle Corporation								*		
Rational	*							*		
R.R. Software, Inc.										MS-Windows
Silicon Graphics, Inc.					*	*				
SL Corporation		*	*			*		*	*	TCP/IP
Software Technology, Inc.				*						
Sunrise Software International									*	
Systems Engineering Research Corporation									*	
Top Graph'X									*	
Verdix									*	
WPL Laboratories, Inc.										GPIB

Repository and Reuse-Library Support

	ASIS	GPEF	GPPF	GKS	IRDS	POSIX	PHIGS	SQL	XWind	others
AJPO						*	*		*	1553, ADAR
AdaNET		*	*	*		*		*	*	TCP/IP
ASSET	*	*	*	*	*	*	*	*	*	ADAR, Adobe, CICS, OSI, PCTE, Secure
FTP										UATL, UNIX XMODEM/ Kermit
COSMIC								*		
DSRS				*			*		*	Paradox
PAL	*			*				*	*	CICS, Adobe, OSI, PCTE

16.2 Ada Semantic Interface Specification (ASIS)

Steve Blake
Alsys, Inc.
10251 Vista Sorrento Parkway - Suite 300
San Diego
CA 92121
USA
Tel: + 1 619 457 2700
Email: sblake@alsys.com

16.2.1 Description and standardisation efforts

The Ada Semantic Interface Specification (ASIS) is a programmatic interface between an Ada compiler's library database and any tool or program requiring information in this library. ASIS is an open and published specification that gives CASE-tool and application developers access to both the syntactic and semantic information contained in an Ada compiler library. ASIS has been designed to be independent of underlying compiler library implementations; thus supporting portability of CASE tools while relieving users from having to understand the complexities of an Ada compiler library's internal representation of data.

ASIS should greatly increase the number of tools available to the end user because tools can be more easily created and ported to environments of competing compiler vendors. Consequently, ASIS will significantly reduce the cost and the risk for a CASE-tool vendor to enter the Ada market. ASIS will also facilitate more powerful and capable tools to support software engineering.

Examples of tools that could benefit from ASIS are symbolic debuggers, test tools, design tools, reverse engineering and re-engineering tools, metrics tools, style checkers, correctness verifiers, and automatic document generators. For example, a metrics tool can use ASIS to evaluate Ada application code. The symbolic name, type, and usage of each Ada object can be obtained through the ASIS interface to support the requirements of the metrics tool.

Examples of other programs that could benefit include client/server communication between Ada programs occurring on separated processors. One application is currently using ASIS to analyze messages transmitted from a satellite to a ground station. The methodology used in this application has a significant cost-savings benefit to any application doing data reduction for post-mission analysis.

ASIS is a unique interface in that it is the only consensus-based "de facto standard" capable of supporting an interface to an Ada library as the library is updated through new compilations. In this manner, CASE tools now have access to the latest information.

ASIS is designed to be implemented on a variety of machines and operating systems by many Ada vendors, and to support Ada semantic requirements for a wide range of client tools. ASIS provides primitive services with the intent that layers of secondary higher-level sophisticated services addressing the variant needs of specific Integrated Software Engineering Environment (ISEE) tools can be created from these primitives.

Plans to standardise ASIS

The latest working draft for ASIS is ASIS 1.1.0, dated August 1993, and is based on the 1983 Ada Specification. The ASIS Working Group (ASISWG), under sponsorship of the Association of Computing Machinery's Special Interest Group on Ada (ACM SIGAda), intends to evolve this working draft into a standard accepted by the International Organisation for Standardisation (ISO), and complementing the Ada 95 standard.

ASISWG hopes to encourage CASE tool builders to use ASIS 1.1 as an important interface for accessing the semantic information in an Ada compiler library. Information gained from the use of ASIS 1.1 will be used to evolve the interface to support Ada 95. The ASISWG plans to seek ISO standardisation for the ASIS interface to support Ada 95 libraries. The ASISWG plans to have an ASIS standard to Ada 95 as an ISO standard approximately six months after Ada 95 becomes an ISO standard.

Products implementing ASIS

To date, product implementations of ASIS are being offered by Alsys, Rational, Verdix, and perhaps others. Contacting these vendors directly is the best way to obtain current product information.

ASIS implementation differences

ASIS 1.1.0 attempts to clearly define the areas where differences are allowed to occur.

This list of potential variations is organised into several categories:

1. Optional & testable functionality: This group includes the optional features that are called out explicitly in the ASIS specification, and for which ASIS provides a query function to test whether the feature is supported by a particular implementation.

2. Bounded untestable variances: This group includes operations or features that are explicitly allowed by the specification to vary in prescribed ways, but for which there is no operation to query the behaviour of a particular implementation.

3. Unbounded & untestable transformations: This group includes transformations, normalisations, and optimisations that may be performed early during compilation and thus affect the view presented via ASIS. There is no way to detect these transformations currently, and they may impact tools.

4. True system dependencies: Operations that it would not make sense to attempt to standardise further. This does not include compiler optimisations.

Information about ASIS

There are two electronic mail forums for the ASISWG. The technical-discussion address is "asis@stars.reston.paramax.com". General high-level nontechical subjects are discussed on "asis-info@stars.reston.paramax.com". Both lists receive all announcements of ASISWG meetings. To have your Email address added to these forums, send Email to

asis-request@stars.reston.paramax.com

    or to

asis-info-request@stars.reston.paramax.com

    and indicate your preferred Email address, name, telephone number, and surface mail address.

    ASIS 1.1 is available for anonymous FTP from ajpo.sei.cmu.edu. It is available, as a series of files, in the public/asis/v1.1.0 directory.

    If you have Internet FTP access, and run your FTP program, your log might look something like this:

```
$ ftp ajpo.sei.cmu.edu
Name (ajpo.sei.cmu.edu:you): anonymous
331 Guest login ok, send ident as password.
Password:you@your-company.com
ftp> cd public/asis/v1.1.0
ftp> binary
ftp> get asis_1.1.asc.zip
200 PORT command successful.
150 Opening data connection for asis_1.1.asc.zip (130.213.1.2,2614)
(611652 bytes).
ftp> bye
```

(The "binary" command is not always necessary. Some host ftp programs drop form-feed characters. The binary command will prevent this behaviour.)

If you have Internet access without FTP, the AJPO host provides mail-server capabilities. To get more information about the mail-server, send Email to "ftpmail@ajpo.sei.cmu.edu", and address your message as:

```
To: ftpmail@ajpo.sei.cmu.edu
Subject: help
```

To get a copy of the /public/asis/v1.1.0/README file, address your Email as:

```
To: ftpmail@ajpo.sei.cmu.edu
Subject: file-request asis/v1.1.0/README
```

To get a "directory" listing of /public/asis, address your Email as:

```
To: ftpmail@ajpo.sei.cmu.edu
Subject: directory asis
```

To get any of the various files, e.g., /public/asis/v1.1.0/asis_1.1.ps.zip, address your Email as:

```
To: ftpmail@ajpo.sei.cmu.edu
Subject: file-request asis/v1.1.0/asis_1.1.ps.zip
```

16.2.2   ASIS resources available from repositories/software-reuse libraries

Asset Source for Software Engineering Technology (ASSET)

The following information was taken from the ASSET Library Repository Catalog. For more information on ASSET, see Appendix C.

```
Ada Semantic Interface Specification (ASIS)
Order Number:       ASSET_A_313
Version:            0.4
Release Date:       21-OCT-91
Producer:           PARAMAX
Author:             Steve Blake
Reference:          CDRL 251901-003, DTIC AD-A257058
Asset Type:         SOFTWARE DOCUMENTATION
Size:               2 Files, 637 Kbytes
Domains:            ADA STANDARDS AND BINDINGS,
                    SOFTWARE ENGINEERING ENVIRONMENT
Keywords:           ADA COMPILER, ADA PROGRAM LIBRARY, ADA SEMANTIC
                    INFORMATION, ASIS, INTERFACE, OPEN ARCHITECTURE,
                    VENDOR-INDEPENDENT
Collection:         STANDARDS AND BINDINGS, STARS CATALOG
Distribution:       Approved for public release,
                    distribution is unlimited
```

The Ada Semantic Interface Specification is a layered vendor-independent open architecture. ASIS queries and services provide a consistent interface to information within the Ada Program Library. Clients of ASIS are shielded and free from the implementation details of each Ada vendor's proprietary library and intermediate representations.

This document consists solely of Ada package (design) specifications with no accompanying software or other documentation.

```
ASIS (Ada Semantic Interface Specification), V. 1.1.0
Order Number:        ASSET_A_686
Alternate Name:      ASIS
Release Date:        09-AUG-93
Producer:            ASIS Working Group
Author:              Gary E. Barnes
Asset Type:          SOFTWARE - BUNDLE
Size:                25 Megabytes
Domains:             ADA STANDARDS AND BINDINGS
Keywords:            ADA, INTERFACE, PROGRAM LIBRARY,
                     OPEN ARCHITECTURE,
                     VENDOR-INDEPENDENT, ADA COMPILER
Distribution:        Approved for public release,
                     distribution is unlimited
```

The Ada Semantic Interface Specification is a layered vendor-independent open architecture. ASIS queries and services provide a consistent interface to information within the Ada Program Library. Clients of ASIS are shielded and free from the implementation details of each Ada vendor's proprietary library and intermediate representations.

Public Ada Library (PAL)

The PAL contains ASIS files in its ../bindings/asis subdirectory, the contents of which are described in that subdirectory's README file. The text of that README file is the same as the text portion of the ASSET catalogue reference given above for ASSET_A_313.

For more information on the PAL, see Appendix C.

16.2.3   ASIS products available from vendors

Alsys, Inc.

Alsys' TRIAD System provides support for ASIS. The TRIAD system is an Ada realtime development environment, used in conjunction with the RISCAda and TeleGen2 product lines. Besides an optimising Ada compiler, TRIAD includes tools such as source-level debugger, profiler, source formatter, automatic builders, cross-referencer, library manager and tools, and a linker that excludes unused subprograms.

For more information, contact: Alsys Sales, Alsys, Inc., 67 South Bedford Street, Burlington, MA 01803, USA; Tel: +1 617/270-0030, Fax: +1 617/270-6882, Email: marketing@alsys.com.

Rational

Rational Apex provides an Ada binding to ASIS.

Rational Apex is an integrated, interactive software-engineering environment for total lifecycle control of Ada projects. It controls large-scale development efforts while lowering project risk. It supports design, development, unit test, maintenance, verification, documentation generation, configuration management and version control. It also supports integration with external front-end CASE tools and external target compilers. In addition, the Rational Environment enables teams of developers to reduce development time by providing syntactic and semantic assistance, incremental compilation, and automation of system builds and releases. The Environment's support of industry-standard protocols simplifies integration with new or existing project support environments. Host/Target: IBM RS/6000 under AIX and Sun SPARC under SunOS as host; targets any third-party platform and operating system.

For more information, contact: Shelly Richard, Rational, 3320 Scott Boulevard, Santa Clara, CA 95054-3197, USA; Tel: +1 408/496-3600; Fax: +1 408/496-3636; Email: shellyr@rational.com.

16.3 Generic Package of Elementary Functions (GPEF)

Gilbert Myers
NCCOSC RDT&E Division (NRaD)
53140 Gatchell Road-Room 335
San Diego
CA 92152-7440
USA
Tel: +1 619 553 4136
Email: gmyers@nosc.mil

16.3.1 Description and standardisation efforts

The proposed standard for the Generic Package of Elementary Functions (GPEF) represents the work of a large number of people in both the United States and Europe who have collaborated to develop specifications for packages of Ada mathematical functions. This development has been difficult and lengthy. The exceptional dedication and perseverance of these people have resulted in the completed specifications for two packages – GPEF, and the Generic Package of Primitive Functions for Ada (GPPF – discussed later).

GPEF is the specification for certain elementary mathematical functions. They are square root, logarithm and exponential functions and the exponentiation operator; the trigonometric functions for sine, cosine, tangent and cotangent and their inverses; and the hyperbolic functions for sine, cosine, tangent, and cotangent together with their inverses.

Background

The Ada-Europe Numerics Working Group (A-ENWG) was formed in 1984 about the same time that an early study proposing standard mathematical packages in Ada was undertaken by Symm and Kok. In 1986, the Numerics Working Group (NUMWG) of the Association of Computing Machinery's Special Interest Group on Ada (ACM SIGAda) was formed, and has met every few months since. During the 1980s, members of A-ENWG met on a regular basis with the NUMWG so that close cooperation was achieved on developing specifications that were joint effort of both groups. The A-ENWG has not met for some three years, but the NUMWG continues informal liaison with key European Ada individuals on continuing work.

Current Status

The work of both groups has resulted in proposed standards for GPEF and GPPF, which have been adopted by the Numerics Rapporteur Group (NRG), a subcommittee of Working Group 9 (Ada) of Subcommittee 22 of Joint Technical Committee 1 of the International Organisation for Standardisation-International Electrotechnical Commission (ISO-IEC JTC1/SC22/WG9 (Ada)). The NRG has proposed GPEF and GPPF for standardisation. WG9 has approved both proposed standards and forwarded them to SC22 for voting. GPEF has been accepted as Draft International Standard (DIS) 11430 and GPFF has been approved as DIS 11729. Work continues to complete the editorial formatting of the documents for final publication and acceptance as international standards.

Copies of the current documents may be obtained from the Ada Joint Program Office (AJPO) or the editor of this section.

16.3.2 GPEF resources available from repositories/software-reuse libraries

AdaNet

The following abstract was taken from AdaNet, and describes software available in source-code form. For more information on AdaNet, see Appendix C.

Title: Generic Math Functions

This is an implementation of the generic_elementary_functions package specified by the ISO Numerics Rapporteur Group, as well as of generic_primitive_functions, generic_algebraic_functions, and math_constants.

Asset Source for Software Engineering Technology (ASSET)

The following information was taken from the ASSET Library Repository Catalog. For more information on ASSET, see Appendix C.

```
Generic Elementary Math Functions
Order Number:        ASSET_A_402
Alternate Name:      MATH FUNCTIONS, PORTABLE GENERIC ELEMENTARY
                     FUNCTION PACKAGE IN ADA AND AN ACCURATE TEST SUITE
Release Date:        01-NOV-90
Producer:            ARGONNE NATIONAL LABORATORIES
Author:              Ping Tak Peter Tang
Reference:           ANL-90/35
Asset Type:          SOFTWARE - BUNDLE
Size:                406 Kbytes, 96 Files
Domains:             ADA STANDARDS AND BINDINGS, MATH UTILITIES
Keywords:            EXPONENTIAL, HYPERBOLIC, MATH FUNCTIONS,
                     MATH LIBRARY, MATH PACKAGE, TRIG FUNCTIONS,
                     TRIGONOMETRIC
Collection:          GENERAL, STANDARDS AND BINDINGS
Distribution:        Approved for public release,
                     distribution is unlimited
```

This set of generic Ada packages provide a set of mathematical functions that conform to the SIGAda Numerics Working Group's proposed standard (which is a proposed secondary ISO standard).

The package as specified consists of 29 functions that can be classified into three families: exponential, trigonometric, and hyperbolic.

The exponential family consists of 5 functions: Sqrt(x), Exp(x), X**Y, Log(X) and Log(x,Base).

The trigonometric family consists of 16 functions: the four usual trig functions Sin(x), Cos(x), Tan(x), and Cot(x) and the four inverses Arcsin(x), Arccos(x), Arctan(y,x), and Arccot(x,y) constitute 8 of the 16. These 8 functions are approximations to the corresponding mathematical functions, with 2pi being the period. The proposed ISO standard also requires 8 other functions that allow the user to specify a period (e.g., 360.0). The calling sequences for the other 8 are Sin(x,cycle), Cos(x, cycle), ..., and Arccot(y,x,cycle).

Finally, the hyperbolic family consists of 8 functions: the commonly used Sinh(x), Cosh(x), Tanh(x), and Coth(x) and the corresponding inverses Arcsinh(x), Arccosh(x), Arctanh(x), and Arccoth(x).

The code has comments defining usage and implementation details, plus an informative README file. Also included are test packages and drivers to test each of the functions.

A Users Manual (ASSET_A_405) for this set of packages is available from ASSET in paper copy.

```
Generic Elementary Math Functions User Manual
Order Number:        ASSET_A_405
Alternate Name:      PORTABLE GENERIC ELEMENTARY FUNCTION PACKAGE IN
                     ADA AND AN ACCURATE TEST SUITE
Availability:        paper only
Release Date:        01-NOV-90
Producer:            ARGONNE NATIONAL LABORATORIES
Author:              Ping Tak Peter Tang
Reference:           ANL-90/35
Asset Type:          SOFTWARE DOCUMENTATION
Size:                37 Pages
Domains:             ADA STANDARDS AND BINDINGS, MATH UTILITIES
Keywords:            EXPONENTIAL, HYPERBOLIC, MATH FUNCTIONS,
                     MATH LIBRARY, MATH PACKAGE, TRIG FUNCTIONS,
                     TRIGONOMETRIC
Collection:          GENERAL, STANDARDS AND BINDINGS
Distribution:        Approved for public release,
                     distribution is unlimited
```

This document describes the background and algorithms used in developing the Generic Elementary Math Functions. It also describes the testing of these and other commercially available math functions, and gives the results of the testing.

This document is a companion to ASSET_A_402: Generic Elementary Math Functions, and is available from ASSET in paper form only.

```
Generic Math Functions
Order Number:        ASSET_A_411
Alternate Name:      MATH FUNCTIONS
Version:             3.25
Release Date:        07-JUN-91
Producer:            NAVAL OCEAN SYSTEMS CENTER
Author:              Vincent Broman
Asset Type:          SOFTWARE - BUNDLE
Size:                57 Files
Domains:             ADA STANDARDS AND BINDINGS, MATH UTILITIES
Keywords:            EXPONENTIAL, HYPERBOLIC, MATH FUNCTIONS,
                     MATH LIBRARY, MATH PACKAGE, TRIG FUNCTIONS,
                     TRIGONOMETRIC
Collection:          GENERAL, STANDARDS AND BINDINGS
Distribution:        Approved for public release,
                     distribution is unlimited
```

This is an implementation of the generic_elementary_functions package specified by the ISO Numerics Rapporteur Group, as well as of generic_primitive_functions, generic_algebraic_functions, and math_constants. As with most software, this carries no guarantees. Single precision and double precision have been pretty well tested on an Apollo (Alsys) and a VAX (DEC). Longest_Float precision is mostly finished, but rough. This will also compile on VAX/UNIX (Verdix), Apollo/SR10.2 (Verdix) and somewhere or other (TeleSoft).

16.3.3   GPEF products available from vendors

Alsys, Inc.

The Alsys Ada Software Development Environment for 386 UNIX is a production-quality Ada environment capable of handling very large Ada applications (over 500,000 lines of code). The product includes the Compiler; Multi-Library Environment, which provides a powerful and flexible way to manage Ada development effort and share program units; Binder, which supports unused subprograms elimination; High- and Low-Level Optimisers for improving code quality and performance; and Run-Time Executive for efficient support for executing Ada programs. Also included is the Developer's Toolset including: Ada Probe, a symbolic source-level debugger and program viewer; AdaXref, a cross-reference generator; AdaMake, a recompilation aid; AdaReformat, a source reformatter.

Alsys currently has Ada bindings to POSIX, X-Windows (OSF Motif), and the Generic Package of Elementary Functions for the Alsys Ada Software Development Environment, running on 386 UNIX 386/486-based machines supported as both host and target and running 386/ix or SCO UNIX. They are also planning a binding to SQL for 386/486 machines. Host/Target: 386/486 PC under IX UNIX, 386/486 PC under SCO UNIX.

The Alsys Ada Software Development Environment for the IBM RS/6000 is a production-quality Ada environment capable of handling very large Ada applications. Hosted on and targeted to the IBM RS/6000 workstation under IBM's AIX operating system, the product includes the Compiler; Multi-Library Environment, which provides a powerful and flexible way to manage Ada development efforts and share program units; Binder; Run-Time Executive; and both a High- and Low-Level Optimiser for improving code quality and performance. Also included is the Alsys Ada Toolset including Ada Probe, symbolic source-level debugger and program viewer; AdaXref, cross-reference generator; AdaMake, recompilation aid; and AdaReformat, source reformatter.

Alsys has bindings currently available to the Generic Package of Elementary Functions and to X-Windows (OSF Motif) for the Alsys Ada Development Environment for the IBM RS/6000 running on any RISC System/6000 machine as both host and target and running IBM's AIX operating system (Alsys's validated Ada compiler 910809W1.11195). Alsys also plans to develop a POSIX binding for the RS/6000. Host/Target: RISC System/6000 under AIX.

The Alsys Ada Software Development Environment for SPARC Workstations is a production-quality Ada environment capable of handling very large Ada applications. Hosted on any SPARC-based workstation under SunOS or SunView, the product includes the Compiler (with High- and Low-Level Optimisers); Binder, which supports unused subprogram elimination; Multi-Library system (Family, Library, and Unit Managers), which provides a powerful and flexible way to manage Ada development efforts and share program units; AdaExec real-time executive, for complete and efficient support for executing Ada programs; and ISO-standard mathematical library. Also included is the Alsys Ada Toolset including AdaProbe, symbolic source-level debugger and program viewer; AdaXref, cross-reference generator; AdaMake, recompilation aid; and AdaReformat, source reformatter.

Bindings to the Generic Package of Elementary Functions and to OSF/Motif are currently available for the Alsys Ada Software Development Environment running on any SPARC-based Workstation as both host and target and running SunOS or SunView. Host/Target: SPARC under SunOS.

For more information, contact: Alsys Sales, Alsys, Inc., 67 South Bedford Street, Burlington, MA 01803, USA; Tel: +1 617/270-0030, Fax: +1 617/270-6882, Email: marketing@alsys.com.

Convex Computer Corporation

Convex Computer Corporation currently offers a binding to GPEF and GPPF for Convex Ada, running under ConvexOS or ConvexOS/Secure on super computers as both host and target. They plan to implement bindings to POSIX and OSF Motif for the same machines and operating systems. Host/Target: Convex under OS, Convex under OS/Secure.

For more information, contact: Brian Allison, Convex Computer Corporation, 3000 Waterview Parkway, Richardson, TX 75083, USA; Tel: +1 214/497-4000.

Encore Computer Corporation

Encore Computer Corporation's Micro Ada Real-Time Executive (MicroARTE) includes Ada bindings to the Generic Package of Elementary Functions (GPEF) and the Generic Package of Primitive Functions (GPPF).

The MicroARTE product is one of several real-time execution environments available on the Encore 90 Family of computers. MicroARTE can be used to provide a real-time execution environment that directly controls processor resources, input/output systems, memory, interrupts, and other functions. MicroARTE eliminates the need to invoke conventional operating-system services and reduces system overhead. Real-time system performance and response are enhanced. Host/Target: Encore 91 under UMAX 3.0.

Encore's Parallel Ada Development System (PADS) includes Ada bindings to the Generic Package of Elementary Functions (GPEF) and the Generic Package of Primitive Functions (GPPF).

The PADS product combines a toolset based on the Verdix Ada Development system and Encore's multi-threaded parallel Ada run-time system to provide a complete environment for the development of Ada language applications.

PADS consists of a validated compiler, run-time libraries, a symbolic debugger, and a set of tools that aid in Ada program generation, analysis, and library management. PADS is hosted by the UMAX V operating system, combining UNIX computing with parallel run-time capabilities. Host/Target: Encore 91 under UMAX 3.0.

For more information, contact: Gary Beerman, Encore Computer Corporation, 6901 West Sunrise Boulevard - Mail Stop 719, Fort Lauderdale, FL 33313-4499, USA; Tel: +1 305/587-2900; Fax: +1 305/795-5546; Email: gbeerman@encore.com.

IBM

The IBM Ada/370 product provides bindings to GPEF and SQL and the Customer Information Control System (CICS – a transaction-processing system). The IBM Ada/370 licensed programs (5706-292 and 5706-295) consist of an Ada language compiler and a run time library for use on various IBM MVS and VM/CMS operating systems. The IBM Ada/370 product provides many development environment aids – such as a source-level debugger (optionally with windowing when using IBM Graphical Data Display Manager Licensed Program for either MVS or VM), a highly configurable source-code formatter to assist in enforcing project coding standards, a dependency lister, a non-intrusive performance profiler, a cross-reference utility and an Ada library-management capability. Ada/370 programs can call VS COBOL II subprograms similar to the calling of VS FORTRAN, C/370, and S/370 assembler subprograms; Ada/370 exported subprograms can be called from VS COBOL II, VS FORTRAN, C/370, and S/370 assembler programs. Additionally, separate features support inter-operation with other major database and transaction-processing subsystems.

One such feature of IBM Ada/370, called the SQL Module Processor for DB2 Database Manager, supports the procedural binding of Ada and SQL.

Another such feature of IBM Ada/370, called the IBM CICS Module Processor/MVS, supports the procedural binding of Ada and CICS, including CICS/OS/VS, CICS/MVS and CICS/ESA. Together with the SQL Module Processor for DB2 Database Manager, powerful Ada applications utilising the combined features of these two subsystems can be productively built.

Host/Target: Ada/370 runs on the IBM 30XX, 43XX, 937X and ES/9000 family processors, which are supported by the following operating systems:

1. VM/System Product (VM/SP) Release 5 or 6 (5664-167) with or without High Performance Option (HPO) (5664-173);

2. VM/Extended Architecture System Product (VM/XA SP) Release 2 (5664-308);

3. VM/Enterprise Systems Architecture (VM/ESA) Release 1 (5684-112);

4. MVS/SP-JES2 Version 2 Release 2 (MVS/XA) (5740-XC6);

5. MVS/SP-JES3 Version 2 Release 2 (MVS/XA) (5665-291);

6. MVS/SP-JES2 Version 3 Release 1 (MVS/ESA) (5685-001);

7. MVS/SP-JES3 Version 3 Release 1 (MVS/ESA) (5685-002);

8. MVS/ESA-JES2 Version 4 Release 1 or 2 (MVS/ESA) (5695-047);

9. MVS/ESA-JES3 Version 4 Release 1 or 2 (MVS/ESA) (5695-048);

Note: All of the above Operating Environments are supported in 31-bit addressing mode with the exception of VM/System Product (VM/SP) Release 5 and 6 which are restricted to 24-bit addressing.

IBM's AIX Ada/6000 product provides a binding to GPEF and IBM AIXWindows (X-Windows ... not Motif). It runs on all models of the IBM RISC System/6000 under the IBM AIX Version 3.2 operating system.

The AIX Ada/6000 licensed programs (5706-291 and 5706-294) consist of an optimising compiler, a run-time environment, a symbolic debugger, an Ada "makefile" generator for use in automating and minimising recompilation, Ada library management tools and Ada language bindings to some key AIX subsystems. With the exception of some system-specific aspects of the language, the Ada language for the AIX operating system is source compatible with the Ada language supported by IBM licensed programs in VM/CMS and MVS. Host/Target: IBM RISC System/6000 under the IBM AIX Version 3.2 operating system.

The IBM products listed above comply with the following standards: ANSI/MIL-STD-1815A – Ada '83; ISO 8652-1987, Programming Languages, Ada; FIPS PUB 119 – Ada; FIPS PUB 127-1 SQL through IBM DB2 Database Manager V2.3; ANSI-X3.135-1986 – Database Language-SQL; ANSI-X3.168-1989 – Procedural Binding of Ada and SQL; CIFO 2.0 & 3.0 Catalog of Interface Features & Options; Validated at current level (1.11) of the ACVC test suite.

For more information, contact: Barry Lee, IBM Corporation, 844 Don Mills Road, North York, Ontario, Canada M3C 1V7; Tel: +1 416/448-3174; Fax: +1 416/448-4810.

MassTech, Inc.

MassTech's MathPack product is an Ada mathematical library that provides more than 350 mathematical subprograms in 20+ generic Ada packages. These subprograms provide solutions to a broad range of mathematical problems including linear systems, eigensystems, differential equations, integration, interpolation, transforms, special functions, elementary functions, polynomials, basic linear algebra, random numbers, probability, and statistics. In addition, there are packages defining data types, numerical, physical and chemical constants. The subprograms in MathPack are based on proven numerical algorithms, such as LINPACK for linear systems, EISPACK for eigensystems, and QUADPACK for integration.

The MathPack provides a binding to the Generic Package of Elementary Functions (GPEF). Host/Target: Convex under UNIX, DEC/VAX under VMS, Digital under Ultrix, Digital under VMS, IBM under UNIX, Silicon Graphics under UNIX, Sun under UNIX, IBM and compatible under DOS.

For more information, contact: MassTech, Inc., 3108 Hillsboro Road, Huntsville, AL 35805, USA; Tel: +1 205/539-8360; Fax: +1 205/533-6730

SL Corporation

SL Corporation provides Ada binding support for its SL-GMS toolkit; this includes support for GPEF, GPPF, POSIX, SQL, TCP/IP, OSF/Motif, and Open Look.

SL-GMS is a toolkit for developing dynamic graphics screens for real-time or highly interactive applications. Non-programmers can design application screens in a standard drawing-tool mode, connect them to real-time data sources and animate screen objects to visualise changing data values. SL-GMS allows the design of custom "GISMOs" to input values or control the application and supports Motif, Open Look and other X toolkit widgets.

SL-GMS is used extensively to provide real-time graphics for applications in the fields of manufacturing, process control, network management, avionics and financial tracking. Host/Target: Validated Verdix and DEC compilers support SL-GMS for the following machines as both host and target: DEC-DECstation/ULTRIX 4.0; DEC-VAXstation/ULTRIX 4.0; DEC-VAXstation/VMS 5.4; DEC-VAXstation/VMS 5.5; DEC Alpha PCs/Windows NT; IBM-RS6000/AIX; HP-9000/300/UNIX; HP-9000/400/UNIX; HP-9000/700/UNIX; HP-9000/800/UNIX; PC-386/IX UNIX; PC-386/SCO

UNIX; PC-386/Lynx; PC-386/0S2; PC-386/System 5.4; SGI-4D/IRIX 3.3; Sun-3/SunOS 4.1; Sun-SPARC/SunOS 4.1 and Solaris; 88 Open/BCS Compliant; and Intel PCs/Windows NT.

For more information, contact: Mike Meagher, SL Corporation, 240 Tamal Vista Boulevard, Corte Madera, CA 94926, USA; Tel: +1 415/927-1724; Fax: +1 415/927-0878.

16.4 Generic Package of Primitive Functions for Ada (GPPF)

Gilbert Myers
NCCOSC RDT&E Division (NRaD)
53140 Gatchell Road-Room 335
San Diego
CA 92152-7440
USA
Tel: +1 619 553 4136
Email: gmyers@nosc.mil

16.4.1 Description and standardisation efforts

The proposed standard for the Generic Package of Primitive Functions for Ada (GPPF) represents the work of a large number of people in both the United States and Europe who have collaborated to develop specifications for packages of Ada mathematical functions. This development has been difficult and lengthy. The exceptional dedication and perseverance of these people have resulted in the completed specifications for two packages – GPPF, and the Generic Package of Elementary Functions for Ada (GPEF – discussed in Section 2).

GPPF is the specification for primitive functions and procedures for manipulating the fraction part and exponent part of machine numbers of the generic floating-point type. Additional functions are provided for directed rounding to a nearby integer, for computing an exact remainder, for determining the immediate neighbors of a floating-point machine number, for transferring the sign from one floating-point machine number to another, and for shortening a floating-point machine number to a specified number of leading radix digits.

Background

The Ada-Europe Numerics Working Group (A-ENWG) was formed in 1984 about the same time that an early study proposing standard mathematical packages in Ada was undertaken by Symm and Kok. In 1986, the Numerics Working Group (NUMWG) of the Association of Computing Machinery's Special Interest Group on Ada (ACM SIGAda) was formed, and has met every few months since. During the 1980s, members of A-ENWG met on a regular basis with the NUMWG so that close cooperation was achieved on developing specifications that were joint effort of both groups. The A-ENWG has not met for some three years, but the NUMWG continues informal liaison with key European Ada individuals on continuing work.

Current Status

The work of both groups has resulted in proposed standards for GPEF and GPPF, which have been adopted by the Numerics Rapporteur Group (NRG), a subcommittee of Working Group 9 (Ada) of Subcommittee 22 of Joint Technical Committee 1 of the International Organisation for Standardisation-International Electrotechnical Commission (ISO-IEC JTC1/SC22/WG9 (Ada)). The NRG has proposed GPEF and GPPF for standardisation. WG9 has approved both proposed standards and forwarded them to SC22 for voting. GPEF has been accepted as Draft International Standard (DIS) 11430 and GPPF has been approved as DIS 11729. Work continues to complete the editorial formatting of the documents for final publication and acceptance as international standards.

Copies of the current documents may be obtained from the Ada Joint Program Office (AJPO) or the editor of this section.

16.4.2   GPPF resources available from repositories/software-reuse libraries

AdaNet

The following abstract was taken from AdaNet, and describes software available in source-code form. For more information on AdaNet, see Appendix C.

Title: Generic Math Functions

This is an implementation of the generic_elementary_functions package specified by the ISO Numerics Rapporteur Group, as well as of generic_primitive_functions, generic_algebraic_functions, and math_constants.

Asset Source for Software Engineering Technology (ASSET)

The following information was taken from the ASSET Library Repository Catalog. For more information on ASSET, see Appendix C.

```
Generic Math Functions
Order Number:         ASSET_A_411
Alternate Name:       MATH FUNCTIONS
Version:              3.25
Release Date:         07-JUN-91
Producer:             NAVAL OCEAN SYSTEMS CENTER
Author:               Vincent Broman
Asset Type:           SOFTWARE - BUNDLE
Size:                 57 Files
Domains:              ADA STANDARDS AND BINDINGS, MATH UTILITIES
Keywords:             EXPONENTIAL, HYPERBOLIC, MATH FUNCTIONS,
                      MATH LIBRARY, MATH PACKAGE, TRIG FUNCTIONS,
                      TRIGONOMETRIC
Collection:           GENERAL, STANDARDS AND BINDINGS
Distribution:         Approved for public release,
                      distribution is unlimited
```

This is an implementation of the generic_elementary_functions package specified by the ISO Numerics Rapporteur Group, as well as of generic_primitive_functions, generic_algebraic_functions, and math_constants. As with most software, this carries no guarantees. Single precision and double precision have been pretty well tested on an Apollo (Alsys) and a VAX (DEC). Longest_Float precision is mostly finished, but rough. This will also compile on VAX/UNIX (Verdix), Apollo/SR10.2 (Verdix) and somewhere or other (TeleSoft).

16.4.3   GPPF products available from vendors

Convex Computer Corporation

Convex Computer Corporation currently offers a binding to GPEF and GPPF for Convex Ada running under ConvexOS or ConvexOS/Secure on supercomputers as both host and target. They plan to implement bindings to POSIX and OSF Motif for the same machines and operating systems. Host/Target: Convex under OS, Convex under OS/Secure.

For more information, contact: Brian Allison, Convex Computer Corporation, 3000 Waterview Parkway, Richardson, TX 75083, USA; Tel: +1 214/497-4000.

Encore Computer Corporation

[Last updated: November 1992] Encore Computer Corporation's Micro Ada Real-Time Executive (MicroARTE) includes Ada bindings to the Generic Package of Elementary Functions (GPEF) and the Generic Package of Primitive Functions (GPPF).

The MicroARTE product is one of several real-time execution environments available on the Encore 90 Family of computers. MicroARTE can be used to provide a real-time execution environment that directly controls processor resources, input/output systems, memory, interrupts, and other functions. MicroARTE eliminates the need to invoke conventional operating system services and considerably reduces system overhead. Real-time system performance and response are greatly enhanced. Host/Target: Encore 91 under UMAX 3.0.

Encore's Parallel Ada Development System (PADS) includes Ada bindings to the Generic Package of Elementary Functions (GPEF) and the Generic Package of Primitive Functions (GPPF).

The PADS product combines a toolset based on the Verdix Ada Development system and Encore's multi-threaded parallel Ada run-time system to provide a complete environment for the development of Ada language applications.

PADS consists of a validated compiler run-time libraries, a symbolic debugger, and a set of tools that aid in Ada program generation, analysis, and library management. PADS is hosted by the UMAX V operating system, combining UNIX computing with parallel run-time capabilities. Host/Target: Encore 91 under UMAX 3.0.

For more information, contact: Gary Beerman, Encore Computer Corporation, 6901 West Sunrise Boulevard - Mail Stop 719, Fort Lauderdale, FL 33313-4499, USA; Tel: +1 305/587-2900; Fax: +1 305/797-5546; Email: gbeerman@encore.com.

SL Corporation

SL Corporation provides Ada binding support for its SL-GMS toolkit; this includes support for GPEF, GPPF, POSIX, SQL, TCP/IP, OSF/Motif, and Open Look.

SL-GMS is a toolkit for developing dynamic graphics screens for real-time or highly interactive applications. Non-programmers can design application screens in a standard drawing-tool mode, connect them to real-time data sources and animate screen objects to visualise changing data values. SL-GMS allows the design of custom "GISMOs" to input values or control the application and supports Motif, Open Look and other X toolkit widgets.

SL-GMS is used extensively to provide real-time graphics for applications in the fields of manufacturing, process control, network management, avionics and financial tracking. Host/Target: Validated Verdix and DEC compilers support SL-GMS for the following machines as both host and target: DEC-DECstation/ULTRIX 4.0; DEC-VAXstation/ULTRIX 4.0; DEC-VAXstation/VMS 5.4; DEC-VAXstation/VMS 5.5; DEC Alpha PCs/Windows NT; IBM-RS6000/AIX; HP-9000/300/UNIX; HP-9000/400/UNIX; HP-9000/700/UNIX; HP-9000/800/UNIX; PC-386/IX UNIX; PC-386/SCO UNIX; PC-386/Lynx; PC-386/OS2; PC-386/System 5.4; SGI-4D/IRIX 3.3; Sun-3/SunOS 4.1; Sun-SPARC/SunOS 4.1 and Solaris; 88 Open/BCS Compliant; and Intel PCs/Windows NT.

For more information, contact: Mike Meagher, SL Corporation, 240 Tamal Vista Boulevard, Corte Madera, CA 94926, USA; Tel: +1 415/927-1724; Fax: +1 415/927-0878.

16.5 Graphical Kernel System (GKS)

16.5.1 Description and standardisation efforts

The Graphical Kernel System (GKS) is an American National Standards Institute (ANSI) standard graphics library, and a superset of the International Organisation for Standardisation (ISO) standard graphics library. GKS contains subroutines for an application programmer to incorporate within a program in order to produce and manipulate graphical images. It is defined independently of any particular language.

Binding Status: The Ada binding to GKS (GKS/Ada) is an ANSI/ISO standard.

Documentation: The ANSI GKS/Ada Binding is published by ANSI as document X3.124.3. The International Standard is published as ISO 8651-3. To inquire about availability of either standard, contact: ANSI, 1430 Broadway, New York, NY 10018; Tel (sales): +1 212/354-3300; general: +1 212/354-3300

For more information, contact: Richard F. Puk, Chairman, X3H3.4, Puk Consulting Services, 7644 Cortina Court, Carlsbad, CA 92009-8206; Tel: +1 619/753-9027; Fax: same as phone; Email: rpuk@ajpo.sei.cmu.edu.

16.5.2 GKS resources available from repositories/software-reuse libraries

AdaNet

The following abstracts were taken from AdaNet, and describe software available in source-code form. For more information on AdaNet, see Appendix C.

Title: Ada Interface to a FORTRAN GKS

Graphical Kernel System implementation, running on an Apollo UNIX workstation with either the Alsys or Verdix Ada compilers, on top of the ULowell GKS implementation. Porting to other environments may take some effort, but this might be a good starting place.

The file 5mar.cdif is provided, which is a patch file for fixing some bugs in the Ulowell FORTRAN code.

This is a Graphical Kernel System level ma, plus higher level functions sufficient to support the BayR-2 application.

Title: Graphic Ada Designer (GAD)

The Graphic Ada Designer is a specialised tool for creating graphical Object Oriented Design Diagrams (OODDs) for Ada programs and the Program Design Language (PDL) representations associated with each OODD. The Graphic Ada Designer is principally targeted towards the interactive development of these block-like diagrams in support of the development of Ada software.

The implementation will use GKS interfaces when possible. Included, are some packages which implements a version of the Graphical Kernel System (GKS) developed by SYSCON Corporation for use with the Graphic Ada Designer. The specification is based on:

1. The Ada Phase I GKS developed by Harris Corp.

2. Draft GKS Binding to ANSI Ada

The implementation and utilisation of those packages will be faithful enough to the real GKS, to permit the Graphic Ada Designer to be easily converted to using a real version of GKS.

Title: Graphic Kernel System (GKS)

This is the Graphical Kernel System (GKS) implemented in Ada. The GKS is an international standard describing high-level graphics functions. This GKS/Ada implementation is the American National Standard (ANS) version of GKS.

Graphic Kernel System (GKS) provides a set of strictly defined graphical procedures which serve as an interface between an application program and physical graphics devices. Using GKS level ma, a programmer can write programs to draw pictures on a display using lines, markers, text, patterned areas, and pixel-filled areas. All of these functions and more are available to the application programmer when using GKS. Because these functions are device independent, the programmer need not specify the particular device that makes up the GKS workstation (physical device(s) in the GKS system). Thus, GKS enable a programmer to write sophisticated graphics programs without learning the scheme for describing graphics on a particular device.

Asset Source for Software Engineering Technology (ASSET)

The following information was taken from the ASSET Library Repository Catalog. For more information on ASSET, see Appendix C.

```
Computer Graphics/Graphic Kernel System (GKS)
Order Number:        ASSET_A_241
Alternate Name:      GKS, SOFTECH2
Release Date:        13-MAR-88
Producer:            SOFTECH INC.
Reference:           SOFTECH2
Asset Type:          SOFTWARE - BUNDLE
Size:                520 files, 6069 Kbytes
Domains:             ADA STANDARDS AND BINDINGS, COMPUTER GRAPHICS,
                     USER INTERFACE
Keywords:            BINDINGS, GKS, GRAPHICS, STANDARDS
Collection:          STANDARDS AND BINDINGS, STARS FOUNDATIONS
Distribution:        Approved for public release,
                     distribution is unlimited
```

This implementation of the international standard for GKS (Graphic Kernel Systems) describes high-level graphics functions, which enable a programmer to write sophisticated graphics programs without learning the scheme for describing graphics on a particular hardware device.

This GKS interface allows the application programmer to make Ada calls to a wide variety of graphics and plotting routines, and supports several types of graphics terminals.

This product was developed as part of the Software Technology for Adaptable, Reliable Systems (STARS) program, sponsored by the Advanced Research Projects Agency (ARPA).

Defense Software Repository System (DSRS)

For the DoD, other Government agencies, and supporting contractors, the Defense Software Repository System (DSRS) lists "GRAFPAK_GKS" (ID cia0795a.1) in its Software Reuse Program's Reusable Asset Catalog. For more information on DSRS, see Appendix C.

Public Ada Library (PAL)

The PAL contains GKS files in its ../bindings/gks subdirectory, the contents of which are described in that subdirectory's README file. The text of that README file is the same as the text portion of the ASSET catalogue reference given above. For more information on the PAL, see Appendix C.

16.5.3 GKS products available from vendors

Advanced Technology Center

The Advanced Technology Center has an Ada binding to GKS. The binding implementation runs on most UNIX-based and VMS systems, and is supported by Verdix, Meridian, TeleSoft, Alsys, and Aetech compilers. The binding to GKS interfaces with ATC's GRAFPAK-GKS. The binding provides full access to level-2C functionality and is linked directly to the GKS internals. Host/Target: under UNIX, VAX under VMS.

For more information, contact: Larry Paulson, Advanced Technology Center, 22982 Mill Creek Drive, Laguna Hills, CA 92653, USA; Tel: +1 714-583-9119 x208; Fax: +1 714/583-9213; Email: comments@atc.com.

Digital Equipment Corporation

Digital Equipment Corporation has bindings available for GKS, PHIGS, SQL, and X/OSF Motif for DEC Ada on OpenVMS VAX, OpenVMS AXP Alpha, and DEC OSF/1 AXP Alpha Systems. The Ada bindings are provided either as part of a compiler product or the services/facilities that are provided by Digital and its suppliers.

Digital Equipment Corporation provides an Ada binding to GKS under OpenVMS VAX Systems, OpenVMS AXP Alpha Systems, DEC OSF/1 AXP Alpha and RISC ULTRIX Systems. Host/Target: DEC VAX under OpenVMS; DEC AXP Alpha under OpenVMS; DEC AXP Alpha under DEC OSF/1; and DEC RISC under ULTRIX.

For more information, contact: Mary Anne Cacciola, Digital Equipment Corporation, 110 Spit Brook Road, Nashua, NH 03062, USA; Tel: +1 603/881-1028; Fax: +1 603/881-1600.

Gallium Software, Inc. (formerly Prior Data Sciences)

Gallium Software's product, Prior GKS, is a high-level two-dimensional graphics development toolkit. It delivers the performance and functionality required for applications such as command and control, computer aided design and drafting, presentation graphics and mapping. Prior GKS, which conforms to the ISO GKS standard, provides application and device portability - protecting software investment. With this toolkit, application developers enjoy reduced development costs, faster time to market and the freedom to select the most effective hardware for a specific application.

This product conforms with the following standards: ISO 7942 and ISO 8651-3. Host/Target: Interactive UNIX, SPARC station as hosts; Interactive UNIX, SunOS as target.

For more information, contact: Peter Hanschke, Gallium Software, Inc., 303 Moodie Drive-Suite 4000, Nepean, Ontario, Canada K2H 9R4; Tel: +1 613/721-0902; Fax: +1 613/721-1278; Email: sales@gallium.com.

Software Technology, Inc.

STI's MicroGKS/Ada provides Ada programmers with 200+ functions to develop GKS-compliant graphics applications; it is supported by the Alsys FirstAda compiler for MS-DOS and the Alsys Ada compiler for 386 UNIX for the interactive UNIX and X11 development environment. It supports windows, graphics segmentation, physical input devices, and hardcopy output. The UNIX version supports an interface to X-Windows. Host/Target: IBM PC/AT under MS-DOS, IBM PC/AT under POSIX / X-Windows.

For more information, contact: Greg Saunders, Software Technology Inc., 1511 Park Avenue, Melbourne, FL 32901, USA; Tel: +1 407/723-3999; Fax: +1 407/676-4510.

16.6   Information Resources Dictionary System (IRDS)

Currie Colket   Clyde Roby
Space & Naval Warfare Systems Command   Institute for Defenses Analyses
Attn: Code 331-1A   1801 North Beauregard Street
CPK 5   Alexandria
Arlington   VA 22311-1772
VA 22245-5200   USA
USA
                                                   Tel: +1 703 845 6666
Tel: +1 703 602 3968   Email: roby@ida.org
Fax: +1 703 602 6805
Email: colket@ajpo.sei.cmu.edu

16.6.1   Description and standardisation efforts

The Information Resource Dictionary System (IRDS)is a series of international standards that specify a software tool that can be used to describe and potentially control an enterprise's information resources. These standards define the structure and part of the content of the data to be maintained at the Information Resource Dictionary (IRD) Definition Level, and the structure of the data to be maintained at the IRD Level. It also defines the services to be provided for maintaining and retrieving data at both levels.

Standards efforts involve both the American National Standards Institute (ANSI) and the International Organisation for Standardisation/International Electrotechnical Commission (ISO/IEC).

Important IRDS international standards include:

- ISO/IEC 10027: 1990; Information Technology – Information Resource Dictionary System (IRDS) Framework.

- ISO/IEC 10032: 1993; Information Technology – Reference Model of Data management.

- ISO/IEC 10728: 1993 (E); Information Technology – Information Resource Dictionary System (IRDS) Services Interface.

The pertinent standard for Ada bindings is the IRDS Services Interface (ISO/IEC 10728). This standard specifies a service interface to give any program full access to all IRDS services through external calls provided by the language in which the program is written. This standard defines the semantics of the interface using ISO Pascal (ISO 7185). Language bindings for other ISO standard programming languages are to be provided as annexes to ISO/IEC 10728. Current work is in process for a C Binding (Annex C) and an Ada Binding (Annex D).

The IRDS Services Interface standard has sections addressing IRDS concepts, IRDS facilities, abstract data structures, service concepts, service facilities, service data structures, and service formats. The Ada binding is primarily concerned with the service data structures (data types used in the interface to IRDS) and the service formats (Ada subprogram calls to the IRDS interface). The Ada binding is syntactic, using the Pascal specification and description in ISO/IEC 10728 for the semantics.

The IRDS Services Interface language binding for the Ada language is presented in the form of an Ada package specification. Equivalent Ada types are used to build data structures. It is expected that the package body will perform the necessary transformations to convert objects of Ada types to objects of IRDS types. Since Ada types are used, separators are not required.

Exceptions are used in lieu of Service Return Codes.

Several IRDS sessions can proceed in parallel using Ada tasking.

The IRDS Ada package specification conforms to the ISO standard for IRDS Services Interface. The package specification contains:

1. Constants defining name length limits, attribute length limits, and control identifier length limits.

2. Type definitions for data types, IRD content status classes, column data types, object names, control identifiers, and column list parameters.

3. Ada Exceptions are used for the diagnostics area in preference to Service Return codes. The invoking of any service (except Get_Diagnostics) can raise the exception called IRDS_Error. The Ada error handler would then invoke the procedure Get_Diagnostics to ascertain the problem. Get_Diagnostics cannot raise exception IRDS_Error, because this would be circular.

4. Procedures are used for specifying operational services, level-independent services, and IRD definition level specific services.

Strategy for the ANSI/ISO Ada Language Binding to IRDS

In the Ada language binding to IRDS, the data names and data structures defined in the IRDS Standard have been adhered to except where the Ada language does not provide an appropriate construct. The binding defined in the package specification provides an interface to the primary Ada types. Time and date abstractions are obtained from Package Calendar. It is expected that the package body will provide the necessary transformations to IRDS types.

In the Ada binding, the procedure names and their parameters have been adhered to except where the Ada language does not provide an appropriate construct.

All names have been spelled out with underscores between logical words. Types as used for data structures have the explicit word "type" added to the simple name.

The "Irds" prefix has been removed from all types, objects, and procedure names. The desired effect is achieved through the use of a package called "IRDS". The fully qualified name will thus include IRDS (e.g., IrdsCreateIRDDefinition becomes IRDS.Create_IRD_Definition, IrdsNameLim becomes IRDS.Name_Limit, IrdsSessId becomes IRDS.Session_Id_Type).

All types end with the suffix "_Type" with the exception of the Ada predefined types of Boolean, Character, and String. This approach provides a means to improve portability between IRDS implementations.

Strings are passed as an access type (a pointer) allowing unbounded lengths. A list structure is used for the Column List Parameters using access types. Access types end with the suffix "Pointer_Type."

Status of the ISO/ANSI Binding

The base IRDS standard is approved by ANSI (X3/H4) and is currently a recommendation to ISO's Joint Technical Committee 1, Subcommittee 21, Working Group 3 (JTC1/SC21/WG3) – reference IRDS Services Interface ISO/IEC 10728:1993(E). The base standard will include the Ada binding specified in a separate Annex. A new standard, colloquially called "IRDS2" includes improvements to IRDS and will incorporate the Ada binding.

Documentation of the ISO IRDS

The ISO standard, ISO/IEC 10728:1993(E), is available from ANSI at a cost of approximately $102. There are additional charges for shipping and handling. Contact: American National Standards Institute, Attn: Customer Service Department, 11 West 42nd Street, New York, NY 10036; Tel: +1 212/642-4900.

When available, the Ada Binding will be Annex D to ISO/IEC 10728. The current Ada binding to IRDS is available in electronic form on the Internet, on the Ada Joint Program Office (AJPO) host in the ../public/irds subdirectory.

Historical Work

The National Bureau of Standards (now National Institute of Science and Technology – NIST) had sponsored a committee in the 1970s to develop Federal Information Processing Standards (FIPSs) for data-dictionary systems. ANSI formed a committee in 1980 to address standardisation of information resource dictionary systems. These committees merged in 1983 with the combined mission to develop a FIPS and an ANSI standard. A framework for IRDS was developed and standardised.

In 1985, the ANSI standard was proposed to ISO for international standardisation and was rejected. For six years the ANSI and ISO IRDS communities worked independently, until 1991 when it was agreed to harmonise their efforts. ISO/IEC 10728 is a partially harmonised standard. The IRDS community is now evolving an object-oriented standard called IRDS2. The ANSI committee responsible for IRDS is JTC1/SC21/X3H4, currently chaired by Dr. Jerry Winkler (Tel: +1 703/425-4558). The ISO IRDS Rapporteur is Mr. David Gradwell (+44 (0) 1276 23519).

16.6.2 IRDS resources available from repositories/software-reuse libraries

When the Ada binding to IRDS is stabilised as a standard, it will be placed into ASSET. Until then, the current version will be available on the AJPO host.

The Ada Joint Program Office host computer on the Internet

The following information was taken from the README file in the ../public/irds subdirectory in the Ada Joint Program Office's host computer (ajpo.sei.cmu.edu). For more information on the AJPO host, see Appendix C.

Information Resource Dictionary System (IRDS)

The latest version of the IRDS Services Interface is the editor's draft, dated 3 July 1992, ISO/IEC 10728: 1993 (E) for the Information Resource Dictionary System (IRDS) Services Interface, Draft International Standard. This document is an editor's draft for the purpose of review by participants in the SC21 editing committee.

This draft standard defines an interface to describe and control an enterprise's information resources. IRDS interfaces to a Software Query Language (SQL) type of database using services in the form of function and procedure calls. The AJPO believes that ISO IRDS will be an important standard.

A draft Ada binding to IRDS has been submitted to the ISO IRDS Rapporteur Group as a proposed Annex D to ISO/IEC 10728. It is currently a working draft. It will be recommended for adoption as Annex D at the next ISO IRDS Rapporteur Meeting in June 1993. If accepted, the Ada binding will be formally incorporated into the ISO/IEC 10728 which will then be registered as a Committee Draft.

This latest draft Ada binding is available in 2 files:

irds_ada.ps Revision 2, draft Ada Binding in Postscript

irds_ada.asc Revision 2, draft Ada Binding in ASCII

Both files are based on the IRDS Standard Services described in ISO/IEC 10728: 1993 (E), 3 July 1992. A copy of the latest IRDS standard can be obtained from:

Mr. David JL Gradwell, Data Dictionary Systems, Limited, 16, Tekels Avenue, Camberley, Surrey, GU15 2LB, United Kingdom; Tel: +44 (0) 1276 23519, Fax: +44 (0) 1276 676670.

Comments on this draft Ada binding were requested by 1 March 1993. However, they are welcome thereafter. Comments can be sent to:

Mr. Currie Colket, Tel: +1 703/602-3968, Fax: +1 703/602-6805,
Email: colket@ajpo.sei.cmu.edu.

Ada Language Binding to the ISO IRDS (Information Resource Dictionary System) Services Interface

Asset Source for Software Engineering Technology (ASSET)

The following information was taken from the ASSET Library Repository Catalog. For more information on ASSET, see Appendix C.

```
Ada Language Binding to ISO IRDS (Information Resource Dictionary System)
Services Interface
Order Number:        ASSET_A_687
Alternate Name:      ADA/IRDS BINDING
Release Date:        06-NOV-92
Producer:            ISO IRDS Working Group
Asset Type:          SOFTWARE - COMPONENT
Size:                25 Kbytes, 3 Files
Domains:             ADA STANDARDS AND BINDINGS
Keywords:            ADA, INTERFACE, IRDS, SQL
Distribution:        Approved for public release,
                     distribution unlimited
```

This is a proposed Ada language binding to the IRDS Services Interface. This Ada/IRDS binding is presented in the form of an Ada package specification.

The binding defined in the package specification provides an interface to the primary Ada types. Time and date abstractions are obtained from Package Calendar. It is expected that the package body will provide the necessary transformations to SQL and IRDS types.

The draft IRDS standard defines an interface to describe and control an enterprise's information resources. IRDS interfaces to a Software Query Language (SQL) type of database using services in the form of function and procedure calls.

16.6.3   IRDS products available from vendors

The AdaIC has not identified any commercial Ada binding products for IRDS.

16.7 Portable Operating System Interface for Computer Environments

David Emery
The MITRE Corporation
Burlington Road
Bedford
MA 01730
USA
Tel: +1 617 271 2815
Email: emery@mitre.org

16.7.1 Description and standardisation efforts

The POSIX Program

The Portable Operating System Interface for Computer Environments (POSIX) is the collective name for a set of standards providing applications portability at the source-code level. Most POSIX standards define either an Application Program Interface (API) or a Profile – which can be used by an applications programmer to write portable applications. An API is a specification of types, operations, etc, to be used by an applications program, along with their associated semantics. A Profile selects one or more standards and identifies options, restrictions, interoperability, etc, to support a specific applications domain.

The POSIX program grew from the effort by UNIX users to develop a "standard" definition of the UNIX system interface. The Institute of Electrical and Electronics Engineers (IEEE) Computer Society's Technical Committee on Operating Systems started work on this project in the 1985-1986 time frame. Later, the International Organisation for Standardisation/International Electrotechnical Commission (ISO/IEC) decided to provide international standardisation for POSIX standards, delegating the development work to the existing IEEE group. Currently, the IEEE group is the Portable Applications Standards Committee (PASC), and the ISO/IEC group is Working Group 15 of Subcommittee 22 of Joint Technical Committee 1 (ISO/IEC JTC1 SC22 WG15). Generally, POSIX standards are developed by a working group within PASC, and submitted for concurrent IEEE and ISO/IEC ballots. The intent is to have a single document as both an IEEE and an ISO/IEC standard.

There are many different POSIX projects currently under way. To date, six POSIX standards have been adopted by the IEEE. These are:

- IEEE Std 1003.1-1990, IEEE Standard for Information Technology – Portable Operating System Interface (POSIX) – Part 1: System Application Program Interface (API), POSIX Basic System Services.

- IEEE Std 1003.2-1992, IEEE Standard for Information Technology – Portable Operating System Interface (POSIX) – Part 2: Shell and Utilities.

- IEEE Std 1003.3-1991, IEEE Standard for Information Technology – Test Methods for Measuring Conformance to POSIX.

- IEEE Std 1003.3.1-1992, IEEE Standard for Information Technology – Test Methods for Measuring Conformance to POSIX – Part 1: System Interfaces.

- IEEE Std 1003.5-1992, IEEE Standard for Information Technology – POSIX Ada Language Interfaces – Part 1: Binding for System Application Program Interface (API).

- IEEE Std 1003.9-1992, IEEE Standard for Information Technology – POSIX Fortran 77 Language Interfaces – Part 1: Binding for System Application Program Interface (API).

Other projects are in varying stages of development, including P1003.4 for real-time extensions, P1003.6 for system security, P1003.7 for system administration, P1003.8 for network file access, P1003.10 for supercomputing profile, P1003.12 for protocol-independent networking, P1003.13 for real-time profile, and at least 10 other projects.

Some (but not all) of the IEEE standards are also ISO/IEC standards. IEEE Std 1003.1 has been adopted by ISO/IEC as ISO 9945-1, and IEEE Std 1003.2 has been adopted by ISO/IEC as ISO 9945-2.

The National Institute for Standards and Technology (NIST) has also adopted POSIX as a Federal Information Processing Standard (FIPS). However, there has been a problem with the FIPS and the IEEE/ISO Standards. IEEE 1003.1 has undergone several revisions since it was first approved by the IEEE in 1988. The current version is ISO/IEC 9945-1:1989/IEEE Std 1003.1-1990, which corresponds to FIPS 151-1. However, a revision to the IEEE/ISO standard is underway. The problem is that the approval cycle for FIPS is not synchronised with the approval cycle for IEEE/ISO POSIX standards. In general, FIPS approval has lagged behind IEEE/ISO approval by at least one year.

Ada Bindings

Initially, because of its UNIX heritage, POSIX API standards were specified in terms of the C language. However, as the POSIX effort grew, it became clear that other languages besides C could make effective use of the POSIX APIs. Projects to develop Ada and FORTRAN bindings were approved around 1986. PASC Working Group P1003.5 was chartered to develop Ada bindings for POSIX standards, with its first project being the Ada binding to IEEE 1003.1.

The P1003.5 Working Group made several initial decisions that influenced the resulting document. The group decided that it was inappropriate for the Ada binding to depend on the C binding, so IEEE Std 1003.5 was specified as a self-contained "thick" binding document. (The alternative, a "thin binding document", would have contained pointers to text in IEEE Std 1003.1). The other major decision was to provide Ada abstractions for the facilities in IEEE Std 1003.1, rather than provide direct Ada analogs to each and every C type and function.

The IEEE approved IEEE Std 1003.5 in July 1992. Due to a disagreement between the IEEE and ISO/IEC on how language bindings would be described, IEEE Std. 1003.5 was not initially accepted by ISO/IEC JTC1/SC22/WG15 for ISO/IEC standardisation. However, IEEE Std 1003.5 is now being submitted to ISO/IEC for standardisation using a "fast-track" approach, and ISO/IEC standardisation is likely in 1993.

The IEEE standard is available from the IEEE as document SH 15354, from the IEEE Services Center, 445 Hoes Lane, Piscataway, NJ 08855, 800/678-4333.

IEEE Std 1003.5 represents only one of many possible Ada bindings for IEEE standards. PASC Working Group P1003.5 is currently working on Ada bindings for the POSIX Real-Time standards, IEEE Projects P1003.4 (real-time extensions), and P1003.4a (threads extensions). The Ada Real-Time bindings project is IEEE P1003.20, and an Ada binding to the facilities in P1003.4 has entered IEEE ballot. This work is being synchronised with both POSIX developments, including balloting of both IEEE P1003.4 and P1003.4a, as well as with Ada 95 and related ISO Ada work.

An overview of IEEE Std 1003.5-1992

IEEE Std 1003.5-1992 (commonly called POSIX/Ada) provides an Ada programmer with access to operating-system services in the area of process control, process environment (including command line parameters), files and input/output (I/O), terminal devices and serial line control, and user and group databases.

The binding is organised as a series of packages, where each package provides access to a set of related services. For instance, facilities for controlling files are contained in the package POSIX_FILES, and the POSIX I/O operations are defined in package POSIX_IO. To avoid library-level name conflicts with user packages, all of the POSIX packages begin with "POSIX_" (except for the one package called "POSIX").

The package POSIX contains several common definitions for the binding, including the type POSIX_CHARACTER. An implementation may provide a character set (such as EBCDIC or IBM-PC character sets) that is different from Ada's predefined set. The type POSIX_CHARACTER allows access to the host environment's character set. The standard defines an interoperable subset of characters that are in both Ada's STANDARD.CHARACTER and POSIX.POSIX_CHARACTER. This package also defines various parameters on the POSIX implementation, such as the maximum number of open file descriptors and the maximum length of a filename.

Error handling is an important part of any binding. Errors are generally reported back to the user via the exception POSIX.POSIX_ERROR. The type POSIX.ERROR_CODE represents the predefined error conditions, such as FILE_EXISTS or PERMISSION_DENIED. When POSIX_ERROR is raised by the call to a POSIX operation, the program can call POSIX.GET_ERROR_CODE to retrieve the error code associated with the failed operation. Error status is kept on a per-task basis, to prevent race conditions between the call to a POSIX operation that fails and the call to GET_ERROR_CODE within a single task.

POSIX models the entire Ada program as a single POSIX process. For instance, all calls to POSIX_PROCESS_IDENTIFICATION.GET_PROCESS_ID from tasks within the same main program must return the same process ID. However, this does not prevent implementations from using multiple processes to support Ada tasking, as long as this does not change the behaviour of POSIX/Ada operations.

Tasking safety was a major concern of the P1003.5 Working Group. In general, POSIX/Ada operations are required to be "reentrant" in the face of tasks. For instance, two calls to POSIX_IO.WRITE should not interfere with each other. (One should be completed before the other starts.) However, POSIX/Ada does not guarantee task-related blocking semantics. If one task performs I/O, the entire process/program may be blocked. The basic definition of POSIX (IEEE Std. 1003.1:1990) does not provide sufficient functionality for POSIX/Ada to require or specify per-task blocking for I/O and other blocking situations. POSIX/Ada does provide a facility that allows the program to determine if the entire program/process or just the calling task will be blocked when doing I/O. A "smart" program can modify its behaviour depending on the facilities provided by the implementation.

The IEEE Standard contains a very detailed rationale explaining the the reasoning and analysis that led to the final shape of the binding. The rationale discusses most of the issues that confront any binding developer, including packaging, documentation style (e.g., "thick" vs "thin") and tasking safety.

Conformance Issues

POSIX conformance is defined both for implementations and for applications. Implementation conformance basically means that the implementation correctly implements the POSIX API and its semantics. Application conformance means that the application uses only facilities defined within POSIX or other IEEE or ISO standards. In particular, a strictly conforming POSIX application may not use implementation extensions to POSIX.

IEEE Std 1003.5 places specific restrictions on conforming implementations. A conforming implementation has to implement the API as defined by the standard – i.e., POSIX_IO.OPEN has to work as described, etc. Since POSIX portability is defined at the source-code level, IEEE Std 1003.5 places restrictions on an implementation's actual definition of the standard POSIX packages. For instance, an implementation may not add an operation to the visible part of a standard package. The intent of these restrictions is to make sure that applications code can be moved from one conforming implementation to another without encountering compiler errors due to inadvertent overloading, etc.

Currently there is no test suite to measure implementation conformance to IEEE Std. 1003.5. (NIST has certified several test suites for measuring conformance for the C binding, IEEE Std 1003.1.) Also, it is possible for an implementor to provide an interface to POSIX that does not claim conformance to IEEE Std 1003.5. Finally, it is quite possible for a system to claim "POSIX conformance" because it conforms to the IEEE 1003.1 (or 1003.9) standard, but no Ada binding is provided. Therefore, when specifying or discussing "POSIX compliance", it is important to ensure that the system provides a conforming implementation of IEEE Std 1003.5. An implementation that claims conformance only to IEEE Std 1003.1 will not be of much use for Ada programming.

Some available resources

Ada Interfaces to POSIX
This report considers the applicability of POSIX in the development of the Defense Department's Software Technology for Adaptable Reliable Systems (STARS) Software Engineering Environment, comparing it to the Common APSE Interface Set, version A (CAIS-A). (This report is available from ASSET as ASSET_A_155. For more information on ASSET, see Appendix C.)
    The POSIX/Ada Binding Tutorial
A tutorial on IEEE Std 1003.5-1992 was presented at the Tri-Ada 1992 and Tri-Ada 1993 conferences, as well as Ada Europe 1993 and Ada UK 1992. Copies of the tutorial slides were printed in the Tri-Ada tutorial proceedings document.
    A Prototype Implementation of the POSIX/Ada Binding
A paper on a prototype of an early verion of POSIX/Ada was presented by David Emery at Tri-Ada 1990. A copy of this paper can be found in the Tri-Ada 1990 proceedings. The paper describes techniques used to implement POSIX/Ada via pragma interface calls to the POSIX C library.

16.7.2 POSIX resources available from repositories/software-reuse libraries

Note: You may also wish to see the section "Other specifications and standards", for the references to the "Ada/Operating System Interface", which provides tools to interface between Ada and an operating system. The package is modeled on the POSIX interface for AIX but may be implemented on other environments as well.

16.7.3 The Ada Joint Program Office host computer on the Internet

The following information was taken from files on the Ada Joint Program Office's host computer (ajpo.sei.cmu.edu). A file name and subdirectory are noted at the beginning of each reference. For more information on the AJPO host, see Appendix C.

POSIX Ada Language Interfaces – package specifications

This file: ajpo.sei.cmu.edu/public/dev-tool/POSIX/README. Last updated: 11/5/93
The following statement is provided by the IEEE and governs the use of this code:
    These package specifications were extracted from IEEE Std 1003.5-1992, IEEE Standard for Information Technology – POSIX Ada Language Interfaces – Part 1: Binding System Application Program Interface by the Institute of Electrical and Electronics Engineers, Inc. These package specifications represent only a portion of the document and are not to be interpreted as the approved consensus standard. The IEEE Std 1003.5-1992 must be used in conjunction with these package specifications in order to claim conformance. The IEEE takes no responsibility for and will assume no liability for damages resulting from the reader's misinterpretation of said information resulting from its out of context nature. To order copies of the IEEE Std 1003.5-1992, please contact the IEEE Service Center at 445 Hoes Lane, PO Box 1331, Piscataway, NJ 08855-1331; Tel: +44 908-981-1393; Fax: +1 908-981-9667.
    Note that these specifications are incomplete, in that the standard identifies some declarations as implementation-defined. In addition, no package bodies are provided.
    This standard was developed by IEEE Working Group P1003.5. For more information on this group, contact the Chairman, James Lonjers, Email: lonjers@vfl.paramax.com; Tel +1 805 987-9457.

Formal requests for interpretations of this standard should be addressed to the IEEE, as specified in the document.

POSIX Ada Run-Time System Librarys (PART)

This file: ajpo.sei.cmu.edu: /public/atip/PART_pointer. Last updated 9/10/93

This is a pointer file to the POSIX Ada Run-Time System Librarys (PART), which contains code from one of the projects supported by the Ada Joint Program Office's FY91 Ada Technology Insertion Program (ATIP).

PART is available to the public from Florida State University (FSU) for non-commercial use. See copyright note near end. PART can be obtained by anonymous FTP from FSU's ftp server (ftp.cs.fsu.edu).

PART Version 1.2: Release on ftp

The POSIX / Ada-Runtime project is happy to announce that the sources of the POSIX Ada Run-Time System Librarys (PART) are now available to the public for non-commercial use (see copyright).
ftp-site: ftp.cs.fsu.edu
internet: 128.186.121.27
directory: /pub/PART
files: part.tar.Z, part_README

Related publications as well as an implementation of POSIX threads are also available on this site in the mentioned directory (see file INDEX).

What is PART?

This is version 1.2 of the POSIX Ada Run-Time System Library (PART) using a CARTS interface [3]. It is implemented over the POSIX 1003.4a Threads Extension (Pthreads) [1], and requires access to an interface compliant with that standard.

The purpose of this release of PART is to demonstrate the feasibility of implementing an Ada '83 run-time system over POSIX threads, and disclose the full details of one such implementation. By mapping Ada tasks onto POSIX threads, this approach should enhance the portability of Ada runtime systems and provide a platform for exploiting shared-memory multiprocessors.

The interface between PART and an Ada compiler is a procedural interface using link-time entries via an external name pragma. The interface is mostly CARTS compliant. Nevertheless, a number of small extensions to the CARTS interface have been added, to allow interaction with a commercial Ada compiler and to provide a base for subsequent extensions such as for Ada 95.

PART has been tested at FSU using a commercial Ada compiler. The specific interface code (glue) to this commercial compiler is NOT part of this release. Also excluded from this release are the bodies of certain machine- and compiler-dependent packages used by the runtime implementation: Compiler_Exceptions, Machine_Specifics, and Compiler_Dependencies. In the testing done at FSU, this release of PART passed the Chapter 9 portion of the ACVC 1.11 validation suite.

PART has only been tested on SunOS running on a SPARCstation, using a library to supply the required Pthreads support. This library is available from the Florida State University by anonymous ftp from ftp.cs.fsu.edu in /pub/PART and is documented in the literature [5]. PART accesses Pthreads operations through a C interface using INTERFACE pragmas. Use of PART on other Pthreads compliant platforms should be possible provided that they can provide all Pthreads operations as procedure calls.

Nevertheless, PART is distributed without any warranty, expressed or implied, including warranty of merchantability or fitness for any particular purpose.

PART is based on previous Ada runtime systems developed at FSU, including CORSET/LACE [6,7], which was developed with funds from Boeing, and MRTSI [2], which was partially funded by the

HQ U.S. Army CECOM, Software Engineering Directorate. The PART runtime system-to-compiler interface is based on the CARTS interface [3], which was derived from the experience gained with MRTSI.

Most of the PART code was produced by FSU students and faculty under the POSIX/Ada Real-Time (PART) project, funded by the Ada Joint Program Office (AJPO) under the Ada Technology Insertion Program (ATIP), through the U.S. CECOM, Software Engineering Directorate, subcontracted through the Telos Corporation.

See the separate file "AJPO.DISCLAIMER" for general term and conditions applicable to software developed under the AJPO's ATIP.

PART project members have included Ted Baker (Principal Investigator), Ted Giering (Chief Programmer), Pratit Santiprabhob (Research Associate), Offer Pazy (Consultant), and Ganesh Rangarajan, R. Ramesh, Frank Mueller, Teguh Ghazalie, Viresh Rustagi, and Seung-jin Moon (Graduate Research Assistants).

This software contains known bugs. The user assumes all risks associated with its use.

Further Information

For information on the CARTS interface, contact solomon@eclus.bwi.wec.com. For information on availability of the PART project final report, contact mbender@ajpo.sei.cmu.edu.

References

1 Threads Extension for Portable Operating Systems (Draft 6). IEEE, Feb 26, 1992, P1003.4a/D6.

2 Ada Runtime Environment Working Group: MRTSI Task Force. A Model Runtime System Interface for Ada. By ACM SIGAda, 1990. Technical Report.

3 T.P. Baker. Requirements Specification for the Common Ada Run-Time System. February 1991. Prepared for Westinghouse Electric Corporation.

4 E.W. Giering, T.P. Baker. Using POSIX Threads to Implement Ada Tasking: Description of Work in Progress. In TRI-Ada '92 Proceedings, November 1992. p. 518-529.

5 Frank Mueller. A Library Implementation of POSIX Threads under UNIX. In Proceedings of the USENIX Conference, Winter 1993. p. 29-41.

6 T.P. Baker. A Corset for Ada. Technical Report TR-86-09-06, Computer Science Department, University of Washington, 1986.

7 T.P. Baker and K. Jeffay. Corset and Lace: Adapting Ada Runtime Support to Real-Time Systems. Proceedings of the Real-Time Systems Symposium, December, 1987. pp. 158-169.

[Note: The AJPO file from which the text above was taken also contains disclaimers from both the AJPO and FSU stating such things as that the software is distributed "as-is", without any warranty expressed or implied, and that general permission to copy and distribute the code is granted provided that this is not done for commercial advantage.]

AdaNet

The following abstracts were taken from AdaNet, and describe software available in source-code form. For more information on AdaNet, see Appendix C.

Title: POSIX Ada Run-Time System Librarys (PART)

This is the POSIX Ada Run-Time System Library (PART) using a CARTS interface. It is implemented over the POSIX 1003.4a Threads Extension (Pthreads), and requires access to an interface compliant with that standard.

The purpose of this release of PART is to demonstrate the feasibility of implementing an Ada '83 run-time system over POSIX threads, and disclose the full details of one such implementation. By mapping Ada tasks onto POSIX threads, this approach should enhance the portability of Ada runtime systems and provide a platform for exploiting shared-memory multiprocessors.

Asset Source for Software Engineering Technology (ASSET)

The following information was taken from the ASSET Library Repository Catalog. For more information on ASSET, see Appendix C.

```
POSIX/Ada Interface Specifications
Order Number:         ASSET_A_395
Alternate Name:       ADA/POSIX BINDINGS
Version:              OCT 93
Release Date:         01-OCT-93
Producer:             IEEE
Author:               IEEE Working Group P1003.5
Reference:            IEEE Standard 1003.5-1992
Asset Type:           SOFTWARE - BUNDLE
Size:                 132 Kbytes, 22 Files
Domains:              ADA STANDARDS AND BINDINGS
Keywords:             ADA, BINDING, IEEE, INTERFACE, POSIX,
                      STANDARD
Distribution:         Approved for public release,
                      distribution unlimited
```

This asset contains Ada package specifications for a binding to POSIX which conforms to the IEEE standard.

These package specifications were extracted from IEEE Std 1003.5-1992, IEEE Standard for Information Technology–POSIX Ada Language Interfaces–Part 1: Binding System Application Program Interface, copyright 1992, by the Institute of Electrical and Electronics Engineers, Inc. These package specifications represent only a portion of the document and are not to be interpreted as the approved consensus standard. The IEEE Std 1003.5-1992 must be used in conjunction with these package specifications in order to claim conformance.

Note that these specifications are incomplete, in that the standard identifies some declarations as implementation-defined. In addition, no package bodies are provided.

16.7.4   POSIX products available from vendors

AETECH, Inc.

Available Ada bindings for AETECH Ada compilers: Microsoft Windows, PHIGS, POSIX, SQL (Supra), X-Windows (Motif, Open Look). Host/Target: 80386 (& 80486) PCs.

For more information, contact: Jim Dorman, AETECH, Inc., 5841 Edison Place, Suite 110, Carlsbad, CA 92008, USA; Tel: +1 619/431-7714; Fax: +1 619/431-0860.

Alsys, Inc.

The Alsys Ada Software Development Environment for 386 UNIX is a production-quality Ada environment capable of handling very large Ada applications (over 500,000 lines of code). The product includes the Compiler; Multi-Library Environment, which provides a powerful and flexible way to manage Ada development effort and share program units; Binder, which supports unused subprograms elimination; High- and Low-Level Optimisers for improving code quality and performance; and Run-Time Executive for efficient support for executing Ada programs. Also included is the Developer's Toolset including: Ada Probe, a symbolic source-level debugger and program viewer; AdaXref, a cross-reference generator; AdaMake, a recompilation aid; AdaReformat, a source reformatter.

Alsys currently has Ada bindings to POSIX, X-Windows (OSF Motif), and the Generic Package of Elementary Functions for the Alsys Ada Software Development Environment, running on 386 UNIX 386/486-based machines supported as both host and target and running 386/ix or SCO UNIX. They are also planning a binding to SQL for 386/486 machines. Host/Target: 386/486 PC under IX UNIX, 386/486 PC under SCO UNIX.

Alsys' RISC Ada/SPARC is a complete Ada development and execution environment combining ease of use, excellent compilation and execution performance, powerful debugging and performance tuning capabilities, support for developing large applications and bindings to industry standards. It includes an X Window-based GUI, an optimising Ada compiler, library manager and tools, the AdaTracer source-level debugger, the ARCS 2.0 Toolbox with graphical system browser, language-sensitive editor and other integrated tools, a dynamic application profiler for isolating performance bottlenecks and Ada bindings to Xview and POSIX. Optionally available are interfaces to X, OSF/Motif, Sybase, Oracle, and TCP/IP.

Alsys' TeleGen2 Ada Host Development Systems contain fast, easy-to-use development tools to create Ada applications while generating efficient applications code. The tools include an Ada compiler with global optimiser, source-level debugger, profiler for dynamic analysis, source formatter, cross-reference, automatic system builders, library manager and tools, etc. Also included are interfaces to standards: POSIX, Macintosh toolbox (Mac only), Sunview (Sun only), and NUMWG math libraries.

For more information, contact: Alsys Sales, Alsys, Inc., 67 South Bedford Street, Burlington, MA 01803, USA; Tel: +1 617/270-0030, Fax: +1 617/270-6882, Email: marketing@alsys.com.

Silicon Graphics, Inc.

Silicon Graphics, Inc.'s (SGI's) MP/Ada 6.2 provides a multiprocess Ada development system built using the POSIX-compliant threads model for Ada tasking. A joint engineering development between Verdix and SGI, MP/Ada is designed to permit full use of SGI's multiprocessor technology and symmetric multiprocessing operating system.

Ada tasks are mapped one-to-one with POSIX-compliant threads. These threads are executed dynamically by a pool of kernel processes that are further scheduled on all available processors (an M-by-N mapping).

Since each task can be bound to an independent kernel process, all of SGI's REACT (realtime extensions to IRIX) capababilities are now accessible to Ada programs. Host/Target: SGI systems under IRIX 4.0.5, IRIX 5.0.1, IRIX 5.1.

For more information, contact: David McAllister, Silicon Graphics, Inc., 2011 North Shoreline Boulevard, Mountain View, 94039-7311, USA; Tel: +1 415/390-3238; Fax: +1 415/390-6218; Email: davemc@sgi.com.

SL Corporation

SL Corporation provides Ada binding support for its SL-GMS toolkit; this includes support for GPEF, GPPF, POSIX, SQL, TCP/IP, OSF/Motif, and Open Look.

SL-GMS is a toolkit for developing dynamic graphics screens for real-time or highly interactive applications. Non-programmers can design application screens in a standard drawing-tool mode, connect them to real-time data sources and animate screen objects to visualise changing data values. SL-GMS allows the design of custom "GISMOs" to input values or control the application and supports Motif, Open Look, and other X toolkit widgets.

SL-GMS is used to provide real-time graphics for applications in the fields of manufacturing, process control, network management, avionics and financial tracking. Host/Target: Validated

Verdix and DEC compilers support SL-GMS for the following machines as both host and target: DEC-DECstation/ULTRIX 4.0; DEC-VAXstation/ULTRIX 4.0; DEC-VAXstation/VMS 5.4; DEC-VAXstation/VMS 5.5; DEC Alpha PCs/Windows NT; IBM-RS6000/AIX; HP-9000/300/UNIX; HP-9000/400/UNIX; HP-9000/700/UNIX; HP-9000/800/UNIX; PC-386/IX UNIX; PC-386/SCO UNIX; PC-386/Lynx; PC-386/0S2; PC-386/System 5.4; SGI-4D/IRIX 3.3; Sun-3/SunOS 4.1; Sun-SPARC/SunOS 4.1 and Solaris; 88 Open/BCS Compliant; and Intel PCs/Windows NT.

For more information, contact: Mike Meagher, SL Corporation, 240 Tamal Vista Boulevard, Corte Madera, CA 94926, USA; Tel: +1 415/927-1724; Fax: +1 415/927-0878.

16.8 Programmer's Hierarchical Interactive Graphics System (PHIGS)

16.8.1 Description and standardisation efforts

The Programmer's Hierarchical Interactive Graphics System (PHIGS) is designed to support computer graphics applications that are highly dynamic and interactive. It supports a hierarchical graphical database that can be edited while elements of the database are being displayed. Such functionality is needed to support such applications as computer-aided design/computer-aided manufacturing (CAD/CAM) systems, command-and-control systems, and modeling of objects, etc.

A complement to PHIGS is the International Organisation for Standardisation (ISO) standard PHIGS Plus (ISO 9592-4). It augments the capabilities of PHIGS with functionality for lighting and shading, as well as for more complex primitives including B-splines. This standard is known as PHIGS PLUS (Plus Lumiere und Shading).

Both PHIGS and PHIGS PLUS are defined independently of any particular language.

Binding Status

The PHIGS/Ada binding has been published as ISO 9593-3 and has been adopted as an American National Standards Institute (ANSI) standard under the same number. Work is underway to develop a PHIGS PLUS/Ada binding, which will be published when available as Amendment 1 to ISO 9593-3.

Documentation

The PHIGS/Ada binding is available from: ANSI, 1430 Broadway, New York, NY 10018; Tel: +1 212/642-4900 (sales), +1 212/354-3300 (general)

For more information, contact: Richard F. Puk, Chairman, X3H3.4, Puk Consulting Services, 7644 Cortina Court, Carlsbad, CA 92009-8206; Tel: +1 619/753-9027

16.8.2 PHIGS resources available from repositories/software-reuse libraries

Asset Source for Software Engineering Technology (ASSET)

The following was taken from information provided by the ASSET Library. For more information on ASSET, see Appendix C.

The following PHIGS-related components are available from the Defense Software Repository System (DSRS), sponsored by the U.S. Department of Defense, Defense Information Systems Agency, Center for Information Management (DISA/CIM), Software Reuse Program, and will be made available from ASSET via library interoperation: 01c00216.1, GRAFPAK_PHIGS; 01d001ym.1, Phigs_Colors; and 01d0020e.1, PHIGS_Error.

Defense Software Repository System (DSRS)

For the DoD, other Government agencies, and supporting contractors, the Defense Software Repository System (DSRS) lists "GRAFPAK_PHIGS" (ID cia0795a.1) and "PHIGS_Error" (ID sif0107a.1) in its Software Reuse Program's Reusable Asset Catalog. For more information on DSRS, see Appendix C.

16.8.3   PHIGS products available from vendors

Advanced Technology Center

The Advanced Technology Center offers an Ada binding to PHIGS and PHIGS PLUS for most UNIX-based and VMS platforms. Verdix, Meridian, TeleSoft, Alsys, and Aetech compilers support the binding. The binding supports a variety of PHIGS and PHIGS PLUS implementations – including TGS FIGARO, Evans and Sutherland PHIGS, graPHIGS, DEC PHIGS, and GRAFPAK-PHIGS. ATC's Ada binding to PHIGS PLUS provides the user with access to PEX libraries. Host/Target: under UNIX, VAX under VMS.

For more information, contact: Larry Paulson, Advanced Technology Center, 22982 Mill Creek Drive, Laguna Hills, 92653, USA; Tel: +1 714-583-9119 x208; Fax: +1 714/583-9213; Email: comments@atc.com.

AETECH, Inc.

Available Ada bindings for AETECH Ada compilers: Microsoft Windows, PHIGS, POSIX, SQL (Supra), X-Windows (Motif, Open Look). Host/Target: 80386 (& 80486) PCs.

For more information, contact: Jim Dorman, AETECH, Inc., 5841 Edison Place, Suite 110, Carlsbad, CA 92008, USA; Tel: +1 619/431-7714; Fax: +1 619/431-0860.

Digital Equipment Corporation

Digital Equipment Corporation has bindings available for GKS, PHIGS, SQL, and X/OSF Motif for DEC Ada on OpenVMS VAX, OpenVMS AXP Alpha, and DEC OSF/1 AXP Alpha Systems. The Ada bindings are provided either as part of a compiler product or the services/facilities that are provided by Digital and its suppliers.

Digital Equipment Corporation provides an Ada binding to PHIGS under OpenVMS VAX Systems, OpenVMS AXP Alpha Systems, and DEC OSF/1 AXP Alpha Systems. Host/Target: DEC VAX under OpenVMS; DEC AXP Alpha under OpenVMS; and DEC AXP Alpha under DEC OSF/1.

For more information, contact: Mary Anne Cacciola, Digital Equipment Corporation, 110 Spit Brook Road, Nashua, NH 03062, USA; Tel: +1 603/881-1028; Fax: +1 603/881-1600.

Silicon Graphics, Inc.

Silicon Graphics, Inc., (SGI) carries Template Software's Figaro product, which includes an Ada binding to PHIGS. Host/Target: host: SGI systems under IRIX 4.0.5, IRIX 5.0.1, IRIX 5.1.

For more information, contact: David McAllister, Silicon Graphics, Inc., 2011 North Shoreline Boulevard, Mountain View, 94039-7311, USA; Tel: +1 415/390-3238; Fax: +1 415/390-6218; Email: davemc@sgi.com.

16.9 Database Language SQL

James W. Moore
Loral Federal Systems
700 North Frederick Avenue
Gaithersburg
MD 20879
USA
Email: moorej@ajpo.sei.cmu.edu

16.9.1 Description and standardisation efforts [August 1993]

This section first describes the ISO/ANSI standard Database Language SQL and its bindings to Ada. It then describes approaches such as the SAME and SAMeDL, which build upon the standard binding. Finally, some issues for a reference model are described.

Database Language SQL and its binding to Ada

Database Language SQL is a language for manipulating relational databases; it is a standard under both the American National Standards Institute (ANSI) and the International Organisation for Standardisation/International Electrotechnical Commission (ISO/IEC). ("SQL" is no longer an acronym. Once it was an acronym for "Structured Query Language", a language associated with a particular vendor's prototype database-management system. When referring to the standard, "SQL" is simply an abbreviation for ANSI's "Database Language SQL".)

SQL provides facilities for defining, manipulating, and controlling data in a relational database. As a standard specification, it promotes the portability of database applications among conforming database management products.

SQL is defined in terms of a reference language called the "module language". In principle, one defines the desired manipulations of the relational database by using the module language to write a number of SQL statements that are then collected as procedures within a "module". Programming-language bindings take either of two forms: a procedural form (which makes application-program subroutine calls on the procedures in the SQL module) or an embedded form (which has the effect of intermixing the SQL statements with the application program). The standard describes the embedded binding in terms of a syntactic transformation of the module and the application program.

Use of the embedded binding involves inserting SQL statements into Ada programs, creating codes that are not pure Ada. These codes are intended to be pre-processed by a vendor-supplied preprocessor that replaces the SQL statements with compilable, but implementation-dependent, subroutine calls. For languages other than Ada, the embedded binding has been the form typically provided by database-management system (DBMS) vendors.

The procedural binding (often called the "module binding") is a thin, direct binding of Ada to an SQL "module" that is a set of SQL statements packaged as procedures. The procedural binding describes how an Ada application program may make Ada subprogram calls upon the procedures of the SQL module. Thus an Ada application using the procedural binding is written in compilable Ada without interleaved SQL statements. Most Ada experts prefer the procedural binding to the embedded binding.

The binding for Ada uses a set of data types that are specified in a package named SQL_STANDARD. The explicit gathering and declaration of the data types provides the Ada binding with an advantage over the bindings to other programming languages. For other languages, the base SQL types are mapped to base types of the programming language. Because the value ranges of the base types are implementation-defined, mismatches can (and do) occur. SQL_STANDARD solves the problem by parameterising the Ada types to match the SQL data types. Other types declared in SQL_STANDARD improve the safety and convenience of error checking.

Status of Database Language SQL and its binding to Ada

The SQL standard has progressed through three generations: a 1986 version (sometimes called SQL/86): a 1989 version (sometimes called SQL/89 or simply SQL); and the recently approved 1992 version (sometimes called SQL2 or SQL/92). Users are likely to encounter both the 1989 and 1992 versions.

The 1989 base SQL standard is approved by ANSI as X3.135-1989 and by ISO/IEC as 9075:1989. The base standard does not include the Ada binding. Instead, the Ada binding is specified in a separate standard, ANSI X3.168-1989. (The procedural binding appears in section 8 of the standard, and the embedded binding in section 9.) Federal Information Processing Standard (FIPS) 127-1, from the National Institute of Standards and Technology (NIST), has the effect of combining X3.135 and X3.168, as well as providing some additional specification for purposes of Federal procurement. As of this writing, many implementations of SQL/89 are available.

The 1992 standard included extensive enhancements to SQL and incorporated an Ada binding. It is both an ISO (9075:1992) and an ANSI (X3.135-1992) standard. Recently, NIST has circulated FIPS 127-2, which describes how the federal government should procure products adhering to the ANSI/ISO standard. Except when waived, FIPS 127-2 will specify procurement of SQL/92 products effective beginning December 1993. Products conforming to FIPS 127-2 are expected to become available in 1994.

Products implementing the Ada binding of SQL

As of the date of this revision (August 1993), no known products offer the 1992 version of SQL or its Ada binding.

The ANSI-standard procedural binding of Ada to SQL/89 has been implemented in products offered by Digital, IBM, Informix, and perhaps others. The embedded binding has been implemented in products offered by Oracle and perhaps others.

Some other vendors provide products including bindings that may be effective but that may not conform to the ANSI standard. It should be noted that vendors may correctly advertise their DBMS as conformant when some of the provided language bindings are not conformant. So, it is important for a buyer to ensure that both the DBMS and the required language bindings conform to the desired level of the standard. NIST performs conformance testing upon SQL products and their bindings. An up-to-date list of conforming products can be obtained by ordering the NIST "Validated Products List" from the National Technical Information Service. Both subscriptions and single copies are available.

Documentation of Database Language SQL and its binding to Ada

The 1992 ANSI standard, X3.135-1992, can be obtained from ANSI at a cost of approximately $225. The ISO standard, ISO/IEC 9075:1992 is also available from ANSI at a cost of $230. The two are substantively identical. There are additional charges for shipping and handling. Contact: American National Standards Institute, 11 West 42nd Street, New York, NY 10036, Attn: Customer Service Department; Tel: +1 212/642-4900.

If still in print, the 1989 ANSI standards, X3.135-1989 and X3.168-1989, can be obtained from ANSI at a cost of approximately $40 and $28, respectively. The ISO standard, ISO/IEC 9075:1989, may be available from ANSI at a cost of approximately $86.

The FIPS standards, FIPS 127-1 and FIPS 127-2, and the NIST Validated Products List (NIS-TIR 5167) can be obtained from: National Technical Information Service (NTIS), U.S. Commerce Department, 5285 Port Royal Road, Springfield, VA 22161; Tel: +1 703/487-4650.

There are several good textbooks describing SQL. The one that I use is: C.J. Date with Hugh Darwen, A Guide to the SQL Standard, 3rd edition (describes SQL/92), Addison-Wesley, 1993.

A tutorial on the use of the procedural binding is provided in: James W. Moore, "The ANSI Binding of SQL to Ada," Ada Letters, XI:5, July/August 1991, published by the Association of Computing Machinery's Special Interest Group on Ada (SIGAda).

During the early 1980's, a proposal variously named as "Ada/SQL" or as the "WIS", "IDA", or "RACOM" approach and described in papers by Friedman and Brykcynski was offered for standardisation. For various reasons that proposal was rejected for standardisation and is now inappropriate for use in new systems.

The SAME approach and the SAMeDL

Although the ANSI standard gives Ada a binding to SQL that is similar to that provided for other languages, some users desire an interface that is more "abstract" and that may be better suited to the software-engineering principles of Ada. To develop this interface, in 1988 the Software Engineering institute (SEI) created an informal, public committee, the SQL/Ada Module Extensions Design Committee (SAME-DC) chaired by Marc Graham. Besides drafting the binding eventually adopted by ANSI and ISO, the committee created a methodology, the SAME approach for layering an abstract module upon the ANSI-standard binding. This abstract module would convert SQL numeric return codes into Ada exceptions, provide for a safe treatment of database nulls, promote basic SQL data types to user-defined types, and group scalar database values into "row-records". It should be noted that the SAME approach provides for data abstraction but not procedural abstraction, i.e., each call from the application maps to a single SQL operation performed on the database. An SEI technical report describes the SAME approach: Guidelines for the Use of the SAME, CMU/SEI-89-TR-16, (DTIC : AD-A223 932). Another SEI report provides suggested conformance criteria intended for use in peer evaluation of application of the approach: Conformance Criteria for the SAME Approach to Binding Ada Programs to SQL, SEI-89-SR-14.

At least two attempts have been made to automate the SAME approach. Under contract by the DoD's Software Technology for Adaptable, Reliable Systems (STARS) program, Lockheed, led by Susan Mouton Phillips, provided Ada programs and a method for generating source code for the SAME abstract module via the declaration, instantiation, and execution of Ada generic packages. Two reports describe the project: an overview of the technical approach is given in General Definition of Project (Ada/SQL Binding), DTIC : AD-A228 481; a more detailed description appears in User's Manual for a Prototype Binding of ANSI-Standard SQL to Ada Supporting the SAME Methodology, DTIC : AD-A228 480.

A more widely known effort, the SAMeDL, is the subject of a standardisation effort. The SQL Ada Module Description Language (SAMeDL) is a language that, when processed by an appropriate tool, generates the SAME abstract module and other code necessary to access a particular database-management system. Although the SAMeDL is defined in terms of the ISO/ANSI binding, an implementation is not constrained to be layered upon the standard binding – and may, in fact, be specific to a particular DBMS product. (Current standardisation work may have the effect of requiring vendors of conformant products to state whether their products are implemented as a layer upon the ANSI/ISO standard SQL interface.) Implementations of the SAMeDL for some specific DBMS products are available from Intermetrics and from Competence Center Informatik.

Efforts to standardise the SAMeDL are underway in ISO/IEC Joint Technical Committee, Subcommittee 22, Working Group 9 (JTC/SC22/WG9), and the language is currently at the Draft International Standard stage, as DIS 12227. The process may be completed in 1994. Although the detailed proposal has been modified as it progresses through ISO, one can find early descriptions in several SEI Technical reports: The SQL Ada Module Description Language – SAMeDL (SEI-90-TR-26; DTIC : AD-A235 781); Rationale for the SQL Ada Module Description Language (SEI-91-TR-4; DTIC : AD-A235 780); and Notes on Applications of the SAMeDL (SEI-91-TR-12; DTIC : AD-A240 851).

Documentation of the SAME and SAMeDL

Any of the SEI reports noted above can be obtained from: Research Access, 800 Vinial Street, Pittsburgh, PA 15212; Tel: +1 800/685-6510.

Reports that have been assigned DTIC accession numbers are available to registered DTIC users from Defense Technical Information Center, Cameron Station, Alexandria, VA 22304-6145; Tel: +1

703/274-7633. Those who are not registered DTIC users may use the DTIC accession numbers to obtain the documents from NTIS at the address noted previously in this section.

Reference Model

The choices available in approaches for binding Ada to SQL suggest the need for a reference model. This thought has occurred to ISO-IEC JTC1/SC22/WG9, but the work to date is quite preliminary in nature. Nevertheless, users should be acquainted with some of the issues involved.

The primary issue for an Ada user is the choice of a portability layer. One might imagine that a SAMeDL processor could generate an abstract module that uses the ISO/ANSI binding for access to the DBMS. Unfortunately, the proposed standard does not require this characteristic, and no current SAMeDL product implements it. Instead, they generate vendor-specific calls to specific DBMS products. So, the user has two choices regarding selection of an interface for portability and vendor-independence. If the user elects to use SAMeDL, then the portability interface is at the SAMeDL layer, and the user chooses among products that generate SAMeDL for some specific subset of DBMS products. If the user elects not to use SAMeDL, then the portability interface is at the ANSI/ISO binding level, and the user chooses among DBMS products that conform to that binding.

The proposed SAMeDL standard would require the vendor of a SAMeDL processor to disclose whether or not the processor generates abstract modules that would layer upon the ISO/ANSI binding.

ANSI SQL/Ada Binding Types

The ANSI standard binding of Ada to SQL/89 is described in ANSI X3.168-1989, which can be obtained as described previously. Section 8 of that standard specifies an Ada code package, SQL_STANDARD, providing the base Ada types to be used for parameters of calls upon the SQL module. The text of that package can be found in element SQL_Standard.ada of ASSET_A_403.

SAME Support Code (ASSET_A_403)

Guidelines for the Use of the SAME, described previously, includes a listing of Ada support code in its Appendix C. Code that is similar (possibly identical) can be found in this asset under the name "SQL/ADA MODULE EXTENSIONS (SAME) STANDARD PACKAGES - CMU VERSION".

Lockheed Prototype of the SAME Method (ASSET_A_159)

The code of the Lockheed prototype for automating the SAME method, described previously, is contained in this asset under the name "ADA/SQL BINDINGS". The documentation described previously can be found in ASSET_A_280 and ASSET_A_281.

SAMeDL Support Code (ASSET_A_406)

Another way to generate an abstract SAME module is to use a SAMeDL compiler conforming to the proposed ISO standard for SAMeDL. The proposed standard includes listings of support code in its Appendices. A copy of some of that code (possibly revised) is contained in this asset under the name "SQL/ADA MODULE EXTENSIONS (SAME) STANDARD PACKAGES – ISO VERSION".

Intermetrics Prototype Module Language Compiler (ASSET_A_225)

Under a STARS Foundation contract, Intermetrics developed a set of tools useful in permitting Ada applications running under the MVS operating system to access CICS and the Datacom/DB database-management system. The SQL Module Language Compiler might be of interest. It appears to process SQL modules (possibly ANSI X3.135-1989 conformant) to produce Ada package specifications and bodies implementing the SQL commands. The specifications appear to be similar to those required by ANSI X3.168-1989. The bodies apparently implement the SQL commands as implementation-dependent calls upon Datacom/DB. Code and documentation is available under the name "ADA INTERFACE TO CICS AND SQL".

16.9.2 SQL resources available from repositories/software-reuse libraries

The Ada Joint Program Office host computer on the Internet

The following information was taken from files on the Ada Joint Program Office's host computer (ajpo.sei.cmu.edu). A file name and subdirectory are noted at the beginning of each reference. For more information on the AJPO host, see Appendix C.

SQL Ada Module Description Language (SAMeDL) Development Environment. This file: ajpo.sei.cmu.edu: /public/atip/samedl/README.

SAMeDL background information

The challenges pertaining to the use of Ada and SQL in a well-engineered information system led to the formation of the SQL Ada Module Extension Design Committee (SAME-DC) at the Software Engineering Institute (SEI). The committee developed the SQL Ada Module Extension (SAME) Methodology to support and extend the modular approach to using Ada and SQL in database applications. The language which is used to implement SAME is the SQL Ada Module Description Language, or SAMeDL.

Using the SAME methodology requires that SQL statements be separated from the Ada application code, and encapsulated in separate modules. The SQL statements are not embedded in the Ada packages, thus isolating the Ada application from the DBMS design and implementation.

SAMeDL is designed to facilitate the construction of Ada database applications that use the SAME methodology.

[Note: The AJPO file from which the text above was taken also contains copyright notice and disclaimers stating such things as that the software is distributed without any warranty expressed or implied, and that general permission to copy and distribute the code is granted provided that this is not done for commercial advantage.]

AdaNet

The following abstracts were taken from AdaNet, and describe software available in source-code form. For more information on AdaNet, see Appendix C.

Title: Ada DBMS Interface (Ada/SQL)

This was the "Proposed Binding Ada to Database Language SQL" presented to the responsible American National Standards Committee (X3H2).

Title: Ada/SQL Test Data Generator (TDG)

The Ada/SQL Test Data Generator (TDG) provides the ability to automatically populate test databases with test data. The TDG is the middle layer of a three-layer WIS IDA Ada/SQL prototype. It builds on the existing WIS IDA Ada/SQL prototype, and reuses most of the original prototype. This original Ada/SQL prototype, of about 6000 loc (lines of code), was built to prove the feasibility of writing schemas and queries in pure Ada, and it is widely available as GFE from a number of sources. It was not intended for production use, and, in fact, it was followed in late 1987-early 1988 by an advanced Ada/SQL prototype. As detailed in part C, the TDG is adding about 6000 loc to the original WIS Ada/SQL prototype.

Title: Prototype Binding of ANSI-Standard SQL to Ada

SQL/Ada binding not only should be standard Ada to promote maintainability and portability between systems with different Ada compilers but it also should be as close to standard SQL as the language permits.

This SQL/Ada binding follows the above guidelines as strictly as possible. This binding allows all checking of data base semantics by the compiler because the binding is valid Ada. Also, the compiler is provided with all needed information to enforce these semantics.

Title: SQL-Ada Interface / SQL Module Compiler

The SQL-Ada module compiler provides a way for application utilities written in SQL module language to be translated into Ada packages that can be used when writing an Ada application for SQL. The SQL-Ada interface package developed for Datacom/DB provides an Ada Interface from which Ada application programs can perform database queries and database manipulations in SQL on Datacom/DB databases.

Asset Source for Software Engineering Technology (ASSET)

The following information was taken from the ASSET Library Repository Catalog. For more information on ASSET, see Appendix C.

```
Ada/SQL Bindings
Order Number:        ASSET_A_159
Alternate Name:      PROTOTYPE BINDING OF ANSI-STANDARD SQL TO ADA
                     SUPPORTING THE SAME METHODOLOGY
Version:             JUN90
Release Date:        14-JUN-90
Producer:            IBM CORPORATION
Reference:           CDRL 02010-001A, DTIC AD-M000059
Asset Type:          SOFTWARE - BUNDLE
Size:                534 Kbytes, 68 Files
Domains:             ADA STANDARDS AND BINDINGS,
                     DATABASE MANAGEMENT SYSTEM
Keywords:            ADA, BINDING, DBMS, SAME, SQL
Collection:          STANDARDS AND BINDINGS, STARS CATALOG
Distribution:        Approved for public release,
                     distribution is unlimited
```

The ANSI Standard binding of SQL to Ada (ANSI X3.168) specifies how Ada programs may access the services of relational databases which conform to ANSI Standard SQL (ANSI X3.135). The ANSI binding uses weak, primitive data types, but most application programs need a binding which deals with strong, user-defined types. To use the ANSI binding in such circumstances, an "abstract module" must be placed between the application program and the ANSI binding in order to raise the level of abstraction of the binding. A specification for such an abstract module is provided by "Guidelines for use of the SAME," Software Engineering Institute Technical Report CMU/SEI-89-TR-16. ("SAME" is an acronym for "SQL/Ada Module Extensions.") Unfortunately, applying the SAME method without any automated support would be a tedious task. "Ada/SQL Bindings" provides the needed automated support. It presumes that an implementation of the module version of the ANSI Ada/SQL binding is provided by the database vendor. It then permits a user to generate an abstract module conforming to the SAME method by instantiating Ada generics and executing the resulting program.

Documents supporting this software are available. They are "General Definition of Project" (ASSET_A_280; DTIC AD-A228481), and "User's Manual for a Prototype Binding of ANSI-Standard SQL to Ada Supporting the SAME Methodology" (ASSET_A_281; DTIC AD-A228 480).

```
Ada/SQL Bindings: General Definition of Project
Order Number:          ASSET_A_280
Alternate Name:        GENERAL DEFINITION OF PROJECT (ADA/SQL BINDING)
Availability:          paper only
Release Date:          31-DEC-89
Producer:              IBM CORPORATION
Reference:             CDRL 02000-001, DTIC AD-A228481
Asset Type:            SOFTWARE DOCUMENTATION
Size:                  16 Pages
Domains:               ADA STANDARDS AND BINDINGS,
                       DATABASE MANAGEMENT SYSTEM
Keywords:              ADA, BINDING, DBMS, DESIGN, SAME, SQL
Collection:            STANDARDS AND BINDINGS, STARS CATALOG
Distribution:          Approved for public release,
                       distribution is unlimited
```

This report presents the background, technical approach, and top-level capabilities of the project to implement an Ada binding to SQL (Structured Query Language). It also discusses such technical problems as storing arbitrary data types in a data base and using SAME (SQL/Ada Module Extensions) without a module language compiler. Ada code is available (ASSET_A_159; Ada/SQL Bindings. DTIC number AD-M000059) to automatically generate the Ada package specifications and bodies to support the SAME Methodology. A User's Manual (ASSET_A_281: User's Manual for a Prototype Binding of ANSI-Standard SQL to Ada Supporting the SAME Methodology. DTIC AD-A228 480) is also available containing installation instructions, compilation order, guidelines for input data, detailed steps to create a specific binding, and information about porting the system to another DBMS.

```
Ada/SQL Bindings: Users Manual
Order Number:          ASSET_A_281
Alternate Name:        USERS MANUAL FOR PROTOTYPE BINDING OF ANSI-STANDARD
                       SQL TO ADA
Availability:          paper only
Release Date:          30-JUN-90
Producer:              IBM CORPORATION
Reference:             CDRL 02020-001, DTIC AD-A228480
Asset Type:            SOFTWARE DOCUMENTATION
Size:                  135 Pages
Domains:               ADA STANDARDS AND BINDINGS,
                       DATABASE MANAGEMENT SYSTEM
Keywords:              ADA, BINDING, DBMS, SAME, SQL, USER MANUAL
Collection:            STANDARDS AND BINDINGS, STARS CATALOG
Distribution:          Approved for public release,
                       distribution unlimited
```

This User's Manual for the Ada/SQL Prototype Binding contains installation instructions, compilation order, guidelines for input data, detailed steps to create a specific binding, and information about porting the system to another DBMS. The Ada software code is available (ASSET_A_159: Ada/SQL Bindings. DTIC AD-M000 059) to automatically generate the Ada package specifications and bodies to support the SAME methodology. Also available is a document, "General Definition of Project" (ASSET_A_280; DTIC AD-A228 481) which presents the background, technical approach, and top-level capabilities of the project.

```
Ada/SQL and CICS Bindings
Order Number:          ASSET_A_225
Alternate Name:        ADA INTERFACE TO CICS AND SQL, INTER-CICSQL2
Version:               1.1
Release Date:          9-AUG-88
Producer:              INTERMETRICS, INC.
```

```
Reference:              INTER-CICSQL2
Asset Type:             SOFTWARE - BUNDLE
Size:                   2532 Kbytes, 362 Files
Domains:                ADA STANDARDS AND BINDINGS,
                        DATABASE MANAGEMENT SYSTEM
Keywords:               ADA, BINDING, CICS, DBMS, SQL
Collection:             STANDARDS AND BINDINGS, STARS FOUNDATIONS
Distribution:           Approved for public release,
                        distribution is unlimited
```

An interface that binds Ada to the IBM CICS transaction-oriented applications. In addition, it provides SQL for future database applications to allow migration to Ada while retaining massive historical databases and existing functional software.

```
SQL/Ada Module Extensions (SAME) Standard Packages - CMU Version
Order Number:           ASSET_A_403
Alternate Name:         SAME STANDARD PACKAGES
Version:                CMU
Release Date:           02-DEC-88
Producer:               SOFTWARE ENGINEERING INSTITUTE
Author:                 Marc H.  Graham
Asset Type:             SOFTWARE - BUNDLE
Size:                   146 Kbytes, 26 Files
Domains:                ADA STANDARDS AND BINDINGS,
                        DATABASE MANAGEMENT SYSTEM
Keywords:               ADA, ADA BINDINGS, BINDING, DBMS, SAME, SQL
Collection:             GENERAL, STANDARDS AND BINDINGS
Distribution:           Approved for public release,
                        distribution is unlimited
```

These software packages support the SAME (SQL/ADA MODULE EXTENSIONS) approach developed by the SAME-DC committee headed by Marc Graham of the SEI. They present strongly typed data types to interface with the SQL Bindings. These packages are tailorable to many applications. The "Installation" document gives complete instructions on how to tailor the packages for the specific database and computer system used, and how to compile the packages.

```
SQL/Ada Module Extensions (SAME) Standard Packages - ISO Version
Order Number:           ASSET_A_406
Alternate Name:         SAME STANDARD PACKAGES
Version:                ISO
Release Date:           02-DEC-88
Producer:               SOFTWARE ENGINEERING INSTITUTE
Author:                 Marc H.  Graham
Asset Type:             SOFTWARE - BUNDLE
Size:                   2 Files, 51 Kbytes
Domains:                ADA STANDARDS & BINDINGS,
                        DATABASE MANAGEMENT SYSTEM
Keywords:               ADA, ADA BINDINGS, ANSI X3.168,
                        BINDING, DBMS,
                        ISO SAMEDL STANDARD, SAMEDL, SQL
Collection:             GENERAL, STANDARDS AND BINDINGS
Distribution:           Approved for public release,
                        distribution is unlimited
```

These software packages support the SAMeDL approach to ANSI standard SQL to Ada bindings, developed by the SAME-DC committee headed by Marc Graham of the SEI. They present strongly typed data types to support the SQL bindings. These packages are similar to the packages in AS-SET_A_403, with subtle differences to conform to ISO standards. One of the packages contains Ada specifications only (no bodies) and the other is written in SAMeDL and requires use of a SAMeDL compiler.

Public Ada Library (PAL)

The PAL contains SQL files under its ../bindings/sql directory, the contents of which are described in subdirectory README files. The text of those README files are the same as the text portions of the ASSET catalogue references given above for SQL/Ada Module Extensions (SAME) Standard Packages – CMU Version, SQL/Ada Module Extensions (SAME) Standard Packages – ISO Version, Ada/SQL and CICS Bindings, and Ada/SQL Bindings.

For more information on the PAL, see Appendix C.

16.9.3   SQL products available from vendors

AETECH, Inc.

Available Ada bindings for AETECH Ada compilers: Microsoft Windows, PHIGS, POSIX, SQL (Supra), X-Windows (Motif, Open Look). Host/Target: 80386 (& 80486) PCs.

For more information, contact: Jim Dorman, AETECH, Inc., 5841 Edison Place, Suite 110, Carlsbad, CA 92008, USA; Tel: +1 619/431-7714; Fax: +1 619/431-0860.

Alsys, Inc.

Alsys' product, RISCAda, includes a graphical debugger (AdaTracer), a productivity tool box (ARCS 2.0), a highly optimised Ada compilation engine and bindings to government and industry standards. Bindings currently available include POSIX, SQL, OSF/Motif, and Open Look. Ada bindings are available for GKS, PHIGS, and TCP/IP. It is supported by the TeleGen2 OCT compiler for SPARC stations. Host/Target: SPARC workstations under Solaris 2.1 and SunOS 4.1 and above.

For more information, contact: Alsys Sales, Alsys, Inc., 67 South Bedford Street, Burlington, MA 01803, USA; Tel: +1 617/270-0030, Fax: +1 617/270-6882, Email marketing@alsys.com.

Competence Center Informatik GmbH (CCI)

The Competence Center Informatik GmbH (CCI) provides the CCI Ada SQL Handler (CASH), a commercial compiler for SAMeDL to support bindings between Ada and SQL.

In its current version, CASH supports Oracle 6.0 as RDBMS. Host/Target: IBM RISCsystem/6000 or Sun SPARCstation; runs under AIX 3 or SunOS. Further host-environments and RDBMSs are in preparation.

For more information, contact: Dr. Peter E. Obermayer, Competence Center Informatik GmbH, P.O. Box 1225, 49792 Meppen, Germany; or: Lohberg 10, 49716 Meppen, Germany; Tel: +49-5931-805-469; Fax: +49-5931-805-100; Email (EUnet): obermaye@cci.de.

Digital Equipment Corporation

Digital Equipment Corporation has bindings available for GKS, PHIGS, SQL, and X/OSF Motif for DEC Ada on OpenVMS VAX, OpenVMS AXP Alpha, and DEC OSF/1 AXP Alpha Systems. The Ada bindings are provided either as part of a compiler product or the services/facilities that are provided by Digital and its suppliers. Host/Target: DEC VAX under OpenVMS; DEC AXP Alpha under OpenVMS; and DEC AXP Alpha under DEC OSF/1.

For more information, contact: Mary Anne Cacciola, Digital Equipment Corporation, 110 Spit Brook Road, Nashua, NH 03062, USA; Tel: +1 603/881-1028.

IBM

The IBM Ada/370 product provides bindings to GPEF and SQL and the Customer Information Control System (CICS – a transaction-processing system). It runs on the IBM 30XX, 43XX, 937X and ES/9000 family processors, which are supported by the following operating systems:

1. VM/System Product (VM/SP) Release 5 or 6 (5664-167) with or without High Performance Option (HPO) (5664-173);

2. VM/Extended Architecture System Product (VM/XA SP) Release 2 (5664-308);

3. VM/Enterprise Systems Architecture (VM/ESA) Release 1 (5684-112);

4. MVS/SP-JES2 Version 2 Release 2 (MVS/XA) (5740-XC6);

5. MVS/SP-JES3 Version 2 Release 2 (MVS/XA) (5665-291);

6. MVS/SP-JES2 Version 3 Release 1 (MVS/ESA) (5685-001);

7. MVS/SP-JES3 Version 3 Release 1 (MVS/ESA) (5685-002);

8. MVS/ESA-JES2 Version 4 Release 1 or 2 (MVS/ESA) (5695-047);

9. MVS/ESA-JES3 Version 4 Release 1 or 2 (MVS/ESA) (5695-048).

Note: All of the above operating environments are supported in 31-bit addressing mode with the exception of VM/System Product (VM/SP) Release 5 and 6 which are restricted to 24-bit addressing.

The IBM Ada/370 licensed programs (5706-292 and 5706-295) consist of an Ada language compiler and a run-time library for use on various IBM MVS and VM/CMS operating systems. The IBM Ada/370 product provides many development environment aids – such as a source-level debugger (optionally with windowing when using IBM Graphical Data Display Manager Licensed Program for either MVS or VM), a highly configurable source-code formatter to assist in enforcing project coding standards, a dependency lister, a non-intrusive performance profiler, a cross-reference utility, and an Ada library-management capability. Ada/370 programs can call VS COBOL II subprograms similar to the calling of VS FORTRAN, C/370, and S/370 assembler subprograms; Ada/370 exported subprograms can be called from VS COBOL II, VS FORTRAN, C/370, and S/370 assembler programs. Additionally, separate features support inter-operation with other major database and transaction-processing subsystems.

One such feature of IBM Ada/370, called the SQL Module Processor for DB2 Database Manager, supports the procedural binding of Ada and SQL.

Another such feature of IBM Ada/370, called the IBM CICS Module Processor/MVS, supports the procedural binding of Ada and CICS, including CICS/OS/VS, CICS/MVS and CICS/ESA. Together with the SQL Module Processor for DB2 Database Manager, powerful Ada applications utilising the combined features of these two subsystems can be productively built.

This product conforms to the following standards: ANSI-X3.135-1986 – Database Language-SQL; ANSI-X3.168-1989 – Procedural Binding of Ada and SQL; ANSI/MIL-STD-1815A – Ada '83; ISO 8652-1987, Programming Languages, Ada; FIPS PUB 119 – Ada; FIPS PUB 127-1 SQL through IBM DB2 Database Manager V2.3; CIFO 2.0 & 3.0 – Catalog of Interface Features & Options; Validated at current level (1.11) of the ACVC test suite.

For more information, contact: Barry Lee, IBM Corporation, 844 Don Mills Road, North York, Ontario, Canada M3C 1V7; Tel: +1 416/448-3174; Fax: +1 416/448-4810.

Ingres Corporation

Ingres Embedded SQL refers to SQL statements embedded in a host language such as Ada. The Ingres Embedded SQL statements available include almost all interactive SQL statements including statements for data definition and data manipulation. In addition, Embedded SQL contains a set of forms statements that allow you to develop forms-based applications.

All embedded SQL/FORMS (Oracle) and SQL statements are processed by the Embedded SQL preprocessor, which converts the statements into host-language source-code statements. These statements call a run-time library that provides the interface to Ingres. Host/Target: UNIX (some), VMS (all)

For more information, contact: Armando Coles, Ingres, 1080 Marina Village Parkway, Alameda, CA 94501, USA; Tel: +1 800/446-4737; Fax: +1 510/748-2545.

Intermetrics, Inc.

Intermetrics offers a SAMeDL compiler that provides an Ada binding to SQL. When using the SAMeDL compiler, the user describes the interface in the SQL Ada Module Description Language, and then invokes the compiler to generate all necessary Ada code and interfacing software.

Because SAMeDL provides a flexible and portable way to interface Ada with SQL applications, it is a requirement for several DoD programs, including LCU, CHS-2 and I-CASE. It is currently a draft ISO standard (ISO/IEC Standard N12227).

The SAMeDL compiler is hosted on a variety of UNIX-based workstations and personal computers. It has been targeted to several DBMSs, including Sybase, Informix and Oracle, and is supported by Verdix and Alsys compilers. Intermetrics will provide tailoring to adapt it to any host platform and any SQL-compliant DBMS. Host/Target: 386/486 PC under UNIX, HP 9000 under UNIX, Sun SPARC under UNIX, RS-6000 under UNIX.

For more information, contact: Bill Zimmerman, Intermetrics, Inc., 733 Concord Avenue, Cambridge, MA 02138, USA; Tel: +1 617/661-1840; Fax: +1 617/868-2843.

Oracle Corporation

Oracle Corporation's Pro*Ada is an SQL/Ada binding that is 100% compliant with the FIPS 127-1 standard for embedded SQL/Ada bindings. Pro*Ada includes both an ANSI standard pre-compiler for SQL and an ORACLE dependent call interface. Programmers can develop systems using either the pre-compiler or the call interface or both. Around the end of 1993, an ANSI-standard Module Language Compiler should be available. Host/Target: The validated Verdix, TeleSoft, Alsys, and DECAda compilers will support Pro*Ada for the following machines as both host and target: IBM RS/6000 (Verdix Ada); SCO (Alsys Ada); SGI Irix (Verdix Ada); HP (Alsys Ada); DEC Ultrix (Verdix Ada); AT&T 3B2 R3 (Verdix Ada); 88open (Verdix Ada (Motorola 88K and DG Aviion)); IBM VMS/VM (IBM Ada); DEC VMS (DEC Ada); and SunOS (SunAda).

For more information, contact: Mr. Amr Assal, Oracle Corporation, MS 659413, 500 Oracle Parkway, Redwood Shores, CA 94065, USA; Tel: +1 415/506-2805.

SL Corporation

SL Corporation provides Ada binding support for its SL-GMS toolkit; this includes support for GPEF, GPPF, POSIX, SQL, TCP/IP, OSF/Motif, and Open Look.

SL-GMS is a toolkit for developing dynamic graphics screens for real-time or highly interactive applications. Non-programmers can design application screens in a standard drawing-tool mode, connect them to real-time data sources and animate screen objects to visualise changing data values. SL-GMS allows the design of custom "GISMOs" to input values or control the application and supports Motif, Open Look and other X toolkit widgets.

SL-GMS is used to provide real-time graphics for applications in the fields of manufacturing, process control, network management, avionics, and financial tracking. Host/Target: Validated Verdix and DEC compilers support SL-GMS for the following machines as both host and target: DEC-DECstation/ULTRIX 4.0; DEC-VAXstation/ULTRIX 4.0; DEC-VAXstation/VMS 5.4; DEC-VAXstation/VMS 5.5; DEC Alpha PCs/Windows NT; IBM-RS6000/AIX; HP-9000/300/UNIX; HP-9000/400/UNIX; HP-9000/700/UNIX; HP-9000/800/UNIX; PC-386/IX UNIX; PC-386/SCO UNIX; PC-386/Lynx; PC-386/OS2; PC-386/System 5.4; SGI-4D/IRIX 3.3; Sun-3/SunOS 4.1; Sun-SPARC/SunOS 4.1 and Solaris; 88 Open/BCS Compliant; and Intel PCs/Windows NT.

For more information, contact: Mike Meagher, SL Corporation, 240 Tamal Vista Boulevard, Corte Madera, CA 94926, USA; Tel: +1 415/927-1724; Fax: +1 415/927-0878.

16.10   X Window System

Christopher M. Byrnes
The MITRE Corporation
202 Burlington Road-M/S A378A
Bedford
MA 01730-1420
USA

16.10.1   Description and standardisation efforts

Ada/X Background

This section first describes the historical background that led to the current Ada/X Window System bindings. Understanding this background is important because potential users of these bindings should check the derivation or "breeding" of a product, as that will help determine the portability and compatibility of the resulting software. Experience has shown that even simple Ada/X applications programs – such as the canonical "Hello, world" example – can be coded in vastly different manners among different bindings. (For a discussion of this, see my "Porting Applications Between Two Commercial Ada/Motif Bindings", Proceedings of TRI-Ada '93.)

Historical Background

There are several different ways of viewing the X Window System. One common way is to view the overall X system architecture arranged in a stack hierarchy:

Application
User Interface Management System (UIMS)
Widget sets
Xt intrinsics
Xlib
X protocol

The lowest level of this stack architecture is the X protocol, which defines the flow and structure of packets of information around a network. A library of subroutines (known as "Xlib") is used to create and receive these packets. These Xlib subroutines provide all the common actions associated with a bit-mapped display terminal, such as drawing a line or being notified that a keystroke was depressed.

Programmers soon realised that trying to write complex applications through these low-level Xlib calls was an extremely complex task. Eventually, a layer on top of Xlib was built, known as the "intrinsics" level, which was written to provide an object-oriented programming (OOP) interface. A major change in an intrinsics layer is the use of event-driven "callback" routines. No longer does the programmer call the windowing system from a "main line" programming loop provided by the application. Instead, the intrinsics layer contains an application's main line routine; the programmer provides the address of subroutines to call back in response to certain events. This completely inverts the flow of control and data in an application, where OOP "message passing" becomes the main programming paradigm. The most popular set of intrinsics functions, used on almost all X applications, are the X toolkit (Xt) intrinsics that are provided by the Athena consortium.

The Xt intrinsics provide just a set of OOP routines and conventions for defining actions such as how workstation events are passed to the application and how changes are propagated through the callback functions. To ensure a common "look and feel" as well as to provide programmers with a large set of reusable components to start with, several organisations have developed reusable widget sets. Some widget sets, such as the Athena widgets, are provided at no extra charge on the X distribution tapes. Other widget sets are developed and maintained for sale by commercial organisations. The two best known of these X widget sets are the Open Software Foundation's (OSF's) Motif widgets and UNIX International's (UI's) Open Look (OL).

Some programmers have found using widget sets such as Motif and OL to be still too low-level to develop programs on. They have chosen the option of using a user interface management system (UIMS) to generate the application program interface (API) calls to a widget set. The highest level of an X architecture remains the application code, which has the option of using one or more of the lower layers. These lower layers are typically provided to the application as program libraries that are connected at link time, based on which API calls were used in the application. Depending on the UIMS, it may make direct bindings to one or more of these X architecture layers, or it may provide a more abstract API (such as a custom-developed binding specific to this UIMS) that provides similar functionality from the underlying widget set and/or intrinsics layer.

Another way of viewing X's architecture is through a client/server model. In this model, an X server is responsible for managing a scarce resource – in this case the workstation's graphical display surface and input devices (keyboard and mouse). The application programs (which sit as the top layer in their earlier stack architecture) are the clients, communicating with the server through X protocol calls. These clients can be local (running on the same workstation the server is) or can be running on another computer (communicating over a network).

The X architectures shown above provide a framework or reference model for describing X software. The actual X Window System software that is sold or distributed can change as new features are added and bugs are fixed. Over time, the Athena Consortium has made both major new versions of X and minor new releases of individual versions available for distribution. At the time of this report's preparation, the current major version of X was 11 and the release level was 5. This is commonly abbreviated as X11R5. Note that even when the Athena Consortium releases a new version of the base (or reference) X server implementation and client libraries (such as X11R6), there may be a lag time before a commercial organisation (such as OSF or UI) or a language-binding developer (such as for Ada/X) will upgrade their products to conform to this new release. Therefore, it is important to understand how "version skew" can affect these X layers and the programming language bindings to them.

There have been a variety of efforts to create Ada/X bindings, below are just some of those the author has heard about:

```
Binding              Developer

Ada/Xlib (R2)   SAIC for original Software Technology for Adaptable
                and Reliable Systems (STARS) Foundations work (1988).

Ada/Windows     DEC's interface to their ''Xlib-like'' DECWindows
                product (1989).

Ada/Xlib (R3)   Early commercial versions of STARS Foundations work
                (1989).

Ada/Xlib (R4)   STARS Ada/Xlib binding from SAIC and Unisys (1991).

Ada/Xt (R2)     Software Productivity Consortium (SPC) proprietary
                binding to Hewlett-Packard (HP) widget set (1989).

Ada/Xt (R3)     STARS Ada/Xt implementation on top of STARS Ada/Xlib
                from both SAIC and Unisys (1991).

Ada widgets     STARS work to populate an Xt widget set on Ada/Xt
                implementation (1991).

Ada/Xt (R4)     Jet Propulsion Laboratory (JPL) work to create Xt
                binding (1991).
```

Ada/Motif (R3)   OSF-funded partial Motif bindings work at University
                 of Lowell (1991).

Ada/Motif   NASA's Transportable Applications Environment Plus
                 (TAE+) UIMS uses Ada bindings to Motif (1991).

Ada/Xt   SEI's Serpent UIMS, generating a direct Ada interface
                 (1991).

Ada/Xt   TRW's Generated Reusable Ada Man-Machine Interface
                 (GRAMMI) UIMS (1991).

Ada/Xt   Advanced Software Engineering Technologies' Agora
                 UIMS based on Serpent.

Ada/Motif   Systems Engineering Research Corporation's (SERC's)
                 SA/Motif binding based on STARS Ada/Xt and Ada/Xlib
                 specifications.

Ada/Motif   Advanced Technology Center (ATC) Ada X Interface
                 binding.

Ada/Motif   TeleSoft's TeleUSE UIMS uses direct Ada bindings to
                 Motif (1991).

Ada/Motif   Objective Interface Systems' Screen Machine UIMS uses
                 abstract Ada interface to Motif (1992).

Ada/Motif   Sunrise Software International's ezX UIMS uses
                 abstract Ada interface to Motif (1992).

Ada/UIMS   Strategies' Heragraph UIMS produces Ada graphics
                 applications conformant to Motif's 'look and feel'.

Ada/UIMS   Sherrill-Lubinski's Graphical Modeling System
                 (SL-GMS) UIMS produces Ada graphics applications
                 conformant to Motif's ''look and feel'' (1992).

In the list above, the "Binding" column indicates which level of the X stack architecture (Xlib, Xt, widget set, and/or UIMS) is being bound to. Note that some of the Ada/UIMS tools do not provide interfaces to the lower layers of the X stack architecture, while other bindings typically provide interfaces to the highest layer named and each lower layer. The "R" number indicates which X release level the Ada API is being provided for, so "R3" indicates X11R3. The "Developer" column indicates who is (or has been) developing this Ada/X binding and what year that binding was first released for use. As can be seen from the dates in the list above, most of the Ada/X binding development work has been done in just the last few years. A number of Ada compiler vendors are reselling one of these bindings (such as SA/Motif and AdaX) as an add-on product to their compilers.

Many of the Ada/X developments discussed above are based on the idea of implementing all or parts of Ada/X as a binding on top of an underlying C/X implementation. Not all Ada developers have agreed with this assumption – some believe that it is possible to develop an all-Ada implementation of the entire X Window System so that their Ada programmers are not tied to what the base C/X implementation provides and so that Ada's built-in object-oriented design (OOD) and OOP constructs can be fully exploited.

Rational Corporation has developed an (almost) all-Ada implementation of Xlib for both their R1000 computers and Sun 3 workstations. This is instead of the more traditional approach of writing a binding to an underlying C/X implementation. They do have some assembler at the lowest layers to interface to the X protocol, where direct calls to network "sockets" are made. Rational donated this 33,000 line Ada/Xlib implementation to the Athena Consortium for distribution on the X11R5 "contributed software" release tape.

Another example of an Ada implementation is XinAda from Top Graph'X.

All the Ada/X development work discussed above concentrates on the client side of X's architecture, providing the Ada interfaces and libraries that an application needs. But there has been work at Lockheed/Sanders to develop an all-Ada implementation of an X server. (For a description of how this Ada/X server implementation was done, see "Ada Implementation of an X Window System Server" by Stuart Lewin, Proceedings of TRI-Ada '89.)

Ada application design issues

One area that has to be considered when developing an application using Ada/X is the software design method(s) being used. The X Window System assumes an OOP approach that is implemented manually in the default C programming language. Ada has its own built-in OOP constructs that OOD often tries to take advantage of. Many of these Ada/X bindings try to straddle the boundary between following what the reference X implementations in C (C/X, with which most existing X programmers will be most familiar with) provides and what an idealised Ada/X binding would provide.

Ada provides a variety of OOP constructs to choose from, and it turns out that many binding developers made different choices in their individual implementations of Ada/X. Experience with different Ada compilers has shown that individual compilers do a good job efficiently handling some Ada constructs but not others. There are variants across compiler vendors, so one compiler might do a good job with one approach but not another. The presence of different Ada/X implementation approaches allows application developers to choose which of the bindings best matches the strengths of their compiler. But this does require detailed knowledge by the application development organisation as to the specific strengths and weakness of their chosen compiler(s).

When assessing a potential Ada binding and/or UIMS to be used with an application, experience with various Ada/X implementations has lead to an initial set of "lessons learned" about using complex Ada applications that vendors should be asked about (if important to the application):

- Interactions with Ada tasking in application program, particularly given the non-threaded nature of many underlying C/X data structures.

- Usability of resulting Ada code with symbolic debugger (Ada, C, etc.), particularly client/server interaction, tasking, and overall memory requirements.

- X resource availability during Ada elaboration and other initialisation order issues.

- Handling of X resources within Ada packages and in the .Xdefaults files.

- Support for Ada generics, which are a means for abstracting some of the Ada/X vendor dependencies out of an application program.

Widget design and implementation issues

A major technical difference among various Ada/X bindings is how Ada/Xt callbacks are implemented. Xt intrinsics use an "event-driven" model of execution; the widget contains a pointer to an application routine that is called when a specified event occurs. The "main" control of the program exists within the internals of Xt; almost all of the application's windowing code will be subroutines that are called from within Xt. Unfortunately, Ada does not handle this particular OOD concept of being able to point to instances of encapsulated code and data very well, so Ada/X vendors had to design something that would simulate this concept.

One approach used within some of the STARS Ada/Xt implementation is to use tasks and task types to encapsulate widget instances. Since Ada allows pointers (access) to task types, it is possible to set up and assign pointers to what to call when certain events occur. Ada task types can be dynamically created and terminated, so the programmer has some flexibility on how and when to construct widgets.

Since Ada tasks exist within Ada's strong typing model, that means there are normally restrictions on how data is passed as parameters to the task's entry points and even how tasks of different types are treated separately. This is a problem with Xt intrinsics because a weak typing model is assumed. Applications programmers and widget developers are supposed to be able to easily construct higher-level widgets from the pieces of lower-level widgets. Xt's "inheritance hierarchy" assures that when an event occurs within one widget, it is propagated up the hierarchy to all the other related widgets that also need to deal with that widget. Widget developers provide default "methods" and "values" that the application programmers can use to control what is done when these events occur. Programmers are free to override these default "methods" through subclassing of a widget class into a new "subclass" and/or by manually setting a new method that is run as an alternative to the old one.

All this dynamic definition and reconfiguration of the structure or architecture of who is allowed to call what tends to conflict with Ada's strong (task) typing model. One solution is to separate the different types of widgets and their associated (underlying) Xt intrinsics into different Ada task types. But instead of different entry points for the different methods of this type of task (widget class), there is only one entry for all tasks (with each defined handle having exactly the same parameter profile). The advantage of this approach is that Ada's Unchecked_Conversion procedure can (hopefully) be used to convert a pointer of one instance of these task types to another. By converting a task access from one type to another, the same calls to the entry can be used to "simulate" the overwriting or subclassing of one Ada/Xt "method" by another.

Other Ada/X vendors have taken a different approach for implementing this callback scheme. Instead of using access to task types, they use pointers to Ada procedures. Since there is no such thing as an access pointer to an Ada subprogram, they use the ADDRESS attribute of the procedures as the values to place and adjust within widget "methods". For example, some of the STARS-based bindings uses a generic callback package, where the "action" routines are passed into it as a generic procedure parameter. The work involved to overwrite default methods will require passing system.addresses around as further parameters. There is a single dispatch subprogram that deals with the "methods", that centralises where these callbacks are handled. As anyone who has programmed in C/Xt can tell you, a variety of terrible things will happen if these pointers become corrupted or set incorrectly.

Another issue to check for in an Ada/X binding is the support for Motif's User Interface Language (UIL). A number of UIMS tools (both Ada and C) will generate UIL in addition to or as a replacement for generated Ada code to an API. This is a more abstract interface to X, but many of the same Ada application program binding issues discussed above remain.

Standardisation issues

Most Ada/X binding developers agree that there needs to be some sort of standards group responsible for just the Ada bindings to the rest of X. But as with the general C/X community, there has been a general lack of progress in developing formal standards (in contrast to de facto standards) in this area. As the vendors listed above generate Ada/Xlib, Ada/Xt, Ada/UIMS, and other specifications, someone needs to transition these specifications to a standards group to be maintained. The incompatible Ada/X systems (differing on even comparatively simple decisions, such as Ada naming conventions) are examples of what can go wrong for the entire Ada/X community that hopes for portability and reusability of software if too many incompatible bindings are developed. The X Window System levels (within the stack architecture) are all in a state of flux as new technical improvements are being added almost continuously. Each of these changes might be implemented differently by the binding developers, hurting overall Ada/X portability. These changes to C/X (at least) are beginning to be controlled by a series of standards groups; some are American National Standards Institute (ANSI) groups (such as X3H3) and some are Institute of Electrical and Electronic Engineers (IEEE) groups, such as POSIX committee P1201.

But progress is slow at the C/X level as well, with Ada/X viewed as an effort that must follow these standards. The use of language-independent specifications (LIS), as has been done in POSIX P1003, would aid an Ada/X binding to underlying X Window System services. But progress to an X, Motif, or OL LIS has been very slow.

Currently there are no clear plans on how (or who) to set up an Ada/X standards group. Any Ada standardisation group would be within the structure of an existing standards group; there is no point in creating some all-new group just for Ada bindings. This means that the Ada group would have to conform to practices being used by its related groups. For example, the POSIX P1201 committee is looking specifically at creating industry standards for X, so it could be a good place to form a subcommittee for dealing just with Ada bindings. POSIX already has a subcommittee that deals with just Ada binding standards to the base operating system (P1003.5), so Ada language-specific bindings are not new to POSIX.

One issue to consider in the timing of the formation of any Ada/X binding standardisation group is the progress being made by the related standards groups. In POSIX, the trend is toward the development first of an LIS for the functionality of some system; with language-specific bindings then developed on top of this standard. For X, this trend leads to some confusion because there are different groups working on different standards (at different rates of completion) for the various layers of X.

At the base of the X Window System is the X protocol defining the bits and bytes that are passed between client and server. The ANSI X3H3.6 subcommittee has developed a standard. Since this protocol layer is well below what any Ada application program would have to deal with (with the possible exception of the Rational Ada/Xlib implementation) and since most other Ada/X bindings abstract away this layer by dealing with the X Window System only through higher layers, there may be no need for an Ada-specific binding standard at the protocol layer.

The next layer up is Xlib. The development of the functionality (specification of behaviour) is done by the Athena Consortium itself, with no formal standards group yet responsible for creating the formal standard. A problem has arisen here in that the Athena Consortium wants to hold off any standardisation (in C, Ada, or anything else) at the Xlib layer until they have come up with a solution to the tricky problem of "internationalisation" (the support of non-Roman alphabets such as Kanji, Hangul, Arabic, and Hebrew).

When moving above Xlib, an Ada programmer moves into X toolkits, widget sets, and controversy. While the X community has settled on using the Xt intrinsics, the widget sets and "look and feel" issues remain highly competitive. POSIX P1201.1 and others are trying again with a very high-level abstract interface known as the Virtual Application Programming Interface (VAPI) that was developed for the XVT commercial virtual toolkit that claims conformance to almost any windowing system (including Motif; and OL). Some progress has been made in developing an Ada/XVT binding.

The Ada/X community will have to address the widget-set issue at some point. The X application development community seems to be lining up behind commercial widget sets such as Motif's and OL's, with older and smaller widget sets such as the Athena and Xray sets falling into disuse. In addition to the size of these commercial widget sets (Ada bindings and/or implementations are a major undertaking), there are nasty copyright and "commercial advantage" issues to consider.

Another standardisation issue to consider is the moving targets being standardised to. The original STARS Foundations Ada bindings were to X11R2; the final STARS Ada/Xlib bindings are to X11R4; and a number of commercial Ada/X bindings support X11R5. Also, there are already rumored plans for future X11 releases (that will include threads, where Ada tasking can really make an impact). The commercial widget sets are also moving targets (such as Motif versions 1.1, 1.2, 2.0, etc.). Note that the commercial X vendors do not always release their products in synchronisation with the latest Athena Consortia releases. (Motif was stuck at X11R3 for a while after X11R4 was released.)

Another question that Ada/X developers should consider is how they should deal with the National Institute of Science and Technology (NIST) Federal Information Processing Standard (FIPS) on user interface models (FIPS 158). NIST has defined a seven-layer reference model (patterned after the Open Systems Interconnection – OSI – network reference model) that is used to organise standards. FIPS 158 defines a user-interface reference model that is closely patterned after the X Window System's architecture "stack":

FIPS 158 model	X11 reality
application	application
dialog	UIMS
presentation	?
toolkit	widgets
subroutine foundation	Xt intrinsics
subroutines	Xlib
byte stream	X protocol

Another standardisation issue to consider for FIPS 158 and Ada bindings are the extensions being made to the X Window System by various developers and researchers. For example, the Programmer's Hierarchical Interface for Graphics Systems (PHIGS) Extensions to X (PEX) defines functionality that some programmers will need but which lie outside the traditional X Window System "reference model". The Ada/PHIGS binding has already gone through its standardisation effort.

Some available resources

In addition to the resources listed below, some additional resources are:
   Ada/Xlib Implementation (Athena)

This is the source code for the X11R3 Ada/Xlib implementation (not binding) developed by Rational and contributed to the Athena Consortium for inclusion on their tapes.
   Ada/Motif Binding (University of Lowell)

This is the partial Ada/Motif binding developed at the University of Lowell and available for FTP access from one of their servers.

16.10.2   X Windows resources available from repositories/software-reuse libraries

AdaNet

The following abstracts were taken from AdaNet, and describe software available in source-code form. For more information on AdaNet, see Appendix C.

   Title: Ada Implementation of the Xt Toolkit (Ada/Xt)

Ada/Xt is an Ada implementation of the MIT X Toolkit (Xt). Xt consists of a set of intrinsic interfaces, which provide operations for construction, arrangement, and manipulation of windows, and a set of widgets, which are window objects ranging from buttons and scrollbars to text editors. Xt is built on top of Xlib, which is a low-level library of window primitives. The routines in Xlib provide window functionality by communicating with the X window server using the X Window System protocol.

   Title: Ada Language Interface to OSF/Motif Toolkit

This is an Ada binding to the OSF Motif toolkit. The Ada widget/function names differ from their C counterparts in that the words are divided by underscores (e.g., XmPushButton ==> Xm_Push_Button). Not all of the functions listed in the reference manual are included in the bindings (the list is provided in file READ_ME).

Asset Source for Software Engineering Technology (ASSET)

The following information was taken from the ASSET Library Repository Catalog. For more information on ASSET, see Appendix C.

```
Ada/X Toolkit (Software)
Order Number:        ASSET_A_162
Alternate Name:      ADA/X WIDGET LIBRARY
Version:             3.3
Release Date:        16-JAN-92
Producer:            PARAMAX
Reference:           CDRL 03716, DTIC AD-A229637
Asset Type:          SOFTWARE - BUNDLE
Size:                7490 Kbytes
Domains:             ADA STANDARDS AND BINDINGS, USER INTERFACE
Keywords:            ADA, BINDING, WIDGETS, X WINDOWS
Collection:          STANDARDS AND BINDINGS, STARS CATALOG
Distribution:        Approved for public release,
                     distribution is unlimited
```

This software package provides an Ada programmatic interface to a set of reusable user interface abstractions known as widgets. The software provides the full functionality of the M.I.T X Consortium Version 11 Release 4 X Window System. The software consists of three components: an Ada binding to the Xlib layer, an Ada implementation of the Xt Intrinsics layer, and an Ada widget library. The Ada binding to the Xlib layer is an upgrade of the STARS Foundations Ada Xlib binding, and provides a protocol interface including a set of graphics drawing primitives. The Xt Intrinsics layer provides a policy-free mechanism for creating and managing user interface objects. User interface objects are contained in the widget library which consists of a small set of commonly used user interface abstractions, such as scroll bars and command buttons.

```
Ada/X Toolkit Architecture
Order Number:        ASSET_A_160
Alternate Name:      ADA/XT ARCHITECTURE: DESIGN REPORT
Version:             1.1
Release Date:        25-JAN-90
Producer:            PARAMAX
Reference:           CDRL 01000, DTIC AD-A228827
Asset Type:          SOFTWARE DOCUMENTATION
Size:                2 Files, 750 Kbytes
Domains:             ADA STANDARDS AND BINDINGS, USER INTERFACE
Keywords:            ADA, ARCHITECTURE, BINDING, INTERFACE, X WINDOWS
Collection:          STANDARDS AND BINDINGS, STARS CATALOG
Distribution:        Approved for public release,
                     distribution is unlimited
```

This report provides a detailed description of the Ada/Xt toolkit architecture. The purpose of this report is to describe the Ada/Xt architecture in terms of system-independent package specifications, and to describe the analysis which contributed to major design decisions. The emphasis on system-independent package specifications rather than language independent specifications derives from recognition that the C language interfaces defined in the X Toolkit (Xt) Intrinsics definition are nearly sufficiently language independent – for languages in the Algol tradition (including Ada). The Ada toolkit design verifies this claim, since there is a very close syntactic mapping of types and interfaces from the Ada specification to the C specification.

```
Ada/X Toolkit Interface Style Guide
Order Number:        ASSET_A_161
Alternate Name:      ADA/X INTERFACE STYLE GUIDE
```

```
Release Date:        20-NOV-90
Producer:            PARAMAX
Reference:           CDRL 01030, DTIC AD-A229350
Asset Type:          SOFTWARE DOCUMENTATION
Size:                2 Files, 688 Kbytes
Domains:             ADA STANDARDS AND BINDINGS, USER INTERFACE
Keywords:            ADA, BINDING, INTERFACE, STYLE GUIDE, TOOLKIT,
                     X WINDOWS
Collection:          STANDARDS AND BINDINGS, STARS CATALOG
Distribution:        Approved for public release,
                     distribution unlimited
```

This technical report defines conventions for development of effective application user interfaces. The guide is intended for use by application developers and user interface developers using the Paramax STARS Ada/X User Interface Software. The intent is to produce a consistent style among Ada applications. The Style Guide addresses three areas of style:

- application/user interactions or dialogues,

- conventions for developing applications, and

- formal and informal user interface standardisation.

```
Ada/X Window System Interface
Order Number:        ASSET_A_240
Alternate Name:      INTERFACE TO THE X WINDOW SYSTEM, SAICX2
Version:             1.1
Release Date:        29-SEP-88
Producer:            SAIC
Reference:           SAICX2
Asset Type:          SOFTWARE - BUNDLE
Size:                2939 Kbytes, 371 files
Domains:             ADA STANDARDS AND BINDINGS, USER INTERFACE
Keywords:            ADA, BINDINGS, INTERFACE, STANDARDS, X WINDOWS
Collection:          STANDARDS AND BINDINGS, STARS FOUNDATIONS
Distribution:        Approved for public release,
                     distribution is unlimited
```

An expression of the various concepts in Ada that provides a full, working Ada specification of the X Window system.

A newer version of this interface is ASSET_A_162: Ada/X Toolkit.

```
Ada/Motif Bindings
Order Number:        ASSET_A_356
Alternate Name:      BCA/STARS MOTIF ADA BINDINGS
Version:             1.0
Release Date:        19-MAR-91
Producer:            BOEING DEFENSE AND SPACE GROUP
Author:              Boeing Commercial Airplanes Avionics
                     Flight Systems Organisation
Asset Type:          SOFTWARE - BUNDLE
Size:                18 Files, 508 Kbytes
Domains:             ADA STANDARDS AND BINDINGS
Keywords:            ADA, BINDING, MOTIF, OSF/MOTIF
Distribution:        Approved for public release,
                     distribution is unlimited
```

Motif is an X-Windows based toolkit for user interface development. The BCA Motif Ada bindings are a binding to (not an implementation of):
– the Motif widget (user interface object) set, and
– a subset of the Motif functions.

You must have the Motif object code libraries to use this software. The bindings were developed using Motif version 1.0.1 and have not been tested under 1.1.

COSMIC

The following information was taken from the 1993 COSMIC Software Catalog. For more information on COSMIC, see Appendix C.

```
Ada to X-Window Bindings
LANGUAGE: ADA ( 99 %); C-LANGUAGE ( 01 %);
MACHINE REQUIREMENTS: UNIX-BASED
PROGRAM SIZE: APPROXIMATELY 90,569 SOURCE STATEMENTS
DISTRIBUTION MEDIA: .25 inch Tape Cartridge in TAR Format
PROGRAM NUMBER: NPO-18760
DOCUMENTATION PRICE: $13.00 PROGRAM PRICE: $500.00
```

(Contract Software Service) The X-Window system and its constituent program libraries were developed almost entirely in the C programming language and, therefore, there are well defined C language interface libraries for all X-Windows functions. The X-Windows programming environment consists of three layers of program libraries: the low level X library, the intermediate layer Xt Toolkit Intrinsics library, and one of various high level widget libraries, with OSF Motif being the most common widget library. Ada to X-Window Bindings was developed to provide Ada programmers with complete interfaces to the Xt Intrinsics and OSF Motif toolkits.

The Xt and Motif programming libraries consist of nearly three hundred C language functions and a large number of C language structure definitions and constants. In order to provide an "Ada view" of Xt and Motif, an entire Ada programming layer was added which hides the interface to the C level libraries. A separate Ada procedure and type definition was written for each C language function and structure definition. The specification presented to the Ada programmer consists almost entirely of Ada types and structures. An effort was made to minimise the amount of type conversions between Ada and C views for which the applications programmer would have to be responsible.

This package is written in Ada and C-language for use with UNIX systems running MIT's X-Window System, Version 11 Revision 4, with the OSF/Motif widget set. Two separate versions of the package are included, one for Motif 1.0 and one for Motif 1.1. This package was developed under ULTRIX on a DECstation 3100 and is designed to be UNIX independent. For some UNIX systems the code may require minor modifications. The standard distribution medium for this package is a .25 streaming magnetic tape cartridge in UNIX tar format. Ada to X-Window Bindings is a copyrighted work with all copyright vested in NASA.

COSMIC, and the COSMIC logo are registered trademarks of the National Aeronautics and Space Administration. All other brands and product names are the trademarks of their respective holders.

Defense Software Repository System (DSRS)

For the DoD, other Government agencies, and supporting contractors, the Defense Software Repository System (DSRS) lists "X_Map" (ID sib0138a.1) and "X_Utils" (ID sia0054a.1) in its Software Reuse Program's Reusable Asset Catalog. For more information on the DSRS, see Appendix C.

Public Ada Library (PAL)

The PAL contains X Windows files under its ../bindings/x11r4 directory, which contains bindings and other documentation on the X Window System, Version 11 Release 4, of the X Consortium at the Massachusetts Institute of Technology. The contents of these files are described in subdirectory README files. The text of those README files are the same as the text portions of the ASSET catalogue references given above for Ada/X Toolkit, Ada/X Toolkit Architecture, and Ada/X Toolkit Interface Style Guide.

For more information on the PAL, see Appendix C.

16.10.3   X Window System products available from vendors

Advanced Technology Center

The Advanced Technology Center (ATC) has an Ada binding to Xlib, Xt, and OSF Motif for their AXI product. AXI is currently available for most UNIX-based platforms, and is supported by Verdix, Meridian, Alsys, and TeleSoft compilers.

AXI is an Ada-to-X-Window System interface that provides the Ada programmer access to the 500+ functions, libraries, and procedures contained in the X library (Xlib), the X Toolkit (Xt), the X Extensible Library, the X Miscellaneous Utilities, the Motif widget set and the Motif Resource Manager.

AXI supports X11R4, X11R5, Motif 1.1, and Motif 1.2. AXI includes STARS-compatibility modukes for Xlib, Xt, and Motif.

For more information, contact: Larry Paulson, Advanced Technology Center, 22982 Mill Creek Drive, Laguna Hills, CA 92653, USA; Tel: +1 714/583-9119 x208; Fax: +1 714/583-9213; Email: comments@atc.com.

AETECH, Inc.

Available Ada bindings for AETECH Ada compilers: Microsoft Windows, PHIGS, POSIX, SQL (Supra), X-Windows (Motif, Open Look). Host/Target: 80386 (& 80486) PCs.

For more information, contact: Jim Dorman, AETECH, Inc., 5841 Edison Place, Suite 110, Carlsbad, CA 92008, USA; Tel: +1 619/431-7714; Fax: +1 619/431-0860.

Alsys, Inc.

The Alsys Ada Software Development Environment for 386 UNIX is a production-quality Ada environment capable of handling very large Ada applications (over 500,000 lines of code). The product includes the Compiler; Multi-Library Environment, which provides a powerful and flexible way to manage Ada development effort and share program units; Binder, which supports unused subprograms elimination; High- and Low-Level Optimisers for improving code quality and performance; and Run-Time Executive for efficient support for executing Ada programs. Also included is the Developer's Toolset including: Ada Probe, a symbolic source-level debugger and program viewer; AdaXref, a cross-reference generator; AdaMake, a recompilation aid; AdaReformat, a source reformatter.

Alsys currently has Ada bindings to POSIX, X-Windows (OSF Motif), and the Generic Package of Elementary Functions for the Alsys Ada Software Development Environment, running on 386 UNIX 386/486-based machines supported as both host and target and running 386/ix or SCO UNIX. They are also planning a binding to SQL for 386/486 machines. Host/Target: 386/486 PC under IX UNIX, 386/486 PC under SCO UNIX.

The Alsys Ada Software Development Environment for the IBM RS/6000 is a production-quality Ada environment capable of handling very large Ada applications. Hosted on and targeted to the IBM RS/6000 workstation under IBM's AIX operating system, the product includes the Compiler; Multi-Library Environment, which provides a powerful and flexible way to manage Ada development efforts and share program units; Binder; Run-Time Executive; and both a High- and Low-Level Optimiser for improving code quality and performance. Also included is the Alsys Ada Toolset including Ada Probe, symbolic source-level debugger and program viewer; AdaXref, cross-reference generator; AdaMake, recompilation aid; and AdaReformat, source reformatter.

Alsys has bindings currently available to the Generic Package of Elementary Functions and to X-Windows (OSF Motif) for the Alsys Ada Development Environment for the IBM RS/6000 running on any RISC System/6000 machine as both host and target and running IBM's AIX operating system (Alsys's validated Ada compiler 910809W1.11195). Alsys also plans to develop a POSIX binding for the RS/6000. Host/Target: RISC System/6000 under AIX.

The Alsys Ada Software Development Environment for SPARC Workstations is a production-quality Ada environment capable of handling very large Ada applications. Hosted on any SPARC-based workstation under SunOS or SunView, the product includes the Compiler (with High- and Low-Level Optimisers); Binder, which supports unused subprogram elimination; Multi-Library system (Family, Library, and Unit Managers), which provides a powerful and flexible way to manage Ada development efforts and share program units; AdaExec real-time executive, for complete and efficient support for executing Ada programs; and ISO-standard mathematical library. Also included is the Alsys Ada Toolset including AdaProbe, symbolic source-level debugger and program viewer; AdaXref, cross-reference generator; AdaMake, recompilation aid; and AdaReformat, source reformatter.

Bindings to the Generic Package of Elementary Functions and to OSF/Motif are currently available for the Alsys Ada Software Development Environment running on any SPARC-based Workstation as both host and target and running SunOS or SunView. Host/Target: SPARC under SunOS.

Alsys' TeleUSE/Ada automates the creation of OSF/Motif graphical user interfaces for Ada applications. It includes a special version of the TeleUse User Interface Management System – which generates Ada source code – and Ada bindings to the TeleUSE run-time routines.

TeleUse/Ada tools allow a GUI to be prototyped and designed using a WYSIWYG editor and a PDL, and also includes tools for debugging, generating production code and maintaining the GUI. TeleUse/Ada can save the developer up to 90 percent of the time required to hand code X Window System GUIs. Host/Target: SPARC under UNIX, Sun-4 under UNIX.

Alsys' TeleWindows is a set of Ada bindings to the X Window System and OSF/Motif. This includes Xlib, XT, X extensions Library, XT+, X miscellaneous utilities, Motif widget set, XM, MWM, Motif resource manager. It supports X-11 R4 and is not based on the public domain version. It closely follows the C Xlib syntax and allows Ada applications to co-exist with C applications. Host/Target: IBM System/370 under VM/CMS.

For more information, contact: Alsys Sales, Alsys, Inc., 67 South Bedford Street, Burlington, MA 01803, USA; Tel: +1 617/270-0030, Fax: +1 617/270-6882, Email: marketing@alsys.com.

Digital Equipment Corporation

Digital Equipment Corporation has bindings available for GKS, PHIGS, SQL, and X/OSF Motif for DEC Ada on OpenVMS VAX, OpenVMS AXP Alpha, and DEC OSF/1 AXP Alpha Systems. The Ada bindings are provided either as part of a compiler product or the services/facilities that are provided by Digital and its suppliers.

Digital Equipment Corporation's DEC Ada product provides X/OSF Motif Ada bindings for OpenVMS VAX, OpenVMS AXP Alpha, DEC OSF/1 AXP Alpha, and RISC ULTRIX Systems. Host/Target: DEC AXP Alpha under DEC OSF/1; DEC VAX under OpenVMS; DEC AXP Alpha under OpenVMS; and DEC RISC under ULTRIX.

For more information, contact: Mary Anne Cacciola, Digital Equipment Corporation, 110 Spit Brook Road, Nashua, NH 03062, USA; Tel: +1 603/881-1028.

EVB Software Engineering, Inc.

Heragraph is a graphics framework that enables development of interactive 2D/3D graphics applications. Use of Heragraph's reusable graphical objects, Motif-style user-interface components, and application framework allows developers to concentrate on the application rather than the graphics primitives. Written in Ada, Heragraph provides a LISP interpreter to facilitate rapid prototyping. All of the Ada functionality of Heragraph is available from the LISP interpreter; however, the user is free to prototype strictly in Ada. The user interface for the application can be ported from X-Windows to

DOS or vice versa by recompiling on the new platform. Host/Target: Available for 386- or 486-based PC with Alsys Ada; Sony NEWS with Alsys; Sun 4 (SPARC) with Alsys, SunAda, TeleSoft; and HP 9000/70 with TeleSoft.

GRAMMI (Generated Reusable Ada Modifiable Machine Interface) is an Ada user-interface toolkit that supports construction of graphical user interfaces (GUIs) using the X-Windows system. GRAMMI's toolkit consists of a user-interface editor, a GRAMMI application environment, a software-generation utility, and a library of graphical components or widgets. With GRAMMI, a user interactively builds the required screens and generates necessary Ada code to implement the user interface. By interactively building the user interface, the developer can do rapid prototyping and evolutionary development of Ada user-interface software. Interfaces built using GRAMMI support all the features of Ada, including the use of multiple Ada tasks to manipulate the user-interface components without conflicts. Host/Target: Available on Sun4 (SPARC) using SunAda 1.11; on Silicon Graphics using SGI Ada 4.1; on HP 9000 using Alsys Ada; and on SCO UNIX using Alsys Ada.

For more information, contact: Patrick Wicker, EVB Software Engineering, Inc., 5303 Spectrum Drive, Frederick, MD 21701, USA; Tel: +1 800/877-1815, 301/695-6960; Fax: +1 301/695-7734.

IBM

IBM's AIX Ada/6000 product provides a binding to GPEF and IBM AIXWindows (X-Windows but not Motif). It runs on all models of the IBM RISC System/6000 under the IBM AIX Version 3.2 operating system. (See also entries for Systems Engineering Research Corporation (SERC) and Advanced Technology Center (ATC) for Motif, GKS or PHIGS bindings for use with IBM AIX Ada/6000 products.)

The AIX Ada/6000 licensed programs (5706-291 and 5706-294) consist of an optimising compiler, a run-time environment, a symbolic debugger, an Ada "makefile" generator for use in automating and minimising recompilation, Ada library-management tools and Ada language bindings to some key AIX subsystems. With the exception of some system-specific aspects of the language, the Ada language for the AIX operating system is source compatible with the Ada language supported by IBM licensed programs in VM/CMS and MVS. Host/Target: IBM RISC System/6000 under the IBM AIX Version 3.2 operating system.

This product conforms to the following standards: ANSI/MIL-STD-1815A – Ada '83; ISO 8652-1987, Programming Languages, Ada; FIPS PUB 119 – Ada; Validated at current level (1.11) of the ACVC test suite.

For more information, contact: Barry Lee, IBM Corporation, 844 Don Mills Road, North York, Ontario, Canada M3C 1V7; Tel: +1 416/448-3174; Fax: +1 416/448-4810.

Integrated Computer Solutions, Inc. (ICS)

The ICS Ada Xcessories provide Ada programmers with the ability to use a Graphical User Interface Builder to build screens. Application developers can use them to build OSF/Motif user interfaces for Ada applications. The ICS Ada Xcessories conform to the STARS bindings recommended by Paramax/STARS.

The ICS Ada Xcessories include BX/Ada, OSF/Motif, and Ada/Motif.

Builder Xcessory (BX) is an interactive graphical tool for building and prototyping OSF/Motif-based user interfaces. BX/Ada generates portable, royalty-free Ada code that does not require any additional run-time libraries. A pull-down menu option allows generation of Ada code in a single step. BX/Ada is supported on Sun 4 OS 4.1.x, HP 700 HPUX 8.07 and 9.01, and IBM RS/6000 OS 3.2 and requires the Ada/Motif bindings.

OSF/Motif is the standard graphical user interface from the Open Software Foundation (OSF). ICS OSF/Motif includes all the enhancements of the latest release from OSF, plus additional bug fixes and testing.

ICS Ada/Motif provides the Ada developer with complete Ada access to the OSF/Motif libraries, and also provides access to the lower-level X libraries.

ICS Ada/Motif corresponds to the standard X and standard OSF/Motif toolkit. ICS Ada/Motif handles tasking issues with the preference package. This package allows the developer to serialise access to the X Window System environment. If the developer uses this package along with the X subroutines, events for handling tasking/blocking will be managed by the bindings. A run-time configurable technology selectable through the preference package also helps to control memory leakage.

Platform	Version	Compiler
Sun4 (Sparc)	4.1.x	SunAda 1.0
Sun4 (Sparc)	4.1.x	SunAda 1.1
Sun4 (Sparc)	4.1.x	TeleGen2 RISC Ada 4.1a
Sun4 (Sparc)	4.1.x	Alsys 5.5
Sun4 (Sparc)	4.1.x	Alsys 5.5.1
HP 700	8.07	Alsys 5.35
HP 700	8.07	Alsys 5.36
IBM RS6000	3.2	Alsys 5.4
IBM RS6000	3.2	AIX Ada 3.0
SGI	4.0.1	SG Ada 4.1

For more information, contact: Integrated Computer Solutions, Inc., 201 Broadway, Cambridge, MA 02139, USA; Tel: +1 617/621-0060; Fax: +1 617/621-9555; Email: info@ics.com.

Objective Interface Systems, Inc.

Objective Interface Systems, Inc., has an Ada binding to X-windows (OSF Motif) for its Screen Machine product. The Screen Machine binding to Motif includes a WYSIWYG drawing tool and an Ada code generator.

Supported by Verdix, SunAda, TeleSoft, IBM Ada, Meridian, DEC, and Rational compilers. Host/Target: SCO UNIX, Irix, SunO/S, HFSI AUX, IBM/AIX, ISC UNIX, DEC Ultrix, Solaris, HP/UX, Windows 3.1.

For more information, contact: Phil Carrasco, Objective Interface Systems, Inc., 1895 Preston White Drive, Suite 250, Reston, VA 22091-5448, USA; Tel: +1 703/264-1900; Fax: +1 703/264-1721; Email: phil.carrasco@ois.com (Internet).

Rational

Rational Apex provides an Ada binding to X-Windows (ASF Motif).

Rational Apex is an integrated, interactive software-engineering environment for total lifecycle control of Ada projects. It effectively controls large-scale development efforts while lowering project risk. It supports design, development, unit test, maintenance, verification, documentation generation, configuration management and version control. It also supports integration with external front-end CASE tools and external target compilers. In addition, the Rational Environment enables teams of developers to significantly reduce development time by providing syntactic and semantic assistance, incremental compilation, and automation of system builds and releases. The environment's support of industry-standard protocols simplifies integration with new or existing project support environments. Host/Target: IBM RS/6000 under AIX, Sun SPARC under SunOS as host; targets any third-party platform and operating system.

For more information, contact: Shelly Richard, Rational, 3320 Scott Boulevard, Santa Clara, CA 95054-3197 USA; Tel: +1 408/496-3600; Fax: +1 408/496-3636; Email: shellyr@rational.com.

SL Corporation

SL Corporation provides Ada binding support for its SL-GMS toolkit; this includes support for GPEF, GPPF, POSIX, SQL, TCP/IP, OSF/Motif, and Open Look.

SL-GMS is a toolkit for developing dynamic graphics screens for real-time or highly interactive applications. Non-programmers can design application screens in a standard drawing-tool mode, connect them to real-time data sources and animate screen objects to visualise changing data values. SL-GMS allows the design of custom "GISMOs" to input values or control the application and supports Motif, Open Look and other X toolkit widgets.

SL-GMS is used to provide real-time graphics for applications in the fields of manufacturing, process control, network management, avionics and financial tracking.

Host/Target: Validated Verdix and DEC compilers support SL-GMS for the following machines as both host and target: DEC-DECstation/ULTRIX 4.0; DEC-VAXstation/ULTRIX 4.0; DEC-VAXstation/VMS 5.4; DEC-VAXstation/VMS 5.5; DEC Alpha PCs/Windows NT; IBM-RS6000/AIX; HP-9000/300/UNIX; HP-9000/400/UNIX; HP-9000/700/UNIX; HP-9000/800/UNIX; PC-386/IX UNIX; PC-386/SCO UNIX; PC-386/Lynx; PC-386/OS2; PC-386/System 5.4; SGI-4D/IRIX 3.3; Sun-3/SunOS 4.1; SunSPARC/SunOS 4.1 and Solaris; 88 Open/BCS Compliant; and Intel PCs/Windows NT.

For more information, contact: Mike Meagher, SL Corporation, 240 Tamal Vista Boulevard, Corte Madera, CA 94926, USA; Tel: +1 415/927-1724; Fax: +1 415/927-0878.

Sunrise Software International

Sunrise Software International's product, ezX, is a rapid application-development tool that automates the creation of graphical user interfaces for OSF/Motif and generates C, UIL, or Ada. ezX provides WYSIWYG screen layout; an easy-to-learn API , and user-extensible dialog-management box.

A prototype can be developed, and using a script language similar to Hypertalk, demonstrated to end-users before the code is written. Then portable Ada, C, or UIL can be generated automatically. Ada bindings are provided. The ezX API simplifies the application program, and eliminates the need to learn the Motif API. ezX also supports direct interfaces from the GUI widgets to another application or hardware device, without programming the callback functions. After the application has been completed and tested, the GUI can still be modified without recompiling (and retesting) the application. Host/Target: Available on Sun, SCO, IBM, DEC (including VMS), HP, SGI.

For more information, contact: Frederick Sells, Sunrise Software International, 170 Enterprise Center, Middletown, RI 02840, USA; Tel: +1 401/847-7868; Fax: +1 401/847-7879.

Systems Engineering Research Corporation (SERC)

SERC's Ada/Motif is a complete binding to X Window and OSF/Motif for the Ada programming language that was based in part upon the SAIC/Unisys (STARS) public domain bindings. That work was leveraged as a starting point for this development; many of the bug fixes and additional capabilities beyond the public domain releases in Ada/Motif have been incorporated. Most noteworthy are the capabilities included in Ada/Motif for Ada tasking, callback registration, memory leak detection/prevention and capabilities for developing customised widgets. Paramax/STARS considers Ada/Motif to be the commercial version of their STARS bindings, according to SERC.

Ada/Motif is supported by the Alsys, Verdix, SunAda, IBM Ada, and SGI Ada compilers. Host/Target: Sun 4, HP 300/400, HP 700, IBM RS 6000, SGI, 386/486 SunOS 4.1.1, Solaris 2.x, HPUX 8.0, SGI 3.2, 4.0, & 5.0, IBM AIX 3.2, SCO 3.2. (Custom ports available on special quotation.)

For more information, contact: Richard Henault, Systems Engineering Research Corporation (SERC), 2555 Charleston Road, Mountain View, CA 94043, USA; Tel: +1 800-ADA-SERC or 415/962-9092; Fax: +1 415/962-0330; Email: Well!sercmail@apple.com.

Top Graph'X

XInAda is not merely "a binding to X Windows". Rather, it is an Ada implementation of X Windows, giving access to the X-Window System for application programs written in Ada. All XInAda software is written completely in Ada.

XInAda-xlibv is a full Ada implementation of the MIT X11 core protocol. It is an Ada equivalent to the MIT C Xlib library available on most UNIX machines. Each Xlib routine has its corresponding facility within XInAda-Xlib. Syntax and procedure names have been chosen to match as closely as possible the original MIT implementation, easing the port of Ada applications previously interfaced with the C Xlib. Supported protocol revisions: 11.4, 11.5, and later.

XInAda-Pexlib is a full Ada implementation of the PEX-5R1 protocol (X Consortium). Its typing is inherited from the PHIGS-Ada norm (ISO 9593-3). It gives direct access to the full set of the Pex facilities. Supported protocol revisions: 5.0P and 5.1P.

XinAda-Widgets is a full Ada implementation of the OSF/Motif widget set. It is based on XinAda-Toolkit and XinAda Xlib; all OSF/Motif widget classes are supported (end of 1994 Q2 release), UIM andMrm also (late 1994). Supported revision: 1.2 of OSF/Motif.

Host/Target: Major compilers are supported, both native and cross-compilation systems; native systems: UNIX, VMS, LYNX, DOS, Windiws NT, OSF1; network transport: TCP/IP, DECNet; network transport for cross-compilers: Alsys AdaConnect and TeleAdaLAN.

For more information contact: Jean-Claude Mahieux, Manager, Top Graph'X, 10 Allee de la Mare Jacob, 91290 La Norville, France; Tel: +33 1 69 26 97 88, Fax: +33 1 69 26 97 89; Email: 100071.45@compuserve.com. (For Alsys compilers, XinAda is also available from Alsys.)

Verdix

The Verdix Ada Development System (VADS), is a complete Ada Compiler System offering a fully validated Ada compiler with chapter 13 support. Verdix supplies VADSself and VADScross. VADSself provides a complete toolset for self-targeted applications. It easily interfaces to databases, windowing systems and program management tools. VADScross provides real-time support for host-to-target system development. VADScross produces small and fast object code. VADS is hosted on the largest number of platforms and targets the greatest number of microprocessors. Host/Target: 88000 BCS under UNIX, DEC VAX under VMS / ULTRIX / UNIX, DECStation (RISC) under UNIX, DECSystem (RISC) under UNIX, HP 9000 Series 300 under HP-UX (UNIX), IBM PS/2 under AIX (UNIX), IBM RISC System/6000 under AIX, SCO Systems V/386 (ABI) under UNIX, Sun SPARC systems under UNIX, Sun-3 systems under UNIX.

Verdix AXI provides an Ada binding to the full Motif, Xt, and Xlib libraries. The product works with user-supplied Motif 1.1 and X11R4 libraries regardless of source. Host/Target: DEC RISC under Ultrix, IBM RS6000 under AIX, MIPS under MIPSos, Sun-4 under SunOS, Sys V386 under ISC UNIX, Sys V386 under SCO UNIX.

For more information, contact: Tim Ruhe, Verdix Corporation, 205 Van Buren, Herndon, VA 22070, USA; Tel: +1 703/318-9304; Email: timr@verdix.com.

16.11   Other specifications and standards

16.11.1   Ada Decimal Arithmetic and Representations (ADAR)

General

The Ada Decimal Arithmetic and Representations (ADAR) were developed under the Ada Joint
Program Office's Ada Technology Insertion Program (ATIP) in order to provide a common approach
for decimal arithmetic in Ada 83.

ADAR resources available from repositories/software-reuse libraries

The Ada Joint Program Office host computer on the Internet

The following information was taken from files on the Ada Joint Program Office's host computer
(ajpo.sei.cmu.edu). The file name and subdirectory are noted at the beginning of the reference. For
more information on the AJPO host, see Appendix C.

Ada Decimal Arithmetic and Representations (ADAR) This file: ajpo.sei.cmu.edu: /pub-
lic/atip/adar/README. Last updated 3/19/93

This is the source code for Ada Decimal Arithmetic and Representations (ADAR), Version 1.0,
January 1993, which is part of the binding project of the Ada Joint Program Office's Ada Technology
Insertion Program (ATIP). The ADAR packages were developed to provide a common approach
for decimal arithmetic and Ada 83. The ADAR package set consists of two related facilities for
decimal arithmetic, one based on discriminant records, and the other on generics, to provide decimal
computation and interoperable representations of decimal quantities.

The ADAR packages include support for decimal data with up to 18 digits of precision, arithmetic
operations with programmer control over rounding versus truncation, conversions to and from common
external representations, and formatted output of decimal values based on COBOL's "picture" clauses.

Asset Source for Software Engineering Technology (ASSET)

The following information was taken from the ASSET Library Repository Catalog. For more information on ASSET, see Appendix C.

```
Ada Decimal Arithmetic and Representations
Order Number:        ASSET_A_347
Alternate Name:      ADAR
Version:             1.0
Release Date:        15-JAN-93
Producer:            MITRE CORPORATION
Author:              Benjamin Brogsol, David Emery,
                     Robert Eachus, The MITRE Corporation
Asset Type:          SOFTWARE - BUNDLE
Size:                124 Files, 291 Kbytes
Domains:             ADA STANDARDS AND BINDINGS, MATH UTILITIES
Keywords:            ADA, ARITHMETIC, COBOL PICTURES,
                     DECIMAL ARITHMETIC, INFORMATION SYSTEMS, MATH,
                     REPRESENTATIONS
Collection:          GENERAL
Distribution:        Approved for public release,
                     distribution unlimited
```

Among the application domains for which Ada is being used or is under consideration, is the traditional
COBOL domain of business data processing. However, Ada's arithmetic type facility does not readily
handle the exact decimal model needed for financial computation, leaving a major impediment to a
successful transition to Ada for Information Systems applications. The ADAR project addresses this

shortcoming by providing a set of packages that define and implement decimal support in Ada 83. The ADAR packages include support for decimal data with up to 18 digits of precision, arithmetic operations with programmer control over rounding versus truncation, conversions to and from common external representations, and formatted output of decimal values based on COBOL's "picture" clauses. The ADAR packages offer a portable interface via a set of unit specifications, and a portable (although not necessarily efficient) reference implementation.

ADAR provides two approaches to decimal arithmetic: one through a discriminated private type, where discriminants establish precision (the number of digits) and scale (the number of digits to the right of the decimal point); and another through generic packages, where the effect of precision and scale is established via generic instantiation. For details on the two approaches, refer to the accompanying report in the SUMMARY.TXT file. Users can employ either or both of the approaches in their programs.

The design and development of ADAR was conducted by Mr. Robert Eachus and Mr. David Emery from the MITRE Corporation, and by Dr. Benjamin Brosgol.

ADAR products available from vendors

The AdaIC has not identified any commercial products for ADAR.

16.11.2   Adobe Font Metrics

General

The Adobe typefonts are widely used in desktop publishing.

Adobe resources available from repositories/software-reuse libraries

Asset Source for Software Engineering Technology (ASSET)

The following information was taken from the ASSET Library Repository Catalog. For more information on ASSET, see Appendix C.

```
Ada Binding to Adobe Font Metrics
Order Number:        ASSET_A_337
Alternate Name:      AFM Binding
Version:             1993
Release Date:        01-FEB-93
Producer:            GENOA SOFTWARE SYSTEMS
Author:              Alex Blakemore
Asset Type:          SOFTWARE - BUNDLE
Size:                4 Files, 77 Kbytes
Domains:             ADA STANDARDS AND BINDINGS
Keywords:            ADOBE, AFM, BINDINGS
Collection:          GENERAL, STANDARDS AND BINDINGS
Distribution:        Approved for public release,
                     distribution is unlimited
```

This set of packages provide an Ada binding to Adobe Font Metrics. They utilise an AFM parser written in C. Together these files provide the functionality to parse Adobe Font Metrics files and store the information in predefined data structures. It is intended to work with an application program that needs font metric information. The program can be used as is by making a procedure call to parse an AFM file and have the data stored, or an application developer may wish to customise the code.

This program is based on the document "Adobe Font Metrics Files, Specification Version 2.0". AFM files are separated into distinct sections of different data. Because of this, the parseAFM program can parse a specified file to only save certain sections of information based on the application's needs.

A record containing the requested information will be returned to the application. AFM files are divided into five sections of data:

1) The Global Font Information
2) The Character Metrics Information
3) The Track Kerning Data
4) The Pair-Wise Kerning Data
5) The Composite Character Data

Basically, the application can request any of these sections independent of what other sections are requested. In addition, in recognising that many applications will want ONLY the x-width of characters and not all of the other character metrics information, there is a way to receive only the width information so as not to pay the storage cost for the unwanted data. An application should never request both the "quick and dirty" char metrics (widths only) and the Character Metrics Information since the Character Metrics Information will contain all of the character widths as well.

Public Ada Library (PAL)

The PAL contains Adobe-support files in its ../bindings/adobe subdirectory, the contents of which are described in that subdirectory's README file. The text of that README file is the same as the text portion of the ASSET catalogue reference given above.

For more information on the PAL, see Appendix C.

Adobe products available from vendors

The AdaIC has not identified any commercial Ada binding products for Adobe font metrics.

16.11.3   Customer Information Control System (CICS)

General

The Customer Information Control System (CICS) is an IBM transaction-processing system.

CICS resources available from repositories/software-reuse libraries

Asset Source for Software Engineering Technology (ASSET)

The following information was taken from the ASSET Library Repository Catalog. For more information on ASSET, see Appendix C.

```
Ada/SQL and CICS Bindings
Order Number:       ASSET_A_225
Alternate Name:     ADA INTERFACE TO CICS AND SQL, INTER-CICSQL2
Version:            1.1
Release Date:       9-AUG-88
Producer:           INTERMETRICS, INC.
Reference:          INTER-CICSQL2
Asset Type:         SOFTWARE - BUNDLE
Size:               2532 Kbytes, 362 Files
Domains:            ADA STANDARDS AND BINDINGS,
                    DATABASE MANAGEMENT SYSTEM
Keywords:           ADA, BINDING, CICS, DBMS, SQL
Collection:         STANDARDS AND BINDINGS, STARS FOUNDATIONS
Distribution:       Approved for public release,
                    distribution is unlimited
```

An interface that binds Ada to the IBM CICS transaction-oriented applications. In addition, it provides SQL for future database applications to allow migration to Ada while retaining massive historical databases and existing functional software.

Public Ada Library (PAL)

The PAL contains the Ada/SQL and CICS Bindings files under its ../bindings subdirectory, the contents of which are described in that subdirectory's README file. The text of that README file is the same as the text portion of the ASSET catalogue reference given above.

For more information on the PAL, see Appendix C.

CICS products available from vendors

IBM

The IBM Ada/370 product provides bindings to GPEF and SQL and the Customer Information Control System (CICS – a transaction-processing system). It runs on the IBM 30XX, 43XX, 937X and ES/9000 family processors, which are supported by the following operating systems:

VM/System Product (VM/SP) Release 5 or 6 (5664-167) with or without High Performance Option (HPO) (5664-173); VM/Extended Architecture System Product (VM/XA SP) Release 2 (5664-308); VM/Enterprise Systems Architecture (VM/ESA) Release 1 (5684-112); MVS/SP-JES2 Version 2 Release 2 (MVS/XA) (5740-XC6); MVS/SP-JES3 Version 2 Release 2 (MVS/XA) (5665-291); MVS/SP-JES2 Version 3 Release 1 (MVS/ESA) (5685-001); MVS/SP-JES3 Version 3 Release 1 (MVS/ESA) (5685-002); MVS/ESA-JES2 Version 4 Release 1 or 2 (MVS/ESA) (5695-047); MVS/ESA-JES3 Version 4 Release 1 or 2 (MVS/ESA) (5695-048);

Note: All of the above Operating Environments are supported in 31-bit addressing mode with the exception of VM/System Product (VM/SP) Release 5 and 6 which are restricted to 24-bit addressing.

The IBM Ada/370 licensed programs (5706-292 and 5706-295) consist of an Ada language compiler and a run-time library for use on various IBM MVS and VM/CMS operating systems. The IBM Ada/370 product provides many development environment aids – such as a source-level debugger (optionally with windowing when using IBM Graphical Data Display Manager Licensed Program for either MVS or VM), a highly configurable source-code formatter to assist in enforcing project coding standards, a dependency lister, a non-intrusive performance profiler, a cross-reference utility, and an Ada library-management capability. Ada/370 programs can call VS COBOL II subprograms similar to the calling of VS FORTRAN, C/370, and S/370 assembler subprograms; Ada/370 exported subprograms can be called from VS COBOL II, VS FORTRAN, C/370, and S/370 assembler programs. Additionally, separate features support inter-operation with other major database and transaction-processing subsystems.

One such feature of IBM Ada/370, called the SQL Module Processor for DB2 Database Manager, supports the procedural binding of Ada and SQL.

Another such feature of IBM Ada/370, called the IBM CICS Module Processor/MVS, supports the procedural binding of Ada and CICS, including CICS/OS/VS, CICS/MVS and CICS/ESA. Together with the SQL Module Processor for DB2 Database Manager, Ada applications utilising the combined features of these two subsystems can be productively built.

This product conforms to the following standards: ANSI-X3.135-1986 – Database Language-SQL; ANSI-X3.168-1989 – Procedural Binding of Ada and SQL; ANSI/MIL-STD-1815A – Ada '83; ISO 8652-1987, Programming Languages, Ada; FIPS PUB 119 – Ada; FIPS PUB 127-1 SQL through IBM DB2 Database Manager V2.3; CIFO 2.0 & 3.0 – Catalog of Interface Features & Options; Validated at current level (1.11) of the ACVC test suite.

For more information, contact: Barry Lee, IBM Corporation, 844 Don Mills Road, North York, Ontario, Canada M3C 1V7; Tel: +1 416/448-3174; Fax: +1 416/448-4810.

16.11.4   General Purpose Interface Bus (GPIB)

General

The General Purpose Interface Bus (GPIB) is an IEEE standard (488.2) for controlling a variety of devices, including power meters, signal-collection devices, etc.

GPIB resources available from repositories/software-reuse libraries

The AdaIC has not identified any Ada binding products for GPIB from repositories/software-reuse libraries.

GPIB products available from vendors

WPL Laboratories, Inc.

WPL Laboratories' AdaGPIB is an Ada device driver for the National Instruments AT-GPIB IEEE-488 board. It is completely implemented in Ada on the IBM PC, supports Alsys Ada, and provides Ada application control of the GPIB and connected devices. Transfer of data is done using direct memory access (DMA); it bypasses DOS by directly communicating with the bare 488 board; it provides support for all GPIB commands. Host/Target: Alsys 5.1 on the PC / NI-AT-GPIB board on the PC.

For more information, contact: William Loftus, Whitehall Offices - Suite 6, 410 Lancaster Avenue, Haverford, PA 19041; Tel: +1 215/658-2362, -2364; Fax: +1 215/658-2361; Email: loftusw@source.asset.com.

16.11.5   Microsoft Windows

General

Microsoft Windows is a graphics-based environment that co-exists with the Microsoft Disk Operating System (MS-DOS). It provides a desktop environment similar to that of the Macintosh. Different applications, or multiples of the same application, are kept active in windows that can be resized and relocated on screen; users can switch back and forth between them.

Microsoft Windows resources available from repositories/software-reuse libraries

The AdaIC has not identified any Ada binding products for Microsoft Windows from repositories/software-reuse libraries.

Microsoft Windows products available from vendors

AETECH, Inc.

Available Ada bindings for AETECH Ada compilers: Microsoft Windows, PHIGS, POSIX, SQL (Supra), X-Windows (Motif, Open Look). Host/Target: 80386 (& 80486) PCs.

For more information, contact: Jim Dorman, AETECH, Inc., 5841 Edison Place, Suite 110, Carlsbad, CA 92008, USA; Tel: +1 619/431-7714; Fax: +1 619/431-0860.

R.R. Software, Inc.

R.R. Software, Inc.'s Janus/Ada Windows Toolkit provides the capability of writing Ada programs that are Windows applications. (In November 1993, R.R. will introduce Janus/Ada Ada 95 for DOS And Windows NT.)

The Janus/Ada Windows Toolkit provides full support to each of three levels of interfaces to Windows. At the lowest level, it provides complete binding to the Windows API. At the intermediate level, it provides an Ada Windows binding for most operations in a form that is more natural to Ada programmers than native Windows API. At the highest level, the Toolkit provides complete support for the standard Ada input/output libraries, allowing existing Ada programs to be recompiled as Windows applications without modification. Modifications to add menus, etc., to applications can be accomplished with Janus/Ada Windows. Host/Target: Intel-based PC under DOS, MS Windows.

For more information, contact: Ian Goldberg, R.R. Software, Inc., P.O. Box 1512, Madison, WI 53701-1512, USA; Tel: +1 608/251-3133; Fax: +1 608/251-3340.

16.11.6   MIL-STD-1553

General

Military Standard 1553 is a data bus used for communications between sensors and computer subsystems on a number of military platforms.

MIL-STD-1553 resources available from repositories/software-reuse libraries

The Ada Joint Program Office host computer on the Internet

The following information was taken from files on the Ada Joint Program Office's host computer (ajpo.sei.cmu.edu). The file name and subdirectory are noted at the beginning of the reference. For more information on the AJPO host, see Appendix C.

Generic Avionics Data Bus Tool Kit (GADBTK)

This file: ajpo.sei.cmu.edu: /public/atip/1553/README

This is the source code for the Generic Avionics Data Bus Tool Kit (GADBTK), which is part of the Ada Joint Program Office's Ada Technology Insertion Program (ATIP) binding project. The GADBTK project is intended to provide a strong Ada software binding to the military standard 1553 data bus. The bus is used for time multiplex data communications between different sensor and computer subsystems on many current military platforms.

The associated documentation will be available through the Defense Technical Information Center (DTIC) and the National Technical Information Service (NTIS).

```
Document                                  Accession No
--------                                  ------------

Software Design Document for
    the Generic Avionics Data Bus Tool Kit    AD-A259 329
Software Programmers Manual for
    the Generic Avionics Data Bus Tool Kit    AD-A259 379
Software Users Manual for
    the Generic Avionics Data Bus Tool Kit    AD-A259 364
Software Requirements Specification for
    the Generic Avionics Data Bus Tool Kit    AD-A260 023


National Technical Information      Defense Technical Information
Information Service (NTIS)          Center (DTIC)
U.S. Dept of Commerce               Cameron Station
5285 Port Royal Road                Alexandria, VA 22314
Springfield, VA 22161               Tel: +1 703/274-7633
Tel: +1 703/487-4650
```

MIL-STD-1553 products available from vendors

The AdaIC has not identified any commercial Ada binding products for MIL-STD-1553.

16.11.7 Ada/Operating System Interface (Ada/OSI)

General

This package provides tools to interface between Ada and an operating system.

Ada/OSI resources available from repositories/software-reuse libraries

Asset Source for Software Engineering Technology (ASSET)

The following information was taken from the ASSET Library Repository Catalog. For more information on ASSET, see Appendix C.

```
Ada/Operating System Interface
Order Number:        ASSET_A_147
Alternate Name:      OPERATING SYSTEM INTERFACE, OSI
Version:             1.0
Release Date:        01-NOV-90
Producer:            SCIENCE APPLICATIONS INTERNATIONAL CORPORATION
Asset Type:          SOFTWARE - BUNDLE
Size:                154 Kbytes, 26 Files
Domains:             ADA STANDARDS AND BINDINGS, OPERATING SYSTEMS,
                     SYSTEM UTILITIES
Keywords:            OPERATING SYSTEM, POSIX
Collection:          GENERAL, STANDARDS AND BINDINGS
Distribution:        Approved for public release,
                     distribution is unlimited
```

This package provides tools to interface between Ada and an operating system. The package is modeled on the POSIX interface for AIX but may be implemented on other environments as well. Functions available include interfaces to files and directories; access to environment variables such as user login name and aliases or logicals; and interfaces to spawn or execute other processes.

Public Ada Library (PAL)

The PAL contains Ada/OSI files under its ../bindings directory, the contents of which are described in that subdirectory's README file. The text of that README file is the same as the text portion of the ASSET catalogue reference given above.

For more information on the PAL, see Appendix C.

Ada/OSI products available from vendors

The AdaIC has not identified any commercial Ada binding products for Ada/OSI.

16.11.8 Paradox

General

Paradox is a widely used database management system.

Paradox resources available from repositories/software-reuse libraries

Defense Software Repository System (DSRS)

For the DoD, other Government agencies, and supporting contractors, the Defense Software Repository System (DSRS) lists "Ada_To_Paradox_Binding" (ID nia0014a.1) in its Software Reuse Program's Reusable Asset Catalog. For more information on the DSRS, see Appendix C.

Paradox products available from vendors

The AdaIC has not identified any commercial Ada binding products for Paradox.

16.11.9 Portable Common Tool Environment (PCTE)

General

The European Computer Manufacturers Association (ECMA) Portable Common Tools Environment (PCTE) is a portability interface based on commercial requirements for integrated project-support environments (IPSEs).

PCTE resources available from repositories/software-reuse libraries

Asset Source for Software Engineering Technology (ASSET)

The following information was taken from the ASSET Library Repository Catalog. For more information on ASSET, see Appendix C.

```
AdaPCTE (Ada PCTE Binding)
Order Number:        ASSET_A_482
Alternate Name:      ADAPCTE
Version:             0.3
Release Date:        24-FEB-93
Producer:            UNISYS
Author:              Michael J. Horton, Robert C. Smith
Reference:           CDRL 05203, STARS-UC-05203/004/00
Asset Type:          SOFTWARE - BUNDLE
Size:                50 Files, 850 Kbytes
Domains:             ADA STANDARDS AND BINDINGS,
                     SOFTWARE ENGINEERING ENVIRONMENT
Keywords:            BINDINGS, ENVIRONMENT, PCTE, PORTABLE COMMON
                     TOOL ENVIRONMENT
Distribution:        Approved for public release,
                     distribution is unlimited
```

This is the Paramax Ada binding to PCTE. The specification of the Ada binding is based on the ECMA (European Computer Manufacturers Association) Ada PCTE specification (Standard ECMA-162 Ada Language Binding, December 1991). The binding uses the GIE Emeraude PCTE 1.5 version 12.2 C libraries. Some changes to the ECMA specifications were made to accommodate the binding to PCTE 1.5. The release includes the AdaPCTE Version Description Document, which describes this version of AdaPCTE and provides installation instructions. These documents are provided in both plain ASCII and PostScript forms.

Public Ada Library (PAL)

The PAL contains PCTE files under its ../bindings/pcte subdirectory, the contents of which are described in that subdirectory's README file. The text of that README file is the same as the text portion of the ASSET catalogue reference given above.

For more information on the PAL, see Appendix C.

PCTE products available from vendors

The AdaIC has not identified any commercial Ada binding products for PCTE.

16.11.10   Secure File Transfer Program (SFTP)

General

BDM Corporation's Secure File Transfer Program provides a means of transferring sensitive information from one computer system to another across a multilevel secure network.

SFTP resources available from repositories/software-reuse libraries

Asset Source for Software Engineering Technology (ASSET)

The following information was taken from the ASSET Library Repository Catalog. For more information on ASSET, see Appendix C.

```
Secure File Transfer Program (SFTP)
Order Number:          ASSET_A_232
Alternate Name:        BDM2, SFTP
Release Date:          28-MAR-88
Producer:              BDM CORPORATION
Reference:             BDM2, CDRL A008
Asset Type:            SOFTWARE - TOOL
Size:                  1014 Kbytes, 86 files
Domains:               ADA STANDARDS AND BINDINGS,
                       NETWORK COMMUNICATIONS
Keywords:              FILE TRANSFER PROTOCOL, RFC:793, SECURITY,
                       TCP, TCP/IP, TRANSMISSION CONTROL PROTOCOL
Collection:            STANDARDS AND BINDINGS, STARS FOUNDATIONS
Distribution:          Approved for public release,
                       distribution unlimited
```

An architecture with the capability to send and receive files across a multilevel secure network, the Secure File Transfer Program is written by the BDM Corporation. It provides a means of transferring sensitive information from one computer system to another. This system implements Transmission Control Protocol (TCP) and conforms to RFC:793. TCP provides a reliable communication between pairs of processes in logically distinct hosts on networks and sets of interconnected networks. The TCP resides in the transport layer of the DoD Internet Model. The system encapsulates messages received from the utility layer protocols, which reside directly above, and passes the packet to the Internet layer (communicates with the Internet Protocol (IP)). The TCP supports the following functions: connection-oriented, reliable data transfer, ordered data transfer delivery, full-duplex, and flow control.

SFTP products available from vendors

The AdaIC has not identified any commercial Ada binding products for SFTP.

16.11.11   Transmission Control Protocol/Internet Protocol (TCP/IP)

General

The Transmission Control Protocol/Internet Protocol (TCP/IP) is a networking protocol suite that forms the core protocol suite used on the Internet network.

TCP/IP resources available from repositories/software-reuse libraries

AdaNet

The following abstracts were taken from AdaNet, and describe software available in source-code form. For more information on AdaNet, see Appendix C.

Title: Package TCP/IP

(February 10, 1988) This package implements the TCP and IP communications protocols as defined in "Military Standard Transmission Control Protocol", MIL-STD-1778, 12 August 1983, and "Military Standard Internet Protocol", MIL-STD-1777, 12 August 1983. These protocols, which are written in Ada, support standardisation efforts in several ways. First, they allow any Ada computing environment to access the DoD networks at a reduced development cost, thereby supporting the DoD standards. Second, they increase the base of existing Ada software, thereby helping to promote Ada as a programming language standard.

Title: Transmission Control Protocol (TCP)

(June 22, 1985) This contains tools and components related to the Defense Data Network, its file transfer, mail, and communications facilities. Implementations of the TCP/IP communications protocol, the FTP file transfer tool, and the SMTP mail handler are included.

TCP/IP products available from vendors

SL Corporation

SL Corporation provides Ada binding support for its SL-GMS toolkit; this includes support for GPEF, GPPF, POSIX, SQL, TCP/IP, OSF/Motif, and Open Look.

SL-GMS is a toolkit for developing dynamic graphics screens for real-time or highly interactive applications. Non-programmers can design application screens in a standard drawing-tool mode, connect them to real-time data sources and animate screen objects to visualise changing data values. SL-GMS allows the design of custom "GISMOs" to input values or control the application and supports Motif, Open Look, and other X toolkit widgets.

SL-GMS is used extensively to provide real-time graphics for applications in the fields of manufacturing, process control, network management, avionics and financial tracking. Host/Target: Validated Verdix and DEC compilers support SL-GMS for the following machines as both host and target: DEC-DECstation/ULTRIX 4.0; DEC-VAXstation/ULTRIX 4.0; DEC-VAXstation/VMS 5.4; DEC-VAXstation/VMS 5.5; DEC Alpha PCs/Windows NT; IBM-RS6000/AIX; HP-9000/300/UNIX; HP-9000/400/UNIX; HP-9000/700/UNIX; HP-9000/800/UNIX; PC-386/IX UNIX; PC-386/SCO UNIX; PC-386/Lynx; PC-386/0S2; PC-386/System 5.4; SGI-4D/IRIX 3.3; Sun-3/SunOS 4.1; Sun-SPARC/SunOS 4.1 and Solaris; 88 Open/BCS Compliant; and Intel PCs/Windows NT.

For more information, contact: Mike Meagher, SL Corporation, 240 Tamal Vista Boulevard, Corte Madera, CA 94926, USA; Tel: +1 415/927-1724; Fax: +1 415/927-0878.

16.11.12   Universal Ada Test Language (UATL)

General

The Universal Ada Test Language (UATL) has been designed as a general multi-purpose test language that provides a consistent framework for testing at all phases of the software/system development, production, and maintenance life cycle.

UATL resources available from repositories/software-reuse libraries

Asset Source for Software Engineering Technology (ASSET)

The following information was taken from the ASSET Library Repository. For more information on ASSET, see Appendix C.

```
UATL (Universal Ada Test Language)
Order Number:        ASSET_A_238
Alternate Name:      ITTAVION-UATL2, UATL
Version:             2
Release Date:        12-JAN-89
Producer:            ITT
Reference:           CDRL, ITTAVION-UATL2
Asset Type:          SOFTWARE - SYSTEM
Size:                14374 Kbytes
Domains:             ADA STANDARDS AND BINDINGS,
                     SOFTWARE QUALITY AND MEASUREMENT
Keywords:            FAULT ISOLATION, IEEE 488, INSTRUMENT CONTROL,
                     MATE-CIIL, SYSTEM DEVELOPMENT
Collection:          STANDARDS AND BINDINGS, STARS FOUNDATIONS
Distribution:        Approved for public release,
                     distribution unlimited
```

A test language that provides a consistent framework for testing complex systems at all stages of the software/system development production and maintenance cycle. The UATL has been designed as a general multi-purpose test language that provides a consistent framework for testing at all phases of the software/system development, production, and maintenance life cycle. It consists of a set of portable Ada packages that provide the user with a complete complement of standardised reusable test functions. These functions include an interactive menu driven test manager, on-line operator controls/displays, real-time "closed loop" test data stimulus/response, instrument control drivers, test data recording, and both ASCII and graphical data reduction analysis. Currently, the UATL supports driving a software unit-under-test (UUT) over internal memory, or a hardware UUT with a set of stimulus and measurement instruments over IEEE 488 and MIL-STD-1553B interfaces. It has been designed to readily support the incorporation of any additional reusable test control or analysis functions in the UATL "test language" library, and allows the user to develop any unique test functions at the Ada code level.

Documentation for this package is available in electronic form in Interleaf format only. Paper copies of the documentation are available by contacting the Librarian.

UATL products available from vendors

The AdaIC has not identified any commercial Ada binding products for UATL.

16.11.13   UNIX

General

UNIX is a widely used operating system developed by AT&T Bell Laboratories.

UNIX resources available from repositories/software-reuse libraries

Asset Source for Software Engineering Technology (ASSET)

The following information was taken from the ASSET Library Repository Catalog. For more information on ASSET, see Appendix C.

```
Paradise
Order Number:          ASSET_A_523
Alternate Name:        ADA INTERFACES TO THE UNIX OPERATING SYSTEM
Version:               3.4
Release Date:          05-JAN-94
Producer:              CENTRE D'ETUDES DE LA NAVIGATION AERIENNE
Author:                Nicolas Courtel
Asset Type:            SOFTWARE - BUNDLE
Size:                  1232 Kbytes, 88 Files
Domains:               ADA STANDARDS AND BINDINGS
Keywords:              ADA, BINDING, FILES, INTERFACE, PIPES,
                       SOCKETS, UNIX
Distribution:          Approved for public release,
                       distribution is unlimited
```

Paradise is a set of Ada packages intended to provide an interface to the UNIX operating system, and more specifically to the communication routines, that are accessed via file descriptors. It lets the Ada programmer use files, pipes, and sockets, as well as signals, error codes, environment variables, etc., using an interface that looks as much as possible like the C interface.

Paradise supports multi-tasking: any input or output is blocking for the calling task only, and not for the entire process.

Paradise is intended to be system-independent and compiler-independent; so far, it works on three environments: - SunOS (Sparc) and SunAda (Verdix 6.1) compiler; - HP-UX (HP9000/700) and HP-Ada (Alsys) compiler; - HP-UX (HP9000/700) and Verdix 6.3d compiler; - SunOS (4.1.3) and Telesoft (V. 4.1.1) compiler.

It is known not to work well on SunOS/Alsys, because of problems on signal handlers;

For people who would like to port it to other environments, information on portability is displayed inside the code. A programmer's guide should appear in future versions.

To install Paradise, you need:

- A supported configuration: - SunOS/SunAda (or Verdix 6.1 or higher); - SunOS/Telesoft (V. 4.1.1); - HPUX/Hp-Ada (or Alsys); - HPUX/Verdix 6.3d or higher.

- A few UNIX tools (may be replaced by the GNU equivalents): - make; - the macro processor m4; - ar and ranlib.

Once you have checked all this, you need to edit the system.mk and compiler.mk files, to make them fit your environment. Default files are provided for SunOS and HP-UX systems, and Alsys and Verdix compilers.

NOTE: there are no Ada sources in the distribution; the source code must be first processed by m4 to become Ada code.

UNIX products available from vendors

The AdaIC has not identified any commercial Ada binding products for UNIX.

16.11.14   XMODEM/Kermit

General

XMODEM and Kermit Network are widely used file-transfer protocols.

XMODEM/Kermit resources available from repositories/software-reuse libraries

Asset Source for Software Engineering Technology (ASSET)

The following information was taken from the ASSET Library Repository Catalog. For more information on ASSET, see Appendix C.

```
Ada Binding to XModem and Kermit Network Protocols
Order Number:        ASSET_A_247
Alternate Name:      NETWORK PROTOCOL, WESTING-NP2
Version:             1.0
Release Date:        30-JUN-88
Producer:            WESTINGHOUSE ELECTRIC CORPORATION,
                     DEVELOPMENT & OPERATIONS DIVISION
Reference:           CDRL A008, WESTING-NP2
Asset Type:          SOFTWARE - BUNDLE
Size:                252 Kbytes
Domains:             ADA STANDARDS AND BINDINGS, NETWORK COMMUNICATIONS
Keywords:            FILE TRANSFER PROTOCOL, KERMIT, TRANSMISSION CONTROL
                     PROTOCOL, X_MODEM
Collection:          STANDARDS AND BINDINGS, STARS FOUNDATIONS
Distribution:        Approved for public release,
                     distribution is unlimited
```

A set of Ada packages that implement the file transfer protocols only (for X_Modem and Kermit protocols).

The documentation is complete and the implementation encourages reuse of this tool in a variety of ways.

XMODEM/Kermit products available from vendors

The AdaIC has not identified any commercial Ada binding products for XMODEM or Kermit.

16.12 Appendix A

Some Other Standards of Interest (Standards for which Ada binding products have not been identified)

The initial questionnaire used to survey vendors about their Ada bindings products addressed a number of standards for which no vendor identified a product. They were:

CASE Data Interchange Format (CDIF)
Government Open Systems Interconnection Profile (GOSIP)
        ISO X.400: Message Handling Service (MHS)
        ISO X.500: Directory Services
Initial Graphics Exchange Specification (IGES)
Standard Generalised Markup Language (SGML)
ISO ISO X.25 Packet-Switching Standard

As we receive information on products available to provide Ada bindings to these standards, we will update the "Available Ada Bindings" report. If you know of any Ada bindings products available for these standards or other, please call the Ada Information Clearinghouse at 1/800-AdaIC-11 (232-4211), or complete the survey form found in Appendix B.

The following subsections provide descriptions of the other standards, and where applicable, a discussion of the current state of the standardisation efforts.

16.12.1 CASE Data Interchange Format (CDIF)

The CASE Data Interchange Format (CDIF) is a developing standard targeted toward analysis and design tools and is based on extensions to the Electronic Data Interchange Format (EDIF).

16.12.2 Government Open Systems Interconnection Profile (GOSIP)

The Government Open Systems Interconnection Profile (GOSIP) defines a common set of data-communication protocols that enable systems developed by different vendors to interoperate and the users of different applications on those systems to exchange information.

ISO X.400: Message Handling Service (MHS) is part of the Open Systems Interconnection standard Email transmission. It establishes procedures for exchanging messages between incompatible Email systems, whether public or private.

ISO X.500: Directory Services is a specification for a global directory system that is flexible enough to hierarchically link the large number and variety of existing directory schemes. The X.500 directory allows users to search for an X.400 address. While X.400 allows users to send Email to any computer user in the world, X.500 will find the address of that person.

16.12.3 Initial Graphics Exchange Specification (IGES)

The Initial Graphics Exchange Specification (IGES) is the neutral file format for the translation of data from one proprietary graphical data base to another. It is an ANSI vector-graphics standard that allows different CAD/CAM systems to interchange product-definition data.

16.12.4 Standard Generalised Markup Language (SGML)

The Standard Generalised Markup Language (SGML) specifies a language for describing documents to be used in office document processing and for interchanging documents between authors and publishers. It provides a coherent and unambiguous syntax for describing the elements within a document and provides other information that makes the markup interpretable.

16.12.5   ISO X.25 - Packet Switching standard

ISO X.25 is a packet-switching standard, and specifies the interface between the user side of the user/network interface and the node processor that serves as an entry and an exit point to the packet-switching network.

16.13   Appendix B

Available Ada Bindings Survey Form

```
        AdaIC QUESTIONNAIRE: PRODUCTS WITH Ada BINDINGS

1.    Name of Product:  _____

2.    For each of the following standards, please indicate if the
      product named above currently provides support for the
      standard or if support will be provided in the future:


=================================================================

|                        | Currently  |Under        |Planned   |
|                        | Available  |Development  |          |
|========================================================|
| ASIS                   |            |             |          |
|------------------------+------------+-------------+----------|
| CDIF                   |            |             |          |
|------------------------+------------+-------------+----------|
| Generic Package of     |            |             |          |
| Elementary Functions   |            |             |          |
|------------------------+------------+-------------+----------|
| Generic Package of     |            |             |          |
| Primitive Functions    |            |             |          |
|------------------------+------------+-------------+----------|
| GOSIP                  |            |             |          |
|------------------------+------------+-------------+----------|
| GKS                    |            |             |          |
|------------------------+------------+-------------+----------|
| IRDS                   |            |             |          |
|------------------------+------------+-------------+----------|
| IGES                   |            |             |          |
|------------------------+------------+-------------+----------|
| Microsoft Windows      |            |             |          |
|------------------------+------------+-------------+----------|
| PHIGS                  |            |             |          |
|------------------------+------------+-------------+----------|
| POSIX                  |            |             |          |
|------------------------+------------+-------------+----------|
| SGML                   |            |             |          |
|------------------------+------------+-------------+----------|
| SQL                    |            |             |          |
|------------------------+------------+-------------+----------|
| TCP/IP                 |            |             |          |
|------------------------+------------+-------------+----------|
| X-Windows (OSF Motif)  |            |             |          |
|------------------------+------------+-------------+----------|
| X-Windows (Open Look)  |            |             |          |
|------------------------+------------+-------------+----------|
| X25                    |            |             |          |
|------------------------+------------+-------------+----------|
| X400                   |            |             |          |
|------------------------+------------+-------------+----------|
| X500                   |            |             |          |
=================================================================
```

AdaIC QUESTIONNAIRE (page 2)
PRODUCTS WITH Ada BINDINGS

3.   Which host system(s)/operating system(s) is/are supported
      by the product?

4.   Which target system(s)/operating system(s) is/are supported
      by the product?

5.   Which validated Ada compiler(s) support(s) the product?

6.   Description of Product (limit 250 words): Indicate the
      numbers of the ISO, ANSI, or other standards to which the
      product conforms.

      _____
      _____
      _____
      _____
      _____
      _____
      _____
      _____
      _____
      _____
      _____

7.   Point of Contact:

Vendor: _____
Name: _____
Address: _____
            _____
Phone :   _____
Fax :   _____
Email: _____

Return completed surveys to Ada Information Clearinghouse,
P.O. Box 46593,
Washington,
DC 20050-6593,
USA;
Tel: + 1 703 685 1477,
Fax: + 1 703 685 7019;
Email: adainfo@ajpo.sei.cmu.edu
CompuServe: 70312,3303.

16.14   Appendix C

Information on Repositories/Software-Reuse Libraries.

16.14.1   The Ada Joint Program Office host computer on the Internet

Besides the bindings software referenced in this report, most Ada Information Clearinghouse (AdaIC) flyers and other publications are available on-line for downloading from the Ada Joint Program Office's (AJPO's) host computer (ajpo.sei.cmu.edu) on the Internet.

The host can be accessed via File Transfer Protocol (ftp), a tool that enables users to transfer files to and from remote network sites. If you are working at a machine that is connected to the Internet and supports ftp, use the procedures outlined below to access files on the AJPO host. If you require additional information about ftp, contact your system administrator.

```
To connect to the AJPO public directories:

1.  At your prompt, type:            ftp ajpo.sei.cmu.edu
2.  At the login prompt, type:       anonymous
3.  At the password prompt, type:    your electronic mail address
                                     (e.g., smith@cc.xsu.edu)
4.  Change to the appropriate
    directory by typing:             cd public/<directory name>
5.  For a list of available
    files, type:                     dir
6.  Get desired file(s) by typing:   get <filename>
                or                   mget <filename1 filename2>
7.  Logout by typing:                bye
```

If you do not have Internet access through your place of business or academic institution, there are hosts that provide accounts to the general public. Some of these are free, some charge, and the services offered vary widely. For more information on public access, see AdaIC flyer S02, "Electronic Mail to the Defense Data Network (DDN) and the Internet Through Public-Access Sites" (AdaIC file MAIL_DDN.HLP).

How to Access Ada Information via "ftpmail"

"ftpmail" can be used by anyone with the capability to send and receive electronic mail over the Internet. To retrieve a specific file, you will need to know the name and directory in which the file resides. To get help, including information on accessing the directories of files, send the following message from your electronic mail account:

To: ftpmail@ajpo.sei.cmu.edu
Subject: help

Items available on the AJPO host

All publically available files are stored in "public" directories. Current offerings are:

```
abwg            information files from Ada Bindings Working Group
                (ABWG)

aces            Ada Compiler Evaluation System (ACES), Version 1.0

acvc-current    current Ada Compiler Validation Capability Test Suite
                (ACVC 1.11)

acvc-9x         pointer file that describes how to obtain the ACVC
```

9X-Basic test suite from the SEI FTP server

ada-adoption-hbk   "Ada Adoption Handbook, A Program Manager's
                    Guide" (Version 2.0, October 1992)

ada-comment   complete listing of Ada Commentaries from the Ada
               Rapporteur Group (ARG)

ada-lsn   Ada Language Study Notes

ada-ui   ISO WG9 Ada Uniformity Issues (UIs) and meeting
               minutes

ada9x   information from the Ada 9X Project Office --
               including Project Reports, announcements, and reports
               from the Ada 9X Project manager

ada9x/mrtcomments full text of comments sent to the Ada 9x
                   Mapping/Revision Team (MRT) mailing list

adastyle   "Ada Quality and Style: Guidelines for Professional
               Programmers, Version 2.01.01, December 1992".
               This is the AJPO's suggested Ada style guide for use
               in DoD programs.

artdata   Ada Runtime Environment Working Group (ARTEWG)
               information and ARTEWG's "Catalogue of Interface
               Features and Options for the Ada Runtime Environment,
               Release 3.0, July 1991" (CIFO 3.0)

asis   "Ada Semantic Interface Specification (ASIS)",
               version 1.1.0, July 1993

atip   source code that was produced under the AJPO's Ada
               Technology Insertion Program (ATIP)

compiler   current list of Validated Ada compilers; information
               about the validation process and evaluating compilers

comp-lang-ada   Frequently Asked Questions (FAQ) files and
                   archived digests from the comp.lang.ada newsgroup
                   on USENET

document   information on how to obtain various documents related
               to the Ada program

dev-tool   customised searches from the AdaIC Products and Tools
               database, information about FREE Ada development tools

ed-train   listing of current Ada classes and seminars, Ada text
               books, and Ada training videotapes. AdaIC report
               "Catalog of Resources for Education in Ada and
               Software Engineering (CREASE) Version 6.0, February
               1992"

ev-info   information files from the APSE Evaluation &
               Validation Team

graphics   graphics of Lady Ada and Ada globe

history   historical information about the Ada program

infoada   "infoada" information files, including digests from
                the info-ada mailing list

irds   draft Ada Binding to the draft ISO Information
                Resource Dictionary System (IRDS) Standard

kitdata   information files from the Kernel Ada Programming
                Support Environment (KAPSE) Interface Team

lrm   "Ada Language Reference Manual, ANSI/MIL-STD-1815A"
                (1983)

news   weekly summary of news about the Ada program, a
                calendar of events, and issues of the AdaIC quarterly
                newsletter

pcis   information from the Portable Common Interface Set
                (PCIS) Programme -- including a draft International
                Requirements and Design Criteria (IRAC), public input
                on IRAC, and an Interface Technology Analyses (ITA2)
                document

piwg   benchmark test suite from ACM SIGAda's Performance
                Issues Working Group (PIWG)

policy   the Congressional Ada mandate, policy letters and Ada
                implementation plans from the Services

rationale   "The Rationale for the Design of the Ada Programming
                Language (1986)"

resource   descriptions of freely available resources for Ada
                information and source code

RRG   documents from the ISO/JTC1/SC22/WG9 Real-Time
                Rapporteur Group (RRG)

survey   AdaIC survey forms. Tell us about your Ada
                application, Ada tools, Ada bindings products, and
                educational offerings.

usage   summaries of Ada's successful use in a variety of
                domains

16.14.2 AdaNET

The AdaNET Repository is the operational part of the Repository Based Software Engineering (RBSE) Program. RBSE is a NASA-sponsored program dedicated to introducing and supporting common, effective approaches to software-engineering practices. The process of conceptualising, designing, building, and maintaining software systems by using existing software assets that are stored in a specialised operational reuse library or repository (AdaNET) is the foundation of the program. The AdaNET Repository contains a comprehensive library of software engineering information and an extensive collection of public-domain software including assets from the Public Ada Library (PAL), the Software Technology for Adaptable, Reliable Software (STARS) Program, many educational institutions, and various other sources. Its non-software information includes relevant research papers, standards, and technical reports.

AdaNET's Client Service distributes assets on diskettes, magnetic tape, and hard copy. Clients can also FTP assets using the output function included as a menu option. The current system, known as ASV3, will be enhanced as ASV4 by the addition of an Internet-based global hypermedia browser known as Mosaic. Part of the World Wide Web (WWW) project, the Mosaic interface allows for the discovery, retrieval, and display of documents, data, images, and sound. Information from within the repository itself as well as from around the world will be interconnected in an hypertext environment. Clients will travel through the information by clicking on links which appear as images, terms, and/or icons. These links point to other related documents and information, thus enabling clients to retrieve any document anywhere on the Internet.

The distinguishing characteristic of the AdaNET system is that the repository will support both the development and sustainment of a system or project life cycle. Unlike traditional software collections consisting almost entirely of source code, AdaNET's assets promote advanced software engineering through reuse, including designs as well as code, and by encouraging the use of processes and standards that will result in more adaptable, extensible, and reliable systems. The adoption the these advances and processes will reduce the costs of sustaining engineering – which accounts for as much as ninety percent of a system's total life cycle cost.

The AdaNET Operations Team includes Client Service, Information Management, Infrastructure Support, and Software Engineering divisions. Each unit within the Op Team is dedicated to facilitating reuse, promoting sound software engineering principles, presenting quality, pertinent assets, and rendering timely, effective client support. The Software Engineering Referral Desk and the Client Service Help Desk are available to all clients. The Help Desk is operated five days a week, 8am -8 pm Eastern Time, and can be reached at +1 304/594-9075. To obtain a client application, software catalogue, or for more information, post a message to:

lacey@rbse.mountain.net
or contact:

AdaNET Client Service
MountainNet, Inc.
2705 Cranberry Square
Morgantown
WV 26505
USA
Tel: +1 304/594-9075

16.14.3   Source for Software Engineering Technology (ASSET)

ASSET, an acronym for Asset Source for Software Engineering Technology, is sponsored by the Advanced Research Products Agency (ARPA) organised under the Software Technology fir Adaptable, Reliable Systems (STARS) program. ARPA tasked Loral Federal Systems (formerly IBM Federal Systems) and its principal subcontractor, Science Applications International Corporation (SAIC) to establish the ASSET Reuse Library to serve as a national resource for the advancement of software reuse across the Department of Defense (DoD).

ASSET's mission is to provide a distributed support system for software reuse within the DoD and to help foster a software-reuse industry within the United States. ASSET's initial and current focus is on software-development tools, reusable components, and documents on software-development methods. ASSET is participating in interoperation with other reuse libraries, such as the Central Archive for Reusable Defense Software (CARDS) and the Defense Software Repository System (DSRS).

Although ASSET's services are currently available without charge to all software practitioners, eventually ASSET will transition to a fee-for-service operation.

ASSET's goals are to create a focal point for software-reuse information exchange, to advance the technology of software reuse, and to provide an electronic marketplace for reusable software products to the evolving national software-reuse industry.

To achieve these goals, ASSET operates the ASSET Reuse Library, and Newsgroup services.

The ASSET staff are constantly working to catalogue and add new reusable software components to the library. Consequently, to determine the latest contents of the library at any time, the ASSET account holder should log on and search the new assets listings.

ASSET Reuse Library (ARL)

ASSET is populating its library with quality reusable software components, which can be distributed to its subscribers. The ARL contains documents, software components, information listings, vendor advertisements, and a reference desk for reuse information. The documents include information on software reuse, software reuse in software engineering, computer-aided acquisition and logistics (CALS) standards and documents, and reuse libraries. The software components are of various sizes, ranging from individual packages and modules to complete tools. Most of the reusable components in the library are available for public distribution, however, there are a few components which have not yet been authorised for distribution beyond government agencies and their contractors. ASSET provides a printed catalogue that contains horizontal domain assets that include Ada Standards and Bindings, Data Base Management Systems, Software Development Process, Software Engineering Environment, and Software Reuse Technologies, as well as others. Also, reuse library interoperability with CARDS and DSRS allows ASSET subscribers access to selected products stored in the CARDS and DSRS libraries.

In addition to library services, ASSET provides a number of additional services to its users at no charge. These include:

- Electronic Mail;

- USENET News (comp.*, news.*, and gnu.* domains only);

- ftp, zmodem, and kermit downloading;

- telnet;

- STARS Bulletin Board System.

Getting an account on ASSET

ASSET accounts are available to all software practitioners including both U.S. and international citizens. An ASSET account allows users to perform customised searching, browsing, extracting, and downloading of the components contained in the ASSET Reuse Library. The ASSET Reuse Library contains both public-domain assets and assets with limited distribution, such as "Government Agencies and Contractors Only". Therefore, when applying for an account, access privileges will be determined and verified, allowing individual users access to all those components for which they have rights.

Contact ASSET for account subscriber information at the folowing address:

ASSET
2611 Cranberry Square
Morgantown
WV 26505 USA
Tel: +1 304 594-3954
Fax: +1 304 594-3951
Email: info@source.asset.com

Connecting to ASSET

There are two methods for users to connect to ASSET. For both of these methods, your terminal emulation should be set to vt100.

Method 1: Telnet
Users may telnet into ASSET at the Internet address source.asset.com (IP Address 192.131.125.10).
Method 2: Dial-In
ASSET maintains a bank of (9) Multitech 9600-baud modems. These can be reached via the following number: +1 304/594-3642
  Your modem settings should be: No Parity, 8 data bits, 1 stop bit (N-8-1), full duplex.

Using the library mechanism

ASSET currently uses the STARS Reuse Library (SRL) mechanism as its library interface. The primary purpose of the SRL is to serve as a library mechanism for the operation of a software-reuse library. It provides a search mechanism, using a combination of faceted and attribute-value classification schemes, for finding candidate assets from the reuse library's collection. Once a list of assets has been obtained, the SRL permits the user to browse through the descriptive material about each asset as well as through the source files of the asset. After browsing, the user may then select assets for extraction from the library. A copy of the files of each asset being extracted is then created for the user and placed in his or her own directory area.

  The SRL User's Guide is available to those with ASSET accounts, and may be browsed on-line or downloaded in both ASCII and Postscript format. This user's guide is also available via anonymous ftp from source.asset.com. The filename is /pub/asset_user_guide.txt.

Library interoperation

ASSET has implemented its initial operating concept of library interoperation. Using TCP/IP protocol, ASSET shares software artifacts with both the CARDS and DSRS repositories, allowing users to extract components from any of the three libraries. These remote library extractions occur transparently to the user. ASSET is continuing efforts to broaden its base of cooperating libraries.

Getting software into the ASSET Library
ASSET has recently begun to include references in the ASSET library to appropriate commercial software and documents. What this really means is that instead of the actual asset (software or document) being included in the library, a user sees information about the asset and how to obtain it. Currently, there is no cost to vendors wishing to include references to their products and services in the Library.

  In addition to commercial assets, ASSET searches the Internet for quality public-domain assets. Staff follow leads received via USENET news articles, published reports and articles, and those provided by our users and 'Netters at large. Suitable assets are culled from selected FTP sites. Assets are also submitted to ASSET by their authors.

ASSET Client Service

The ASSET staff is trained to provide assistance and support to all software practitioners and suppliers of reusable software. There is a user-hotline telephone number (+1 304/594-3954), and also Email (problem@source.asset.com).

16.14.4 COSMIC

COSMIC is the National Aeronautics and Space Administration's (NASA's) Computer Software Technology Transfer Center, the central repository for software developed under NASA funding. Programs are made available for re-use by domestic industries, government agencies, and universities under NASA's Technology Utilisation Program. Educational discounts may apply.

In addition to its catalogue, released in January of each year, COSMIC offers the following services (at no charge): 1) A nine-month subscription to the quartly publication Software Technology Transfer; 2) a custom search of the inventory, based on key words of your selection; 3) a monthly Email listing of new and updated programs, sent to your Internet address; 4) Email User Group Conferences via Internet for the computer programs: CLIPS, TAE+, NETS, FEAT, and NQS.

To use any of these services, contact:

COSMIC Customer Support
The University of Georgia
382 East Broad Street
Athens
GA 30602-4272
USA
Tel: +1 706 542 3265
Fax: +1 706 542 4807
Email: service@cossack.cosmic.uga.edu

16.14.5 Defense Software Repository System (DSRS)

DSRS accounts are available for Government employees and contractor personnel currently supporting Government projects. The following is taken from the "Defense Software Repository System (DSRS) Services Guide".

The DISA/CIM Software Reuse Program (SRP) is a member of the DoD Software Reuse Initiative under the Defense Information Systems Agency/Center for Information Management (DISA/CIM). The SRP is the organisation responsible for the Defense Software Repository System (DSRS). The DSRS is an automated library of Resuable Software Assets (RSAs) available to the DoD, other Government Agencies, and supporting contractors.

SRP Mission

The SRP mission is to implement a software reuse engineering program which supports DoD Information Management and C2 domains. This includes encouraging software reuse practices by providing software reuse operational support to users, quality RSAs, and access to the DSRS. The SRP includes coordination and support of DoD Software Reuse Support Centers (SRSC) at the Service and Agency levels within DoD.

SRP Goals

- Improve the quality and reliability of software-intensive systems;

- Provide earlier identification and improved management of software technical risk;

- Shorten system development and maintenance time; and

- Increase cost effectiveness and productivity through better utilisation and optimisation of the software industry.

The DSRS

The DSRS is an automated repository for storing and retrieving Reusable Software Assets (RSAs). The DSRS software now manages inventories of reusable assets at seven software reuse support centers (SRSCs). The DSRS serves as a central collection point for quality RSAs, and facilitates software reuse by offering developers the opportunity to match their requirements with existing software products.

The DSRS is written in Ada, utilises the ORACLE database-management system, and now operates in a UNIX (SUN OS) environment.

Although primarily used to support reuse and development of object-oriented Ada development products, the DSRS will also support storage and retrieval of products generated using any standard programming language. The DSRS will also support storage and retrieval of other information assets, including data elements, documents, and standards.

Using the DSRS

Users describe their requirements, using the faceted cataloging ("classification") method, through a series of menu-driven screens. The repository identifies one or more suitable RSAs from its collection. The user may browse an individual RSA or analyze a group of RSAs. An abstract is provided, which includes a summary of the component and its characteristics, classification description, supporting documentation, and numerical measures. The user may then select reusable assets for immediate extraction. An RSA may be extracted to the user's PC, or a tape or hardcopy may be requested.

Additionally available is an on-line help facility, RSA relationship and dependency information, session maintenance, and user suggestion and feedback facilities.

The RSAs

RSAs maintained by the DSRS form a broad-based aggregate of products whose potential for reuse has been clearly identified through domain analysis or customer demand. Various categories of RSAs (Government, public domain, and commerical-off-the-shelf) are available through the DSRS. RSAs may be virtually any product generated during a software development project – such as requirements, design specification, architectures, design diagrams, source code, documentation, and test suites.

Each RSA is catalogued ("classified"), abstracted, and installed in accordance with SRP published standards and guidelines.

All RSAs in the DSRS are catalogued by SDRP staff according to a uniform method. The method is faceted. RSAs are catalogued with a set of facets (groups of term values) which reflect properties an RSA may have. They represent multiple ways of looking at a component, i.e., "aspects" or "views".

In conducting certification of RSAs, multiple levels are recommended as a practical way of providing desirable assets for potential reuse. The following levels are currently in use by the SRP for code assets:

Level 1 – identifies the RSA as approved for installation, based on user demand only. No testing or documentation beyond that originally provided by the donor is required. Completeness of RSC functionality is unknown.

Level 2 – identifies the RSA as released to users and verified for completeness. Offers a greater level of confidence than Level 1, but does not receive the validation required to assure quality testing or documentation.

Level 3 – identifies the RSA as having met the requirement of Level 2 and also having complied with reusability criteria, and functional validation and verification.

Level 4 – identifies the RSA as meeting all Level 3 requirements plus documentation standards. These RSAs offer the highest level of quality assurance, completeness, and reusability. Non code asset certification categories include training, document, and library support.

Submitting RSAs

Before submitting a component for placement in the DSRS, the donor is encouraged to prepare an abstract and select cataloging terms for the RSA as directed in SRP standards and guidelines, to aid the staff. Information on acceptable formats for submitting components may be obtained by contacting the Customer Assistance Office (CAO).

DSRS accounts

DSRS accounts are available for Government employees and contractor personnel currently supporting Government projects. The Account Request Form must be approved and signed by the requestor's Government Project Manager prior to submission to the SRP. Completed forms may be mailed or faxed to the CAO at the address or fax number listed below.

The Customer Assistance Office (CAO)

The CAO is the SRP point of contact for both technical and non-technical information and support. The staff is available Monday through Friday between 8am and 4pm Eastern Time. Calls are received via voice mail during off-hours, weekends, and holidays.

Please contact the CAO by telephone or mail correspondence to:

DISA/CIM Software Reuse Program
Customer Assistance Office
500 North Washington Street, Suite 101
Falls Church
VA 22046
USA
Tel: +1 703 536 7485
Fax: +1 703 536 5640

16.14.6 The Public Ada Library (formerly the Ada Software Repository)

Since 1984, the Ada Software Repository (ASR) has been a major, publicly available source of Ada code. Now called the Public Ada Library (PAL), it provides more than 100 megabytes of programs, components, tools, general information, and educational materials on Ada. It also contains materials on the Very High Speed Integrated Circuit (VHSIC) Hardware Description Language (VHDL), which is based on Ada.

For those with access to the Internet, the PAL can be accessed via the widely available File Transfer Protocol (FTP).

The PAL is located on the wuarchive.wustl.edu host, and on mirror sites at ftp.cnam.fr and ftp.cdrom.com. Also, the PAL can be obtained on disk, tape, and compact-disk read-only memory (CD-ROM).

(Additionally, the PAL can be accessed by means of such Internet services as: the Network File System (NFS), which allows computers to share files across a network; archie, a system of querying anonymous-FTP sites; and gopher, via gopher servers wuarchive.wustl.edu and gopher.wustl.edu.)

16.14.7 From ASR to PAL

Originally, the ASR was stored on the SIMTEL20 host computer at White Sands Missile Range, N.M.; over the Internet, and the ASR's resources were available for downloading directly from SIMTEL20, from ASR mirror sites, and via AdaNet.

By early 1993, however, the SIMTEL20 host was an aging machine and had been faced with increasing costs; it was believed likely that it would cease operation later in the year. Facing this, Rick

Conn, the ASR Manager, had to choose between alternatives: "I was faced with a choice of stopping my activities or going on under a different environment."

Fortunately, such an environment was available, and he chose to proceed – establishing a new Ada repository at Washington University, St. Louis. He decided to call this facility the Public Ada Library (PAL), and it would still be accessible over the Internet.

Previously the University's host (wuarchive.wustl.edu) had been a mirror site for the ASR. Effective early June, it became the principal site for the PAL.

With a new disk drive installed, the WUARCHIVE host was up to over 14 gigabytes of disk space, with over 3 Gbytes free for expansion. Mr. Conn expressed his appreciation both to Washington University at St. Louis and to Digital Equipment Corporation (DEC) for their generous donation of the ALPHA AXP system that WUARCHIVE runs on.

The existing ASR is now a subdirectory tree under the PAL. Mr. Conn reports that "users familiar with UNIX should be pleased in that the PAL is on an OSF/1 machine. UNIX naming conventions apply, so there is no longer a need to learn the TOPS-20 conventions used on SIMTEL20." If users wish to access the ASR through the PAL, they need only do a simple translation: directories such as PD7:<ADA.COURSEWARE> on SIMTEL20 are now available as languages/ada/ASR/courseware or /archive/languages/ada/ASR/courseware on the PAL.

As before, everything is available via anonymous FTP. If you have an account on the Internet, and it supports FTP (File Transfer Program), it's "ftp wuarchive.wustl.edu" – logging in as "anonymous", and giving your Email address as the password.

16.14.8   Acquiring the ASR or PAL

You can acquire the contents of the ASR (or the PAL) through the following four methods.

(Note, however, that prospective purchasers should check with each source about the version, extent, etc., of the ASR or PAL software in any particular offering.)

Tape Distribution – available from the Program Library of the Digital Equipment User's Society (DECUS).

PC floppy disks – 1.2-megabyte 5.25" floppy disks are available from Advanced Software Technology, Inc.

CD-ROM distribution – from Alde Publishing, DECUS, Rush River Software, and Walnut Creek CDROM.

On-line – through the WUARCHIVE host, its mirror sites, and through AdaNET. There is no charge for either service; however, access to WUARCHIVE and its mirror sites requires an account on the Internet.

(Report of a product, service, or event is for information purposes only, and does not constitute an endorsement by the Ada Joint Program Office or by the Ada Information Clearinghouse.)

On tape from DECUS

The DECUS Library maintains four collections of software from the SIMTEL20 host. They are offered in VMS Backup Format. The Ada Collection is a copy of the ASR; the collections are from the March 1990 SIMTEL20.

VS0091 SIMTEL20 Ada Collection
VS0089 SIMTEL20 MS-DOS Collection, Part 1
VS0090 SIMTEL20 MS-DOS Collection, Part 2

The tapes range from $140–$160, depending on the medium requested. The address and phone number for the DECUS Library is: DECUS Program Library; DECUS U.S. Chapter; 334 South Street, SHR3-1/T25; Shrewsbury, MA 01545-4195.

On floppy disks

Advanced Software Technology, Inc., offers the ASR on 5.25" floppy disks – in high-density (1.2-MB) MS-DOS format only. Due to the compression of files on distributed diskettes, you will need a hard disk to download the files. All software is offered on an "as is" basis.

AST offers 36 different diskettes at $10 each, including shipping and handling. All international orders must include $2 per disk, and payment must be in the form of a bank check from a U.S. branch.

The diskettes are grouped according to applications, which include: database management and SQL, Ada software components, tools, educational information, CAIS, DDN, editors, metrics, graphic kernel system, management tools, a math library, one disk with simulation, AI and internal tools, benchmarks, Ada program design language, miscellaneous tools, style checkers, menu or form generator and program stubber, spelling checkers and pretty printers, communications programs, new components, a two-disk set with an Ada to X-windows binding; Ada manuals; PIWG benchmarks; a two-disk set with a COBOL-to-Ada translator; and others.

For further information, contact: Jeffrey Hickey; Advanced Software Technology, Inc.; 5 Patricia Lane; Patchogue, NY 11772, USA; Tel: +1 516/758-6545. (No telephone orders.)

On CD-ROM from Alde

Alde Publishing offers "Ada White Sands" for $99. The disk can be used with an IBM PC XT/AT/PS2 or compatible and a compact-disc read-only memory (CD-ROM) player. It is in High Sierra format. Alde sells Ada White Sands for $99 alone, or bundled with a CD-ROM player for $639.

The ASR is also part of Alde's "Ada Buffet" ($239.50), which additionally contains the Ada Reference Language Manual (LRM) in a Window Book format and the Software Repository Index (SRI). The "Ada Graduate" ($895) includes the ASR, SRI, Hypertext LRM, and adds the Integrada programming support environment for Z248 and Z184 PCs; the larger "Ada Master" ($1395) is for 80386/80486 PCs.

For more information, contact: Alde Publishing; 6520 Edenvale Boulevard, Suite 118; Eden Prairie, MN 55346; Tel: 612/934-4239.

On CD-ROM from DECUS

DECUS is in the process of making CDROMs of the entire WUARCHIVE, including the PAL. They intend to create new versions periodically. When contacting DECUS, be sure to check on the date of the CDROM release.

You can get an application for membership in the DECUS U.S. Chapter by calling 508/841-3500.

Sites that wish to get DECUS CDROMs should contact their DECUS Local User Group or: the DECUS Library, 333 South Street, SHR1-4/D33, Shrewsbury, MA 01545-4112; Tel: +1 508/480-3418.

On CD-ROM from Rush River

Rus River Software publishes the "Ada Collection" collected by the Grebyn Corporation. A two-CD-ROM collection of Ada material, it includes Ada software and utilities, documentation and commentary on various aspects of Ada, and materials from university and government repositories of Ada material adding up to approximately 1.2 gigabytes of Ada material.

To introduce the Ada Collection, Rush River Software is bundling the CD-ROM repository with Object-Oriented Design with Ada: Maximising Reusability for Real-Time Systems, by Kjell Nielsen, and Developing with Ada: Life-Cycle Methods, by Bruce E. Krell. Both books are published by Computer Literacy Bookshops.

The Ada Collection can be ordered for $79.95 through Computer Literacy Bookshops, Inc. Tel: +1 703/734-7771; Email: info@clbooks.com).

The Ada Collection can also be ordered directly from Rush River Software (Email order-rr@comm-data.com). For a detailed listing of the CD-ROM contents, send an Email request to info-rr@comm-data.com.

On CD-ROM from Walnut Creek CDROM

Walnut Creek offers its "Ada CDROM" for $39.95. It contains over 560 Mbytes of documentation, information, and source code, including the ASR.

For more information, contact: Walnut Creek CDROM; 1547 Palos Verdes Mall, Suite 260; Walnut Creek, CA 94596; Tel: +1 510/674-0783, Fax: +1 510/674-0821, Email: info@cdrom.com.

Walnut Creek is also sponsoring a mirror site of the PAL. To access this site, FTP to the host ftp.cdrom.com and log in using the anonymous FTP login convention. Then cd to the directory pub/languages/ada or pub/languages/vhdl. There is no charge for this service.

On-line through AdaNET

The ASR is also available on-line through AdaNET, an information and software-reuse project designed to provide public-domain Ada software and information from libraries obtained from the National Aeronautics and Space Administration, the Department of Defense, and other Federal sources.

AdaNET is sponsored by NASA, and there is no charge for an account. While this does not provide full Internet access, Internet Email facilities are available. For further information, contact: AdaNET; c/o MountainNet; Eastgate Plaza, 2nd Floor; P.O. Box 370; Dellslow, WV 26531-0370; Tel: +1 304/296-1458.

On-line through the WUARCHIVE Host

If you have an account on an Internet host computer, you may be able to use FTP to download source code from the ASR to your computer.

FTP allows a user to transfer files to and from a remote network's host site. FTP will work for any hosts on the Internet, which includes such nets as ARPANET and MILNET. (If you need to transfer files to or from a site that is itself only a remote site connected to an Internet host, then you may have to ask the owner of the file at that remote site to send you the file via electronic mail.)

The Internet host with which FTP will communicate can be specified on the command line that invokes FTP (e.g., "ftp wuarchive.wustl.edu"). In that case, FTP will immediately attempt to connect to the host. Once the connection has been established, FTP enters its command interpreter, which is indicated by the ftp> prompt. If FTP is invoked without a host argument, you will enter its command interpreter right away.

What to get first

To begin using the PAL, read the PAL's file for Frequently Asked Questions (FAQs). It's available in the languages/ada/userdocs/faqfile subdirectory as file PAL.FAQ. (It's also posted on USENET.) It is highly recommended that users also obtain the current PAL Catalog (named PALCAT.DOC in the subdirectory languages/ada/userdocs/catalog).

(Users wishing to access the PAL by FTP via one of the mirror sites should note that the languages/ada tree on WUARCHIVE corresponds to the pub/Ada/PAL tree on cnam and the pub/languages/ada tree on cdrom.)

Is the software in the PAL free of defects?

The software in the PAL is an outstanding collection from all over the world, but it comes with a warning: like any such collection, there are outstanding items, good items, average items, and poor items. This software contains items that are really useful, items that you cannot live without, and items that simply may not work in your environment. So you, as a user, must not come into this thinking that everything is perfect.

So how do you know in advance what software is good and what is bad?

Study.

This problem came up over and over again with the ASR, and it was answered by adding a REVIEW CODE field to all the items in the ASR Master Index.

Chapter 1 of the Master Index gives the keys for this field (e.g., CS means Compiled Successfully, ES means Executed Successfully, NR means Not Rated (PAL staff doesn't know whether it is good or bad), etc.). Every item in the Master Index book has an associated REVIEW CODE field. Look at this when you consider using the item.

Also, look for Comment (CMM) files throughout the ASR. They tell success/problem stories. They are text files, so you can just read them. Finally, if you find an item marked with a CS and ES, note the compilers/platforms noted with this mark (e.g., CS(DEC Ada), etc.). If a number of compilers/platforms are named, you probably have a very portable item.

The PAL as a whole has a document called the PAL Catalog (similar in nature to the Master Index of the ASR). It weighs in at nearly two Mbytes, and it's found in file PALCAT.DOC in the languages/ada/userdics/catalog subdirectory. The PAL Catalog has a similar REVIEW CODE field, and CMM files are also supported in the PAL. In phase 2 of the PAL, one or more automated static code-analysis tools will be used to analyze the Ada source code in the PAL and report on it.

User documentation

The subdirectory userdocs in the PAL contains a number of subdirectories of interest to the users of the PAL. Key user documents include:

PAL.FAQ – the Frequently Asked Questions list;

PALCAT.DOC – as noted above, a softcopy catalogue of the contents of the PAL;

PALDB.DOC – a listing of PAL files in a Comma-Separated-Value (CSV) text file suitable for reading by database managers and spreadsheets;

PALHDR.DOC – field-length information for PALDB.DOC; and

PALTAX.DOC – a taxonomy of the PAL.

Other files in the userdocs/catalog and userdocs/faqfile subdirectories are used to create these key files. Additionally, the user is invited to look in the following directories for additional useful information:

userdocs/alt_srcs – alternative sources carrying PAL items; and

userdocs/internet – information on using the Internet.

Information-distribution lists

Users of the PAL are supported by three electronic information-distribution lists on the wunet.wustl.edu host computer. (Note that this is not wuarchive.wustl.edu, the host for the PAL.)

- PAL-ANNOUNCE is an announcement list for users of the Public Ada Library. The purpose of PAL-ANNOUNCE is to distribute information on additions to the PAL, changes to the PAL, and other announcements of interest to the users of the Public Ada Library. PAL-ANNOUNCE is an announcement-only list and will not accept general postings for redistribution.

- WUARCHIVE-ANNOUNCE is an announcement list for users of WUARCHIVE. The purpose of WUARCHIVE-ANNOUNCE is to distribute information on the status of WUARCHIVE, planned downtime, and other items of interest to users of WUARCHIVE. Like PAL-ANNOUNCE, WUARCHIVE-ANNOUNCE is an announcement-only list and will not accept general postings for redistribution.

- ADA-TRAIN is a discussion list for people involved in Ada education and training. The purpose of ADA-TRAIN is to provide a forum for communication between college and university professors, people involved in Ada-oriented education and training in commercial, corporate, and government organisations, and high school teachers. ADA-TRAIN is a discussion list, unlike the two ANNOUNCE lists, and it will accept general postings for redistribution.

If you wish to subscribe to PAL-ANNOUNCE, WUARCHIVE-ANNOUNCE, or ADA-TRAIN, send an electronic-mail message to:

listserv@wunet.wustl.edu

Leave the subject line blank and place the following line into the body of this message:

subscribe <list name: pal-announce, wuarchive-announce, ada-train>

Example:

subscribe pal-announce

Begin this line in column 1. Your return address will be used as the address to which announcements will be sent. You will receive a message back from the listserv software, telling you of the success or failure of your request. After you have subscribed, you may wish to send another message to the listserv address, placing the following line into the body of the message:

help

This will result in instructions on the use of the listserv software being sent back to you.

For further information, contact pal-announce (described above).

17

Ada references

17.1   Calendar of events for 1995

7-9 Feb.   **AFCEA Computing Conference & Exposition ACCE '95**
USA
                Location: Arlington, Virginia
                Contact: Carol Busey, AFCEA Exhibits Department
                Tel: +1 703 631 6200
                Fax: +1 703 631 9177

14-16 Feb.   **Software Development '95 West**
USA
                Location: San Francisco
                Contact: SD '95 West
                Tel: +1 214 245 8874
                Fax: +1 214 245 8700

28 Feb - 4 Mar. **1995 ACM Computing Week**
USA
                Location: Nashville, Tennessee
                Contact: Don Nowak
                Tel: + 1 212 626 0512
                Email: nowak@acm.org

13-16 Mar.   **13th Annual National Conference on Ada Technology**
USA
                Location: Valley Forge, Pennsylvania
                Contact: Ms. Chris Braun
                Tel: +1 703 818 4475
                Email: braun@europa.eng.gtefsd.com

21-23 Mar.   **FOSE '95**
USA
                Location: Washington D.C.
                Contact: Jean Lucas, Reed Exhibition
                Tel: +1 301 495 7115
                Fax: +1 301 495 7148

29 Mar - 1 Apr.   **8th Conference on Software Engineering Education**
USA

        Location: New Orleans, Louisiana
        Contact: Rosalind Ibrahim, Conference Chair
        Tel: +1 412 268 3007
        Email: education@sei.cmu.edu
            rli@sei.cmu.edu

9-14 Apr.   **7th Annual Software Technology Conference**
USA

        Location: Salt Lake City, Utah
        Contact: Dana Dovenbarger, Conference Management
        Tel: +1 801 777 7411
        Fax: +1 801 777 8069
        Email: dovenbar@oodis01.hill.af.mil

24-26 Apr.   **Joint Workshop on Parallel and Distributed Real-Time Systems**
USA

        Location: Santa Barbara, California
        Contact: Theodore Baker, Florida State
        Email: baker@cs.fsu.edu

24-28 Apr.   **17th International Conference on Software Engineering**
USA

        Location: Seattle, Washington State
        Contact: David Norkin
        Tel: +1 908 582 7550
        Email: dep@research.att.com

10-12 Oct.   **International Ada-UK Conference**
UK

        Location: York
        Contact: Ada UK
        Tel: +44 (0) 1904 412 740
        Fax: +44 (0) 1904 426 702

Information provided by:

        Ada Information Clearinghouse (AdaIC)
        P.O. Box 46593
        Washington
        DC 20050-6593
        USA
        Tel: + 1 703 685 1477
        Fax: +1 703 685 7019
        Email: adainfo@ajpo.sei.cmu.edu
          : adainfo@mtc.iitri.com

17.2   Booklist

Only books published in the last five years are included.*

1990

Distributed Ada: Developments and Experiences
> Judy M. Bishop (ed)
> Cambridge University Press
>
> Proceedings of the Southampton symposium with comprehensive papers by the leading
> experts in distributed Ada.

Exploring Ada, Volume I
> Douglas L. Bryan and Geoffrey O. Mendal
> Prentice-Hall
>
> Describes Ada's type model, statements, packages and subprograms. Includes pro-
> gramming features such as information hiding, facilities to model parallel tasks, data
> abstraction, and software reuse.

Practical Visual Techniques in System Design in Ada
> R.J.A. Buhr
> Prentice-Hall
>
> Offers a personal statement on how to use visual techniques to organise one's thinking
> during the design process.

Real-Time Systems and Their Programming Languages
> A. Burns and A. Wellings
> Addison-Wesley
>
> Provides a study of real-time systems engineering, and describes and evaluates the
> programming languages used in this domain.

Ada Software Repository (ASR)
> R. Conn (ed)
> Zoetrope
>
> Describes how to use the Ada Software Repository, which contains Ada programs,
> software components, and educational materials, and resides on the host computer of
> the Defense Data Network (DDN).

Selecting an Ada Compilation System
> J. Dawes et al (eds)
> Cambridge University Press, Ada Companion Series
>
> Presents the findings of the Ada-Europe specialist group for compiler assessment.

Resources in Ada
> Gerry Fisher (Intro.)
> ACM Press
>
> Complete compendium of Ada information.

---

*Some of the entries in this section are taken from the Ada Information Clearinghouse report Ada BOOKS.

Software Reuse with Ada
R.J. Gautier and P.J. Wallis (eds)
Peter Peregrinus

Contains three sections: 1) general reuse issues, comprises a collection of papers on various aspects of Ada software reuse; 2) case studies of Ada reuse in practice; and 3) Ada Reuse Guidelines.

Ada Applications and Administration, 2nd edn
Phillip I. Johnson
McGraw-Hill

Explains how to ensure the reliable, error-free, cost-effective operation of large computer systems with Ada.

Ada: Experiences and Prospects
Barry Lynch (ed)
Cambridge University Press

Proceedings of the Ada-Europe Conference, Dublin 1990.

Programming with Specifications: An Introduction to Anna, a Language for Specifying Ada Programs
David C. Luckham et al
Springer-Verlag, Texts and Monographs in Computer Science

Offers an in-depth look at ANNA, a form of the Ada language in which specially marked comments act as formal annotations about the program to which they are attached.

File Structures with Ada
Nancy Miller and Charles Peterson
Addison-Wesley

Uses packages to implement a range of file structures.

Ada in Distributed Realtime Systems
Kjell Nielsen
McGraw-Hill

Emphasises design paradigms and heuristics for the practicing software engineer. Provides important background material for the builder of operating systems and runtime support environments for distributed systems.

Computer Systems Techniques: Development, Implementation, & Software Maintenance
J. Sodhi
Tab Books, a division of McGraw-Hill

Managing Ada Projects Using Software Engineering
J. Sodhi
Tab Books, a division of McGraw-Hill

Describes some of the practical aspects of developing a flawless project in Ada.

Programming in Ada
J. Tremblay
McGraw-Hill

Explains computer science concepts in an algorithmic framework, with a strong emphasis on problem solving and solution development.

Introduction to Programming Using Ada
Dennis Volper and Martin D. Katz
Prentice Hall

Uses the spiral approach as the presentation methodology in this introductory course in Ada programming.

Parallel Processing & Ada
Y. Wallach
Prentice-Hall

1991

Programming Languages: Paradigm & Practice - Ada Mini-Manual
D. Appleby
McGraw-Hill

Object-Oriented Reuse, Concurrency and Distribution; An Ada-Based Approach
C. Atkinson
Addison-Wesley

Provides and introduction to DRAGOON, the object-oriented language that combines the power of object-oriented languages with the software engineering features of Ada.

Software Engineering with Abstractions
V. Berzins and Luqi
Addison-Wesley

Uses a formal specification language ("Spec") to lead readers through the software-development process to develop large, real-time, and distributed systems in Ada.

Introduction to Ada
D. Bover
Addison-Wesley

Software Design Techniques for Large Ada Systems
William Byrne
Digital Press (Simon and Shuster)

Introduces design strategies for controlling complexities inherent in large computer programs and in software systems as groups of large computer programs executing concurrently.

Programming in Ada, A Beginner's Course
David Bover, Michael Oudshoom and Kevin Maclunas
Addison-Wesley

Covers a subset of Ada for beginners, with software engineering included.

Ada: The Choice for '92
Dimitris Christodoulakis (ed)
Springer-Verlag

Proceedings of the Ada-Europe Conference, Athens 1991.

Ada Problem Solving & Program Design
M.B. Feldman and E.B. Koffman
Addison-Wesley

Designed to introduce the novice to a number of Ada features, such as subprograms, packages, operator overloading, enumeration types, and array-handling operations.

Ada: Concurrent Programming
N. Gehani
2nd edition, Silicon

Offers a large collection of concurrent algorithms, expressed in terms of the constructs provided by Ada, as the support for concurrent computation. Explains the concurrent programming facilities in Ada and shows how to use them effectively in writing concurrent programs.

Ada Programmer's Handbook
D. Gonzalez
Benjamin-Cummings

Adopts a reference-oriented approach to describing key Ada concepts.

Ada Programmer's Handbook and Language Reference Manual
D. Gonzalez and W. Dean
Benjamin-Cummings

Presents information intended for those professionals transitioning to Ada.

Rationale for the Design of the Ada Programming Language
J. Ichbiah
Cambridge University Press

Presents the rationale behind the design and development of the Ada programming language.

Ada Yearbook 1991
Fred Long (ed)
Chapman & Hall

The first issue of the book you are now reading.

Exploring Ada, Volume II
Geoffrey O. Mendal and Douglas L. Bryan
Prentice-Hall

A method of presentation based on the Socratic method, provides coverage and the semantics of Ada. Discusses focused problems individually. The second volume expands on the larger issues dealing with Ada's more advanced features.

Annotated Ada Reference Manual, 2nd edition
Karl A. Nyberg
Grebyn Corporation

Contains the full text of ANSI/MIL-STD-1815A with inline annotations derived from the Ada Rapporteur Group of the International Organisation for Standards responsible for maintaining the Ada language.

Move up to Ada
C.G. Peterson and N. E. Miller
P&M

Developing Safety Systems with Ada
Ian C. Pyle
Prentice-Hall

A presentation of concepts for practicing engineers or programmers involved with the development of safety-related computer-based systems.

Software Engineering: Methods, Management, and CASE Tools
J. Sodhi
Tab Books, A division of McGraw-Hill

1992

Mission Critical Operating Systems
A.K. Agrawala et al (eds)
ISBN: 9-051-99069-3

This book explores the design and implementation of mission critical operating systems (MCOS) and mission critical computing systems (MCCS).

Understanding Ada: A Software Engineering Approach
G. Bray and David Pokrass
(Reprint of 1985 edition.) Krieger

Towards Ada 9X
A. Burns
IOS Press

This book is a collection of edited papers on the general theme of Ada 9X.

Ada: A Developmental Approach
Culwin
Prentice-Hall

Intended for use on courses which teach Ada as the first programming language. The book is designed to take the reader from the basic principles of programming to advanced techniques.

Ada: Moving Towards 2000
J. van Katwijk (ed)
Springer-Verlag (LNCS 603)

Proceedings of the 11th Ada-Europe Conference, Zandvoort, The Netherlands, 1992.

Developing with Ada: Life-Cycle Methods
B. Krell
Computer Literacy Bookshops

Dr. Krell offers his opinion on the key to using Ada to its fullest potential: a tested development methodology for implementing real-time Ada systems quickly and efficiently, from requirements and code through design and test.

Ada Yearbook 1992
   Fred Long (ed)
   Chapman & Hall

   The second issue of the book you are now reading.

Exploring Ada, Volume 2
   G. Mendal and D.L. Bryan
   Prentice-Hall

   A method of presentation based on the Socratic method, provides coverage and the semantics of Ada.

Abstract Data Types & Ada
   R. Mitchell
   Prentice-Hall

Object-Oriented Design with Ada/Maximising Reusability for Real-Time Systems
   Kjell Nielsen
   Computer Literacy Bookshops

   Shows Ada programmers how to design, implement, and maintain reusable real-time software systems using object-oriented methods.

Reusable Ada Components Sourcebook
   A. Orme et al
   Cambridge University Press

   The authors consider how the Ada software components that may be found in this book could be used.

Ada: An Introduction to the Art and Science of Programming
   W.J. Savitch
   Benjamin-Cummings

   Written specifically for the first programming course.

Ada: in Transition
   W.J. Taylor (ed)
   IOS Press

   This book reviews the current practice in Ada applications, innovative developments in Ada technology, how Ada can be applied in more demanding systems in the safety-critical area and reports on the Ada 9X revision effort.

Ada, The Enchantress of Numbers: A Selection from the Letters of Lord Byron's Daughter and Her Description of the First Computer
   B. A. Toole
   Strawberry

   The author states that she selected and arranged the letters to enable the reader to follow a loose story line of Lady Ada Lovelace's life. In her letters, Ada describes her thoughts of the first computer, and Ms. Toole relates these descriptions to the modern software language, Ada.

1993

Concurrent Programming with Ada
E. Andrews (ed)
Benjamin-Cummings

Ada 9X: Towards Maturity
L. Collingbourne (ed)
(Studies in Computer & Communication Systems, Vol. 6) IOS Press

Introduction to Ada
J.E. Cooling
Chapman and Hall

Introduction to Ada gives a comprehensive introduction to the subject, covering all the basic aspects of the language with reference to the particular strengths of Ada in real-time systems.

A First Course in Computer Science with Ada
N.J. Delillo
Richard D. Irwin, Inc.

This book is intended for a first course in computer science that emphasises programming and problem-solving methodology using the Ada programming language.

Ada Yearbook, 1993
Chris Loftus (ed)
IOS Press

The third edition of the book you are now reading.

Design of Dependable Ada Software: The Use of Exception Mechanisms
G. Motet and A. Marpinard
Prentice-Hall

Introduction to Software Design & Development with Ada
D. Rudd
West

Introduction to Programming Concepts and Methods with Ada
Smith
McGraw-Hill

Explains the fundamentals of programming concepts and methodology, and presents a major part of the Ada language (exclusive of concurrency and low-level features) as a vehicle for applying these concepts and methods in practice. The book does not assume any prior programming experience.

Data Structures with Abstract & Ada
D. F. Stubbs and N. W. Webre
PWS

Data Structures & Algorithm Analysis in Ada
Mark Weiss
Benjamin-Cummings

1994

Programming in Ada Plus an Overview of Ada 9X
J.G.P. Barnes
Addison-Wesley

The fourth edition, while remaining focused on the current ANSI 83 standard, reflects the imminent Ada 9X standard in three ways: all features of Ada that will be affected by the Ada 9X standard are highlighted with icons and their design rationale described in detail; a full chapter on Ada 9X provides a tutorial and summary of the most important changes, including the increased support for object-oriented programming, the introduction of a hierarchical library structure and the inclusion of protected objects; full details of the syntax changes are provided in the appendices for easy reference.

Object Oriented Design with Applications
G. Booch
Benjamin-Cummings

Software Engineering with Ada
G. Booch
Benjamin-Cummings

Introduces Ada from a software engineering vantage. Addresses the issues of building complex systems. Includes new features in this second version: a more thorough introduction to Ada syntax and semantics, an updated section on object-oriented techniques to reflect the current state of knowledge, and improved examples that illustrate good Ada style for production systems development.

Programming and Problem Solving with Ada
N. Dale, C. Weems and J. McCormick
D.C. Heath and Company

Designed for University Level 1 courses with a strong emphasis on problem solving, early use of Ada procedures and Ada packages, extensive and varied exercises including Quick Check, Exam Preparation, and Programming Warm-up.

Software Design Methods for Concurrent and Real-Time Systems
Hassan Gomaa
Addison-Wesley

Gomaa outlines the characteristics of concurrent, real-time, and distributed systems, describes the concepts most important in their design, and surveys the design methods available for them.

Ada Yearbook, 1994
Chris Loftus (ed)
IOS Press

The fourth edition of the book that you are reading.

Software Systems Construction with Examples in Ada
B. Sanden
Prentice-Hall

Primarily intended for readers with practical experience in software construction. It targets graduate or upper-level undergraduate students of software engineering as well as practitioners.

Ada Byron Lovelace: The Lady & the Computer
   M. D. Wade
   Macmillan Child

1995

Ada Yearbook 1995
   Mark Ratcliffe (ed)
   IOS Press 1995.

   The book that you are now reading

17.3   Publications

There are many regular journals, magazines and newsletters devoted to Ada. These carry articles, views, reports of meetings and conferences as well as advertising for compilers, courses, software etc. Some of the most effective are listed here.

Ada-Belgium Newsletter
> To provide the Belgian Ada Community with information about Ada activities in Belgium as well as in the rest of the world. Distributed to all members of Ada-Belgium. Quarterly.
> Contact: Ada-Belgium, Université Libre de Bruxelles (ULB), Boulevard du Triomphe, Campus de la Plaine CP 202, B-1050 Bruxelles, Belgium.
> Tel: +32 2 650 56 11 and +32 2 650 56 14. Fax: +32 2 650 51 13.

Ada Companion Series
> A series of books on special Ada topics, published in conjunction with the Commission of the European Communities.
> Contact: Cambridge University Press, The Edinburgh Building, Shaftesbury Road, Cambridge CB2 2RU, UK.
> Tel: +44 1223 315052.

AdaData
> Newsletter with emphasis on commercial significance of new Ada developments and the Defense Department's policies. Monthly.
> Contact: International Research Development, 21 Locust Avenue, #1C, New Canaan, CT 6840-4735, USA.

Ada-Europe News
> Newsletter to provide the European Ada Community with information about Ada activities in Europe as well as in other parts of the world. Distributed to all Ada-Europe members. Distribution to indirect members is through their national associations. Subscriptions are available on request for individuals or institutions outside Europe only. Quarterly.
> Contact: Ada-Europe, Weiveldlaan 41/B32, Zaventem, B-1930, Belgium.

Ada Information Clearinghouse Newsletter
> This is the official publication of the Ada Joint Program Office (AJPO). It contains news about Ada's official progress, events and lists of validated compilers. Quarterly. Free.
> Contact: Ada Information Clearinghouse, c/o IIT Research Institute, 4600 Forbes Boulevard, Lanham, MD 20706-4320, USA.
> Tel: +1 703 685 1477.

Ada Letters
> One of the most useful Ada publications, with articles, reports, events, tutorials and compiler information. Published by the ACM's Special Interest Group on Ada (SIGAda). Bimonthly.
> Contact: Ada Letters, ACM Headquarters, 11 W 42nd Street, New York, NY 10036, USA.
> Tel: +1 212 869 7440.

Ada Strategies

Newsletter focusing on competitive strategies in the Ada marketplace. Monthly.
Contact: Cutter Information Corp. 1100 Mass Ave, Arlington, MA 02174, USA.
Tel: +1 617 648 8700.

Ada User

Publication of Ada UK with information of events and products connected with Ada.
Quarterly.
Contact: IOS Press, Van Diemenstraat 94, 1013 CN Amsterdam, Netherlands.
Fax: +31 20 620 34 19.

Info-Ada Newsletter

A newsletter that contains information on current events in the Ada community, plus
lists of validated compilers. Monthly.
Contact: Karl A Nyberg, Grebyn Corporation, P O Box 1144, Vienna, VA 22180-1144,
USA.
Tel: +1 703 281 2194, Email: karl@grebyn.com

Journal of Pascal, Ada and Modula-2

A journal that provides an international forum for research, developments, applications
and new products in these languages. Bimonthly.
Contact: JPAM Corp, P O Box 968-B, Ft Washington, PA 19034, USA.

La Lettre Ada

Published in French, with information about products and events in France and Europe.
Monthly.
Contact: Jean-Claude Rault, EC2, 269-287 rue de la Garenne, 92000 Nanterre, France.
Tel: +33 47 8 70 00.

SpAda

Newsletter of Ada-Spain, distributed freely to its members. Quarterly.
Contact: Francisco Perez-Zarza, Ada-Spain, P.O. Box 50.403, E-28080 Madrid, Spain.
Fax: +34 1 656 5887, Email: fperez@ada.es.

17.4   Contributors and contacts

Ada 9X Project Office
Project Manager: Christine M. Anderson
PL/VTES
Kirtland AFB
NM 87117-5776
USA

Tel: +1 505 846-0817 / 0461
Fax: +1 505 846-2290
Email: andersonc@plk.af.mil

Ada Association of Australia
Clive Boughton
Ferranti Computer Systems Pty Ltd
GPO Box 2888
Canberra City ACT 2601
Australia

Ada-Belgium
President: Luc Bernard
Offis S.A.
Atlas Park
Weiveldlaan 41 B.32
B-1930 Zaventem
Belgium

Tel: +32 2 725 4025
Fax: +32 2 725 4012

Ada in Denmark
Jorgen Bundgaard
c/o DDC-International A/S
Gl. Lundtoftevej 1B
DK-2800 Lyngby
Denmark

Tel: +45 45 87 11 44
Fax: +45 45 87 22 17
Email: jb@ddci.dk

Ada-Deutschland
Dr Peter Wehrum
Rational GmbH
Rosenstrasse 7
Grosshesselohe
D-8023 Pullach im Isartal
Germany

Tel: +49 89 797 021
Fax: +49 89 799 343
Email: rpw@Rational.com

Ada-Europe
Secretary: Karlotto Mangold
ATM Computer GmbH
Büecklestr. 1-5
D-7750 Konstanz
Germany

Tel: +49 7531 807 235
Fax: +49 7531 807 585
Email: ada-euro@atmkn.uucp

Ada-France
Jean-Pierre Rosen
AdaLOG
27, Avenue de Verdun
F-92170 Vanves
France

Tel: +33 1 46 45 51 12
Fax: +33 1 46 45 52 49
Email: rosen@enst.enst.fr

Ada-Greece
Apostolos Coucouvinos
Intrasoft
Athens Tower
2, Mesogion Str
Athens 115.27
Greece

Tel: +30 1 770 1692
Fax: +30 1 778 2444

Ada Information Clearinghouse
PO Box 46593
Washington DC
20050-6593
USA

Tel: +1 703 685-1477
Email: adainfo@ajpo.sei.cmu.edu

Ada-Ireland
Barry Lynch
Tirion Software
95 Haddington Road
Ballsbridge
Dublin 4
Ireland

Tel: +353 1 609011
Fax: +353 1 609828

Ada-Italy
President: Paolo Panaroni
Intecs Sistemi S.p.A.
Via Gereschii 32
56126 Pisa
Italy

Tel: +39 50 545 233
Fax: +39 50 545 200
Email: paolo@pisa.intecs.it

Ada Joint Program Office
Acting Director: Major Dirk Rogers
Room 3E114 (1211 Fern Street/C-107)
The Pentagon
Washington
DC 20301-3081
USA

Tel: +1 703 614-0208
Email: rogersd@ajpo.sei.cmu.edu

Ada Joint Users Group (AdaJUG)
Chairperson: Mike Ryer
Intermetrics, Inc.
733 Concord Avenue
Cambridge
MA 02194
USA

Tel: +1 617 661 1840
Fax: +1 617 868 2843
Email: ryer@inmet.inmet.com

Ada-Nederland
Mr P. Verduin
Bagijnhof 80
Postbox 3318
2601 DH Delft
The Netherlands

Tel: +31 15 123 190
Fax: +31 15 147 889
Email: ada-nederland@west.nl

Ada in Norway
Anton B. Leere
Norwegian Defence Research
    Establishment
P.O. Box 25
N-2007 Kjeller
Norway

Tel: +47 680 7394
Fax: +47 680 7212
Email: leere@ndre.no

Ada Resource Association
Bob Mathis
4719 Reed Road
Suite 305
Columbus
OH 43220
USA

Tel: +1 614 442 9232
Fax: +1 614 442 0055

Ada-Scotland
Bob Duncan
Napier University
Sighthill
Edinburgh EH11 4BN
UK

Tel: +44 131 444 2266
Fax: +44 131 458 5089
Email: bob@cs.napier.ac.uk

Ada-Spain
Secretary: Francisco Perez-Zarza
P.O. Box 50.403
E-28080 Madrid
Spain

Fax: +34 1 656 5887
Email: fperez@ada.es

Ada in Sweden
Secretary: Elsa-Karin Boestad-Nilsson
National Defence Research Institute
S-10254 Stockholm
Sweden

Tel: +46 8 631500

Ada in Switzerland
Magnus Kempe
Chair, Ada in Switzerland
Swiss Federal Institute of Technology
in Lausanne
EPFL-DI-LGL
CH–1015 Lausanne
Switzerland

Tel: +41 21 693 2580
Fax: +41 21 693 5079
Email: Magnus.Kempe@di.epfl.ch

Ada UK
Helen Byard
Ada UK Administrator
PO Box 322
York
YO1 3GY
UK

Tel: +44 1904 412740
Fax: +44 1904 426702

Address for parcels:
Rose Bank
Garrow Hill
Green Dykes Lane
York
YO1 3HL

Ada Validation Office
Ms Audrey Hook
Institute for Defense Analysis
1801 N Beauregard Street
Alexandria
VA 22311
USA

Tel: +1 703 824 6639

AFCET
156, Bld. Pereire
75017 Paris
France

Tel: +33 1 47 66 24 19
Fax: +33 1 42 67 93 12

Alsys
Ian Campbell
Partridge House
Newtown Road
Henley-on-Thames
Oxon
RG9 1EN
UK

Tel: +44 1491 579090
Fax: +44 1491 571866

Angel Alvarez
Depto. Ing. Sist. Telemáticos
E. T. S. Ing. Telecomunicación
Univ. Politécnica de Madrid
Ciudad Universitaria
E-28040 Madrid
Spain

Tel: +34 1 336 7349
Fax: +34 1 336 7333
Email: aalvarez@dit.upm.es

Jorge Amador-Monteverde
See European Space Agency

**American National
    Standards Institute**
1430 Broadway
New York
NY 10018
USA

Tel sales: +1 212 642 4900
Tel general: +1 212 354 3300

Christine M. Anderson
See Ada 9X Project Office

John Aspinall
See GEC-Marconi Software Systems

**Association for Computing
    Machinery Incorporated**
11 West 42nd Street
New York
NY 10036
USA

**Association for Computing
    Machinery Special Interest
    Group on Ada (ACM/SIGAda)**
Chairperson: Hal Hart
TRW, R2/2062
One Space Park
Redondo Beach
CA 90278
USA

Tel: +1 310 812-0661
Email: hart@ajpo.sei.cmu.edu

BAeSEMA Ltd
Mike Christie
Biwater House
Portsmouth Road
Esher
Surrey
KT10 9SJ
UK

Tel: +44 1372 466660
Fax: +44 1372 466566

Alan Baldwin
See MOD (PE)

Judy Bamberger
'Ada Follies'
Software Engineering Institute
Pittsburgh
PA 15213
USA

Tel: +1 412 268 5795
Fax: +1 412 268 5758
Email: bamberg@sei.cmu.edu

John G.P. Barnes
Chairman, Ada UK
President, Ada-Europe
John Barnes Informatics
11 Albert Road
Caversham
Berkshire
RG4 7AN
UK

Tel: +44 1734 474125
Fax: +44 1734 483474

Bernard Banner
NYUADA9X Project
Courant Institute of Mathematical
    Sciences
New York University
251 Mercer Street
New York
NY 10012
USA

Email: banner@cs.nyu.edu

Patrick Bazire
Télécom Paris – ENST
Département Informatique

Email: bazire@inf.enst.fr

John Bennett
See Ferranti Naval Systems

Luc Bernard
See Ada-Belgium

Elsa-Karin Boestad-Nilsson
See Ada in Sweden

Frank Bott
Department of Computer Science
University of Wales, Aberystwyth
Penglais
Aberystwyth
Dyfed
SY23 3DB
UK

Tel: +44 1970 622424
Fax: +44 1970 622455
Email: mfb@aber.ac.uk

Clive Boughton
See Ada Association of Australia

Dave Brookman
SIGAda Object-Oriented WG
E-Systems
PO Box 41241
St. Petersburg
FL 33743
USA

Tel: +1 813 381-2000 (x2678)

Benjamin M. Brosgol
SIGAda Commercial Ada Users WG
Brosgol Consulting and Training
79 Tobey Road
Belmont
MA 02178
USA

Tel: +1 617 489-4027
Fax: +1 617 489-4009
Email: brosgol@ajpo.sei.cmu.edu

Jorgen Bundgaard
See Ada in Denmark

Alan Burns
Real-Time and Distributed Systems
        Research Group
Department of Computer Science
University of York
York
UK

Email: burns@minster.york.ac.uk

Helen Byard
See Ada UK

CADRE Technologies Ltd
Joanne Cooling
Edenfield
London Road
Bracknell
Berkshire
RG12 2XH
UK

Tel: +44 1344 300003
Fax: +44 1344 360079

Ian Campbell
See Alsys

Bernard Carré
See Program Validation Ltd

Mike Christie
See BAeSEMA Ltd

Andrew Clarke
See Harris Systems Ltd

Ed Colbert
SIGAda, Vice Chair for Liaison
Absolute
4593 Orchid Drive
Los Angeles
CA 90043-3320
USA

Tel: +1 213 293 0783
Email: hermix!colbert@rand.org

Cyrille Comar
Computer Science Department
New York University
USA

Email: comar@cs.nyu.edu

**Commission of the European
    Communities**
Karel de Vriendt
DG XIII, A25 9/6A
Rue de la Loi 200
B-1049 Brussels
Belgium

Tel: +32 2 235 7769
Fax: +32 2 235 0655

Joanne Cooling
See CADRE Technologies Ltd

Apostolos Coucouvinos
See Ada-Greece

Mike Curtis
ICL Secure Systems
Eskdale Road
Winnersh
Wokingham
Berkshire
RG11 5TT
UK

Tel: +44 1734 693131
Email: mikec@win.icl.co.uk

**Data Analysis Center for Software
    (DACS)**
RADC/COED
Griffis AFB
NY 13441-5700
USA

Tel: +1 315 336 0937

Martin Davies
BSI Quality Assurance
PO Box 375
Linford Wood
Milton Keynes
MK14 6LE
UK

John Dawes
ICL Secure Systems
Eskdale Road
Winnersh
Wokingham
RG11 5TT
UK

Tel: +44 1734 693131
Fax: +44 1734 693131 Extn. 6004
Email: sjd@win.icl.co.uk

**Defense Technical
    Information Center**
Cameron station
Alexandria
VA 22304-6145
USA

Tel: +1 703 274-7633

Richard De Morgan
De Morgan Associates
Evesden
Chapel Lane
Padworth Common
Reading
RG7 4QE
UK

Tel: +44 1734 700326

Robert B.K. Dewar
SIGAda Standards WG
73 5th Avenue
New York
NY 10003
USA

Tel: +1 212 741-3722
Email: dewar@cs.nyu.edu

Jorge L. Diaz-Herrera
SIGAda Artificial Intelligence WG
Software Engineering Institute
MSE Program
Carnegie Mellon University
4500 Fifth Avenue
Pittsburgh
PA 15213-3890
USA

Tel: +1 412 268-7636
Email: jldh@sei.cmu.edu

Digital Equipment Co. Limited
Philip Heslin
Digital Park
Imperial Way
Reading
RG2 OTE
UK

Tel: +44 1734 202378
Fax: +44 1734 202129

Kenneth W. Dritz
Mathematics and Computer Science
    Division
Argonne National Laboratory
Argonne
Illinois 60439
USA

Email: dritz@mcs.anl.gov

Bob Duncan
See Ada-Scotland

The Secretary General
ECMA
114 Rue du Rhone
CH-1204 Geneva
Switzerland

Tel: +41 22 735 3634
Fax: +41 22 786 5231

EDS
Dave Jacobs
Pembroke House
Pembroke Broadway
Camberley
Surrey
GU15 3XD
UK

Tel: +44 1276 415000
Fax: +44 1276 415333

Rod Ellis
School of Comp. Sci. & Info. Sys. Eng.
University of Westminster
115 New Cavendish Street
London
W1M 8JS

David Emery
Technical Editor, IEEE P1003.5
The MITRE Corporation
MS A155
Bedford
MA 01730
USA

Tel: +1 617 271 2815
Fax: +1 617 271 2607
Email: emery@mitre.org

Encore Computer (UK) Limited
Vincent Rich
Marlborough House
Mole Business Park
Leatherhead
Surrey
KT22 7BA
UK

Tel. +44 1372 363363
Fax. +44 1372 362926

European Space Agency
Jorge Amador-Monteverde
Software Engineering &
    Standardisation Section (WME)
ESA-ESTEC
PO Box 299
2200 AG Noordwijk
The Netherlands

Tel: +31 1719 84388
Fax: +31 1719 85420
Email: amador@wm.estec.esa.nl

Mike Feldman
SIGAda Education WG
Dept. of Electrical Engineering
    and Computer Science
The George Washington University
Washington
DC 20052
USA

Tel: +1 202 994-5253
Email: mfeldman@seas.gwu.edu

Ferranti Naval Systems
John Bennett
A division of GEC-Marconi Limited
Mountbatten House
Jackson Close
Cosham
Hampshire
PO6 1UD
UK

Tel: +44 1705 383101
Fax: +44 1705 326589

Moving to a new site in spring of 1995 to:
Fitzherbert Road
Farlington
Hampshire

Tel: +44 1705 701701

Peter Fitzpatrick
See VSEL Electronics and Software
    Products

Franco Gasperoni
Télécom Paris – ENST
Département Informatique

Email: gasperon@inf.enst.fr

**GEC-Marconi Software
    Systems**
John Aspinall
Elstree Way
Borehamwood
Hertfordshire
WD6 1RX
UK

Tel: +44 181 732 0238
Fax: +44 181 732 0362

Mark S. Gerhardt
IALC Convenor
TRW/ESL M/507
495 Java Drive
Sunnyvale
CA 90488-5310
USA

Tel: +1 408 738 2888 (x2459)
Email: gerhardt@ajpo.sei.cmu.edu

G. Giannino
See NATO NACISA/AdaSCC

Ian Gilchrist
See IPL

J.G. Glynn
Company Secretary, Ada UK
IALC Secretary
Department of Computing
University of Brighton
Watts Building, Lewes Road
Moulescoombe
Brighton
East Sussex BN2 4GJ
UK

Lewis Gray
SIGAda Software Development Standards
    and Ada WG
Ada PROS, Inc.
12224 Grassy Hill Court
Fairfax
VA 22033-2819
USA

Tel: +1 703 591-5247
Email: adapros@grebyn.com

Steve Grinham
GEC-Marconi Combat Systems
Station Road
Addlestone
Weybridge
Surrey
KT15 2PW
UK

David Guaspari
Odyssey Research Associates
Ithaca
NY 14850
USA

Keith Hardy
See Ultra Electronics Command
    and Control Systems

Harris Systems Ltd
Andrew Clarke
Computer Systems Division
Riverside Way
Watchmoor Park
Camberley
Surrey
GU15 3YD
UK

Tel: +44 1276 686886
Fax: +44 1276 678733

Hal Hart
See ACM SIGAda

Philip Heslin
See Digital Equipment Co. Limited

Alec Hill
Nuclear Electric Plc
Location 94
Barnett Way
Barnwood
GL4 7RS
UK

Tel: +44 1452 652045
Fax: +44 1452 653244

Harry Hughes
See i-Logix UK Ltd

IDE UK Ltd
Adrian Jones
1 Stirling House
Stirling Road
The Surrey Research Park
Guildford
Surrey
GU2 5RF
UK

Tel: + 44 1483 579000
Fax: + 44 1483 31272
Email: adrian@ideuk.co.uk

i-Logix UK Ltd
Harry Hughes
1 Cornbrash Park
Bumpers Way
Chippenham
Wilts
SN14 6RA
UK

Tel: +44 1249 446448
Fax: +44 1249 447373

IPL
Ian Gilchrist
Eveleigh House
Grove Street
Bath
BA1 5LR
UK

Tel: +44 1225 444888
Fax: +44 1225 444400

Integral Solutions Ltd
Ben Rabau
3 Campbell Court
Bramley
Basingstoke
RG26 5EG
UK

Tel: + 44 1256 882028
Fax: + 44 1256 882182

Integrated Systems Inc Ltd
Hamid Mirab
Gatehouse
Fretherne Road
Welwyn Garden City
Hertfordshire
AL8 6NS
UK

Tel: + 44 1707 331199
Fax: + 44 1707 391108

Dave Jacobs
See EDS

Adrian Jones
See IDE UK Ltd

Martyn Jordan
See Tartan Inc.

Mike Kamrad
SIGAda Ada Run-Time Environment WG
Unisys Corporation
MS U2F13
PO Box 64525
St. Paul
MN 55164-0525
USA

Tel: +1 612 456-7315
Email: mkamrad@ajpo.sei.cmu.edu

Jim Kelly
See Program Analysers Limited/LDRA

Magnus Kempe
See Ada in Switzerland

Anton B. Leere
See Ada in Norway

Stanley H. Levine
SIGAda Reuse WG
Army Project Manager
Common Hardware/Software
Attn: SFAE-CC-CHS
Ft. Monmouth
NJ 07703
USA

Tel: +1 908 544-2603
Email: levinest%doim6.monmouth@
   emh3.army.mil

Bill Loftus
SIGAda Ada Bindings WG

Email: loftusw@source.asset.com

Chris Loftus
Department of Computer Science
University of Wales, Aberystwyth
Penglais
Aberystwyth
Dyfed
SY23 3DB
UK

Tel: +44 1970 622435
Fax: +44 1970 622455
Email: cwl@aber.ac.uk

Fred W. Long
Department of Computer Science
University of Wales, Aberystwyth
Penglais
Aberystwyth
Dyfed
SY23 3DB
UK

Tel: +44 1970 622440
Fax: +44 1970 622455
Email: fwl@aber.ac.uk

James P. Lonjers
Chair, IEEE P1003.5
Paramax Systems Corporation
MS 02-B208
5151 Camino Ruiz
Camarillo
CA 93011
USA

Tel: +1 805 987 9457
Email: lonjers@prc.unisys.com

M.J. Looney
Defence Correspondent, Ada UK
Room 402, Block 2
DRA Portsmouth
MCO2
Portsmouth
PO6 4AA
UK

Barry Lynch
See Ada-Ireland

Karlotto Mangold
See Ada-Europe

Markus Meier
See Ada in Switzerland

Regis Minot
Emeraude
153, bureaux de la colline
92213, Saint Cloud
France

Fax: +33 1 49 11 72 40
Email: regis.minot@emeraude.syseca.fr

Hamid Mirab
See Integrated Systems Inc Ltd

The MITRE Corporation
James W. Moore
7525 Colshire Boulevard
W534 McLean
Virginia 22102
USA

Tel: +1 703 883 7396
Email: moorejw@ajpo.sei.cmu.edu

MOD (PE)
Alan Baldwin
CIS (Eng) 31a
MOD (PE)
Turnstile House
98 High Holborn
London
WC1V 6LL

Tel: +44 171 218 9050
Fax: +44 171 218 9055

James W. Moore
See The MITRE Corporation

Gilbert Myers
SIGAda Numerics WG
Naval Ocean Systems Center
Code 413
271 Catalina Boulevard
San Diego
CA 92152-5000
USA

Tel: +1 619 553-4136
Email: gmyers@ajpo.sei.cmu.edu

**National Institute for
        Standards and Technology**
Nat. Computer Systems Laboratory
Software Standards Validation
        Group
Bldg. 255/Rm. A-266
Gaithersburg
MD 20899
USA

Tel: +1 301 975 2490

**National Technical
        Information Service (NTIS)**
5285 Port Royal Road
Springfield
VA 22161
USA

Tel: +1 703 487 4600

NATO NACISA/AdaSCC
G. Giannino
Rue de Genève, 8
B-1140 Brussels
Belgium

Tel: +32 2 728 8388

Objective Interface Systems, Inc
Phil Carrasco
1985 Preston White Drive
Suite 250
Reston
Virginia
22091-5448
USA

Tel: +1 703 264 1900
Fax: +1 703 264 1721

John Palmer
See SQL Software Ltd

Paolo Panaroni
See Ada-Italy

Ian Pascoe
See Rational

Francisco Perez-Zarza
See Ada-Spain

M.J. Pickett
Treasurer, Ada UK
"Norvu"
60 New Road
Twyford
Berkshire
RG10 9PT
UK

Ron Pierce
See York Software Engineering Limited

Prof. Erhard Ploedereder
University of Stuttgart
Institute for Informatics
Breitwiesenstr. 20-22
D-70565 Stuttgart
Germany

Email: ploedere@orchidee.informatik.
uni-stuttgart.d400.de

Program Analysers Limited/LDRA
Jim Kelly
56A Northbrook Street
Newbury
Berkshire
RG13 1AN
UK

Tel: +44 1635 528 828
Fax: +44 1635 528 657
Email: sales@ldra.com

Program Validation Ltd
Bernard Carré
26 Queen's Terrace
Southampton
Hants
SO1 1BQ
UK

Tel: +44 1703 330001
Fax: +44 1703 230805

Richard F. Puk
Chairman, X3H3.4
Puk Consulting Services
7644 Cortina Court
Carlsbad
CA 92009-8206
USA

Tel: +1 619 532 9027

Ben Rabau
See Integral Solutions Ltd

Dev Raheja
SIGAda Safety and Security WG
Technology Management Inc.
9811 Mallard Drive
Laurel
MD 20708-2317
USA

Tel: +1 410 792-0701
Fax: +1 301 953-2213

Mark Ratcliffe
Department of Computer Science
University of Wales, Aberystwyth
Penglais
Aberystwyth
Dyfed
SY23 3DB
UK

Tel: +44 1970 622435
Fax: +44 1970 622455
Email: mbr@aber.ac.uk

Rational
Ian Pascoe
Olivier House
18 Marine Parade
Brighton
East Sussex
BN2 1TL
UK

Tel: +44 1273 624814
Fax: +44 1273 624364

Vincent Rich
See Encore Computer (UK) Limited

Bob Risinger
See TLD Systems

Clyde Roby
SIGAda Environment WG
Institute for Defense Analysis
1801 N. Beauregard Street
Alexandria
VA 22311-1772
USA

Tel: +1 703 845-6666
Email: croby@ajpo.sei.cmu.edu

Major Dirk Rogers
See Ada Joint Program Office

Jean-Pierre Rosen
See Ada-France

Dan M. Roy
SIGAda Performance Issues WG
Software Engineering Institute
Carnegie Mellon University
Pittsburgh
PA 15213
USA

Tel: +1 412 268-6180
Email: royd@ajpo.sei.cmu.edu

Mike Ryer
See Ada Joint Users Group (AdaJUG)

Edmond Schonberg
NYUADA9X Project
Courant Institute of Mathematical
    Sciences
New York University
251 Mercer Street
New York NY 10012
USA

Email: schonberg@cs.nyu.edu

Thomas E. Shields
SIGAda Ada Semantic Interface
    Specification WG
Unisys Corporation
Information Systems
Dept 7670
12010 Sunrise Valley Drive
Reston
VA 22091
USA

Email: shields@stars.reston.paramax.com

Jun Shimura
Treasurer, Japan SIGAda
Alsys-KKE
Technowave 1-1-25
Shin-Urashima
Kanagawa-ku
Yokohama 221
Japan

Prof. D. Simpson
Editor Ada User, Ada UK
ITRI, University of Brighton
Watts Building, Lewes Road
Moulescoomb
Brighton
BN2 4AT
UK

Tel: +44 1273 642450
Fax: +44 1273 642405
Email: ds33@unix.bton.ac.uk

**Software Engineering
    Institute**
Carnegie Mellon University
Pittsburgh
Pennsylvania 15213-3890
USA

Tel: +1 412 268 7700
Fax: +1 412 268 5758

SQL Software Ltd
John Palmer
Northbrook House
John Tate Road
Hertford
SG13 7NN
UK

Tel.: +44 1992 501414
Fax: +44 1992 501616

Prof. Alfred Strohmeier
Liaison officer, Ada in Switzerland
Swiss Fed Inst of Technology Lausanne
EPFL-DI-LGL
CH-1015
Switzerland

Tel: +41 21 693 4231
Fax: +41 21 693 5079
Email: alfred.strohmeier@di.epfl.ch

Bob Sutherland
MOD(PE) CIS(Eng) 31a
Room 408
98 High Holborn
London
WC1V 6LL
UK

Tel: +44 171 305 8547
Fax: +44 171 305 8531

Tartan Inc.
Martyn Jordan
European Sales Office
Little Langtree
Hill Bottom
Whitchurch Hill
Reading
RG8 7PU
UK

Tel: +44 1734 843260
Fax: +44 1734 841014

Tartan Inc.
Pittsburgh Corporate Office
300 Oxford Drive
Monroeville
PA 15146
USA

Tel: +1 412 856 3600
Fax: +1 412 856 3636

Bill Taylor
Conference Co-ordinator, Ada UK
Transition Technology Ltd
5 Lark Hill Rise
Badger Farm
Winchester
Hants
SO22 4LX
UK

Tel: +44 1962 877466 / 860767
Fax: +44 1962 877467
Email: taylorb@ajpo.sei.cmu.edu

TLD Systems
Bob Risinger
3625 Del Amo Boulevard, Suite.100
Torrance
CA 90503
USA

Tel: +1 310 542 5433
Fax: +1 310 542 6323
Email: tld@cerf.net

Bob Risinger
See TLD Systems

Brian C. Tooby
Director, Ada UK
High Integrity Systems Ltd
Astras Centre
Edinburgh Way
Harlow
CM20 2BE
UK

Tel: +44 1279 450000

**Ultra Electronics Command
    and Control Systems**
Keith Hardy
Knaves Beech Business Centre
Loudwater
High Wycombe
Buckinghamshire
HP10 9UT
UK

Tel: +44 1628 530000
Fax: +44 1628 524557

Mr P. Verduin
See Ada-Nederland

Karel de Vriendt
See Commission of the
    European Communities

VSEL Electronics and Software Products
Peter Fitzpatrick
Technology & Marketing Division
Barrow-in-Furness
Cumbria
LA14 1AF
UK

Tel: +44 1229 873993
Fax: +44 1229 873846

Dr Peter Wehrum
See Ada-Deutschland

Rob Westermann
Ada-Nederland
West Consulting BV
Delft
The Netherlands

Tel: +31 15 123 190
Fax: +31 15 147 889
Email: rob@west.nl

York Software Engineering Limited
Ron Pierce
University of York
York
YO1 5DD
UK

Tel. +44 1904 433741
Fax. +44 1904 433744

Indexes

There are three indexes. The first is a general index. The second is an index of names of people, organisations and publications and the third is an index of computer systems and tools which are mentioned in the book. However, the list of validated Ada compilers in Section 12.2 is not indexed here nor is the Ada 9X Compatibility Guide (Chapter 15). All the indexes are arranged alphabetically.

An entry should appear in only one index. Inevitably, it is not always clear-cut in which index an entry should appear. For example, should 'HOOD' appear in the general index, the index of names or the index of systems? (In fact, it appears in the general index.)

If you are looking for an index entry but cannot find it in the general index, don't forget to look in the other two indexes. Of course, mistakes do happen, and some entries that you might have expected will have been omitted altogether.

General index

Index of names

Index of systems and tools

Feedback page

Please send comments, on any aspects of this book, to the editor at the address given below. All suggestions about what should, or should not, be included in future issues are welcome. If there is something you particularly like, or dislike, about the way the book is presented, please let me know.

If you have any comments or suggestions, please send them to:

Mark Ratcliffe
Department of Computer Science
University of Wales, Aberystwyth
Penglais
Aberystwyth
Dyfed
SY23 3DB
UK

Tel. +44 (0) 1970 622441
Fax. +44 (0) 1970 622455
Email: mbr@aber.ac.uk